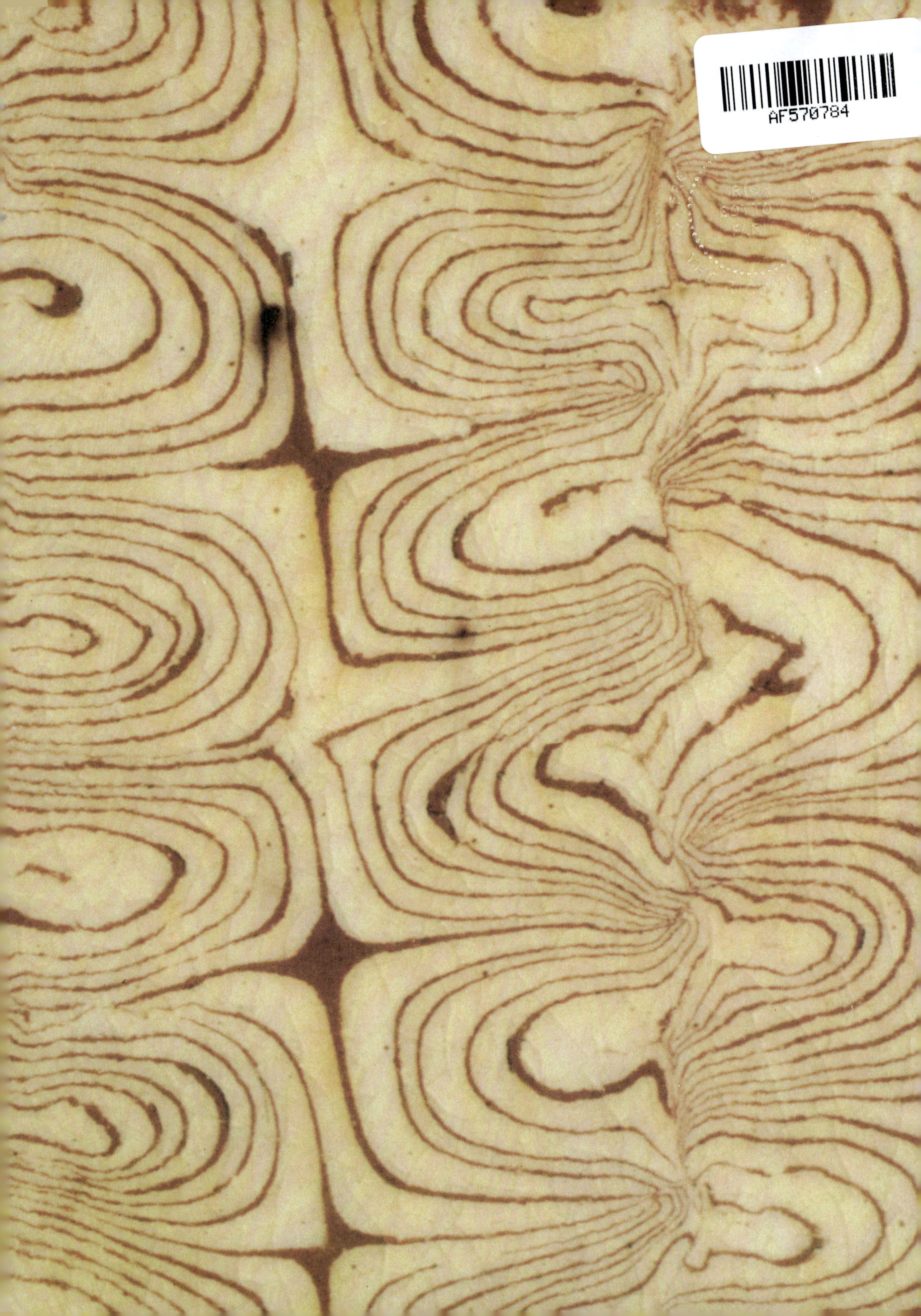

Ceramics in America

CERAMICS IN AMERICA 2003

Edited by Robert Hunter

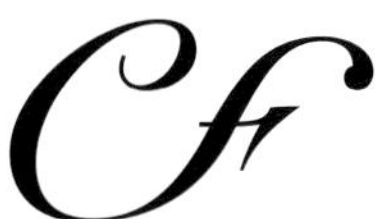

Published by the CHIPSTONE FOUNDATION

Distributed by University Press of New England

Hanover and London

Cover Illustration: Detail of Staffordshire slipware dish, 1720–1740. (Courtesy, State Museum of Pennsylvania; photo, Gavin Ashworth.)

Design: Wynne Patterson
Copyediting: Alice Gilborn
Printing: Meridian Printing
Type: Aardvark Type

Published by the Chipstone Foundation, 7820 North Club Circle, Milwaukee, WI 53217

Printed in the United States of America 5 4 3 2 1
ISSN 1533-7154
ISBN 0-9724353-1-X

Contents

Editorial Statement

Ceramics in America is an interdisciplinary journal intended for collectors, historical archaeologists, curators, decorative arts students, social historians, and contemporary studio potters. Authors are encouraged to submit articles on the broad role of historical ceramics in the American context including essays on ceramic history, archaeological research, ceramic technology, social history, studio pottery, and ceramic collecting. Short illustrated notes on new ceramic discoveries are particularly wanted. References to be compiled in an annual bibliography, including electronic sources, may also be submitted. Manuscripts must be typed, double-spaced, illustrated with high-quality color transparencies, and prepared in accordance with the *Chicago Manual of Style*. Computer disk copy is requested but not required. The Chipstone Foundation will offer significant honoraria for manuscripts accepted for publication and reimburse authors for all photography approved in writing by the editor.

Robert Hunter

Robert Hunter

Introduction

▼ AMERICA'S EXTRAORDINARY ceramic heritage results from ideas and ceramic technologies brought to this country through centuries of European immigration. The articles in *Ceramics in America* 2003 are linked by the themes of cultural innovations, migrations, and adaptations. Although these presentations deal with eighteenth- and nineteenth-century ceramics, the concept of cultural diffusion—the flow of styles and conventions from one region or social group to another—also applies to the study of America's earliest ceramics.

Pottery in the New World appeared in the Amazon Basin nearly 7,000 years ago. By the third millennium B.C., native populations in southeastern North America were making and using a variety of clay vessels. Since these early cultures left no written record, their fragments of clay pots provide the only evidence to learn about their ceramic history. Ceramics specialists try to decode the silent language encapsulated in the wares by studying clay constituents, manufacturing techniques, and functional and stylistic attributes. Unfortunately, this is not easy research as the various permutations of these cultural traditions are endless. For example, even the most basic questions of how and where pottery making originated in the New World have yet to be fully answered.

We do know that European ceramics first appeared in America with the arrival of the early Spanish explorers. America's ceramic legacy took on a truly global perspective in the sixteenth and seventeenth centuries with the influx of English, Dutch, and French settlers. Chinese and Japanese porcelain from the Far East found its way here as well.

Those of us who restrict our ceramic research to America's historic period usually expect to have an easier task than prehistorians in studying cultural innovation, adaptation, migration, borrowing, mixing, and outright appropriation. But do we? Almost everyday a new ceramic object is excavated—or discovered at the flea market or sold at a major New York or London auction—that confounds even the most self-assured expert. These unexpected finds continue to stimulate and energize us as collectors and scholars, forcing us to develop new methods for looking at old pots. Some of these strategies will be evident in this year's journal articles.

After two hundred years of dependence on British and European ceramics, a true American industry began to develop in the nineteenth century. This development coincided with western expansion, growing transportation networks, an emergent middle-class market, and the wholesale immigration of Staffordshire-trained potters to America. Miranda Goodby examines the correspondence of some of these Staffordshire potters who presented first-person accounts of their experiences in a new country. These surviving documents illustrate the debt owed to the Staffordshire potters, and, perhaps more importantly, their letters remind us of the people behind the anonymous pots made in America in the 1800s.

Among the products produced by these potters was a brown glazed ceramic type known as Rockingham. Rockingham wares were America's first mass-produced domestic ceramics, made in factories from the Mid-Atlantic to the Midwest beginning in the 1830s and 1840s. Documentary and archaeological evidence indicates that Rockingham products were mostly plain and utilitarian. However, a number of decorative molded forms were produced using techniques directly borrowed from the Staffordshire potteries. Arthur Goldberg presents an overview of the major Rockingham producers, illustrated with examples from his collection.

Barbara Magid and Bernard Means examine another type of American pottery that was made in late eighteenth-century Alexandria, Virginia. The potters are members of the Henry Piercy family from Saarbrücken, Germany, and the ceramic type is a slip-decorated redware. Most scholars have been exposed to the more widely published slipwares of Philadelphia. Magid and Means discovered that both Alexandria and Philadelphia products share many characteristics that make them virtually indistinguishable. To help solve this dilemma, the authors employed Mössbauer spectroscopy to distinguish the Philadelphia clay body from the Alexandria clay body. Not only is their article important for their comprehensive color presentation of the range of the Alexandria slipwares, Magid and Mean's research confirms the value of material science to help sort out the products of other American regional potteries.

Immigrant potters arrived in America with only their experience and technological repertoire as they adapted to the local clays and fuel resources. Particulars of their technical secrets were often lost. In an effort to rediscover one such technique, Michelle Erickson and this author explore the mysteries of agateware, a ceramic type that blends two or more colors of solid clay to create the illusion of a marble or agate stone. In searching for the origin of this specialized ceramic technique, they argue that eighth-century T'ang dynasty ceramics served as the prototypes for mid-eighteenth-century Staffordshire agateware, underscoring the international nature of stylistic borrowing.

For ceramic historians to fully understand the differences and similarities in various cultural traditions, comparative analysis of ceramic assemblages is essential. The importance of archaeology in providing primary data for this type of analysis is demonstrated by Peter Williams' documentation of a significant late seventeenth- and early eighteenth-century tavern group recovered from Tetbury, England. Distinguished by a preponderance of nearly complete mugs, this collection of early English tavern wares affords the opportunity for researchers to make direct comparisons with wares from other English and American taverns.

Cultural traditions can also be studied by tracing the evolution and use of a single artifact type through time and space. In an encyclopedic voyage through several centuries of ceramic history, Ivor Noël Hume elevates the humble chamber pot from an object of derision to a vital cultural artifact. The ownership and use of this universal receptacle transcended many economic and social boundaries possibly qualifying it as the most democratic of all ceramic forms.

If chamber pots are among the least personalized forms, then ceramic grave markers have to be the most individualized. Reflecting their owners' social status as well as their identity, ceramic grave markers are common in a number of cultures. Richard Veit and Mark Nonestied have identified the unique use of terracotta in a New Jersey community that fashioned architectural elements for the building of late nineteenth- and early twentieth-century New York City. Their study expands the traditional view of the medium and highlights the aesthetic contribution of this fascinating form of mortuary art.

Collecting ceramics continues to be a recurring topic in journal articles. Graham Hood reminisces on the ceramic highlights from his multi-faceted curatorial career at some of America's most important decorative arts museums. Although he might be termed a "professional" collector relying upon rational accessions needs, his poetic essay belies an academic approach and reveals the passionate attraction to the ceramic medium that many of us share but struggle to express.

Both passion and rational thought are apparent in Anthony Butera's essay on collecting Long Island redware. Focusing on the production of the Huntington potteries, Butera draws upon a number of historical, archaeological, and comparative sources, relying on "informed conjecture" to make his attributions and assertions. In the absence of institutional interest, regional typologies will continue to be built by dedicated collectors such as Butera.

The best tool for any collector or ceramic scholar remains his or her library. Towards that end, New Discoveries editor Merry Outlaw has assembled a variety of short contributions on important new research. An anthropomorphic theme pervades her selections wherein some aspect of the human figure is portrayed. Book review editor Amy Earls has again compiled a wide range of book reviews along with a comprehensive bibliography of ceramic scholarship published during the last year.

Many of the themes addressed in this third *Ceramics in America* will be revisited in future issues. More regional studies of American redware and stoneware potteries will be presented during the next few years. In addition, some exciting new information about eighteenth-century English porcelain in the American context will be forthcoming. Comments on articles or suggestions for future topics can be submitted via email at <CeramicJournal@aol.com.> Selected articles from previous volumes can also be accessed on the Chipstone Foundation's website <http//:www.chipstone.org.>

Ceramics in America

Miranda Goodby

"Our Home in the West": Staffordshire Potters and Their Emigration to America in the 1840s

▼ IN 1845 A SERIES OF polemical verses titled "The Pioneers Song" appeared in a union newspaper, *The Potters' Examiner and Workman's Advocate,* published in Hanley, Stoke-on-Trent. They called for British potters to forsake the tyranny of their homeland and emigrate to America:

Hark Hark to that strain! Let us hear it again!
From a bark that is bearing away from the quay:
It's a pioneer band, that departs from the land,
To establish a home for the brave and the free.

"Farewell!" sing the crew, as they sail from our view,
"The land of the pauper is not for the free:
"We sail for the west, where the weary shall rest:
"And the 'Bastile' of England, no more shall we see.

"The tyrants of state, in their pride and their hate
"Have driven their thousands to premature graves;
"The lives of the poor, they think of no more
"Nay less than the Planters would think of their slaves.

"Farewell, and away o'er the bright bounding spray"
Sing the bold pioneers, as they dash o'er the wave'
"There's health in the gale, as it fills every sail,
"And bears us away to the home of the brave.

"The dear friends, we leave, for them, we may grieve,
"And may offer a tribute to memory dear;
"For the sorrow and care, they are all doomed to bear
"Will ever call forth to our eye-lids a tear.

"But away with the pain—we shall see them again!
"We are only preparing a way for the rest:
"Then blow! Breezes blow! As onward we go-
"The Potters shall yet have a home in the West!"[1]

Whether inspired by the poem or not, hundreds of British potters emigrated to the United States in the early nineteenth century. This is not an exhaustive study but rather an examination, through their own words, of those potters who left during the first sustained period of emigration in the 1840s, looking at the state of the Staffordshire pottery industry at the time, the hardships endured by the workers there, and the reasons that prompted them to leave their homes for a new country. It is also an attempt to show what their opinions of America were and how they sought to establish themselves and their families. It makes use predominantly of one full and detailed—if biased—source, the Staffordshire weekly newspaper, *The Potters' Examiner and Workman's Advocate*.[2]

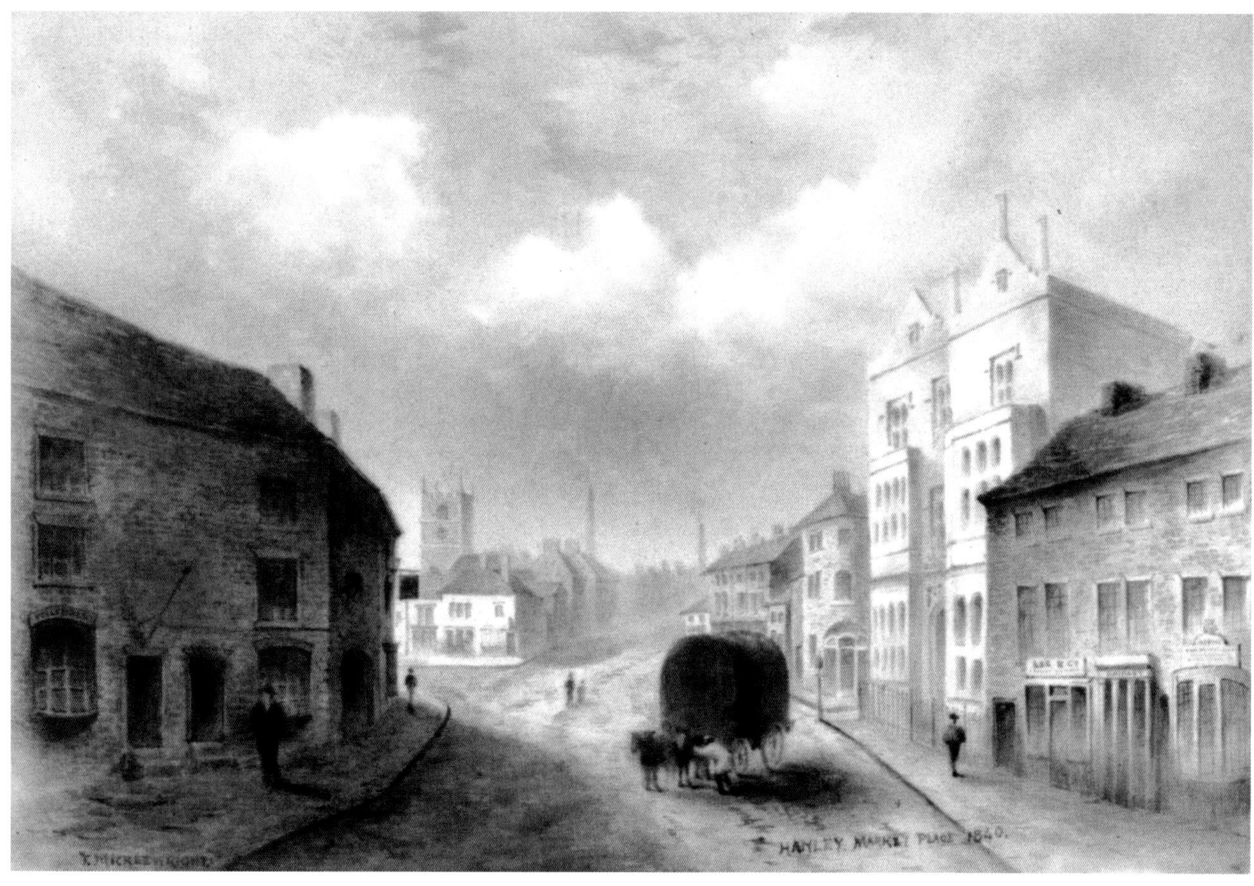

Figure 1 F. Micklewright, *Hanley Market Place, 1840*. Enamel painting on bone china. (Courtesy, The Potteries Museum & Art Gallery, Stoke-on-Trent; photo, David Barker.)

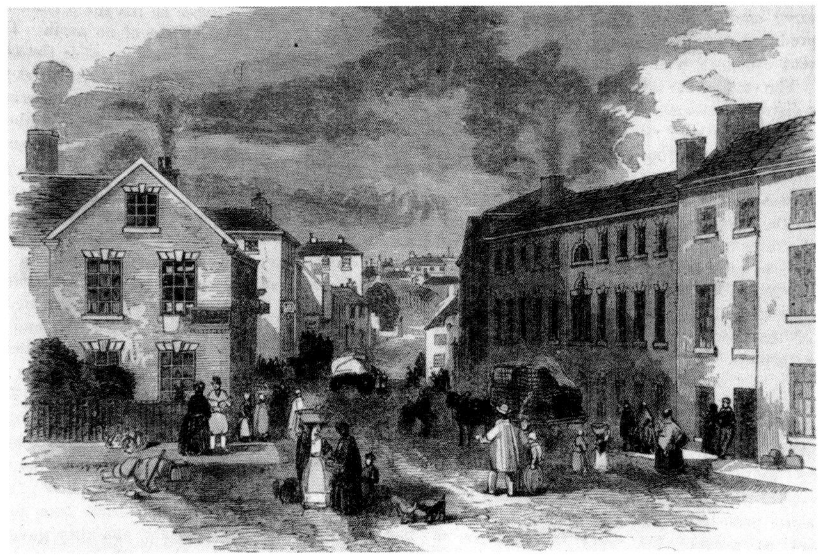

Figure 2 *Church Street, Stoke-upon-Trent,* ca. 1840. Colored engraving. 6¼" x 4¾". (Private collection.)

In the early years of the American colonies, pottery making was not high on the list of desirable immigrant skills or crafts. It was a specialized trade requiring skilled workers and access to raw materials of clay, fuel, and lead for glazing. Necessary ceramics could be supplied from Britain, including European wares shipped through British ports. In addition, the British government prohibited the establishment of certain manufacturing trades or industries in the colonies in order to protect English interests.

Nonetheless, as America became more settled and the population pushed westward, there was an increasing demand for pottery, along with the discovery of new deposits of raw materials, some suitable for making coarse kitchen and dairy wares, others—white-firing clays—for making the more highly regarded stonewares, creamwares, and even porcelains. It became harder to enforce the restrictive regulations against competition. Demand for certain products encouraged the development of trade skills and the establishment of workshops on a large and small scale. By the end of the eighteenth century, numerous potters from Britain and the European continent worked along the eastern seaboard. Their products reflected both the raw materials available in various regions and consumer demand.

Meanwhile, across the Atlantic, pottery production in Britain was expanding massively. By 1762 about one hundred and fifty factories existed in north Staffordshire alone with employment at around seven thousand;[3] by 1800 employees numbered fifteen to twenty thousand.[4] There was job security for all who had the necessary skills. Indeed, skilled labor was so scarce that a system of annual hiring was instituted, enabling employers to contract potters for a period of twelve months, from Martinmas to Martinmas. Employers could be sure they had skilled workers for the year ahead.

This was not a climate in which pottery workers were likely to consider emigration. Opportunities for master potters were limited in the North American colonies where the market was still small and pottery workers would have to be imported. In addition, there was no infrastructure to provide the necessary fuel, clay, or other essential materials for fine wares.

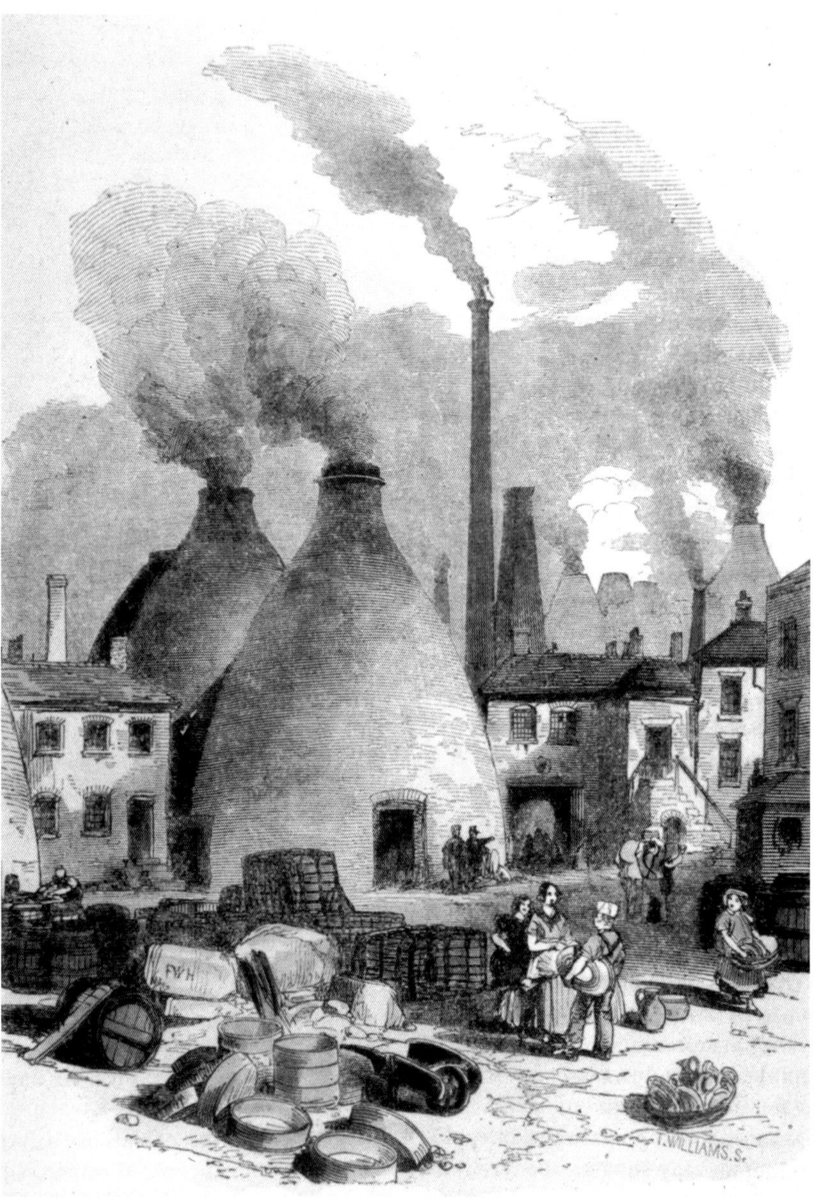

Figure 3 T. Williams, Sr., *The Bank*, ca. 1840. Colored engraving. 5" x 6". (Private collection.) Packing the finished ware for sale.

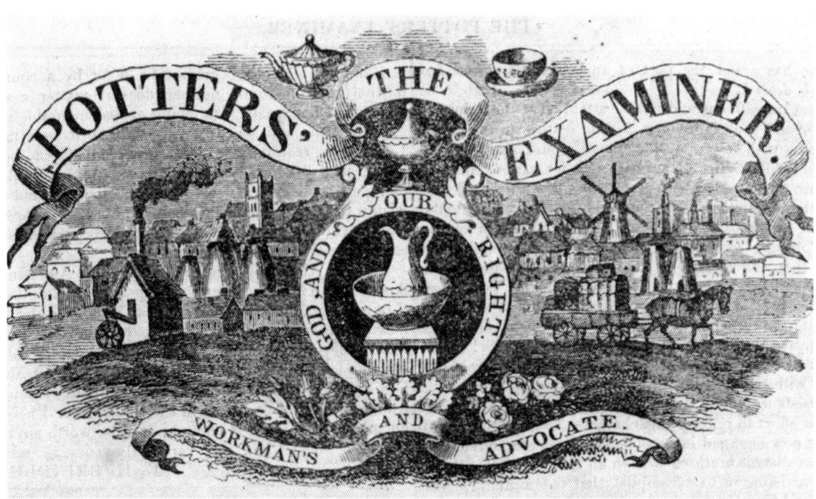

Figure 4 Masthead of *The Potters' Examiner and Workman's Advocate*, published 1837–1847.

Manufacturers in north Staffordshire benefited from the local availability of skilled labor, as well as from a close-knit society that provided financial support and social and political connections. As America expanded, however, it became potentially more attractive to British potters.

Since the middle of the eighteenth century, it was known that fine clays were available in America. The first patent for Bow porcelain mentioned the use of "unaker," or white clay from Carolina also known as "Cherokee clay."[5] William Cookworthy, who took out a patent for hard-paste porcelain in 1768, was also interested in clay from Carolina,[6] and Josiah Wedgwood paid Thomas Griffiths to search Carolina for suitable clays for his creamware factory.[7]

None of these mid-eighteenth-century ventures took root commercially. The difficulties of negotiating for access rights, transport problems, and costs meant supplies were intermittent, and potters turned to English clays instead. However, one Staffordshire master potter was sufficiently intrigued by the possibilities of "Cherokee clay" to move to South Carolina, establish a factory, and encourage workers to join him. This was John Bartlam, who, according to a 1783 pamphlet written by Josiah Wedgwood:

> Went to South Carolina, and by offers made from thence . . . prevailed upon some of our workmen to leave their country and come to him . . . the men, puffed up with the expectations of becoming gentlemen soon, wrote to their friends here what a fine way they were in, and this encouraged others to follow them. But change of climate and manner of living, accompanied perhaps with a certain disorder of mind to be mentioned hereafter, (which have always made great havock among the people who have left this country to settle in remote parts) carried them off so fast, that recruits could not be raised from England sufficient to supply the places of the dead men . . . they fell sick as they came, and all died quickly.[8]

This pamphlet, partnered with other lurid tales of American life, was designed to emphasize the risks involved in going to work abroad. According to Wedgwood, emigration would lead to almost certain poverty and despair, probably culminating in an early death: "Like plants removed into a soil unnatural to them, they dwindled away and died."[9]

Proclaiming that Britain was "a land truly flowing with milk and honey" Wedgwood addressed himself to those contemplating emigration:

> Let me prevail upon you to pause here awhile—to compare the country and situation you have left, with those in which you now find yourselves. In . . . Staffordshire, you [are] happily placed amidst populous and thriving towns and manufacturers; amongst people of the same religion, speaking the same language, and brought up in the same habits of life as yourselves—among neighbours, who knew you from your infancy . . . . You [would be] outcasts in a strange land . . . [people] must look upon you as unworthy members of the community you had before belonged to as having deserted its cause, endeavoured to ruin its manufacturers as having disregarded the interest of your neighbours and friends whom you left behind . . . . And . . . there is a disease of the mind, peculiar to people in a strange land; a kind of heart-sickness and despair, with an unspeakable longing after their native country, not to be described, and of which no one can have a just idea but those who have been under its influence. Most travellers have felt it, in greater or lesser degree; many have died of it; and those who have recovered declare it to be worse than death itself.[10]

Wedgwood concluded by pointing out Parliamentary acts decreeing that "a manufacturer or artificer," such as a potter, would be committing a criminal act, liable to a fine of £500 or twelve months imprisonment, if he left "His Majesty's dominions" in order to "use, exercise or teach any of the said trades" to foreigners and did not return to Britain after being given notice to do so. Such persons would be excluded from taking any legacy devised to them, prevented from administering to anyone's estates, and would forfeit all lands, goods, and chattels. In addition, they would be regarded as "an alien and out of His Majesty's protection." Wedgwood ended his address by offering a bounty of fifty guineas for every person "apprehended by you who shall be convicted of endeavouring to entice or to hire any of our potters into foreign service."[11] The two acts of Parliament mentioned in Wedgwood's pamphlet were sufficiently draconian on their own, without Wedgwood's additional fifty guineas and ominous warnings, to explain why relatively few potters were immigrating to America at the end of the eighteenth century.

The eighteenth and early nineteenth centuries were a period of intense political upheaval. Continental wars spread from Europe to the Americas, while the insurrection of the colonists, which brought Wedgwood's nephew Thomas Byerley unexpectedly home from America, further dissuaded Englishmen from immigrating to the United States for some time.[12] Once the relationship between the new nation and Britain was stabilized, the sympathy of America for the regicides of France and the Napoleonic Wars discouraged many potential immigrants from abandoning England for unknown conditions, a situation which was reinforced with the War of 1812.

It was not just fear that kept the Staffordshire potters at home. In the early nineteenth century, the British pottery industry continued to grow and, despite some setbacks, it was a prosperous time for potters, both masters and workmen.[13] In 1824 the Combination Acts were repealed.[14] For the first time, potters were able to organize into unions and negotiate collectively for improved hiring practices, working conditions, and wages.

Although operating from a strong negotiating position, the diversity of skills among the potters made it difficult for workers to band together; each trade had its own concerns. However, there were a number of grievances in common: annual hiring abuses, payments "good from oven," and the allowance and truck systems.

Annual hiring was a long-established system whereby, in the autumn, employees were hired for the coming year. Although employees were bound to the employer for twelve months, the latter was not obliged to find work for his laborers for more than one day per week. Despite this, potters could not give notice and work elsewhere without written authorization from their contracted employer. At slack times, the employer could lay off his workforce for as long as he wanted, knowing that they would be available as soon as conditions improved.

At the annual hiring, the rates of pay for piecework were also fixed for the year.[15] This meant that only those rates in place at Martinmas were agreed upon; any prices for making wares or patterns introduced during the remainder of the year could be imposed by the manufacturer without negotiation. This was frequently a way to effect a wholesale reduction in prices paid for work and, therefore, in wages.

Another major grievance was paying "good from oven." In this instance, workers were only paid for what was deemed good, saleable ware—not at the point when the ware left their hands as is the present system but after it had been fired in the biscuit oven. For example, a thrower or plate maker might do his work well, yet if the firing failed and his work was ruined, he was not paid. Since the manufacturer established what was "good from oven," the system was open to abuse. Employees alleged that employers, having refused to pay them for work done, were then selling their wares as seconds or even thirds.[16]

A third indignity was the allowance system. Another way of cutting wages, the workman "allowed" his employer one, two, or three pence in the shilling. The term itself was misleading, for it was the employer who settled the rate, and the deduction was compulsory.

Some manufacturers had an additional way of cheating their employees: the truck system. Rather than paying their employees in cash, they paid them in goods. However, poor quality or useless goods—lengths of cloth or cheap jewelry—could not take the place of cash to pay the rent or buy food and fuel. Of all the ways to lower wages, this practice raised the most indignation among the workers.

It was not surprising that once unions had been legalized a series of strikes erupted specifically to rectify these problems. In the main, they were successful, but in 1836 the National Union of Operative Potters overreached itself, and after a twenty-week stoppage of work, union members were forced by starvation to return. As a result, they were in debt, demoralized, and unwilling for a number of years to "turn-out" against the employers. The strike was followed by a serious downturn in trade in the

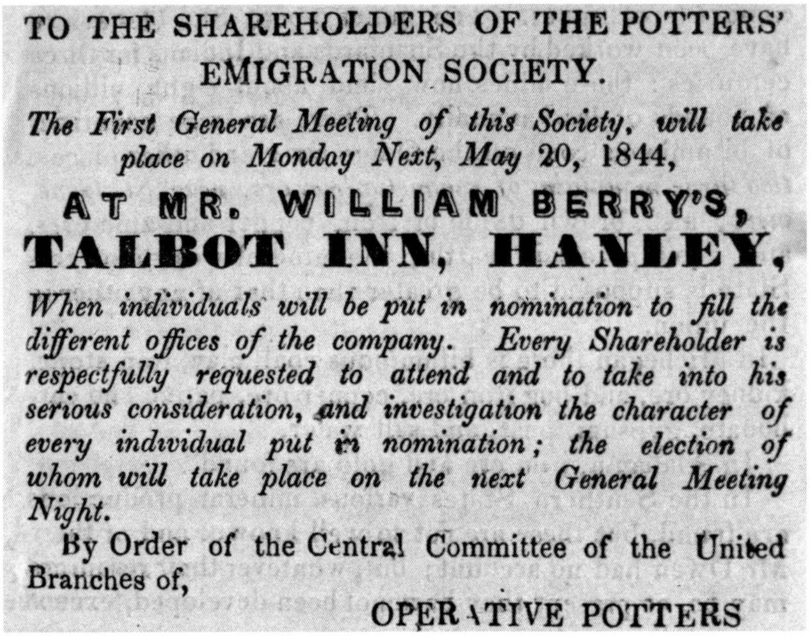

TO THE SHAREHOLDERS OF THE POTTERS' EMIGRATION SOCIETY.

The First General Meeting of this Society, will take place on Monday Next, May 20, 1844,

AT MR. WILLIAM BERRY'S,

TALBOT INN, HANLEY,

When individuals will be put in nomination to fill the different offices of the company. Every Shareholder is respectfully requested to attend and to take into his serious consideration, and investigation the character of every individual put in nomination; the election of whom will take place on the next General Meeting Night.

By Order of the Central Committee of the United Branches of,

OPERATIVE POTTERS

Figure 5 Notice to the "Shareholders of the Potters' Emigration Society" in *The Potters' Examiner and Workman's Advocate*, May 18, 1844. In May 1844 the United Branches of Operative Potters union formed The Potters' Joint Stock Emigration Society and Savings Fund.

1840s. Unemployment was on the rise, as were former hiring and wage abuses, including the now illegal truck system. A new union—the United Branches of Operative Potters—was formed in 1843. As an alternative to direct, aggressive action against employers, the new union proposed emigration to remove surplus labor from the market and give the remaining workers a better bargaining position.

In May 1844 the union's Central Committee formed The Potters' Joint Stock Emigration Society and Savings Fund.[17] They decided to raise a levy of one pound per man for the purchase of 12,000 acres of land in one of America's western states.[18] This acreage would be divided into allotments of twenty acres, with five acres of each to be fenced, planted, and provided with a house before the immigrants' arrival. Union members, and their families, would receive an allotment of land by lottery and have all their emigration expenses paid to settle them in a new life, not as potters, but as farmers.

This was the era of the "Hungry Forties" in Britain. Trade and the economy were bad. In the same year that the Emigration Society was founded, machinery was introduced by the pottery employers. The plight of the hand-loom weavers of the neighboring county of Lancashire was making national headlines. Replaced by mechanically operated looms, these workers, who only a few years earlier had been the highest paid workers in the massive textile industry, were now starving by the hundreds. In 1844 *The Potter's Examiner and Workman's Advocate* reported that the manufacturer C. J. Mason of Fenton had openly installed a "jigger," or plate-making machine, capable of turning out sixty to one hundred dozen saucers a day. The machine did not require a skilled plate maker but could be operated by a woman. The article went on to say that factories in northeast England already had cup-making machines. Operated by two women, they were as productive as "six middling workmen"; so that one woman could produce sixty dozen cups for two shillings, whereas a man's wages for making the same number without machinery would range from fifteen to seventeen shillings.[19] The fear aroused by the introduction of this new technology was another argument in favor of the union's emigration scheme.

The skilled men who, as throwers and flat ware and hollow ware pressers, made up a great part of the potters' union rallied to support the Central Committee in opposing the introduction of machinery, while *The Examiner* wholeheartedly promoted the cause of emigration.[20] The editor, William Evans, filled the paper with articles and editorials recommending emigration, with poetry and dramatic sketches eulogizing "Our Home in the West," and, more practically, with advertisements aimed at emigrants.[21]

The tone of the newspaper was utterly different than that of Wedgwood's pamphlet written sixty years earlier. Wedgwood had stressed the dangers of overseas travel, the unfamiliar qualities of a foreign country, the uncertain prospects in a new land, and the alienation and homesickness that the emigrant would experience. Under Evans' editorship, there was an almost religious fervor in depicting America as a promised land, an earthly paradise, and emigration itself as a means of salvation for the working potter.

Although the Potters' Emigration Society intended to send people overseas to become farmers, it could see that many might choose to emigrate, with or without the support of the society, to become potters. "And why not?" asked *The Examiner*:

> It has been stated, that to remove the surplus labourers of the potting districts of this empire to agricultural homes on the free prairies of America will be to ruin the potting trade of this country, by sending individuals away who would ultimately take our trade from us by commencing potting themselves . . . [this] has no foundation in truth from the following several reasons:
>
> 1st. The thirty-per-cent duty placed on all imported potting goods, entering the American market, amounts almost to a prohibition, and, consequently, denies to us an extensive market, which we might otherwise possess.
>
> 2nd. These establishing of the manufacture of porcelain and earthenware in the United States of America would be to create a demand for British potters, without the slightest injury to the potting business of this empire. The thirty-per-cent duty excludes our goods to a certain extent from the American market; consequently there is a large population in the United States who are in want of our goods, and whom a few hundreds of potters from this country would be able to supply, with benefit to themselves, and without injury to us.
>
> 3rd. In an operative point of view, it matters little to us, as working men, to what quarter of the globe our trade may go, so that that quarter be healthy in climate, free in its institutions, and pays a good price for labour; for wherever pots are to be made, there must be potters to make them. Potters are not the production of a day; and if the potting business of this country is to be removed, those who remove it must take potters to establish it.
>
> 4th. The United States does not require any further information for the establishing of potting:—it is already established: the principles are there, and there are hundreds of potters working those principles.[22]

The Examiner was perfectly correct. In the 1840s emigration was in the air and, without waiting for the Potters' Emigration Society to begin its operations, many potters were emigrating independently. Few were possessed of sufficient funds to consider setting up as master potters; most would seek employment in the growing American industry.

Enoch Bradshaw was a union member who, with five colleagues—William Mountford, Thomas Cartwright, George Garner, John Howson, and a Mr. Stacey—set out for America in June 1844.[23] Bradshaw gave some idea of the spirit that moved the small group in a letter published by *The Examiner* shortly before departing:

> My mind is cheered with the prospect of realizing by honest industry, that position in society, and those comforts of life, denied to me in the land of my birth. Nevertheless, although my mind is cheered, I feel a heaviness at heart in leaving the companions of my youth; leaving them to the same ruthless power, and the same necessitous circumstances, that are forcing me across the broad Atlantic. For them I feel that the hand of tyranny will still be raised, that the strugglings for bread will still be hard, and that the same monotonous rounds of toil and ill requited labour will be their fate until home, rural homes, are secured for the redundant hands

> of the potting business. For myself I feel there is a home for me in the land of my adoption. Already I feel that I am free from the trammels and tyrannies of English factory existence;—that I may exercise the *dignity of a man* without *offending* the creatures of commerce. A purer atmosphere and a freer existence are before me: and whether I settle in the city, or on the prairie, my prayers will be for you; that we may meet again under more happy circumstances, is the deep-felt wish of my heart.[24]

Bradshaw had been an ovenman living and working in Hanley. A member of the Ovenmen's branch of the Union of Operative Potters, he was presented by his fellow members with five pounds on his departure for America, a significant gift considering the sum was equal to more than a skilled man's monthly wage.[25] His departure had been precipitated by dismissal from his job because of union affiliation and, presumably, for being an active correspondent to *The Examiner*.[26] From the first, one of the aims of the emigration society was to help prevent starvation and provide asylum for those union members blacklisted by their employers:

> We intend to send the most industrious and honest men there are in the Potteries, as we intend this colony to be an asylum for those who have the BLACK mark put upon them, or, in other words, for those who are turned adrift for their integrity to the Union.[27]

Bradshaw's letter was one of a number, written by intending or actual emigrants, printed by *The Examiner* to support the society. The letters were drawn from a wide variety of sources—from Staffordshire men who had emigrated independently to become farmers or potters, as well as from members of other emigration societies. Although the letters had been carefully selected by *The Examiner*'s editor to support the union's argument in favor of emigration, they are illuminating for other reasons. They depicted the urgency of the emigrants, not only to give an account of their new way of life but also to encourage their friends and relatives to join them.

The letters fall into two main groups: those from emigrants who had become farmers and those who had found journeyman's work as potters at established workshops, or who had set up in business for themselves. The latter are some of the most interesting since they reveal the difficulties and triumphs attendant on establishing their industry in a new country.

In the United States, many Staffordshire potters settled near the Mississippi River. The towns of Alton, Chester, and Nauvoo, Illinois, were popular in the early 1840s as were St. Louis, Missouri, and the surrounding district.[28] Some settled farther east at East Liverpool and Zanesville, Ohio. The existence of pottery making and the presence of other Staffordshire people in the Alton and St. Louis areas of the Mississippi attracted other immigrants.

Two letters from brothers Walter and Thomas Croxton, who were working as potters at Alton in the early 1840s, offer interesting information about their business:[29]

> From its drawing toward Martinmas, we thought proper to take stock. When we found that the value of our goods, at the factory, amounted to

about eight hundred dollars.[30] We are worth about four hundred dollars in clear property! Tell William he may sell my violin and appropriate the money towards defraying his expences in coming to us, for we want him to be here as soon as he can make it convenient to come.

Mr Robinson and Mr Goodwin[31] and families, Mr Berrisford[32] and Mr James came all in good health, and the day after their arrival, we had a goose for supper—and joyful time we had with the exception of Mrs Robinson, who, not having previously heard of her son William being lost, was very unhappy. They will have to live with us until they can procure houses for themselves: houses are very scarce at present. We have engaged Mr Tams to work for us.

The first time we drew our kiln, I wish you had been here to have seen the sight. There was such a one that I never expected to see. There were three potsellers, with their waggons, waiting for the ware, as it came out of the kiln. All the ware was drawn, packed, and sold before dinner. The weather is milder now than it was at this time last year, for we were obliged then to cease work, from the frost being so severe; but now we are as busy as we can be. Give our love to my father, mother, brothers and sisters; and tell them all, they must come to us as soon as they can for we want them to be with us. Tell my father that he must not think of farming for the first twelve months after he come here, as he will do better by potting, for we often want his assistance. If he were with us, we should do much better than we are doing, although we are in good circumstances as could be expected, from our being but young men, and in a strange land.[33]

The next edition of *The Examiner* printed a second letter from the brothers.

I had better proceed at once to let you know how we are progressing in potting. First, then, we have built our new kiln, and a very pretty one it is, too; and, as the Americans say, "I guess it will shine when it is fired, full of glost ware;" which circumstance will not be long before it takes place; and then I should like for the whole of you to be here, that you may see the reward of persevering industry. Our old slip kiln, not being large enough for our present purposes, we have built another this week, which is 21 feet long by 5 feet wide. We have engaged a saggar-maker, a dish-maker, a hollow-ware presser, a man to throw coarse ware, and now we are going to send to St. Lewis for a slip maker. I will now tell my brother B. a few of our prices, so that, if he thinks he can earn at those prices sufficient to purchase a little bread and a few potatoes, we should like him to come, as we will undertake to find him plenty of beef and pork to them; although, perhaps, when he comes here, we shall find him something else to do. For ewers we pay 4*s*. per dozen,[34] for chambers 4*s*.6*d*.; for cover-dishes, 3*s*.3*d*.; for 4's jugs, plain, 3*s*.3*d*. per dozen,[35] and 12's French, 2*s*.11*d*.; for round nappies 12*s*.5*d*. per dozen,[36] 11's, 4 1/2*d*.; 10's, 4*d*.; 9's, 3 1/2*d*.; 8's, 7's, 6's, 2 1/2*d*. per dozen; and for plates, twifflers, and muffins, 4*s*.2*d*. per score.[37] Such are our prices! You must excuse my not writing sooner, as I have been waiting for the finishing of our kiln.[38]

Although the Alton potters' surname is not given in the two letters, they were mentioned by a number of Staffordshire men writing home including Benjamin Berrisford. Thomas Gotham settled at St. Louis in 1842 and wrote home about the pottery being made nearby:

About six miles from the city there is China clay, flint stones and coals. At Commerce, 400 miles from St. Louis, in the state of Illinois, there is plenty of clay. In Alton there is also plenty of clay, it belongs to a native American named Harrison.[39]

Figure 6 "Important to Emigrants" in *The Potters' Examiner and Workman's Advocate,* November 2, 1844. The editor filled the paper with articles and editorials recommending emigration, with poetry and dramatic sketches eulogizing America as a promised land, and, more practically, with enticing advertisements.

EXAMINER,

IMPORTANT TO EMIGRANTS!!!

For New Orleans, and the Western part of the United States of America, the fine

Fast Sailing American Ship "Chatham,"

CAPTAIN NASON,

470 ***Tons Register,*** 800 ***Tons Burthen, will Sail from Liverpool for New Orleans, on the 6th November,***

Which will take Passengers, and furnish them with all necessary Provisions for the Voyage, at the following low rates:- ***Forward Steerage, £4:—After Steerage, or Second Cabin, £5:—Separate Rooms in ditto, (for Families desirous of being more select,) £6:—Children under 14 years, Half Price; Infants under twelve months, Free.***

LIST OF PROVISIONS SUPPLIED.

Biscuit	35	Pounds.	Beef and Pork	12	Pounds.
Flour	10	..	Tea	¼	..
Oatmeal	10	..	Coffee	1	..
Potatoes	90	..	Sugar	4	..
Barley	2	..	Butter	5	..
Rice	2	..	Cheese	3	..
Peas	2	..			

The above Fares include Head Money at New Orleans, and every other charge. Parties intending to avail themselves of the above opportunity, must remit £1, by Post Office Order, or otherwise, on, or before Nov. 3rd, stating which place they wish to have Berths secured in.

Those engaging earliest, will have the best Berths reserved for them. Another Ship will be despatched for New Orleans, on the above terms, on the 20th of November.

APPLY TO

ROBERT E. WALKER,

No. 11, Goree Piazza, Liverpool,

Who continues to despatch fine first-class Ships, to New York, Boston, Baltimore, and Philadelphia.

Thomas and Walter Croxton are pot-making in Alton; they have been having as much clay as they wanted of Harrison; but Harrison has lately got a man from the Potteries, whose name is Robinson,[40] to make pots for him, and since he came, Harrison won't let them have any more clay. I have seen Thomas and Walter Croxton; they have told me that they should have done well had they contrived to get more clay from Harrison. I have seen the ware that they have made, it is a very good yellow ware. A man could do very well if he could get a good glaze; the china clay is got from Commerce; and there are plenty of coals at fourpence a bushel. There is plenty of clay in Indiana, where James Clews was potting. Thomas Croxton is going to Indiana to see if he can take the Pottery that James Clews was at.[41]

Figure 7 "Notice to Emigrants" in *The Potters' Examiner and Workman's Advocate*. This advertisement, with minor changes, appeared every week from April 6, 1844, to October 26, 1844.

NOTICE TO EMIGRANTS.

FITZHUGH, WALKER, AND Co., 12, GOREE PIAZZAS,

LIVERPOOL,

Despatch Fine First-class American Ships,

Of large Tonnage, for the following Ports, viz:

NEW YORK,	**BOSTON,**
PHILADELPHIA,	**and**
BALTIMORE,	**NEW ORLEANS,**

And which are intended to sail punctually on their appointed days, They are fitted up expressly for the comfort and convenience of Cabin, Second Cabin, and Steerage Passengers. Persons about to emigrate, may save themselves the expense and delay of waiting in Liverpool, by writing a letter addressed as above, which will be immediately answered, the lowest Price of Passage told them, and they will be enabled to go direct on board the Ship, immediately on their arrival in Liverpool, thus saving the Expense of Lodging, &c. And should F. W. and Co., detain any Ship after the appointed Time, Passengers will be paid for detention.

Passengers will be found by the Ships with the full quantity of Biscuit, Flour, Oatmeal, Rice, and Potatoes, according to Act of Parliament, without extra charge.

☞ Every information will be given by applying as above, or to Mr. Thomas Coward, King Street, Burslem.

Another member of the Croxton family, Elijah, was potting across the river at St. Louis:

> You will be wanting to know how we are getting along: well I can tell you; we are doing very well. I am receiving every week—no play weeks—£1 9*s*.2*d*.; and provisions being so cheap here, you will conclude that we are not wanting for much.[42] We are quite busy at work, burning as fast as we can make. There are twelve men and four boys at work; we are doing a good business, considering all things.
>
> Thomas Biddulph . . . is making uncovered Chamber Pots at 3*d*. each. I heard him say last week that a waggon and horses should not draw him back. He is very comfortably fixed; he can get twenty-five shillings a week without hurting himself. He can get more than that if he likes; there is no stint.[43]

Although many families emigrated together, very often the husband would go ahead to establish himself and send money home to his family for their journey. In 1845 John and Elisha Poole emigrated from Cobridge, Stoke-on-Trent, to Missouri. Both quickly gained employment at a country pottery and wrote home with accounts of how they found America and their plans:

> We found out [Elijah] Croxton's family, [at St. Louis] from John Ridgway's Manufactory.[44] We dined with them several times. They could have found us work, had they had a thrower . . . . We met at Croxton's with an American, who wanted a Turner. He lived about eighty miles from St. Louis. I engaged to go with him to see what could be done. When I got there I found a poorly constructed lathe and throwing wheel,

> and every thing in a rough state for Potting. He was a coarse ware manufacturer. Well, we engaged to begin to make pots, he finding fixtures and every thing to our use. He is also finding Board and Lodging till we have ware ready for the market; we are then to take half of the profits. We have built a slip kiln, and a small oven; and have put the lathe and wheel in repair. We have fired a biscuit oven, and very well it looks. The oven will hold one hundred dollars' worth, or twenty pounds in your money. At the least calculation we shall make a Oven a week; but it is very likely that we shall make three a fortnight. We get plenty of good clay for the fetching from a short distance; and plenty of good decomposed flint that wants no grinding. We have nothing to pay for, except glaze, and that costs us very little, as we grind it ourselves. Ours is the only white ware Pottery in the state of Missouri. We get three shillings for a fours jug; two shillings for six cups and six saucers, and for other things accordingly. This is the place for Potting; if a Potter has a chance of making his fortune it is now. We have plenty of government land, containing potting materials at five shillings an acre.
>
> I happened to go in a store in the small Town in which we live. To my surprise, I saw at the bottom of a printed mug "T. J. and J. Mayer."[45] I began to look about me and I saw Albert Cups of my own turning from Mayer's!
>
> Give our love to our Wives and tell them to kiss the children for us. Tell them the reason why we did not write to them first was, we resolved to either send for them this fall, or to send something to support them on till we could send for them . . . . Tell our Wives to keep up their hearts. In a few weeks money will tumble in upon us, and we shall be able to send each of them a letter worth receiving.[46]

Months later Elisha Poole added, "I say if a Potter cannot make his fortune here, he does not deserve the name of a Potter."

It is also possible, through the letters published in *The Examiner,* to follow the careers of Enoch Bradshaw and his five companions once they arrived in America. Bradshaw's departure may have been precipitated by his employers finding disfavor with his union activities, but two of his companions, George Garner and John Howson, had contemplated their departure for some time. Howson was the third of his family to emigrate, joining his brothers, Bernard, who was already working in East Liverpool, Ohio, and Thomas, then working in Louisville, Kentucky. Bernard Howson had written to John from East Liverpool in September 1843:[47]

> Dear Brothers and Sisters
>
> After a long silence I, at last, commence writing to you . . . . I received a letter by Mrs Goodwin, and was glad to hear of your being all well . . . . I understand that times are very bad with you. You said nothing in your last letter about coming to America. If you think of doing so you need not be afraid. You may , if you can, sell my interest in that house at Newcastle, and receive what rent there is due to me, and devote the whole to your own use . . . .[48] Times are rather dull except in Potting. There are in this place, three small Factories; I am throwing at one. John Goodwin, a handler from Ashby Wolds,[49] is throwing at another, and a Turner from the same place, named Edward Bennett, is throwing at the third. I am getting 87 cents per score for throwing and 7 cents for turning; so now you can judge in regard to price and whether a thrower be wanted here or not. There is no thrower in this (western) country, except G. Nixon, and he is at Troy.[50] I think Potting has just taken a start. There is as good ware made in this place as ever I saw, with the exception of being short of

Colours. If you come, bring with you such things that you know are useful for Colouring. I wrote to my brother [Thomas Howson] about a week ago, requesting him to come up here as a presser and a handler are wanted badly. I have not received any answer at present. He is at Louisville, making stoneware. If you can purchase and bring with you some black printing colours and a plate ready for using, I think they would be of great use. If you should not come, I wish you would send me those articles by some friend that is coming near to this place, which is about 45 miles below Petersburg.

Since writing the above, Mr Goodwin and Mr Potts, have each received a letter; according to which I am at a loss to know what you do to make a living . . . . After reading both letters, and seeing the price of provision and witnessing the fact that Potters, good workmen, are obliged to work on a road leading from Burslem to Leek for one shilling per day, and hundreds I understand cannot get work at that price, some of them finding their own tools, I say, at once, leave such a country: for what I ask, can be the prospect of yourself and children under circumstances like these . . . . If you can sell the property, hesitate not one moment to make use of it to escape from such distress, for you may be convinced that you cannot make worse your condition if you share any in the misery that is abroad in your land . . . . Mr Potts and family wished me to remember them to their Father and Mother . . . . They have removed to Pittsburgh and are doing well at Potting.[51]

John Howson, in Stoke-on-Trent, also received a letter from a Rockingham ware potter at Utica, New York, a Mr. Walker, who was operating a small-scale workshop:

I have done full as well as I expected by myself; but could have done much better by having an assistant. You will see what a perplexing job I have had, having had everything to do myself. I've been bricklayer and carpenter and smith; I've put up my shop and built my kiln; have been modeller and mould-maker, sagar-maker, brown-dipper, plain slip-maker and presser and have gone up and down the country for miles, seeking &c. &c. Now, by this time, I think you will say, I must have been pretty busy these last twelve months.

I have also further to add, I've succeeded in making an excellent and beautiful common earthenware, the best in the United States, and as fine a glaze as ever you saw, even on that of the great Wedgwood Rockingham! I am quite satisfied, there is a comfortable business to be done here, preferable to any thing you can do in England with a small capital, against so powerful a competition as there is in the British market. I do not wish to entice you away; but should you think well to come to this country, I should always be glad to see you; and if you did not think well to stop here, this would not be out of the road for your going to Kentucky, to your brothers; for by this route, you would have rivers and canals all the way, and the expenses would be about one halfpenny per mile! My place is but small but very convenient; and could soon be made large enough for a thrower. My ware sells well, and at good prices, and, I think, I can do much better this way than working journeyman's work. I am making Tea-Pots, Sugars, Milks, Pitchers, Flower-Pots, Bowls, Cups, Saucers, and some Toys. I could sell Chamber-ware and thrown Tea-Pots would come cheaper than pressed ones.

Here is an extensive and wealthy country of more than one thousand miles in length, all inland and without any opposition in fine kind of ware! Surely the little ware made at one works, would only be like a crab in a coal-pit! Here is some red-ware works, but the ware is bad beyond descriptions, and can never do me any harm. I fire with wood the same as the Americans, and have got to be a pretty good Fireman, buiscuit and glaze! This is a beautiful little City, about fifteen thousand inhabitants, and provisions very cheap. It lies on the Erie canal, about 250 miles from New York; water all the way. The Americans have put a good duty on English pottery—30 per cent. This and carriage and breakage make a good profit to a works here and the good can be made as cheap here as in the Potteries. The best Ball Clay is about 25 *s*[hillings] per ton; and the clay I am useing, I get, for carriage;—1s *6d* per ton . . . . I've found clays that make as good ware as any in the Potteries! But will require a little capital to bring them into the market.

The winter is setting in, frost and snow. I've gotten a good stove and a close little room, and plenty of wood for fire; and hope not to be stopp'd by the weather. I've gotten clay, down in the celler, to last me though the winter; I hope to be pretty busy.

Please to let me here from you soon and remember me to all old friends. I think John Bailey would be a useful hand to me. Ask him if he should like to come to America.[52]

Walker also wrote to George Garner who was contemplating emigration, again showing how well his business was doing and how he was thriving:

Dear Sir

Your favour of the 26th February I've just received. I beg to say, I am in treaty with a potter, a neighbour of yours, as a partner and fellow-workman [John Howson], but should he not come, I shall be happy to treat with you. I am in expectation of his final reply every day: until then I cannot speak positively or conclusively. However, I will say this much, I should have no objection to a second partner, should he be agreeable. I have no doubt of plenty of business for three of us. My place is small; only one potting room, and a small kiln, holds seven bungs of saggars; saggarhouse, and wood shed, and a little house I live in; it's plenty large enough for me, but must be enlarged when more come. I shall want a larger potting room, and larger kiln. The ware I am making at present is common red earthen, with a fine Rockingham glaze on; it sells well; it is the best ware in the United States of the kind. I can make any other kind of ware here; but would require more capital. You did not name any capital you could employ in the business. I judge you have some spare money, by you naming land or farming for that will require a little money . . . . Before you can receive this my partner will have left the Potteries, otherwise I would have expected you to have called on him.[53] The mould you name would be very useful, in case you should come. I think potting would suit you better than farming; working on the land is very hard work for a person that has not been used to it. I should like to see a good large establishment here! There is plenty of scope for business here. You name making bowls without the lathe: this would be desirable and they are things that would sell here . . . . You name coming out in the fall. I beg to say you cannot do anything on a farm, new lands particularly, in winter: you will have to live out of your pocket altogether till next summer. You can think of this . . . . My partner that is coming is a working man, but he has gotten a little money to put in the business; and as soon as he arrives I will name your business to him. In the mean time you had better write me again, when you have thought the contents of this letter over, and let me know what money you think you can put in the business, and you may rely on an immediate reply, conclusively.[54]

Knowing of Walker's arrangement with John Howson, Garner decided against going to Utica. Instead he, Enoch Bradshaw, and Thomas Cartwright traveled to East Liverpool, Ohio. He wrote to a correspondent giving an account of how they had fared:

> We were well received at East Liverpool by a many that came from the Potteries, together with others from Ashby-wholds.[55] In three days after we got in, Bradshaw, Cartwright and myself began to work. Cartwright was turning after me;[56] and Bradshaw began in the kiln at John Goodwin's. John Goodwin wanted me to take a share with him, in the business, but I declined. I told him I did not intend to go into business until spring. By that time I shall know a little more of the country. It would be unwise of me to commence in business as soon as I got in. There are those that have, and have lost their money to teach them sense.
>
> But I feel more favourable to the potting business, and have determined to enter into the business in spring. And, in order to gain information respecting the sale of the ware, I have been through Pittsburgh, and the surrounding markets, and I find there are markets open to receive every cup of ware that is made. The Derbyshire ware cannot come into these markets, under one dollar per dozen, that is unhandled ware—handled, a deal higher. Now there can be as good a body as your citron body got up here, and sold at thirty per cent less than the Derbyshire. This you may easily infer, because there is a duty of 30 percent on your English pottery. This, with breakage, makes it higher. I have seen in one of the respectable houses in Pittsburgh, white cream-coloured dishes sold at six dollars per dozen. Now there can be good yellow-ware dishes got up here and sold at 70 cents per dozen—2*s*.4*d*. your money.
>
> East Liverpool is full of clay and coal and contains about 7,000 inhabitants; lying on the Ohio River, 45 miles from Pittsburgh. It lies well for shipping to Cincinnati; also to New Orleans, and a many other markets. I have engaged with the Bennetts, that were potting there, to do their throwing until spring. Cartwright has engaged with them also, to turn for them. They, together with us, have left East Liverpool, and have come to Birmingham. The Bennetts have built a factory, to the amount of 4,000 dollars which is now in operation at Birmingham. I shall have a good situation. I will not recommend any potters to come out, unless they have situations to come to; but as the trade spreads potters will be wanted. But there are none wanted at present. If any potters come here they will only be in each other's way and give to the masters an opportunity of reducing wages.[57]

Trade did spread, and by 1846 Garner was back in East Liverpool working for himself.[58] Cartwright had returned to East Liverpool by March 1845, where he worked for Benjamin Harker.[59]

John Howson went, with his companions Mountford and Stacey, to join his correspondent Mr. Walker of Utica, New York. Despite Walker's promises to him of finding a successful Rockingham ware pottery on his arrival, Howson was disappointed. Eighteen months after arriving in America, he wrote to his friends in Stoke-on-Trent:

> You have often thought it strange that I have not written to you sooner; but circumstances, over which we have no control, made things very different to what we expected, when we left friends and home, so, I hope, you will excuse me, for not having written to you before. We had a pretty good passage over the Atlantic, of about 45 days and arrived safely and in

good health at New York . . . we proceeded up the Erie Canal, 90 miles, to Utica; where we stopped about nine months and where I lost about ninety dollars, beside my work, and then left . . . from whence . . . to Zanesville, where I still remain.[60]

> Things here are a little better with me. Zanesville is a pleasant town; situated on the Muskingham river; and steamboats come and go which makes it more pleasant . . . . We do not get much money; but we have every comfort that our hearts can desire; that is, in meat. We keep as good a table as any parson does; and you know they don't keep bad ones; and a good warm house, and plenty of coals to put on the fire; and plenty to cook by that fire, wishing you had only such a table to set before your family . . . . We can trade our ware for every article we want, except flour. But money is becoming more plentiful; and I think it will be greater in a little time, as the inhabitants are about to establish a State-Bank; and then we shall be better off.

> I made up my mind to give America a fair trial before I started; or else, I have had enough to have made me come back since I came to this county. But now, I am more at home, with a prospect of gaining what I have lost and my two children have the opportunity of getting a good education—far better than if they had staid in England.

> Tell Old — — — — - he might have plenty of Whiskey if he were here. But I do not drink any now as the people here are very sober; and they think very little of men that get drunk. So I have given it up altogether; and feel a deal better for having done so, both in body and mind.[61]

Although he scarcely mentions potting in his letter, John Howson was in partnership with his brother Bernard, who had joined him from East Liverpool to make yellow and Rockingham wares. The partnership, Howson and Brother, was not a success and was dissolved in December 1846. The firm continued as Howson & Hallam until about 1850,[62] and then as Howson and Son until John Howson's death in 1863. His temperance did not last; a letter written in 1851 by Sarah Tunnicliffe, wife of another English pottery owner in Zanesville, said Howson "is drunk nearly all the time and it seems to be general opinion is going to ruin very fast."[63]

Both of John Howson's partners—his brother Bernard and John Hallam—went to work at the Tunnicliffe's Pottery in Zanesville before the latter left for Kewanee, Illinois, in 1853.[64] According to Robert Adams, a descendant of the Howson family, Bernard Howson moved to Mineral, Ohio, where he started another pottery.

Mountford and Stacey went to Utica with Howson, but Mountford soon moved on, eventually settling in Whitewater, Wisconsin, where he wrote to his parents:

> I left Ohio in October 1845, for Wisconsin. I commenced work here last April 27th at pressing. I am pressing, glazing, and firing now, and I suppose I shall have to go to throwing for throwers are very scarce. I tried some of the glazes that you sent me and they work very good. I am getting one dollar a day and my board . . . I understand Mr Cartwright was come back to England and gives America a very bad account;[65] but you must not be discouraged with that; he has not travelled so far as I have in the country; he knows nothing about the country, because he did not give it a fair trial. It was just the same with me before I left Utica, but since that I have never been homesick . . . . Almost everybody that comes

> here does not like the country for the first twelve months because they are green and don't understand the customs of the country. I know you would be the happiest man alive if you were here and had a piece of land and a small pot-shop upon it.[66]

Mountford's letter crossed in the post with one from his father, which he answered within a week:

> I am sorry that my mother is so obstinate about coming to America. But I suppose the salt water is what makes her afraid. I would have liked you to have come out, very much, next Spring, as I was about to buy a house and 83 acres of land; and a brick yard; and a pottery. I could have bought the whole for two thousand dollars by paying half in ware and half in cash. The property is very cheap and all ready for business. But as you are not coming out at present I shall decline buying it.
>
> As regards C—- coming back you need not place any dependence on what he says, because he came right over and went right back, without giving the country a fair trial.[67] It was just the same with me, when I first came over I was as home sick as a dog. But when I left the State of New York the disease left me entirely; and I have never been troubled with home-sickness yet.[68]
>
> Father I know that if you should be here six months you would not return for all England is worth . . . you would not have your tyrannical masters tyrannising you to death. The masters here are not higher in station than the men who work for them. If ever I should come back, I should be mad enough to whip all the master potters that come within my reach . . . . I love the land of my birth but I utterly detest its contemptible laws and the foolish and selfish men, such as master potters, and other masters who govern the country. I mean such men as live on the fruits of poor men's labour and not satisfied with that, but they will tyrannise a poor man all but to death; pull him down in the price of his labour; cheat him out of his hard earnings; and the next will be they will kick him off their premises.[69]
>
> I hope George will come out . . . . My master has agreed to furnish him with work, if he come, at his own business. But he will have to learn to turn his own wheel.[70] I am glazing and burning, but now I have engaged to go to throwing for the coming season. I have got one more oven to fire and then I commence. Our oven holds about 400 dollars worth. I settled up with my master on the 1st of January last; and got a due bill of 139 dollars and I have earned 36 dollars since, besides my board, I can throw 100 gallons a day now; and turn my own wheel. Our ware runs from 1/2 to 4 gallons and I can throw the largest ware we make.[71]

Despite the promising letters and articles published in *The Examiner,* the union's own scheme to send potters to Wisconsin and to found an agricultural settlement was not a success. Fewer than one hundred families emigrated under the scheme, which was under funded and badly advised. The scheme was fatally wounded when it was discovered that the land purchased did not belong to the Potters' Emigration Society. It was, in fact, Indian land that had not been surveyed for settlement.[72] After six years, the society was effectively dead, and its demise brought down the United Branches of Operative Potters, which, under William Evans' guidance, had devoted much of its funds to the scheme.

Nonetheless, potters, especially those skilled workers who had managed to accumulate a small amount of capital, continued to emigrate. The majority

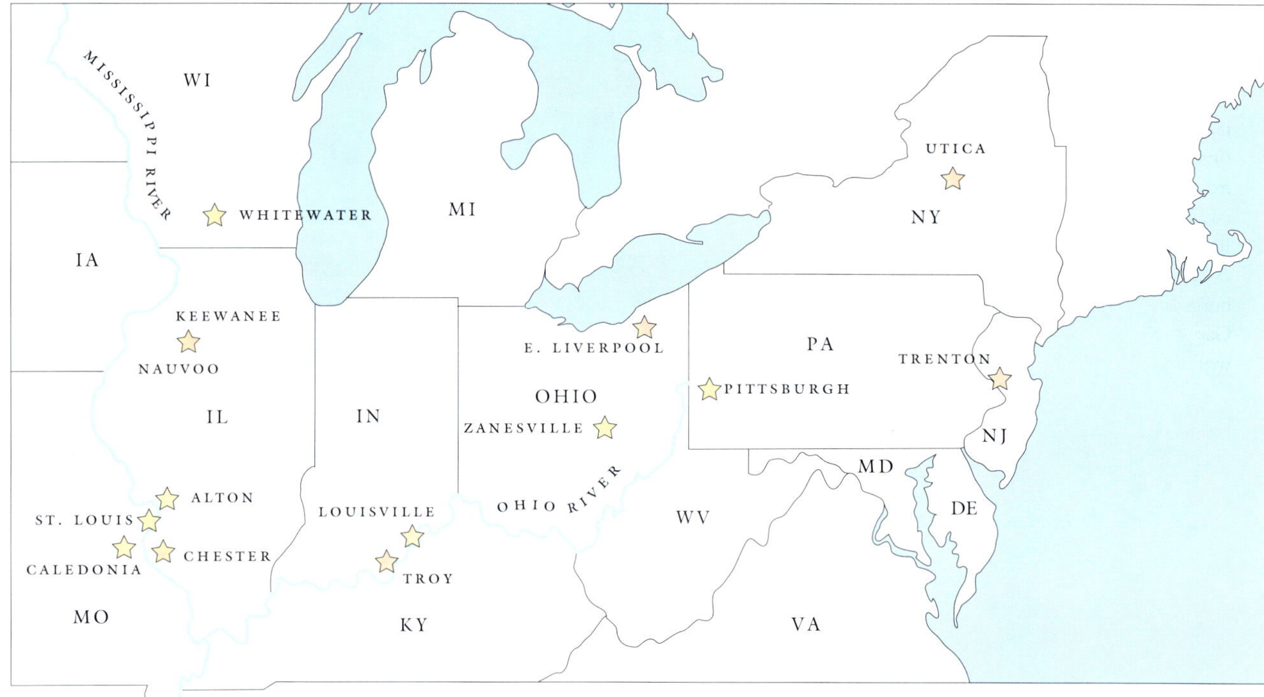

Figure 8 Map showing the locations where various immigrants mentioned in the article worked.

did not aspire to produce china or even white earthenwares. Whatever their background, almost without exception, they made what the local materials dictated.

The adaptability of the immigrant master potters, most of whom had been raised in the Staffordshire tradition, to local conditions in a foreign country must be admired. The majority of emigrating potters, however, were not master potters. These journeyman potters sought employment at established production centers, such as East Liverpool, Ohio, where by 1850 English-born potters composed over seventy percent of the workforce.[73]

Some of the unfavorable conditions left behind in England were also found in America. In 1845 Thomas Cartwright, and many others, were paid partly in cash and partly in goods due to the lack of ready money, and during the 1840s and 1850s there were several disputes and turn outs or strikes over paying in truck.[74] Annual hiring and payment "good from oven" were not applied, however, in the United States, although they remained part of the Staffordshire hiring practice until the twentieth century.[75]

It was economic necessity that drove most potters and their families to emigrate. The 1840s saw the first major wave, but potters continued to travel to America throughout the century. The rate of emigration fluctuated, reflecting both the state of the English economy and the time of year. One hopeful mother wrote:

> I should think potting is good in America—there is going a great many potters there—there went seventy in one lot from Longport Station about five weeks ago—they went to East Liverpool. There went two young men from the factory where my son works a few months ago—they went to Trenton, New Jersey. It is hiring time here with the potters—they have all had notice of a reduction.[76]

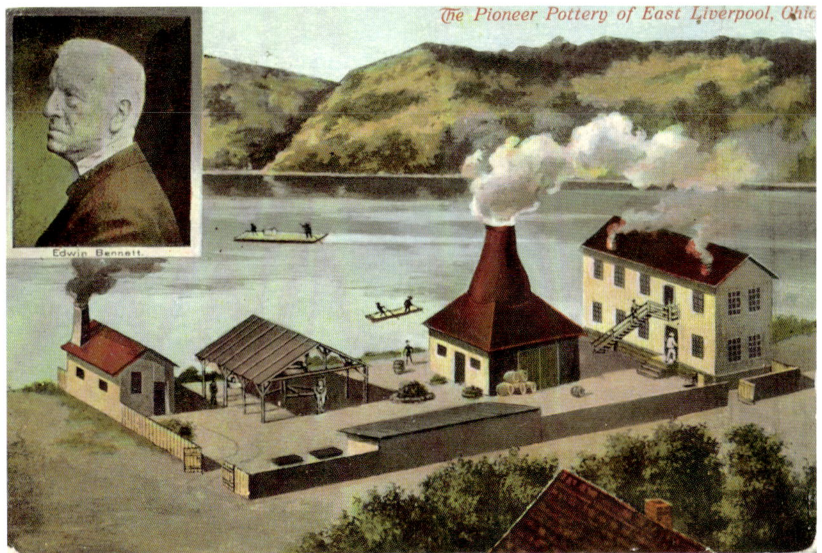

Figure 9 Postcard, ca. 1915. *The Pioneer Pottery of East Liverpool, Ohio.* (Private collection.) This single-kiln pottery was built by James Bennett on the Ohio River in 1840. Bennett's three brothers, Edwin (inset), Daniel, and William, emigrated from England the following year. Bennett and Bros. produced yellow ware and Rockingham ware in East Liverpool until 1844, when the firm moved to the Pittsburgh area. There thrower George Garner, a Staffordshire immigrant, worked for the Bennetts in 1844.

In the latter part of the nineteenth century, American factories were actively seeking workers from Stoke-on-Trent, especially as those factories introduced white wares. In 1879 during a strike at East Liverpool, manufacturers sent for workers from Staffordshire, and more than thirty emigrated to be joined later by their families.[77]

By this date immigrant potters were finding that in the United States working conditions were comparable to those they were leaving, as well as having higher pay and a better standard of living. There was an established industry to take them in with the same division of labor and familiar types of ware: common earthenware, white granite, and china. In addition, travel was much easier and faster; railways and steamships had replaced canal boats and sailing ships.

What is clear from the letters published in *The Examiner* between 1843 and 1847 was the reliance of pioneers on a network of family and neighborly ties to establish themselves in their new country, at least initially. The letters also reflected the immigrants' mood. Whether they went to work in existing factories, or had hopes of setting up their own workshop, they were without exception happy that they had left the British class system behind. The main theme of the letters was the high standard of living that the immigrants found in America. Cash payments might be in short supply, and manufactured goods expensive in remote areas, but food was cheap and plentiful. These positive aspects of American life were constantly stressed by *The Examiner,* giving an almost evangelical tone to the argument for emigration. Even though the distance and costs involved meant that many immigrants would never see their English homes again, most urged their relations not to fear the ocean but to have the courage to join them. Perhaps, most significantly, the published letters reveal the authentic, but rarely heard, voices of a number of ordinary working men and women who were bold enough to seek their "Home in the West."

ACKNOWLEDGMENTS

For assistance with this article the author thanks Robert Adams, Margaret Beard, Chris Latimer, and all the staff of the Stoke-on-Trent Archive Service at Hanley Library, and Don Carpentier of the Eastfield Foundation, East Nassau, New York.

1. J. M., "The Pioneers Song," dated Tunstall April 9, 1845, printed in *The Potters' Examiner and Workman's Advocate* 3, no. 21 (April 19, 1845): 168. "The Bastille" was a common name for the workhouse in Victorian England; the institution to which those unable to support themselves through old age, sickness, or unemployment were sent by their parish authorities to receive "indoor relief" from their poverty.

2. The weekly newspaper was founded in Hanley, Stoke-on-Trent, by the United Branches of Operative Potters and published from 1837 to 1847. It ceased publication briefly and then reappeared as *The Potters' Examiner and Emigrants' Advocate* (hereafter *PE&WA*).

3. "Petition to Parliament from the Staffordshire Potters, 1762," quoted in Arnold R. Mountford, *The Illustrated Guide to Staffordshire Salt-Glazed Stoneware* (London: Barrie & Jenkins, 1971), p. 11.

4. Frank Burchill and R. Ross, *A History of the Potters' Union* (Stoke-on-Trent, Eng.: Ceramic & Allied Trades Union, 1977), p. 27.

5. Elizabeth Adams and D. Redstone, *Bow Porcelain* (London: Faber & Faber, 1981), pp. 80–81.

6. William Cookworthy to Richard Hingston, May 30, 1745, in Hugh Owen, *Two Centuries of Ceramic Art in Bristol* (Gloucester, Eng.: privately printed for the author by J. Bellows, 1873), p. 7.

7. Josiah Wedgwood to Thomas Bentley, May 20, 1767, to June 15, 1767, *Letters of Josiah Wedgwood,* edited by Lady K. E. Farrer, 3 vols. (Manchester, Eng.: Morten, Ltd., 1903), 1:138–56. See also Bradford L. Rauschenburg, "'A Clay as white as Lime of Which There is a Design formed by Some Gentlemen to Make China': The American and English Search for Cherokee Clay in South Carolina 1745–1775," *Journal of Early Southern Decorative Arts* 17, no. 2 (November 1991): 67–79.

8. Josiah Wedgwood, *An Address to the Workmen in the Pottery, on the Subject of Entering into the Service of Foreign Manufacturers,* 1783, reprinted in full in Bradford L. Rauschenburg, "John Bartlam Who Established 'new Pottworks in South Carolina' and Became the First Successful Creamware Potter in America," *Journal of Early Southern Decorative Arts* 17, no. 2 (November 1991): appendix 1, 50–57.

9. Ibid.

10. Ibid.

11. Ibid.

12. Josiah Wedgwood to Thomas Bentley, June 23, 1775, Farrer, ed., *Letters of Josiah Wedgwood,* vol. 2, pp. 227–28.

13. The pottery industry had continued to expand in the early nineteenth century with exports to America alone rising from £59,665 in 1805 to £326,3393 by 1815. The postwar slump had seen exports fall by more than three-quarters to £76,552 in 1820, but within five years rose to £182,642. Neil Ewins, "Supplying the Present Wants of Our Yankee Cousins: Staffordshire Ceramics and the American Market 1771–1880," *Journal of Ceramic History* 1 (Stoke-on-Trent, Eng.: City Museum and Art Gallery, 1997), 15: 7.

14. Designed to prevent workers combining together and forming unions.

15. Piecework was, and still is, the usual method of pay in the Staffordshire potteries. Workers do not receive a set weekly wage but are paid by how much ware they produce by the end of the week.

16. Burchill and Ross, *A History of the Potters' Union,* pp. 9–11.

17. The Potters' Joint Stock Emigration Society and Savings Fund was one of only a number of similar schemes, including the Temperance Emigration Society founded at Sheffield in 1842. It was unusual in being trade specific.

18. Wisconsin was decided on and the settlement of Pottersville established in 1845.

19. "Candour," "A Few Thoughts on Machinery, Addressed to the United Branches of Operative Potters," *PE&WA* 2, no. 24 (November 9, 1844): 186–87.

20. There were approximately two thousand union members in the district. Burchill and Ross, *A History of the Potters' Union,* p. 84.

21. "Our Home in the West" was a term regularly used in the pages of *The Examiner.* Notably it is the heading of a play by "Quizicus" subtitled "A Dialogue between Old Tom Potts and his Brother Joe" in *PE&WA* 2, no. 9 (July 27, 1844): 67–69; and the title of a poem in ibid., nos. 23 and 24 (November 2 and 9, 1844).

22. Editorial article by "Mentor" (William Evans' pseudonym) in *PE&WA* 2, no. 8 (July 20, 1844): 57–59.

23. Stacey's Christian name is not given in *The Examiner* article, nor in the subsequent letters from his companions. Their departure was marked by a dinner given by the United Branches of Operative Potters to "Messrs. Howson, Garner and Bradshaw," and notice that "Messrs. Cartwright, Stacey and Mountford" had also announced their emigration. *PE&WA* 2, no. 3 (June 15, 1844): 20.

24. Letter from Enoch Bradshaw of Hanley, dated June 9, 1844, in *PE&WA* 2, no. 3 (June 15, 1844): 19–20. On arriving in America, Bradshaw, Garner, and Cartwright made their way to East Liverpool, Ohio, where they quickly got employment. Bradshaw thrived there. In 1854 he was commissioned to conduct a mid-decade census of the city. In 1889 he started the *East Liverpool Democrat,* which was published until 1876, and he was still writing to the town council in 1884. William C. Gates, Jr., *City of Hills and Kilns: Life and Work in East Liverpool, Ohio* (East Liverpool, Ohio: East Liverpool Historical Society, 1984).

25. Approximately $25, a significant gift when a skilled man's wage averaged $5 to $8 per week.

26. A letter from the Central Board of Ovenmen in *PE&WA* 2, no. 5 (June 29, 1844): 39 stated: "Your Central Committee have responded to your generally expressed wish, in rendering to our worthy friend and brother Enoch Bradshaw, some little pecuniary assistance, to enable him to exchange this land of persecution and mental thraldom, for one of liberty, where he may speak or write an honestly conceived opinion without fear of being proscribed or marked by his fellow men as a dangerous member of society. Your Committee feel assured that you will feel individually as they do an inward indescribable satisfaction . . . in having assisted a brother in the time of need—in contributing your mite towards frustrating the machinations of those who wished to throw him upon our funds; in fact to assist a fellow creature to earn a livelihood by honest industry in a foreign land which was denied to him in his fatherland . . . .

Your Committee would further state if others of their brethren are discharged for no visible conclusive cause, any further than being connected with our Union, as they believe was the case with brother Bradshaw, they shall again call upon you to unite your energies to assist us in sending [them] after him, in full assurance that such call will not be made in vain."

27. "Chat," "Dialogue Between Two Operative Potters on the Subject of Emigration," *PE&WA* 1, no. 24 (May 11, 1844): 189–90.

28. "I have seen plenty of people here from Longport and Burslem [districts of Stoke-on-Trent], but the place I saw most at was at Nauvoo." Letter from Leonard Brown of Paddock's Prairie, near Alton, Illinois, dated March 11, 1844, in *PE&WA* 1, no. 24 (May 11, 1844): 191–92.

29. Letter from Walter and Sarah Croxton of Alton, Illinois, dated November 1, 1841, in *PE&WA* 1, no. 21 (April 21, 1844): 167.

30. In Stoke-on-Trent the annual hiring of potters and fixing of wages for the coming twelve months was fixed at Martinmas. It is interesting to see that, as Staffordshire men, the brothers clung to that time of year to take account of their business.

31. James Goodwin, a potters' miller from Stoke-on-Trent. He stayed only three years, returning to England in December 1844, shortly after his brother Thomas had joined him in Illinois. Thomas became a successful farmer. Letters to Thomas Goodwin from his relations in Stoke-on-Trent, including James, were published in *Of What We Potters Are: A History of Some Descendants of John Goodwin of Cheddleton, Staffordshire, England, Based upon Letters from England and Other Family Letters, 1845–98,* edited by W. L. Goodwin (n.p., privately printed, 1975).

32. Benjamin Berrisford returned to Stoke-on-Trent in 1844 with James Goodwin. A letter from Berrisford to his wife and children dated December 19, 1843, was published in *PE&WA* 2, no. 6 (July 6, 1844): 46.

33. Letter from Walter and Sarah Croxton of Alton, Illinois, dated November 1, 1841, in *PE&WA* 1, no. 21 (April 20, 1844): 167.

34. "4*s* per dozen." Before the decimalization of British currency in the 1970s, money was divided in pounds, shillings, and pence, frequently abbreviated to *£.s.d*. There were twelve

pence to a shilling and twenty shillings to a pound. At this time the pound–dollar exchange rate was approximately five dollars to the pound.

35. "4's jugs, plain." In Stoke-on-Trent the size of flat wares were reckoned by the inch, hollow wares were reckoned by the dozen, but a potter's dozen was rarely twelve. "4's" were therefore large jugs as there would be only four to the dozen, "12's French" referred to as the next item were smaller vessels, counted as twelve to the dozen. The potter's dozen could be as few as four or as many as forty-eight to the dozen. Walter and Thomas carried their familiar way of reckoning with them in their new venture.

36. Nappies were shallow dishes. As flatware they were reckoned by the inch. "12's" were therefore twelve inches in diameter.

37. Twifflers were plates between 8½ to 9⅜ inches. Muffins were plates between 7½ and 8⅜ inches.

38. Letter from Walter and Sarah Croxton of Alton, Illinois, dated September 12, 1843, in *PE&WA* 1, no. 22 (April 28, 1844): 175–76.

39. Gotham presumably meant that Harrison was born in America, rather than being an immigrant as were so many settlers in Illinois.

40. Possibly the Robinson mentioned in Walter Croxton's letter (see note 33).

41. James Clews of Cobridge, Stoke-on-Trent, was a master potter who had been declared bankrupt in 1834. He came to Troy, Indiana, in 1837 to establish a white ware manufactory but failed. It was taken over by Jabez Vodrey, another Englishman, from 1837–1846. Frank Stefano, Jr., "James Clews, 19th century Potter," parts 1 and 2, *Antiques* 105, no. 2 (February 1974): 324–328; no. 3 (March 1974): 553–555. Letter from Thomas Gotham of St. Louis, Missouri, December 18, 1842, to Mr. Michael Hill, Clayton, Newcastle-under-Lyme, Staffordshire, in *PE&WA* 4, no. 23 (November 1, 1845): 189–90.

42. "Play" was the north Staffordshire term for being idle through lack of work. It was often used ironically by potters when their employers would not provide work for them.

43. Letter from Elijah and Charlotte Croxton of St. Louis, Missouri, dated April 30, 1843, to "Father, Mother, Brothers and Sisters," in *PE&WA* 4, no. 24 (November 8, 1845): 189–90.

44. William Ridgway, a pottery manufacturer from Hanley, Stoke-on-Trent, came to Kentucky in the early 1840s to set up a factory there. He failed, and the sale notice for his American property was advertised in the *Staffordshire Advertiser* newspaper, August 12, 1848. Geoffrey Godden, *Ridgway Porcelains* (Wappingers Falls, N.Y.: Antique Collectors' Club, 1985), p. 169.

45. John, Thomas, and Jos Mayer had an earthenware manufactory at Longport from 1843 to 1855. They exported much of their ware to the United States.

46. Letter from John Poole of Washington County, Missouri, dated July 17, 1845, to John Mould, Cobridge, Stoke-on-Trent, in *PE&WA* 5, no. 1 (November 29, 1845): 213.

47. There were four Howson brothers. Three immigrated to America, while the fourth, George, remained in Burslem, Stoke-on-Trent, and opened his own pottery as a sanitary ware manufacturer.

48. Newcastle-under-Lyme, Staffordshire, was the main market town of north Staffordshire, about five miles from Burslem where the Howson family lived.

49. A pottery-making district of Derbyshire from which a number of men emigrated to America.

50. Presumably at Vodrey's factory.

51. Letter from B. Howson, East Liverpool, Columbia City, Ohio, to Mr. John Howson, dated September 12, 1843, in *PE&WA* 1, no. 16 (March 16, 1844): 125.

52. Letter from J. Walker of Utica, New York, to Mr. John Howson, undated, in *PE&WA* 1, no. 12 (February 17, 1844): 95–96.

53. In fact Howson left Stoke-on-Trent in June 1844, only a few days before Garner. In light of their subsequent actions, it is very probable that they discussed Walker's letters: both were published in *PE&WA* before the two men left England.

54. Letter from S. [*sic*] Walker of Utica, New York, to Mr. Garner, dated March 25, 1844, in *PE&WA* 2, no. 10 (August 3, 1844): 78–79.

55. Ashby-wholds was a center for pottery making, near Burton-on-Trent, Derbyshire. A number of potters at East Liverpool, including the Bennett brothers and the Tunnicliffes, were from Derbyshire, rather than the neighboring county of Staffordshire.

56. Garner was a thrower; Cartwright was presumably turning Garner's ware for him.

57. Letter from George Garner of Birmingham, Allegany County, State of Pensilvania [*sic*], dated December 25, 1844, in *PE&WA* 3, no. 12 (February 15, 1845): 93–94.

58. *Posthumous Letter of a Pioneer Potter* (East Liverpool, Ohio: Simms Printing Co., 1934).

59. Gates, *City of Hills & Kilns,* p. 44.

60. According to George Garner's letter in *PE&WA* 3, no. 12 (February 15, 1845): 93–94, Howson landed in New York early in August 1844. If he stayed nine months at Utica he would have left for Zanesville in May 1845.

61. Letter from John Howson, Zanesville, Muskingham County, Ohio, to Mr. Thomas Lloyd, dated February 8, 1846, in *PE&WA* 5, no. 25 (May 16, 1846): 197–98.

62. *Zanesville Courier,* December 5, 1846. Richard Hallam, the new partner, was also from England.

63. Letter from Sarah Tunnicliffe to an unknown correspondent, dated April 21, 1851, and reproduced in the *Sunday Times Signal,* Zanesville (Ohio), June 26, 1949.

64. The Tunnicliffes, like Howson, produced Rockingham and yellow wares. Bernard Howson had known the family from the time when both had worked in East Liverpool for the Bennett brothers. He joined the Tunnicliffes as a thrower. *Sunday Times Signal,* Zanesville (Ohio), November 17, 1957.

65. Possibly the Thomas Cartwright who went to East Liverpool and Birmingham.

66. Letter from Thomas Mountford of Whitewater, Wallworth County, Wisconsin Territory, dated November 1, 1846, to Barnet Mountford, in *PE&WA* 6, no. 24 (August 8, 1846): 190.

67. Possibly another reference to Thomas Cartwright.

68. An interesting contrast with Wedgwood's comments.

69. It is possible that Enoch Bradshaw was not the only potter to have been turned off for his radical beliefs.

70. Throwers in Staffordshire invariably used the "Great Wheel" in which the motive power was provided by a child or woman. This type of wheel was clearly not used in Wisconsin where Mountford was using a type of kick wheel.

71. Letter from Thomas Mountford of Whitewater, Wallworth County, Wisconsin Territory, dated February 19, 1847, to Barnet Mountford in *PE&WA* 7, no. 26 (June 26, 1847): 198.

72. *The Staffordshire Advertiser,* August 17, 1850, and March 1, 1851.

73. Gates, *City of Hills & Kilns,* p. 89, Table 4.

74. Ibid., pp. 44–45. Cartwright was one of the six men who emigrated in June 1844.

75. Annual hiring contracts were abolished in 1866, although Martinmas remained the time when wage rates were set for the following year until 1888. Payment "good from oven" was finally abolished in 1964. It had lingered in the sanitary ware trade after being abolished in other branches in 1919.

76. Letter from Sarah Eardley, Staffordshire, 1879, quoted in Gates, *City of Hills & Kilns,* p. 88.

77. Ibid.

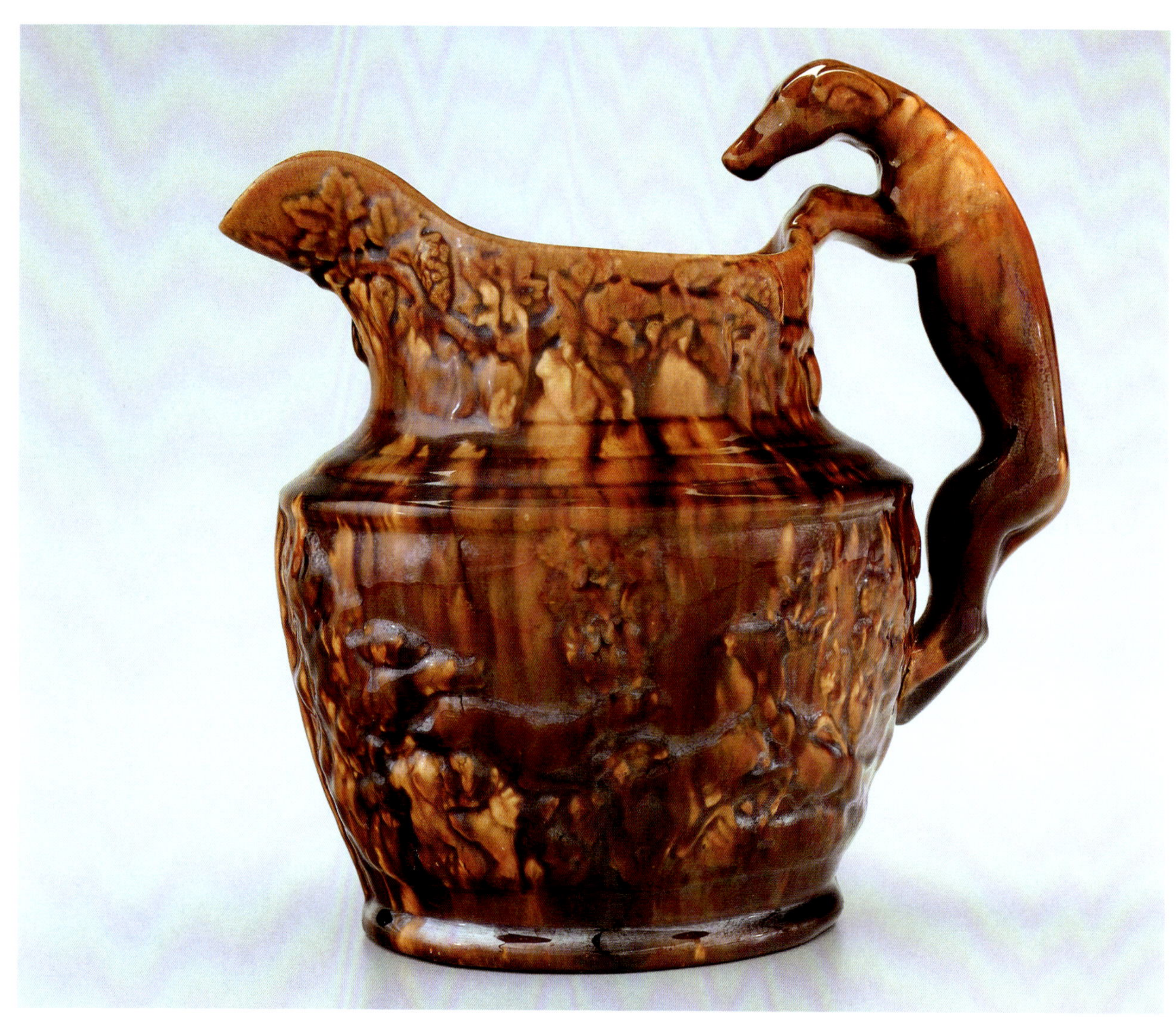

Figure 1 Hound-handle pitcher, Harker, Taylor & Co. East Liverpool, Ohio, 1847–1851. Rockingham glazed earthenware. H. 9¾". (All objects from the Arthur F. Goldberg collection; photos, Gavin Ashworth).

Arthur F. Goldberg

Highlights in the Development of the Rockingham and Yellow Ware Industry in the United States—A Brief Review with Representative Examples

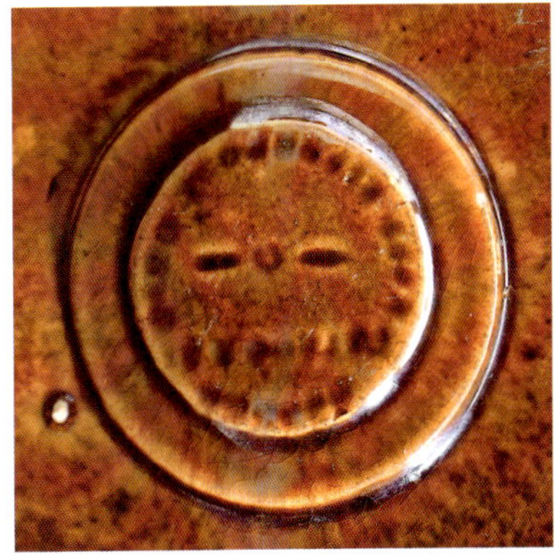

Figure 2 Detail of the Harker, Taylor & Co. mark on the bottom of the pitcher illustrated in fig. 1.

▼ YELLOW AND ROCKINGHAM ware potteries were established in the United States primarily by Staffordshire potters who learned their trade before immigrating to America. Many were master potters and modelers, whose serviceable wares were widely used throughout the United States for the better part of the nineteenth century. These immigrants faced serious challenges, as there were fires that burned down their works; shortages of clay, mineral components, and labor; and financial difficulties. Some failed economically; others rebuilt their potteries, joined different potteries locally, or moved elsewhere.

The story of these potters and their potteries represents the history of an American industry led by a small number of intelligent, creative, hard working, and skillful individuals. Most significantly, their newly adopted country provided an environment of freedom and opportunity that encouraged the expression of their entrepreneurial spirit. Raw materials, transportation facilities, and markets were available, and the potters became successful and secure in their new lives. When Rockingham and yellow ware were no longer popular or economically viable, substitutions became necessary for survival, a necessity that eventually led to the growth of the whiteware and porcelain industries.

The American Pottery Company of Jersey City, New Jersey, was the initial employer of a number of potters when they emigrated from England beginning in 1828. Some of these early potters later moved on to make significant contributions to the American ceramic industry. Daniel Greatbach worked in Bennington, Vermont, and Peoria, Illinois; James Bennett in East Liverpool, Ohio; James Taylor and William Bloor in East Liverpool and Trenton, New Jersey; Charles Coxon in Baltimore, Maryland, and South Amboy, New Jersey; Thomas Locker and James Carr in South Amboy and New York City.[1]

Before discussing the more important potters and potteries of the period and their east-west association, however, a definition of Rockingham and yellow ware is in order. The name Rockingham was first used for a late-eighteenth-century, dark brown glaze created at the Swindon works in Yorkshire, England, on the estate of the Marquis of Rockingham.[2] Ever since, the glaze, with slight variations, has been copied by both English and American potteries. Somewhat confusingly, later Swindon potteries made an excellent porcelain which was also called Rockingham. Later on in the United States, the term was applied to yellow *earthenware* that, covered with a similar colored glaze, constituted a major generic group.

Although the Americans applied the glaze in a uniform overall fashion like the English, their techniques varied in many ways, including the amount of glaze used and the contrasting patterns employed to create something new and beautiful. The glaze was dabbed, spattered, or dripped in long, spreading streaks down the vessel's side. Thinner coatings produced shadows outlining the molded designs and highlights to contrast or reveal the underlying yellow clay. Also attractive was the application of the glaze in a random pattern. In addition, some potteries used different metallic oxides in the glazing process, enhancing the overall appearance with variegated colors. This pottery is often referred to as flint enamel ware.

The term Rockingham has been equally applied to stoneware using the same glaze. Various potteries modified the glaze formulas creating different shades of brown, some with a reddish tint. Stoneware was almost always uniformly glazed, and some vessels were embellished with a double dip.

Just as there had been an earlier craze for glossy, black Jackfield-type ware and black basalts, the Rockingham glaze also stimulated the imagination of the potters and captivated America's public taste for more than three-quarters of a century. Brown had become beautiful, and brown ware had become fashionable.

Yellow ware is earthenware made from native yellow clay. The potteries produced utilitarian wares—baking dishes, pie plates, bowls, custard cups, milk pans, cake molds, soap dishes, pitchers, chamber pots, and bedpans—for households. The yellow ware was covered with a clear, lead-based glaze allowing the underlying clay to show through.

In contrast, two methods were used for applying the Rockingham glaze to these earthenware and stoneware forms. In the first, potters air-dried the green ware, applied the Rockingham glaze all over uniformly, and then fired the vessel in the kiln. In the second, the green ware was bisque fired, immersed in an underglaze, and air-dried, producing a glossy film. The Rockingham glaze was then applied and refired.[3]

At the appropriate temperature, the glaze, consisting of silica in combination with a flux and metallic oxide, vitrified and fused to the ceramic surface (glost firing). Adding more manganese or iron to the Rockingham glaze would darken its brown color to black. Earthenware was fired to about 1200 degrees centigrade; stoneware, from about 1200 degrees to 1300 degrees centigrade. Determining the chosen method is as easy as examining the pottery's base. The second method deposited a shiny coating of underglaze, absent in the first process. The second firing method produced wares of exceptional quality; the resulting glaze was a brilliant, lustrous brown having great transparency. Until replaced by whiteware, these Rockingham glazed earthenwares and stonewares became the most popular American wares during the mid-nineteenth century.

In America, the popularity and availability of English ceramics was widespread. It was believed that pottery was more marketable if made in the English fashion. Along with the expertise of these immigrant Staffordshire potters, a permissive intellectual and moral climate and lax copyright laws allowed American potteries to literally pirate another potter's design.

East Liverpool

East Liverpool, Ohio, was the major center for the production of Rockingham and yellow ware during the 1840 and 1850s.[4] In fact it was in East Liverpool that James Bennett created the first American Rockingham ware. Some of the potters working there later left to establish their own businesses in Trenton, New Jersey, and Baltimore, Maryland. Others had links with Jersey City and South Amboy, New Jersey, and Bennington, Vermont.[5] As a result of this close relationship, the midwestern and eastern potteries laid the foundation for the development of Rockingham and yellow ware manufacture.

The genesis for the American production of this ware began when master potter James Bennett left Derbyshire, England, for America in 1834. He initially worked for D. & J. Henderson at the American Pottery Company in Jersey City, New Jersey, but in 1837 he moved to Troy, Indiana, to work with the famous Staffordshire potter James Clews. In 1839 he established his own pottery in East Liverpool, Ohio, with his younger brother, Edwin, and two other brothers who joined him in 1841. Their partnership, called Bennett Brothers, made the first Rockingham and yellow ware in the United States.

In 1842 Englishman Benjamin Harker, Sr., although not a potter, created East Liverpool's second pottery for the manufacture of Rockingham and yellow ware. The business failed until James Taylor, who had previously worked at the American Pottery Co., joined the firm, forming Harker, Taylor & Company (1847 to 1850), also called Etruria after Josiah Wedgwood's works in Staffordshire.[6]

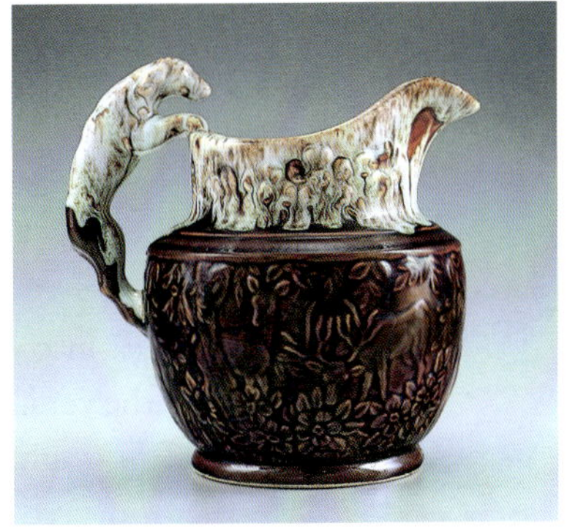

Figure 3 Hound-handle pitcher, East Liverpool, Ohio, ca. 1965. Rockingham glazed earthenware. H. 9¾". The upper portion and hound are covered with an off-white glaze. The impressed mark reads: "Reproduction Harker Rockingham/Mfg 1848/U.S.A. 1965."

The company's most noted ceramic piece was an unusual and large, hound-handled pitcher, circa 1847–1851 (figs. 1, 2). Although slight changes were made, the pottery copied the earlier New Jersey Boar and Stag Hunt pitcher made by the American Pottery Company and the Salamander Works. About 1965 the Harker Pottery Company, a derivative enterprise, manufactured a Rockingham semivitreous reproduction. Although advertised as an authentic reproduction of the original pitcher, it was not. Besides adding an off-white glaze over the hound and the vessel's upper portion, the violent scenes on its sides were replaced to show stags and does grazing in a peaceful, bucolic forest. The transformed images indicate a changing cultural climate, superseded by political correctness (fig. 3).[7]

Two other East Liverpool potteries of the period deserve mention. Jabez Vodrey, a Staffordshire potter, immigrated to the United States in 1827, operated a pottery in Pittsburgh, Pennsylvania, later worked in Louisville, Kentucky, and in 1839 took charge of James Clews' Indiana Pottery Company. Clews, a Staffordshire potter, had left his English works and moved to Troy, Indiana, in 1837. He hoped to produce fine whiteware like the English, but was unsuccessful. As a substitute, Clewes made Rockingham and yellow ware. Vodrey added different metal oxides to his glaze, producing multiple colors.

Because local problems developed while Vodrey was in Indiana, he moved to East Liverpool, where in 1848, with the help of financial backers, he established his own successful Rockingham and yellow ware pottery.

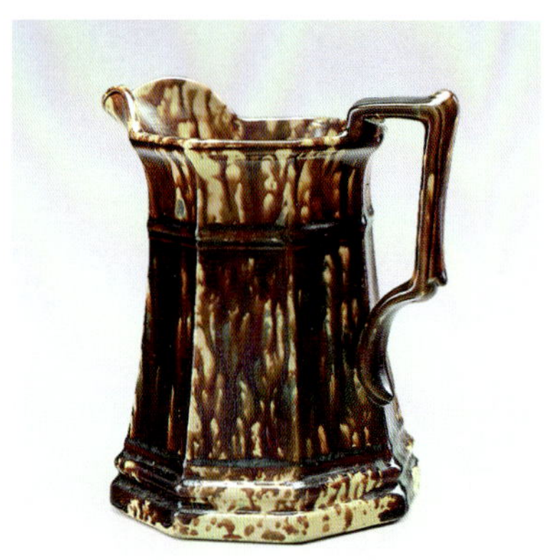

Figure 4 Octagonal paneled pitcher, attributed to Bennett & Brothers, East Liverpool, Ohio, or Pittsburgh, Pennsylvania, ca. 1844. Rockingham glazed earthenware. H. 7⅜". Powdered flint was added to the Rockingham glaze to produce the streaks of green and blue. A similar pitcher with a different Rockingham glaze is in the collection of the East Liverpool Museum of Ceramics, East Liverpool, Ohio.

Although a fire destroyed his small enterprise, Vodrey rebuilt it and symbolically renamed it the Phoenix Pottery. By 1852 the company had grown to five buildings, three large kilns, and about seventy-five employees. The Phoenix Pottery was one of the largest potteries in East Liverpool, manufacturing some of the finest quality ware.[8]

John Goodwin emigrated from Burslem, England, in 1842 and initially worked for Bennett and Harker in East Liverpool. In 1844 he formed his own very successful Eagle Pottery making an extensive line of Rockingham and yellow ware (1844–1853). After a ten-year hiatus, he started another pottery but left in 1870 to purchase an interest in the Trenton Pottery Company, which manufactured ironstone and sanitary ware.[9]

Baltimore

In 1844 Edwin Bennett left East Liverpool and moved to Birmingham (Pittsburgh), Pennsylvania, with three other brothers (fig. 4). Shortly after, in 1847, Edwin and his brother William formed their own pottery, E. & W. Bennett, in Baltimore, Maryland. Their modeler, master potter Charles Coxon (1850–1858), designed a number of fine ceramic pieces, among them his Boar and Stag Hunt, Gypsy, and Heron pitchers, and a Toby shaving mug.[10]

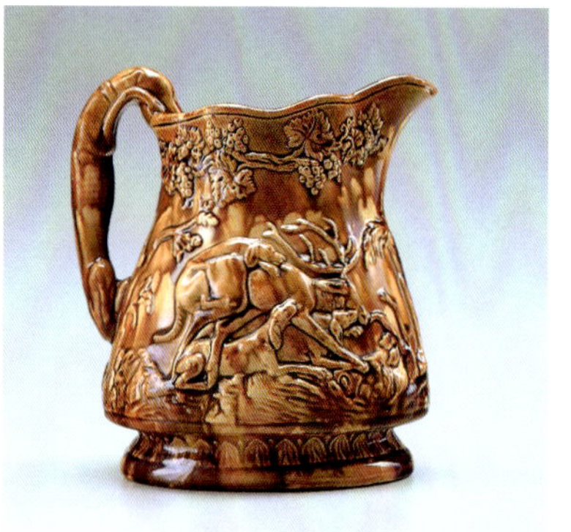

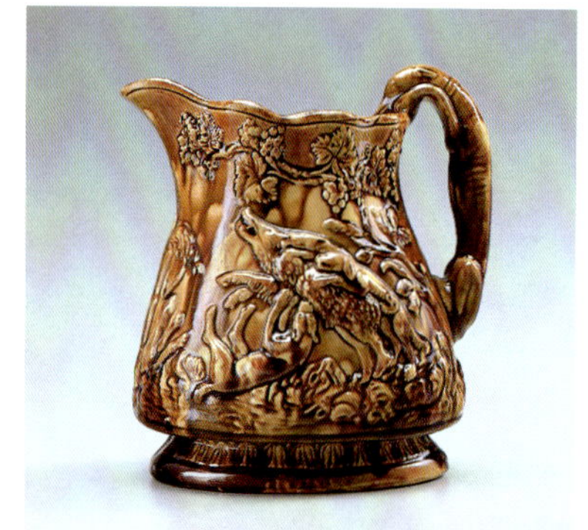

Figure 5 "Boar and Stag Hunt" pitcher with hound handle, E. & W. Bennett, Baltimore, Maryland, 1850–1858. Rockingham glazed earthenware. H. 7⅞".

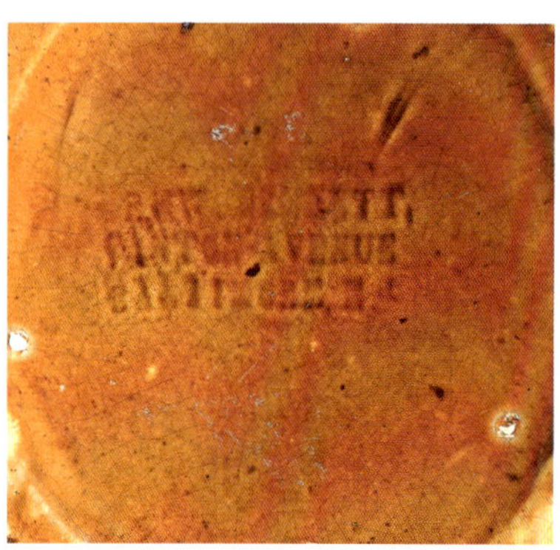

Figure 6 Detail of the mark "E. & W. BENNETT / CANTON AVENUE / BALTIMORE, MD". in large rectangle on the base of the pitcher illustrated in fig. 5. Two of the three stilt marks are visible.

The relief on the Boar and Stag Hunt pitcher contrasts two compelling images: violent and grisly hunt scenes against lushly encompassing, grape-clustered vines (figs. 5, 6). A similar pitcher was first made in stoneware by Phillips & Bagster of Hanley, England, about 1840, and was essentially duplicated by both the American Pottery Company and the Salamander Works of New Jersey in the 1840s and 1850s. With slight variations, especially of the hound handle, it was copied—in both Rockingham ware and stoneware—by many others including, most particularly, potteries in New York State and New England. Hunting pitchers have had a long tradition in England and America and were popular, judging from the number of extant pitchers. Coxon's pitcher was copied by John Bell of Waynesboro, Pennsylvania, and Solomon Bell of Strasburg, Virginia (1845–1880).[11]

The Gypsy pitcher shows a panorama of life on the road (fig. 7). Its prototype was made in 1842 by James Walley and Samuel Alcock in England, and is almost an exact match with Coxon's design. To date, there is no doc-

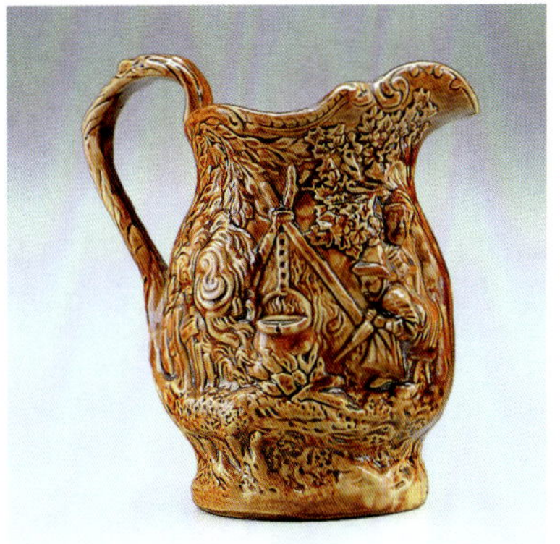

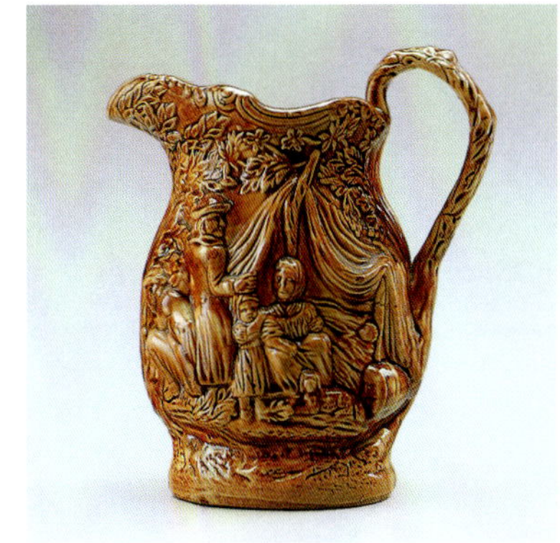

Figure 7 "Gypsy" pitcher, E. & W. Bennett, Baltimore, Maryland, 1850–1858. Rockingham glazed earthenware. H. 8⅝". This pitcher has a modified branch handle with very crisp defined details. It is marked "E. & W. BENNETT / CANTON AVENUE / BALTIMORE, Md." in small rectangle and has three stilt marks in a triangular pattern on the base.

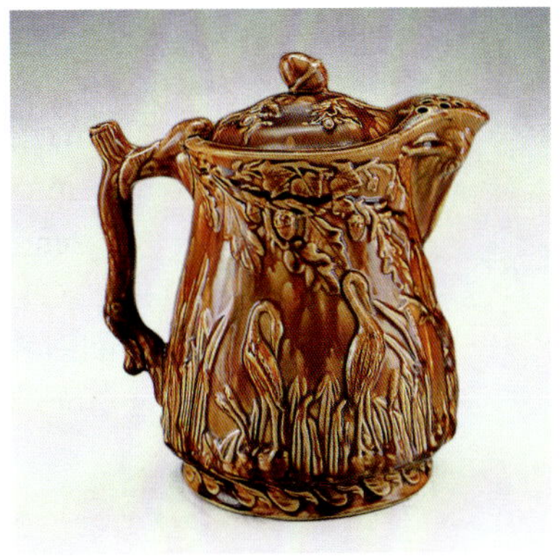

Figure 8 "Heron" pitcher, attributed to E. & W. Bennett, Baltimore, Maryland, 1850–1858. Rockingham glazed earthenware. H. 10". This is a molded covered ale pitcher with a branch handle.

umentation that Coxon designed his version of this pitcher before arriving in Baltimore.

An original Coxon design is his Rockingham-glazed, Heron ale pitcher. This pitcher incorporates long-billed, long-legged herons posed against a backdrop of tall reeds and cattails on both sides. The naturalistic imagery is further embellished with an entwining snake, the head of a boar, and a broad band of oak branches. The cover, with acorn finial, is similarly decorated. To date, no marked Heron pitcher has been found (fig. 8).

The Rockingham-glazed shaving mug with a branch handle was designed in the English manner and with the characteristic image of Toby on both sides but without his traditional ale pitcher and mug (fig. 9). The overall design is remarkably similar to the flint enamel Toby snuff jars made in Bennington, Vermont, marked "Lyman, Fenton & Co.'s Fenton's Enamel 1849."[12]

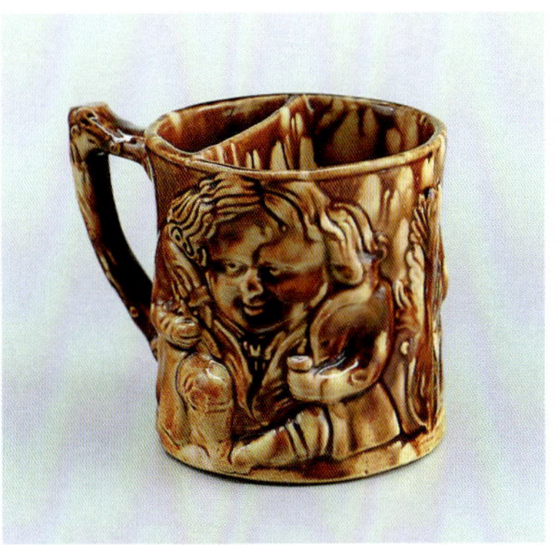

Figure 9 Shaving mug, E. & W. Bennett, Baltimore, Maryland, 1850–1858. Rockingham glazed earthenware. H. 4⅜". This molded mug has the image on both sides of Toby seated holding a razor in one hand with a mug in his other. It is marked "E. & W. BENNETT / CANTON AVENUE / BALTIMORE/ Md." and has three stilt marks in a triangular pattern on the base.

Potter Edward Bennett claimed that he designed his most popular vessel, the Rebekah-at-the-Well teapot (fig. 10) about 1850. This assertion has been challenged by the suggestion that it was actually designed and modeled by his chief modeler, Charles Coxon. Regardless of who claims credit, the prototype for the teapot was a covered ewer made by the English pottery of Samuel Alcock and Company, circa 1847. Coxon left Bennett and moved to South Amboy, New Jersey, to run the Swan Hill Pottery (1858–1860), which manufactured Rockingham and yellow ware. In 1863 he established his own pottery, Coxon & Co., in Trenton, New Jersey.[13]

The Rebekah-at-the-Well teapot became so popular that it was copied by many American potteries, and was still in production at the Bennett pot-

Figure 10 Teapot, attributed to E. & W. Bennett, Baltimore, Maryland 1851–1857. Rockingham glazed earthenware. H. 10". This teapot has the molded inscription "REBEKAH AT THE WELL" on the front and a flower finial on the lid. Three spur marks in a triangular pattern are on the base.

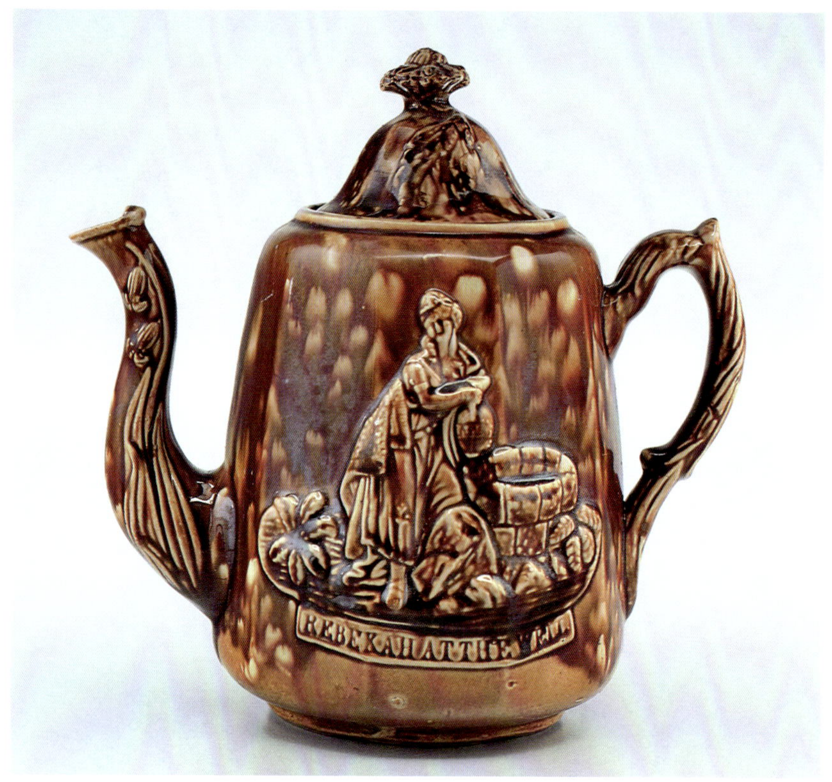

tery (although with different glazes) into the mid-1930s. Other companies modified the design, using less detail and modeling definition, as well as different Rockingham glaze shades and techniques. These copies never achieved the beauty and quality of those made in the early production of E. & W. Bennett.

All of the Bennett pieces exhibit characteristic coloring and glazing. The Rockingham glaze achieved its greatest beauty when it was lightly applied over the molded decorations leaving thin highlights on the low relief design, exposing the yellow clay. The relief outline and deeper grooves, pooled with additional glaze, delineated the design.

Besides the lustrous surface colored with shades of light and dark brown, the beauty of the overall glazing is its clarity, brilliant sheen, and transparency. No glazed vessel is alike due to the innumerable random applications of the glazes and the way they flow down the vessel's surface to reveal and contrast with the clay. Nevertheless, in spite of variations, there is an overall balance and harmony between the glaze and clay body. Bennett produced some of the finest designs, modeling, and Rockingham glazes.

Bennington

During the period that Ohio potteries were developing, there was similar activity in New England. Christopher Webber Fenton joined the older Norton Pottery (established in 1793) in Bennington, Vermont, about 1839. In 1847, along with salt-glazed stoneware production, the first parian ware in the United States was made just two years after it was produced by W. T. Copeland in England. The Norton and Fenton firm was dissolved in 1847.[14]

About 1848 or 1849, Fenton created a new enterprise called Lyman, Fenton & Co., producing some of the finest American Rockingham ware marked "Fenton's Enamel, Patented 1849." The ware had a brilliant glaze with variegated colors of yellow, orange, blue, green, olive, brown, and red. The company's name later changed to the United States Pottery Company, and primarily concentrated on parian ware and porcelain until 1858, when it closed for economic reasons. Initially its biscuit wares were covered with a transparent glaze. Later, the surface was sprinkled with various metallic oxides in amounts designed to produce different color intensities, yet leaving some openings for the clay to show through. The pottery was then glazed and refired. During the firing, the oxides melted fusing to the glaze in an abstract, flowing, or spotted pattern.[15]

Some have used the English terms, "Whieldon" or "tortoise shell," to describe the American flint enamel ware. Thomas Whieldon (1740–1780) splattered metallic oxides on some of his earthenwares to create a mottled color effect. With the exception of flowing, variegated colors, the two were aesthetically different. One of the finest examples of this ware was a sculptural lion, believed to have been designed by modeler Daniel Greatbach, a major achievement of American ceramic production for the time (fig. 11).[16]

Stimulated by the reports of travelers taking the Grand Tour in Italy and the growing awareness of classical antiquities, many Staffordshire potters made ceramic lions. In particular, they were inspired by a pair of marble lions at the entrance to the stairs of the Loggia de Lanzi in Florence, Italy.[17] The Bennington Pottery modified earlier English ceramic designs using shredded clay, called "coleslaw," to create a realistic, and charming, lion's mane.

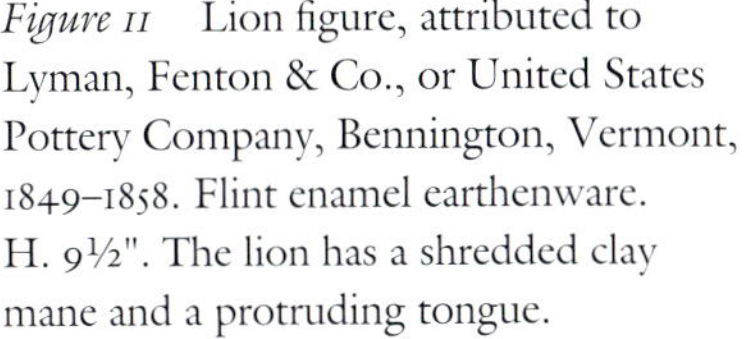
Figure 11 Lion figure, attributed to Lyman, Fenton & Co., or United States Pottery Company, Bennington, Vermont, 1849–1858. Flint enamel earthenware. H. 9½". The lion has a shredded clay mane and a protruding tongue.

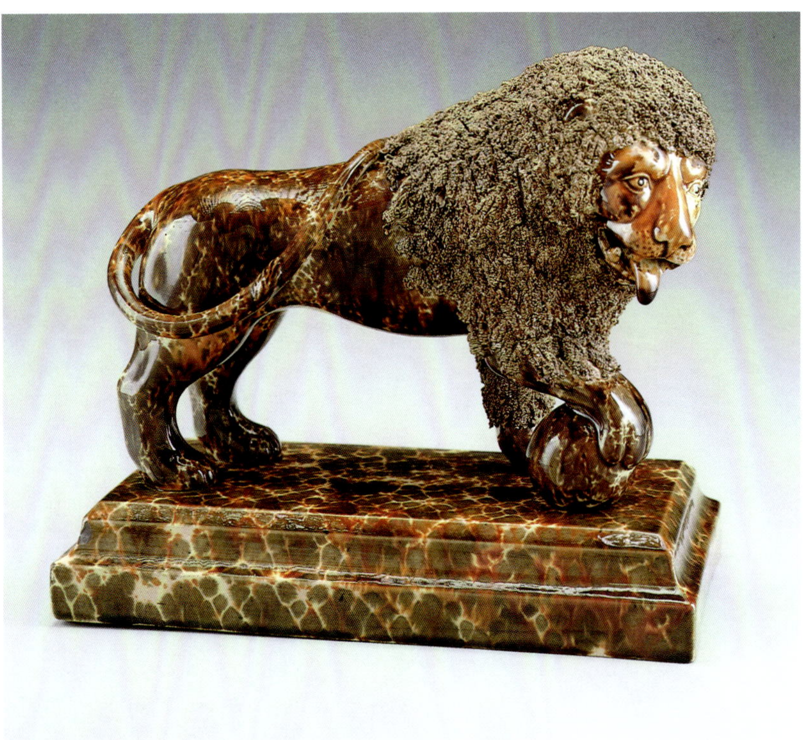

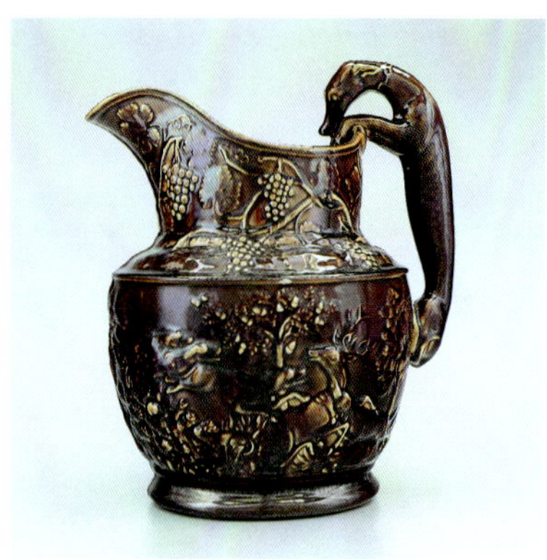

Figure 12 Hound-handled pitcher, United States Pottery Company, Bennington, Vermont, 1852–1856. Rockingham glazed earthenware. H. 12⅛". There are three stilt marks in a triangular pattern on the base.

Brown-glazed earthenware, called dark lusterware, was also made. One example is the popular hound-handled pitcher designed and modeled by Daniel Greatbach. With some variation, this pitcher is similar to the one he designed for the American Pottery Company (fig. 12). To date, no marked pitcher has been found.

New Jersey

After purchasing the short-lived Jersey Porcelain and Earthenware Company in 1828, Scotsman David Henderson and his brother established a successful pottery using Staffordshire mold-making techniques to manufacture stoneware, Rockingham, and yellow wares. As a result, he revolutionized the American pottery industry by transforming the production of hand-turned pottery to a factory production system, and at prices competitive with imported wares. In 1833 their name changed from D. & J. Henderson Flint Stoneware Manufactory to the American Pottery Manufacturing Company, or the American Pottery Company, about 1840. Henderson's pottery also played an important role in the formative years of the American pottery industry, employing immigrant Staffordshire potters when they first arrived in the United States. A number of them learned his methods and went on to establish important and successful potteries elsewhere.[18]

A very important figure in American pottery design during this period was Daniel Greatbach. Like his grandfather William Greatbach, who worked for Thomas Whieldon and Josiah Wedgwood, Daniel was a skillful modeler and a designer. In 1838 the younger Greatbach emigrated from Staffordshire to work for David Henderson's American Pottery Company of Jersey City, New Jersey.

Around 1828, D. & J. Henderson obtained an original mold belonging to the English firm of Phillips and Bagster, and reproduced its version of a hound-handle hunt pitcher about 1828. Greatbach redesigned the Phillips and Bagster pitcher and also created many other original ceramic forms. For the next ten years, he designed and modeled a number of important pieces, including many Toby pitchers.[19]

The hound-handle hunt pitcher and other wares are high quality items, with exquisite modeling and an elaborate, inventive vocabulary of decorative designs (figs. 13–16). The skillful modeling and manufacturing techniques produced a product with crisp details. As well, the hound-handle pitchers have a strong sculptural image; the proportional open space

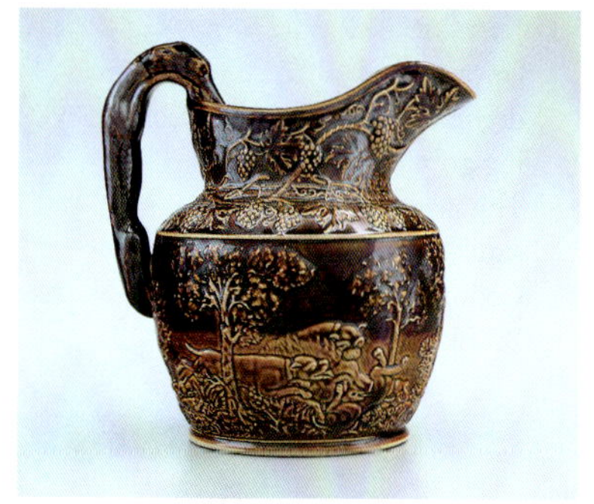

Figure 13 Hound-handle pitcher, American Pottery Company, Jersey City, New Jersey, 1840–1845. Rockingham glazed stoneware. H. 9¼". This molded pitcher has double dipped brown glaze on its upper portion and a putty colored glaze inside. The neck and shoulder have an undulating vine with leaves, tendrils, and grape clusters. A scene of hounds attacking a stag is on one side and a boar being attacked by mastiffs is on the other.

Figure 14 Detail of the mark on the bottom of the pitcher illustrated in fig. 13.

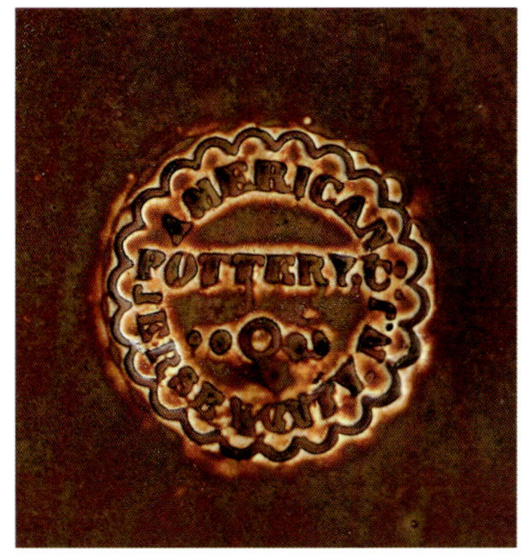

Figure 15 Hound-handle pitcher, American Pottery Company, Jersey City, New Jersey, 1840–1850. Rockingham glazed stoneware. H. 8½". This molded pitcher has a reddish brown glaze outside and a putty colored glaze inside. A vine with leaves, tendrils, and grape clusters is on its neck and shoulder.

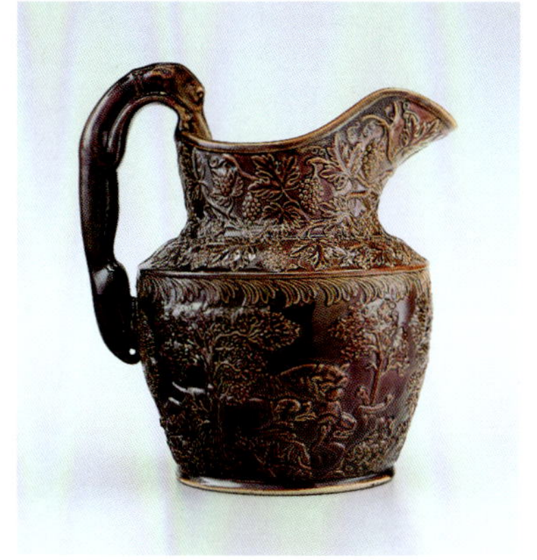

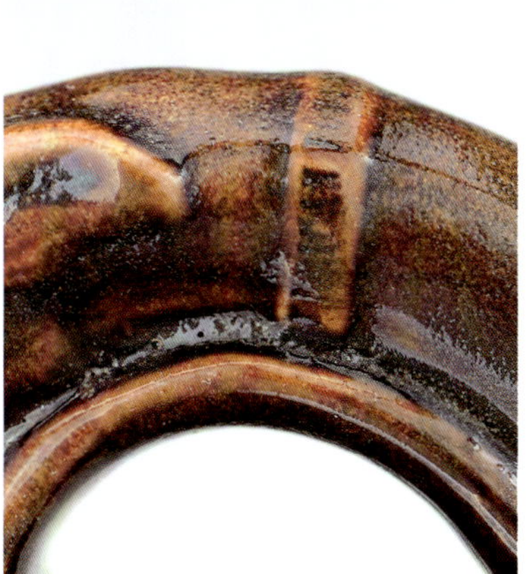

Figure 16 Detail of the "AMERICAN POTTERY" mark on the collar band of hound-handle pitcher illustrated in fig. 15.

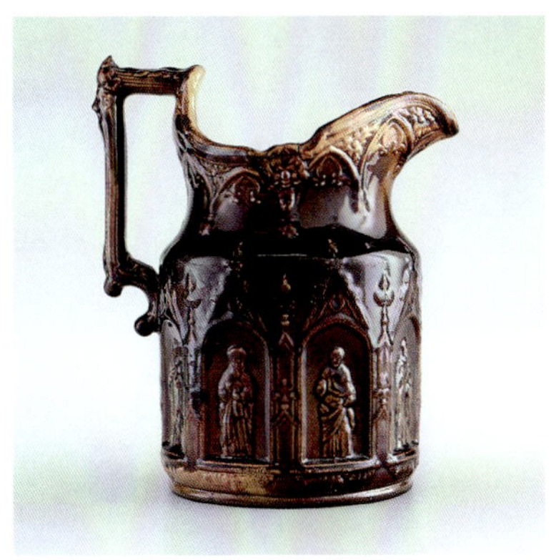

Figure 17 Pitcher, attributed to the American Pottery Co., Jersey City, New Jersey, ca. 1845. Rockingham glazed earthenware. H. 9¼". This molded pitcher is decorated with an elaborate design featuring gothic architecture and eight apostles. This example is unmarked although a similar pitcher with the American Pottery Co. mark is in the Clement Collection, Brooklyn Museum of Art.

between the hound and vessel body enhance their three-dimensional form. Their brown Rockingham glaze is rich and lustrous, and the smaller pitcher has a reddish hue. In areas where the glaze is thin, the underlying clay highlights the surface design. Greatbach's contemporaries recognized the pitcher's outstanding design, and it became so popular that it was copied by many potteries for years to come.[20]

Interest in the Gothic Revival is represented by another Rockingham glazed pitcher that Greatbach designed for the American Pottery Company. Except for some simplifications and added decoration, it is a copy of the "Apostle Pitcher," a stoneware jug made by Charles Meigh of Hanley, England, in 1842. A gothic arcade and a canopy with eight sections, each containing a standing apostle, surrounds the pitcher's body. Further decoration includes a dictionary of other gothic architectural motifs, from fine tracery to ornamental finials to pointed arches and satyr heads in place of gargoyles. In spite of its complexity, the dynamic interplay of individual parts unifies the design (fig. 17).[21]

In 1852 Greatbach left New Jersey for Bennington, Vermont, to work for Christopher Webber Fenton's United States Pottery Company. There he designed their hound-handle pitchers along with many other ceramics. Later, he put in a short stint at the Swan Hill Pottery (1840–1875) in South Amboy, New Jersey, where he ran the pottery with Samuel Riley from 1856 to 1857. When Bennington's United States Pottery closed in 1858, Greatbach joined

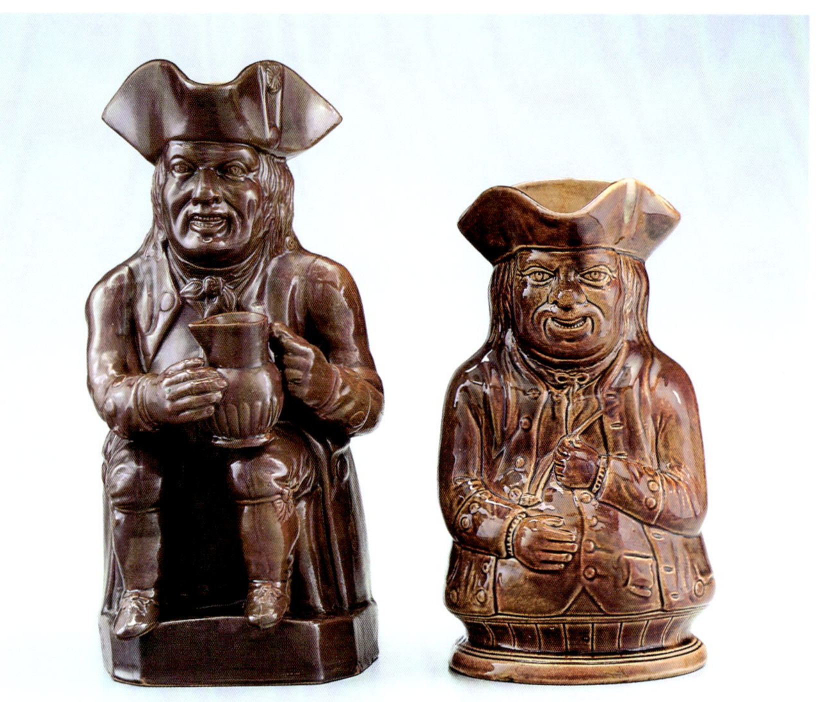

Figure 18 Toby Philpott pitchers. Left: attributed to the Salamander Works, New York City or Woodbridge, New Jersey, 1837–1850s. Rockingham glazed stoneware. H. 13". This example has a reddish brown glaze, double dipped on its upper body, and a putty colored glaze inside. This form probably represents pattern J on the Salamander Works' 1837 price list. Right: attributed to the American Pottery Company, Jersey City, New Jersey, 1840. Rockingham glazed stoneware. H. 9". This pitcher has a rustic branch handle and a reddish brown, putty colored glaze inside.

Christopher Fenton and Decius Clark, his superintendent in Peoria, Illinois, to found the American Pottery Company. There, as at Bennington, Greatbach was chief designer and mold maker. In 1865 the enterprise failed and he moved to Trenton, New Jersey, where he eventually died in poverty.[22]

Another pottery, the Salamander Works, was making stoneware in New York City from about 1835 to 1839 or 1840 when it relocated to Woodbridge, New Jersey, and continued to make similar wares. Salamanders' stoneware production changed to industrial items around 1857, although an exact date is not known. M. Lelyn Branin believed that their high point was the late 1830s to the 1840s and continued into the 1850s. Alice Cooney Frelinghuysen cites the active dates of the pottery as 1836–1855. She further illustrates stoneware examples in her article made circa 1837 to 1842 or 1845. Both Branin and Frelinghuysen recognized the production of stoneware in New York City before going to Woodbridge, New Jersey. Frelinghuysen correctly lists the stoneware illustrated in her section as Salamander Works, New York City or Woodbridge, New Jersey.[23]

Earlier authors believed that all Salamander Works pieces were made in Woodbridge, dismissing pieces marked New York and the 54 Cannon St., New York City address as representing only their sales office and not the site of ceramic production. There are two known hound-handle pitchers with the inscription "Salamander Works/Woodbridge/N. J." on their bases.[24]

The Salamander Works received a diploma in 1835 from the American Institute of the City of New York for "a fine specimen of flint stoneware." The following year they received another diploma at the Ninth Annual Fair for "a beautiful specimen of stoneware." The judges noted that their ware "of all descriptions, [was] not to be surpassed by other manufacturers, either in America or abroad." Silver medals were also awarded in 1838 and 1839.

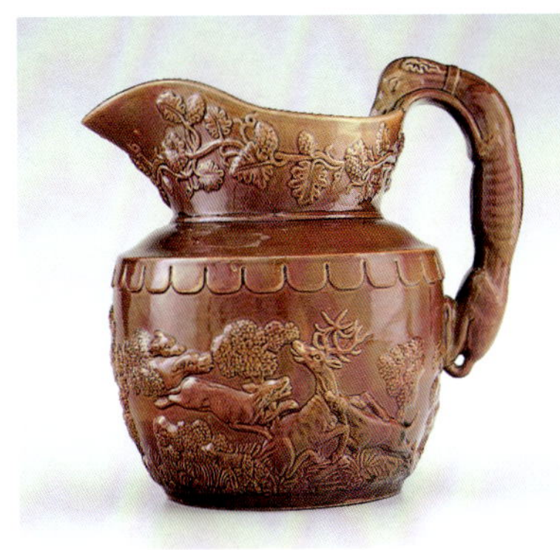

Figure 19 Hound-handle pitcher, attributed to Salamander Works, New York City or Woodbridge, New Jersey, 1837–1850s. Rockingham glazed stoneware. H. 11". A hunt scene of hounds attacking a stag is on one side and a boar being attacked by mastiffs is on the other. The pitcher has a leafy hop vine with flowers around the neck and a scalloped design around the shoulder.

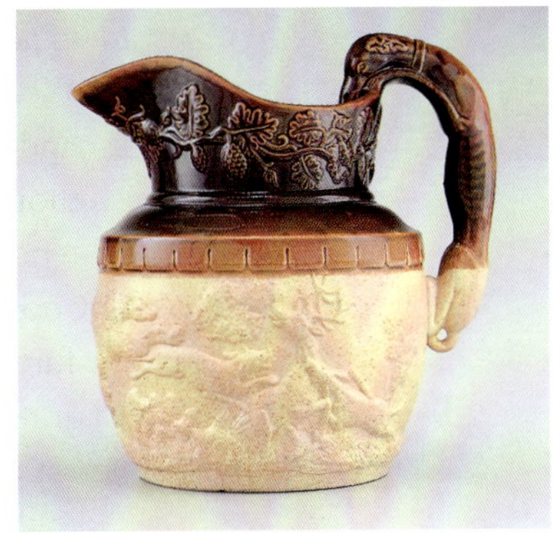

Figure 20 Hound-handle pitcher, Salamander Works, New York City or Woodbridge, New Jersey, 1837–1850s. Rockingham glazed stoneware. H. 10". A hunt scene of hounds attacking a stag is on one side and a boar being attacked by mastiffs is on the other. The lower half of the pitcher is not glazed, and the interior is putty colored. The neck has a leafy hop vine with flowers, and the shoulder has a square scalloped fringe. The base is embossed "B2." This pitcher is called the "Hound Pattern" on the Salamander Works' 1837 price list.

An 1837 illustrated handbill showing pottery being made at Salamander Works in New York City helps identify existing ceramics. A sign of a major enterprise, it lists forty-five different items, many in multiple sizes. Besides fourteen different pitcher patterns, there were coffee and teapots, washbasins, water ewers, chamber pots, bed and foot pans, spittoons, table and kitchenware, spitting cups, inkstands, and toys.[25] Today, only about a dozen different items are known. Pitchers are the most common.

The imposing pitcher shown on the left in figure 18 was made by the Salamander Works of New York City or Woodbridge, New Jersey.[26] It is a commanding sculptural piece and is taller than its English counterparts, which usually measure nine to ten inches in height. This pitcher corresponds to what is called the Ordinary English Toby and was copied from this prototype. The tricorn hat makes an excellent pouring spout. The mold details are crisp and exquisite, from the fine details of the teeth, eyes, furrowed brow, crow's feet, and fingernails to the knotted bow on the breeches and shoes.

A contrasting Toby pitcher was made by the American Pottery Company of Jersey City, New Jersey, also about 1840 to 1850 (fig. 18). Here is a new American form designed and modeled by Daniel Greatbach. Atypically, Toby is not seated, and the jolly tippler motif is absent. Similar fine modeling is present, exemplified by the lace blouse and the vertical design lines on the pipe bowl. The pooling effects of the Rockingham glaze enhance the beauty of the piece and accentuate the deeper modeling lines, creating a more three-dimensional figure.

Figures 19 and 20 represent two other examples of Salamander's hound-handle pitchers. As competitors to the American Pottery Company, the Salamander Works recognized a popular form and design, and acted to capitalize on it. With the exception of a few minor changes, they copied the original Phillips and Bagster pitcher. However, they did appropriate Greatbach's hound, although adding more details. Both pitchers are handsome examples, each having different colored lustrous glazes. The hops in the neck design suggest the pitchers were used to hold beer.

It is often difficult to distinguish unmarked, hound-handle hunt pitchers made by the American Pottery Company and Salamander Works based solely on their exterior and interior glazes. A simple and quickly discernable sign for differentiating between the two is Salamander's inclusion of one to three incised lines, indicating digits, on the back of the hound's paws. In addition, the ears of the hound on Salamander Works pitchers have multiple folds, whereas the ears of the hound on American Pottery Company pitchers are simpler. Close examination reveals further differences.

1. Both potteries tried to cover the seam of the two-part body mold with a tree. On the Salamander pitcher it is fully leaved with branches obscuring the seam. The tree's short trunk is on a mound of earth with no brush on either side. In contrast, the American Pottery Company pitcher has a tall trunk over the seam, considerably fewer leaves on top, no earth mound, and usually has large leaved brush at either side. Usually in the rear below the hound handle is a tree over the seam similar to the one in front of the Salamander pitcher. In the American Pottery version, there is no tree and the seam is visible.

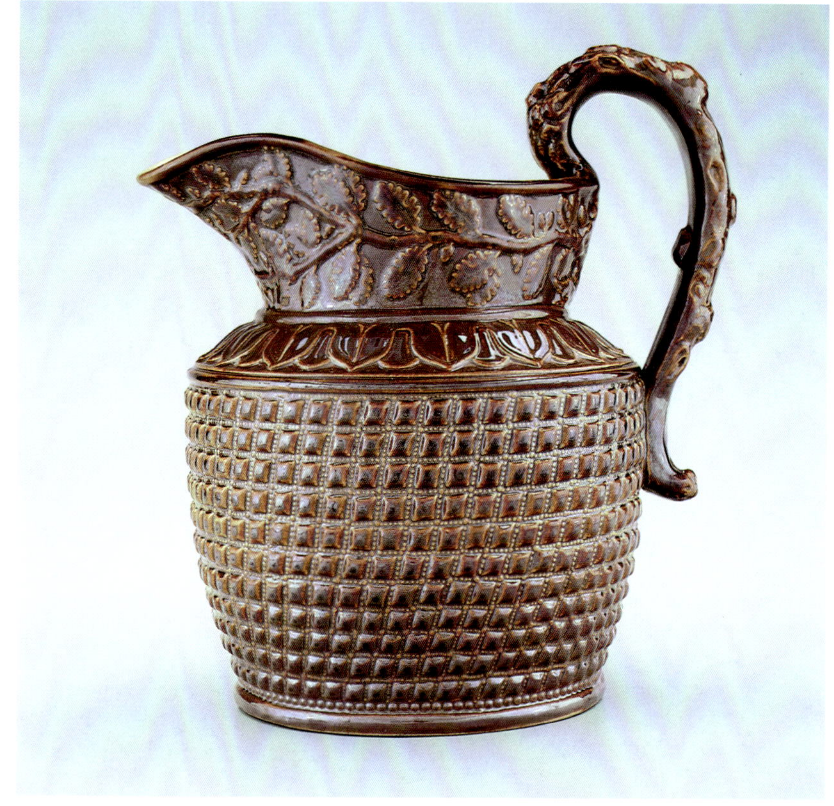

Figure 21 Pitcher, Salamander Works, New York City or Woodbridge, New Jersey, 1837–1850s. Rockingham glazed stoneware. H. 11½". This example is a reddish brown color with a putty colored glaze inside; an oak leafed branch with acorns is around its neck, a lotus leaf design on its shoulder, and its body surface is covered with elaborate parallel rhomboids surrounded by a delicate dot-like design simulating a pineapple. It has a branch handle and is embossed N1 on the base.

2. On the Salamander Works pitcher, the deer's head points upward and its antlers terminate in a five pointed star formation. On the American Pottery Company pitcher the deer turns laterally and its longest antler has a bifid end.

3. The dogs on the Salamander Works pitcher are far behind the central hound, whereas those on the American Pottery Company pitcher are closer.

4. The fox hiding in the foreground brush of the Salamander Works pitcher has no tail, whereas the one on the American Pottery Company pitcher has a long tail.

5. There is a prominent dog's head peering at the fox to its right on the Salamander Works pitcher. The dog's head is barely visible on the American Pottery Company example.

6. The left forelimb of the central mastiff is outstretched and clearly visible on the Salamander Works pitcher. It is partially seen below the dog's head on the American Pottery Company pitcher.

7. The small mastiff attacking the rabbit on the Salamander Works pitcher has long ears, whereas the one on the American Pottery Company pitcher has small ears.

8. Leafy foliage extends across the middle of the central mastiff on the Salamander Works pitcher, whereas a tree trunk extends across the middle of the dog on the American Pottery Company pitcher.

9. There are other details separating the two pitchers—from the width of the hound's collar and variations in the forest floor foliage to tree and leaf designs in the open spaces as well as the detailed treatment of leaf clusters.

If a pitcher has white glazed letters spelling a dedicated name on its shoulders, those of the Salamander Works are smaller whereas the American Pottery letters are much larger, filling most of the width of the shoulders' rim.

One particularly distinctive stoneware pitcher from the Salamander Works is unlike any other design made at that time (fig. 21). It has complex, finely molded details with a broad, rustic-branch handle enhancing its overall sculpted form. The embossed "N1" on its base identifies its maker and represents a non-titled pattern in the 1837 Salamander Works bill head. The design, simulating a pineapple, emulates a prototype from eighteenth-century Staffordshire wares.

Some of the finest American yellow ware was made during the earliest manufacturing period, as was this one from the Swan Hill Pottery of Hanks and Fish of South Amboy, New Jersey (1850–1852). An elaborate yellow ware ale pitcher (figs. 22, 23) shows a bold, bifid branch handle extending across its body. Its cover is embellished with a grape and vine design, all the details delicately sculpted. The beauty of the pitcher's low relief design is best appreciated in raking light, which creates shadowing that outlines the sculptural surface and delineates its three dimensionality. The naturalistic design of the pitcher was an inventive form, free from English influence, and introducing a strainer at the spout. This pitcher was also made with a Rockingham glaze.[27]

Hanging-game pitchers were a popular subject. Figure 24 shows an elaborate eight-paneled example with a hound handle and a Rockingham, flint enamel glaze. An eagle postures below its spout, and suspended from its sides are ducks, rabbits, boars, and stags—all animals that were hunted in the countryside. Another example features suspended pheasants, deer, and rabbits. To hide the mold line, an expansive tree trunk covers both the front and rear seams. The pitcher's branch handle cleverly rises from the trunk (fig. 25).

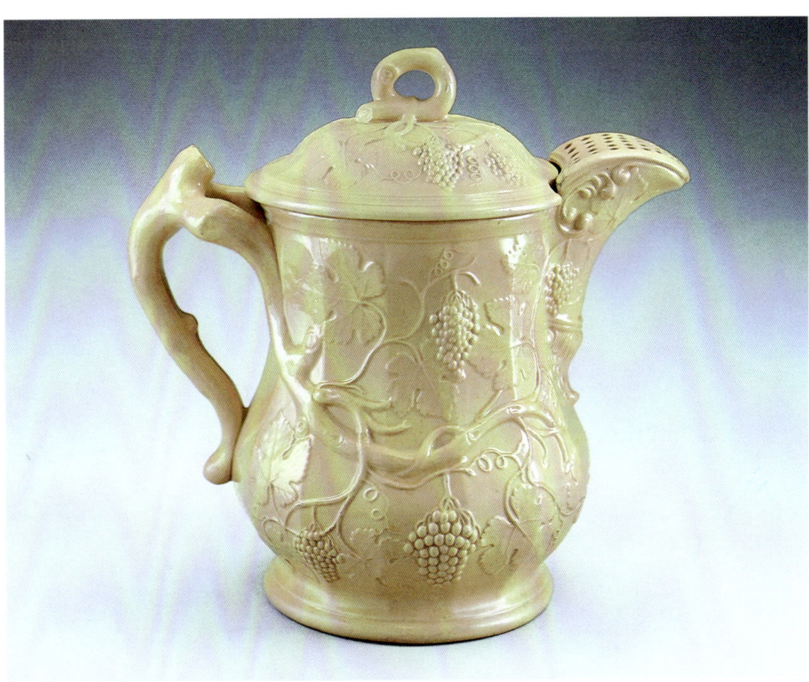

Figure 22 Covered pitcher, Swan Hill Pottery, Edward Hanks and Charles Fish, South Amboy, New Jersey, 1850–1852. Yellow ware. H. 11⅞". This example has a strainer spout and an elaborate bifid branch handle with a branch finial on the lid.

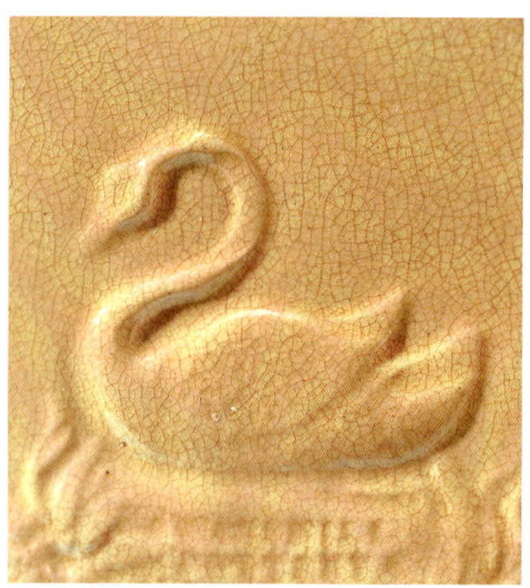

Figure 23 Detail of the mark on the base of the yellow ware pitcher illustrated in fig. 22. It is impressed "SWAN HILL/ POTTERY/SOUTH AMBOY."

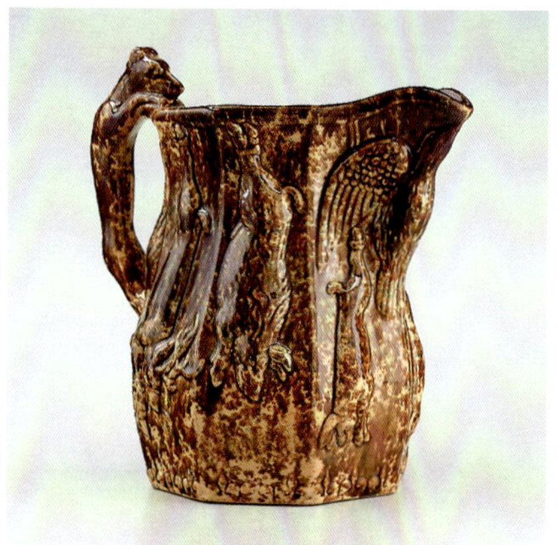

Figure 24 Hound-handle pitcher, possibly East Liverpool, Ohio, mid-nineteenth century. Rockingham glazed earthenware. H. 9¾". This eight sided pitcher has a molded eagle beneath its spout and is colored with a speckled blue flint glaze.

A molded Rockingham presentation pitcher with a colored enamel frog inside was made by the potter Daniel Regan while he was working at John L. Rue and Company, one of the successors to the Swan Hill Pottery (1860– ca. 1871) (fig. 26). On one side of this pitcher are two mounted hunters and on the other a confrontation between the proverbial (and violent) stag and hounds. Charles Coxon first designed this piece while working at Bennett's Baltimore Pottery (1851–1858), and later reproduced it when he ran the Swan Hill Pottery (1858–1860). It continued to be made for many years after.[28]

Dedicated to Mrs. John Webb, yet another Rockingham frog presentation pitcher created a new, elaborate American design with the addition of a central medallion, and is attributed to the Swan Hill Pottery, South Amboy, New Jersey (fig. 27). Somewhat similar designs were also made at

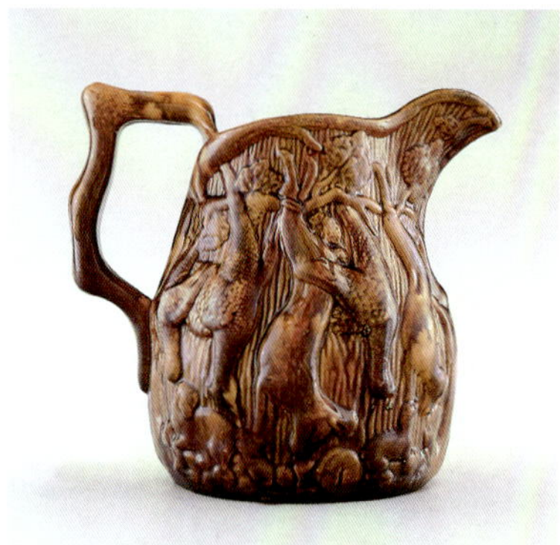

Figure 25 Pitcher, American, mid-nineteenth century. Rockingham glazed earthenware. H. 10". This molded pitcher has a hanging game scene and a branch shaped handle. Three stilt marks in a triangular pattern are on the base.

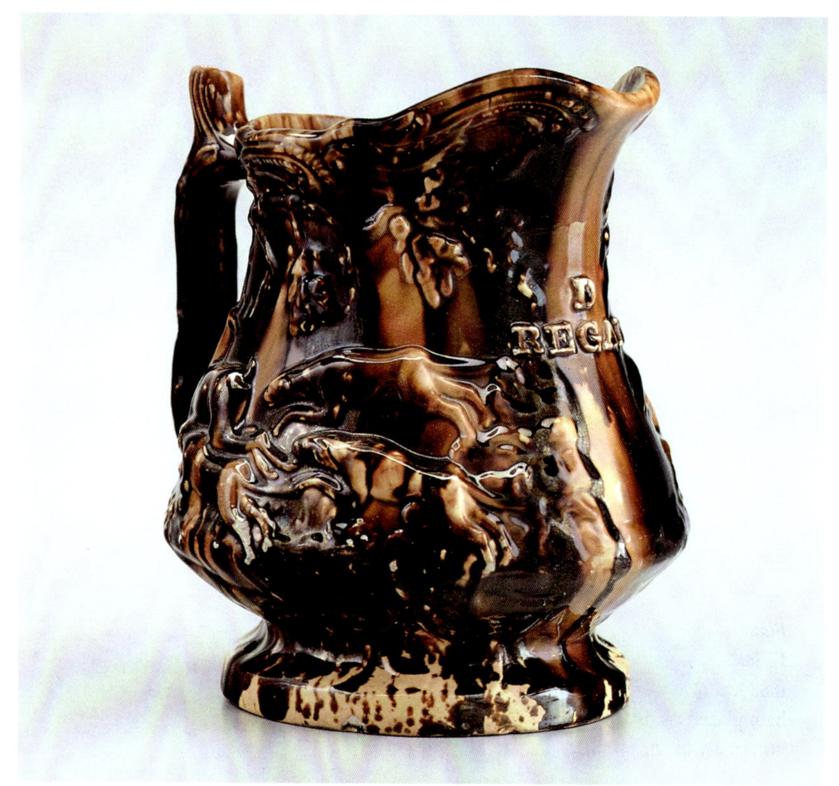

Figure 26 Presentation pitcher, attributed to John L. Rue and Company, 1870. Rockingham glazed earthenware. H. 9". The pitcher has a branch-shaped handle and a flint enamel glazed frog inside on the bottom. The name "D. REGAN" in raised white glazed letters is on the front with "Daniel Regan" and "August 3, 1870" incised on the base.

Figure 27 Presentation pitcher, probably South Amboy, New Jersey, 1860–1870. Rockingham glazed earthenware. H. 10". This pitcher may have been made by John L. Rue and Company, the Swan Hill Pottery, or a later firm copying their work. It has an elaborate filigree-like design around a circular medallion with a bearded man's head. On the front, in white letters, is the name "MRS JOHN WEBB." The inside has a white glaze and a molded Rockingham glazed frog on the bottom.

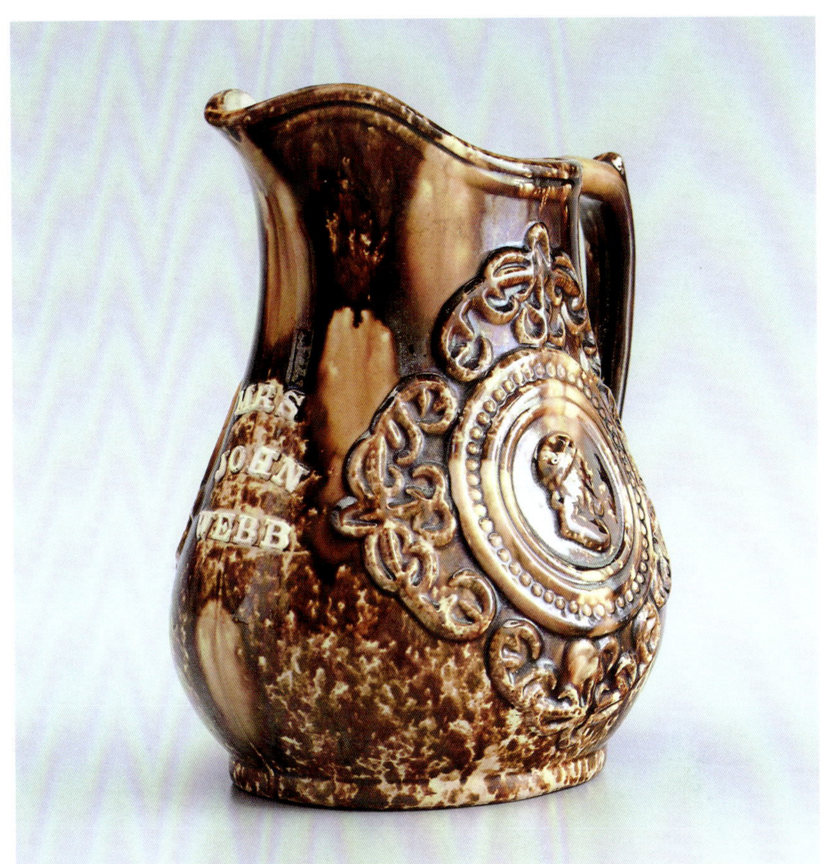

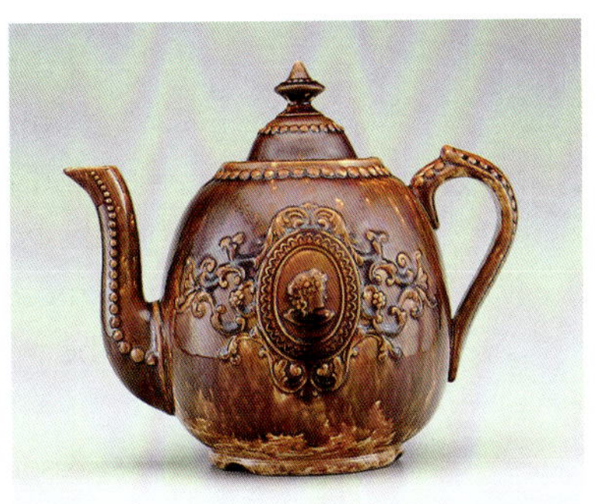

Figure 28 Teapot, attributed to John E. Jeffords and Company, Philadelphia, 1868–ca. 1876 and possibly later. Rockingham glazed earthenware. H. 9¾". A medallion of a woman's head is on both sides.

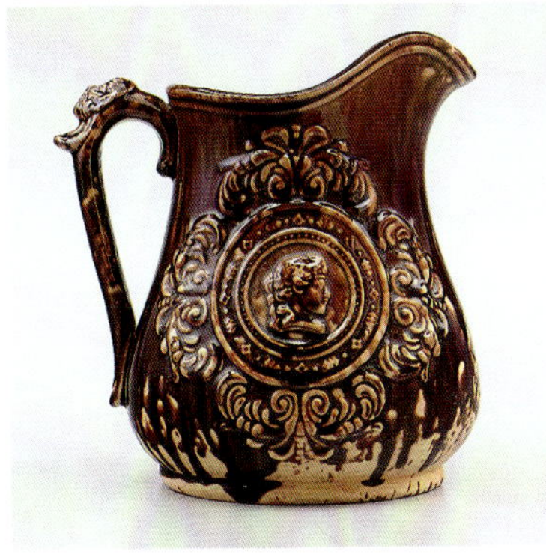

Figure 29 Pitcher attributed to John E. Jeffords and Company, Philadelphia, 1868–ca. 1876 and possibly later. Rockingham glazed earthenware. H. 8". A medallion of a woman's head is on both sides.

the John E. Jeffords and Company of Philadelphia, Pennsylvania: one, a teapot (fig. 28), and the other, a pitcher (fig. 29), both with beautiful Rockingham glazes.[29]

In 1852 potters James Taylor and Henry Speeler moved to Trenton, New Jersey, to form the first factory making white ironstone dinnerware. They primarily made Rockingham ware, porcelain, Queensware, and stoneware. In 1855 English potter William H. Bloor joined them. Earlier, Bloor had worked at the D. & J. Henderson Pottery in Jersey City, and in 1849 he was making Rockingham and yellow ware with William Brunt, Sr., in his East Liverpool pottery.[30]

Bloor worked in Trenton until 1859 and then returned to East Liverpool, where he purchased part of the Phoenix Pottery and made the city's first ironstone ware, as well as Rockingham and yellow ware. By 1861 he had established the East Liverpool Porcelain works, making fine porcelain and parian ware, another first for the region. Because of financial difficulties and loss of labor to the Civil War effort, Bloor was forced to sell his pottery in 1862. Returning to Trenton in 1863, he joined in partnership with Joseph Ott and Thomas Booth under the name of Bloor, Ott, and Booth, also called the Etruria Pottery Works. This firm was the forerunner of the renowned firm of Ott and Brewer, which continued to produce some of the finest porcelain and parian ware in the United States. Bloor's role and achievement in both East Liverpool and Trenton established him as one of the major pioneers in the American ceramic industry.[31]

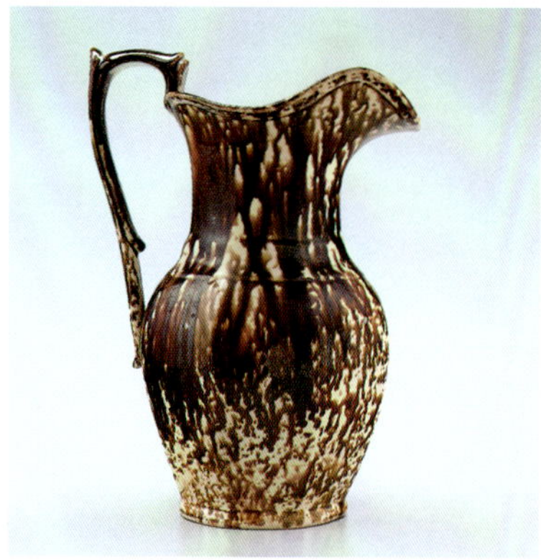

Figure 30 Pitcher, American, mid-nineteenth century. Rockingham glazed earthenware. H. 11⅛".

The Rockingham Aesthetic

Besides its different glaze application, Rockingham ware displays a quality and variety of molded designs, from low relief with intricate modeling or rounded smooth edges to the fine detailing of delicately carved grapes, the underside of a leaf, wavy hair, or a wrinkled brow. All of these complexly designed vessels, to one degree or another, present their own aesthetic. However, there are many Rockingham glazed utilitarian vessels that do not have a sculptural surface embellishment. Others achieve great beauty beyond their useful value.

An example of this is a pitcher (fig. 30) that displays a long, graceful neck extending from an eight-paneled body. Its overall form is narrow, not globular, and has the appearance of a vase. The lip and rim have a gentle curve and a delicate dentilated edge. The handle, long, narrow, and slightly curved, accentuates its height. Independent of the shape, the vertical, flowing lines of Rockingham glaze acts to unify the overall design and accentuate its form. Its translucent glistening brown glaze contrasting with the underlying yellow clay adds to its beauty, singularly dependent on form and glaze.

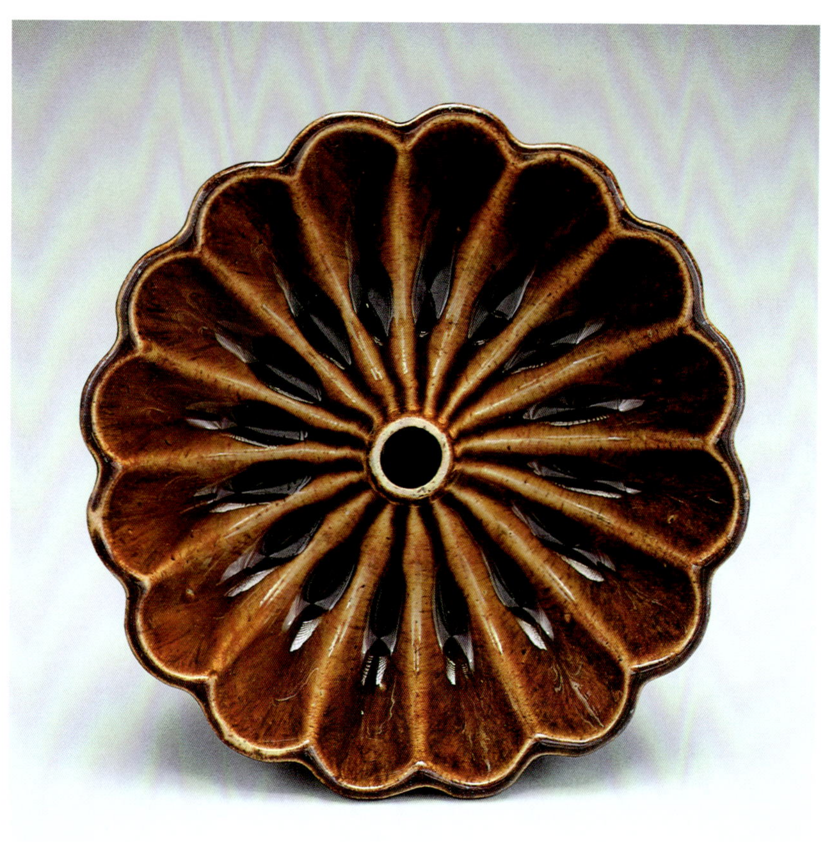

Figure 31 Cake mold, American, mid-nineteenth century. Rockingham glazed earthenware. D. 10".

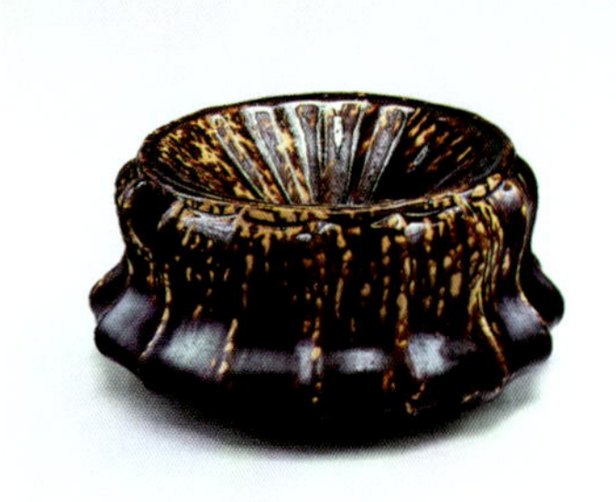

Figure 32 Spittoon, Harker, Taylor & Company, East Liverpool, Ohio, ca. 1852. Rockingham glazed earthenware. D. 8½". Impressed mark on base: "ETRURIA WORKS / EAST LIVERPOOL" in circle with "1852" in center.

Another example is a cake mold enhanced by a lustrous glaze (fig. 31) that arrests the viewer with its overall shape and blended colors. The gently swirled and fluted interior is accentuated by intense glaze pooling in its lower portion and up its central fluted column. One could not ask for a more translucent lustrous glaze, its tonalities of brown contrasted in more thinly applied areas with the underlying yellow clay.

Spittoons were a common product, a logical byproduct for the widespread habit of chewing and spitting tobacco. An early Rockingham example made by Harker, Taylor & Company's Etruria Pottery (1847–1850) in East Liverpool is illustrated in figure 32. Conversely, a rare ceramic form, a flint enamel glazed candlestick made in Bennington about 1850 is pictured in figure 33.[32]

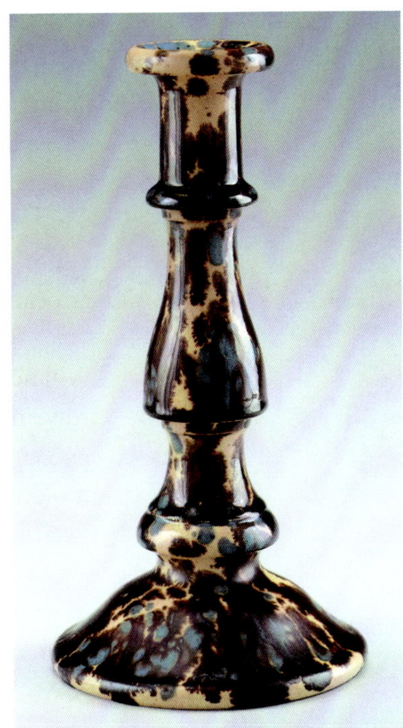

Figure 33 Candlestick, Lyman, Fenton & Co. / United States Pottery Company, Bennington, Vermont, 1849–1858. Rockingham glazed earthenware. H. 9⅜". Flint enamel was added to the glaze.

During the mid-nineteenth century, few people owned sculptural figurines like the Scottish lad and lassie illustrated in figure 34. Made of Rockingham-glazed yellow ware, this pair was inspired by similar Staffordshire examples. The quality of the mold shows in its detail—the young couple's facial features, fringes on dress, plumed feathers, the lamb's wool, and bag pipes, which, in some examples, are obscured by a thick glaze.[33]

Some yellow ware figures were also colored with a darker brown or a mottled glaze; others, made of stoneware, were salt glazed with highlights of cobalt blue. A broad line of utilitarian Rockingham and yellow earthenware, as well as stoneware, was also in production at a number of potteries in upstate New York and other parts of the country.

By the 1840s and 1850s, potteries had grown in size, numbers, efficiency, and industrialization. More modern mass production methods were introduced, and potteries were able to meet the demands of growing markets. As the popularity of Rockingham and yellow ware declined, the potteries were able to compensate by introducing new utilitarian products: whitewares for home table use, hotel china, and sanitary wares. American

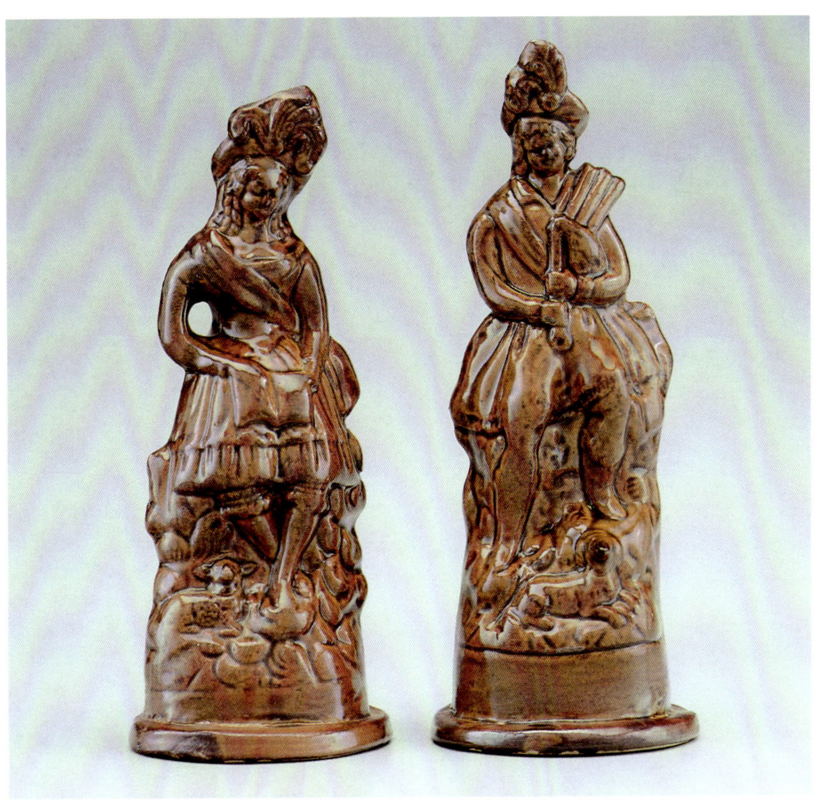

Figure 34 Figures probably by W. H. Farrar, Geddes (Syracuse), New York, ca. 1840–1857, or made in Lyons, New York, by Nathan Clark or Thompson Harrington in the 1850s. Rockingham glazed molded earthenware H. 9⅞" and 10¼". These unmarked figures have a quarter inch central hole in the base.

potteries were on their way to produce wares economically competitive with English manufactories. Later, fine porcelain art pottery and parian wares were made. Credit for this is largely due to the infusion of experienced immigrant potters primarily from Staffordshire and a few from elsewhere. As a result, major pottery centers were created in East Liverpool, Trenton, Jersey City, Woodbridge, Baltimore, and Bennington.

1. James Carr, who was born in England, worked at the American Pottery Company from 1844 to 1852. He left to rent Charles Fish's Swan Hill Pottery at South Amboy and worked there with Thomas Locker and Joseph Wooten until 1853 making yellow, Rockingham and whiteware until 1853. One of their billheads is illustrated in both M. Lelyn Branin, *The Early Makers of Handcrafted Earthenware and Stoneware in Central and Southern New Jersey* (Cranbury, N.J.: Associated University Presses, 1988), p. 200, and Joan Liebowitz, *Yellow Ware* (Atglen, Pa.: Schiffer, 1993), p. 33. Carr subsequently moved to New York City where he formed the New York City Pottery, initially making opaque china, while later making granite and majolica and then excellent bone china and parian ware. See Edwin Atlee Barber, *The Pottery and Porcelain of the United States* (1893 and 1909; reprint, New York: Feingold and Lewis, 1979), pp. 179–80. Branin, *The Early Makers of Handcrafted Earthenware and Stoneware,* p. 198, and Arthur W. Clement, *Notes on American Ceramics, 1607–1943* (New York: Brooklyn Museum, Brooklyn Institute of Arts and Sciences, 1944), p. 19, have Carr working at South Amboy until 1855. Thomas Locker continued to work at the Swan Hill Pottery after Carr's departure. See Branin, *The Early Makers of Handcrafted Earthenware and Stoneware,* p. 99.

2. Arthur A. Eaglestone and T. A. Lockett, *The Rockingham Pottery,* new revised ed. (Rutland, Vt., and Tokyo, Japan: Charles E. Tuttle Company, Inc., 1973), pp. 89, 90; Frederick Litchfield, *Pottery and Porcelain: A Guide to Collectors* (New York: M. Barrows and Company, Inc., 1951), p. 217; Lura Woodside Watkins, *Early New England Potters and Their Wares* (1950; reprint, Hamden, Conn.: Archon Books, 1968), pp. 7, 212; Richard Carter Barret, *Bennington Pottery and Porcelain: A Guide to Identification* (New York: Crown Publishers, 1958), pp. 18, 19.

3. John Spargo, *The Potters and Potteries of Bennington* (1926; reprint, New York: Dover Publications, 1972), pp. 172, 173.

4. Not to be overlooked as well is the origin of utilitarian, salt-glazed stoneware manufacture, which was simultaneously made in the Midwest. Those potters working in Indiana were also primarily English, with only a small percentage from Germany. By 1840 at least twenty-three potters operated in Illinois making stoneware. The most famous were the Kirkpatrick family potteries established in 1836. See Eva Dodge Mounce, "Checklist of Illinois Potters and Potteries," *Historic Illinois Potteries* 1, no. 3 (1989), p. 3.

5. William C. Gates and Dana E. Ormerod, "The East Liverpool, Ohio Pottery District; Identification of Manufacturers and Marks," *Historical Archaeology: Journal of the Society for Historical Archaeology* 16, nos. 1–2 (1975): 15; Barber, *The Pottery and Porcelain of the United States,* pp. 192–96; Edwin Atlee Barber, *Marks of American Potters* (1904; reprint, New York: Feingold and Lewis, 1976), p. 143; Eugenia Calvert Holland, *Edwin Bennett and the Products of His Baltimore Pottery* (Baltimore, Md.: The Maryland Historical Society, 1973), p. 2.

6. Gates and Ormerod, "The East Liverpool, Ohio Pottery District," p. 79; Barber, *The Pottery and Porcelain of the United States,* p. 199; Barber, *Marks of American Potters,* p. 105.

7. Their advertising sheet states it was made by the Harker China Company/The Oldest Pottery in America/Established 1840 as an "authentic reproduction of the first Harker Rockingham Hound Handled 2 Qt. Jug, produced in 1948." They also created a hound-handle mug similarly glazed and a "Rebekah-at-the-Well" teapot with an overall dark brown glaze.

8. Gates and Ormerod, "The East Liverpool, Ohio Pottery District," p. 300; Barber, *The Pottery and Porcelain of the United States,* p. 199; Barber, *Marks of American Potters,* pp. 160, 161, 201. An 1864–1865 price list of the Vodrey Pottery Works of his Rockingham and varigated ware and yellow ware is illustrated in Joan Liebowitz, *Yellow Ware* (West Chester: Pa.: Schiffer, 1993), p. 45.

9. Gates and Ormerod, "The East Liverpool, Ohio Pottery District," p. 52; Barber, *The Pottery and Porcelain of the United States,* p. 200. An 1850 price list of his yellow and Rockingham ware is illustrated in Liebowitz, *Yellow Ware,* p. 43.

10. Holland, *Edwin Bennett and the Products of His Baltimore Pottery,* pp. 2–13. David Goldberg, "Charles Coxon, Nineteenth Century Potter, Modeler-Designer and Manufacturer," *American Ceramic Circle Journal* 9 (1994): pp. 28–64.

11. H. E. Comstock, *The Pottery of the Shenandoah Valley Region* (Chapel Hill: University of North Carolina Press for the Museum of Early Southern Decorative Arts, 1994), p. 122, fig. 4.117, p. 220, figs. 8.62–8.64.

12. Barret, *Bennington Pottery and Porcelain: A Guide to Identification,* p. 320, pl. 417, p. 321, pl. 418. John Bell also copied this mug (see Comstock, *The Pottery of the Shenandoah Valley Region,* p. 130, fig. 4.143). Coxon continued to make this mug with slight variations when he was at the Swan Hill Pottery, ca. 1858–1860.

13. Gary Stradling, "Puzzling Aspects of the Most Popular Piece of American Pottery Ever Made," *Antiques* 151, no. 2 (1997): 332–37; Goldberg, "Charles Coxon," pp. 30, 31, 37–43. Branin, *The Early Makers of Handcrafted Earthenware and Stoneware,* p. 202; Goldberg, "Charles Coxon," pp. 59, 60.

14. Alice Cooney Frelinghuysen, "Empire City Entrepreneurs: Ceramic and Glazes in New York," in *Art and the Empire City, New York 1825–1861,* edited by Catherine Hoover Voorsanger and John K. Howat (New Haven and London: Yale University Press, 2000), pp. 136, 142; Watkins, *Early New England Potters and Their Wares,* p. 212.

15. John Spargo, *Early American Pottery and China* (New York: The Century Co., 1926), p. 317; Watkins, *Early New England Potters and Their Wares,* pp. 211–13.

16. Spargo, *Early American Pottery and China,* p. 306; Spargo, *The Potters and Potteries of Bennington,* pp. 180–84; Watkins, *Early New England Potters and Their Wares,* p. 218.

17. I am grateful to Leslie B. Grigsby for this citation and for sending me photographs of examples of early Staffordshire earthenware lions from her book *The Henry H. Weldon Collection, English Pottery, Stoneware and Earthenware 1650–1800* (New York: Sotheby's Publications, 1990).

18. Diana Stradling, *Jersey City: Shaping America's Pottery Industry, 1825–1892* (Jersey City, N.J.: Jersey City Museum, 1997); Ellen Denker, "Exhibition Checklist," in ibid. Watkins, *Early New England Potters and Their Wares,* p. 211.

19. Diana Stradling, *Jersey City: Shaping America's Pottery Industry, 1825–1892*; Barber, *The Pottery and Porcelain of the United States,* pp. 21, 438–40; Lura Woodside Watkins, "Henderson of Jersey City and His Pitchers," *Antiques* 50, no. 6 (December 1946): 390, 391.

20. Diana Stradling and Ellen Denker have an excellent enlarged copy of the D. and J. Henderson 1830 price list, first reproduced in *Antiques* 26 (September 1934): 109. In copying Greatbach's design, other potters modified the hound, its arched back, and the floral decoration, leaving the hunt scene usually unchanged. All have an Albany slip interior not seen in the American Pottery Company examples. The glazing and modeling details of the copies are inferior compared with the original ones.

21. New Jersey State Museum, *The Pottery and Porcelain of New Jersey, 1688–1900* (Newark, N.J.: Newark Museum, 1947), p. 48, no. 113, pl. 26. It is also listed in Clement, *Notes on American Ceramics,* p. 17, pl. 24; Watkins, "Henderson of Jersey City and His Pitchers," p. 392, fig. 14; and Barber, *The Pottery and Porcelain of the United States,* p. 124.

22. Barber, *The Pottery and Porcelain of the United States,* pp. 438, 439; Diana Stradling, *Jersey City: Shaping America's Pottery Industry, 1825–1892.*

23. Branin, *The Early Makers of Handcrafted Earthenware and Stoneware,* p. 189; Frelinghuysen, "Empire City Entrepreneurs: Ceramic and Glazes in New York," p. 336.

24. Clement, *Notes on American Ceramics,* p. 18; New Jersey State Museum, *The Pottery and Porcelain of New Jersey, 1688–1900,* p. 46; *Early Arts of New Jersey, The Potters Art, c. 1680–c. 1900* (Trenton, N.J.: New Jersey State Museum, 1956), p. 30; *New Jersey Pottery to 1840* (Trenton, N.J.: New Jersey State Museum, 1972). Barber, *Marks of American Potters,* pp. 75–77. Barber was unaware at this time of the Salamander Works at Woodbridge. New Jersey State Museum, *The Pottery and Porcelain of New Jersey, 1688–1900,* p. 47, no. 138, and *New Jersey Pottery to 1840,* fig. 119.

25. Frelinghuysen, "Empire City Entrepreneurs: Ceramic and Glazes in New York," p. 334, fig. 273.

26. Ibid., p. 49, pl. 39, cat. no. 146.

27. The usual Hanks and Fish Swan Hill mark described in the literature is larger, a bit more elaborate, and the swan faces right. Illustrated in Clement, *Notes on American Ceramics,* pl. 54; Lois Lerner, *Lerner's Encyclopedia of U. S. Marks on Pottery, Porcelain & Clay* (Paducah, Ky.: Collector Books, 1988), p. 452; Ralph M. and Terry H. Kovel, *Dictionary of Marks–Pottery and Porcelain* (New York: Crown Publishers, 1995), p. 161. There are two pitchers with Rockingham

glazes which have a mark similar to this one. These are illustrated in Jane Perkins Clany, "Rockingham Ware in America, 1830–1930: An Exploration in Historical Archaeology and Material Culture Studies" (Ph.D diss., University of Pennsylvania, 2000). This is a long-awaited work on Rockingham ware. Besides chapters on archaeology and material cultures, there is an excellent comprehensive history and definition of the term Rockingham as used in England and the United States. Arthur W. Clement, *New Jersey Pottery to 1840* at New Jersey State Museum, Trenton, New Jersey Collection. There is also a known spittoon with the same mark. Branin, *The Early Makers of Handcrafted Earthenware and Stoneware,* pp. 197, 198.

28. Branin, *The Early Makers of Handcrafted Earthenware and Stoneware,* p. 201.

29. "J. E. Jeffords & Company, Philadelphia, Pa., Illustrated List of Yellow, Rockingham, White Lined, Lava and Buff Stoneware," *Crockery and Glass Journal* 3, no. 17 (1876).

30. Gates and Ormerod, "The East Liverpool, Ohio Pottery District," p. 79; David Goldberg, *Preliminary Notes on the Pioneer Potters and Potteries of Trenton, N.J.: The First Thirty Years, 1852–1882* (Trenton, N.J.: Trenton Museum Society, ca. 1983), p. 24.

31. Gates and Ormerod, "The East Liverpool, Ohio Pottery District," p. 16; Goldberg, *Preliminary Notes on the Pioneer Potters and Potteries of Trenton, N.J.,* pp. 24, 25, 40–42.

32. Barret, *Bennington Pottery and Porcelain: A Guide to Identification,* pp. 134–35.

33. A different Rockingham glazed pair of these figures in a private collection has W. H. F. Geddes, N.Y., incised on the back of the young girl, presumably for W. H. Farrar who worked at the Geddes pottery ca. 1840–1857. A similar pair is known made of cobalt blue decorated stoneware and marked "Lyons" in bluish script on their bases. See Vicki and Bruce Waasdorp, *American Pottery Auction* (September 22, 2002), no. 272. Both Nathan Clark (ca. 1822–1852) and Thomas Harrington (ca. 1852–1872) worked in Lyons, New York, during this period. Their pottery's name was stamped under their respective names and "Lyons" on their stoneware. William Ketchum, Jr., *Potters and Potteries of New York State, 1650–1900,* 2d. ed. (Syracuse, N.Y.: Syracuse University Press, 1987), p. 481. Ketchum does not list Lyons as an isolated mark.

Barbara H. Magid

and

Bernard K. Means

In the Philadelphia Style: The Pottery of Henry Piercy

▼ THE EARLIEST EARTHENWARE manufactured in Alexandria, Virginia, is linked both historically and stylistically with Philadelphia, Pennsylvania, 150 miles to the north. Alexandria's first potter, Henry Piercy, arrived there in 1792, having learned the trade at his brother Christian's Philadelphia pottery where he worked from 1769 until at least 1776. Piercy's first advertisement in the *Alexandria Gazette* boasts that his wares are "equal to any work in Philadelphia or elsewhere."[1] Indeed, the wares of Henry Piercy and his Alexandria contemporaries are stylistically identical to some of the Philadelphia earthenware produced during the last three decades of the eighteenth century (figs. 1–4).

The Philadelphia pottery industry was well established by the mid-eighteenth century, and "Philadelphia Earthenwares" were advertised up and down the East Coast. Philadelphia-style earthenwares, including slip-

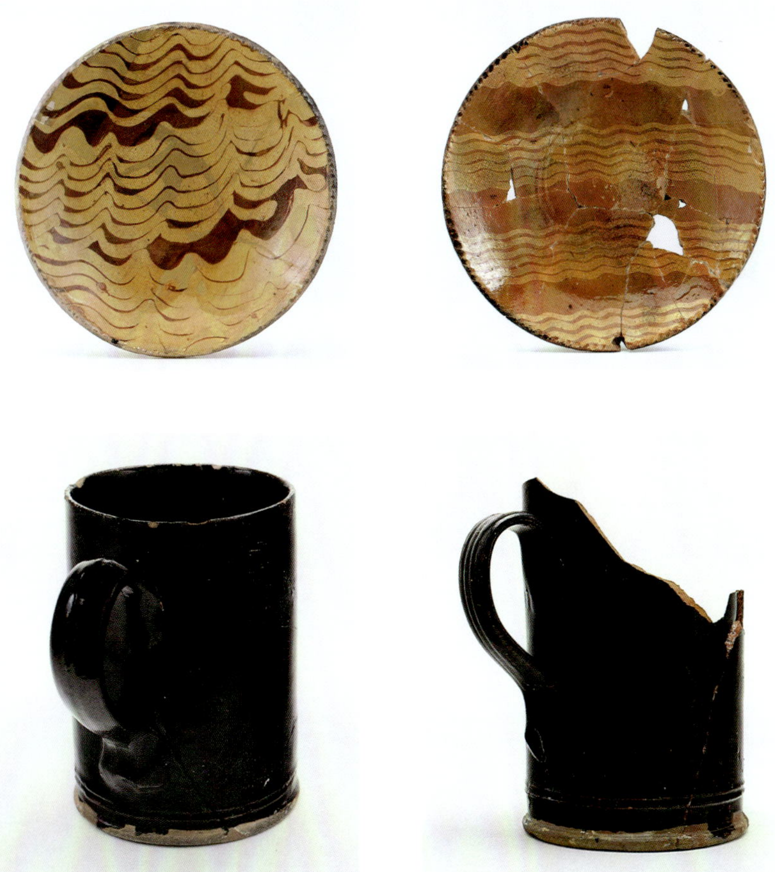

Figure 1 Dish, Henry Piercy, Alexandria, ca. 1792–1796. Slipware. D. 10". (All objects courtesy Alexandria Archaeology unless otherwise noted; photos by Gavin Ashworth unless otherwise noted.)

Figure 2 Dish, Topham/Miller Pottery, Philadelphia, ca. 1795–1815. Slipware. D. 13½". (Courtesy, Dr. Richard J. Dent, Department of Anthropology, American University.)

Figure 3 Tankard, Henry Piercy, Alexandria, ca. 1792–1795. Lead-glazed earthenware. H. 6¼".

Figure 4 Tankard, Philadelphia, ca. 1770s. Lead-glazed earthenware. H. 6¼". (Courtesy, National Park Service, Independence National Historical Park, Inde-57732.)

decorated bowls and trailed and combed wares, have been found in excavations from the Fortress of Louisbourg in Nova Scotia to St. Augustine, Florida, and as far away as Bermuda and Barbados.[2] Philadelphia pottery thus gained a sound and widespread reputation, and was the basis for comparison in advertisements for many potters of the time.

Philadelphia-style pottery was not only imitated in Alexandria but also in Providence, Rhode Island; New York City; and even in rural St. Mary's County, Maryland. In 1767 Joseph Wilson of North Providence (a town northwest of the capital city) advertised "Earthen Ware at a cheap Rate, made in the best Manner and glazed in the Same Way as Practiced in Philadelphia."[3] In 1773, a New York advertisement for potter Jonathan Durrell, "the manufacturer late from Philadelphia," announced that he was making "Philadelphia Earthenware" and that "the ware is far superior to generality, and equal to the best of any imported from Philadelphia, or elsewhere."[4] As early as 1756, Thomas Baker of St. Mary's County advertised earthenware "of the same Kind as imported from Liverpool, or made in Philadelphia, such as Milk-Pans, Butter-Pots, Jugs, Pitchers, Quart-Mugs, Pint-Mugs, Porringers, Churning-Pots, painted Dishes, Plates, etc. with sundry other Sorts of small Ware too tedious to mention" made by his "good workmen from Liverpool and Philadelphia."[5]

When Philadelphia-style pottery is recognized in archaeological contexts, it is generally thought to represent imports from Philadelphia. However, in Alexandria, the locally produced pottery is visually indistinguishable from Philadelphia pottery. This raises interesting questions: How much Philadelphia-style pottery found in archaeological sites throughout America was actually produced in Philadelphia? And how much was produced in other towns, either by potters of Philadelphia origin or by others who learned to emulate the desirable Philadelphia wares?

Archaeologists from Alexandria and physicists from American University are working together to provide the answers and determine if a process called Mössbauer spectroscopy can differentiate between Alexandria and Philadelphia pottery by assessing clay composition and firing conditions.[6] For this study, sherds were analyzed from a waster pile at Alexandria's Piercy Pottery site and from the Topham Pottery at the Metropolitan Detention Center site in Philadelphia. This research will lay the framework for the study of Philadelphia-style earthenware from other cities, as well as establish a method for distinguishing locally produced wares from those that have been imported from Philadelphia.

Philadelphia Antecedents

The Piercy family came to Philadelphia in 1769 as part of a large influx of German immigrants. Over 100,000 German-speaking people had arrived in Pennsylvania by 1760. This migratory trend began nearly a century before, when William Penn's agents enticed European redemptioners to come to Philadelphia for land and religious freedom. Although the first known Philadelphia potters were English, several potters emigrated from Germany in the eighteenth century, including French Huguenot Michael Hillegas

(1727), Jacob Roat (ca. 1739), Matthias Meyer (ca. 1740), and Jacob Utteree/Udery (ca. 1745). Christian Piercy later purchased land from Hillegas for his pottery in the Northern Liberties section of Philadelphia.[7]

Soon, Philadelphia pottery became an amalgam of English and German styles. The ethnic fusion that took place in the industry was a continuation of that which took place in England a century earlier, when English potters were influenced by potters of the lower Rhineland.[8] Philadelphia's pottery industry bustled, supplying local needs and markets throughout the Northeast. The city's archaeological sites reveal that after 1780, wares of local manufacture all but replaced English coarse earthenwares.

The urban potting tradition in Philadelphia predates the rural Pennsylvania German slipware tradition of the late eighteenth and nineteenth centuries. German immigrant potters settled in the rural communities of Bucks and Montgomery Counties around 1760 and produced highly decorated sgraffito and slip-decorated wares, often depicting tulips, birds, and other culturally symbolic motifs. Some of these wares were also made in Philadelphia but are outside the tradition that made its way to Alexandria (figs. 5, 6). The

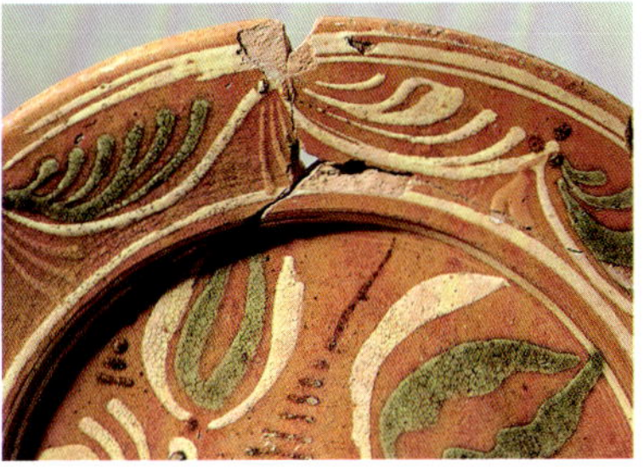

Figure 5 Dish, Philadelphia, ca. 1769. Slipware. D. 9". (Courtesy, National Park Service, Independence National Historical Park, Franklin Court V-627.) This Moravian-style vessel, with a multicolored slip-trailed tulip design, shows a strong Germanic influence.

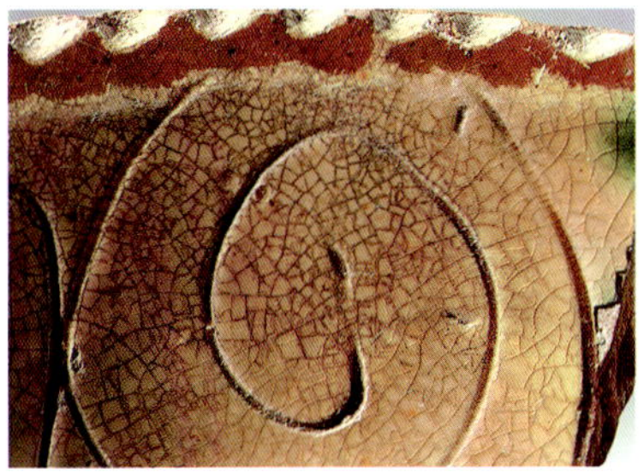

Figure 6 Dish, Philadelphia, ca. 1769. Slipware. D. 8¾". (Courtesy, National Park Service, Independence National Historical Park, Inde-24523.) The sgrafitto technique of scratching a design through a layer of slip was commonly used in England.

rural Pennsylvania potters migrated south through Pennsylvania to rural Virginia and West Virginia, while urban Philadelphia potters often moved to other urban areas. Consequently, Shenandoah Valley pottery shows more similarity to Pennsylvania folk traditions, and Alexandria pottery follows the simpler Philadelphia pottery types.[9]

Earthenware Types Common to Philadelphia and Alexandria

Collections from three archaeological sites in Philadelphia were examined for comparison to the Alexandria wares (fig. 7). The first collection consisted of kiln-related waster sherds from the Topham Pottery (1766–1783), which was studied in the Mössbauer spectrographic analysis. The second was a collection of kiln wasters from an unknown pottery from a Franklin Court deposit dating to 1769. The third collection, from the Chiller Plant

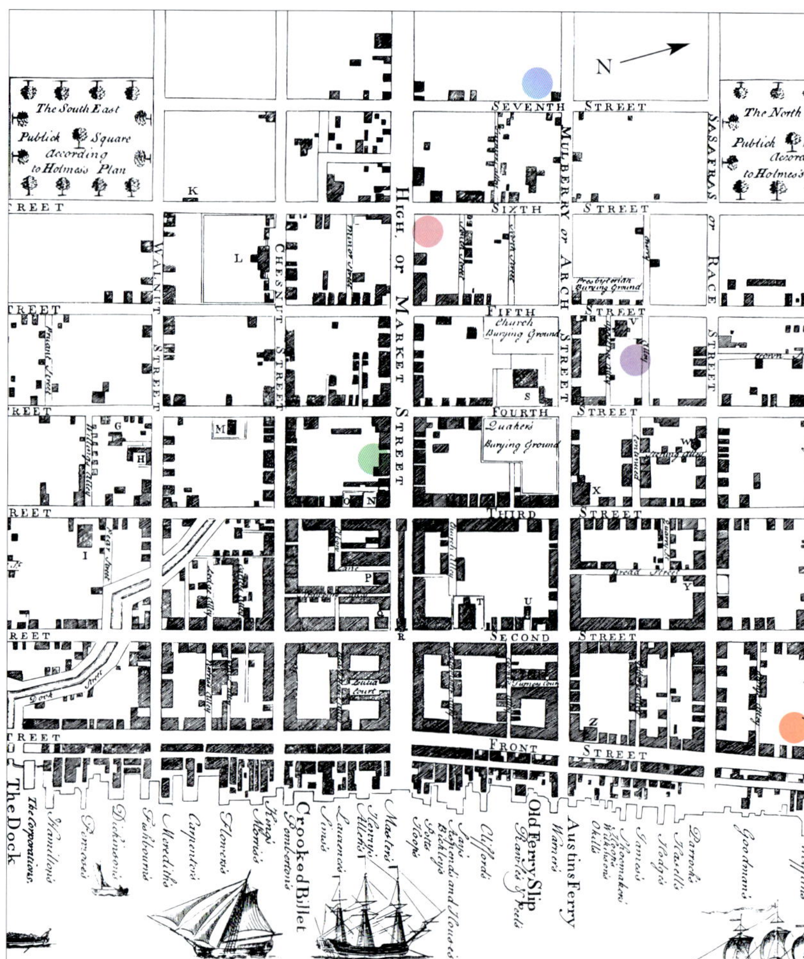

Figure 7 Philadelphia earthenware-related sites, superimposed on Nicholas Scull's plan of Philadelphia, 1762.

A. The Topham/Miller Pottery at the Metropolitan Detention Center site (36PH91).

B. Pottery waster deposit at the Franklin Court site.

C. The Chiller Plant site at Independence National Historical Park.

D. The approximate location of Christian Piercy's pottery, where Henry Piercy worked before moving to Alexandria.

E. Source of clay deposit used in Mössbauer spectroscopy.

site at Independence National Historical Park, was a deposit of domestic trash from a privy shaft dated circa 1770. These collections yielded many parallels for each of the earthenware types found at the sites of Piercy's pottery and retail shop.

Slip-Decorated Wares

PANS: Pans, or basins, are wheel-thrown vessels with sloping sides and narrow, everted rims. Although Piercy's pans (fig. 8) commonly range in diameter from ten to fourteen inches, examples as small as seven-and-three-quarter inches were found in the Philadelphia collections (fig. 9). The pans are decorated with yellow spirals or bands against an orange or red surface. After the pan was formed and dried to a leather-hard state, the decoration was added by turning the vessel as the slip trailed from a slip cup.[10] The vessel's surface was then covered with a lead glaze, giving a yellow hue to the raised lines of white pipe-clay slip. Piercy was adept at creating finely executed spiral bands that are evenly and closely spaced (fig. 10). The bands of slip generally extend over the pan's rim and sides, but they may also continue onto the base. A wavy line may decorate the rim or, like the example from Alexandria, display a chain pattern made of two intersecting wavy lines (fig. 11). Pans may be further embellished with powdered copper

Figure 8 Pans, Henry Piercy, Alexandria, ca. 1792–1796. Slipware. D. 11½", 12½" and 12¾". These vessels were found in a privy behind a china and glass shop that Henry Piercy owned from 1795 to 1796.

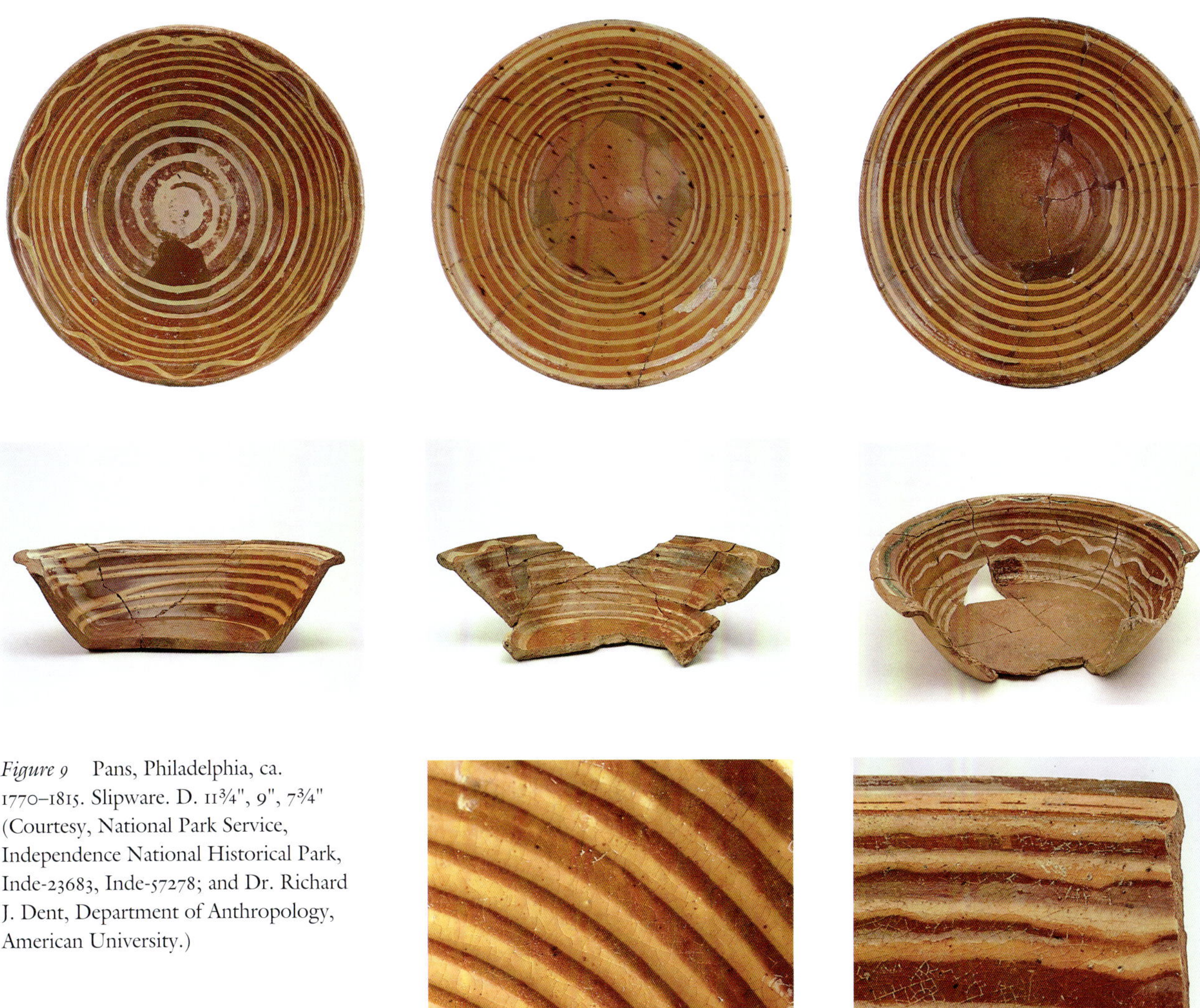

Figure 9 Pans, Philadelphia, ca. 1770–1815. Slipware. D. 11¾", 9", 7¾" (Courtesy, National Park Service, Independence National Historical Park, Inde-23683, Inde-57278; and Dr. Richard J. Dent, Department of Anthropology, American University.)

Figure 10 Detail of pans showing slip-trailed spiral decoration. (Courtesy, Alexandria Archaeology; and National Park Service, Independence National Historical Park, Inde-57278.) The example on the left, from the Piercy kiln site, shows the even, finely executed spirals found on Alexandria slipware. The example on the right is from Philadelphia, ca. 1770s.

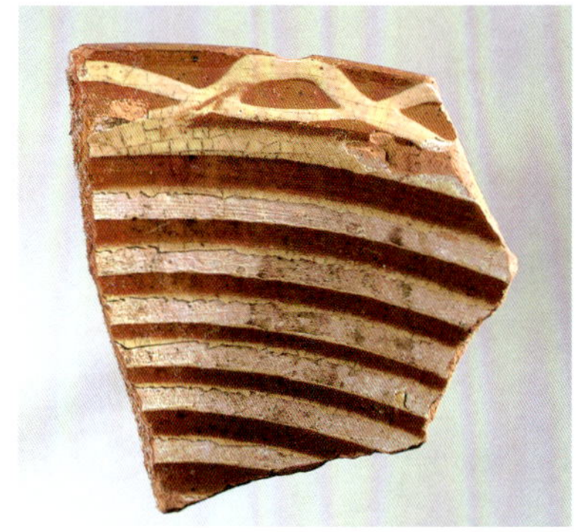

Figure 11 Pan fragment, Henry Piercy, Alexandria, 1792–1809. Slipware. This rim from the Piercy waster dump is embellished with a chain pattern made of two intersecting lines of slip. A plain line or single wavy line is more common.

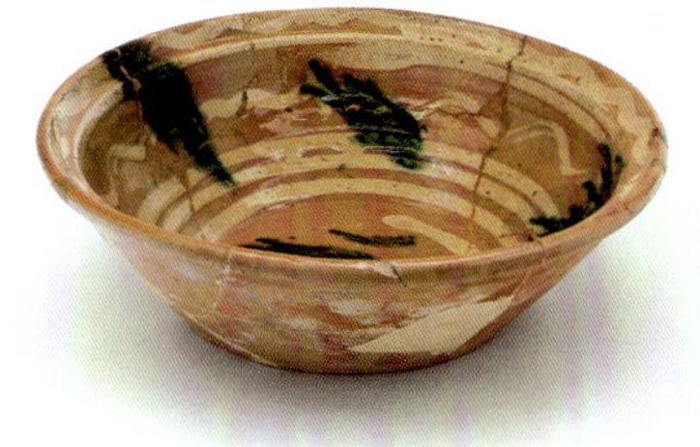

Figure 12 Pan, Alexandria, ca. 1792–1809. D. 10¼". Slipware with green copper-oxide splotches.

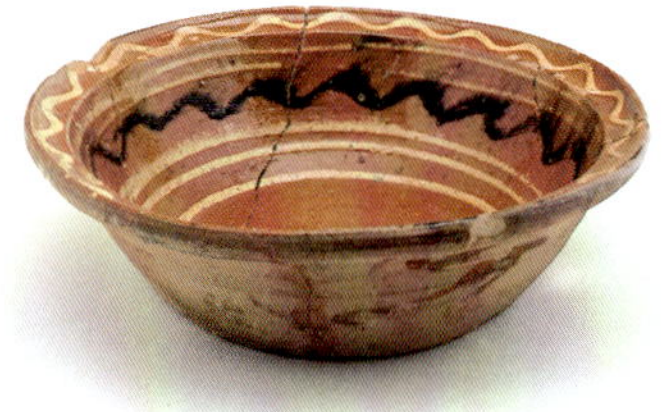

Figure 13 Pan, Philadelphia, ca. 1770s. Slipware with black and yellow trailed slip. D. 8½". (Courtesy, National Park Service, Independence National Historical Park, Inde-57209.) Similar black slip is used by Shenandoah Valley potters, but not in Alexandria.

oxide daubed over areas of the vessel (fig. 12). Some Philadelphia pans include bands of black slip (fig. 13). The latter ornamentation is commonly found on pottery from the Shenandoah Valley, but not seen on Alexandria wares.

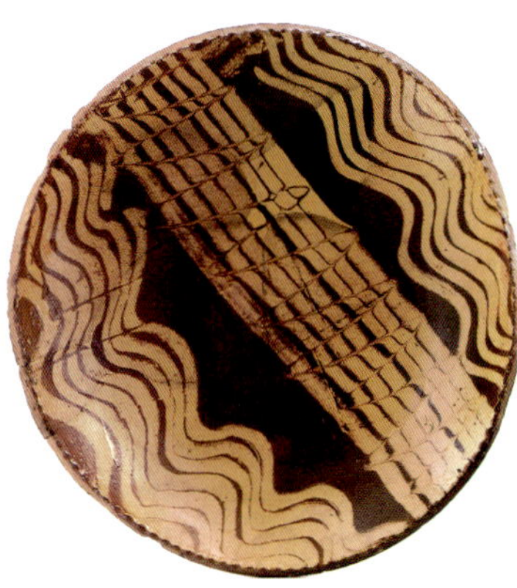

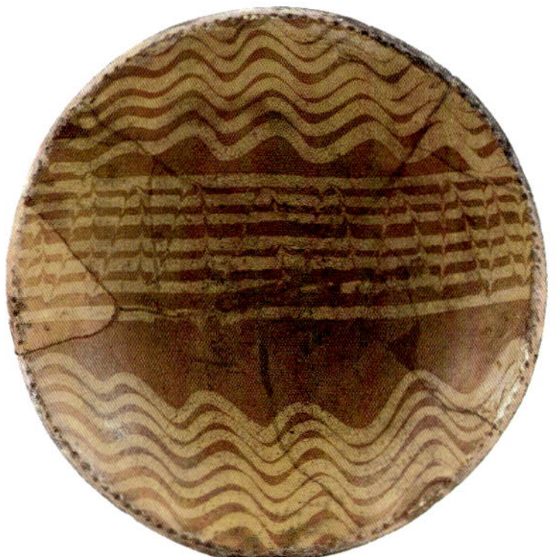

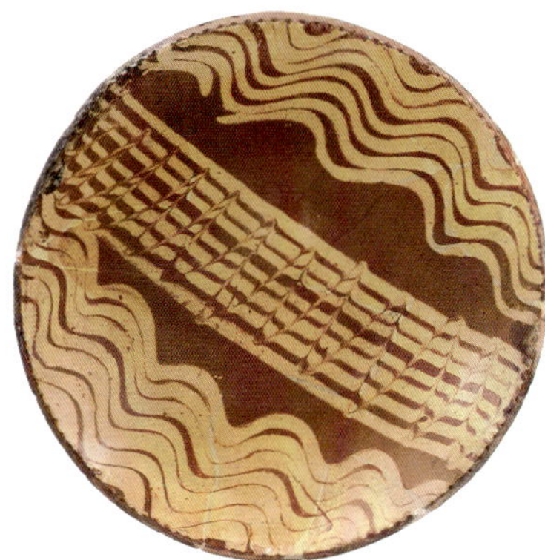

Figure 14 Chargers, Henry Piercy, Alexandria, ca. 1792–1796. Slipware. D. 13", 12½", 13". These large dishes were among more than eighty of Piercy's manufacture that were found in a privy behind his King Street retail shop, occupied for only six months from 1795 to 1796.

CHARGERS: Chargers are shallow, rounded vessels with coggled piecrust rims (figs. 14, 15). These large dishes or plates were drape molded, not wheel-thrown. In this process, the potter rolled a circular slab of clay, decorated it, placed it face down over a domed form called a drape mold, and trimmed the edges.[11] On some of the Philadelphia examples, a faint circle from the mold can be seen in the vessel's center (fig. 16). The mold-drape technique was used on earlier examples of English slipware when the white slip was most often applied over a dark glaze. The slip's flat surface—rather than the raised bands of slip seen on pans—is proof that the slip was applied before the slab was draped over the mold to achieve the curved shape.

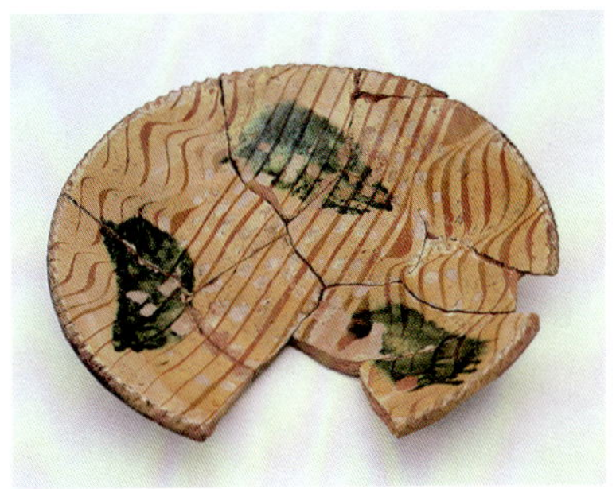

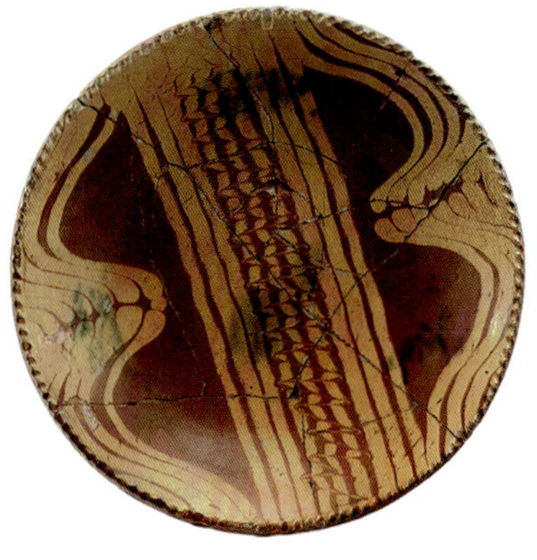

Figure 15 Chargers, Philadelphia, ca. 1770s. Slipware with green copper-oxide daubings. D. 11¾" and 9½". (Courtesy, National Park Service, Independence National Historical Park, Inde-57214 and Franklin Court V-279.)

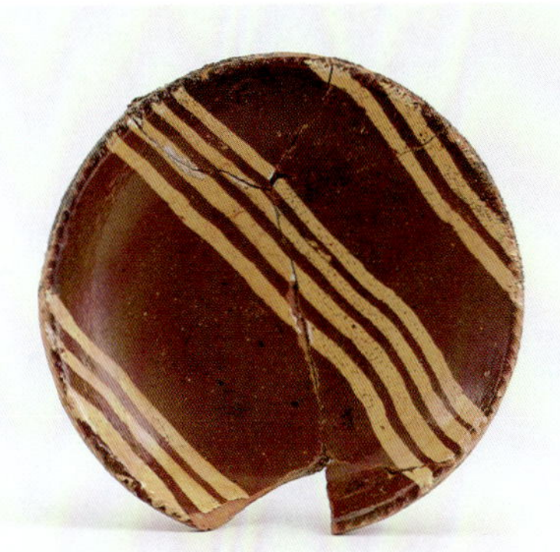

Figure 16 Dish, Topham/Miller Pottery, Philadelphia, ca. 1795–1815. Slipware. D. 7½". (Courtesy Dr. Richard J. Dent, Department of Anthropology, American University.) A faint circle from the drape mold can be seen in the center.

Figure 17 Detail of a dish, Henry Piercy, Alexandria, 1792–1796. This dish clearly shows the use of a multiple-spouted slip cup.

Figure 18 Detail of the combed slip on a dish from the Henry Piercy site, Alexandria, 1792–1796.

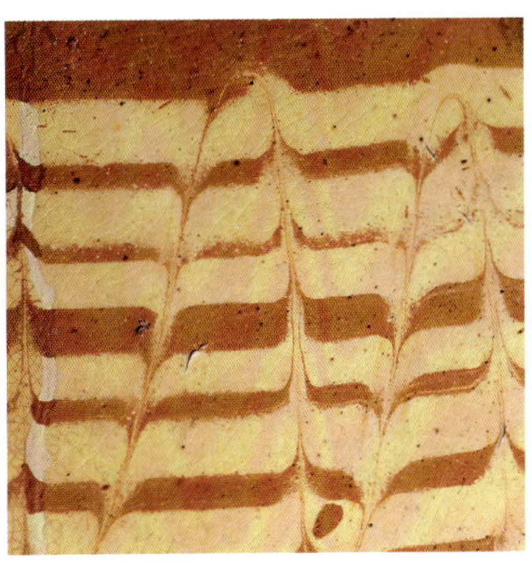

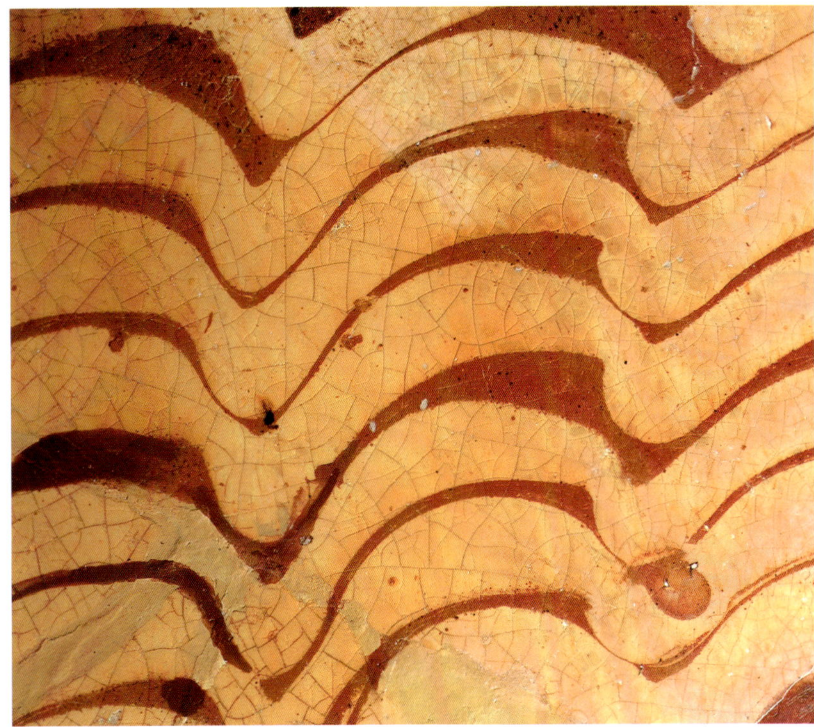

The most common Alexandria pattern is a band of seven combed, straight lines flanked by multiple wavy lines (fig. 17). Some of the bands of slip were combed through while still damp to create a marbled effect (fig. 18). Sometimes green copper-oxide was also applied to examples from

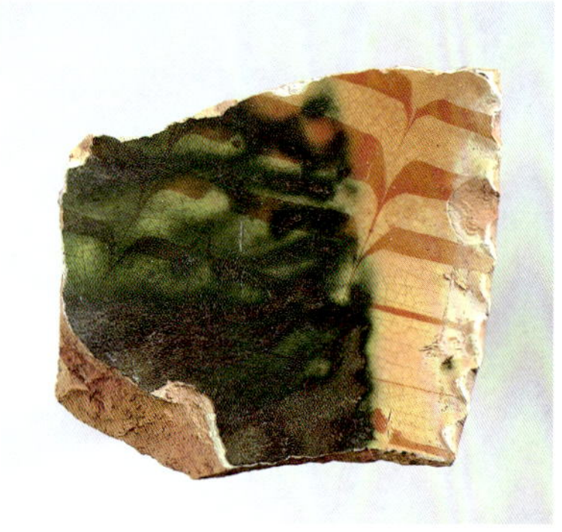

Figure 19 Dish fragment, Henry Piercy, Alexandria, 1792–1809. Slipware. This sherd from the Piercy kiln site is decorated with combed slip and copper-oxide splotches.

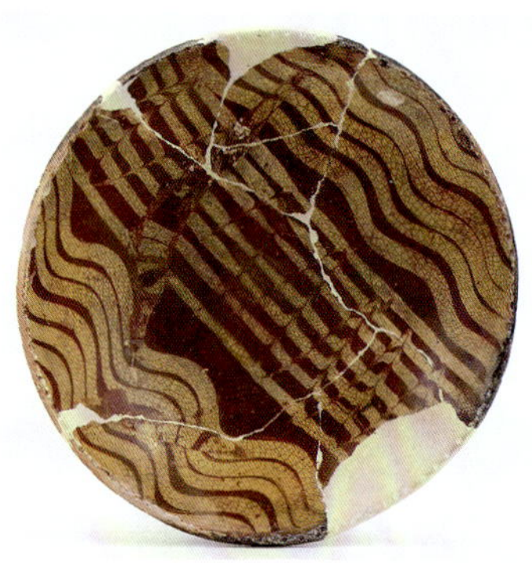

Figure 20 Dish, Henry Piercy, Alexandria, 1792–1796. Slipware. D. 10".

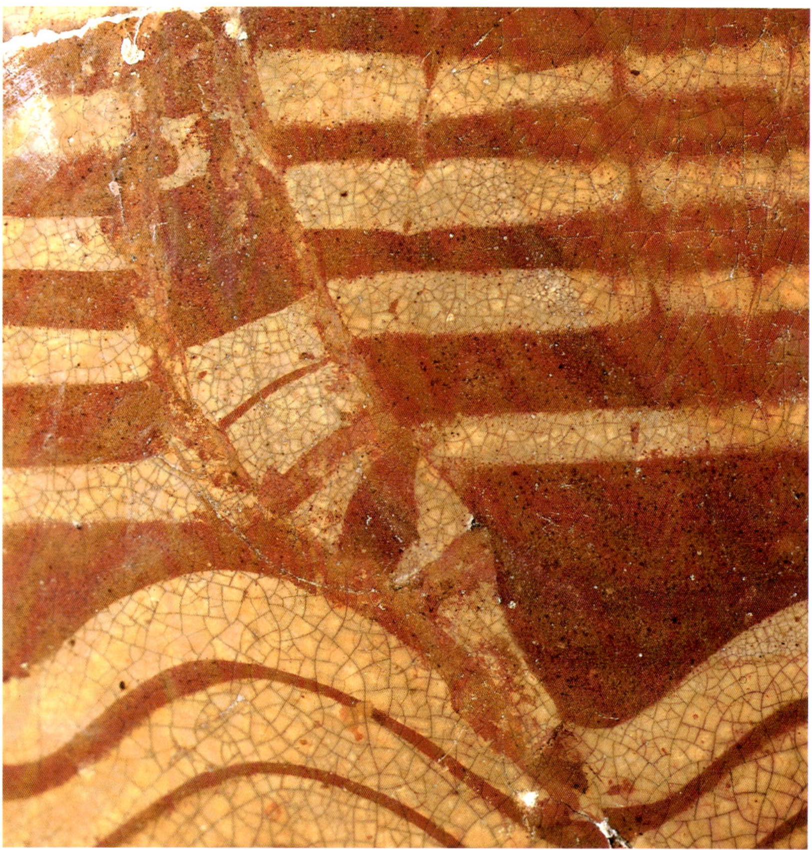

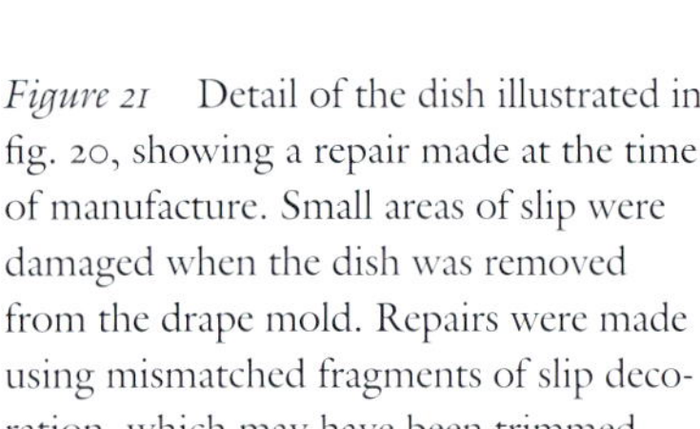

Figure 21 Detail of the dish illustrated in fig. 20, showing a repair made at the time of manufacture. Small areas of slip were damaged when the dish was removed from the drape mold. Repairs were made using mismatched fragments of slip decoration, which may have been trimmed from the edge of the dish.

both Alexandria and Philadelphia (fig. 19). One piece from Alexandria shows repairs made at the time of manufacture. Small areas of slip were damaged when the vessel was removed from the mold, and repairs were made using mismatched fragments of slip decoration, perhaps from the trimmings of this or another vessel (figs. 20, 21).

BOWLS: A brown or orange glaze provides a background for slip-decorated bowls (figs. 22, 23). The bowls' interiors were covered in slip, leaving a narrow band at the rim. The slip, appearing yellow, usually was further embellished with brown splotches. Slip was applied in overlapping lobes on bowls from Philadelphia, but it was evenly applied over the interiors of the Alexandria examples.

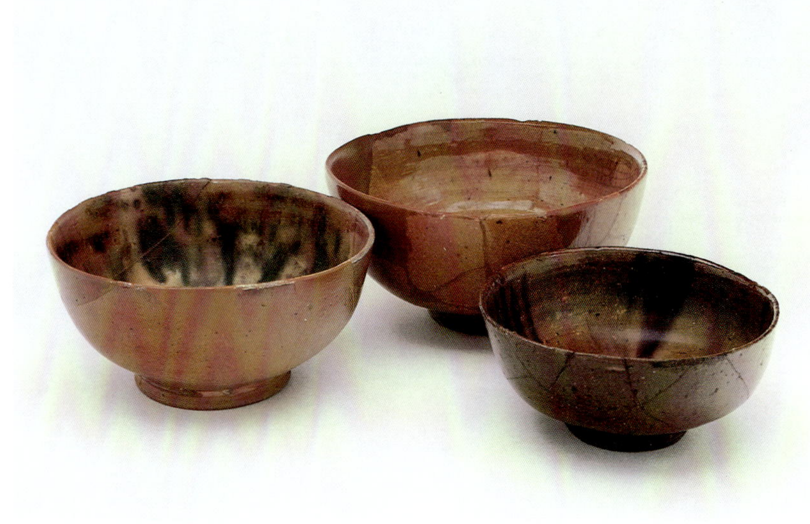

Figure 22 Bowls, Henry Piercy, Alexandria, ca. 1792–1796. Slipware. D. 5½", 6", 5". Note the variation in slip decoration.

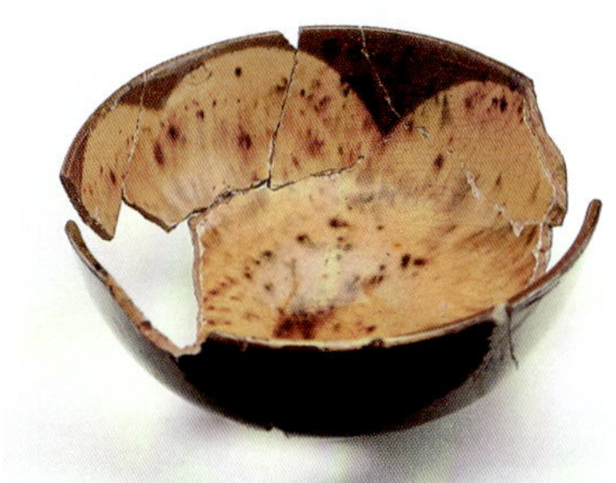

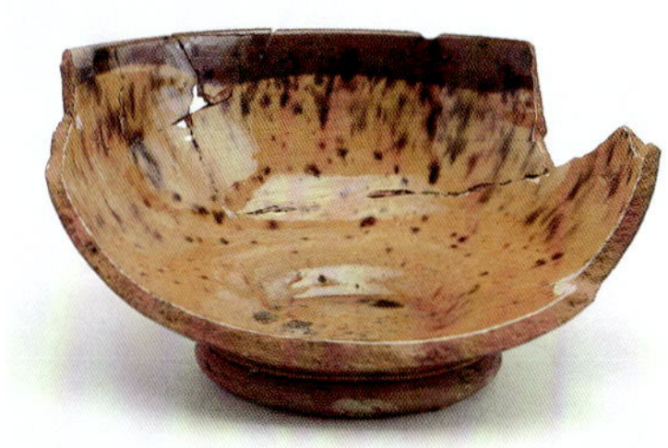

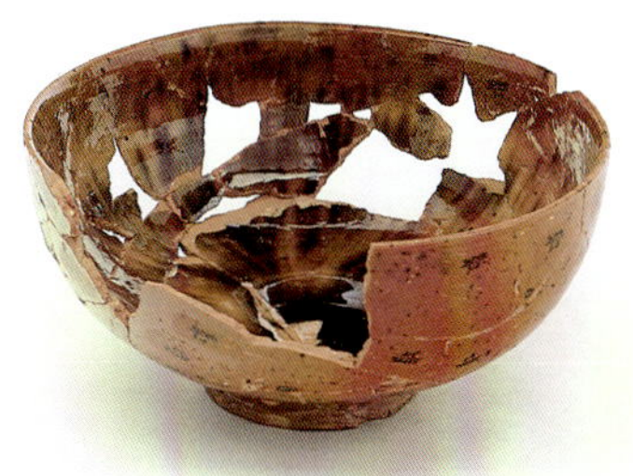

Figure 23 Bowls, Philadelphia, ca. 1770–1815. Slipware. D. 6¼", 5¼", 6". (Courtesy National Park Service, Independence National Historical Park, Inde-54233 and Inde-60183; and Dr. Richard J. Dent, Department of Anthropology, American University.) The application of the slip in lobes, or "petals," can be clearly seen on the example from Franklin Court (left).

Black-Glazed Wares

The black or dark brown wares can be divided into three major groups based on their general shape. The presence of wheel marks helps identify function.

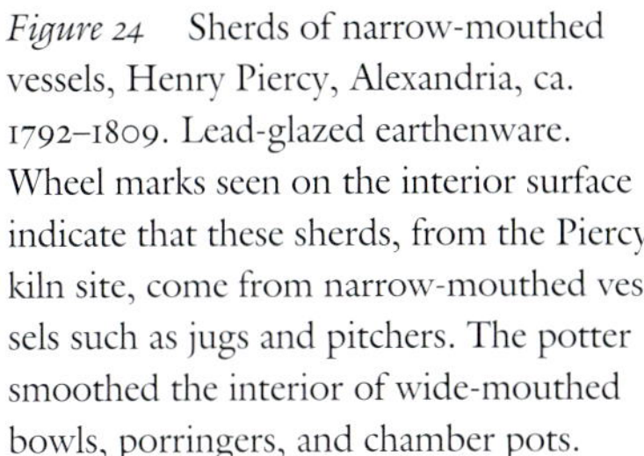

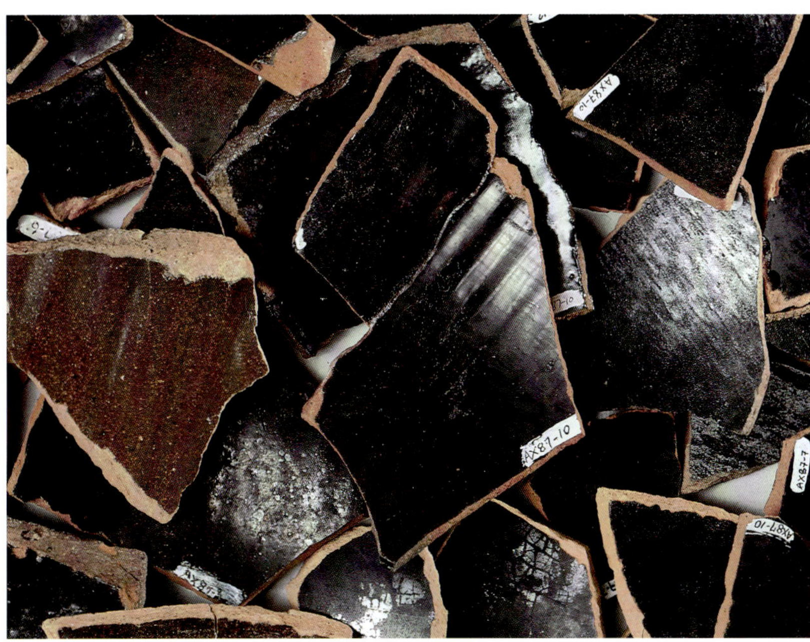

Figure 24 Sherds of narrow-mouthed vessels, Henry Piercy, Alexandria, ca. 1792–1809. Lead-glazed earthenware. Wheel marks seen on the interior surface indicate that these sherds, from the Piercy kiln site, come from narrow-mouthed vessels such as jugs and pitchers. The potter smoothed the interior of wide-mouthed bowls, porringers, and chamber pots.

Figure 25 Syrup jugs, Henry Piercy, Alexandria, ca. 1792–1796. Lead-glazed earthenware. H. 7". These examples are from the site of Piercy's shop.

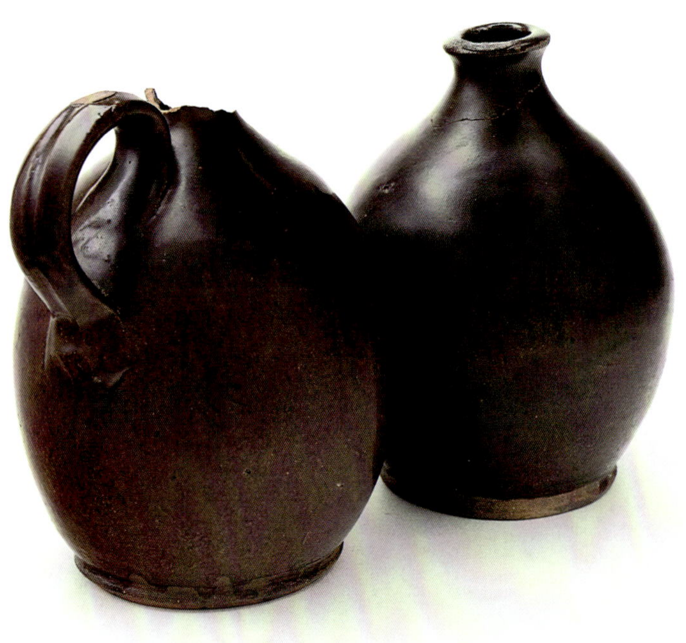

NARROW-MOUTHED VESSELS: Bulbous-shaped jugs and pitchers have clearly visible wheel marks on the interior (fig. 24), indicating that the potter could not reach inside to smooth the pot's surface after it was thrown. Syrup jugs (fig. 25), or bottles, have bulbous bodies, strap handles, and narrow necks with round lips and no pour spout. Pitchers have similar bases and lower bodies but wider necks and pour spouts (fig. 26). Some pitchers in both Philadelphia and Alexandria have a pronounced ridge embellishing the neck of an otherwise plain vessel.

Figure 26 Pitchers, Henry Piercy, Alexandria, ca. 1792–1796. Lead-glazed earthenware. H. 9". Both styles are also found in Philadelphia. These examples are also from the site of Piercy's shop.

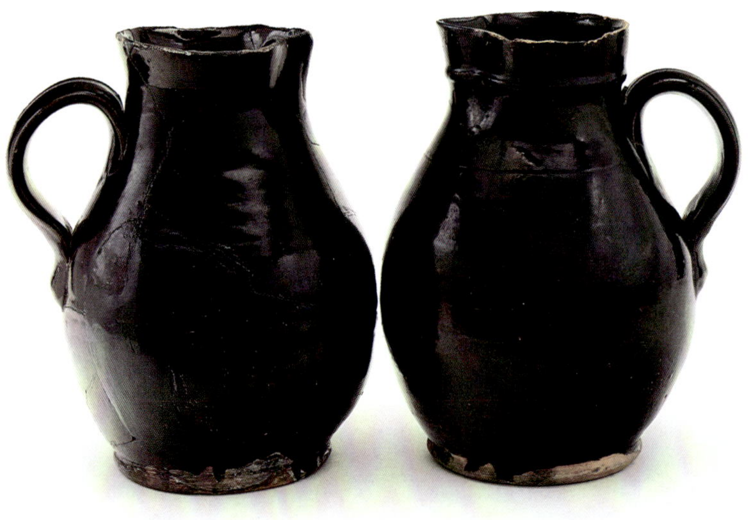

WIDE-MOUTHED VESSELS: A second group consists of rounded vessels with footed bases and smooth interiors. The smooth interior indicates wide-shape vessels—chamber pots, porringers, and bowls—which enable the potter to reach inside and smooth the surface. Chamber pots have either rolled or flat, everted rims (fig. 27). Porringers have strap handles and curved, everted rims (figs. 28, 29). Undecorated bowls generally range in size from five to seven inches in diameter and have a small well in the bottom resulting from the formation of the footring (figs. 30, 31).

Figure 27 Chamber pot, Henry Piercy, Alexandria, ca. 1792–1796. Lead-glazed earthenware. D. 7½".

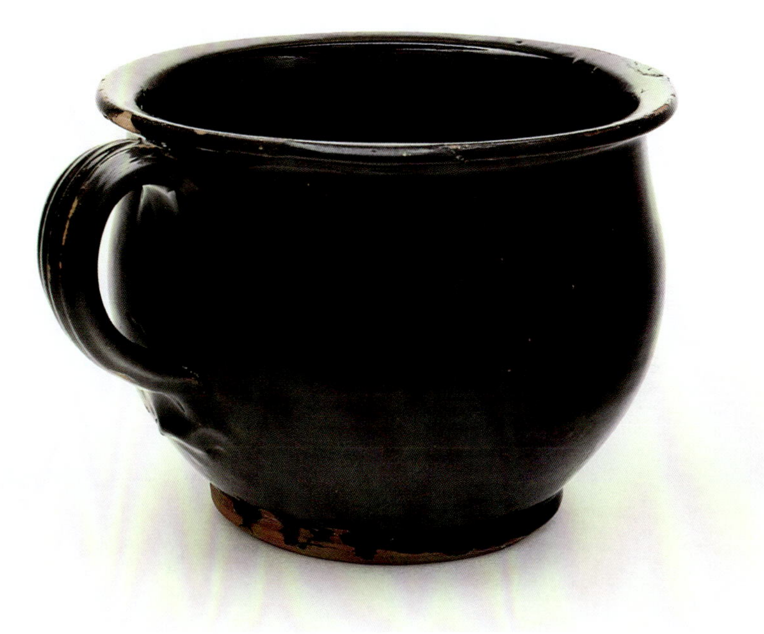

Figure 28 Porringer, Henry Piercy, Alexandria, ca. 1792–1796. Lead-glazed earthenware. D. 5½".

Figure 29 Porringer, Philadelphia, ca. 1769. Lead-glazed earthenware. D. 5½". (Courtesy, National Park Service, Independence National Historical Park, Inde-23705.)

Figure 30 Bowl, Henry Piercy, ca. 1792–1809. Lead-glazed earthenware. D. 6½". This black-glazed bowl is from the Piercy kiln site.

Figure 31 Bowl, Philadelphia, ca. 1770s. Lead-glazed earthenware. D. 8". (Courtesy, National Park Service, Independence National Historical Park, Inde-59910.) Note the well formed by shaping the footring.

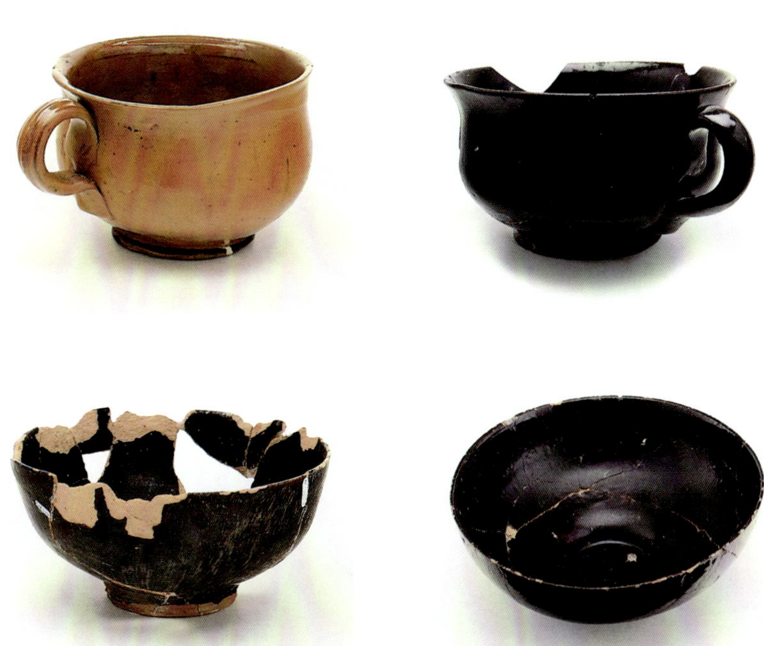

STRAIGHT-SIDED VESSELS: A third group of black-glazed wares includes straight-sided tankards with strap handles and plain rims (see figs. 3, 4), and preserve jars with a cylindrical shape, flat or slightly sloping shoulders, and plain or rolled rims (fig. 32).

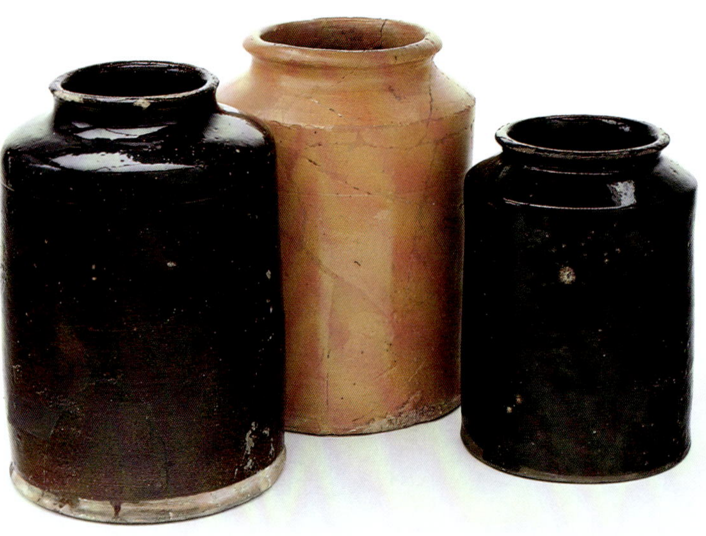

Figure 32 Jars, Alexandria, ca. 1792–1809. Lead-glazed earthenware. H. 8½", 8½", 7".

Utilitarian Wares

Utilitarian wares are unglazed on the exterior, with a dark brown-black (or, rarely, orange) glaze on the interior. The glaze was poured into the vessel and the excess poured out. Smears of glaze can usually be seen on the exterior, below the rim.

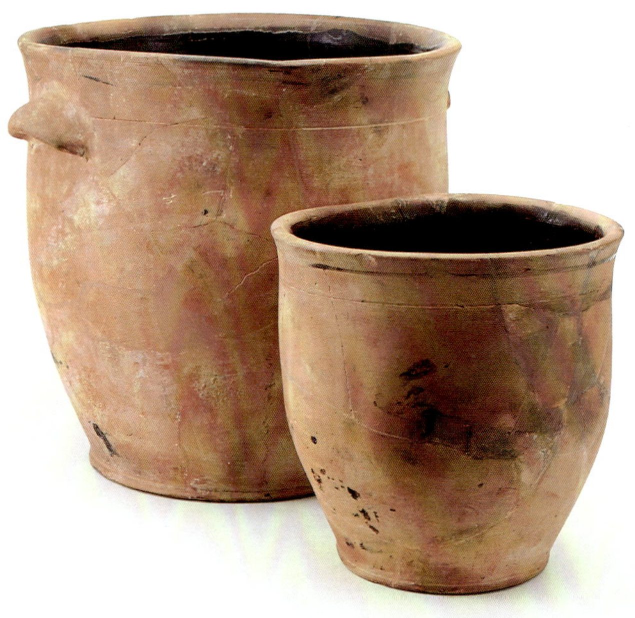

Figure 33 Utilitarian pots, Henry Piercy, Alexandria, ca. 1792–1796. Lead-glazed earthenware. H. 13", 9". The largest pots have lug handles.

Figure 34 Utilitarian pot, Philadelphia, ca. 1770s. Lead-glazed earthenware. H. 10". (Courtesy, National Park Service, Independence National Historical Park, Inde-57294.)

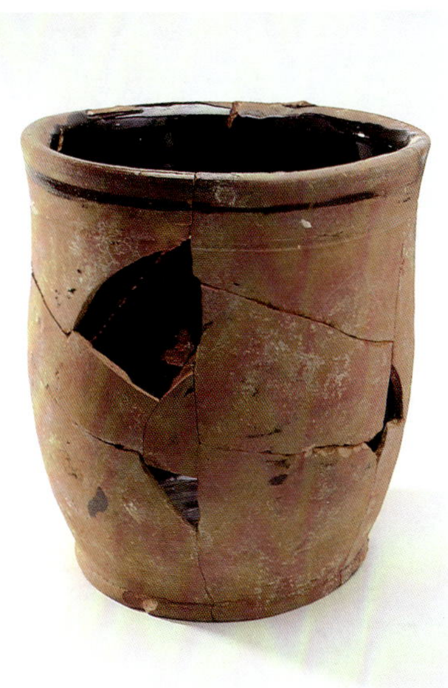

POTS: The pots range in size from five to thirteen and one-half inches in height and six to fourteen inches in diameter. The largest pots have lug handles. These vessels held a variety of food products and may have been covered with muslin tied on with string (figs. 33, 34).

MILK PANS: Milk pans are also glazed on the inside and exhibit smears of glaze beneath the exterior rim. These shallow pans have sloping sides and a pour spout, and range from ten to fifteen and one-half inches in diameter (fig. 35).

Figure 35 Milk pan, Henry Piercy, Alexandria, ca. 1792–1809. Lead-glazed earthenware. D. 11". Milk pans are glazed on the inside of the vessel and have a pouring spout, seen at lower left. They range in size from 10" to 15½" in diameter. Most are shallow like this example, but a few have steeper sides.

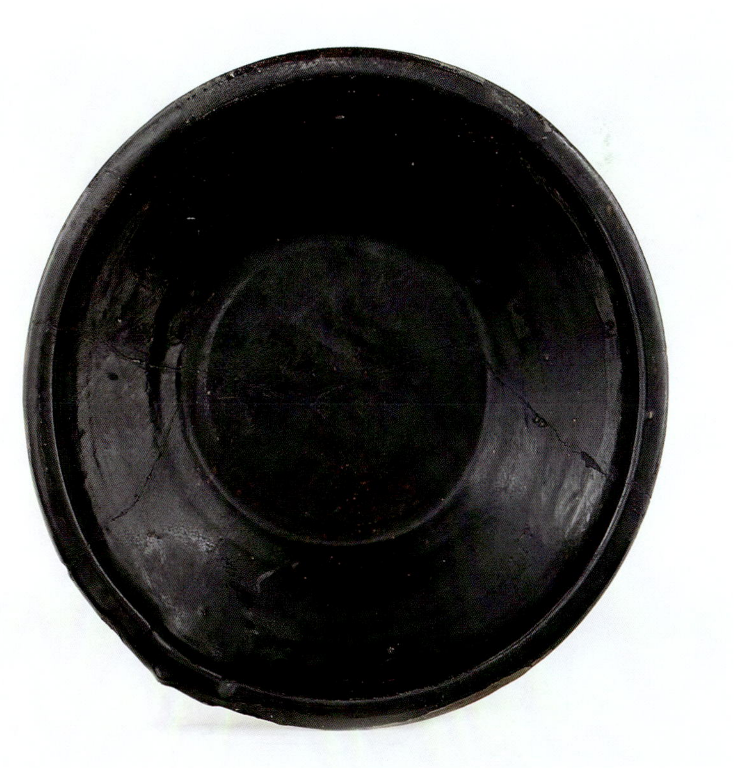

PIPKINS: Pipkins are long-handled cooking pots with a flat or tripod base and a pour spout (fig. 36).

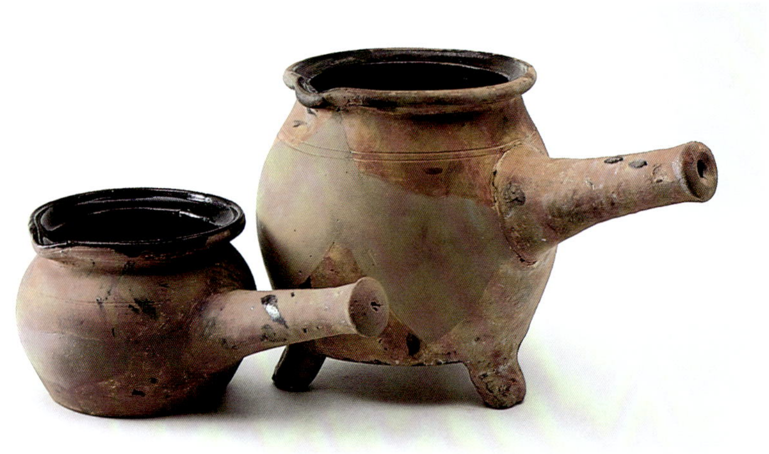

Figure 36 Pipkins, Henry Piercy, Alexandria, ca. 1792–1809. Lead-glazed earthenware. H. 5", 8½". The small pipkin on the left, from Piercy's shop, has a flat bottom. An example from a privy on Market Square has tripod feet to raise it above the hot ashes on the hearth.

Unglazed Wares

Unglazed flowerpots are decorated with piecrust rims and flanges, and may display combing. Some examples have round holes pierced through the side, similar to modern-day strawberry pots. Flowerpot trays were also found (figs. 37, 38).

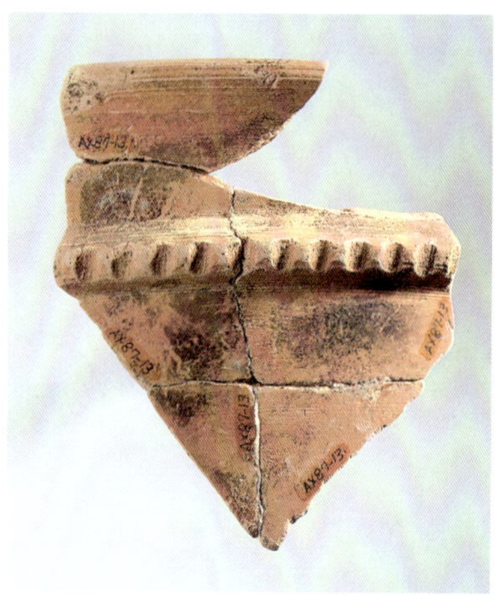

Figure 37 Flowerpot fragment, Henry Piercy, Alexandria, ca. 1792–1809. Unglazed earthenware. D. 10". This sherd from the Piercy kiln site displays a piecrust flange. Some Alexandria flowerpots also have a piecrust rim and wavy combed lines on the body.

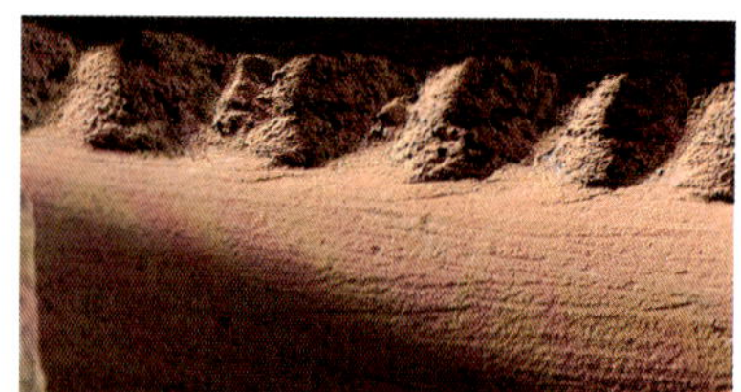

Figure 38 Detail of the piecrust flange of a flowerpot, Philadelphia, ca. 1769. (Courtesy, National Park Service, Independence National Historical Park, Inde-24490.)

Earthenware from the Topham Pottery

Metropolitan Detention Center Site (36PH91)

The Metropolitan Detention Center site is located in Philadelphia's Center City, on the west side of North Seventh Street, between Arch and Filbert Streets (see fig. 7).[12] Data recovery investigations by Louis Berger & Associates, Inc. focused on the mid-eighteenth- through early nineteenth-century components, although the site saw mixed residential, commercial, and light industrial uses until the mid-twentieth century. One of the site's most significant finds was an extensive buried landscape surface. The landscape contained evidence of various domestic and craft-related activities, including the manufacture of earthenware pottery.[13] Evidence was also found for the manufacture of brass tacks and straight pins, bone buttons, leather shoes, and wooden furniture.

From 1766 until his death in 1783, Daniel Topham operated a pottery at 50 North Seventh Street, near what is now Filbert Street in Philadelphia. Historical sources indicate that Topham used local clays that were probably obtained from deposits in or near the Metropolitan Detention Center site.[14] He petitioned in 1780 for "The Privilege of Digging clay for the purpose of making bricks and Potter's Ware on a Certain Lot Situate on the North Side of Race Streets, and between Tenth and Eleventh Streets in the City."[15]

Topham's pottery consisted of a "dwelling, pott house, stable and two sheds."[16] His business was purchased by Andrew Miller in 1785 and operated as a pottery by members of the Miller family until 1840.[17] Although Topham was in debt when he died, by the 1820s Miller and his sons had expanded the business from craft to industrial production, including the manufacture of fire brick, tile, furnaces, and sugar molds. The family was also experimenting with the manufacture of white earthenware and lusterwares.[18]

Daniel Topham was a contemporary of Henry and Christian Piercy in Philadelphia and was influenced by the same stylistic traditions. Traces of pottery produced by Topham were recovered from a group of excavation units (designated Block 2) located in the rear of the 710 and 712 Arch Street lots.[19] These fragments were attributed to Topham, rather than Miller, because of the earlier date of deposition.[20] The highest percentage of redware sherds at the Metropolitan Detention Center site was identified from this area, as was kiln furniture and sherds that were interpreted as possible kiln wasters.[21] These material remains represent indirect evidence of Topham's pottery, since construction of a department store probably destroyed his kiln and pot house. Topham apparently disposed of his broken kiln furniture and wasters near the kiln in an attempt to fill a low-lying and swampy area.[22]

The kiln furniture from Block 2 is similar in form to that found at the Piercy site in Alexandria. Glazed pots were fired inside of the saggers, which came in two basic shapes. One form was cylindrical, like the Alexandria saggers, and the other had in-sloping sides. Their base diameters ranged from six to twelve inches, with most in the eight- to nine-inch range. Other types of kiln furniture included tiles, fire bars, and small wedges, many of which showed fingerprints.[23] A total of 464 fragments of kiln furniture was recovered, along with 193 sherds of coarse earthenware.

Of the earthenware sherds, some were clearly domestic trash; some had charring on the exterior, indicating their use over an open fire; and a few were recognized as imported wares. Most, however, were thought to be kiln wasters: sherds with glaze on the broken edges from breakage in the kiln; sherds adhering to other vessels from explosions in the kiln; or sherds from severely warped vessels. Many of the other earthenware sherds are also likely to be wasters, although they only exhibit breakage from the disposal process.[24]

Topham's inventory, recorded at his death in 1783, included "a quantity of burndt earthen ware, such as Pints, Basons, bowls, juggs, potts, etc."[25] The sherds—remnants from slip-trailed pans ("Basons" in the inventory) and chargers ("dishes" in the site report)—recovered from Block 2 are clearly similar to Alexandria wares in rim forms, basic decorative types, and appearance of the clay body and glazes (fig. 39). Although many fragments

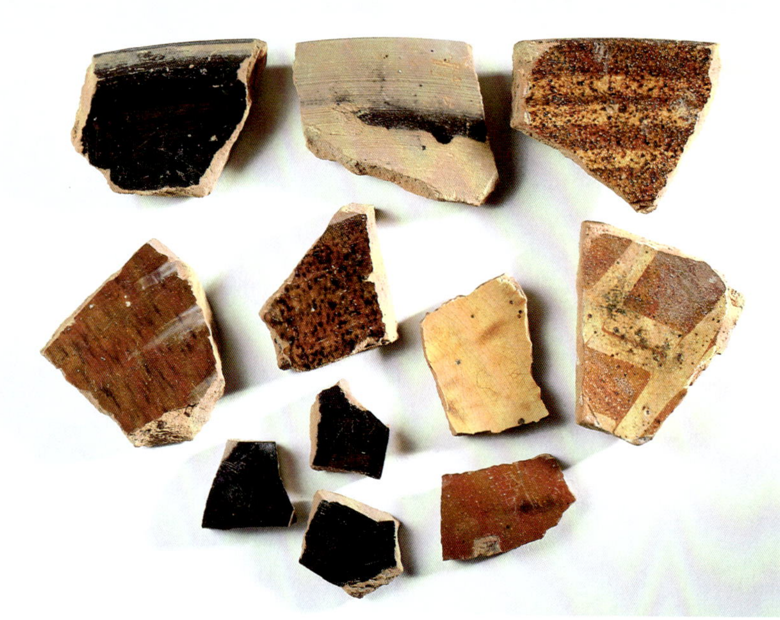

Figure 39 Waster sherds attributed to Daniel Topham, Philadelphia, 1766–1783, recovered from the rear of 711 and 712 Arch Street (Block 2 of the Metropolitan Detention Center site in Philadelphia). (Courtesy, Dr. Richard J. Dent, Department of Anthropology, American University.) Included are fragments of utilitarian pots; a slipware pan, dish, and bowl; and black-glazed vessels.

are decorated similarly to the Alexandria wares, there is some variation, such as a criss-cross pattern seen on one charger sherd. Black- or dark brown-glazed milk pans were the next most common form retrieved. Slip-decorated bowls, dark-glazed jars, porringers, pitchers, chamber pots, tankards ("Pints" in the inventory), and utilitarian pots were also found.

Similar forms and decoration were found on earthenware recovered from Feature 19, a privy at 702 Arch Street. These fragments, however, are from a deposit of domestic trash dating to circa 1795–1815, and may be associated with Andrew Miller or another potter from this later period. The earthenware from Feature 19 also exhibits a wider range of decorative styles of slipware than found in Alexandria, but it includes similar chargers, pans, bowls, syrup jars, and chamber pots.

With the cooperation of the lead investigator at the Metropolitan Detention Center site, Professor Richard J. Dent, samples were selected for physical analysis and clay sourcing from among the kiln wasters in a single unit in Block 2.[26] The selected earthenware wasters were produced by Daniel Topham and are similar in form and shape to Henry Piercy's wares.

Earthenware from Franklin Court

Independence National Historical Park

Three mid-eighteenth-century privy deposits (Features 9, 22 and 25) from the Franklin Court site (see fig. 7) revealed large assemblages of artifacts

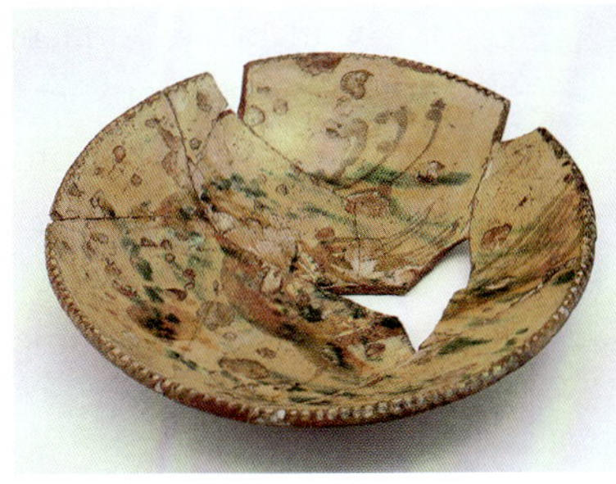

Figure 40 Dish, Philadelphia, ca. 1769. Slipware. D. 11¾". (Courtesy, National Park Service, Independence National Historical Park, Inde-24234.) This vessel from Franklin Court has a bird motif.

from a local pottery, including earthenware wasters and kiln furniture.[27] These artifacts were found in association with other trash dating to circa 1740–1765. The kiln-related material was thought to have been brought from nearby, around 1769, as privy drainage base fill. Similar kiln-related materials were found under the paving of Oriana Street from extensive filling and grading for the site of Franklin's new house.[28]

The range of decoration on these colonial Philadelphia wares was broader than that used in Alexandria in the 1790s, and included more clearly Germanic forms. However, many of the wares are similar to those later made by Henry Piercy. A similarly dated domestic deposit from the Chiller Plant site on Independence Mall contained many of the same wares.[29]

The Philadelphia chargers from the Franklin Court site are marbled, sponged, striped, or combed, while Alexandria wares are limited to striped or combed lines. Trailed-slip designs, used primarily on shallow pans with sloping sides, include examples with floral, foliate, or bird motifs, as well as the yellow banding or spirals found in Alexandria (fig. 40). Slip is applied to bowls in the lobed, or "petal," pattern.

Some examples of sgraffito or scratched decoration (see fig. 6) were found at Franklin Court, but this technique is little used by the end of the eighteenth century and is not found in Alexandria. Sgrafitto, used in England and Northern Europe and common in the rural Pennsylvania Dutch tradition, was also used in the Shenandoah Valley.[30] Also recovered from Franklin Court are vessels covered by white slip with applied trailed-

Figure 41 Detail of a hollow ware vessel, Philadelphia, ca. 1769. Slipware. (Courtesy, National Park Service, Independence National Historical Park, Inde-23688.) This vessel from Franklin Court has black on white slip decoration on the exterior.

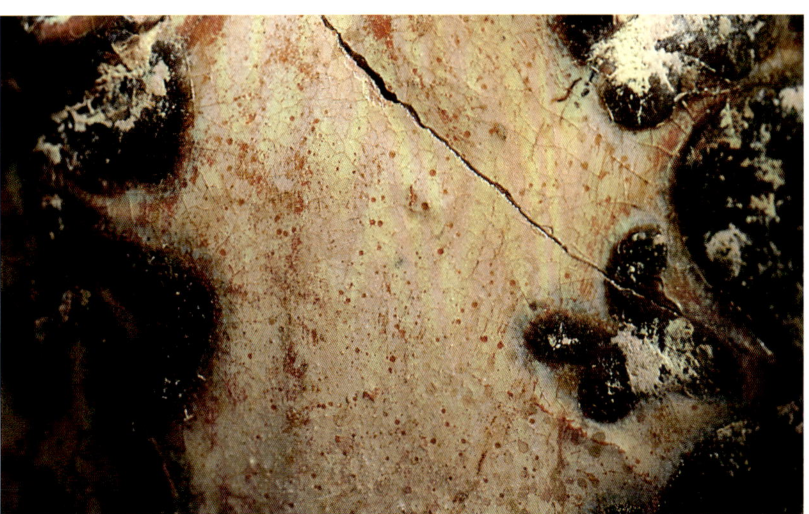

slip designs in black (fig. 41). Sgraffito and the slip-trail technique often depict birds or flowers. Decoration applied over white slip was later used by Shenandoah Valley potters such as John Bell and J. Eberly.[31]

In both Philadelphia and Alexandria, handled porringers, tankards, chamber pots, pitchers, and syrup jugs (round bottles) are black glazed on both interior and exterior. Some of the Philadelphia examples, like those from Alexandria, have no ornamentation. Others have a ribbed midsection (fig. 42) reminiscent of Buckley ware (a contemporary English coarseware with an agate clay, thick black glaze, and, often, ribbing).[32] Bowls appear in both plain and slip-decorated versions. Utilitarian milk pans, pots, and pipkins are glazed only on the interior.

Although the Franklin Court assemblage has more variety in both style and form, nearly all of Henry Piercy's wares are identical to examples found at Franklin Court. More than twenty-five years after the Franklin Court kiln wasters were discarded, a well-entrenched Philadelphia style was still evident in Philadelphia as well as in Alexandria. A later assemblage of household debris at Franklin Court (Feature 26), with a date range of circa 1780–1800, contained vessels similar to the earlier kiln-related assemblages.[33] Piercy continued to make wares in Alexandria in the 1790s that had been in vogue upon his arrival in Philadelphia in 1769, but these same styles also continued to be made in Philadelphia at the century's end.

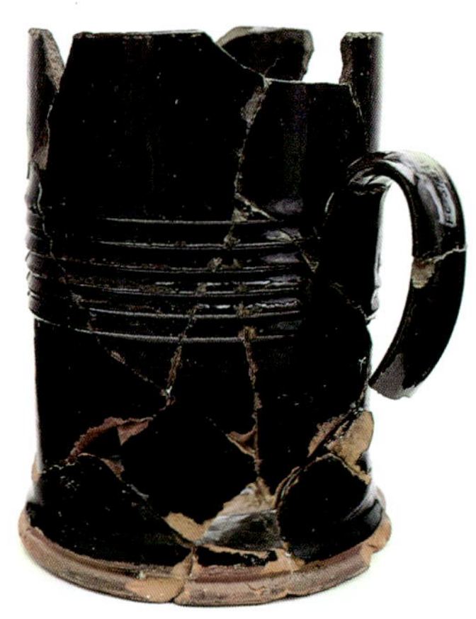

Figure 42 Tankard, Philadelphia, ca. 1769. Lead-glazed earthenware. H. 4¾". (Courtesy, National Park Service, Independence National Historical Park, Inde-23646.) This vessel from Franklin Court has a ribbed midsection reminiscent of Buckley ware.

Henry Piercy and the Alexandria Potters

The Piercy Family

Henry Piercy was born in Saarbrücken, in Germany's lower Rhineland, in 1756 (fig. 43). At age thirteen, he immigrated to Philadelphia with his family. His parents, John Jacob Piercy (1707–1769) and Anna Cunigundo Piercy, had six children. Christian, Jacob, and Henry Piercy were potters. There was another brother, George, and two sisters whose names are unknown.[34]

At age twenty-five, Christian became head of the household when his father died the same year the family arrived in Philadelphia. Christian's home was in the Northern Liberties section of Philadelphia, at 296–298 North Front Street.[35] His pot house was nearby (see fig. 7). Christian's first mention in the *Pennsylvania Gazette* was in 1774, when he offered a reward for a runaway apprentice.[36] As Captain of the Fifth Philadelphia Militia, he served at Valley Forge during the winter of 1777 to 1778.

Henry Piercy, the youngest brother, learned the pottery trade from Christian and worked with him for seven years before enlisting in the Revolutionary army in 1776 at age twenty. He was promoted to lieutenant in February 1777. Henry was an aide-de-camp to George Washington and an original member of the Society of the Cincinnati.[37]

Christian's great-grandson Joseph Fornance recalls a family story "that while at Valley Forge, being a potter, he built a kiln and made a lot of dishes for the soldiers. But the needs of the soldiers were so great that when the kiln was opened they rushed in and took all the dishes, leaving him none for his own use."[38] (Brothers Jacob and Henry also served at Valley Forge.)

After the war, Christian returned to his successful pottery business in Philadelphia. He and potter Michael Gilbert led twenty potters in the Grand Federal Procession in Philadelphia in 1788. Along with one of his eight children, he died in the yellow fever epidemic of 1793 at age forty-nine. On January 4, 1794, the *Pennsylvania Packet* announced the public sale of his potting business and household effects, but notices in May 1794 and July 1795 stated that the business would continue.[39]

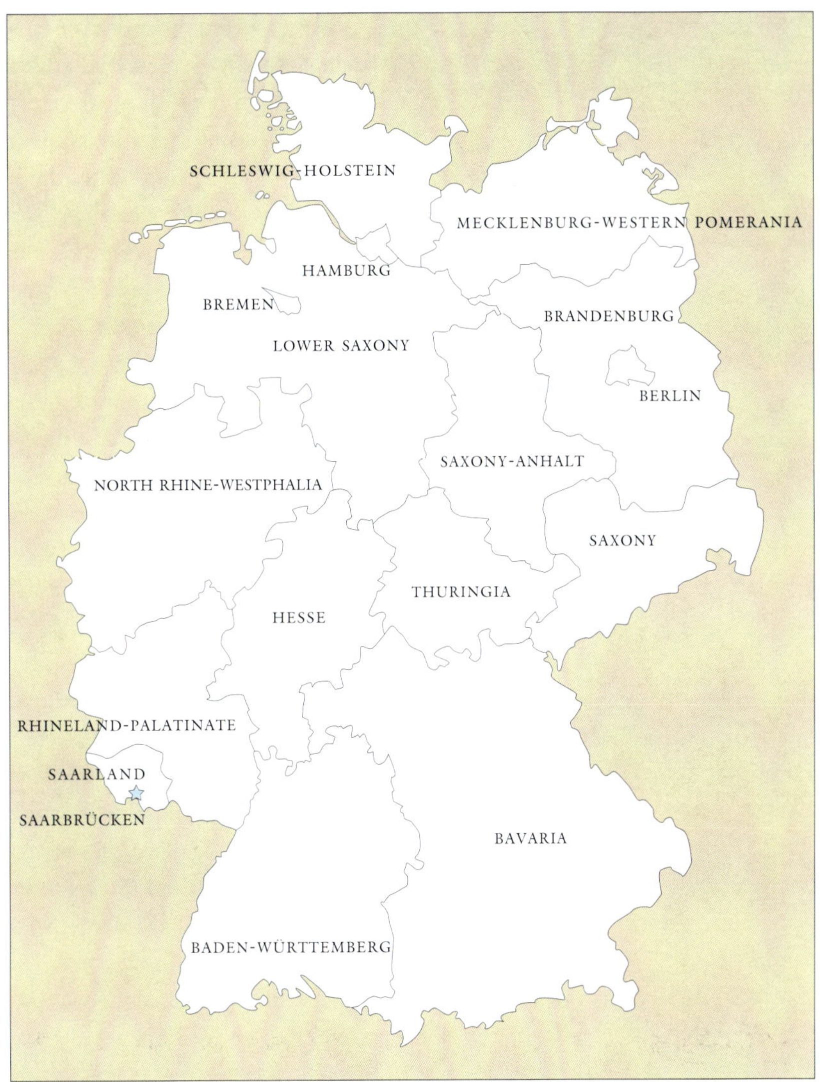

Figure 43 Piercy's homeland in Saarbrücken, Germany, was a major center of earthenware production. (Artwork by Nichole Drgan and Wynne Patterson.)

Henry may have returned to Philadelphia with his brother after the war, but he was not listed in the 1790 census. In April 1792, he was living in Trenton, New Jersey, and had been appointed a master mason in Trenton Lodge #5. By November of that year, he had moved to Alexandria and opened his "Manufactory of Earthen Ware."[40]

After Henry moved to Alexandria, he married Mary Burroughs. He had no children but took in his niece Catherine and nephew John after their father Christian's death. "Henry Piercy/Lewis Plumb/John Piercy" was recorded on the 1797 tax rolls, indicating John's involvement in the pottery. In 1798 John was back in Philadelphia, listed in the city directory as a potter at 324 North Front Street.[41] At age twenty-one, John may have returned to run his late father's business or another nearby pottery.

Henry Piercy was a prominent member of Alexandria society, serving on three grand juries between 1795 and 1797. As a Mason, he was elected junior warden of Alexandria Lodge #22 in 1793, and was senior warden from 1797 until 1801. He also commanded a company of military volunteers, the Independent Blues of Alexandria, whom he paraded in honor of

George Washington's visit to Alexandria on November 6, 1798, and again the following year at Washington's funeral. Henry leased his pottery business in 1799, apparently no longer active in the business. That same year, he received a commission as captain in the Eighth Infantry Regiment. When Henry died in June 1809, the Lodge marched with a military escort to the Old Presbyterian Meeting House for the funeral, and he was buried in the Episcopal burial grounds.

The Town of Alexandria

The town of Alexandria was established in 1749 after a group of merchants and landowners petitioned the General Assembly for creation of a market town. But even before this, seventeenth- and eighteenth-century plantations dotted the countryside. Waterworn ceramics from the third quarter of the seventeenth century, which were found in fill beside a later wharf, are indicative of ships ballast and suggest port activity more than fifty years before the town's establishment.[42] By the 1730s Hugh West had established a tobacco warehouse, a ferry service, and a tavern on the bluff overlooking the city's bay. And Philip and John Alexander farmed the surrounding land. In 1749 a street grid was established over a sixty acre area, and eighty-four half-acre lots were sold at auction. In 1752 the Fairfax County Courthouse moved to Alexandria, establishing the new town as the regional center of northern Virginia. Over the next half century Alexandria continued to grow, expanding to the west with the sale of new lots. The steep bluffs on the Potomac were cut down to fill the shallow half-moon bay, increasing valuable commercial property and deepening the harbor. The town was incorporated in 1779, and in 1789 some of its area was included in the parcel given by Virginia to form part of the new District of Columbia.

By the end of the eighteenth century, Alexandria's designation as an official port of entry enabled foreign ships to land and unload without registering elsewhere. Fronting the Potomac River, the city became one of the ten busiest ports in America, with one thousand ships arriving each year.[43] Henry Piercy was one of many settlers from Philadelphia who was attracted to the thriving town. In 1792, the year that he arrived, a law was passed exempting artisans, mechanics, and handcrafters who migrated to Virginia from taxes on implements of trade and from other taxes apart from those assessed on land. This exemption was in effect until 1826 and encouraged the migration of skilled craftsmen.[44] That many of the craftsmen came from Philadelphia is alluded to in an 1816 issue of the *Alexandria Gazette:* "The houses are generally built of brick and upon the less modern Philadelphia plan, the most of the mechanics having been from that place."[45] In 1816 Alexandria potter Lewis Plum was also still producing earthenware of the "less modern Philadelphia" style.

Before 1792, when Piercy and other craftsmen were encouraged to move to Virginia, Alexandria homes and businesses used utilitarian pottery imported from England, Germany, and other parts of America, including, most likely, Philadelphia. Archaeological excavations primarily show German and English stoneware and English earthenware before circa 1790. In Piercy's first advertisement in 1792, he asks for "the patronage of all those who wish to encourage home manufactures."[46] Home manufactures were indeed encouraged by Alexandrians, and utilitarian wares found on archaeological sites dating from the 1790s through the 1870s appear mostly to be of local manufacture. Chemical analysis to determine the clay source of Philadelphia-style earthenware found on residential sites (beyond the scope of our current research) will be necessary to determine whether the wares are indeed of local manufacture, or if they were imported from Philadelphia even after Piercy's business was well established.

Henry Piercy's Business Ventures

As Alexandria's first known potter, Henry Piercy introduced the Philadelphia style of pottery to other potters who worked alongside or in competition with him. Slip-decorated pans and other Philadelphia forms continued to be made with little change for around thirty years, until stoneware had all but replaced earthenware. Between 1792 and 1876, Alexandria had at least seventeen potters working at nine different potteries, producing earthenware and, later, stoneware.[47]

Piercy built his pot house on a quarter-block lot on the northeast corner of Washington and Duke Streets. At the time, the location was on the outskirts of town, where noxious fumes from the kiln and danger of fire would be of less concern (fig. 44).[48] In 1795 Thomas Fisher built a second pot house opposite Piercy's, on the southwest corner. As demonstrated from wasters discovered in test excavations in the 1960s, these potteries produced similar wares in the Philadelphia style.[49]

Piercy was also involved in retail ventures. On November 1, 1792, he advertised "for sale at his house, the upper end Prince Street, a large assortment of CHINA QUEEN's WARE and GLASS."[50] He also sold china and glass from a shop on King Street, between Royal and Pitt Streets, which was in operation for only ten months. On June 20, 1795, the local newspaper advertised:

> PIERCY AND GRAHAM Have Just Received and Now Opening for Sale Opposite Mr. McNight's Tavern, King Street, a neat and general assortment of DRY GOODS . . . Amongst which are a beautiful assortment of NANKEENS . . . Also an Assortment of China and Glass.[51]

Significantly, a well behind this shop was excavated in 1974, and the eighty vessels of Piercy's manufacture that were recovered can be dated to the brief ten-month time period.[52]

According to tax records, Piercy formed a partnership with his nephew John Piercy and potter Lewis Plum in 1797, while Fisher went into partnership with potters Thomas Hewes and James Miller. Henry Piercy and Fisher were working together by March of 1797 when they advertised the opening of their Alexandria "Delfware manufacture" in a Norfolk, Virginia, newspaper. Nothing resembling tin-glazed delftware has been found, however, at the Piercy or Fisher Potteries, or in any Alexandria pottery site.[53] Tax records of 1798 confirm the Piercy and Fisher partnership. The

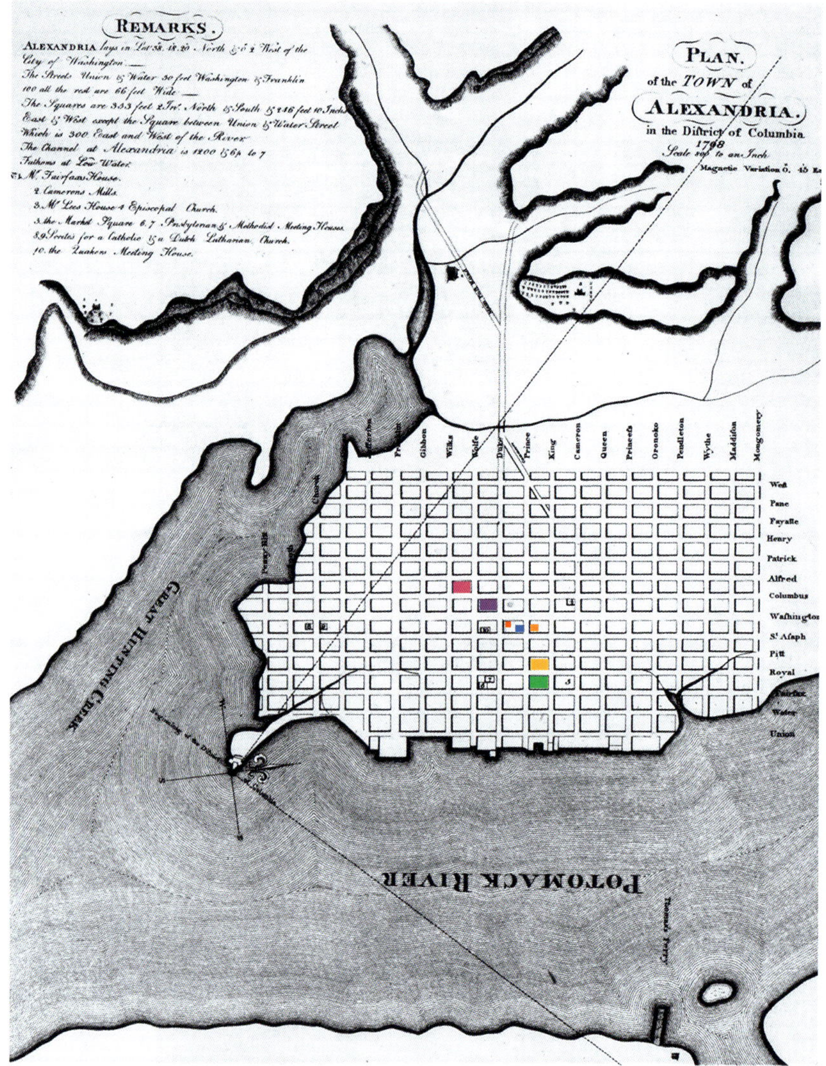

Figure 44 Sites related to Henry Piercy, and other Alexandria potters, superimposed on the Gilpin map of Alexandria, 1798.

- A. Piercy Pottery, 1792–1809 (44AX87).
- B. Piercy waster pile, 1792–1809 (also 44AX87).
- C. Piercy and Graham's china and glass shop, 1795–1796 (44AX91 4KSW-15).
- D. Piercy's house, 1796 (127 S. Fairfax Street).
- E. The Fisher Pottery, 1795–1798 (44AX80).
- F. The Plum Pottery, 1800–1803.
- G. The Plum Pottery, 1814–1828 (44AX7).

two operated the Piercy Pottery for a year before renting it to their former partners Lewis Plum and Thomas Hewes. The Fisher Pottery is not mentioned in tax records or other documents after 1798, and may have been closed. Piercy may no longer have been actively engaged in potting by then, but he continued to own the pot house until his death in 1809.[54] Plum and Hewes rented the pot house for just one year (1799–1800), and then Plum opened a competing pottery one block away, on the northwest corner of Prince and St. Asaph Streets.

The Piercy Pottery was rented next to Joseph Hibberd. Hibberd had apprenticed with David Brown in Baltimore. He moved to Waterford, Virginia, just a few months after the following announcement appeared in the *Alexandria Advertiser* on October 13, 1801:

> Joseph Hibberd, Late from Baltimore, Respectfully informs the public that he has commenced the Potting Business at the pot-house formerly occupied by Capt. Henry Piercy where he manufactures & has for sale at the most reduced prices for case, by wholesale or by retail, a large assortment of coarse Earthenware of the best quality.

In 1805 the next—and last—known tenants were Thomas Hewes and James Miller. They both had worked at the pottery previously as partners with Fisher in 1797. Hewes had also rented the Piercy Pottery in 1799 with Lewis Plum, while Miller worked at Plum's new pot house on Prince Street in 1800.

Two months after Piercy's death, the property was offered for lease. The advertisement described "three frame buildings, one has been used as a pot house, but could easily be altered into anything else, as it is a large and strong building."[55] A month later, on November 1, 1809, a public sale was held on the premises for "The POT HOUSE, formerly occupied by Captain Piercy, with the Kiln, Mill, etc., the whole must be removed before the 10th of November next."[56] On November 1, 1810, the land was deeded to Jonathan Scholfield in return for an annual ground rent. The property, with two wooden buildings and three new brick houses fronting on Washington Street, was offered for lease in April 1811. The property was expanded to six brick houses, which survive today, and are known as Lloyd's Row. The pot house, the third frame building mentioned in the 1809 advertisement, had apparently been removed. It has been conjectured that Scholfield may have moved it two blocks south to Washington and Wilkes Streets, where he was assessed for a pot house in 1812.[57] John Swann, Lewis Plum's apprentice from 1803 until 1810, purchased the Wilkes Street lot containing this pot house in 1813. Salt-glazed stoneware was manufactured there until 1876, first by Swann and later by B. C. Milburn and his sons.

Excavation of the Alexandria Potteries and Related Sites

Test Pits at the Piercy and Fisher Potteries

In 1968, a test pit was excavated on the Piercy Pottery site (44AX87) in the backyard of one of the Lloyd's Row townhouses (fig. 45), and in 1969 another was excavated on the Fisher Pottery site (44AX80). Artifacts from the Piercy site include slip-decorated chargers, pans, and bowls; dark

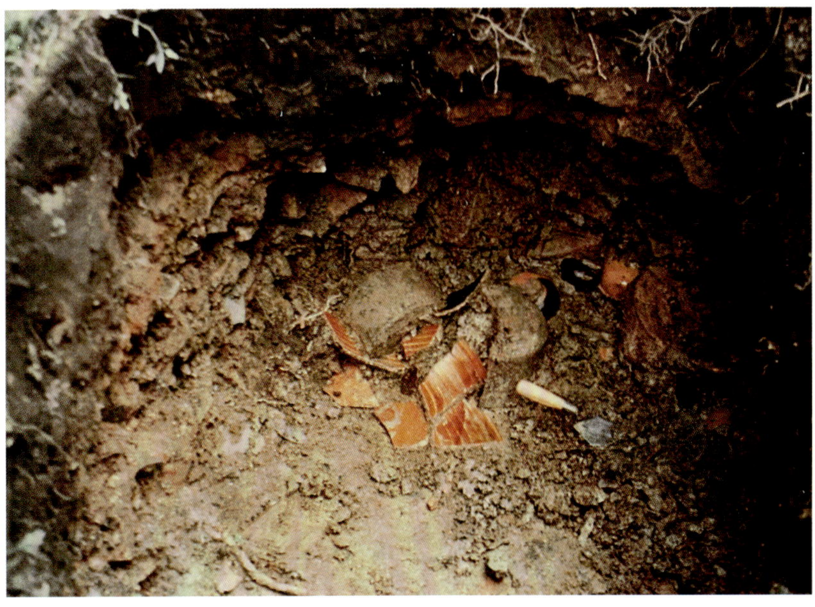

Figure 45 Test excavation at the Piercy Pottery site (44AX87), 1968. (Photo, Richard Muzzrole, Smithsonian Institution.) Note fragments of slipware pans and bowls and black-glazed bowls.

brown-glazed chamber pots, porringers, tankards, jugs, and pitchers; and utilitarian pots and milk pans, glazed on the interior. Similar wares were excavated at the Fisher Pottery along with some flowerpot fragments. These same forms, and the same decorative motifs, are found at all of the Alexandria pottery sites, and in Philadelphia.[58]

Fragments of a molded teapot were found at the Fisher site. The sherds, obvious kiln wasters, have glaze on the broken edges. Fragments of two similar teapots were found at another Piercy property at 127 South Fairfax Street. The black-glazed teapots are oval in shape, with molded fluting in imitation of silver teapots (figs. 46, 47). Similar sherds have been found at domestic sites in Alexandria. Teapots were made in Philadelphia as early as the mid-eighteenth century, but they were not a common American product until the 1820s.[59] The imitation of silver teapots in clay reached its zenith later in the nineteenth century with the production of silver luster or "Poor Man's Silver." This English ware displayed a platinum wash applied to the surface of a molded, black-glazed pot.

Figure 46 Teapot fragment, Thomas Fisher, Alexandria, ca. 1795–1798. Lead-glazed earthenware. These sherds from the Fisher site have glaze on a broken edge, an indication that the pot broke in firing.

Figure 47 Teapot fragments, Henry Piercy, Alexandria, ca. 1796. Lead-glazed earthenware. These sherds were found at Piercy's property at 127 S. Fairfax Street. Some have a poorly fired glaze and display marks from contact with kiln furniture or other pots.

Sherds of gray, salt-glazed stoneware were also found at both sites (fig. 48). Some are obvious wasters and might be attributed to Lewis Plum, who first worked at the site in 1797. Similar wares were absent from the 1795–1796 deposit associated with Piercy and Graham's shop, but were found at Plum's later pottery on Wolfe Street and at the Wilkes Street Pottery, which was opened by Plum's apprentice, John Swann, in 1813 (fig. 49).

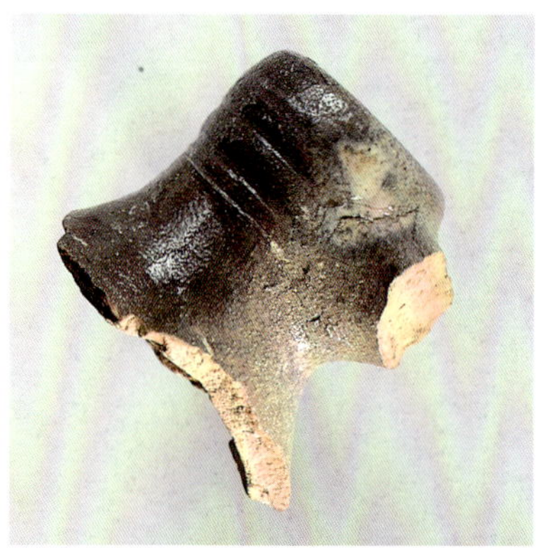

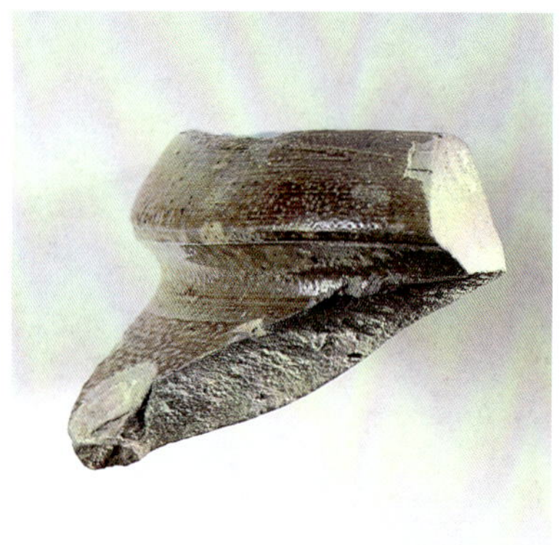

Figure 48 Bottle and jar fragments, probably Lewis Plum, Alexandria, ca. 1799–1809. Salt-glazed stoneware with iron-oxide wash. These wasters were found at the Piercy kiln site.

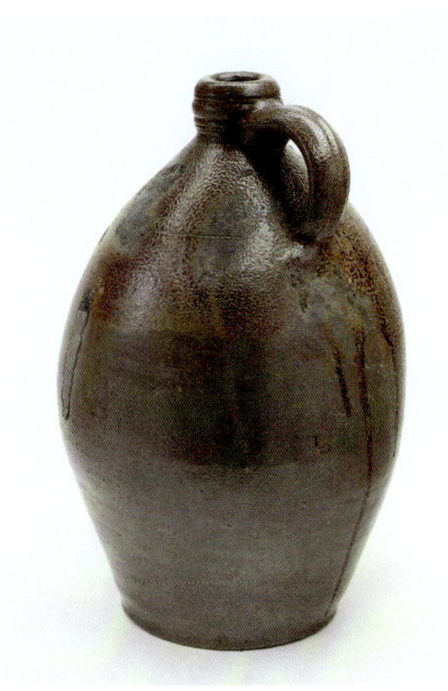

Figure 49 Jug, John Swann, Alexandria, ca. 1813–1820. Salt-glazed stoneware with iron-oxide wash. H. 12". This example is from a domestic site, but many similar wares were found at Swann's pottery on Wilkes Street. The reeded neck and iron wash are also found on bottle, jug, and jar wasters from the Piercy Pottery. These vessels are attributed to Lewis Plum who rented the pottery in 1799 and with whom Swann apprenticed.

Recovered forms include bottles, chamber pots, jars, and jugs. Some jars are covered with a brown iron wash. One fragment from a pitcher or jug from the Piercy site has a loopy line of slip-trailed cobalt that may represent the hair of a figure in profile, like the one on a pitcher from a nearby site (figs. 50, 51). Slip-trailed cobalt is not seen again in Alexandria until it is made by B. C. Milburn after 1841. However, this bulbous-shaped pitcher appears to be earlier than the forms produced by Milburn.[60]

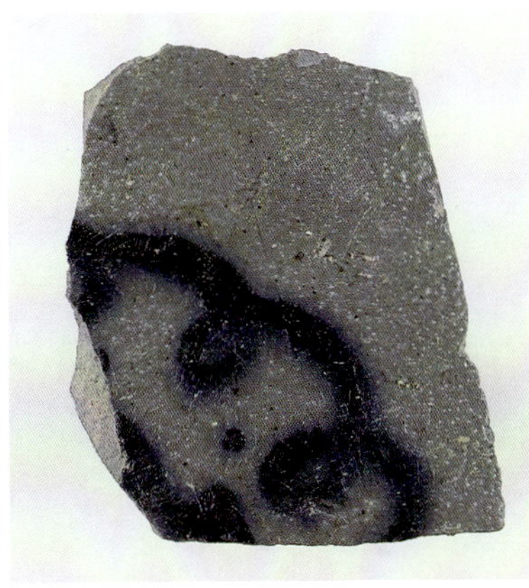

Figure 50 Stoneware fragment, probably Lewis Plum, Alexandria, ca. 1799–1809, from the Piercy kiln site. Salt-glazed stoneware with slip-trailed cobalt.

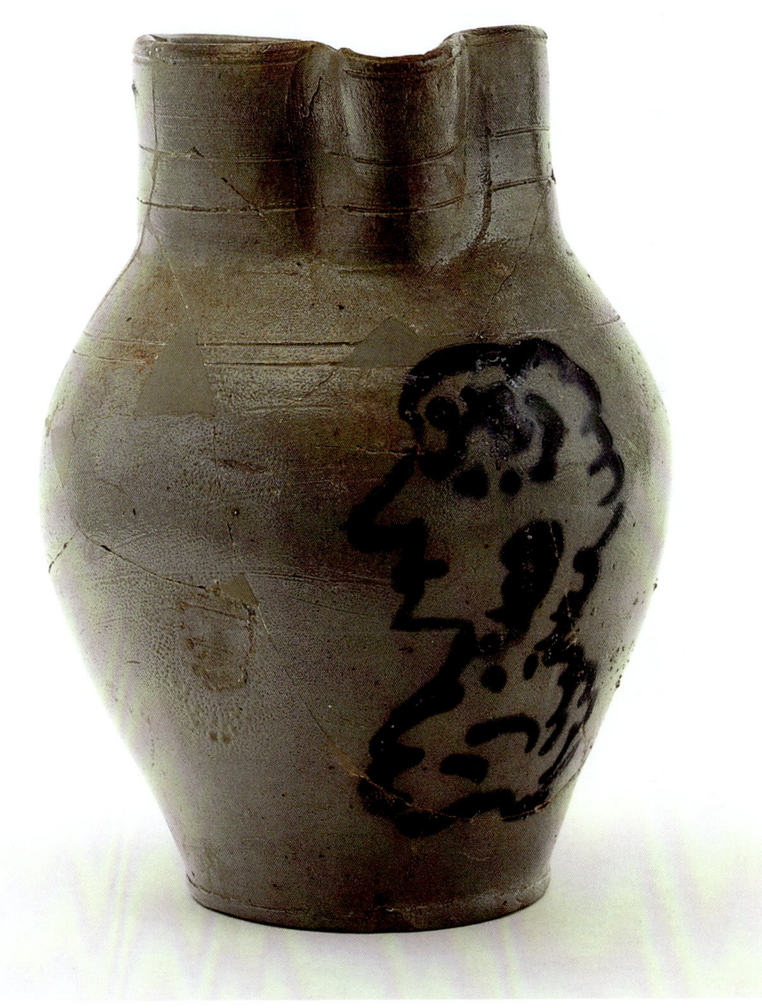

Figure 51 Pitcher, possibly Alexandria, ca. 1799–1820. Salt-glazed stoneware with slip-trailed cobalt. H. 8½". This pitcher from a privy on Market Square has decoration similar to the fragment from the Piercy kiln site illustrated in fig. 50.

The Piercy Waster Pile

A much larger collection of Piercy wasters was recovered in 1999, when an extensive waster dump (also part of 44AX87) was encountered during construction of a house addition at 211 South St. Asaph Street (fig. 52). The

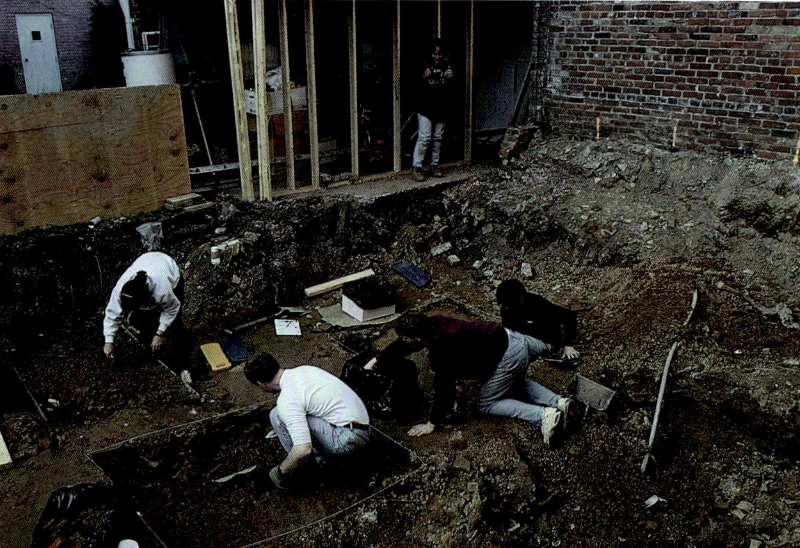

Figure 52 Excavations at the Piercy waster dump (44AX87), 1999. (Photo, Bernard K. Means, Alexandria Archaeology.)

house lot lies just outside the quarter block that was occupied by Piercy's pot house, and the property was never owned or rented by Piercy or the other potters.[61] At the Franklin Court site, pottery wasters and kiln furniture were used in extensive filling and grading to solve drainage problems.[62] The waster pile at 211 South St. Asaph may have served a similar need. Alexandria Archaeology collected artifacts from a construction backhoe pile and excavated three five-foot square excavation units. More than 6,000 waster sherds (fig. 53), representing at least 250 vessels, were recovered from this area. In addition, 7,800 fragments of kiln furniture were found.[63] Excavations covered one-third of the area impacted by the addition. The huge waster pile extended beyond the limits of the new addition and under an earlier addition at the rear of the house. In fact, a new foundation had to be constructed for the addition because it rested directly on the unstable waster pile. A few sherds of creamware, pearlware, glass, bone, oyster shells, and other artifacts from the 1790s were found among the wasters and kiln furniture.

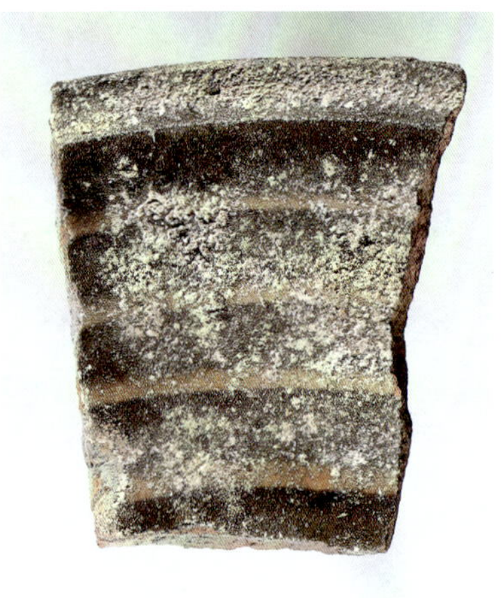

Figure 53 Pan, Henry Piercy, Alexandria, ca. 1792–1809. Slipware. Many wasters from the Piercy Pottery were overfired and discolored, or have a bubbled or pitted glaze. Some, like this slipware pan fragment, are severely burned.

Earthenware

Slipwares include at least twenty pans (fig. 54), eight chargers (fig. 55), and thirty-two bowls. The only known dated Alexandria earthenware—a ten-inch punch bowl—was found at this site (figs. 56, 57). The bowl has yellow-appearing white slip on the interior and the upper half of the exterior, and is spattered with brown manganese or iron oxides. The vessel is similar in appearance to eighteenth-century Staffordshire slipware.[64] However, the English examples were made from a white clay, the lower half of the vessel

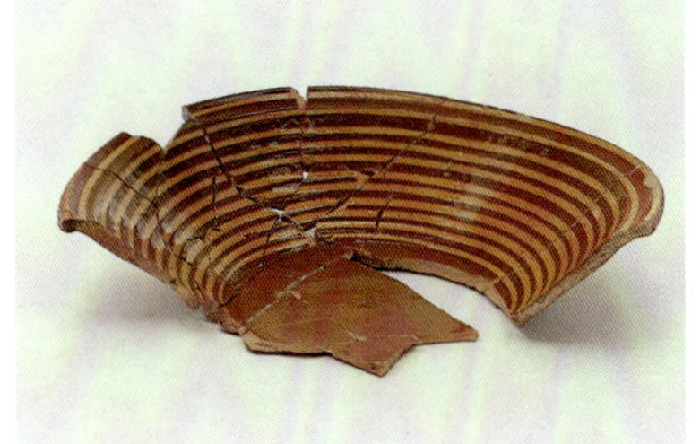

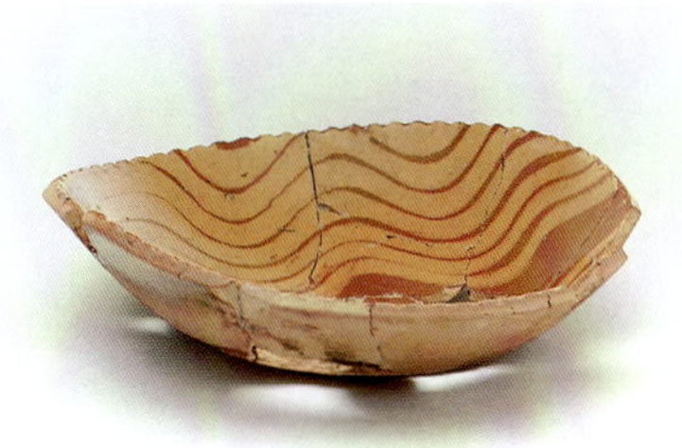

Figure 54 Pan, Henry Piercy, Alexandria, ca. 1792–1809. Slipware. D. 13". This vessel from the Piercy waster pile shows his well-executed, tightly spaced spiraling slip.

Figure 55 Dish, Henry Piercy, Alexandria, ca. 1792–1809. Slipware. D. 7½". This vessel is from the Piercy waster pile.

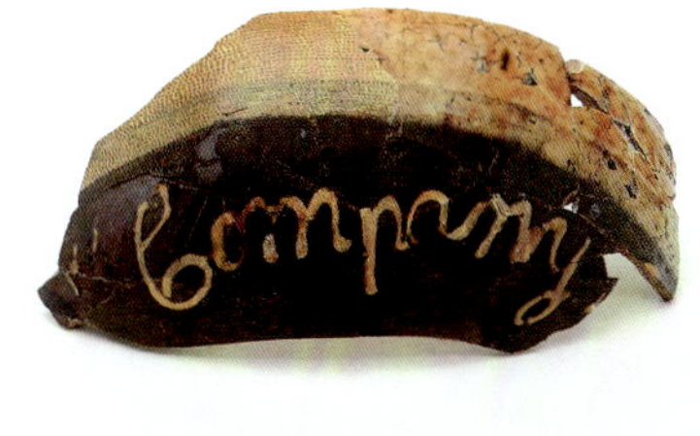

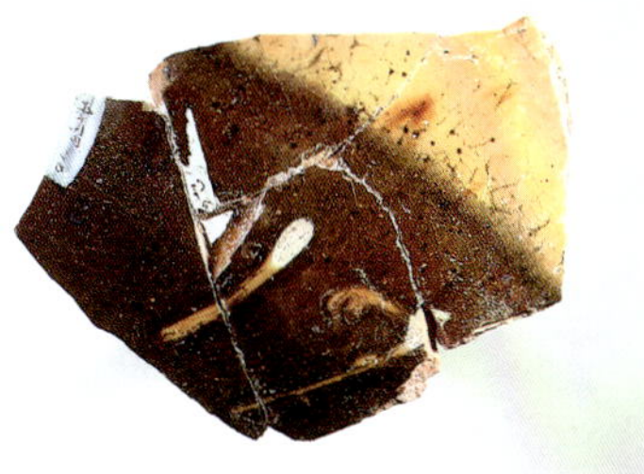

Figure 56 Punch bowl, Henry Piercy, Alexandria, ca. 1792–1799. Slipware. D. 10". The incomplete inscription includes the partial date "17—" and the word "Com(p)any." This vessel from the Piercy waster pile is the only dated piece of Alexandria earthenware. The stippled surface denotes areas of restoration.

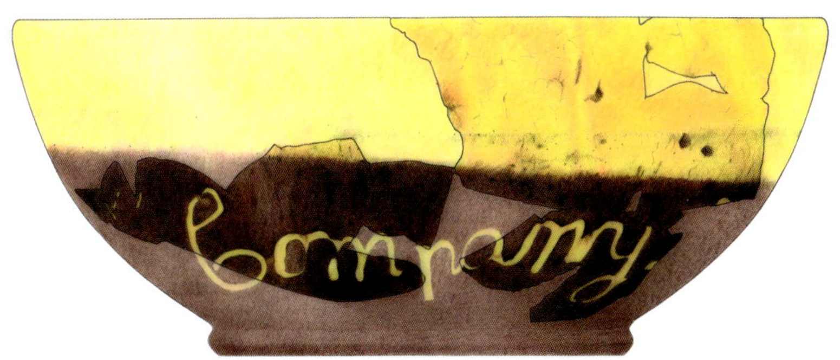

Figure 57 Reconstruction of the Piercy punch bowl illustrated in fig. 56. (Illustration, Andrew Flora.)

dipped in a black slip. The Alexandria bowl has a black glaze underlying the white slip. Below its yellow band, an inscription in yellow-trailed slip encircles the pot. Although incomplete, the recovered fragments read simply "17—" and "Com(p)any." The partial lettering may refer to an organization or military company, or may be part of a saying, such as "In Good Company." A similarly shaped punch bowl, plain with a yellow interior and rolled rim, was found at the nearby site of McKnight's Tavern.

Black-glazed wares represent the largest group of wasters from this site, with ninety-three vessels identified. Of thirty-nine narrow-mouthed vessels showing visible wheel marks on the interior, at least fifteen were identified as syrup jugs and four as pitchers. Of the wide-mouthed vessels, there were at least twenty-three chamber pots, including seven with rolled or flat, everted rims. This group also includes ten porringers and five bowls. Straight-sided vessels include ten tankards and seven preserve jars. A few orange-glazed vessels were also found. Evidence from Piercy's shop and other sites indicates that some of these shapes, including milk pans, pots, jugs, jars, bowls, and porringers, were also produced with a glaze that appears bright orange. From the kiln site, only one porringer and one bowl with brown splotches displayed the orange glaze. Four more bowls with a dark olive-green glaze and grayish body were probably intended as orange, but overfired.

At least fifty utilitarian milk pans and pots were found, and are still undergoing analysis at the time of publication. All examples have a black or dark brown-glazed interior and streaks of glaze near the rim of the unglazed exterior. Pots with orange glaze are known from the Piercy shop site. The larger pots have lug handles, like the ones found at the shop site. Milk pans have shallow, sloping sides and pour spouts. Two examples of unglazed flowerpots and a flowerpot tray were also found. These pieces have flanges and piecrust rims, and are similar to ones later produced at the Plum pottery and found on domestic sites in Alexandria.

Stoneware

Fragments of only five stoneware vessels—some obvious kiln wasters—were found in the recent dig, but eighteen were found in the 1968 dig. They are thought to have been made by Lewis Plum who rented the pottery site in 1799, and who went on to produce both earthenware and stoneware at another site. Bottles were found in the waster dump, and bottles, jars, jugs, and a chamber pot in the earlier dig. Some have a gray, salt-glazed surface, and some are covered with a brown iron-oxide wash.

Kiln Furniture

The kiln furniture consisted of saggers, tiles, fire-bars, and wedges. Most common (nearly 7,000 fragments) were heavy clay saggers used to protect the more delicate pottery in the kiln during firing (fig. 58). These vessels are easily distinguished from the pottery product itself, having straight sides, plain flat rims, no glaze, and a notch, or air vent, in the rim that allows heat to enter and fire the pots evenly. Ranging in size from seven to ten inches in diameter and five to eight inches high, they were reused and show effects of the heat. Some even show evidence of the vessels that were fired inside them. Occasionally, the shadow of a pot's base or small puddles of glaze

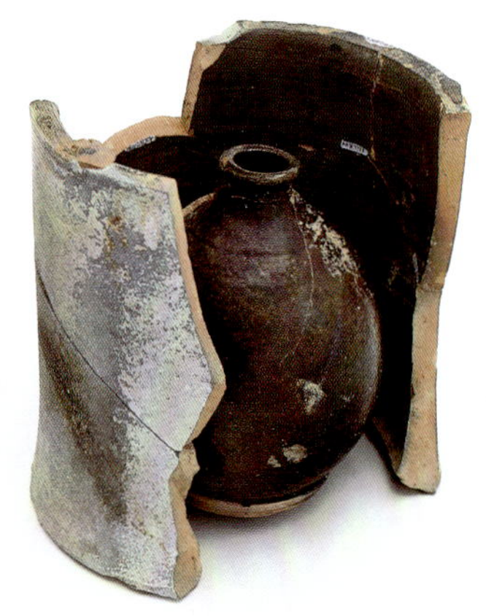

Figure 58 Sagger with syrup jar, Henry Piercy, Alexandria, ca. 1792–1809. H. 8½". The glazed wares were placed in saggers for protection in firing.

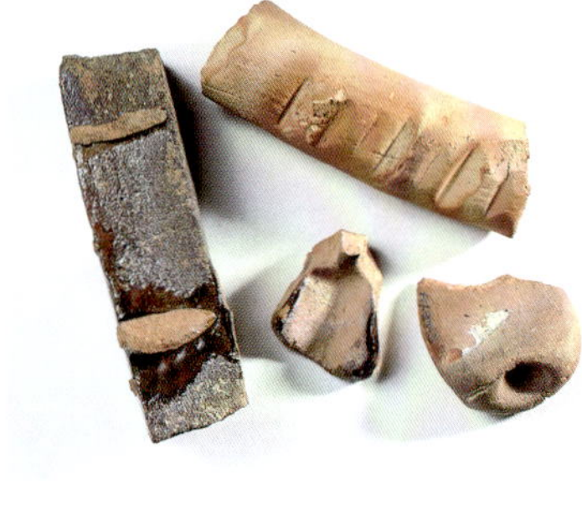

Figure 59 Kiln furniture, Henry Piercy, Alexandria, ca. 1792–1809. Fire bars and wedges were used to separate large pots with heavy rims and to steady the stacks of pottery in the kiln. Small wads of clay were pinched between the potter's fingers and used to support the pots as they were stacked in the kiln.

can be seen. Bowl rims adhere to the sides of a number of saggers. And on one, the top of a syrup jar adheres to the interior of the sagger's base, indicating the sagger was placed upside down over the jar.

Heavy, one-inch thick flat tiles were used to support stacks of pottery or saggers in the kiln. More than 550 fragments were found, representing around 250 tiles. Shadows, or glaze spills, ranging from two to fifteen inches in diameter, indicate the size of vessels or saggers that sat on many of the tiles. For instance, many of the footed bowls have two-inch diameter bases, while pan rims may be as large as fifteen inches. Most shadows are eight to ten inches in diameter and may show contact with saggers. Several tiles have distinctive shadows from syrup jar rims, indicating that they were placed inside saggers, with a tile placed on the sagger's top to support another layer of pottery in the kiln. Fragments of pottery vessels, other tiles, saggers, wedges, and brick were found adhering to the tiles.

Larger pots with heavier rims were stacked one upon the other, and separated and steadied as needed with kiln furniture and small wads of clay. One hundred and nine rectangular fire bars and 190 wedges show signs of reuse and repeated firings. Sixteen rounded fire bars and thirty-five small wads of clay were probably used once, then shaped and placed directly on the pot rims to separate them in the kiln (fig. 59).

The Piercy and Graham Shop

The brick-lined privy shaft excavated in 1974 at the rear of 406 King Street (44AX91 4KSW-15) was five feet wide, five feet deep, and contained several hundred vessels of Piercy's manufacture. The vessels date from the short period, June 1795 to April 1796, when Piercy and Graham operated a dry goods shop at this location. The ceramics in the collection—slip-decorated bowls, pans and chargers; black-glazed bowls, porringers, pitchers, syrup jugs, jars, chamber pots; and an orange-glazed porringer—are identical to those from the Piercy kiln site and waster pile. Utilitarian forms, glazed on the inside, include pots from five to fourteen inches tall, the larger with lug handles; milk pans; and a flat-bottomed pipkin.

A few more unusual pieces can probably be attributed to Piercy. An oil lamp has crimped edges on the base and yellow slip at the rim (fig. 60).

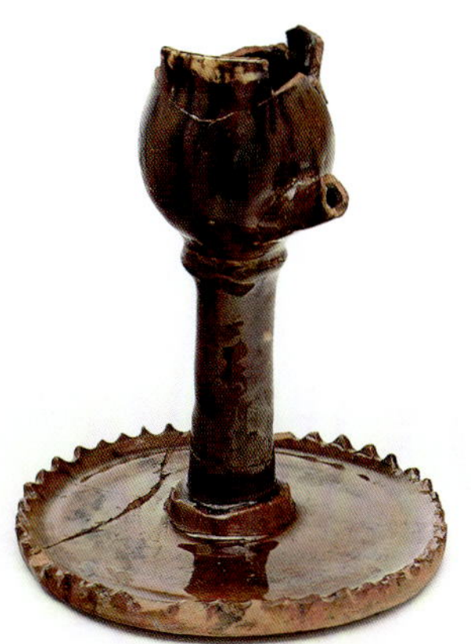

Figure 60 Oil lamp, Henry Piercy, Alexandria, ca. 1792–1809. Lead-glazed earthenware. H. 7½". This lamp is from the Piercy shop. Fragments from a similar vessel were found at the kiln site.

Figure 61 Jar, lid, and vase, Henry Piercy, Alexandria, ca. 1792–1809. Lead-glazed earthenware. H. 5½", H. 2½", Base D. 3¼". These atypical vessels with swirls of slip are from the Piercy shop site.

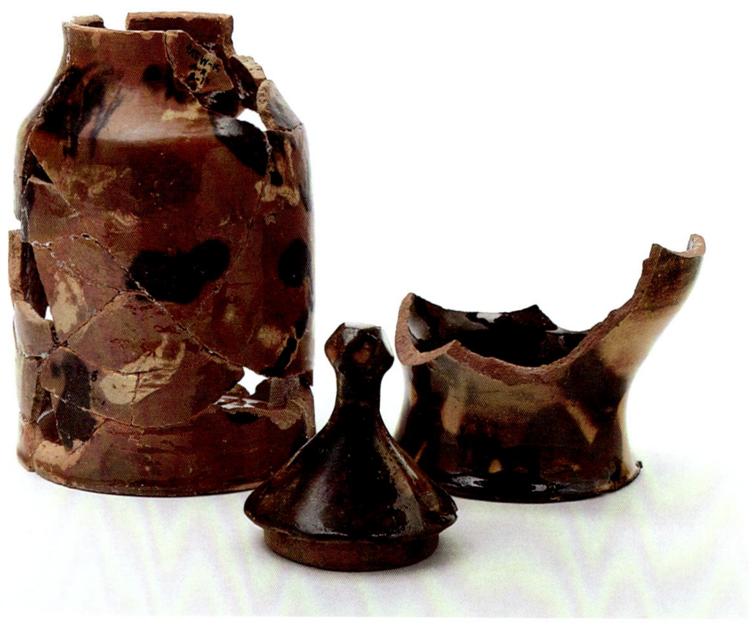

Figure 62 Pan, dish, and dish fragments, possibly Alexandria, ca. 1792–1809. Slipware. D. 11½", 10", and 6½" (extrapolated). A pan from the Piercy shop and a small dish from nearby McKnight's Tavern have atypical yellow on brown decoration. These pieces were thought to be imported, but similar sherds were found at the Piercy waster dump.

Fragments of what appears to be the bowl of a similar lamp were found at the kiln site. A preserve jar has the typical cylindrical shape, but is decorated with brown and yellow slip on an orange glaze. A lid, perhaps from a small teapot, is the only one known from Alexandria. A vase shaped like a Chinese garniture urn is decorated similarly to Piercy bowls, with a brown glaze and yellow slip topped with brown oxides (fig. 61). Fragments from the base of a similar vessel were found at the assemblage of Piercy

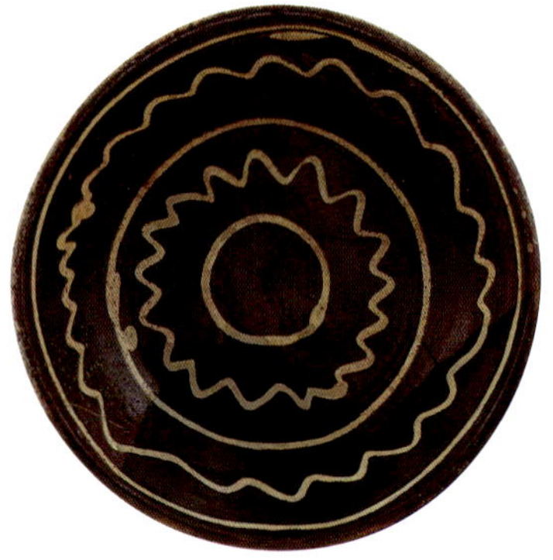

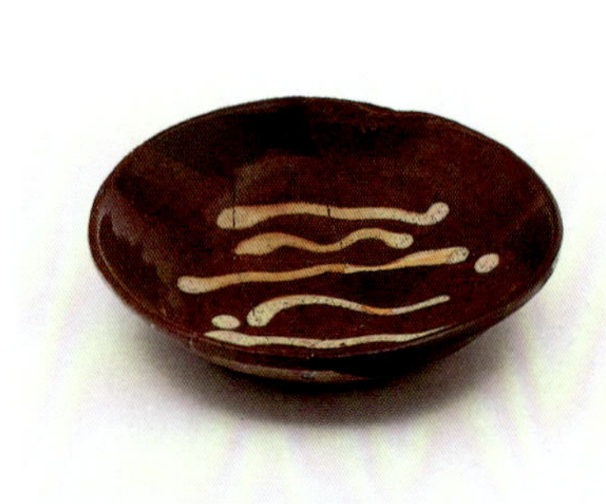

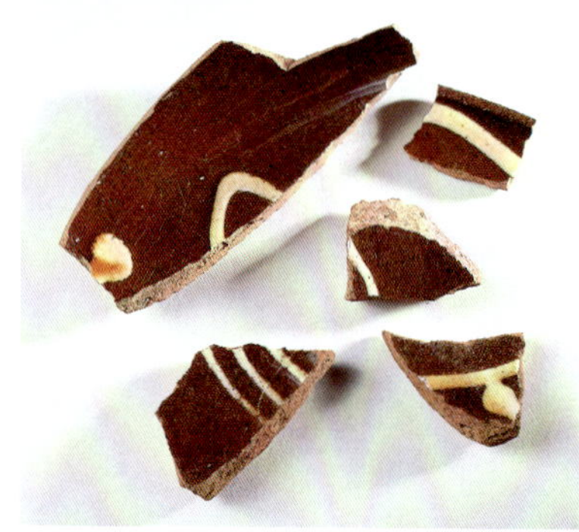

pottery from 127 South Fairfax Street. Despite its similar shape and clay body, a pan with atypical yellow on brown decoration was thought to be an import until similar sherds were found at the Piercy waster dump (fig. 62).

Piercy's Property at 127 South Fairfax Street

In June 1796, Piercy advertised a store and cellar for rent at 127 South Fairfax Street.[65] In 1974, a contractor found "a half barrel of large Piercy sherds in one pile that apparently had been a yard clean up." These 289 sherds, representing a minimum of forty-one vessels, are in the collection of the

Alexandria Archaeology Museum. Plain pots, milk pans, and slip-decorated pans make up more than half of the collection. Other common Piercy forms include slip-decorated chargers (one with green copper-oxide splotches) and bowls; brown-glazed bowls, large pitchers or jugs, and a jar; and an orange-glazed porringer. Three of the vessel forms have not been found on other Alexandria sites. One small outward-sloping vessel is probably a glazed flowerpot with brown speckling on both the yellow-slipped exterior and orange-glazed interior. The others, all with brown-glazed interiors, include a vessel with a thin handle that, perhaps, is a ladle or papboat (feeding dish); and a lidded jar or churn with an everted rim to support the lid. Fragments of two molded teapots, one a kiln waster, were also found. The teapots are similar to one found at the Fisher kiln site (see figs. 46, 47).

The Plum Pottery

In 1975 a twenty-foot backhoe trench was excavated on the southwest corner of Wolfe and South Columbus Streets (44AX7). Pieces of kiln flooring and earthenware wasters more than six feet beneath the ground surface were uncovered. Lewis Plum, who had rented the Piercy Pottery in 1799, purchased this property in 1801. He produced pottery here at least as early as 1814, after operating another manufactory on the northwest corner of Prince and St. Asaph Streets. After Plum's death in 1821, the pot house was operated by Evans and Griggs until 1828. Earthenware and stoneware wasters, similar to those found at the Piercy site, were recovered from this site, but the collection awaits further analysis. Most of the waster sherds, however, appear to be of utilitarian and black-glazed wares. The assemblage also includes slip-decorated wares and stoneware.

Differentiating Between Philadelphia and Alexandria Earthenware

Visual Appearance

The visual appearance of the fired clay, glazes, vessel forms, and decoration of the standard forms produced by Henry Piercy and his contemporaries in Alexandria is identical to that of Philadelphia pottery (figs. 63–65). The wares include slip-decorated pans, chargers and bowls; black-glazed syrup

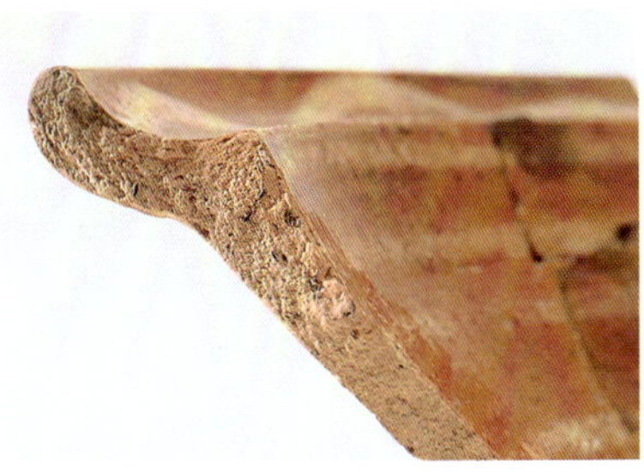

Figure 63 Detail of a pan, Philadelphia, ca. 1770s. Slipware. D. 10½". (Courtesy, National Park Service, Independence National Historical Park, Inde-60179.)

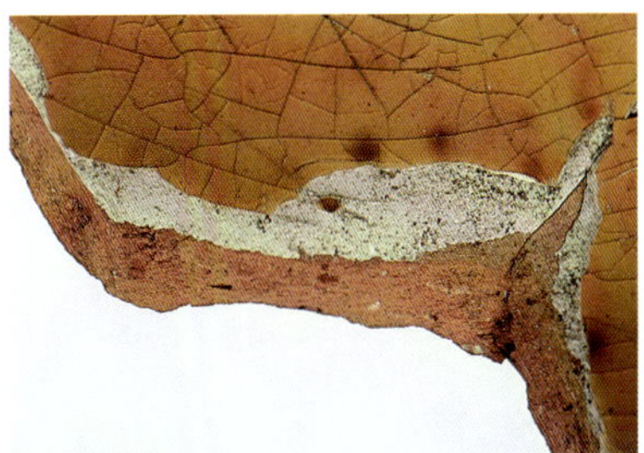

Figure 64 Detail of a bowl, Philadelphia, ca. 1770s. Slipware. (Courtesy, National Park Service, Independence National Historical Park, Inde-60183.)

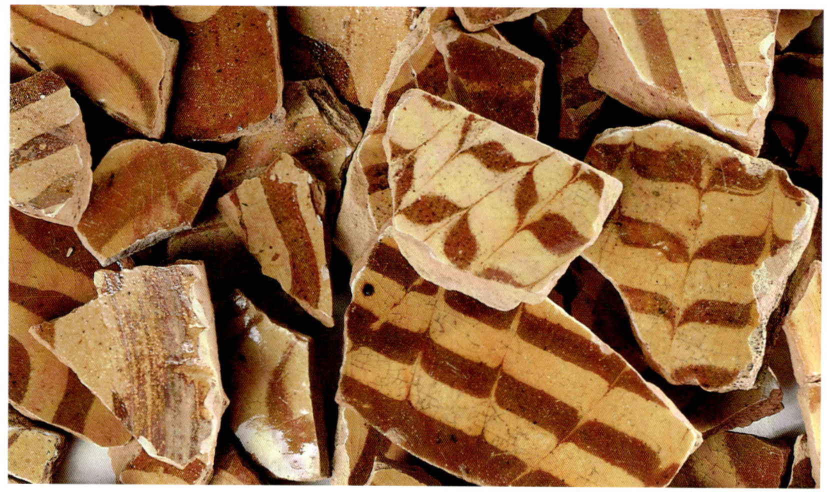

Figure 65 Dish fragments, Henry Piercy, Alexandria, ca. 1792–1809. Slipware. The appearance is similar to that of Philadelphia wares.

jugs, pitchers, preserve jars, tankards, chamber pots, bowls and porringers; and utilitarian pots and milk pans. In order to differentiate between Philadelphia and Alexandria versions of these wares, and those produced elsewhere "in the Philadelphia style," archaeologists need to turn to physical analysis and clay sourcing.

Physical Analysis and Clay Sourcing

The physical structure and appearance of coarse earthenware ceramics, such as those of the types manufactured by Henry Piercy and various potters in Philadelphia, are susceptible to the vagaries of the production process and the clay sources used. Temperature fluctuations, differential air flow, variations in vessel shapes and thickness, and, of course, raw clay drawn from a variety of sources, are a few of the factors that can result in visually distinct differences in the clay bodies of coarse earthenwares. Vessels produced during the same firing episode at the same kiln may look subtly different from one another, and even different parts of individual vessels can exhibit recognizable distinctions.

Despite these factors, the coarse earthenwares manufactured by Henry Piercy have an overall consistency in the appearance of their clay bodies. They are generally very porous and light in weight, with a light buff-orange color and no visible inclusions. We initially expected that coarse earthenware pottery manufactured in Philadelphia would appear clearly distinct from Piercy's wares, since different local clay sources were used. Unfortunately, when we had the opportunity to examine a large assemblage of coarse earthenware ceramics from an archaeological site in Philadelphia, we quickly determined that, on a macroscopic level, the coarse earthenwares manufactured by the Philadelphia potters are indistinguishable from the stylistically similar pottery produced by Piercy.[66] The need to find an empirical way to differentiate between the wares became apparent, and a joint investigation was undertaken by physicists Dr. Romeo Segnan and Dr. J. P. Auffret from American University.[67]

Archaeologists have increasingly turned to the physical sciences when facing questions related to the composition of ceramic artifacts that can only be addressed through analysis on microscopic and even molecular or atomic levels. Prudence Rice, in her 1987 *Pottery Analysis,* detailed a number of "the more commonly used techniques [that] focus on the mineralogical and chemical constituents of the ceramic."[68] These techniques include petrographic analysis, X-ray diffraction, thermal analysis, neutron activation analysis, atomic absorption spectroscopy, and Mössbauer spectroscopy.[69] Fortunately, since we are dealing with pottery manufactured at local kilns, we are not concerned with the manufacturing process but are concerned with distinguishing the sources of clay used to produce earthenwares in Philadelphia and Alexandria.[70]

Mössbauer Spectroscopy

While pondering the difficulty of distinguishing between Philadelphia-style earthenwares, the authors were informed that physicists at American University were looking for samples from American earthenware manufacturing sites to use in a study employing Mössbauer spectroscopy, and that a comparative collection of earthenware from Philadelphia was available in the Anthropology Department at American University, where it is curated by Dr. Richard J. Dent. Drs. Romeo Segnan and J. P. Auffret had previously used Mössbauer spectroscopy to analyze protohistoric ceramics from Venice, and were seeking new avenues to expand their research.[71] Segnan and Auffret suggested that, on a molecular level, the process might distinguish between earthenwares manufactured in Alexandria and Philadelphia (fig. 66). Thus began a collaborative effort between American University and the Alexandria Archaeology Museum. The study is still underway, but preliminary results of Segnan and Auffret's analysis are offered here.

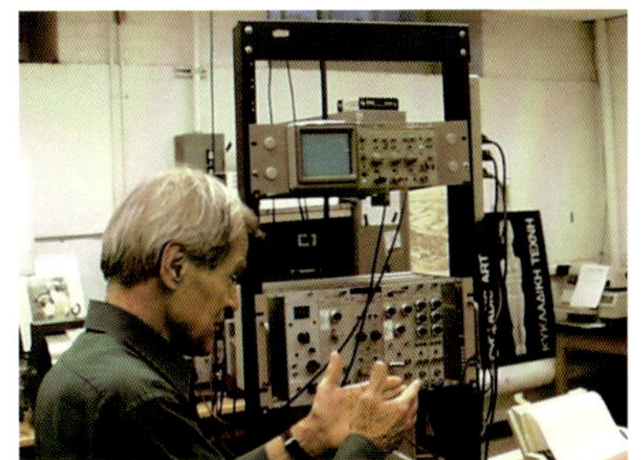

Figure 66 Dr. Romeo Segnan explains Mössbauer spectroscopy in his physics laboratory at American University. (Photo, Bernard K. Means, Alexandria Archaeology.)

At this juncture, it is appropriate to provide a few details on Mössbauer spectroscopy. At the risk of oversimplifying, the Mössbauer effect essentially rests on the fact that when a gamma ray is emitted from a radioactive source into certain solids, it is absorbed in characteristic ways and causes energy shifts that can be measured using spectroscopy.[72] Mössbauer spectroscopy of solids containing iron, tin, antimony, iodine, europium, and dysprosium show strong results that are relatively easy to interpret.[73]

Mössbauer spectroscopy has applications in solid-state physics, metallurgy, chemistry, and biochemistry.[74] In ceramic analysis, Mössbauer spectroscopy has been able to characterize raw and fired clays or pigments, estimate firing temperatures, determine if ceramic vessels were fired in kilns or in open air sites, and has also been useful in provenience studies.[75] This research is possible because most clay minerals contain iron. Thus, Mössbauer spectroscopy can be used to learn about the character and location of iron in clay minerals.[76]

For the current study, eleven potsherds and a single sagger, kiln tile, and brick fragment from the Piercy Pottery waster pile at the rear of 211 South St. Asaph Street (44AX87) in Alexandria are being compared with ten fragments of similar wares from the Topham Pottery site on the Metropolitan Detention Center site's Block 2 (36PH91) at the rear of 710–712 Arch Street

Figure 67 The central peak for the Alexandria clay spectrum shows larger splitting than the corresponding peak in the Philadelphia clay spectrum. (Courtesy, Drs. Romeo Segnan and J. P. Auffret, Department of Physics, American University.)

in Philadelphia. These pottery samples include slip-decorated wares, glazed wares, and utilitarian wares with glazed interiors. Additional clay samples were analyzed from the Piercy waster pile and from a block in Philadelphia's Independence National Historical Park between 5th and 6th Streets and Arch and Race Streets.[77] This location is two blocks east of the Topham Pottery and five blocks east of where Topham had petitioned to dig clay, on the north side of Race Street between 10th and 11th Streets (see fig. 7).

Drs. Segnan and Auffret have completed the initial testing of unfired clay samples, ceramic vessel fragments, and kiln furniture from Alexandria and Philadelphia. Visual inspection of the clay samples alone suggested that the reddish Philadelphia clay had a higher iron content than the yellower Alexandria sample, and Mössbauer spectroscopy confirmed the assesment. The Mössbauer spectrum from the Philadelphia clay sample showed the characteristic sextet splitting indicative of a greater iron oxide content; the sextet splitting was absent in the Alexandria clay spectrum, indicating little or no hematite (iron oxide). The two clay sample spectra also had differences in their central peaks: the central peak for the Alexandria clay spectrum showed larger splitting than the corresponding peak in the Philadelphia clay spectrum (fig. 67).

When clays are fired, visual distinctions such as those seen between the Alexandria and Philadelphia raw clays disappear, and the use of techniques,

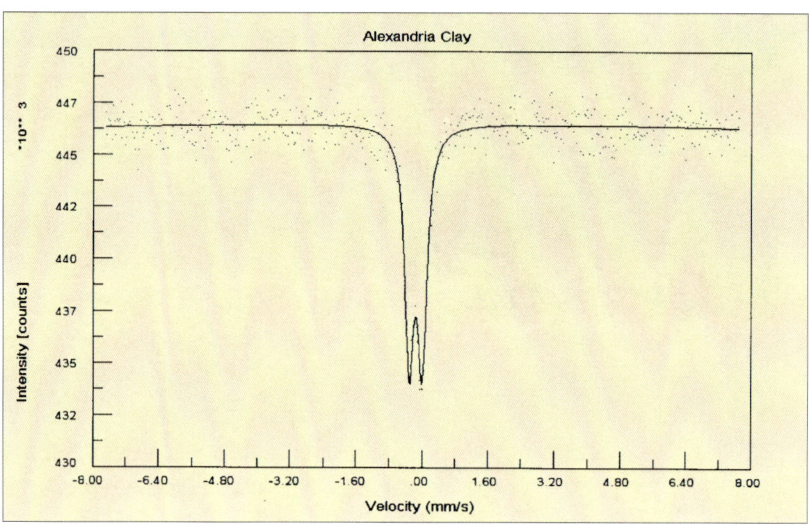

such as Mössbauer spectroscopy, become essential. The split in the central peak of the Mössbauer spectra for the ceramic vessel fragments and kiln furniture from Alexandria showed the same splitting in the raw Alexandria clay sample. Other samples are being studied using Mössbauer spectroscopy, which will provide further information about the elemental composition of clays and ceramic artifacts from both cities.

Future Directions

Mössbauer spectroscopy appears to be a useful addition to the tools available for the study of period earthenwares. Archaeologists from Alexandria and the physicists from American University hope to extend this study to samples of clay and ceramics from other cities with similar Philadelphia-style earthenware. This will, we hope, address questions of how much Philadelphia-style pottery was actually produced in Philadelphia, and how much was produced in other towns throughout America.

ACKNOWLEDGMENTS

The authors thank their colleagues at Alexandria Archaeology, especially Dr. Pamela J. Cressey, Dr. Steven J. Shephard, and Francine Bromberg for their work on the site of the Piercy waster pile and their support and encouragement on the writing of this paper. This research would not have been possible without the assistance of staff and volunteers who helped to excavate the site and the lab volunteers who worked thousands of hours to process and catalog the artifacts. We are also indebted to the late Jack Pickens and C. Malcolm Watkins for their research on Henry Piercy and other Alexandria potters. Professor Richard J. Dent of American University and Robert L. Giannini III, Museum Curator for Independence National Historical Park, were instrumental in providing access to comparative collections from Philadelphia. And thanks especially go to American University physicists Drs. Romeo Segnan and J. P. Auffret, who undertook the physical analysis of the earthenware from Alexandria and Philadelphia.

1. EARTHENWARE MANUFACTORY

> The subscriber has lately, at a very considerable expense erected a Manufactory of Earthen Ware in the Town, which he now carries on, on a very extensive plan, where Merchants & others can be supplied at the shortest notice, & their orders carefully executed. He flatters himself that the quality of his wares is, & will constantly be, equal to any work in Phil. or elsewhere, & that his assiduity to please, & the goodness of his ware, will assure him the patronage of all those who wish to encourage home manufactures. He has also for sale at his house, the upper end, Prince St., a large assortment of CHINA, QUEEN'S WARE & GLASS.
>
> *Alexandria Gazette,* November 1, 1792

2. Carl Steen, "Pottery, Intercolonial Trade, and Revolution: Domestic Earthenwares and the Development of an American Social Identity," *Historical Archaeology* 33, no. 3 (1999): 62–63.

3. Lura Woodside Watkins, *Early New England Potters and Their Wares* (Cambridge, Mass.: Harvard University Press, 1950), p. 209.

4. *New York Gazette and Weekly Mercury,* March 15, 1773, cited in Susan H. Myers, *Handcraft to Industry: Philadelphia Ceramics in the First Half of the Nineteenth Century* (Washington, D.C.: Smithsonian Institution Press, 1980), p. 105.

5. *Maryland Gazette*, September 2, 1756, cited in Myers, *Handcraft to Industry,* p. 105.

6. This work is being undertaken by physicists Dr. Romeo Segnan and Dr. J. P. Auffret of American University.

7. Beth A. Bower, "The Pottery-Making Trade in Colonial Philadelphia: The Growth of an Early Urban Industry," in *Domestic Pottery of the Northeastern United States, 1625–1850,* edited by Sarah Peabody Turnbaugh (Orlando, Fla.: Academic Press, 1985), pp. 268–71. The first known Philadelphia potter was William Crews of Southwark in Surrey.

8. David R. M. Gaimster, Mark Redknap, and Hans Helmut Wegner, *Zer Keramik des Mittelaters und der beginnenden Neuzeit im Rheinland* (Oxford, Eng.: BAR International Series 440, 1988), p. 174, as cited in Patricia E. Gibble, "Continuity, Change and Ethnic Identity in Eighteenth-Century Pennsylvania Red Earthenware" (Ph.D. diss., American University, 2001), p. 183.

9. Elizabeth Cosans, "1974 Franklin Court Report, Volume VI: Catalog and Remarks" (Philadelphia: National Park Service, Independence National Historical Park, 1974), pp. 52–56; H. E. Comstock, *The Pottery of the Shenandoah Valley Region* (Winston-Salem, N.C.: Museum of Early Southern Decorative Arts, 1994), pp. 4–8 and fig. 1.3.

10. English slipware technology is illustrated in Michelle Erickson and Robert Hunter, "Dots, Dashes, and Squiggles: Early English Slipware Technology," in *Ceramics in America,* edited by Robert Hunter (Hanover, N.H.: University Press of New England for the Chipstone Foundation, 2001), pp. 95–114. A discussion of slipware methodology can also be found in Leslie B. Grigsby, *English Slip-Decorated Earthenware at Williamsburg* (Williamsburg, Va.: The Colonial Williamsburg Foundation, 1993), pp. 16–19.

11. Erickson and Hunter, "Early English Slipware Technology," pp. 95–114.

12. Richard J. Dent et al., *Archaeological and Historical Investigation, Metropolitan Detention Center Site (36PH91), Philadelphia, Pennsylvania,* Occasional Publication 2, The Cultural Resource Group, Louis Berger & Associates, Inc., Washington, D.C., for the U.S. Department of Justice, Federal Bureau of Prisons, Washington, D.C. (1997), I-I.

13. Dent et al., *Metropolitan Detention Center,* p. i.

14. Dent et al., *Metropolitan Detention Center,* part III, pp. 35 and 86.

15. *Records of the Supreme Executive Council,* April 4, 1780, as quoted in Beth A. Bower, "The Pottery-Making Trade in Colonial Philadelphia," in *Domestic Pottery of the Northeastern United States 1625–1850,* p. 275.

16. As quoted in Dent et al., *Metropolitan Detention Center,* part III, p. 37.

17. Ibid.

18. Ibid., part V, p. 181.

19. Ibid., part IV, p. 53.

20. Ibid., part V, p. 126.

21. Ibid., part V, p. 88.

22. Ibid., part V, p. 126.

23. Ibid., part V, p. 129.

24. Ibid., part V, p. 132.

25. *Philadelphia Deed Book D* 44 (1783): 347, cited in Dent et al., *Metropolitan Detention Center,* part V, pp. 126 and 132.

26. Ten sherds were selected for analysis, from excavation Block 2, Unit 6, Stratum B (buried A horizon). These were found in association with kiln furniture.

27. In 2001 the author viewed materials from these Franklin Court features at Independence National Historical Park, courtesy of Robert L. Giannini III, Museum Curator.

28. Cosans, "1974 Franklin Court Report," part VI, pp. 4–5 and 57–59. In 1962 archaeologists excavated an assemblage of kiln-related materials on the same block, under the granite paving of disused Oriana Street, and surmised that they related to Deborah Franklin's first husband, potter John Rogers, who left Philadelphia in 1727. As reported in John L. Cotter, Daniel G. Roberts, and Michael Parrington, *The Buried Past: An Archaeological History of Philadelphia* (Philadelphia: University of Pennsylvania Press, 1992), pp. 93–94 and 453. Cosans, however, thought it more likely that the Oriana Street deposit, along with that in the wells, related to drainage problems on the block and the extensive filling and grading that took place in 1769 at the site of Franklin's new house.

29. The author viewed materials from the Chiller Plant site (INDE 4037) in 1999, courtesy of Paul Inashima, while they were undergoing analysis and conservation at the National Park Service's Denver Service Center in Rockville, Maryland, and again in 2001 at Independence National Historical Park, courtesy of Robert L. Giannini III, Museum Curator.

30. Comstock, *Shenandoah Valley,* p. 84.

31. Ibid., pp. 106–44, 225–74.

32. Ivor Noël Hume, *A Guide to Artifacts of Colonial America* (New York: Alfred A. Knopf, 1969), p. 135.

33. Cosans, "1974 Franklin Court Report," part VI, p. 52.

34. Documentary research on Piercy and other Alexandria potters was conducted by John K. Pickens, the first chairman of the Alexandria Archaeological Commission, and by C. Malcolm Watkins, Richard Muzzrole, and Betty J. Walters, under the auspices of the Smithsonian Institution. John K. Pickens, "Early American Craftsmen: Captain Henry Piercy, Patriot and Master Potter" (1979), files of the Alexandria Archaeology Museum and the Pickens Papers (box 57), Alexandria Library, Special Collections; C. Malcolm Watkins, "The Pots and Potteries of Alexandria, Virginia: 1792–1876," (n.d.), files of the Alexandria Archaeology Museum.

35. Directories of 1791 and 1793, cited in Harrold E. Gillingham, "Pottery, China and Glass Making in Philadelphia," *The Pennsylvania Magazine of History and Biography* 54 (1930): 114.

36. *Pennsylvania Gazette,* December 21, 1774, cited in Gillingham "Pottery, China and Glass Making," p. 113.

37. The Society of the Cincinnati was organized in 1783 by officers of the Continental Army. George Washington was the society's first president. Membership in the society passed to the eldest son upon the member's death.

38. Joseph Fornance, Esq., "The Lonely Grave near Woodstown, N.J.," Papers of John K. Pickens, in the files of Alexandria Archaeology Museum. Fornance was a great-grandson of Christian Piercy.

39. Gillingham, "Pottery, China and Glass Making," p. 113. The procession included a flag with the motto "The Potter hath power over his clay" (Romans 9:21) as well as an image of a kiln burning and several men at work, a horse-drawn carriage with a potter's wheel that could produce cups, bowls, and mugs during the parade, and a group of twenty potters led by Piercy and Gilbert.

40. *Virginia Gazette and Alexandria Advertiser,* November 1, 1792.

41. Gillingham, "Pottery, China and Glass Making," p. 114.

42. Alexandria Archaeology discovered the waterworn ceramics beside the Carlyle-Dalton Wharf, 44AX81. The wharf, at the foot of Cameron Street, was built by two of the town's founders in 1759. The artifacts from the fill consisted of some mid-eighteenth-century ceramics that were not waterworn, and the waterworn ceramics from the third quarter of the seventeenth century.

43. James C. Mackay, "A Brief History of Alexandria, Virginia" (Alexandria, Va.: The Lyceum, Alexandria's History Museum, 1996), <http://oha.ci.alexandria.va.us/lyceum/ly-historic.html>; and Donald K. Shomette, "Maritime Alexandria: An Evaluation of Submerged Cultural Resource Potentials at Alexandria, Virginia" (1985), pp. 67–69, files of the Alexandria Archaeology Museum.

44. Samuel Shepherd, *The Statutes at Large of Virginia, From October Session 1792, to December Session 1806, Inclusive, in Three Volumes, (New Series,) Being a Continuation of Hening* (New York: AMS Press, Inc., 1970), p. 149.

45. T. Michael Miller, ed., *Pen Portraits of Alexandria, Virginia, 1739–1900* (Bowie, Md.: Heritage Books, 1987), p. 60, quoting *The Alexandria Gazette Commercial & Political* of July 26, 1816.

46. *Virginia Gazette and Alexandria Advertiser,* November 1, 1792.

47. The following table summarizes ownership and partnerships at Alexandria Potteries that produced earthenware in the Philadelphia style. Stoneware potters John Swann (1813–1825), who had apprenticed with Lewis Plum, and Tildon Easton (1841–1843) also produced some undecorated, utilitarian earthenware.

Date	*Piercy Pottery*	*Fisher Pottery*	*Plum Pottery*
1792–1809	Owner: Henry Piercy		
1795–98		Owner: Thomas Fisher	
1797	Partners: Henry Piercy Lewis Plum John Piercy (nephew)	Partners: Thomas Hewes James Miller	
1798	Partners: Henry Piercy Thomas Fisher	Partners: Henry Piercy Thomas Fisher	
1799	Tenant: Lewis Plum Thomas Hewes		
1800	Tenant: Joseph Hibberd		Prince Street Partners: Lewis Plum James Miller Apprentice

Date	*Piercy Pottery*	*Fisher Pottery*	*Plum Pottery*
1803			Prince Street: Owner: Lewis Plum Apprentice: John Swann
1805	Tenant: Thomas Hewes James Miller		
1809	Property offered for sale at Piercy's death		
1811	Property divided into house lots		
1814–21			S. Columbus Street: Plum moves to new Pottery on S. Columbus near southwest corner of Wolfe
1822			S. Columbus Street: Owners: Evans and Griggs (after Plum's death)
1828			Pottery no longer in operation

48. The location of potteries was not regulated in Alexandria at this time but was of concern. A letter to the editor published in the *Columbian Mirror & Alexandria Gazette* on May 31, 1800, expresses concern about an unknown pot house that apparently underlies the nineteenth-century Alexandria City Hall on Cameron Street between Fairfax and Royal Streets:

> Mr. Price:
> I Wish to call the attention of the citizens to a subject, which appears to me to require their immediate interposition. A pot-house has lately been erected, nearly in the center of the improved part of the Court House square: it is surrounded on all sides by wooden buildings, some of which are within three or four feet of the blaze of the oven. Connected as it is, and exposed to every wind that may blow, a terrible conflagration must be rightly expected, as long as the evil is permitted to exist.

49. From 1968 to 1969, test excavations were conducted at the Piercy (44AX87) and Fisher (44AX80) potteries. These excavations were conducted by Richard J. Muzzrole, Museum Specialist, the Department of Cultural History of the National Museum of History and Technology (now the National Museum of American History), Smithsonian Institution, under the direction of curator C. Malcolm Watkins. This undertaking was part of an effort by the Smithsonian to conduct salvage archaeology in the area of a large urban renewal project in the center of Old Town Alexandria. A large number of Philadelphia-style wares were found in privy deposits, and Watkins and his staff searched documentary evidence, and then the pottery sites, for evidence that the earthenwares were locally produced.

50. *Virginia Gazette and Alexandria Advertiser,* November 1, 1792.

51. *Columbia Mirror and Alexandria Advertiser,* June 20, 1795. On March 3, 1796, another ad offered for rent as of April 1, "A brick house in King Street now occupied by Captain Pearcy [*sic*]."

52. A brick-lined privy behind the shop at 406 King Street (44AX91, feature 4KSW-15), was excavated in 1974 by Richard Muzzrole for the City of Alexandria. All artifacts are in the collection of the Alexandria Archaeology Museum.

53. Although not found at the Alexandria pottery sites, tin-glazed wares were made by

potters in the Shenandoah Valley. *American Gazette & General Advertiser* (Norfolk, Va.) March 17, 1797, 3: 3, cited in Bradford L. Rauschenberg, "American Tin-Glaze: The John Bell Inkstand," *Journal of Early Southern Decorative Arts* 3, no. 1 (May 1977): 34. A color illustration of the Bell inkstand, dated 1825, appears in Comstock, *Shenandoah Valley,* p. 109, fig. 4.71.

54. Alexandria City Land and Personal Property Tax Assessments 1796–1800. Microfilm, Alexandria Library, Special Collections.

55. *Alexandria Daily Gazette, Commercial and Political,* August 28, 1809:

> TO LEASE . . . A Valuable half acre Lot of Ground, situated on Washington and Duke streets, with a fine corner lot. There is on the said property three frame buildings, one has been used as a pot house, but could easily be altered into anything else, as it is a large and strong building—the others are dwelling houses.
>
> M'Knight and Stewart

56. *Alexandria Daily Gazette, Commercial and Political,* November 1, 1809.

57. Pickens, "Captain Henry Piercy," p. 22b.

58. Wasters and kiln furniture from the Smithsonian's 1968 excavation at the Piercy Pottery site are in the collections of the Alexandria Archaeology Museum and the Department of Ceramics and Glass at the National Museum of American History, Smithsonian Institution.

59. Susan H. Myers, "Marketing American Pottery: Maulden Perine in Baltimore," *Winterthur Portfolio* 19, no. 1 (Spring 1984): 56.

60. The loopy, slip-trailed lines resemble a figure's hair, drawn in profile, on a pitcher from Market Square, AX94 MB-C, 67.1783A.

61. Deed research for the 200 block of South St. Asaph Street provided by T. Michael Miller, Research Historian, Office of Historic Alexandria, City of Alexandria, Virginia.

62. Cosans,"1974 Franklin Court Report," citing Barbara Liggett, "1971 Franklin Court Report."

63. The site (44AX87) was excavated over a five-day period in February 1999 under the direction of archaeologists Steven J. Shephard and Francine Bromberg of Alexandria Archaeology, a division of the Office of Historic Alexandria, City of Alexandria, Virginia.

64. For example, Erickson and Hunter, "Early English Slipware Technology," p. 103.

65. Pickens, "Captain Henry Piercy," p. 13a. The property was advertised in the *Columbia Mirror and Alexandria Gazette* on June 6, 1796:

> TO BE RENTED–A Store and Cellar, and, if required, a Country Room. They are situated in Fairfax Street near Prince Street. Inquire of H. PIERCY

66. The authors examined Philadelphia earthenware from excavations at 6th and Market Streets on Independence Mall, with thanks to National Park Service archaeologist Paul Inashima and conservator Lisa Young of Alexandria Conservation Services, Ltd. The site was excavated by archaeologists Rebecca Yamin and Jed Levin of John Milner Associates.

67. Dent et al., *Metropolitan Detention Center,* part III, p. 36.

68. Prudence Rice, *Pottery Analysis: A Sourcebook* (Chicago: University of Chicago Press, 1987), p. 371.

69. Ibid.

70. Ibid., p. 413.

71. Mariangela Bertelle et al., "Firing Techniques of the Impasti from the Protohistoric Site of Concordia Sagittaria (Venice)," *Journal of Cultural Heritage* 1 (2000): 261–79.

72. R. L. Cohen, "Mössbauer Spectroscopy: Recent Developments," *Science* 178 (1972): 828; Gary S. Collins, "Point Defects in Solids Studied by Hyperfine Methods," Defects in Solids Group, Hyperfine Interactions Laboratory, Department of Physics, Washington State University, Pullman, Washington (1977), <http://defects.physics.wsu.edu/ME-setup.html>; The Danish Mars Project, "Mössbauer Spectroscopy" (University of Copenhagen: The Danish Mars Project at the Niels Bohr Institute for Astronomy, Physics, and Geophysics, 2000), <http://www.fys.ku.dk/mars/moss_long.htm>; Gunther Wertheim, "Mössbauer Effect in Chemistry and Solid-State Physics," *Science* 144 (1964): 253.

73. Cohen, "Mössbauer Spectroscopy: Recent Developments," p. 828.

74. Ibid.

75. Bertelle et al., "Firing Techniques of the Impasti," pp. 262–77; Rice, *Pottery Analysis: A Sourcebook,* p. 400.

76. Bertelle et al., "Firing Techniques of the Impasti," p. 262; Charles Weaver, J. M. Wampler, and T. E. Pecuil, "Mössbauer Analysis of Iron in Clay Minerals," *Science* 156 (1967): 504.

77. The clay sample from excavations at the site of the National Constitution Center's future home on Independence Mall was provided by archaeologists Thomas Crist and Peter Glumac of Kise Straw & Kolodner, Inc.

Michelle Erickson and Robert Hunter

Swirls and Whirls: English Agateware Technology

▼ PREVIOUSLY THE AUTHORS reviewed the use of slips—liquid clays—to create a *marbled* effect on the surface of a clay object.[1] In this article, we examine how two or more colors of clay are used to make a variegated ceramic body generally known as *agateware*. Although these two terms are sometimes confused, marbled decoration implies a surface treatment whereas agateware refers to a solid clay fabric.

Semiprecious stones, such as agate, are some of the most beautiful of all substances. They were prevalent as design elements in Chinese, Greek, and Roman societies and often associated with nobility. The use of multiple colored clays to imitate agate can be traced to antiquity as well. Beginning in the late seventeenth century, this technique was used to fashion a class of English ceramics recognized as agateware.

English agateware has been made for useful and ornamental purposes, collected, and written about for several centuries. However, only limited discussions of production methods have been published, which run the gamut from fairly accurate to wildly speculative. In addition, these descriptions have not contained illustrations of agateware techniques.[2]

Our approach to decoding and recreating English agateware began with the information contained in the actual wares themselves. Careful examination and considerable trial and error experimentation produced results that we are now able to demonstrate. Insights gained from this preliminary exploration should help frame further questions about the manufacture of agateware and its place in eighteenth-century consumer society.

Agateware can be divided into two broad categories: *thrown agate* and *laid agate*. *Thrown agate* describes a vessel formed on a wheel using a prepared mixture of various colored clays. *Laid agate* refers to an object created from a thin sheet or bat made of agate clay. This thin sheet is draped or laid in the mold and pressed into shape—hence our use of the term *laid*.[3] Both types of agateware continue to be produced commercially as well as employed in the repertoire of the contemporary studio potter.[4]

History of Production

English Thrown Agate

The earliest documented agateware is found among the products of John Dwight (even though he himself referred to it as marbled). Considered by many as the father of English pottery, Dwight is well known in the annals of ceramic history for his innovations (fig. 1). He conducted numerous

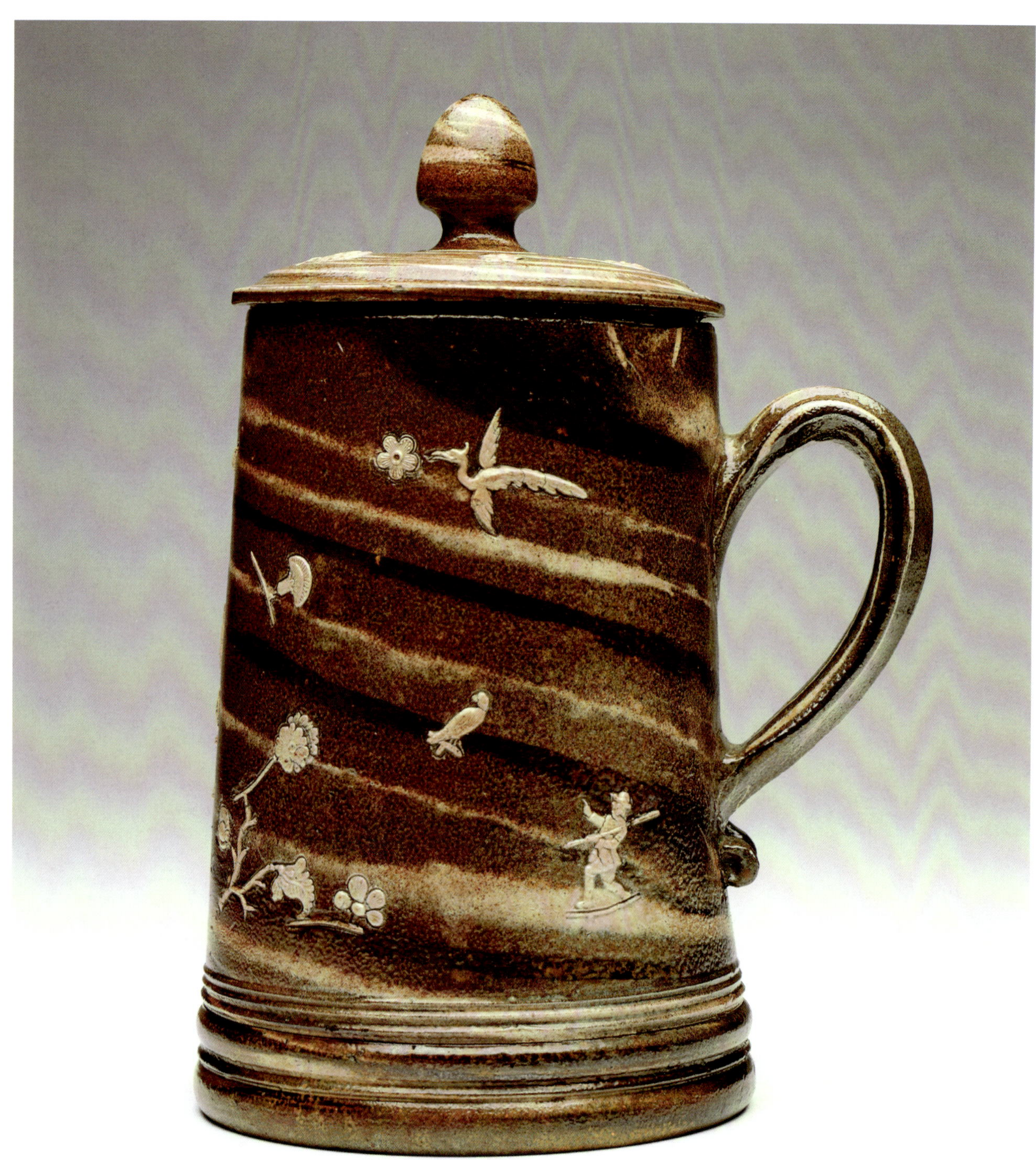

Figure 1 Covered mug, John Dwight, London, ca. 1688. Salt-glazed agateware. H. 10⅛". (Courtesy, Nelson Atkins Museum of Art, Kansas City, Missouri; gift of Mr. Frank P. Burnap.) This thrown agate mug is embellished with fine sprig moldings including a conjoined bust of William and Mary.

ceramic experiments beginning in the 1670s, delved into the mysteries of porcelain, and recorded his recipe to produce "marbled" stoneware:

> A dark colour'd Cley for marbled dishes and Teapots to endure boiling Water
>
> Take fine dark Earth ten pounds
> fine white Earth Eleaven pound
> Cley Sifted one & twenty pounds
> White Sifted through Cyprus Sieve
> Six pounds, mingle & tread

Included with the instructions are these comments:

> Note y t this dark colours; the mouse colourd, & the dish white Cleyes, agree best together to marke marbled Vefsells, that will burne Every where, & Endure boiling Water.
>
> But to make marbled gorges or Cans, the gorge white may be used instead of the dish-white, because it works Stronger upon ye wheel.[5]

Dwight's notes reveal two important material considerations in making an agate body: clay color and clay compatibility.

To create the illusion of agate striations, different color clays must be obtained naturally or by modification, adding pigments or coloring agents. The tone of a natural clay can also be altered by sieving to remove impurities such as iron and sand.

Creating a successful variegated appearance also depends on the proportions of clay colors used. Dwight's recipe required equal parts of dark (ten pounds) and white (eleven pounds) clay and an additional six pounds of white clay passed through a Cyprus sieve. Named for the silk material used for the mesh, this type of sieve had the smallest or finest opening available at the time. For the first of these colors, Dwight's notebooks contain instructions for making "a dark earth"—a clay artificially stained with iron oxides obtained from the hammer scale of a blacksmith's forge. The second color, the fine white, may be a natural pale- to mid-gray clay. Research shows that specimens of the final color—the six pounds of sifted white clay—are pure white and have virtually no macroscopically visible inclusions.[6]

Clues for understanding problems related to combining multiple clays are also contained in Dwight's formula. These include shrinkage rates, firing temperatures, density, plasticity, elasticity, and strength. All of these properties must be considered when mixing dissimilar clay bodies.

When Dwight writes that these "dark colours; the mouse colourd, & the dish white Cleyes, agree best together to marke marbled Vefsells, that will burne Every where, & Endure boiling Water," he is referring to the ability of clays to blend successfully to throw properly, to survive the firing without splitting or warping, and, as a finished product, to withstand the thermal shock from boiling water. In considering the agate clay's working capabilities, Dwight prescribes that "the gorge white may be used instead of the dish-white, because it works Stronger upon ye wheel." The term "Stronger" means that the clay could be better pulled up on the wheel and into a cylinder without distortion or collapse.

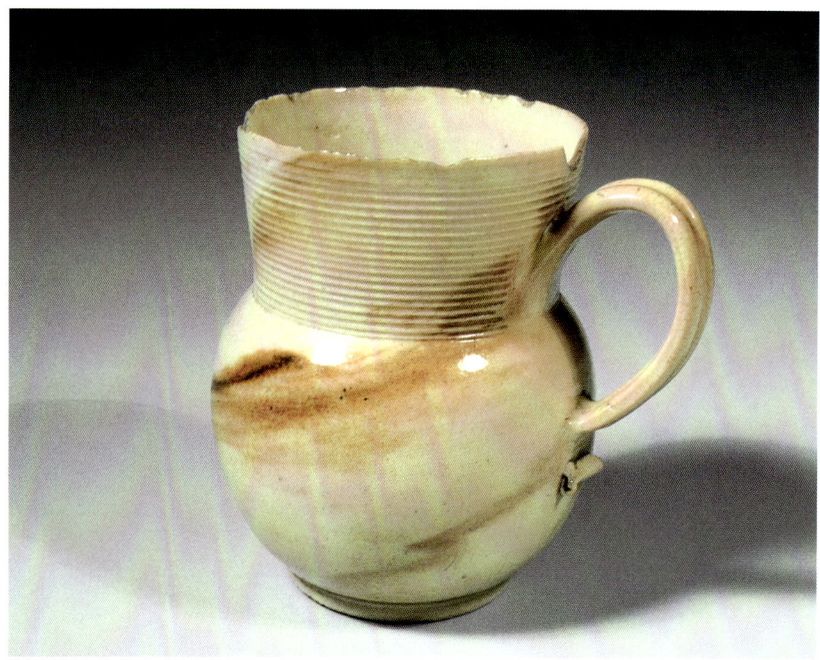

Figure 2 Mug, Francis Place, Yorkshire, ca. 1680. Salt-glazed stoneware. H. 3½". (Courtesy, Mint Museum of Art, Charlotte, North Carolina. Gift of the Delhom Service League; photo, David Ramsey.)

Today, only a few of Dwight's "marbled" or agatewares survive.[7] In addition, some agateware fragments have been recovered from archaeological excavations of his pottery site in Fulham. These fragments include examples of a tankard, a gorge (or mug), a cappuchine (coffee cup), and a teapot. The discovery of a teapot underscores Dwight's concerns expressed in his recipe note that the clay could "Endure" boiling water.[8]

It is hard to judge whether Dwight's agateware was received as a novelty or as an important scientific discovery. Evidence for the latter may be suggested by the "marbled" salt-glazed stoneware of Francis Place of York (fig. 2). Primarily an artist and engraver, Place was also a dilettante with eclectic interests, and he prominently included a mug in the foreground of his circa 1680 self-portrait. As part of a growing group of gentlemen-artists who studied every new artistic and scientific inquiry in English society, Place was undoubtedly inspired by the growing national interest in new ceramic discoveries which would lead to many technological breakthroughs in the eighteenth-century English ceramic industry.[9]

Commercial production of English agateware does not begin in earnest until the second quarter of the eighteenth century. In 1729, Samuel Bell, at the Lower Street potworks, Newcastle-under-Lyme, was granted a patent to produce "red marbled stoneware with mineral earth found within this kingdom which being firmly united by fire will make it capable of receiving a gloss so beautiful as to imitate if not compare with ruby."[10] Like Dwight's agate, the Bell products were thrown on the wheel. After being initially formed, the wares were turned on the lathe to thin the body and concurrently create a clean variegated surface. These wares typically had a red and off-white clay body even though a black colored clay was used.

Contrary to the wording of the patent, Bell's agateware is earthenware rather than stoneware. These wares are distinguished for being the earliest

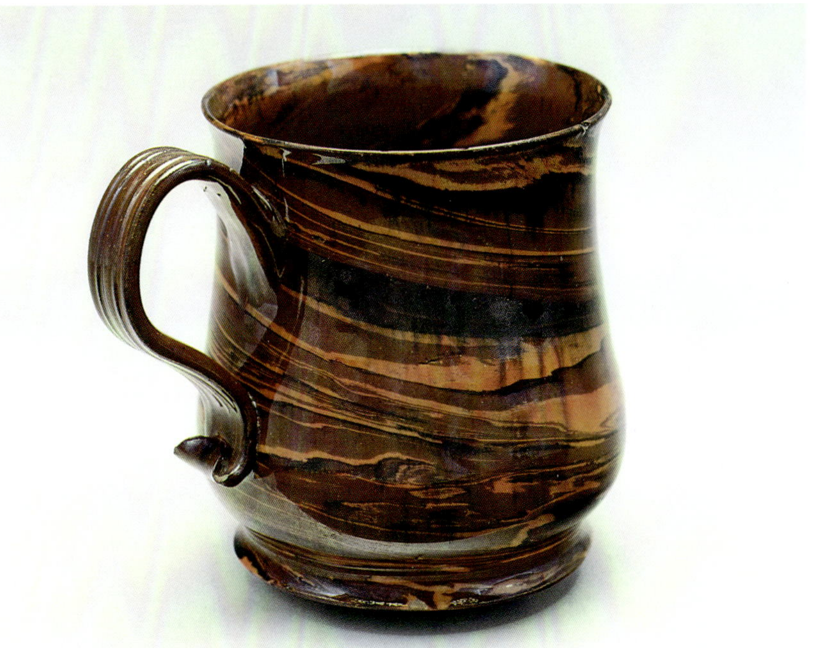

Figure 3 Mug, attributed to Samuel Bell, Staffordshire (Newcastle-under-Lyme), ca. 1740. Lead-glazed agateware. H. 4½". (Courtesy, Troy D. Chappell Collection; photos by Gavin Ashworth unless otherwise noted.)

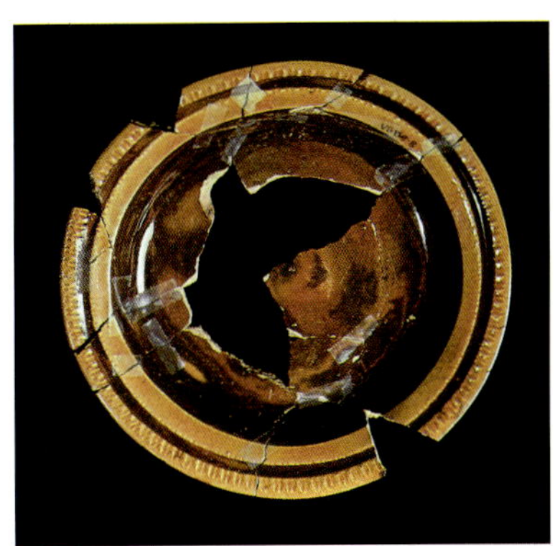

Figure 4 Dish, Staffordshire, ca. 1780. Lead-glazed agateware. D. 6½". (Photo, Robert Hunter.) Dishes of this type appear to have been imported into America in large quantities as they are commonly found in archaeological excavations of the last quarter of the eighteenth century. It is uncertain if the agate effect was intentional or the result of using a mixture of different clays intended to create a better body. Precedent for the latter is found in the so-called Buckley wares made in North Wales from ca. 1720 to 1780, although this ware was covered in a thick black glaze and the agate body is generally not visible.

known twice-fired earthenware in Staffordshire, first being fired to a biscuit state then dipped into a liquid lead glaze and fired again. The wording in his patent "being firmly united by fire" may reflect Bell's recognition of the potential problems of successfully integrating different clays into a single ceramic body.

Archaeological evidence from the excavation of Staffordshire factory sites, including that of John Bell and of John Astbury at Shelton Farm, shows that many potters made this type of thrown agate. Tea wares were the most common forms made, although mugs and bowls were also produced (fig. 3). Thrown agate reached its height of popularity in the 1750s and continued in production into the early 1770s.[11]

At that time, a coarser type of thrown agateware was introduced in Staffordshire. Used primarily for plates, dishes, and bowls, these wares frequently included rouletted bands of white slip decoration. This utilitarian agateware is commonly found in American archaeological sites of the 1770s and 1780s (fig. 4). Thrown agate production all but disappeared in Staffordshire by the late eighteenth century but continued sporadically in other pottery centers such as Sussex in the nineteenth century.[12]

English Laid Agate

The second quarter of the eighteenth century saw many innovations in the Staffordshire potteries. One of these was the use of molds for creating forms either by slip casting or pressing. Press molding permitted new possibilities for developing agate bodies (figs. 5–7).

Laid agateware is inherently different from thrown agateware in that the pattern must first be prepared before the shape is made. In other words, the decoration is made before the pot. It is uncertain exactly when the laid agate technique was developed in Staffordshire. Ceramic historian Simeon Shaw mentions Dr. Thomas Wedgwood of Burslem (1695–1737) as

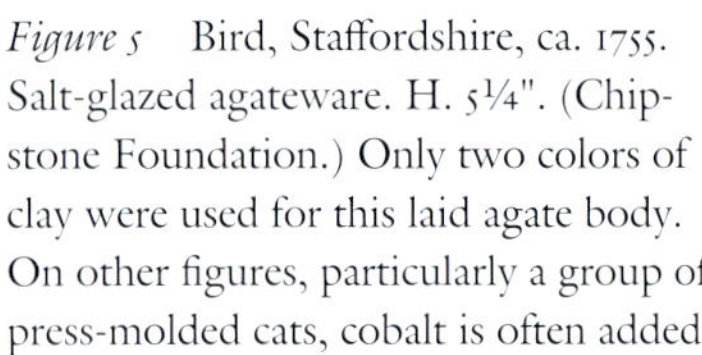

Figure 5 Bird, Staffordshire, ca. 1755. Salt-glazed agateware. H. 5¼". (Chipstone Foundation.) Only two colors of clay were used for this laid agate body. On other figures, particularly a group of press-molded cats, cobalt is often added.

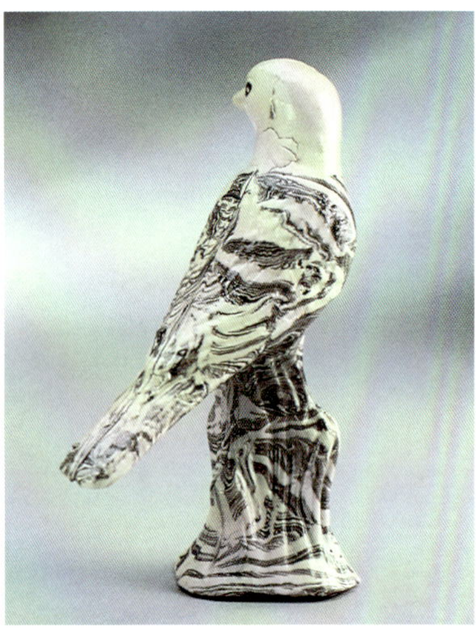

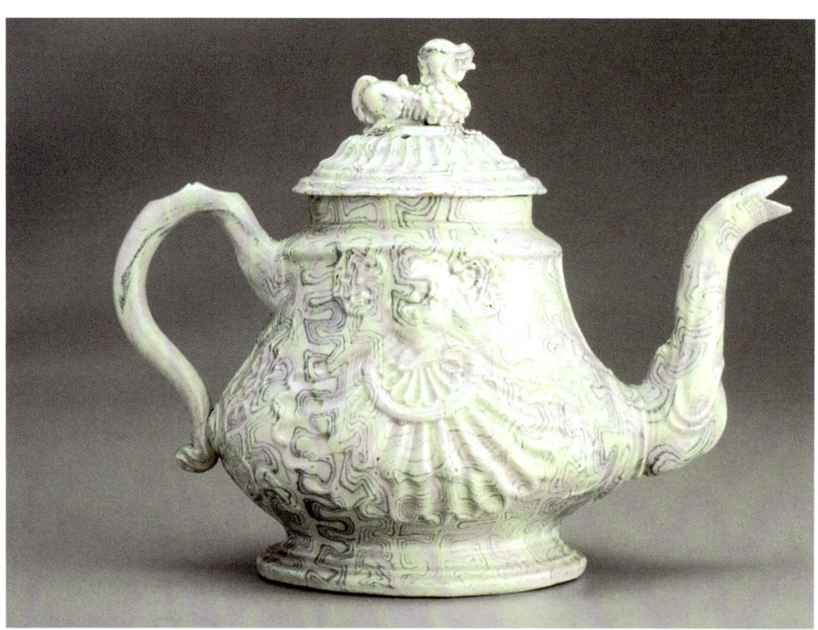

Figure 6 Teapot, Staffordshire, ca. 1755. Salt-glazed agateware. H. 5⅝". (Chipstone Foundation.) Most of the salt-glazed laid agateware consisted of two colors although three-color examples exist. The orientation of this relatively simple agate pattern, sometimes called "elephant's tooth" by collectors, is arranged in vertical strips.

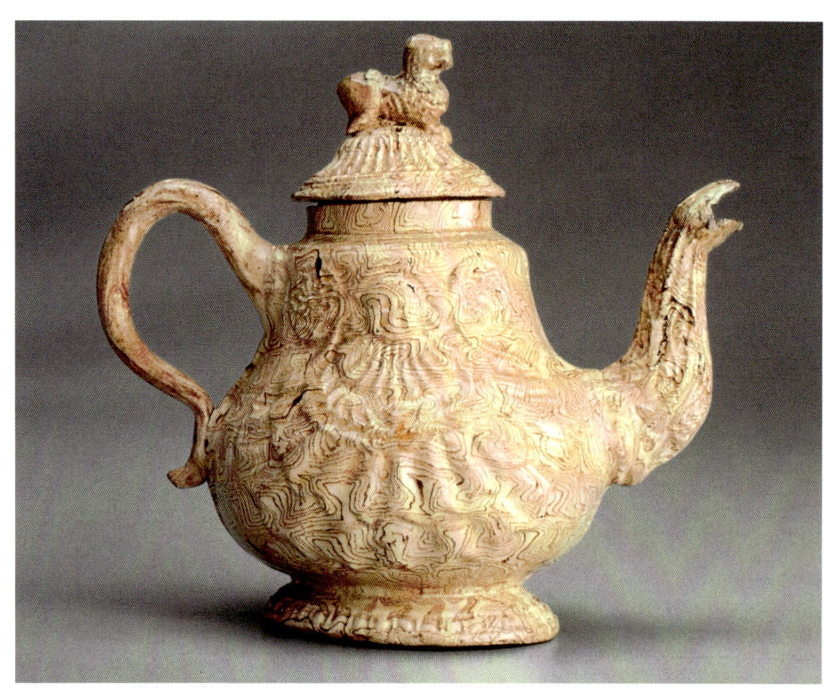

Figure 7 Teapot, Staffordshire, England, ca. 1755. Lead-glazed agateware. H. 5¾". (Chipstone Foundation.) Two colors of earthenware clay were used for this shell shaped teapot. This is similar to the pattern illustrated in fig. 6, but with a horizontal orientation.

the earliest potter associated with the process. Apparently his products included "Coffee and Tea Pots, of clays compounded and mixed to resemble agate, marble, and other natural bodies, . . . in various shapes; some glazed with lead ore; and the white, all salt glaze." Shaw continues, "Had the agate rising genius of that day been adequately encouraged, doubtless many important improvements would have resulted."[13]

Another likely candidate is Thomas Whieldon of Fenton Low (1719–1795). Whieldon is most often recognized for his improvements in agateware undertaken in the 1740s, including the use of white clays stained with metallic oxides.[14] Still, a firm date for the beginning of laid agate in Staffordshire has yet to be established, although an agateware dish with the inscribed date of 1746 may be the earliest documented example that exists.[15]

Beyond the date of its introduction, however, the source of the laid agate pattern is perhaps the more important inquiry. Several writers have been hesitant to make this correlation, but, for us, it is clear that eighth-century T'ang dynasty Chinese wares inspired many eighteenth-century Staffordshire laid agatewares. The relationship is most obviously visible in the form of globular censers, or incense burners, which are of the same size and shape as the Staffordshire teapots (figs. 8, 9).[16]

Figure 8 Footed censers, China, T'ang Dynasty. Agateware. H. 3" and 2⅞". (Courtesy, Bonhams & Butterfields Auctioneers.)

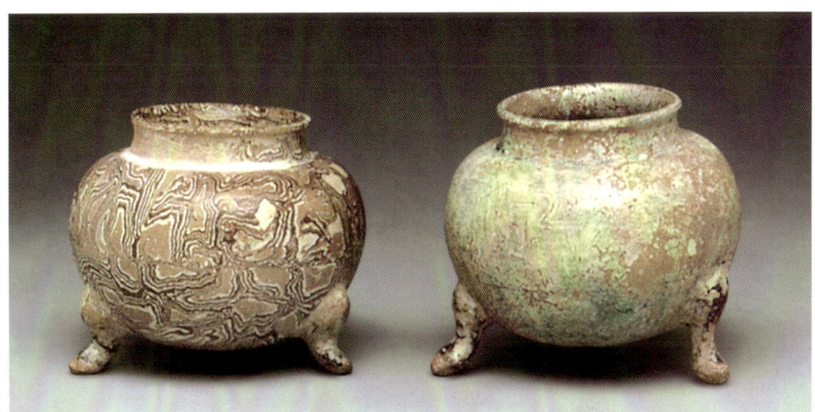

The imitation of eighth-century Chinese ceramics by Staffordshire potters is not as improbable as it may seem at first. It is known that contemporary Chinese porcelains and Yixing stonewares served as direct prototypes for many eighteenth-century Staffordshire tea wares. It is likely that older Chinese wares resided in European and English antiquarian collections. Such antique wares were sought for the "cabinets of curiosities" of the English cognoscenti. Intriguingly, the cabinets belonging to these scientifically minded collectors often included "agates, onyxes and intaglios."[17]

If Thomas Whieldon is responsible for deciphering the Chinese laid agate technique and introducing it in the Staffordshire potteries, he must have studied antique examples at length. In 1754, Whieldon entered into a partnership with young Josiah Wedgwood. Excavations at Whieldon's manufactory at Fenton Vivian revealed a number of laid agate wasters, which appeared to have been manufactured during the period of the part-

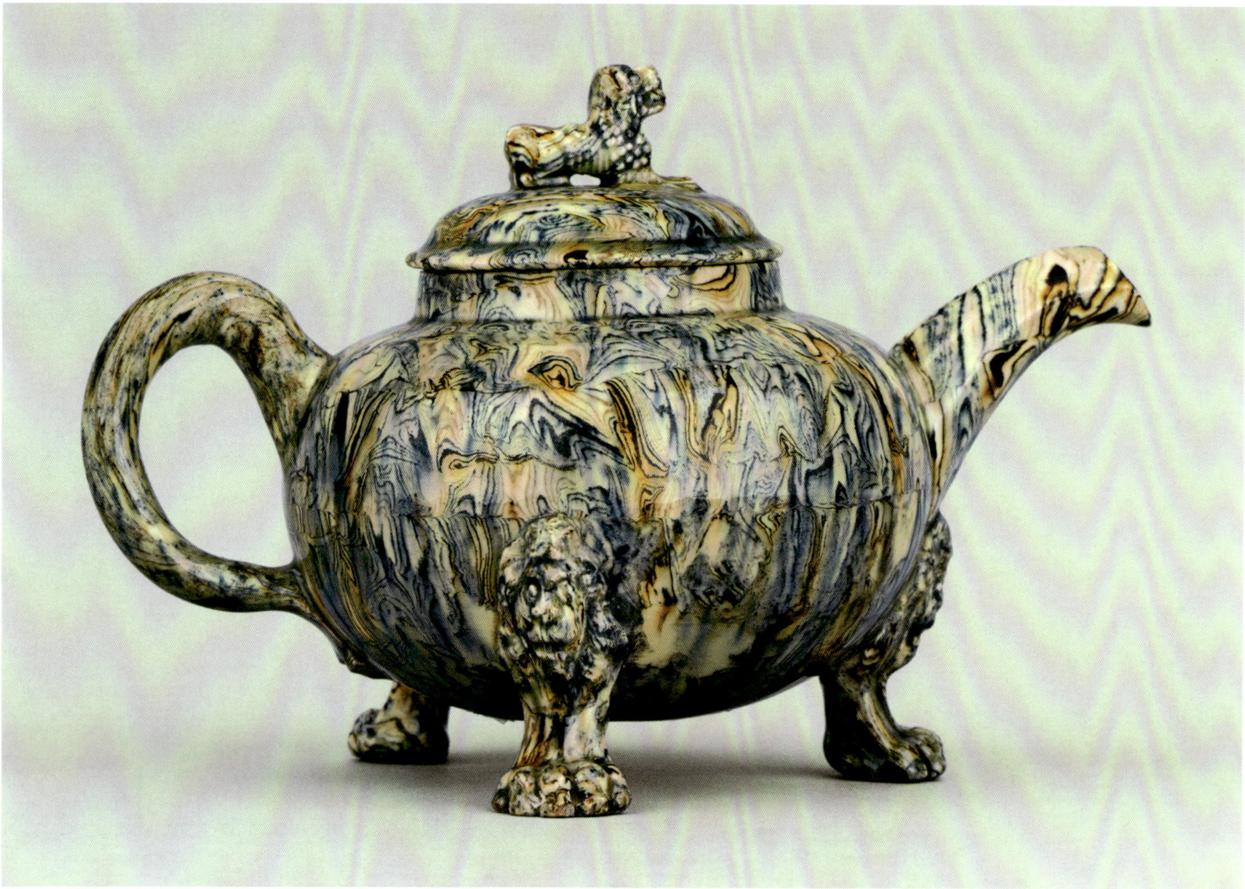

Figure 9 Teapot, Staffordshire, ca. 1750. Lead-glazed agateware. H. 5". (Courtesy, Colonial Williamsburg Foundation.) Note the identical shape to the Chinese censers illustrated in fig. 8.

nership.[18] One of the most often cited agateware references comes from Josiah Wedgwood's experiment book on March 23, 1759: "I had already made an imitation of Agat which was esteem'd very beautiful, and a considerable improvement . . . ."[19] Just how much he improved the agateware process and whether he had a direct hand in copying Chinese prototypes is undocumented.

Josiah Wedgwood concluded his partnership with Whieldon that year and went into business for himself. He continued to refine the agate technology for decorating his ornamental vases. Wedgwood used both solid agates and marbled slip techniques at his Etruria factory into the 1780s. Rather than copies of Chinese prototypes, the vases were directly inspired by antique Etruscan and Roman examples.[20]

Agateware made on the Continent is occasionally confused with Staffordshire specimens (fig. 10). Close examination usually reveals both significant differences in the agate veining and vessel forms. In addition, the earliest known French agateware made by Francius Moulina and Jacques Barthelemy in Apt, France, beginning in 1768, was almost two decades later than the main production period in Staffordshire. Other laid agateware was made through the nineteenth century at several European centers.[21]

In the later part of the eighteenth century, some Staffordshire potters applied laid agate to utilitarian creamwares and pearlwares. Used in conjunction with mocha-type slip decoration, these examples had an agate

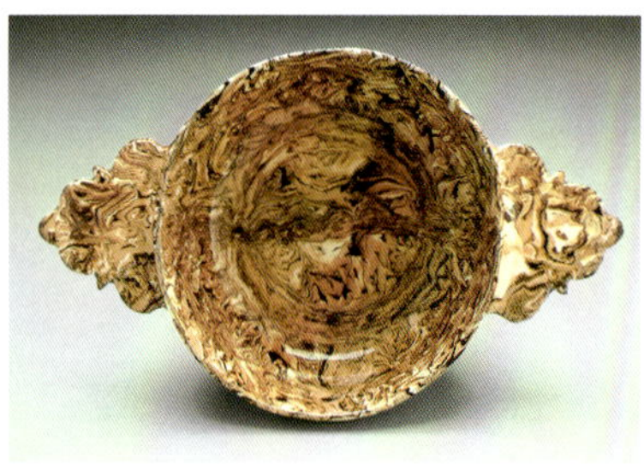

Figure 10 Porringer, Apt, France, ca. 1770. Lead-glazed agateware. L. 9½". (Chipstone Foundation.)

Figure 11 Mug and jug fragments, Staffordshire, ca. 1785. Pearlware. (Courtesy, Alexandria Archaeology.) Fragments from these similarly slip-decorated vessels are highlighted with a sheet of agate inlaid in the bodies.

Figure 12 Detail of the agate inlay in the fragments illustrated in fig. 11. This pattern is created with alternating black-and-white and red-and-white squares of agate clay.

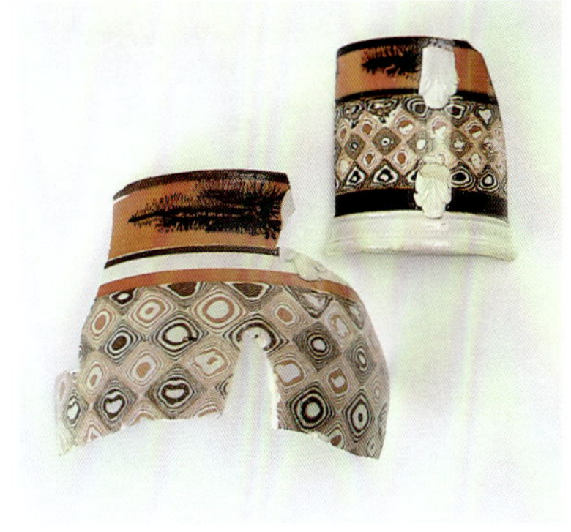

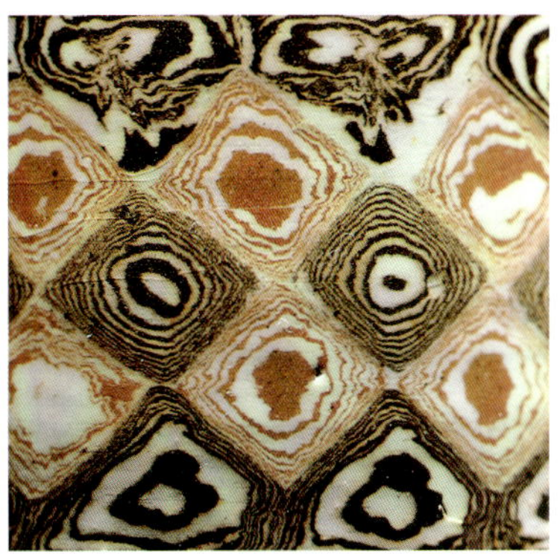

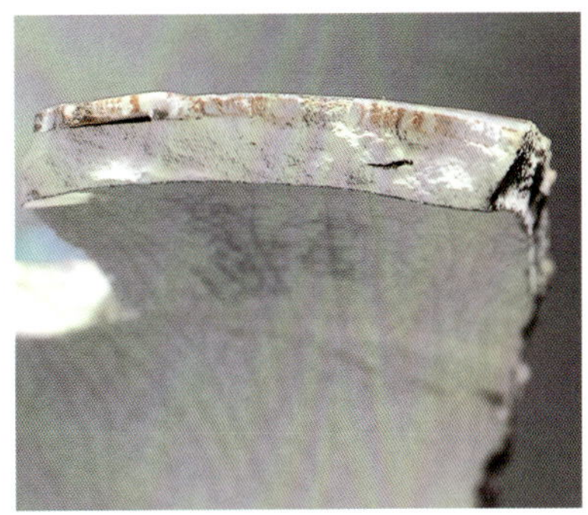

Figure 13 Detail of the fragment section illustrated in fig. 12 showing the thin solid sheet of agate veneered to the surface of the pearlware body. After the agate sheet was inlaid, the vessel was trimmed on a lathe to reveal this distinct pattern.

sheet laminated to the surface (figs. 11–13). This so-called *surface agate* or *inlaid agate*, although seemingly a laborious method of decoration, was still practical enough to embellish these inexpensive earthenwares.[22]

American Agateware

In America the use of agate clays is occasionally seen on domestically produced redware in the seventeenth and eighteenth centuries. Indeed, the earliest documented use of agateware technology comes with the circa 1650–1669 tobacco pipe kiln of Emanuel Drue in Maryland (fig. 14).[23] However, the best-known examples of American agateware are the nineteenth-century products of the U. S. Pottery Company in Bennington, Vermont, termed "scroddled ware," although the company called the ware "Lava" (fig. 15).[24]

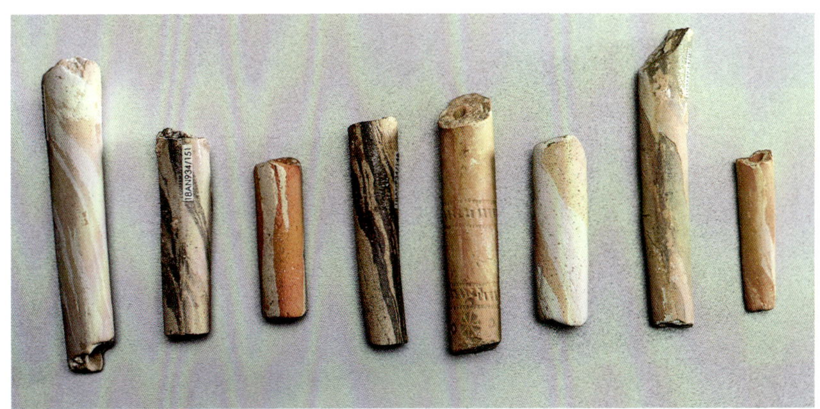

Figure 14 Tobacco pipes, Emanuel Drue, Maryland, 1650–1669. Earthenware. (Courtesy, Al Luckenbach.) These pipe fragments probably represent the earliest use of the agate technique in colonial America. The agate pattern was created using naturally occurring colored clays. Similar examples of Dutch tobacco pipes have been found in a circa 1620 context at Martin's Hundred in Virginia.

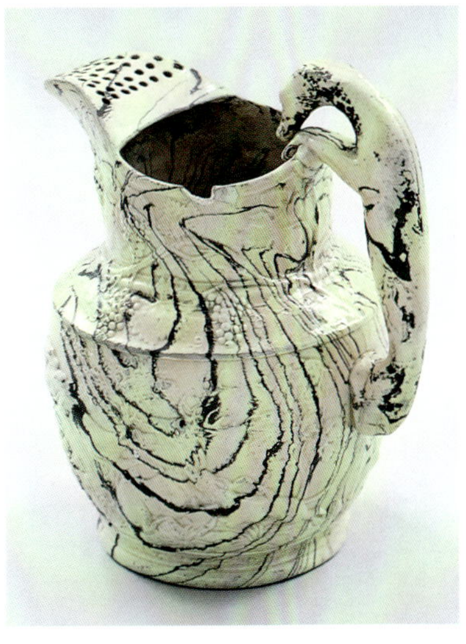

Figure 15 Pitcher, U.S. Pottery Company, Bennington, Vermont, ca. 1853. Lead-glazed agateware. H. 11⅜". (Courtesy, The Bennington Museum.) This pitcher was designed by Daniel Greatbach. Ceramics historian John Spargo writes that scroddled ware was manufactured in the nineteenth century exactly as it was in eighteenth-century Staffordshire.

Figure 16 Vase, Evans Pottery, ca. 1950. H. 10½". (Private collection.)

Figure 17 Vase, North State Pottery, North Carolina, ca. 1930. H. 9½". (Private collection.) This thrown agate vase demonstrates extremely vigorous striations of clays. The interior is lead glazed.

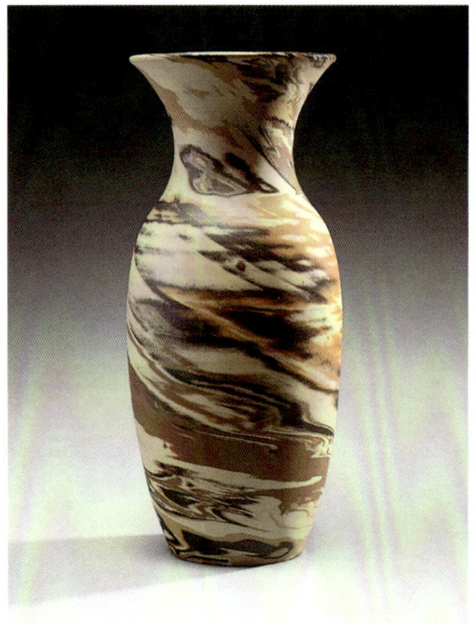

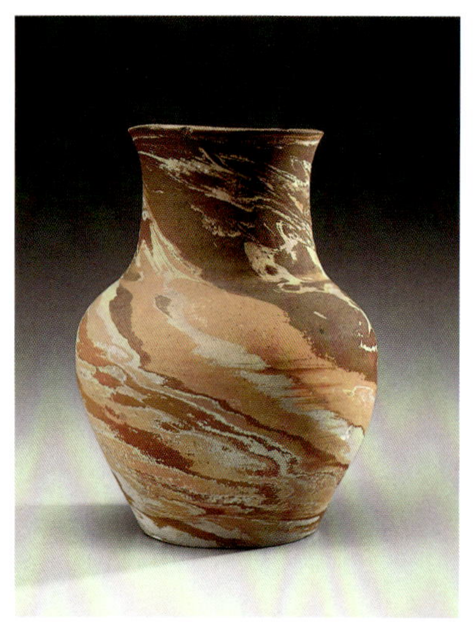

A number of nineteenth-century American potteries used agate clays to manufacture doorknobs covered with a Rockingham glaze. In the twentieth century, agateware makes a brief appearance in the arts and crafts movement, most notably in the "Mission Swirl" line of the Niloak Pottery Company in Benton, Arkansas (fig. 16). Another thrown agate of this general type was produced by North State Pottery of North Carolina (fig. 17) in the 1920s and 1930s.

Demonstration of Agateware Techniques

Thrown Agateware Techniques

The key step in creating an agateware body can be summed up in three words: preparation, preparation, preparation! For creating thrown agate, the initial selecting and mixing of clays is critical (fig. 18). To begin, clay slabs are built up, alternating the colors (fig. 19). This stack is then wedged

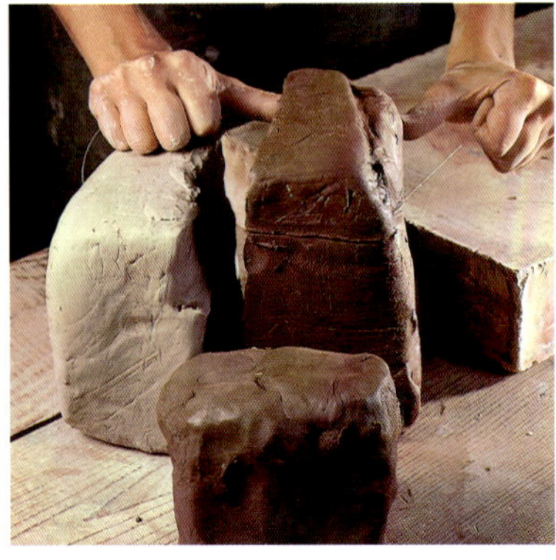

Figure 18 In preparing the clay for throwing an agateware mug, slabs of varied colored earthenware clays are cut and stacked. At this stage the proportion of the colored clays determine the intensity of the agate patterning. Three colored clays are selected for making a mug: a white clay, a red iron clay, and an iron manganese body.

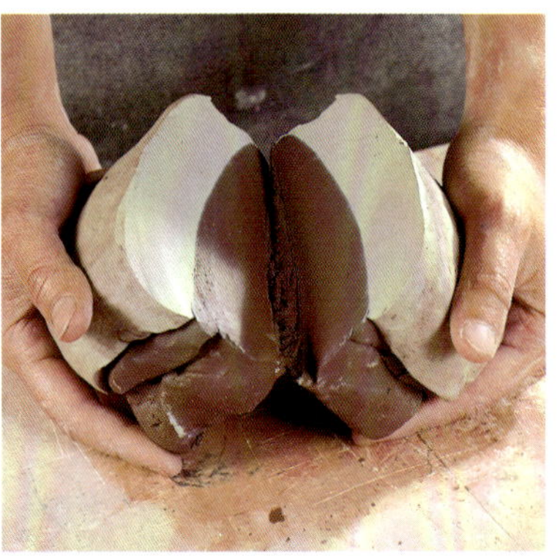

Figure 19 The slabs are then stacked in alternating colors. After the initial stacking, the clay is sliced in half and restacked to start with an even distribution of layers.

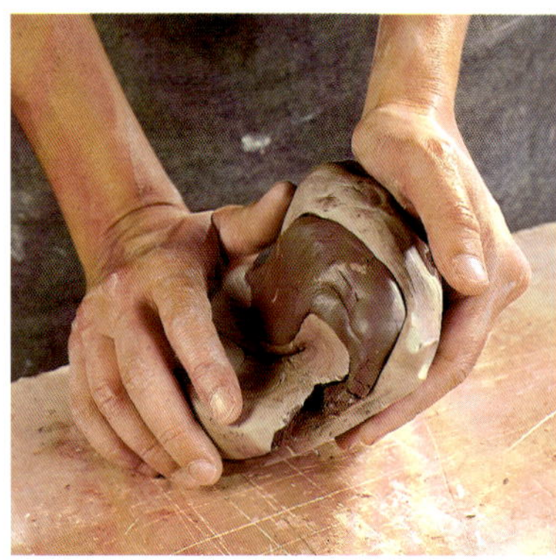

Figure 20 The clay is carefully wedged or kneaded to prepare it for throwing. Care has to be taken at this stage to expel air from the clay without overworking the clays. The more the clays are wedged the less distinct the resulting agate pattern.

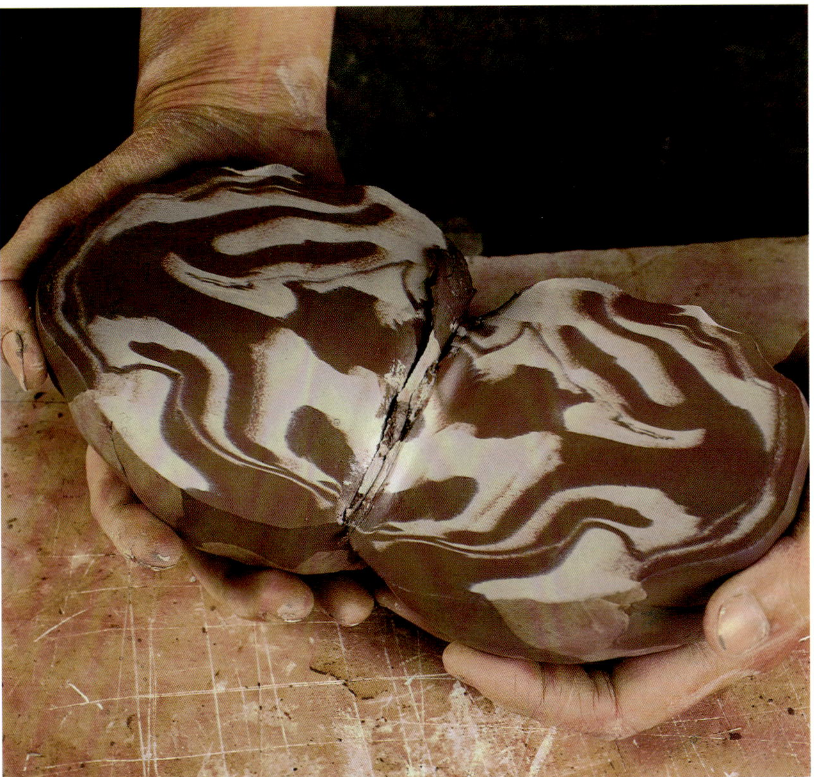

Figure 21 For demonstration purposes, the wedged ball is cut to show the pattern prior to throwing. Restacking these halves can improve the quality of the agate patterning in the finished product.

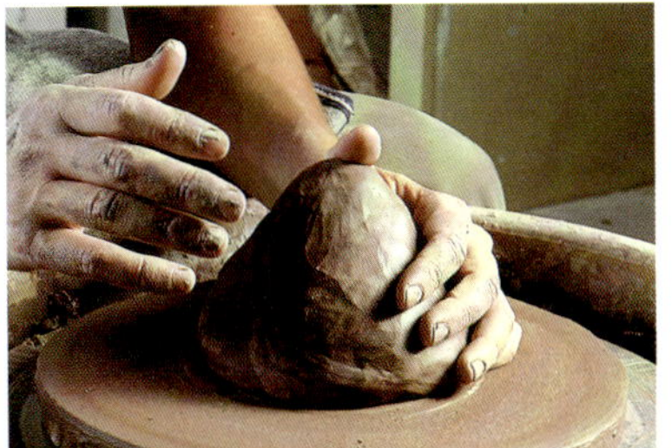

Figure 22 The prepared agate clay ball is centered on the wheel.

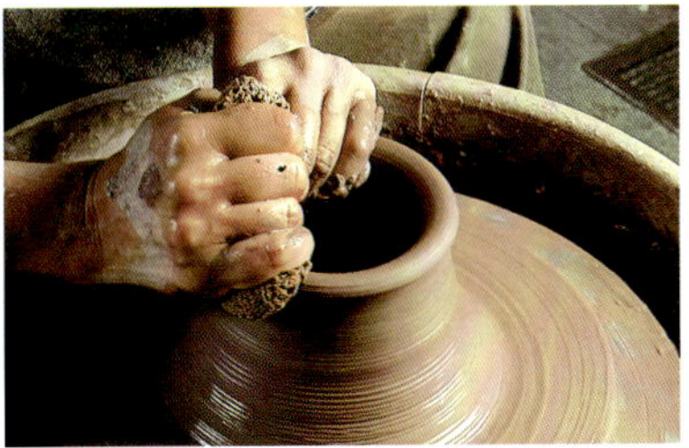

Figure 23 Once centered, the clay ball is opened and pulled quickly into a cylinder. During the throwing process it is important not to overwork the clay as this will lessen the distinctions between the colors.

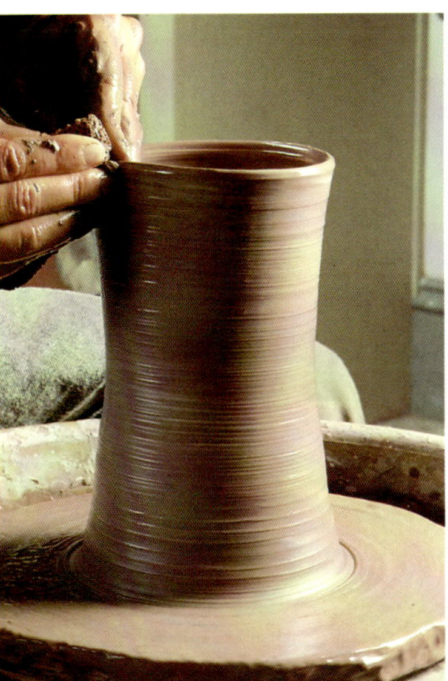

Figure 24 The cylinder is shaped into the final mug form. Note how the muddy surface has concealed the agate patterning.

or folded to form a ball that can then be thrown on the wheel (fig. 20). Care has to be taken during wedging to ensure the clays are mixed without overly distorting or blurring the resultant agate pattern (fig. 21). The degree of success in an agate pattern comes from the initial wedging process as well as the throwing.

The prepared clay ball is then centered on the wheel (fig. 22). During throwing, the surface of the clay body becomes smeared so that agate patterning is obscured (figs. 23–28). Care has to be exercised during throwing

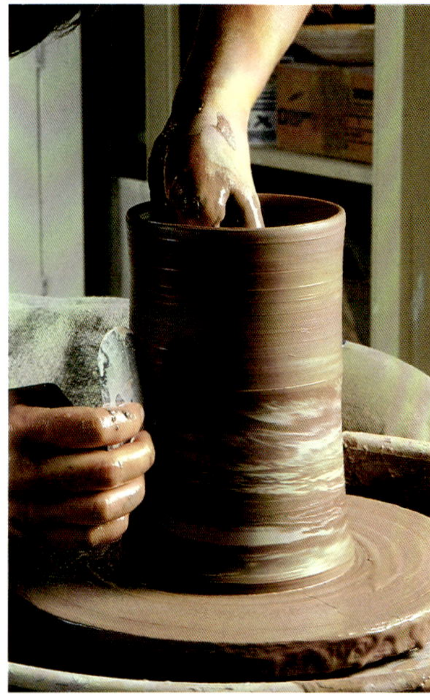

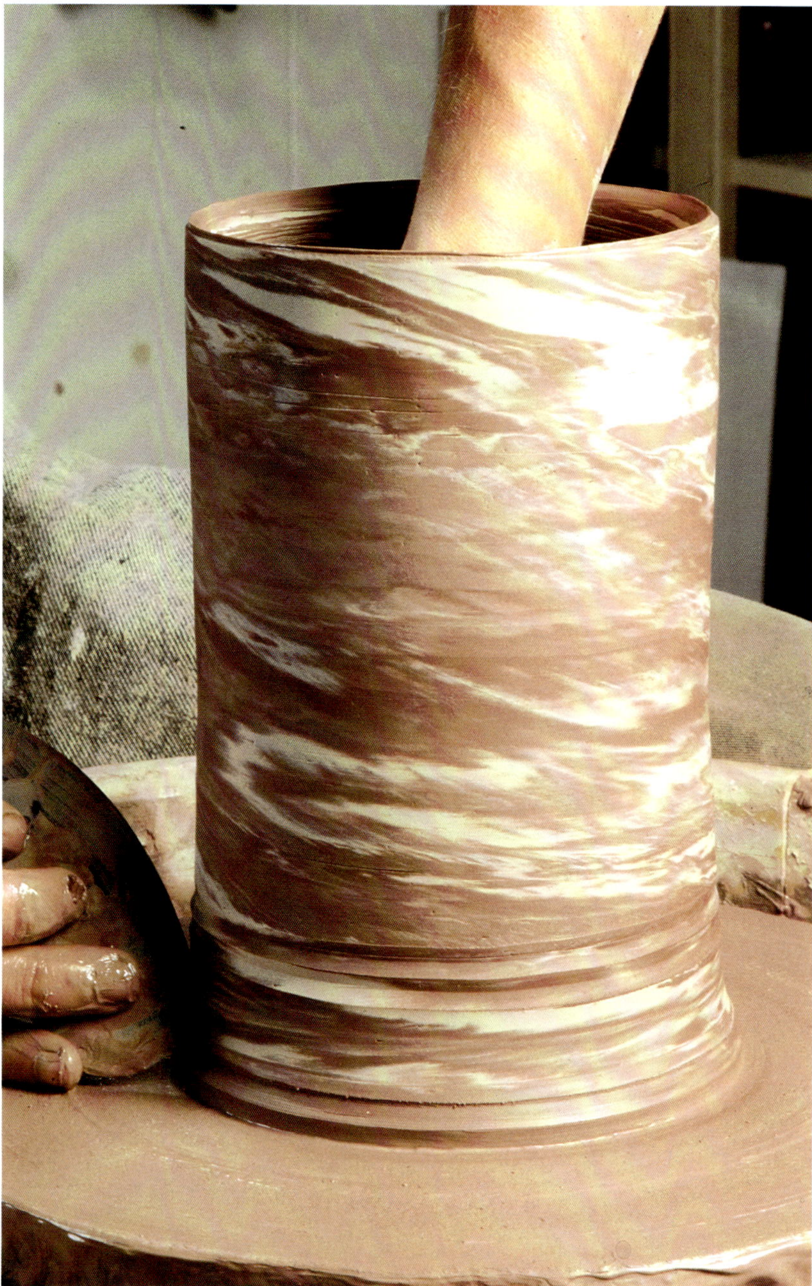

Figure 25 The final contours are shaped using a metal rib, and the muddy exterior of the thrown mug is scraped away, revealing the agate pattern.

Figure 26 Final finishing of the thrown mug.

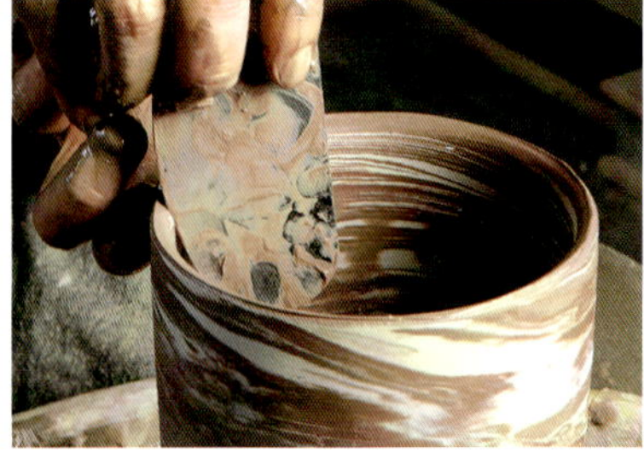

Figure 27 Interior of the mug being scraped to reveal the agate pattern.

so as not to overwork the clay; otherwise, the pattern becomes muddled. Since nearly all Staffordshire thrown agate was subsequently trimmed on the lathe, the veining usually appears sharp and crisp (fig. 29). Later smearing and smudging can occur at the attachment points of handles or spouts as evidenced on some antiques.

Laid Agateware Techniques

Making a laid agate vessel requires a different set of skills than competent throwing. Deciphering the techniques behind the process required direct examination of extant pots and subsequent experimentation (fig. 30). Ceramic historian Pat Halfpenny wrote, "There is no 18th-Century manual

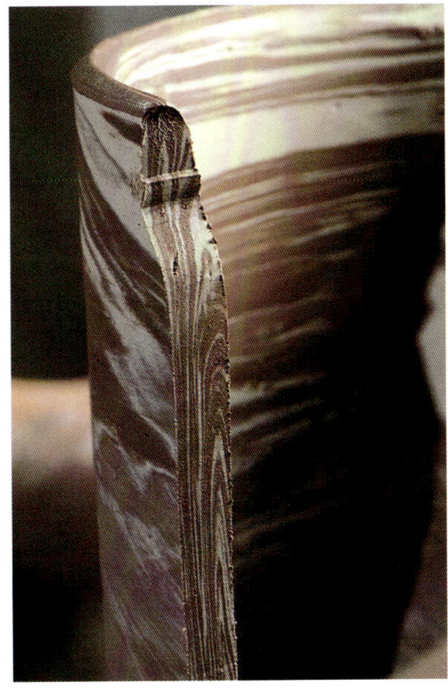

Figure 28 The thrown mug is sliced to reveal a cross-section of the body that shows the solid agate pattern and uniform thickness of the wall. Even wall thickness is important to the success of the next step.

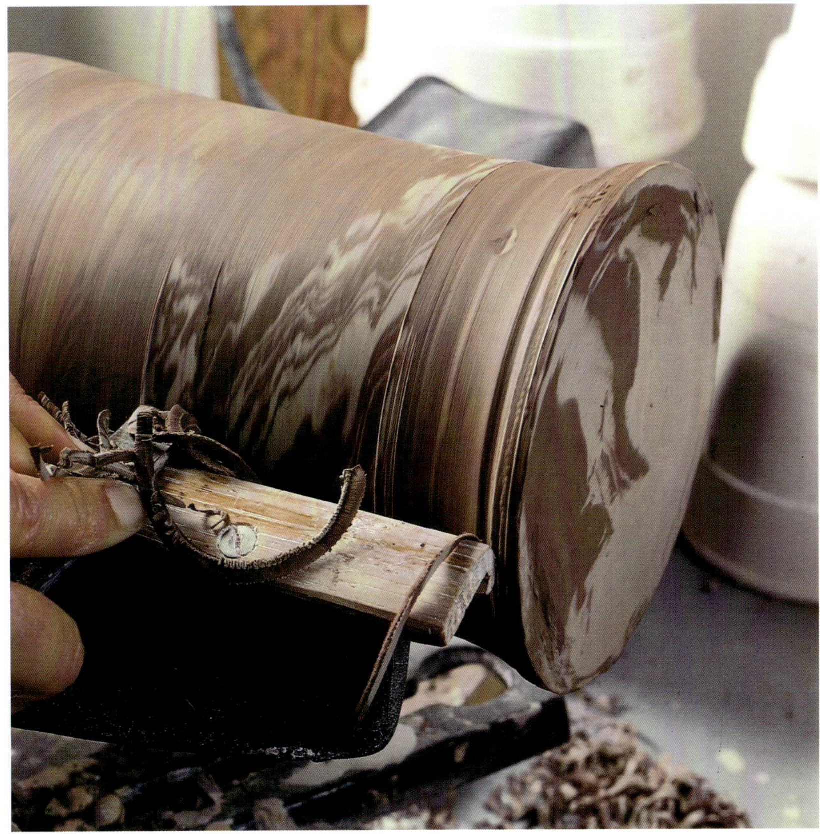

Figure 29 In the production of eighteenth-century Staffordshire hollow wares, the forms are affixed to a lathe for final trimming. After this stage, a handle is pulled or extruded from an agate clay ball and attached to the mug. Subsequently, the mug is dried, fired to biscuit, glazed, and refired.

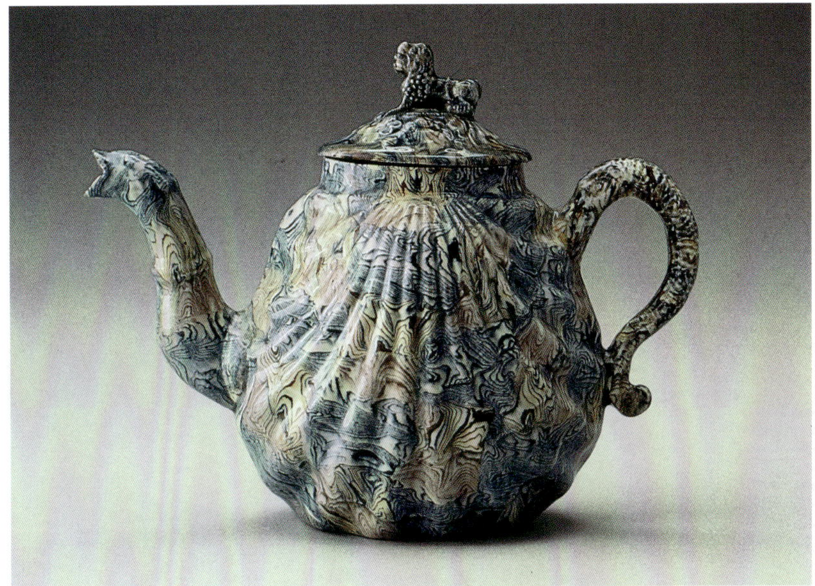

Figure 30 Teapot, Staffordshire, 1745–1755. Lead-glazed agateware. H. 5⅛". (Chipstone Foundation.) An example of a press-molded pecten shaped teapot. Note the seemingly naturalistic patterning of the laid agate which exhibits alternate squares of cobalt colored clay. This antique specimen serves as the prototype for the demonstration of the laid agate techniques.

on ceramic technology." What we do have, instead, are secondary descriptions by ceramic writers since the mid-nineteenth century.[25] One account by the ceramic historian Louis Solon explains the procedure:

> Agate-ware was a complicated process; the marbling, instead of being produced on the surface, went through the body. It was thus practiced: Thin laminae of yellow and red clay were laid alternately upon each other until they formed a thick mass; from that mass thin slices were

> transversely cut with a wire, making thin bats which showed the veining produced by the superimposed layers of clay; these were then used to press the piece, the neatest side being placed against the mould. The bat required careful handling, as a pressure sideways in the wedging in or a too rough pressing in the mould destroyed the fineness in the marbling.[26]

Solon's description makes clear that the making of agateware is a "complicated" process. That his account is over simplified, however, is suggested by our research. As noted earlier, the initial preparation of clay is the key for creating laid agateware (fig. 31). Using naturally colored clays and those colored with metallic oxides, the clay slabs are first stacked in a selected sequence (fig. 32). Rather than wedging, the stacks are slammed onto a hard surface to elongate and consequently thin the slabs (fig. 33). The process continues with cutting and restacking the slabs, thinning and increasing the numbers of layers (figs. 34–38). The ultimate success of the agate patterning lies in the care taken at this initial stage.

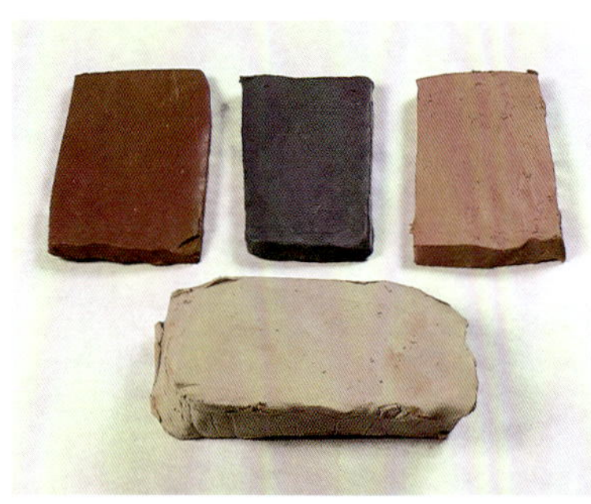

Figure 31 Four colors of clay slabs. A base white earthenware is in the foreground. The other slabs have been colored with (left to right): iron oxide, manganese oxide, and cobalt carbonate.

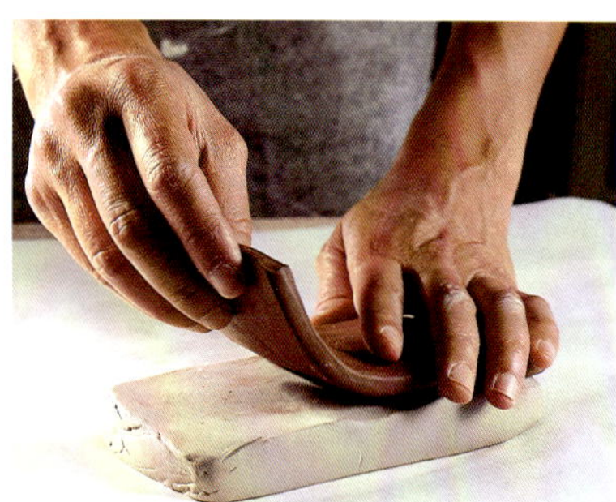

Figure 32 A slab of iron enriched red clay is laid onto a base white clay of the same length and width. The slab of white clay is approximately three times as thick.

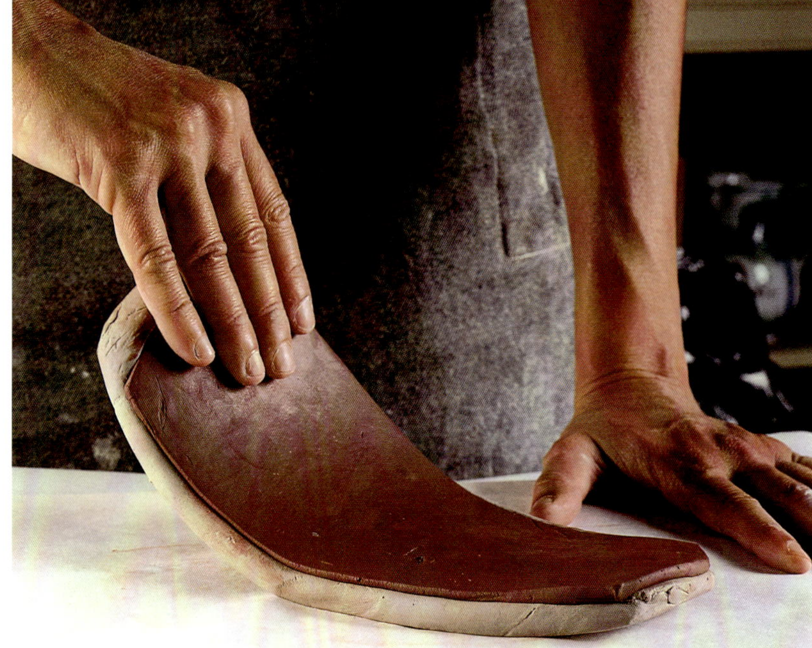

Figure 33 The combined slabs are repeatedly slammed on the table to stretch and thin the layers. This process of using the clay's natural properties to achieve the thinning is a simple but elegant solution.

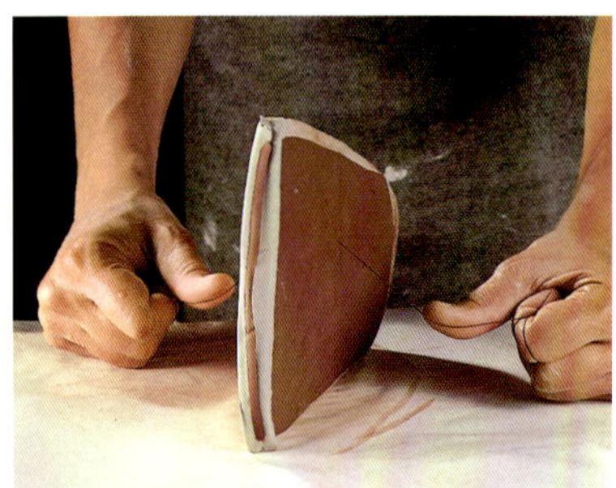

Figure 34 The combined clay slab is cut in half and the two pieces restacked. This process is repeated, continuously adding and thinning the layers.

Figure 35 The slab after cutting the second time showing two layers.

Figure 36 Cutting the slab in half after several repeated steps of stacking and thinning.

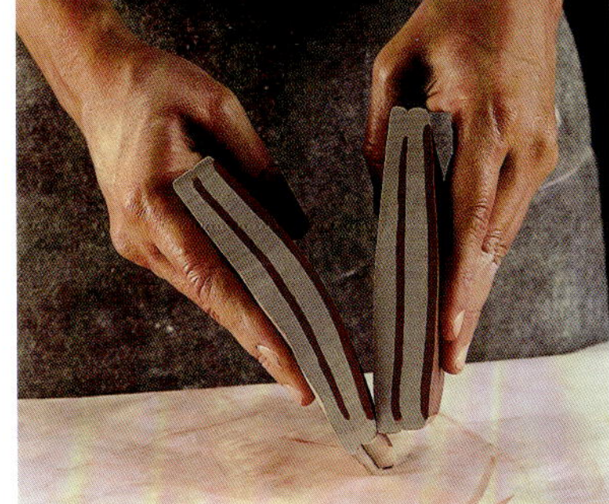

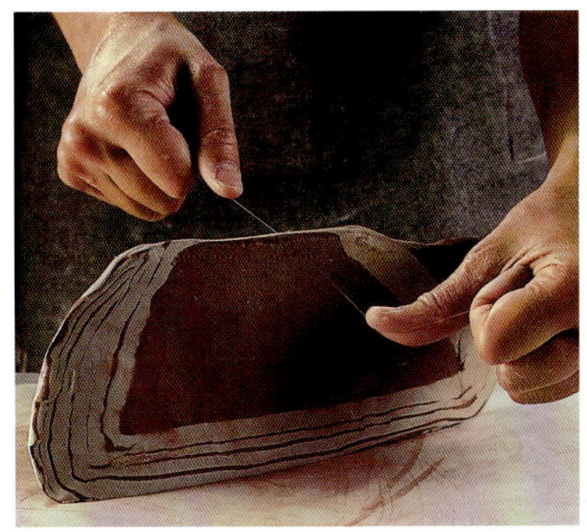

Figure 37 Cross-sections of the stacking and thinning process.

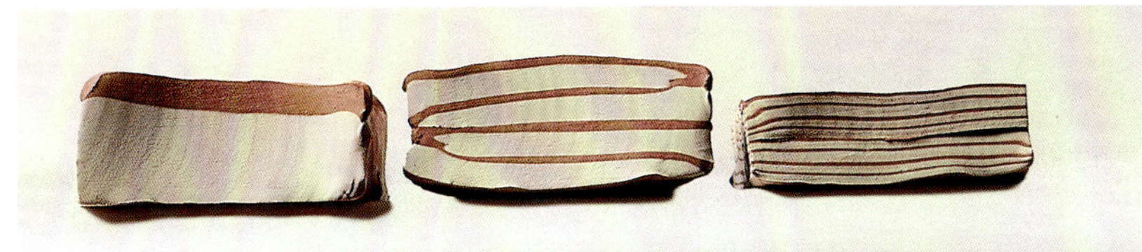

Figure 38 The three color clay slabs are prepared in the same way. The layered slabs are then trimmed to equal rectangular sizes.

Figure 39 A coil is formed with each slab and cut from the slab. Several coils can be made from each slab.

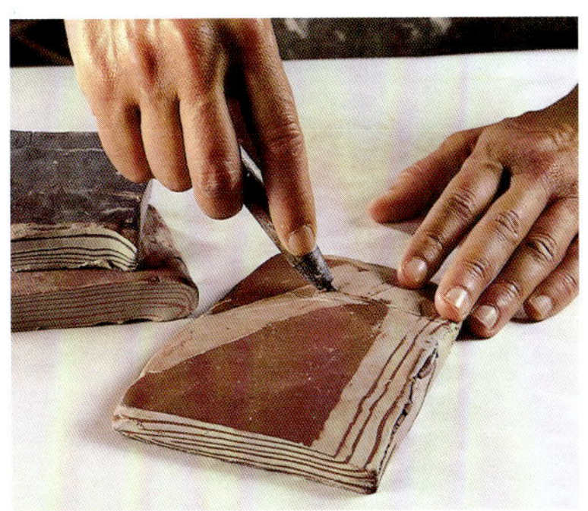

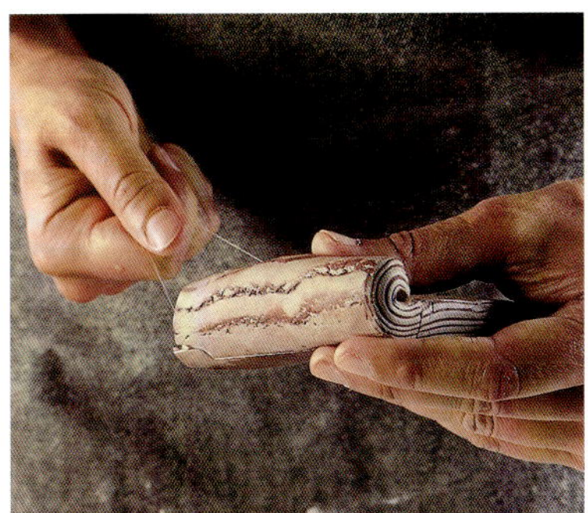

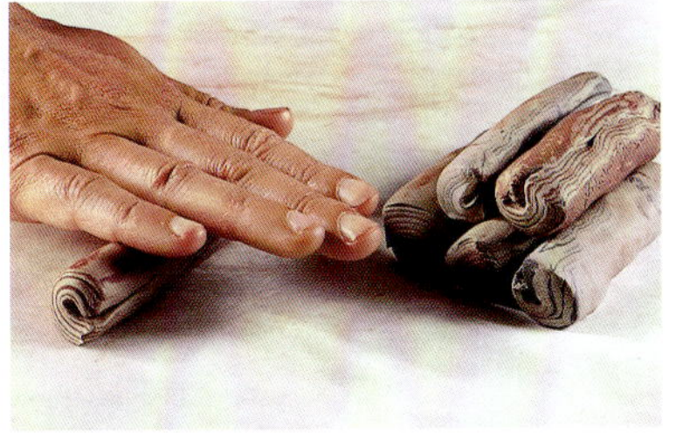

Figure 40 The coils are further rolled into cylindrical shapes.

Figure 41 The rolled coils are arranged in alternating colors. At this stage, particular attention is paid to the arrangement of the individual colors. Note the similarities to the laid agate pattern illustrated in fig. 11.

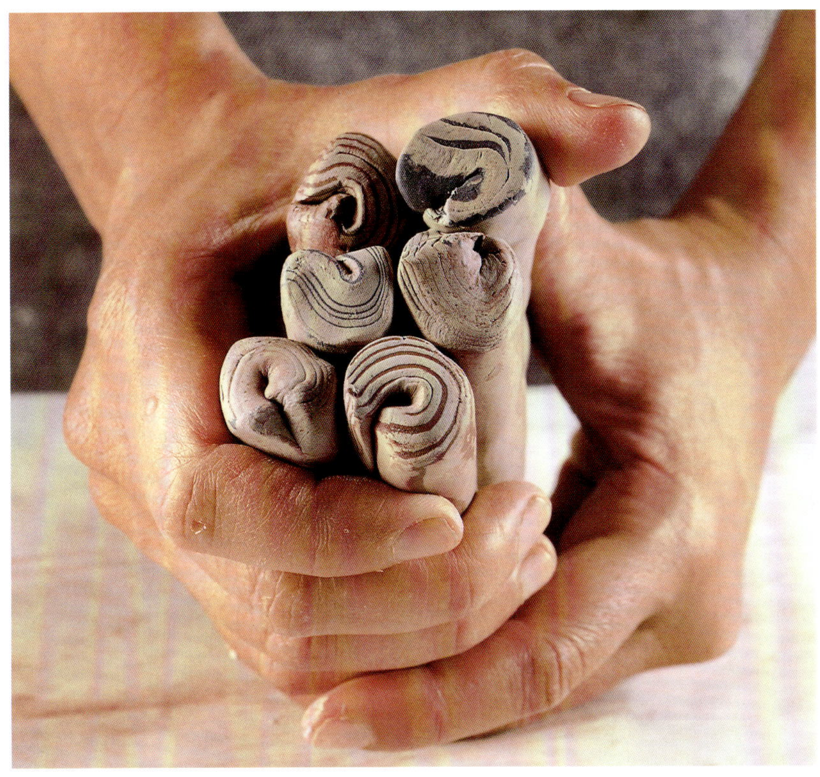

After these slabs of thinly layered clays are prepared, they are rolled into tight coils (figs. 39, 40). These coils are then arranged, sometimes by alternating colors, and carefully pressed into a single mass (figs. 41, 42). From this amalgamated mass, thin slabs are then cut and arranged on a flat surface to begin forming a sheet (figs. 43–45). At this point, the outcome of the agate striations can be controlled by the placement of the slabs. Once a reconstituted clay sheet is made, it is cut into strips and reassembled to emulate the arbitrary nature of the agate pattern (figs. 46, 47). Examination of antique pots suggests that such strips were cut and rearranged several times on both a horizontal and vertical plane (figs. 48–51). In working through this technique, it is clear that a number of variations are possible through the deliberate arrangement of the agate pattern.

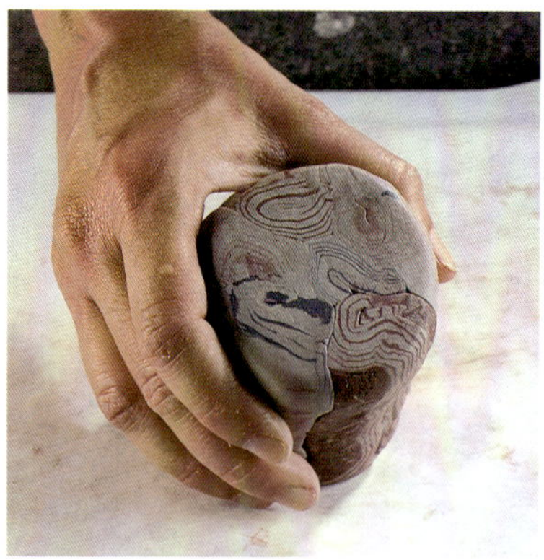

Figure 42 The coils are pressed into a solid cylindrical mass.

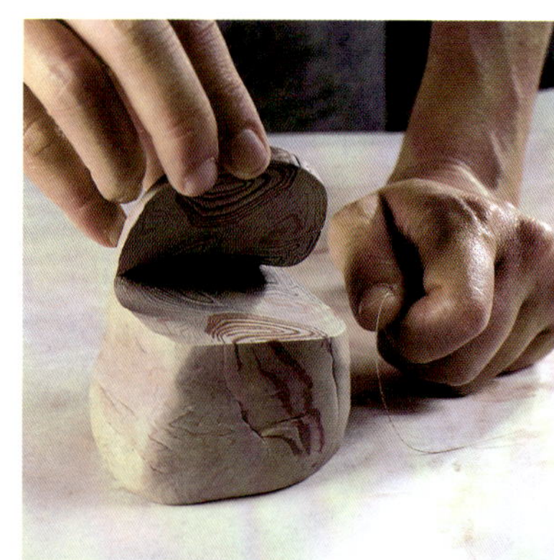

Figure 43 The mass is squared off and thin sections are cut from the stack revealing the beginnings of the agate pattern.

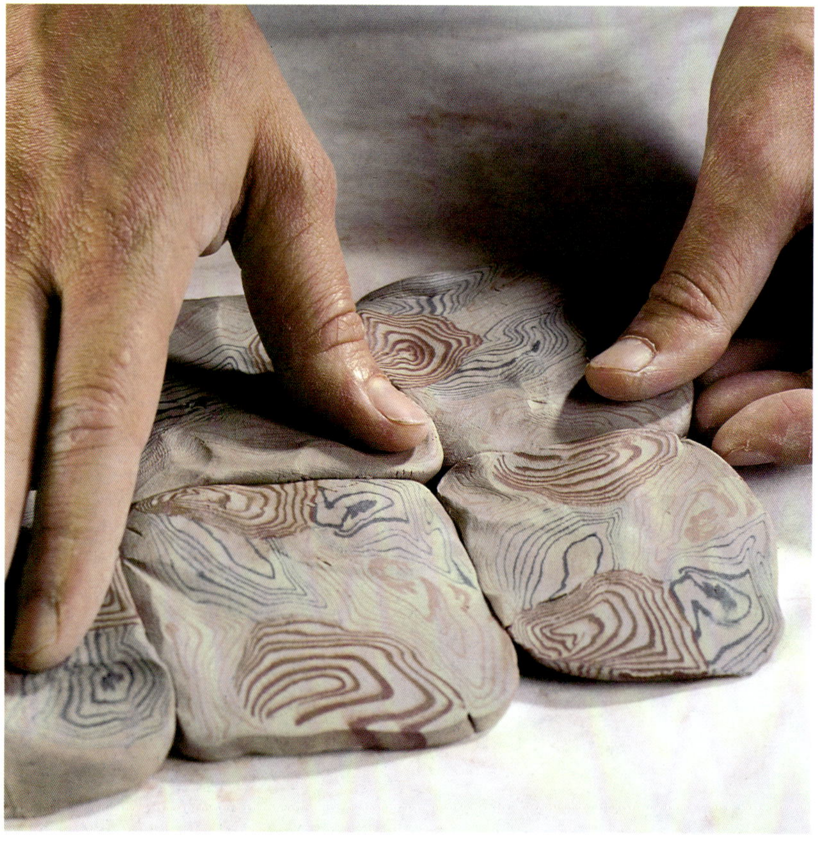

Figure 44 The sections are arranged and carefully pushed together on a flat surface alternating the patterns.

Figure 45 The sections are joined and flattened using a rolling pin. The paper provides a barrier to keep the pattern crisp and the clay from sticking to the rolling pin. The paper will be changed frequently during the next several steps to prevent smudging the surface.

Figure 46 After a flat slab is prepared, regular strips of clay are cut in a horizontal plane.

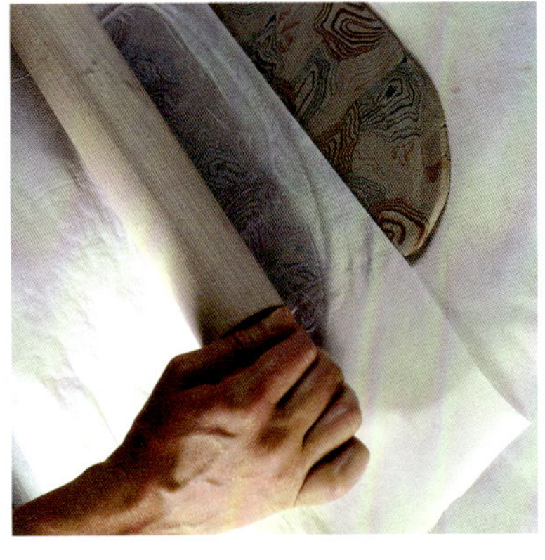

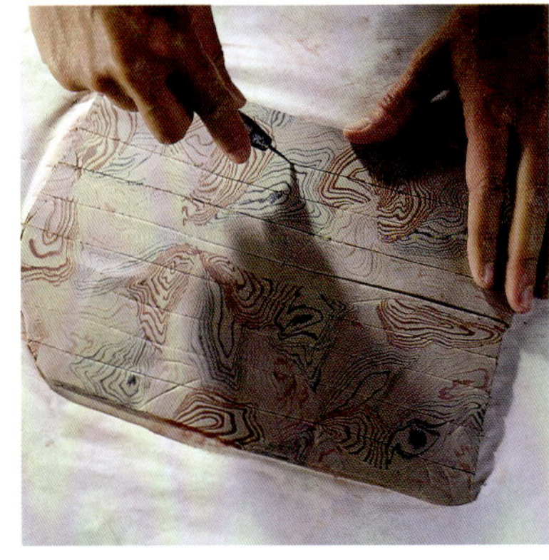

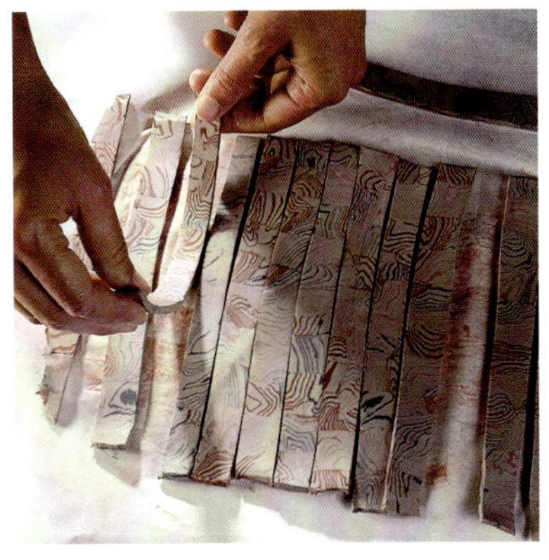

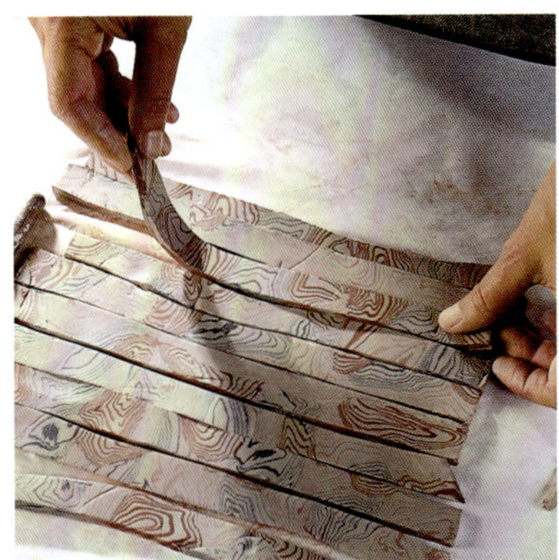

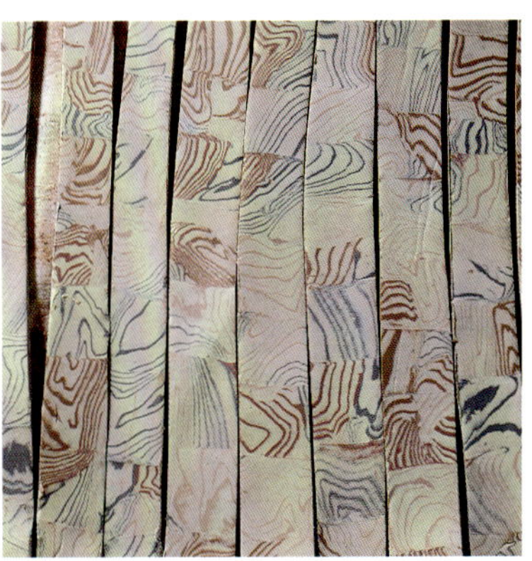

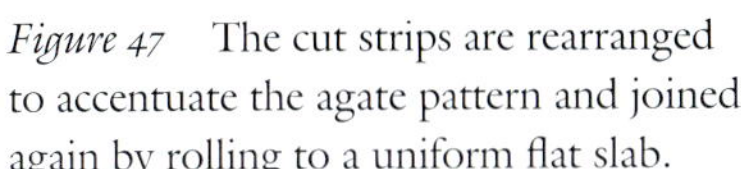

Figure 47 The cut strips are rearranged to accentuate the agate pattern and joined again by rolling to a uniform flat slab.

Figure 48 Strips of clay are once again cut from the newly made slab, this time in a vertical plane.

Figure 49 The strips are rearranged to intensify the agate pattern and rolled again.

Figure 50 Cream jug, Staffordshire, ca. 1750. Lead-glazed agateware. H. 10". (Chipstone Foundation.) The body of this jug was formed in a two piece press mold. The cabriole feet were molded separately and applied, as was the handle.

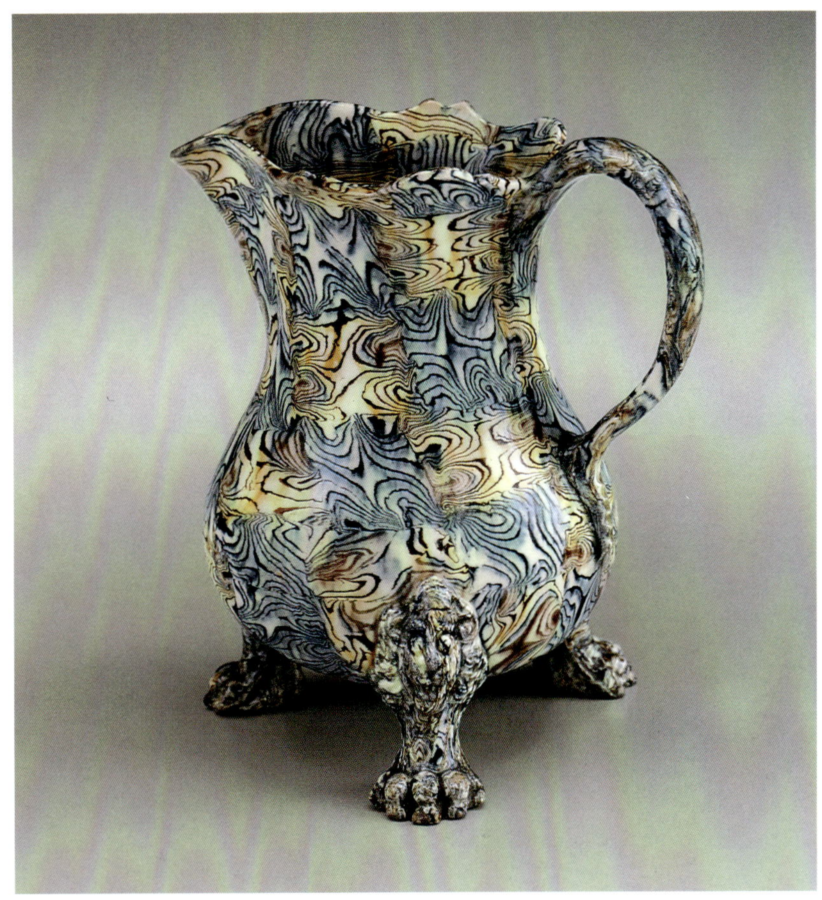

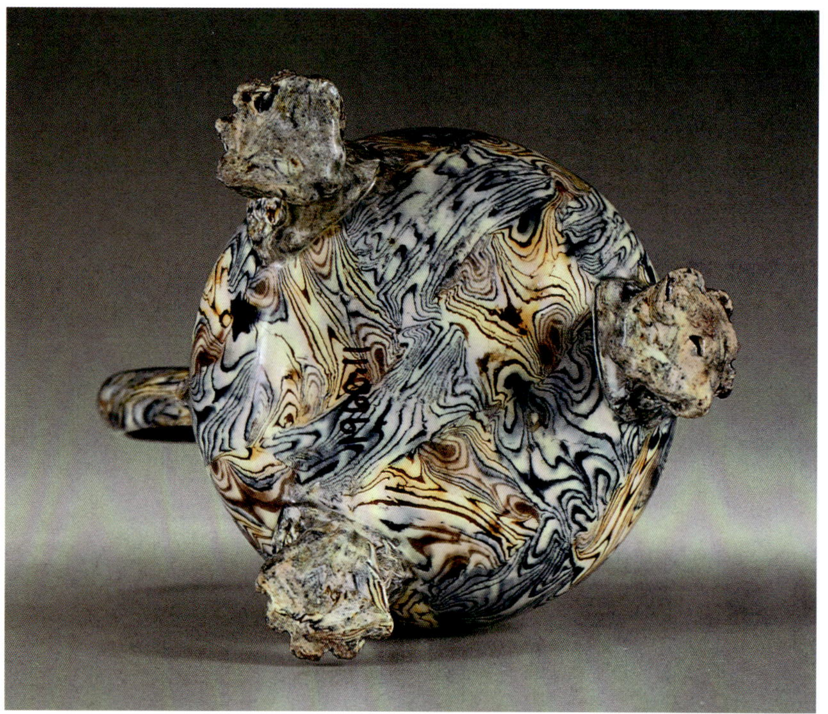

Figure 51 Bottom view of the cream jug illustrated in fig. 50. Note the checkerboard patterning of the agate strips which have been arranged in an alternate pattern. This view also shows the smeary patterning of the molded cabriole feet.

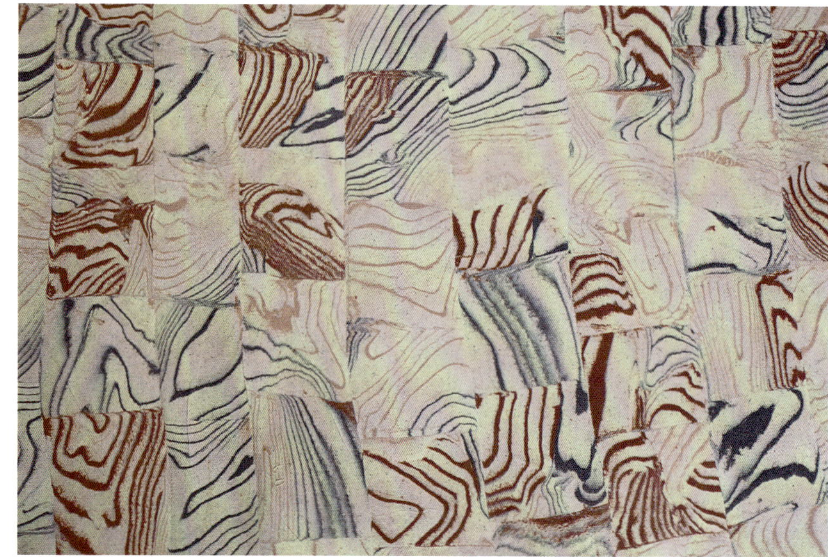

Figure 52 The final agate slab. At this stage, the checkerboard pattern created by both horizontal and vertical cutting is readily observed. For the demonstration, the patterning of the agate has been left moderately coarse so that is it easily observable in the photographs. The slab is now usable.

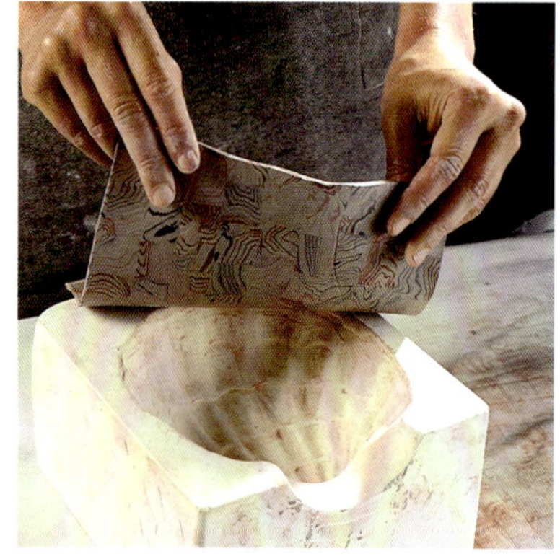

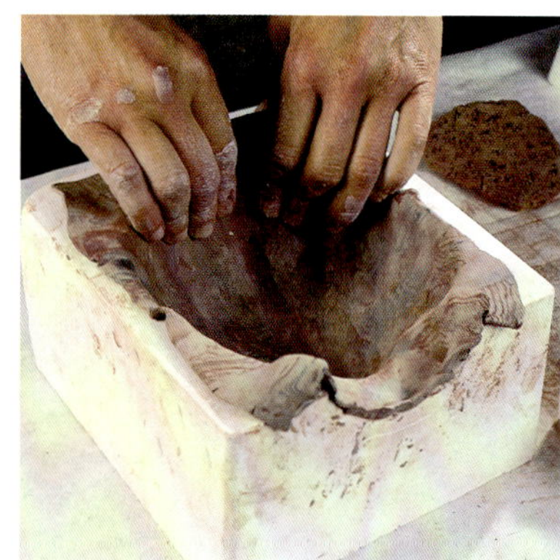

Figure 53 The thin agate slab being laid into the plaster press mold.

Figure 54 The slab is then pressed firmly into the concavities of the mold. Great care is taken to work the clay gradually into the recesses of the mold without tearing along the many seams in the agate sheet. Pressure from the fingers muddies the interior of the agate surface.

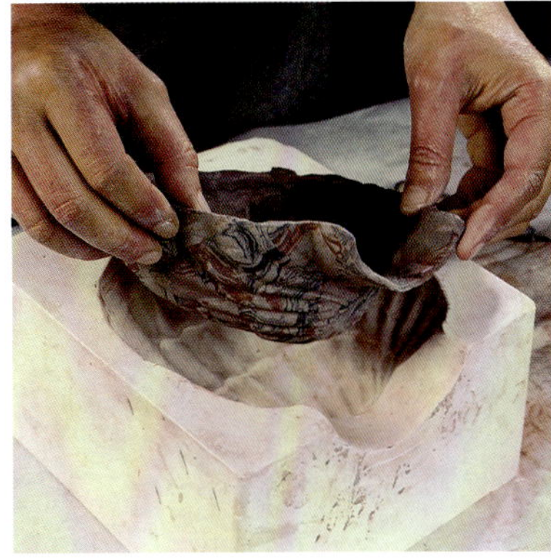

Figure 55 The slab is allowed time to firm up within the mold so the completed teapot half being removed is without distortion.

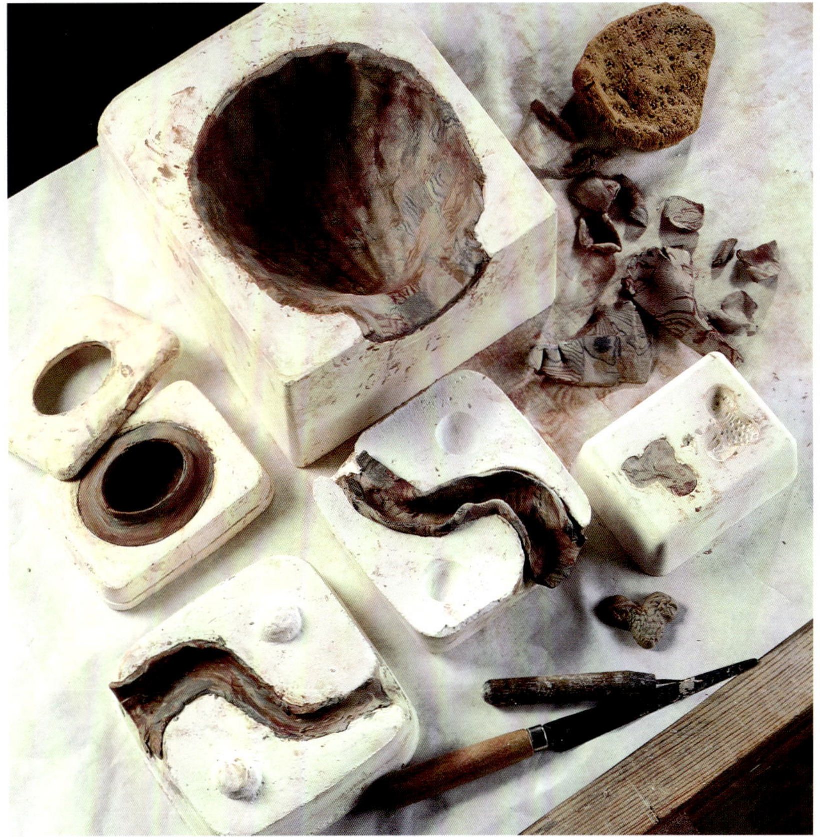

Figure 56 The two piece molds necessary for producing a pecten shell teapot including the body, spout, handle, and Fo Lion finial. These molds were taken from original master models sculpted by Michelle Erickson.

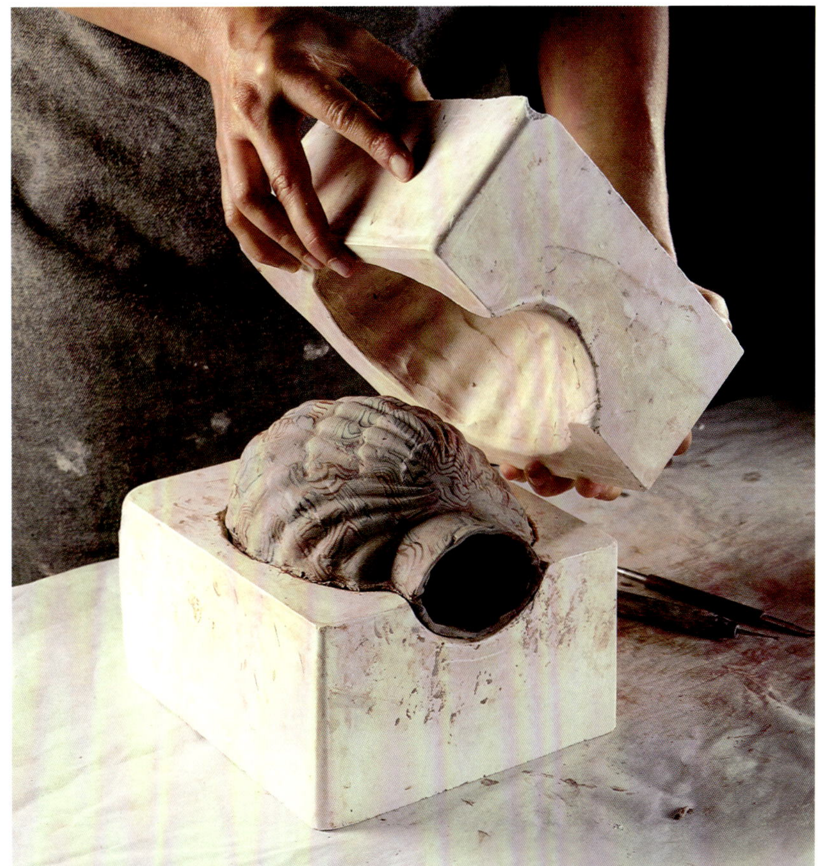

Figure 57 Once two halves are pressed in separate molds, they are ready to be joined. The edges are lightly scored and moistened. The two molds are aligned, and the seam is closed by working from the inside through the opening in the neck. After being joined, the teapot body is removed from the molds and the exterior seam is carefully smoothed and finished before attaching the spout and handle.

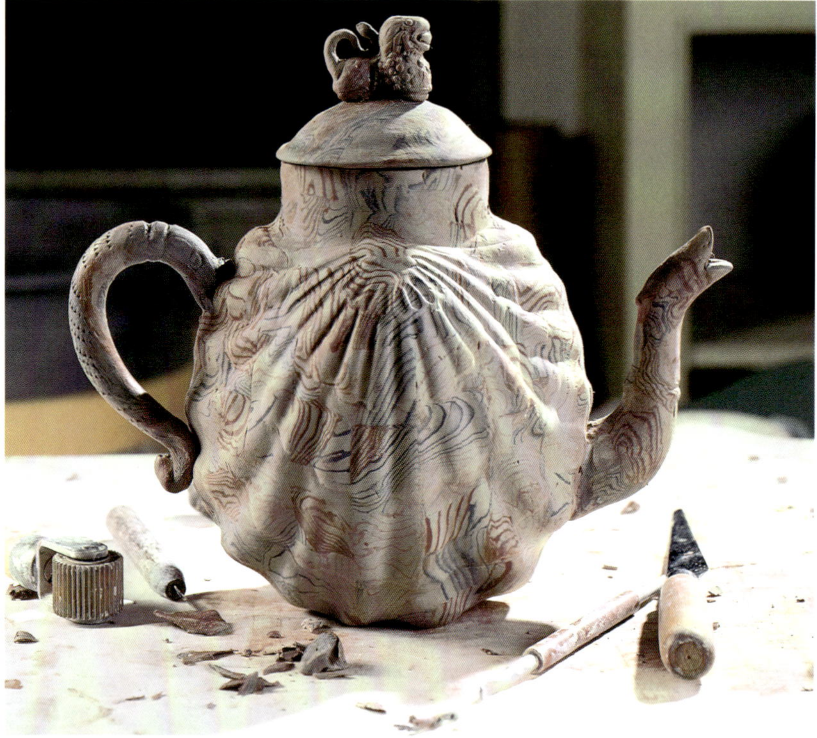

Figure 58 The assembled pecten shell teapot. The pot is now slowly air dried. Once dried, it is possible to enhance the agate surface with a light scrubbing using the equivalent of a fine steel wool. Any heavy smudging or distortion cannot be altered. The pot is fired to biscuit, glazed, and fired again.

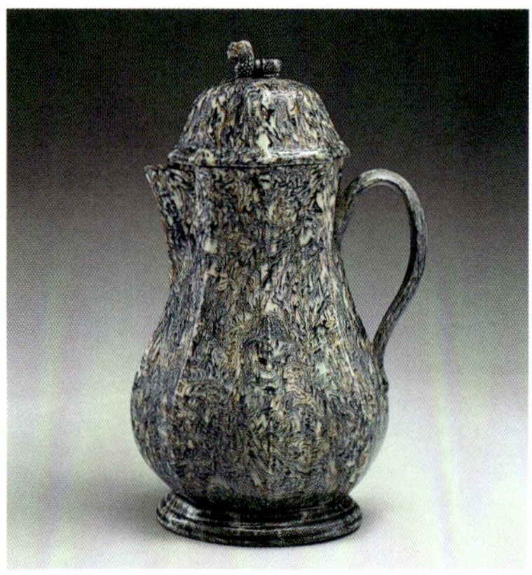

Figure 59 Coffee pot and lid, Staffordshire, ca. 1750. Lead-glazed agateware. H. 7⅝". (Chipstone Foundation.) The body of this eight paneled coffee pot was made in a press mold. The handle, spout, and foot were molded separately and applied. The matching lid and the Fo Lion finial were molded separately as well. Note that this agate pattern was created using a variation on the technique.

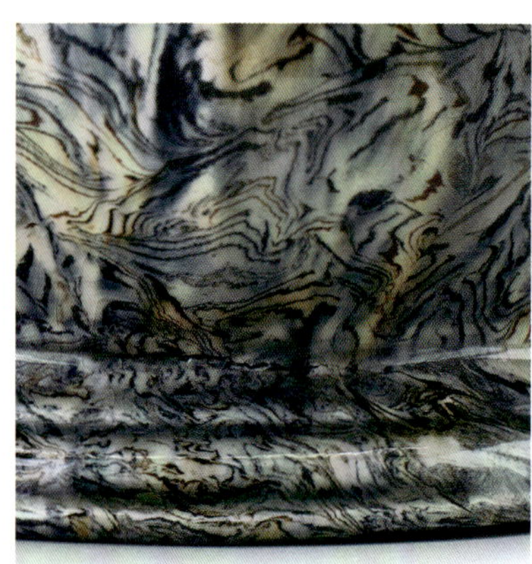

Figure 60 Detail of the applied foot on the coffee pot illustrated in fig. 59. The foot was separately molded and applied. The point of attachment can be distinguished by the discontinuities in the agate patterning and the slight separation crack that opened during later drying or firing.

Once a suitable agate pattern is created, the thin sheet of clay is ready for molding (fig. 52). In most cases, it appears that all elements of laid agateware were created by press molding (figs. 53–58). This process requires a separate plaster or clay mold for each component of a pot. This would include the body, foot rim or feet, lid, finial, spout, and handles. As with the thrown agate, joins may show smearing, or distortion (figs. 59–62).

Discussion and Summary

We hope this overview of English agate techniques will provide the basis for continued research. The laid agate technique is an extremely complicated procedure. Indeed, the replication of the processes presented here required nearly two years of trial and error research.

A rich opportunity exists to further study the production history of English agateware. Although Josiah Wedgwood's "marbled" vases inspired

Figure 61 Waste bowl, Staffordshire, ca. 1750. Lead-glazed agateware. D. 5". (Chipstone Foundation.) A form that is typically thrown, this bowl had to be press molded using laid agate clays. Examination of antique agateware bowls and sauce boats indicate that two thin sheets of agateware clay were laminated during the molding process to create the interior and exterior patterns.

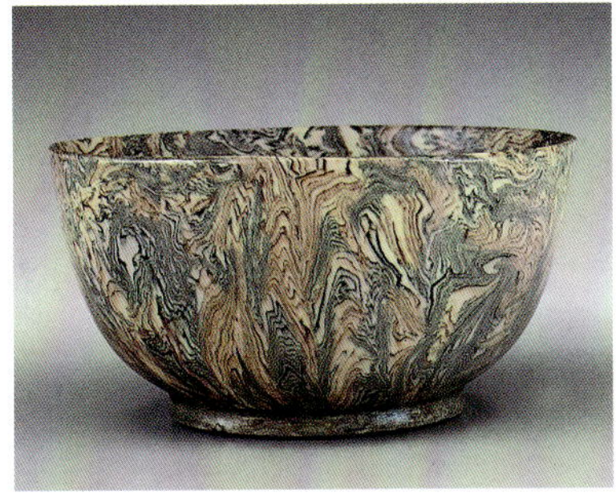

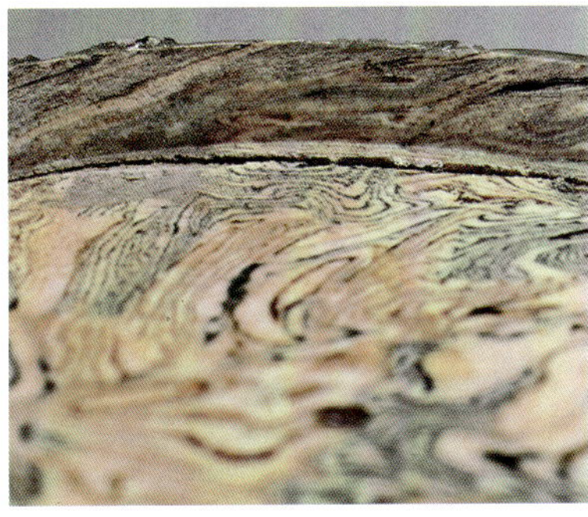

Figure 62 Detail of the foot attachment to the bowl illustrated in fig. 61. Note the distinct separation where the foot pulled away from bowl during the finishing process. Also note the distortion of the agate pattern on the interior of the foot.

by classical antiquities have been discussed at length in the literature, the origin of the Staffordshire laid agate techniques needs further examination. In addition, as we have demonstrated, a great deal of idiosyncratic behavior is reflected in the agateware process. For thrown agate this behavior manifests itself in the initial mixing of clays and the orientating of the prepared clay ball on the wheel. In her recent studies of the agateware fakes once associated with the Henry H. Weldon Collection, Pat Halfpenny observed differences in the agate striations in the contemporary imposters, which she attributed to possible differences in eighteenth-century versus twentieth-century wheel technology.[27] Further research along these lines could identify variability among period factory sites and perhaps individual potters.

For laid agate, although the patterning is often described as random, we have concluded that it is very deliberate. This deliberateness can be seen in a variety of other agate patterns that have yet to be fully classified (figs. 63–66). As more information becomes available from the excavation of Staffordshire production sites, perhaps an explicit typology can be developed using the agate "fingerprints" that may be inherent in each example.

A larger issue to discuss is why agateware, although intermittently fashionable within the last three hundred years, has never been made in large quantities compared to other decorative ceramics types. Some ceramics historians have typically characterized agateware as costly and labor intensive in order to explain the relatively small production levels.[28] From the consumer side, in contrast, examination of American invoices from the 1770s suggests that agateware was only moderately more expensive than undecorated creamware.[29] Even when the Staffordshire potters produced an inexpensive transfer-printed version of agateware in the nineteenth century, the pattern was not popular.

Beyond costs, however, consumer demand for agateware must also be considered. A long-term view of agateware shows peaks of production in between extended periods when more austere ceramic styles were in vogue. In effect, this trend suggests that agateware was more a novelty than a product with staying power. Archaeological evidence helps with this. At John Dwight's factory few agateware sherds were recovered from the many tons of waster fragments found.[30] The recent 1997–1998 excavation at the U.S. Pottery Factory in Bennington only revealed 309 agateware sherds out of the 27,000 ceramic fragments recovered.[31] These numbers do not suggest a popular ceramic type.

Archaeological evidence from domestic sites also hints at a low volume of public consumption. Without question, the English thrown agateware of the 1740s and 1750s far outnumber those of laid agates encountered in American sites. Although quantification has yet to be conducted, only a handful of laid agateware is present among the hundreds of thousands of eighteenth-century ceramic fragments excavated in Williamsburg, Virginia. This scarcity has been noted at other American archaeological sites as well.[32]

Why, then, does laid agateware appear to have survived in relatively large numbers in ceramic collections? Has it always been considered the "holy grail" among ceramics types and thus cherished and protected?

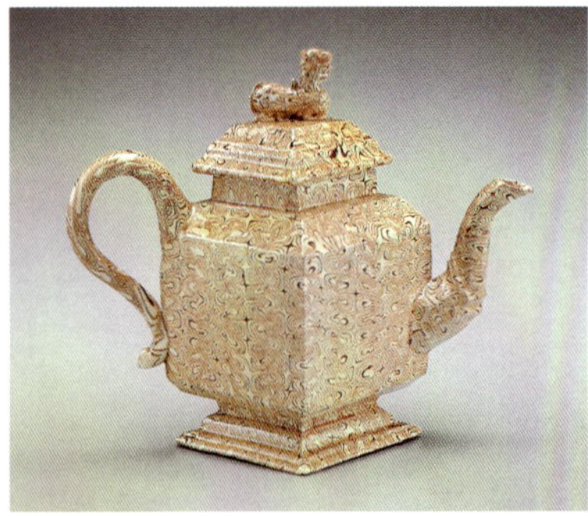

Figure 63 Teapot, Staffordshire, 1745–1750. Lead-glazed agateware. H. 5¾". (Courtesy, Troy D. Chappell Collection.) The two-colored agate pattern used for this diamond shaped teapot has been commonly called "elephant's tooth" by collectors.

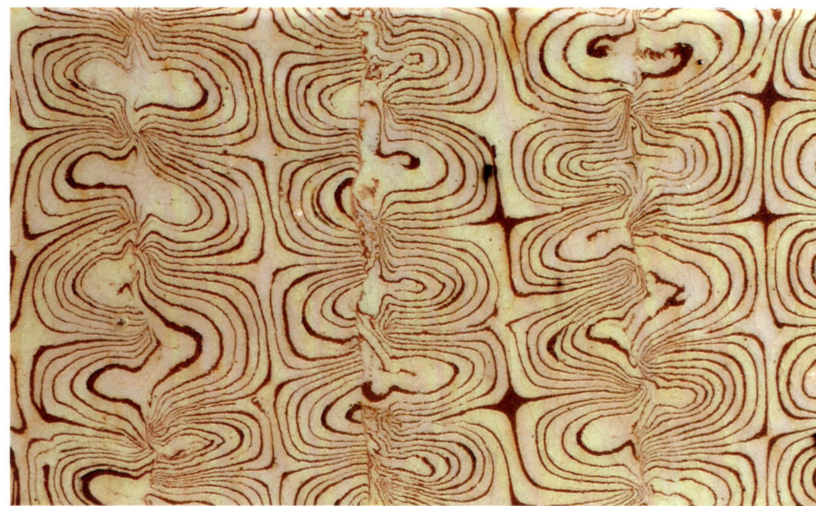

Figure 64 Detail of the agate pattern on the teapot illustrated in fig. 63. Note the purposeful placement of both vertical and horizontal strips. Compare this relatively simple agate pattern with the stage of preparation illustrated in fig. 41.

How can this dichotomy be explained? Perhaps Josiah Wedgwood can help answer these questions when we look at the second part of his statement written in 1759: "I had already made an imitation of Agat which was esteem'd very beautiful, and a considerable improvement, but the Country had been surfeited with variegated colours." The *Oxford English Dictionary* defines surfeit as "to oppress or nauseate with overabundance of something."[33] Wedgwood himself ultimately turned his attention to his extraordinarily plain creamware.

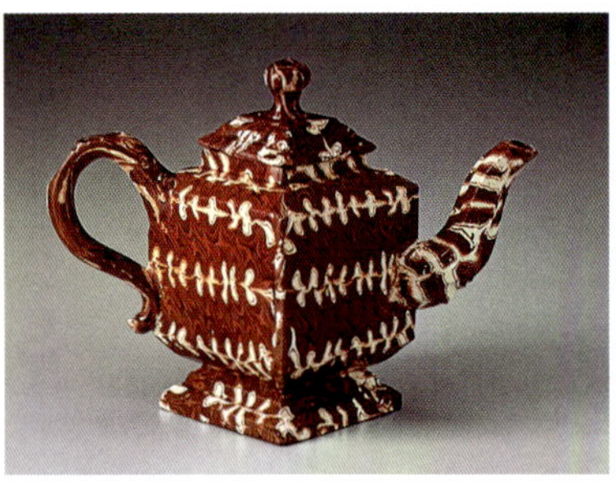

Figure 65 Teapot, Staffordshire, 1745–1755. Lead-glazed agateware. H. 5⅛". (Chipstone Foundation.) Although the form of this teapot is similar to that illustrated in fig. 63, an unusual three colored agate pattern is used. The effect is that of matched veneers similar to what one may see on furniture construction. The actual technique used to create this pattern needs further exploration.

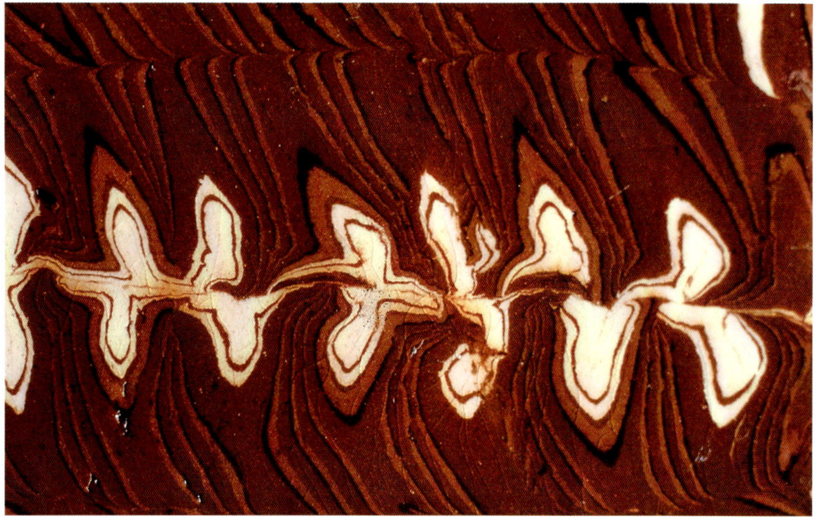

Figure 66 Detail of the agate pattern from the teapot illustrated in fig. 65.

Without question, agateware can generate a kaleidoscopic effect that some may find dizzying. Although the general public has never embraced agateware products, a fierce competition for antique examples exists among a small cadre of collectors—past and present. Perhaps this fact alone substantiates the often heard claim that agateware is considered "the ultimate refinement of the pottery's art."[34] We hope this demonstration has provided some insight into the mysteries of the potter's art and that new research on the history of agateware can be conducted with fresh eyes.

ACKNOWLEDGMENTS

The authors thank Abe Addonizio, Gavin Ashworth, Bob Barth, Amy Earls, Rodney Hampson, Al Luckenbach, Ivor Noël Hume, George Miller, Frank Russo, and Janine Skerry. We are especially grateful to Troy D. Chappell for his comments and suggestions.

1. Michelle Erickson and Robert Hunter, "Dots, Dashes, and Squiggles: English Slipware Technology," in *Ceramics in America,* edited by Robert Hunter (Hanover, N.H.: University Press of New England for the Chipstone Foundation, 2001).

2. One exception is Mireille De Reilhan's *Agateware Pottery Magic* (London: Andre Deutsch Ltd., 1995), which demonstrates some general techniques of making agateware intended primarily for the contemporary studio potter.

3. Other writers have also used the term *solid agate* to make a distinction from surface slip marbling. We think a further distinction is necessary since both thrown and laid agates have a mixture of solid clays. The term *press molded agate* is also commonly used to refer to the class of wares that we term laid agate.

4. See the contemporary agateware by David Hewitt at his website: <http://www.dhpot.demon.co.uk/agate.htm>. This link includes his recipe for making agate and throwing agateware. Also Tony Bouchet of Bouchet Agateware Pottery, Jersey, France, at website: <http://www.agateware.co.uk/index2.htm>. See also Robert Hunter, "The Stylized Works of Michelle Erickson," *Ceramics: Art and Perception,* no. 46 (2002): 46–51.

5. Dennis Haselgrove and John Murray, "John Dwight's Fulham Pottery: a Collection of Documentary Sources, *Journal of Ceramic History* 11 (1979): 80. This recipe was recorded in 1693 although Dwight was making agateware earlier.

6. Chris Green, *John Dwight's Fulham Pottery Excavations 1971–79* (London: English Heritage, 1999), p. 340.

7. These include a thrown gorge, bottles, and a press molded flask. Most notable is a large covered agate tankard with white clay sprigging over the agate body in the Burnap Collection at the Nelson-Atkins Museum. See Robin Hildyard, *Browne Muggs, English Brown Stoneware* (London: Victoria and Albert Museum, 1985), p. 29, and Julia E. Poole, *English Pottery* (Cambridge: Cambridge University Press, 1995), pp. 36–37. Ross E. Taggart, *The Frank P. and Harriet C. Burnap Collection of the English Pottery in the William Rockhill Nelson Gallery* (Kansas City, Mo.: Nelson Gallery/Atkins Museum, 1967).

8. Green, *John Dwight's Fulham Pottery,* p. 127.

9. Patricia M. Korry,"Francis Place, Seventeenth-Century English Potter and Man of the Enlightenment," *Ars Ceramica,* no. 16 (2000): 40–49, and Richard E. G. Tyler, "Francis Place's Pottery," *English Ceramic Circle* (1972): 203–12.

10. David Barker and Pat Halfpenny, *Unearthing Staffordshire* (Stoke-on-Trent, Eng.: City of Stoke-on-Trent Museum & Art Gallery, 1990); David Barker, *A New Perspective of the Staffordshire Potteries* (London: Jonathan Horne Publications, 1998); Paul Bemrose, "The Pomona Pot Works, Newcastle, Staffordshire, Part II. Samuel Bell: His Red Earthenware Production, 1724–44," *English Ceramic Circle Transactions* 9, pt. 3 (1975): 292–303. The citation for Samuel Bell's patent is the 1729 Patent at the British Public Records Office C66/3577.

11. Barker and Halfpenny, *Unearthing Staffordshire,* p. 31.

12. Ivor Noël Hume, *A Guide to Colonial Artifacts* (New York: Alfred A. Knopf, 1976), pp. 134–35; Ivor Noël Hume, *If These Pots Could Talk: Collecting 2000 Years of British Household Pottery* (Hanover, N.H.: University Press of New England for the Chipstone Foundation, 2001), p. 281; Leslie B. Grigsby, *English Slip-Decorated Earthenware at Williamsburg* (Williamsburg, Va.: The Colonial Williamsburg Foundation, 1993), pp. 62–63 and pp. 68–69.

13. Simeon Shaw, *History of the Staffordshire Potteries* (1829; reprint, New York: Praeger Publishers, 1970), pp. 211–15; J. C. Wedgwood, *A History of the Wedgwood Family* (London: St. Catherine Press, 1908). On pp. 149–51, he gives details of Dr. Thomas Wedgwood born June 25, 1695, died February 20, 1737. Much research is needed to clarify the development and products of this enigmatic potter.

14. Bernard Hughes, *English and Scottish Earthenware 1600–1860* (London: Abby Fine Arts, 1960), pp. 60–62. Other agateware potters cited by Hughes include Thomas Astbury, Daniel Bird, Ralph Wood, Josiah Spode, and Ralph Brown.

15. Taggart, *The Frank P. and Harriet C. Burnap Collection,* p. 101.

16. Ibid. Although Taggart illustrates several T'ang dynasty agate vessels in his discussion of English agateware, he concludes that "any suggestion of a direct connection is untenable," p. 101.

17. Gertrude Z. Thomas, *Richer Than Spices* (New York: Alfred A. Knopf, 1965), p. 76.

18. Arnold Mountford, "Thomas Whieldon's Manufactory at Fenton Vivian," *English Ceramic Circle* (1972): 164–82.

19. Wedgwood's experiment book on March 23, 1759.

20. Elizabeth Bryding Adams, *The Dwight and Lucille Beeson Wedgwood Collection at the Birmingham Museum of Art* (Birmingham, Ala.: Birmingham Museum of Art, 1992).

21. De Reilhan, *Agateware Pottery Magic,* p. 3.

22. Donald Carpentier and Jonathan Rickard, "Slip Decoration in the Age of Industrialization," *Ceramics in America,* edited by Robert Hunter (Hanover, N.H.: University Press of New England for the Chipstone Foundation, 2001), pp. 116–17.

23. Al Luckenbach, "The Swan Cove Kiln: Chesapeake Tobacco Pipe Production (ca. 1650–1669)," forthcoming in *Ceramics in America* (2004).

24. John Spargo, *The Potters & Potteries of Bennington* (Boston: Houghton Mifflin Company and Antiques Incorporated, 1926; reprint, Dover, N.Y.: Dover Publications, Inc., 1972). Spargo's description of the scroddled technique is as follows: "A lump of clay, prepared much as for ordinary white body, was first thoroughly kneaded; upon this was pressed, or 'wedged,' a similar lump into which coloring matter derived from oxides of iron, manganese, and cobalt had been thoroughly mixed; upon this, again, was placed still another lump, colored in the same manner, and of the same materials, but lighter or darker in shade, as required. The entire mass was then pounded and hammered, so that, when it was flattened out, a cross-section of it presented the appearance of stratified rock. Pounded back into a single cake, the mixed clay was sliced by drawing a strong wire through it. These slices were 'thrown' upon the wheel and worked or moulded into the desired forms. Treated to a clear glaze composed mainly of flint and feldspar, it was subjected to great heat for a much longer time than most other ware."

25. Pat Halfpenny, "Collector Beware" in Peter Williams and Pat Halfpenny, *A Passion for Pottery: Further Selections from the Henry H. Weldon Collection* (New York: Sotheby's Publications, 2000), p. 339.

26. Louis Marc Solon, *The Art of the Old English Potter* (London: Bemrose & Sons, 1883), p. 212.

27. Halfpenny, "Collector Beware," p. 337.

28. Leslie B. Grigbsy, *The Henry H. Weldon Collection of English Pottery 1650–1800* (New York: Sotheby's Publications, 1990), p. 36.

29. Nancy S. Dickinson, "'Of Other Sorts of Ware, Too Tedious to Particularize': The Rhinelanders as Ceramic Merchants in Eighteenth Century New York City" (report, Colonial Williamsburg Foundation, January 1988). An examination of orders placed between 1775 and 1781 suggests that agateware was higher than undecorated creamware but often the same price as "Cauliflower," "Pineapple," "Melon," and other common wares of the period. Appendix 12a, p. 116.

30. Green, *John Dwight's Fulham Pottery,* pp. 61–62 and 127–28.

31. Catherine Zusy, "Archaeology at the United States Pottery Company Site in Bennington, Vermont," in *Ceramics in America,* edited by Robert Hunter (Hanover, N.H.: University Press of New England for the Chipstone Foundation, 2002), pp. 221–23.

32. Robert Barth, personal communication, Portsmouth, New Hampshire, 2002.

33. *The New Shorter Oxford-English Dictionary on Historical Principles,* edited by Lesley Brown, 2 vols. (Oxford: Clarendon Press, 1993), 2:3157.

34. De Reilhan, *Agateware Pottery Magic,* back cover.

Peter Williams

The Talbot Hotel Pit Group

▼ FOR CENTURIES, the Talbot Hotel was one of the foremost taverns in the picturesque and historic Cotswold town of Tetbury, Gloucestershire.[1] Situated at No. 14 Market Place, the hotel is primarily a seventeenth-century building that was refronted in the early nineteenth century (fig. 1). A popular gathering place for travelers and locals alike, the Talbot enjoyed a reputation for the best of food, services, atmosphere, and all-night parties. In 1971, it even appeared in *Dulcima,* a Sir John Mills movie drama. Since 1594, when Richard Biddle bought and paid an extra two-pence rent for "A Taverne Head with a shoppe," there has been a tavern on the Talbot Hotel site; that is, until April 5, 1986.[2] On this date, after nearly 400 years of welcoming guests, the Talbot closed its doors to the public. Today, the celebrated landmark is a private residential property (fig. 2).

Set in the midst of quiet, green countryside, Tetbury, nevertheless, was the center of much marching and fighting during the English Civil War, a conflict between Royalists and Parliamentarians, which began in 1641. The cloth manufacturing areas of the Stroudwater were strongly in favor of the parliamentary forces, and the towns of Malmesbury, Tetbury, Beverston, and Wotton-under-Edge were fortified posts for the crown on the edge of these disaffected districts.[3] In 1643, a royalist garrison was established in Tetbury. In fact, on his way from Bristol to Gloucester, King Charles I dined there—reputedly at the Talbot Hotel itself. Favorably impressed, perhaps, the king issued an order to his officers to "spare" the town. Other monarchs recorded as passing though Tetbury include Charles II (in 1664), James II (in 1687), and Queen Anne (in 1702).

The first mention of the Talbot Hotel by name does not occur until 1656, when the following entry appeared among the presentments of the borough court roll:

> We order that the incroachment at the Inne called the Talbott beinge a penthouse that the Landlord and Tenent or one or either of them nor there successors shall molest or hinder any person or persons in standinge & selling of Cheese or any other commodity on the Market day there upon the fforfeiture for everie day ________________ v s. [5 shillings]

Local directories record the more recent Talbot landlords, but early information is difficult to find. For example, the Talbot is listed as one of the oldest inns in Tetbury, but no information is given about earlier owners

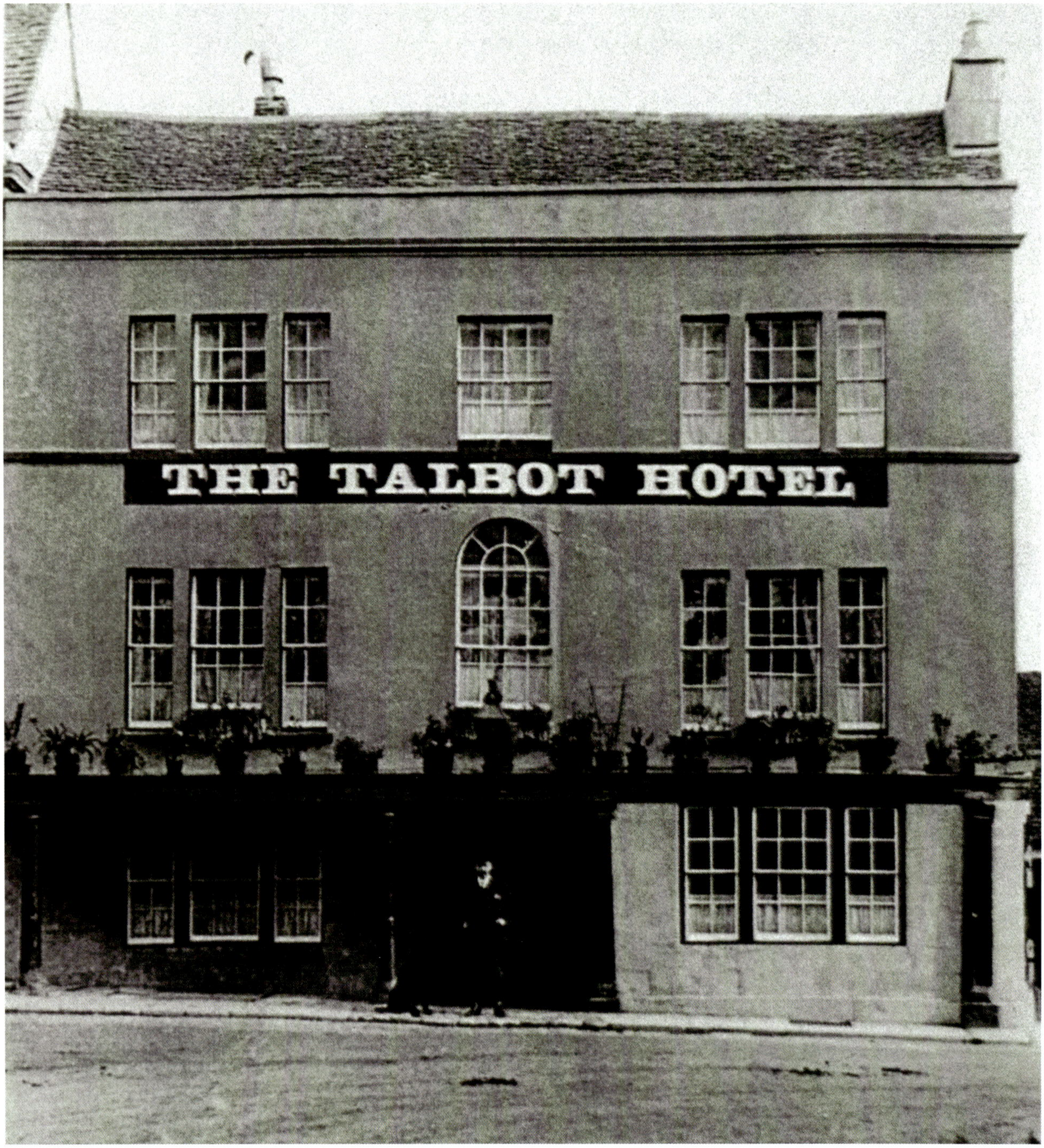

Figure 1 Photograph of the Talbot Hotel, Tetbury, England, ca. 1910. Edwin Webb, the landlord and captain of the Tetbury Fire Brigade is in the foreground. (Courtesy, Peter Williams.)

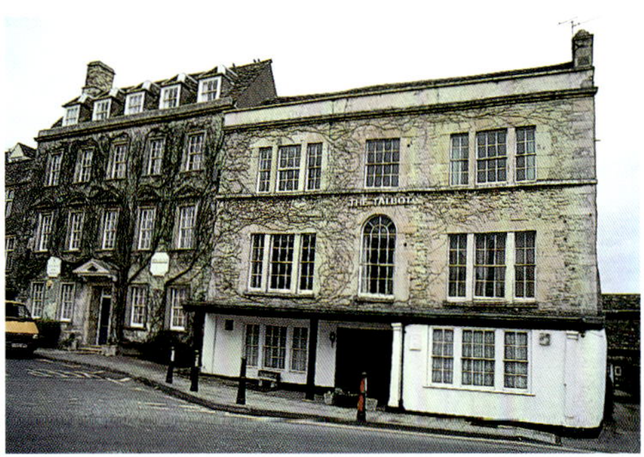

Figure 2 The Talbot Hotel today. (Photo, Peter Williams.)

or tenants.[4] As well, most of the alehouse recognizances for Gloucestershire were destroyed in the mid-nineteenth century. Unfortunately, none of the surviving records in the Gloucestershire Record Office include information on the Longtree Hundred, the parish in which Tetbury lay. Archaeology would tell us much more—at least about tavern life.

An Account of the Investigations at the Talbot Hotel

In May 1985 alterations to properties adjacent to the Talbot led the hotel owners, Mr. and Mrs. Roy Speakes, to explore their cellars. According to the hotel's deeds, the Talbot contained five wells. Three were uncovered, including one lying under the dining room floor and another under a flagstone in the gent's toilet (fig. 3).

The small, rough stone-built room, opening off the main cellar, was investigated by archaeologists Nigel Spry and Harold Wingham, and a short report on the exploration was published.[5] The stone room was located about five yards back from the hotel's front wall, and had for many years been used for the disposal of rubbish. Clearance revealed a collapsed floor of reused oolite limestone flags, which had sealed either a large well, holding tank, or soak-away pit about two yards square and partially filled with water. Limited exploration yielded a great deal of dense, soft organic material, reminiscent of that encountered in medieval cesspits. Farther below, a more recent, final fill of large stone fragments and yellow-brown, clayey loam was uncovered. The final fill accumulation was extracted and a layer of the soft deposit was then removed to a depth of about eight inches. It was found to contain fragments of pottery, clay pipes, and glass wine bottles, including a complete onion-shaped bottle, identified as Flemish and pre-1710. Added to the mix were animal—mainly lamb—bones, corks, nuts, straw sweepings, leather, and preserved timber wainscoting. Oyster

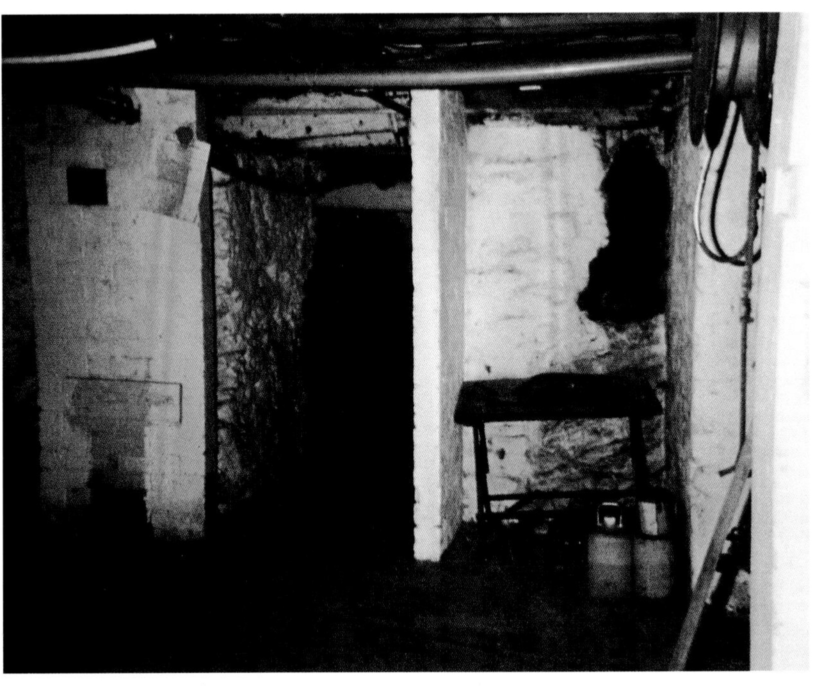

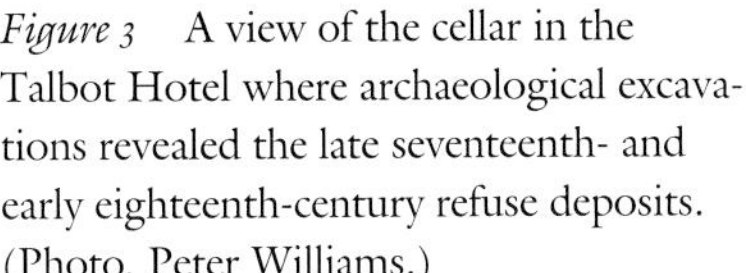

Figure 3 A view of the cellar in the Talbot Hotel where archaeological excavations revealed the late seventeenth- and early eighteenth-century refuse deposits. (Photo, Peter Williams.)

shells were also recovered. Since there are no records of oyster beds in the nearby River Severn, it is possible that the oysters were transported in seawater from the Kent coast.

Further explorations of the pit took place during the summer of 1985, down to a depth of about two yards where hard stones were encountered. Among the recovered items were two small pieces of jewelry engraved with a Tudor rose. These small items looked like cuff links, but were probably used as dress fasteners. Also recovered was a shoe heel and silver buckle, countless clay pipes, and more wine-bottle fragments, one with a seal initialed "T H."

The recovered pottery and clay pipe fragments were received by local dealer and conservator, Peter Wain, who had assisted personally with the investigations. The pottery was considered to be from the late seventeenth century to the early eighteenth century. Since the ceramic fragments were found at the top of the pit, Wain deduced that it was sealed some time between 1720 and 1725. It was also concluded that if the pit had originally been a well, it probably dried up before this date, and was then used as a receptacle for rubbish from the hotel's public rooms—a common practice of the period.

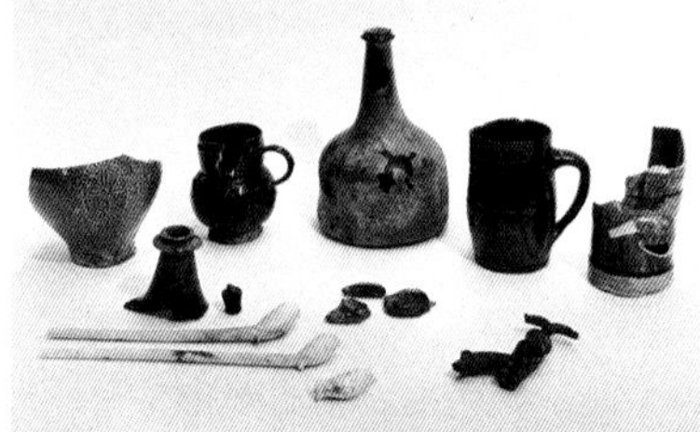

Figure 4 A selection of archaeological objects exhibited at the Corinium Museum shortly after their recovery. (Courtesy, Peter Williams.)

Three of the recovered clay pipes bearing maker's marks were identified as having been made in Bristol. One was marked "R TIP" for Robert Tippett who was active from circa 1680. Another was marked "ANDRE— —," possibly for Andrews, a known pipe maker from 1739, although the date is inconsistent with other pipes found in the same layer. The large collection of clay pipes, including many by previously unrecorded makers, was donated to the Gloucester City Museum.

Other finds from the Talbot Hotel were passed to the Corinium Museum, Cirencester, where in December 1985 a collection of the best discoveries was put on display as "A Picture of Pub Life" (fig. 4). The glassware, including a previously unrecorded seventeenth-century Venetian fluted wine glass, was later donated to the Corning Museum of Glass in Corning, New York.

A Review of the Pottery Finds from the Talbot Hotel

Peter Wain initially reconstructed many of the salvaged pottery finds from the Talbot Hotel pit. The entire ceramic assemblage was subsequently reanalyzed with additional mending and refitting of fragments. The assemblage is presently in a private collection where it is being maintained intact. What follows is an overview and discussion of the ceramics organized by ware type from this virtually unparalleled assemblage of early English tavern wares.

Lead-Glazed Earthenware

COARSE EARTHENWARE

Only a handful of late-sixteenth- and seventeenth-century lead-glazed coarse earthenware fragments were recovered (figs. 5, 6). It is assumed that these remnants are probably all of local manufacture.

Figure 5 Fragments of a pitcher or chamber pot, England, ca. 1680. Lead-glazed coarse earthenware. (All artifact photos by Gavin Ashworth unless otherwise noted.) These fragments represent a vessel with a rounded body and an internal mottled olive-brown glaze. The flared lip has traces of pinching, and the unglazed exterior has a wheel-turned double-grooved shoulder-band. The handle upper junction is at the lip, the lower junction with a thumbed attachment. Excavated evidence shows that chamber pots were not always used in the generally suspected manner. Many unearthed examples show signs of having been heated, as if they had been used for cooking purposes.

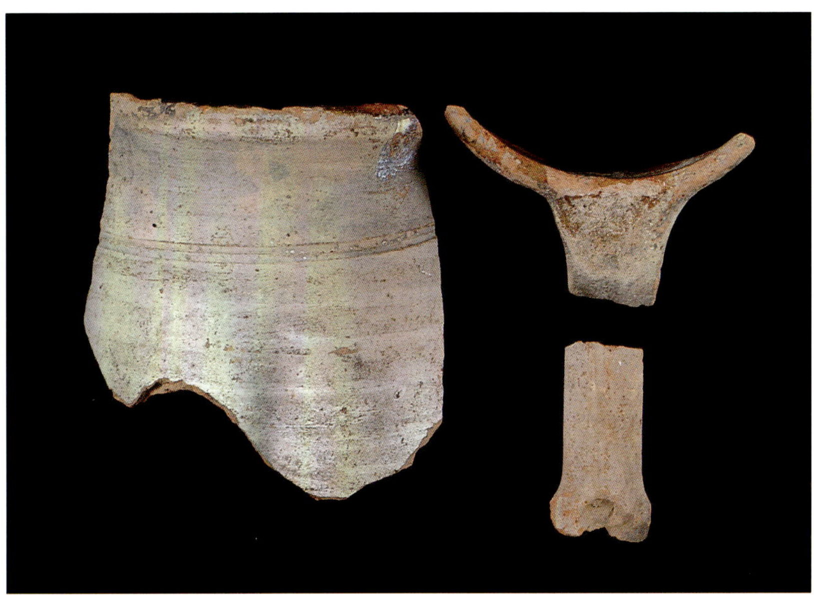

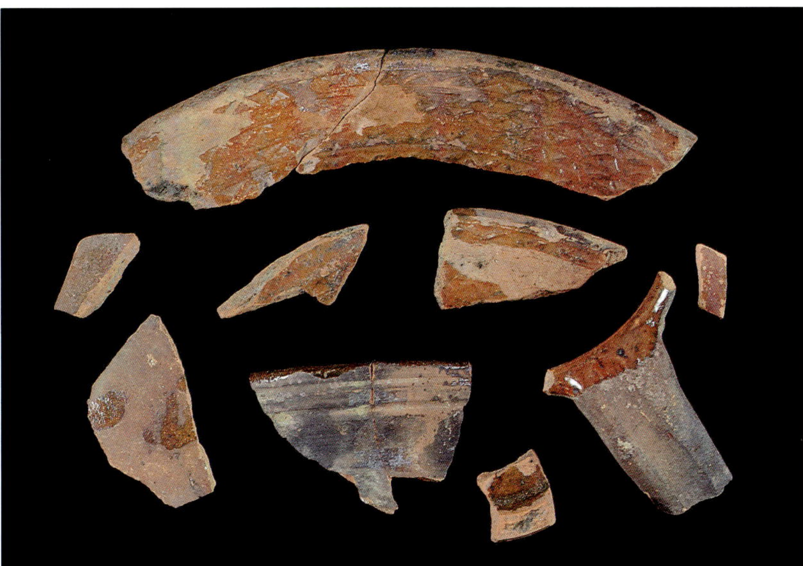

Figure 6 Various fragments, England, ca. 1680. Lead-glazed coarse earthenware. Diameter of this dish is estimated to be 16¾". The flange of this large dish has a rouletted, relief border of at least five concentric bands of zigzags reserved within concentric line borders. The upper surface is glazed. Fragments of various other vessels, including part of a lip with a wheel-turned, double-grooved band; part of a handle; and a small base fragment were recovered.

ASHTON KEYNES EARTHENWARE

A distinctive recovered group of lead-glazed red earthenware jugs was identified as having been made at the village of Ashton Keynes, North Wiltshire, situated some ten miles to the west of Tetbury (figs. 7–12). These late seventeenth-century jugs are almost medieval in character and are representative of a traditional localized pottery industry that had been prevalent in rural Britain for centuries.

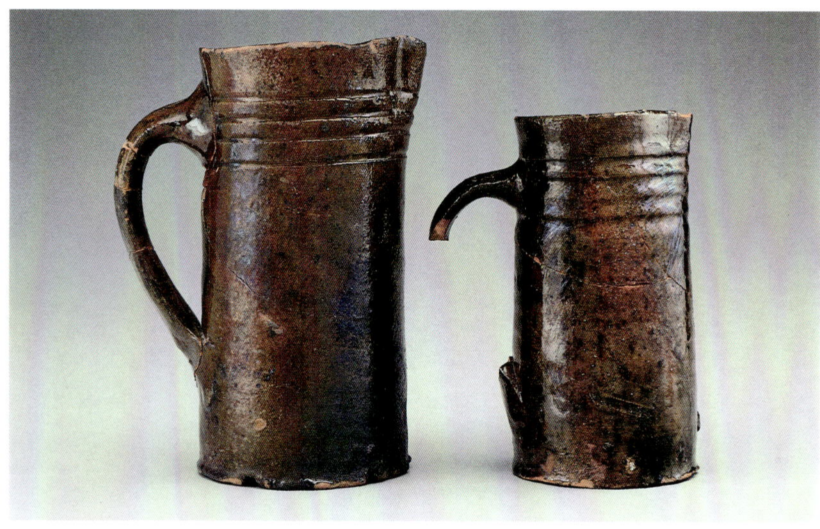

Figure 7 Jugs, Ashton Keynes, North Wiltshire, England, late seventeenth century. Lead-glazed coarse earthenware. H. 7¼" and 6". These jugs have a mottled olive-brown glaze on a tall, cylindrical body. The rims have been pinched to create pouring lips. The shoulder-bands are formed by wheel-turned grooves. The flat, circular bases are unglazed except for slight glaze flooding.

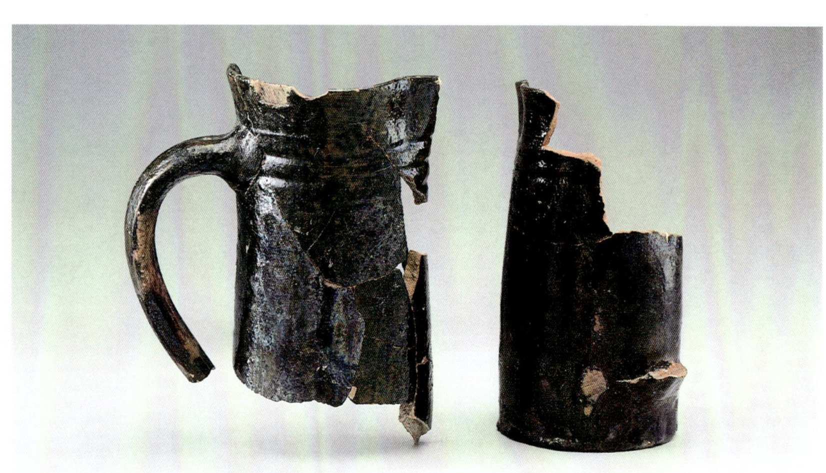

Figure 8 Jug fragments, Ashton Keynes, North Wiltshire, England, late seventeenth century. Lead-glazed coarse earthenware. H. 5¾". These fragments are from jugs with tall, cylindrical bodies with lip-pinch and shoulder-band formed by wheel-turned grooves. The jug on the left has a green glaze fired with a lustrous metallic appearance. The other has an olive-brown glaze, also fired with a lustrous metallic appearance. The flat, circular base is unglazed except for slight glaze flooding.

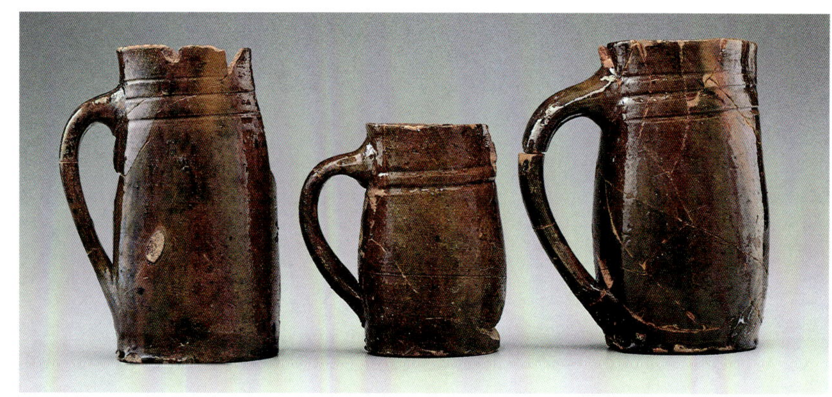

Figure 9 Jugs, Ashton Keynes, North Wiltshire, England, late seventeenth century. Lead-glazed coarse earthenware, H. 6¾", 5", and 6½". These three jugs, each with a mottled olive-brown glaze, have slightly rounded, tall, cylindrical bodies. The flat, circular bases are unglazed except for slight glaze flooding. The jug on the right has a pinched lip for pouring.

Ashton Keynes was renowned for its leather glove-making industry, which probably developed because of the parallel growth of the woolen industry and tanning, which offered a good supply of raw material. Gloving flourished in the village in the nineteenth century, but the industry dates back in Wiltshire as early as the thirteenth century.

Evidence of early potters at work in Ashton Keynes has been found at a medieval settlement near Flood Hatch Copse (a half-mile stretch of gravelly

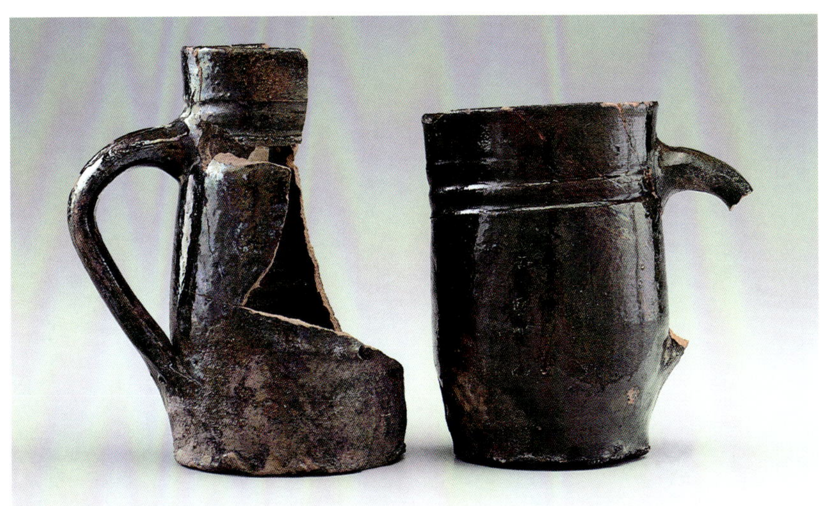

Figure 10 Jugs, Ashton Keynes, North Wiltshire, England, late seventeenth century. Lead-glazed coarse earthenware. H. 5½" and 4⅝". Examples of two jugs with a mottled green glaze. The flat, circular bases are unglazed except for slight glaze flooding. The jug on the right has a pinched lip for pouring.

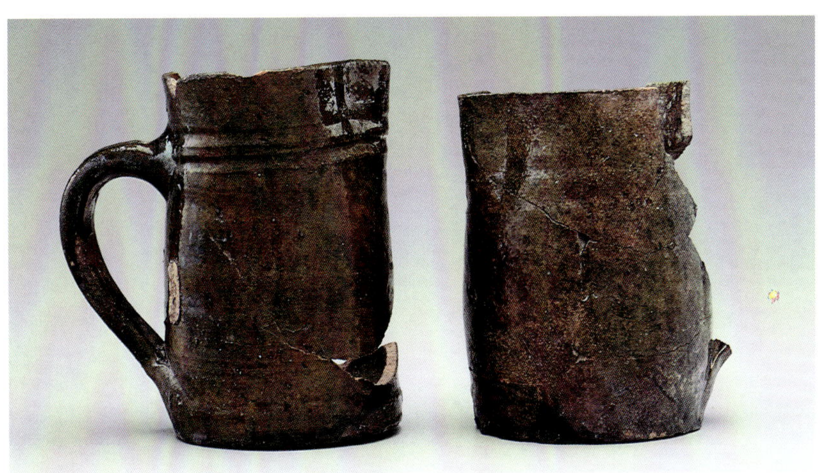

Figure 11 Jugs, Ashton Keynes, North Wiltshire, England, late seventeenth century. Lead-glazed coarse earthenware. H. 4⅝" and 4¼". These jugs have a mottled green glaze on a slightly rounded, tall, cylindrical body with pouring lips. The flat, circular bases are unglazed except for slight glaze flooding.

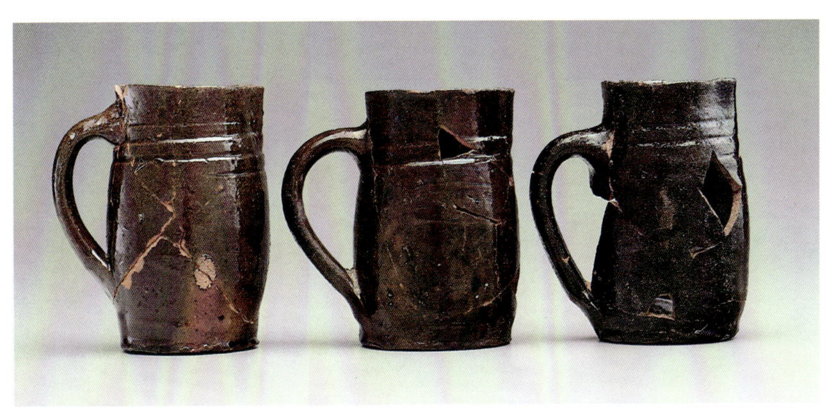

Figure 12 Jugs, Ashton Keynes, North Wiltshire, England, late seventeenth century. Lead-glazed coarse earthenware. H. 5". These three jugs have a mottled, olive-brown glaze, although the glaze on the central jug has fired with a slight luster. The glaze on the far right jug has fired with a metallic lustrous appearance. Its base is also covered with glaze. The flat, circular bases of the other two jugs are unglazed except for slight glaze flooding.

water) and at many other sites within the village. The village is built mainly on Thames gravel, but to the north the land rises over clay. The interface seems to be behind the houses built in Back Street, and several closes in that area are called "Clay Piece" or the like. A brickyard existed at North End in the eighteenth and nineteenth centuries.

Documentary evidence about the villagers' occupations does not commence until the seventeenth century, but it appears that there was never enough room in the village for more than one pottery at a time. The earliest record of a potter at Ashton Keynes is the will of Barbar Vincent, potter, proved November 13, 1661. Barbar was married in the village on January 23, 1629, and was buried there on September 25, 1661. Although the exact location of his premises is not known, it is thought to have been in the Kent End area at the eastern end of Back Street. The next record is the inventory of Richard Vincent taken in 1663 by his son Richard, potter, and including a quantity of "unburned potts" and "one potters oven to burn potts in." Richard Vincent's house also contained a shop described as an "inner room," presumably therefore not facing the street. Richard Vincent's relationship to Barbar is unknown, but they were possibly brothers. There are no further records of the Vincents as potters, though they remained in the village until at least 1700.

It is possible that the Vincents' business was passed, or sold to the Taylor alias Corver family. The inventory of Anne Taylor als Corver, widow, dated May 15, 1684, includes "clay, potts, earthenware, and raw potts unburned," clearly implying that she was running a pottery business. A few years later the parish registers reported the occupations of the villagers between 1700 and 1707, and listed the two following entries:

> 1701 Anne, the wife of Thomas Taylor alias Corver (potter), buried June 19th.
>
> 1705 John, the son of Henry Corver als Taylor (potter), baptized March 28th.

Later in the eighteenth century a series of records confirm that the family was still potting:

> 1750 Thomas Taylor is assessed for Land Tax at 15s 3¾d.
>
> 1761 Thos. Taylor, potter, is recorded in the Freehold Books. (He also appears in earlier books back to 1743, though occupations are not recorded in earlier years.)
>
> 1763 Deeds of 12/13 August include Thos. Taylor als Corver, potter.
>
> 1773 A deed of August 9 for the sale of land involves Thomas Taylor als Corver of Ashton Keynes, potter, as well as his son Robert, also a potter.

No further records of the Taylor alias Corver family as potters are known, but they did continue in the village for some decades afterwards and were clearly moderately well off.

It seems likely that the maker(s) of the group of Ashton Keynes earthenware jugs recovered from the Talbot Hotel would have been either Thomas or Henry Taylor alias Corver, or both. Although the surrounding road system was not particularly good in the late seventeenth and early eighteenth centuries, Ashton Keynes was only a few miles from the great Roman roads through Cirencester; thus transportation to Tetbury would not have proved too difficult at that time.

Other than two clay pipe manufacturers, the only other mention of a potter in the village in the eighteenth century seems to be a marriage settlement of October 18, 1775, concerning the Carter family, which mentions a messuage occupied by John Millard, potter. The Carters owned property at the top of Clay Hill at North End, near the brickyard, and Millard may have worked there.

Interestingly, amongst the entries in the 1851 census, which listed everyone in the village, together with their occupation, are:

Agricultural Labourers	122
Boot & Shoe Makers	14
Farmers	19
Glovers	55
Masons	14
Paupers	13
Potters	3

The principal of the three noted potters was Charles Gardner, who carried on a pottery at Harberts Cottage. However, while still described as a potter in 1851, he was by then blind and presumably retired. The two other potters were John Weaver, a potter journeyman who may have taken over Harberts Cottage from Charles Gardner, and Edward Turner, living in the family of Thomas Turner, brick manufacturers at Coxes Lane brickyard.[6] Sadly, any reference to the production of pottery at Ashton Keynes had disappeared by 1867, and the most notable local modern industries are those based on gravel extraction for concrete-based products.

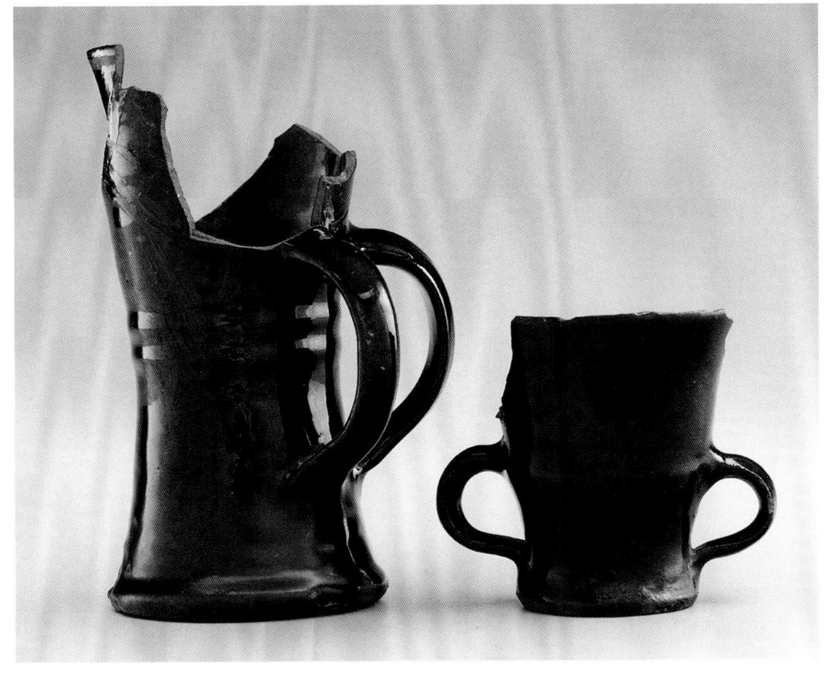

Figure 13 Mug and cup, Staffordshire, 1660–1680. Lead-glazed red earthenware. H. 6" and 3⅛". The waisted mug on the left has a cylindrical body with two cordons around the middle. The slightly concave, circular base is unglazed except for slight glaze flooding. There are three clay-pad marks, one mark having glaze and clay adhesions. The two elongated loop handles are set at approximately twenty-two degrees to one another, attaching above the waist and midway between the waist and base. The cup illustrated on the right has a flared, cylindrical body with a rib encircling the waist. The base is unglazed except for slight glaze flooding, and there are two clay-pad marks. Base and handle fragments of another mug, or mugs, were also found each similar to the recovered beaker-shaped mug.

BLACKWARE

A mid-seventeenth-century mug and cup made from red, iron-bearing, earthenware with a dark black iron and lead glaze were recovered, together with two small fragments of another mug, or mugs, found in the excavation (fig. 13). All appear to have been made in North Staffordshire and seem to have been influenced by earlier "Cistercian" wares.[7] Several mugs similar to the Talbot Hotel example were excavated from the Marquis of Granby Hotel site in Burslem, Stoke-on-Trent, in 1956.[8] The site was previously occupied by a house and oven, which could have been part of "Ralph Allon's Red-Ware Work." Similar blackware vessels are commonly found in excavations in the Stoke-on-Trent area (fig. 14) and on numerous other sites throughout Great Britain.[9]

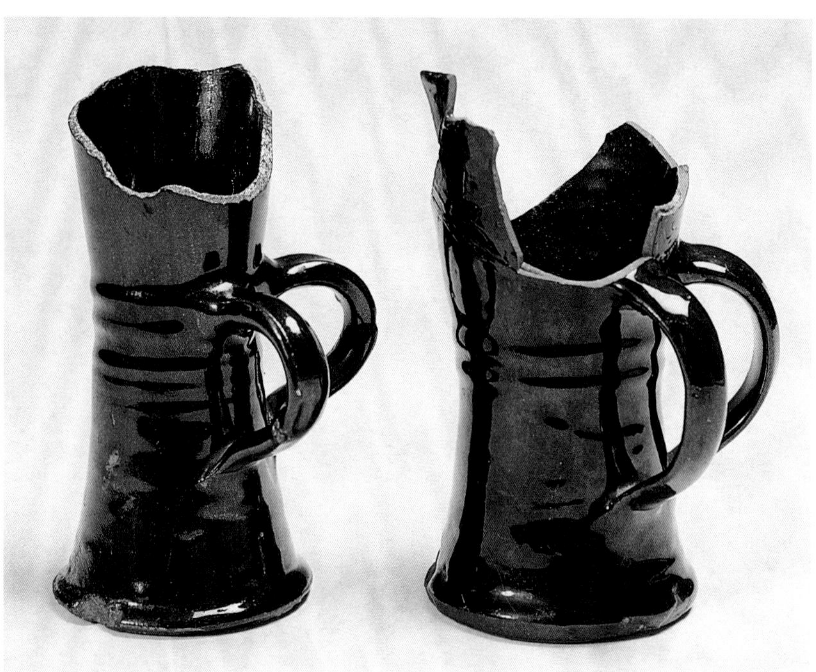

Figure 14 Mugs, Staffordshire, 1660–1680. Lead-glazed red earthenware. (The example on the left courtesy, Potteries Museum.) Similar vessels are commonly found in excavations in the Stoke-on-Trent area and on numerous other sites throughout Great Britain.

MOTTLED WARE

A comprehensive group of thrown and turned lead-glazed, pale-buff earthenware vessels with mottled brown coloring was recovered from the Talbot Hotel (figs. 16–36). This assemblage—mainly cylindrical mugs—appears to be solely of North Staffordshire manufacture and dates from circa 1700–1720.

This type of pottery was referred to as "manganese-glazed ware" in excavation reports of the 1970s and 1980s. The glaze's streaked appearance suggests that, possibly, it is the "Motley-colour" referred to by Robert Plot, "which is procured by blending the *Lead* with *Manganese,* by the *Workmen* call'd *Magnus*."[10] However, it is conjectured that Plot, or the workmen he interviewed, could have been confusing manganese with magnas, an iron-ore.[11]

There was widespread production of mottled ware throughout Stoke-on-Trent, as evidenced by the excavations of kiln sites at Albion Square and Old Hall Street, Hanley. Significant groups of mottled ware were also

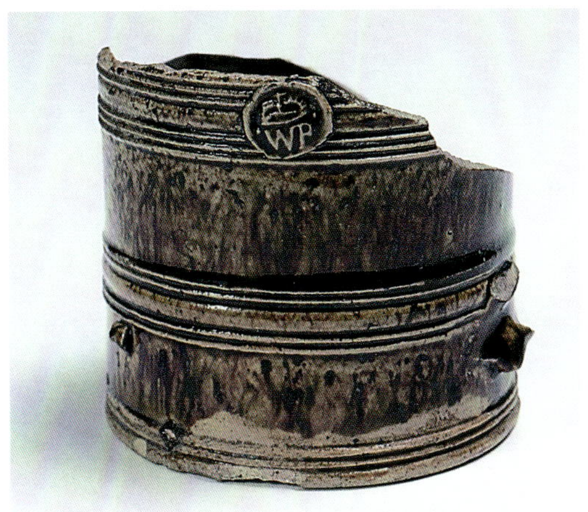

Figure 15 Mug fragment, Staffordshire, 1700–1720. Manganese-mottled earthenware. (Courtesy, Potteries Museum.) Applied, or sometimes impressed, ale-measure marks are commonly found on "mottled ware" tavern mugs, these bearing the initials of the reigning monarch, namely "WR" for William III, "AR" for Queen Anne, and "GR" for George I.

recovered from Swan Bank, Burslem, and Town Road, Hanley.[12] The majority of the excavated production waste appears to date from the period 1700–1720.

Domestic groups of mottled ware were common during the eighteenth century. An ample assemblage of this early-eighteenth–century ceramic type was found at Temple Balsall, Warwickshire, at South Castle Street, Liverpool, and at Mount Street, Stafford. Although there is no conclusive evidence for Staffordshire production of mottled ware into the second half of the eighteenth century, a Stafford pit group dating to circa 1770 contained several late examples of mostly kitchen and food preparation vessels, as well as chamber pots.[13]

Mottled ware appears to have been made at other major potting centers during the eighteenth century, including Buckley, Prescot, Sheffield Manor, Bristol, Ironbridge, and Derby. Many examples are known to have forms that differ considerably from those found in Stoke-on-Trent, and widespread production is therefore indicated.

Applied, or sometimes impressed, ale-measure marks are commonly found on mottled-ware tavern mugs bearing the initials of English monarchs, "WR" for William III (see fig. 15), "AR" for Queen Anne, and "GR" for George I.[14] Several of the mugs recovered from the Talbot Hotel bear "AR" ale-measure marks. Interestingly, although utilitarian mottled ware vessels were obviously in common use at the time, examples are rarely found today, other than in an excavated context.

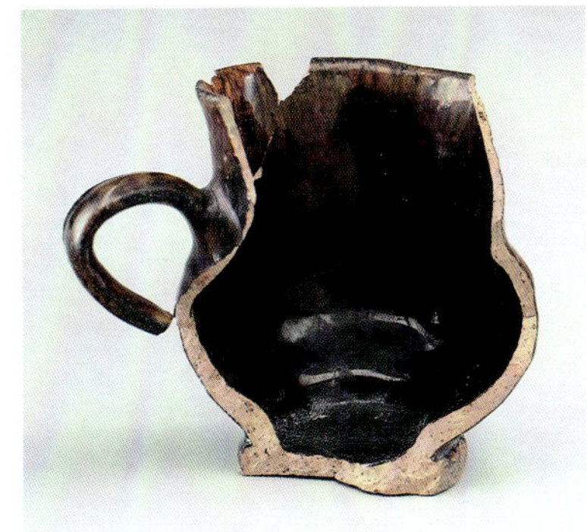

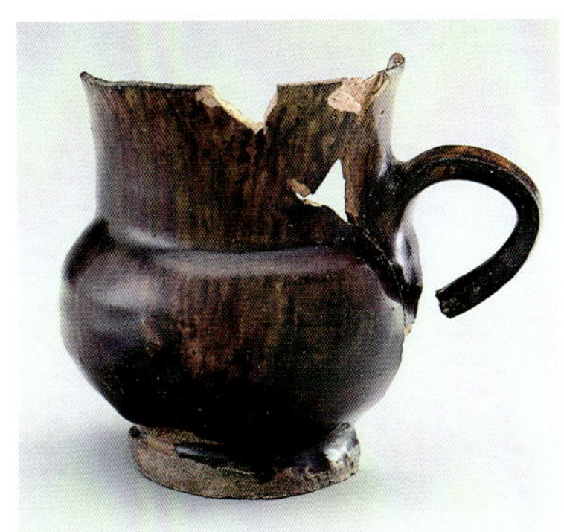

Figure 16 Cup, Staffordshire, 1700–1720. H. 2⅞". Manganese-mottled earthenware. This "thistle" shape cup has a compressed spherical body, a flared cylindrical neck, an unglazed short cylindrical foot and an unglazed flat circular base. The earthenware fabric is a pinkish buff. Slipware cups of similar shape were recovered from the same site (see fig. 47). A "mottled ware" triple fuddling cup is recorded, formed by conjoined vessels of the same shape.

Figure 17 Mugs, Staffordshire, 1700–1720. Manganese-mottled earthenware. H. 3⅞" and 4". Mugs of similar shape, referred to at the time as a "gorge," were also produced in German and English stoneware, delftware, and metalware, in the late seventeenth and early eighteenth centuries. The mug on the left has a short angular foot that is unglazed, as is the flat circular base (save for slight glaze flooding). The mug is rather heavily potted. The mug on the right also has a spherical body smaller than the body of the foregoing mug. Likewise, its slightly flaring cylindrical neck is taller and narrower. There is a glaze flaw on the extremity of the body where it has touched against another vessel in the kiln. The flared foot is unglazed, as is the flat circular base. The mug has been professionally reconstructed and has two small areas of restoration.

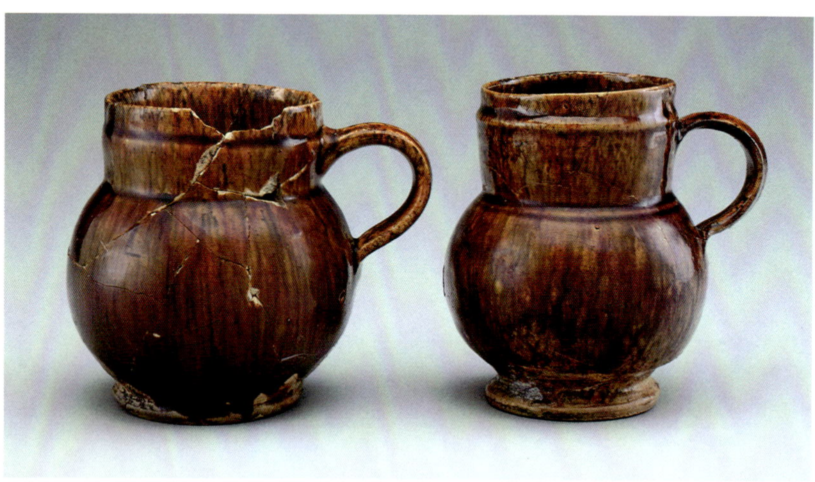

Figure 18 Mug fragments, Staffordshire, 1700–1720. Manganese-mottled earthenware. Several other fragments of these gorge shaped mugs were recovered.

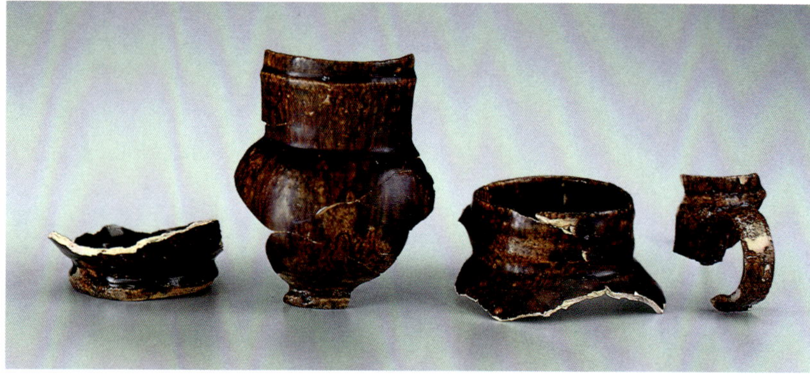

Figure 19 Mugs, Staffordshire, 1700–1720. Manganese-mottled earthenware. H. of right mug: 3¾". These two mugs have a half-pint capacity. Each has a cylindrical body with a slightly tapering cylindrical neck and a single shoulder-band formed by ten deep wheel-turned grooves. The partially glazed foot-band is formed by five deep wheel-turned grooves, and the flat circular base is unglazed. The mug on the right has a ribbed "ear" shaped handle with the upper junction at the shoulder-band and the lower junction just above the foot-band. The mug on the left lacks the handle, but the junctions are in the same position. Both mugs are by the same maker. A number of other fragments of similar mugs were also recovered.

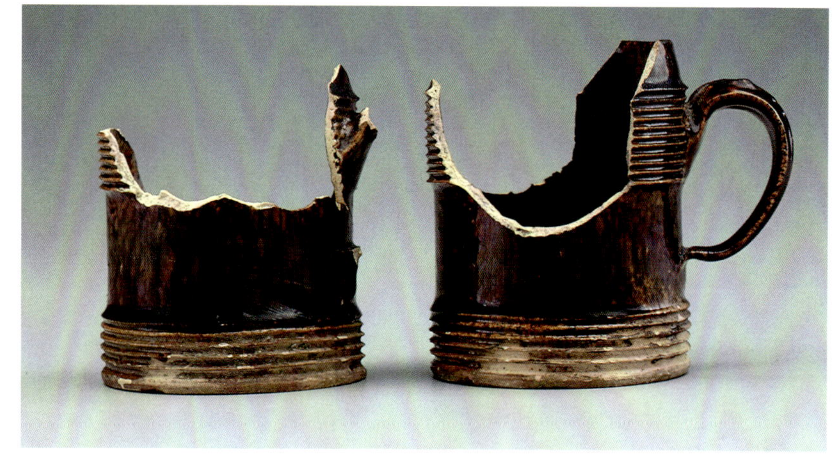

Figure 20 Mugs, Staffordshire, 1700–1720. Manganese-mottled earthenware. H. 4" and 5¾". The base of the half-pint mug on the left displays numerous parallel straight, string-mark lines. The elongated ribbed loop handles attach at the shoulder-band and just above the foot-band. The lower junction shows a tightly thumbed terminal that has excess clay folded over and up. The body of the pint mug on the right is misshapen, where it was accidentally squashed between the handle junctions before firing. The partially glazed foot-bands have been formed by numerous wheel-turned grooves, and the flat, circular bases are unglazed. Both mugs were probably made by the same potter.

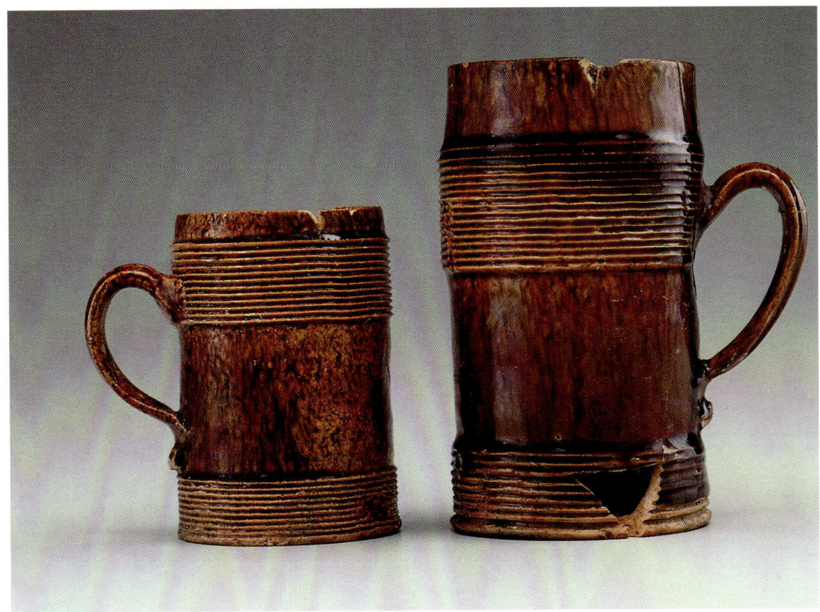

Figure 21 Mugs, Staffordshire, 1700–1720. Manganese-mottled earthenware. H. 5¾" and 5½". The mug on the left shows the reverse of the mug illustrated in fig. 20 (right). The mug on the right has a cylindrical body, slightly tapering cylindrical neck, and a single shoulder-band formed by numerous wheel-turned grooves. The unglazed, flared foot-band is also formed by numerous wheel-turned grooves, and the flat, circular base is unglazed. The same potter possibly made this and the two mugs illustrated in fig. 20.

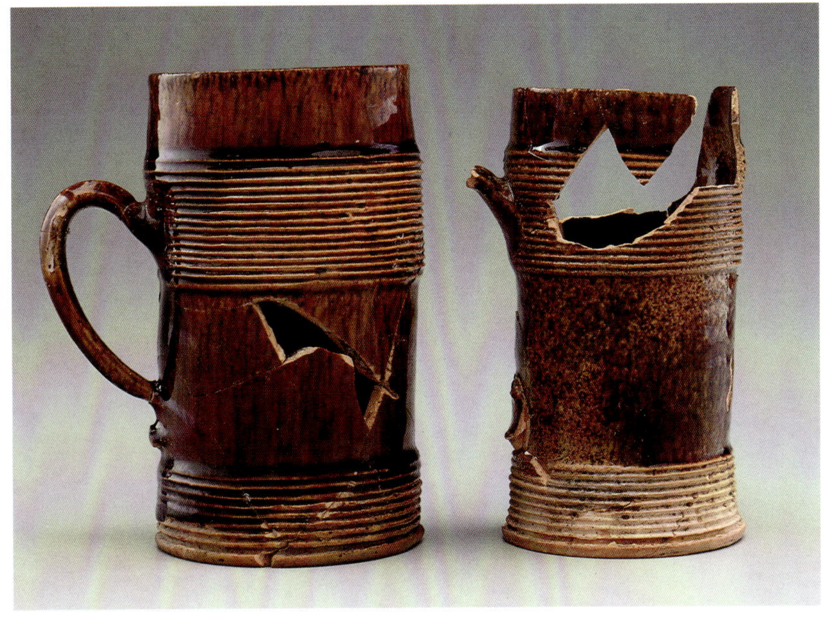

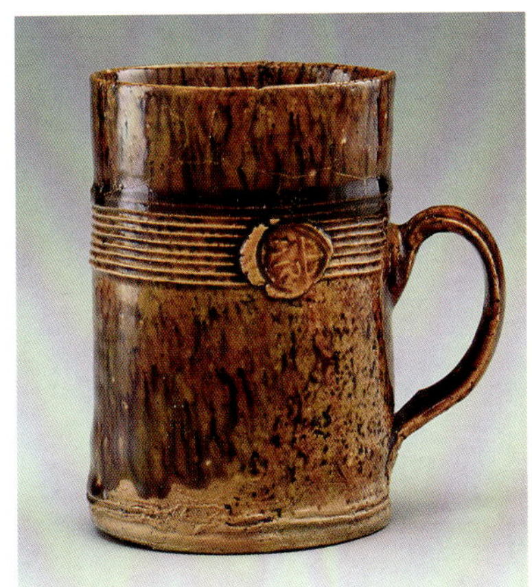

Figure 22 Mug, Staffordshire, 1702–1714. Manganese-mottled earthenware. H. 3⅞". This half-pint mug's cylindrical body has a single shoulder-band formed by numerous wheel-turned grooves. The shoulder-band incorporates an applied clay pad stamped with a crowned "AR" ale-measure mark with relief details. The elongated ribbed loop handle attaches at the lower part of the shoulder-band and just above the narrow, mainly unglazed, foot-band. The unglazed flat, circular base has clay adhesions from another vessel or kiln furniture. The mug has been professionally reconstructed, with only minor restoration.

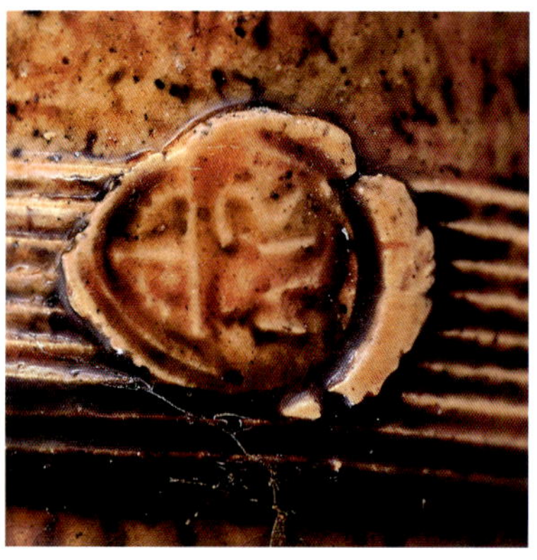

Figure 23 Detail of the "AR" excise mark on the mug illustrated in fig. 22.

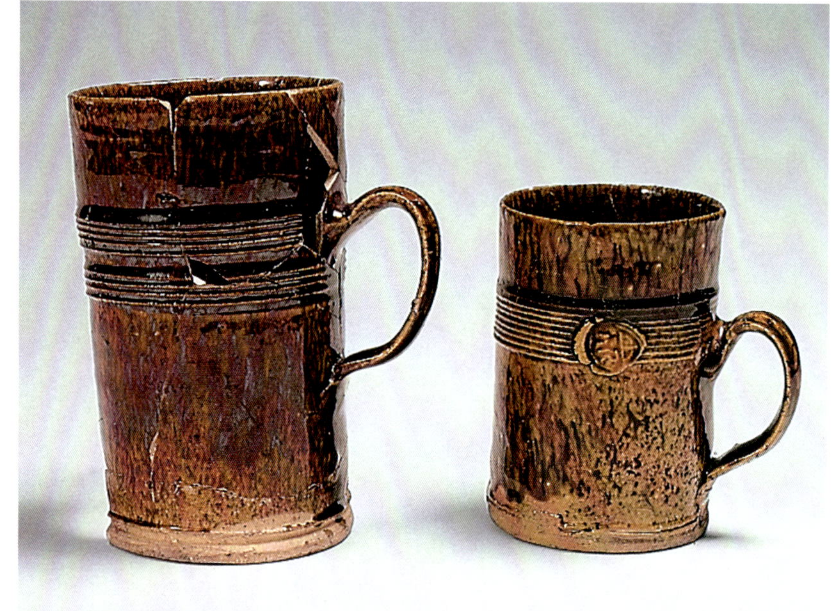

Figure 24 Mugs, Staffordshire, 1700–1720. Manganese-mottled earthenware. The mottled-ware mug on the left was excavated in Town Road, Hanley, Stoke-on-Trent, and is shown for comparison with the mug illustrated in fig. 22.

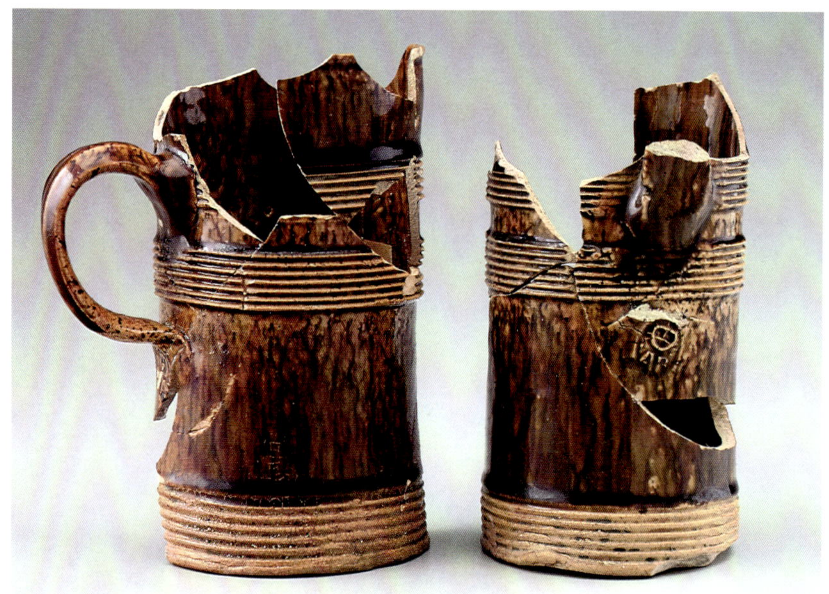

Figure 25 Mugs, Staffordshire, 1702–1714. Manganese-mottled earthenware. H. (left) 5¾". The half-pint mug on the left shows a narrow, raised band around the rim with an underlying groove about ⅛ inch below. The double shoulder-bands and the unglazed foot-bands were formed by numerous wheel-turned grooves, and the flat, circular bases are unglazed. The handle's lower junction is stamped with a crowned "AR" ale-measure mark. The same potter made both mugs, although the "AR" marks are different.

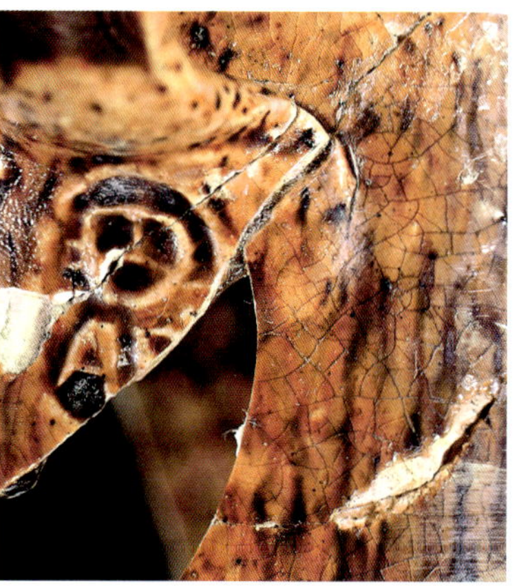

Figure 26 Detail of the "AR" mark on the mug illustrated on the left in fig. 25.

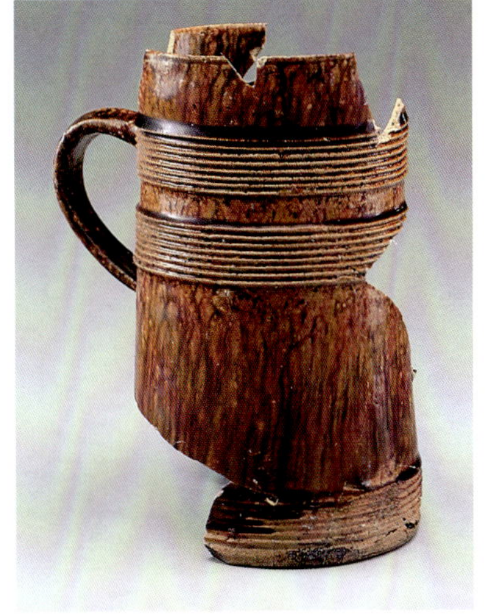

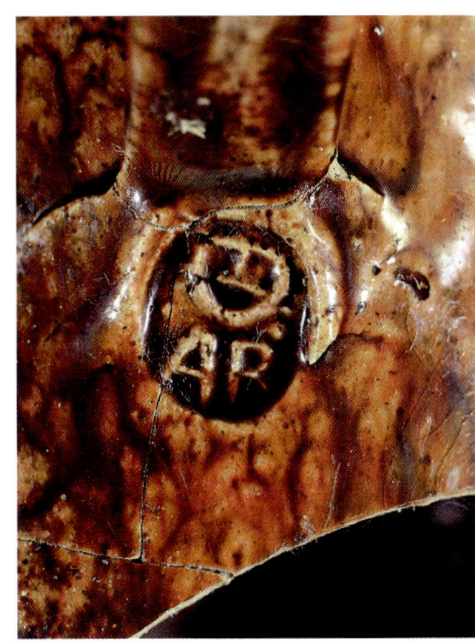

Figure 27 Mug, Staffordshire, 1702–1714. Manganese-mottled earthenware. H. 6⅝". This quart sized mug is very similar to the smaller pint mugs illustrated in fig. 25 and probably was thrown by the same potter. It is stamped with a crowned "AR" ale-measure mark.

Figure 28 Detail of the "AR" mark on the mug illustrated in fig. 27.

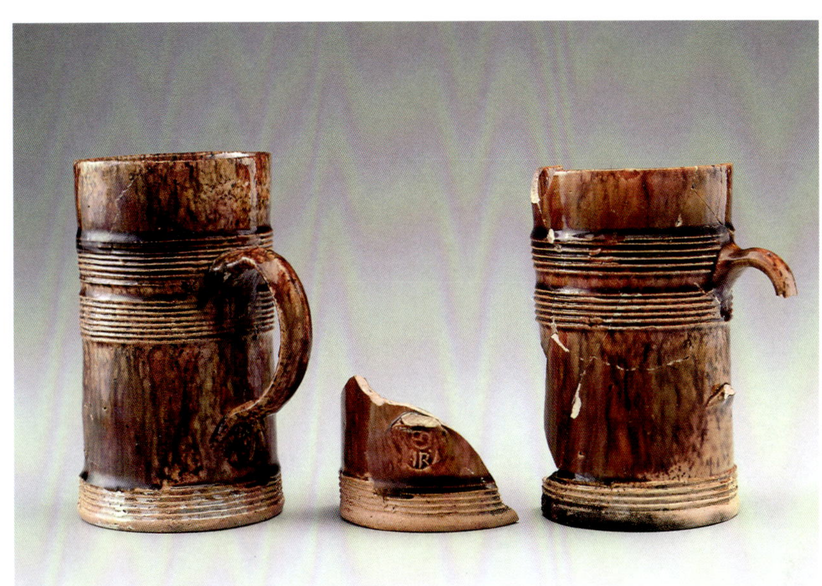

Figure 29 Mugs, Staffordshire, 1700–1720. Manganese-mottled earthenware. H. 5½" and 5¼". The two nearly complete pint mugs display a double shoulder-band and an unglazed foot-band formed by numerous wheel-turned grooves. One mug (left) handle's lower junction is stamped with an indistinct crowned "AR" ale-measure mark terminal with relief details. The same stamped terminal appears on the mug fragment (center). The mug on the left has been professionally reconstructed.

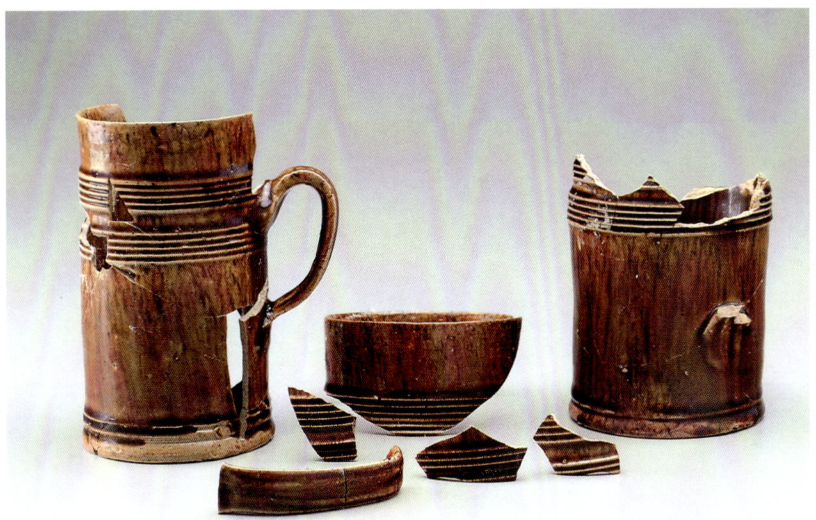

Figure 30 Mugs, Stafffordshire, 1700–1720. Manganese-mottled earthenware. H. (left) 5⅛". Each of these pint mugs has a cylindrical body and a double shoulder-band formed by numerous wheel-turned grooves.

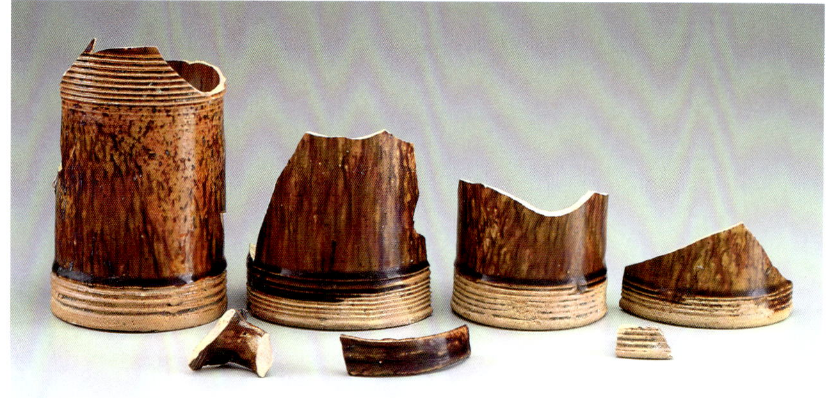

Figure 31 Mug fragments, Staffordshire, 1700–1720. Manganese-mottled earthenware. H. (left) 5¾". Each of these fragments of four mugs has a cylindrical body and an unglazed foot-band formed by numerous wheel-turned grooves.

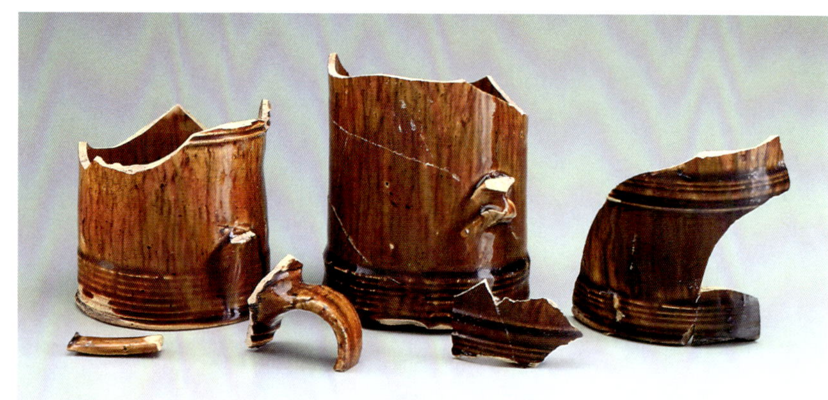

Figure 32 Mugs, Staffordshire, 1700–1720. Manganese-mottled earthenware. D. (left) 3⅝". Each of these fragments of four mugs has a cylindrical body and a glazed foot-band formed by numerous wheel-turned grooves.

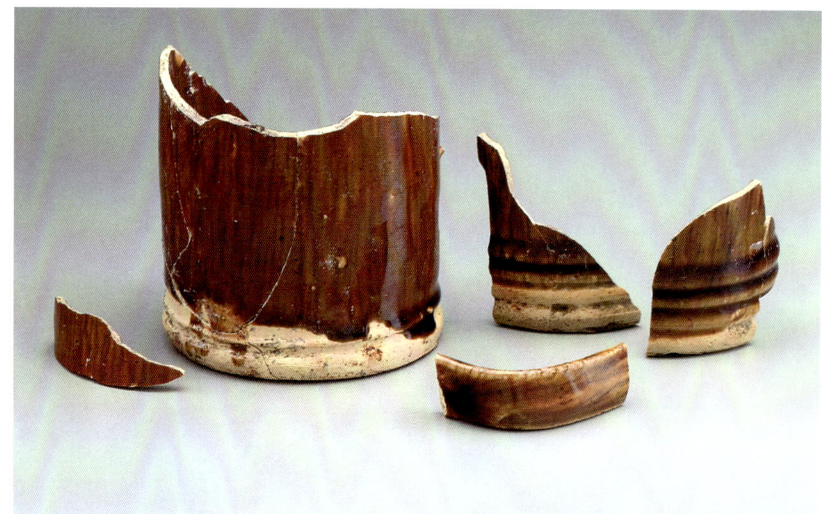

Figure 33 Mug fragments, Staffordshire, 1700–1720. Manganese-mottled earthenware. D. of base: 3⅛". The base fragment has an unglazed rounded foot displaying a single wheel-turned groove. The flat, circular base is unglazed.

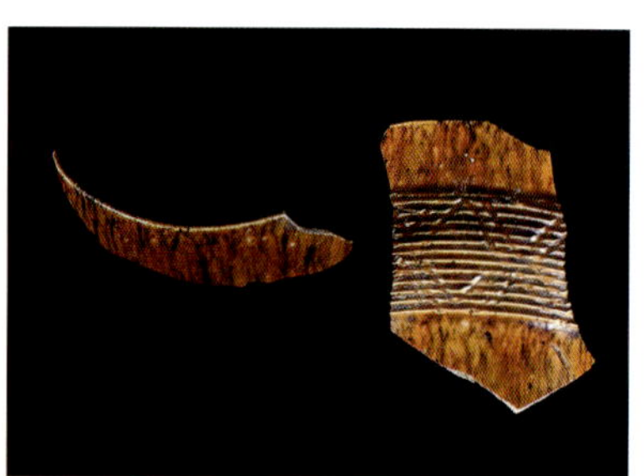

Figure 34 Mug fragments, Staffordshire, 1700–1720. Manganese-mottled earthenware. The rim fragment on the left is from a thinly potted mug being 1⁄16" to 3⁄32" thick and has a mottled olive-brown glaze. The fabric is a high-fired gray earthenware, which does not appear to correspond with any of the other recovered "mottled" wares from the Talbot Hotel. The fragment on the right has a shoulder-band formed by numerous wheel-turned grooves that are additionally hand-incised with linked double-lined saltire crosses.

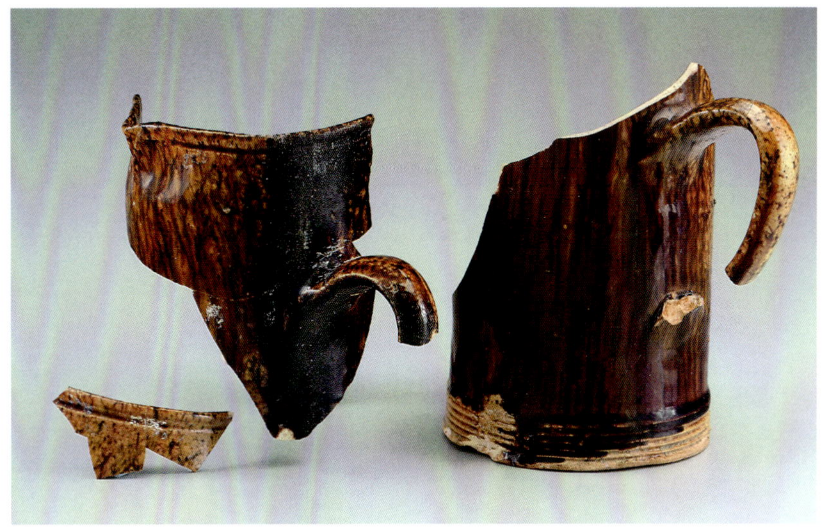

Figure 35 Jug fragments, Staffordshire, 1700–1720. Manganese-mottled earthenware. D. of base: 3¾". One jug (left) has a neck with a lip-pinch and a single groove running about 3/16 inches below the rim. A section of its elongated loop handle is set at ninety degrees to the lip-pinch. The second jug has a section of an elongated loop handle matching the handle of the first, and the handle's upper junction is assumed to be in a similar position. The flat, circular base is unglazed.

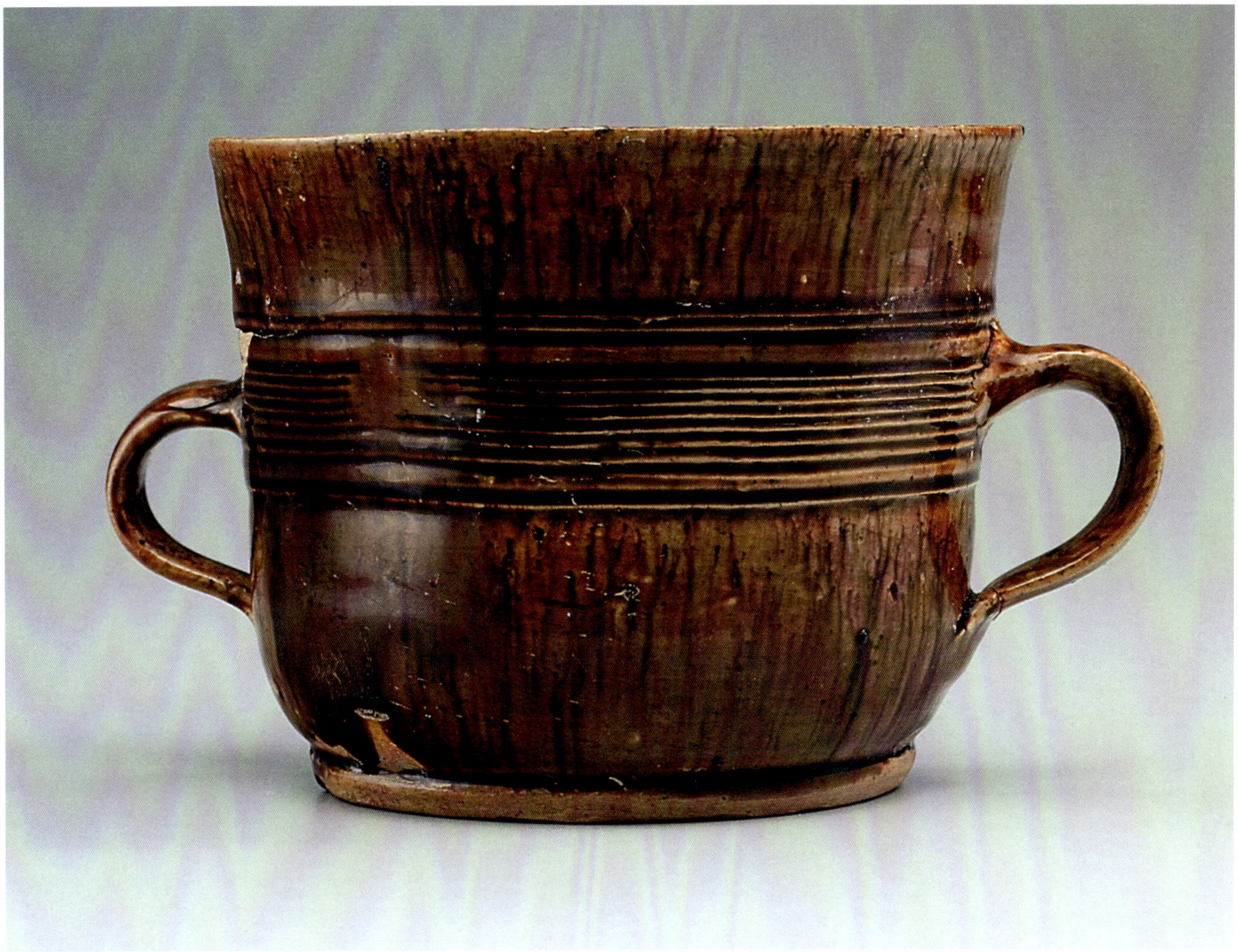

Figure 36 Cup, Staffordshire, 1700–1720. Manganese-mottled earthenware. H. 5". This large cup has a rounded body with a widely flared cylindrical neck above a wide shoulder-band formed by numerous wheel-turned grooves, and incorporating a prominent cordon near the top and bottom. The short, angular foot is partially glazed, whereas the flat, circular base is unglazed. The fabric is grayish-buff earthenware. The glaze shows scratching and wear, particularly on the interior.

English Salt-Glazed Stoneware

WHITE-DIPPED STONEWARE

The majority of the recovered white, salt-glazed stoneware has an off-white, pipe-clay slip dip over a pale gray stoneware fabric (figs. 37–39). The group appears to be of North Staffordshire manufacture and dates from circa 1720.

Similar white-dipped stoneware vessels have been excavated in Stoke-on-Trent, including one mug found at Fenton Vivian when the Thomas Whieldon factory site was investigated. A Staffordshire white-dipped stoneware mug was also found at Wetherburn's Tavern in Williamsburg, Virginia, in a mid-eighteenth-century context.[15]

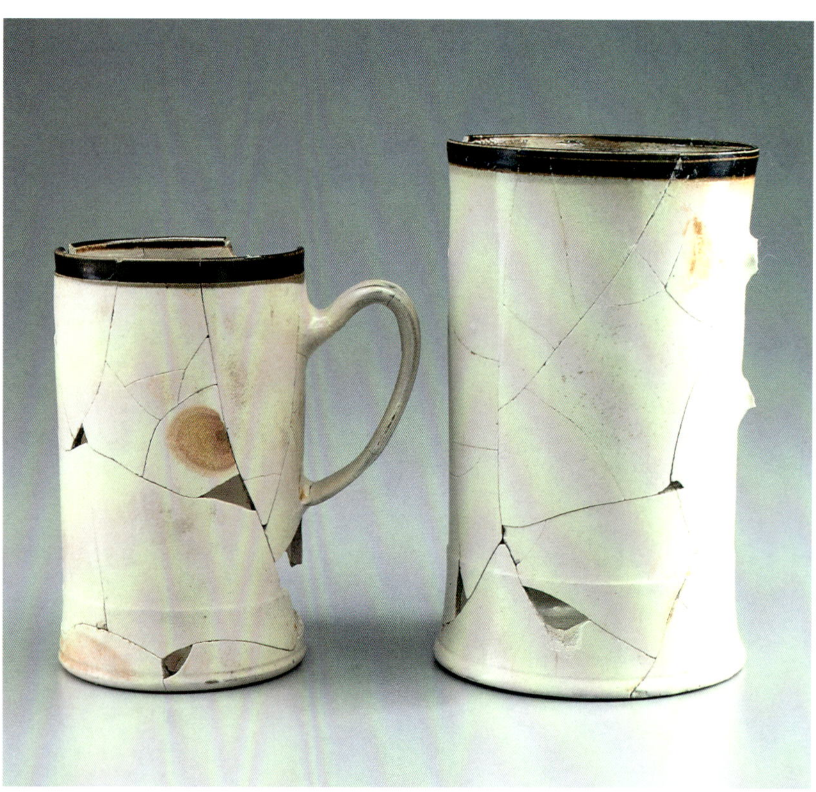

Figure 37 Mugs, Staffordshire, ca. 1720. Salt-glazed stoneware. H. 5⅜" and 6⅝". These white dipped mugs have the addition of an iron-rich slip around the rim. Both mugs have areas of iron contamination, and the quart mug (right) has small areas of the white pipe-clay slip pulling away just below the rim interior.

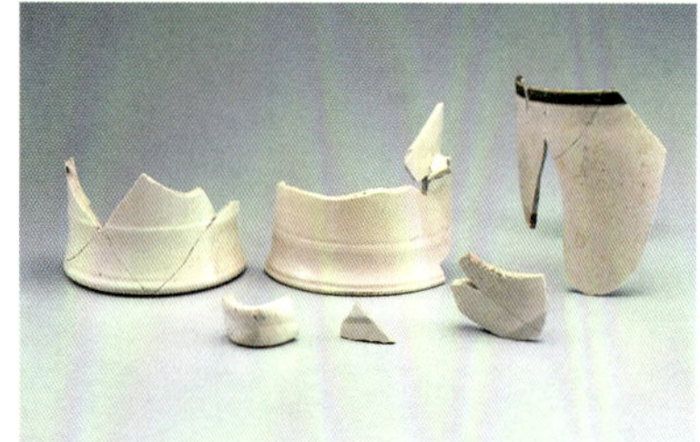

Figure 38 Mug fragments, Staffordshire, ca. 1720. Salt-glazed stoneware.

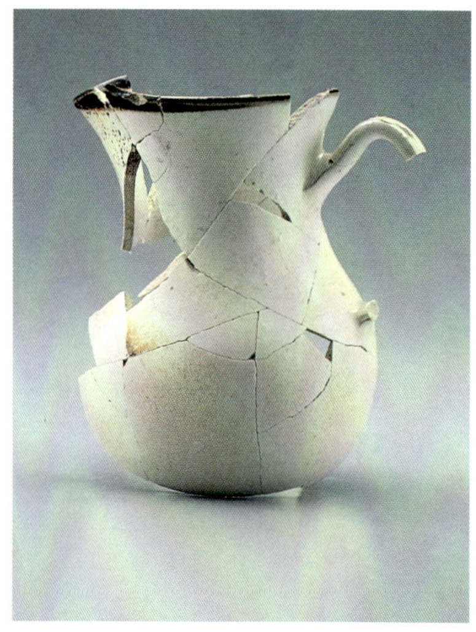

Figure 39 Jug, Staffordshire, 1700–1720. Salt-glazed stoneware. H. 5½". The spherical body has a flared neck, pinched lip, and band of iron-rich slip around the rim. A similar excavated jug is in the Potteries Museum and Art Gallery, Stoke-on-Trent, and at Rummey's Tavern in London Town, Maryland.

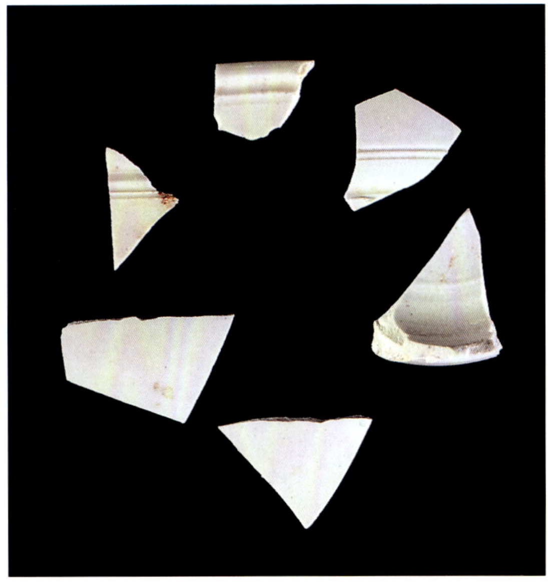

Figure 40 Fragments, Staffordshire, ca. 1725. Salt-glazed stoneware. These small fragments represent one or more vessels including a base fragment and a rim fragment, with wheel-turned grooved banding.

WHITE STONEWARE

Only a few small fragments of high-fired, salt-glazed white stoneware were recovered (fig. 40). These appear to be of North Staffordshire manufacture and date from circa 1725, or possibly later. These few fragments are the latest ceramic types in this assemblage suggesting the terminus date for the deposit.

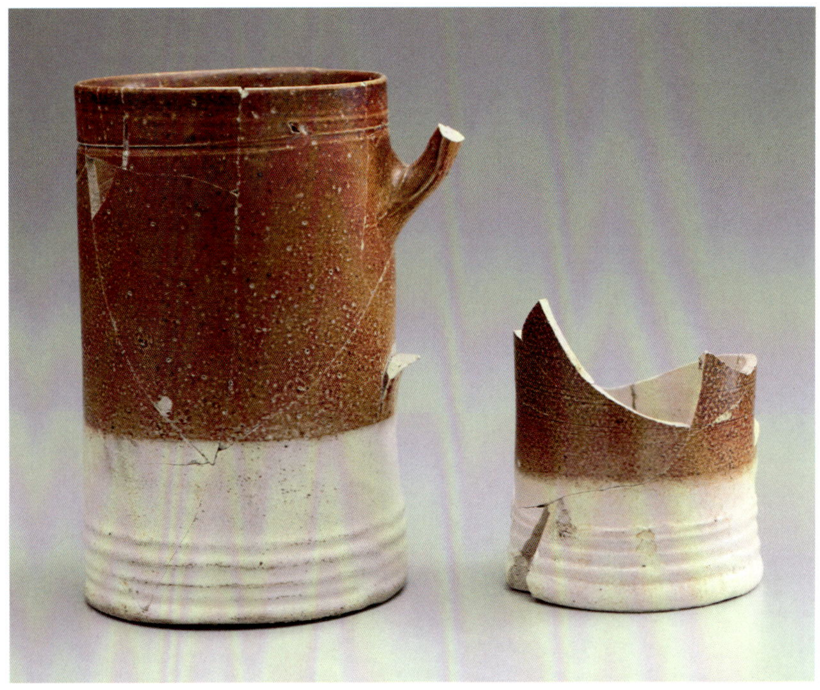

Figure 41 Mugs, Staffordshire, 1700–1720. Salt-glazed stoneware. H. 5". The pint mug on the left has a foot-band formed by four wheel-turned cordons above a rounded foot-rim. The lower part of the pint has an off-white pipe-clay slip dip on the exterior, over a pale gray fabric, and there are areas of slip on the slightly concave base where the slip has run from the foot-rim. The upper part of the pint mug has a freckled iron-rich dip that also continues down from the rim on the interior about ¾ inch (1.9 cm.) and on the remaining sections of the grooved handle. The half-pint mug on the right has a white-slip dip on the interior, on the lower part of the exterior and over the base. Both mugs are probably by the same maker. These mugs were included in Jonathan Horne's 1985 *Exhibition of English Brown Stoneware,* in Kensington Church Street, London. Similar mugs were recovered from Swan Bank, Burslem.

BROWN STONEWARE

The salt-glazed brown stoneware mugs and fragments recovered from the Talbot Hotel are from various centers of manufacture, but all date from the early eighteenth century (figs. 41–46).

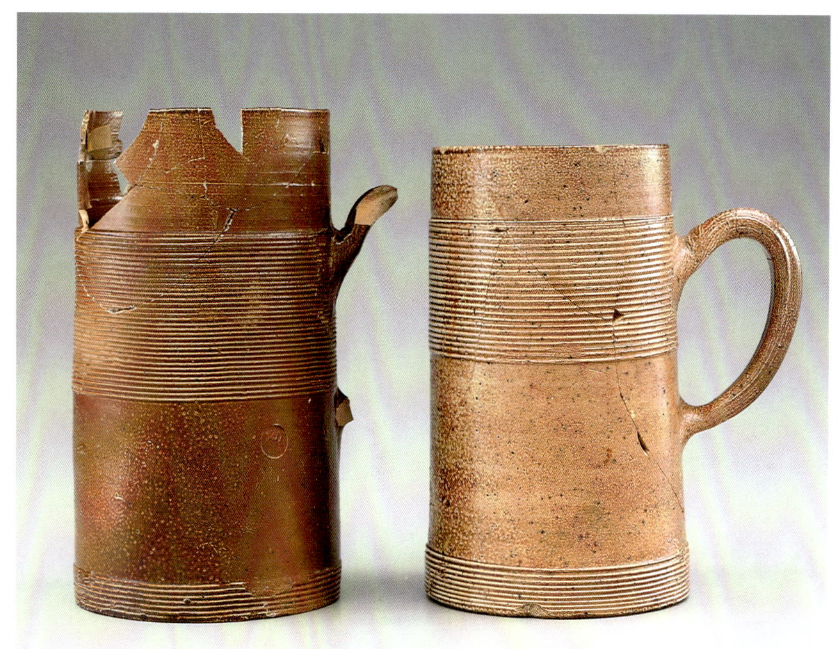

Figure 42 Mugs, England, ca. 1710. Salt-glazed stoneware. H. 7" and 6½". The quart mug on the left was probably made in Nottingham and has an impressed circular ale-measure mark below the wide band, with the uncrowned conjoined initials "AR" in relief. The mug on the right was possibly made in Bristol. The pale gray fabric has a freckled iron-rich dip overall. These mugs were included in Jonathan Horne's 1985 *Exhibition of English Brown Stoneware,* in Kensington Church Street, London.

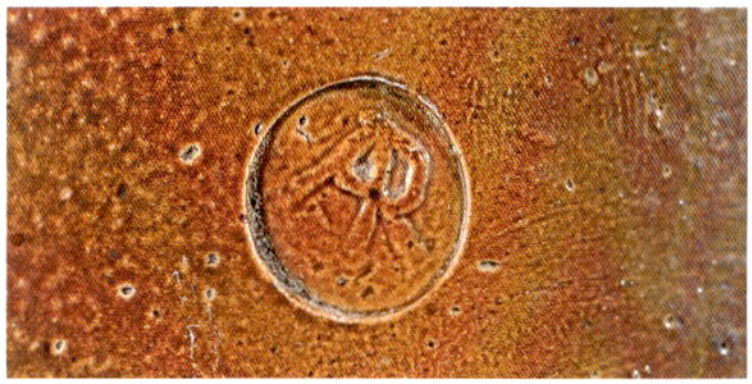

Figure 43 Detail of the impressed "AR" on the mug illustrated on the left in fig. 42.

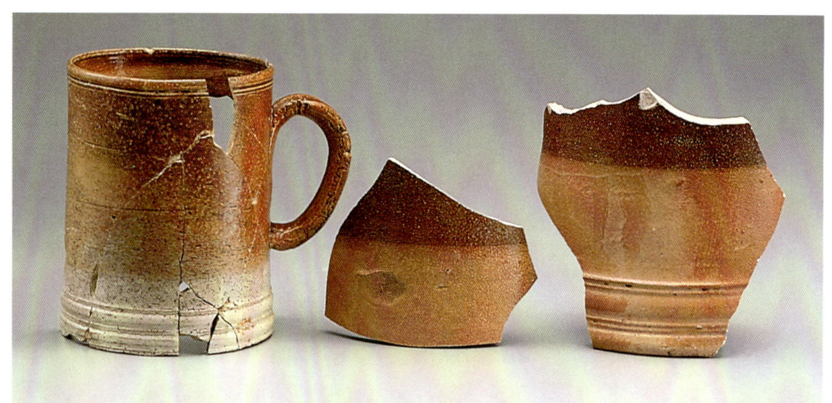

Figure 44 Mug and mug fragments. Salt-glazed stoneware. Left: Possibly Bristol, H. 3¾". The top three-quarters of the exterior of the mug, including the handle, has a freckled iron-rich dip over the pale gray stoneware fabric. The interior is partially wiped in dark brown. This mug was included in Jonathan Horne's 1985 *Exhibition of English Brown Stoneware,* in Kensington Church Street, London. Right: Two large fragments of a Staffordshire mug, one fragment with a foot-band formed by a central cordon between wheel-turned grooves, above a rounded foot-rim. A white-slip dip over the pale gray fabric and the overall freckled iron-rich dip on the exterior is divided into two distinct tones by the white-slip base dip.

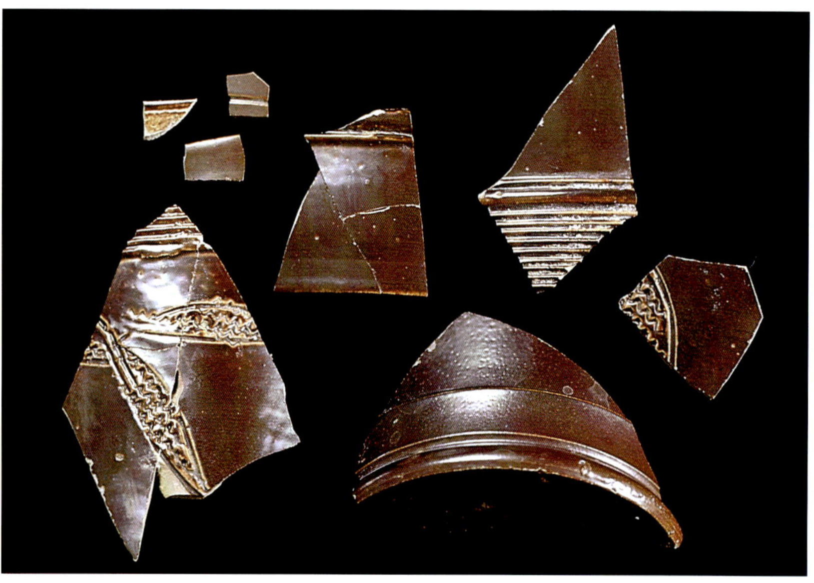

Figure 45 Mug fragments, Staffordshire, ca. 1710. Stoneware with a solid lustrous iron-rich dip on the exterior, matt mid-brown overall on the interior. The banded decoration is formed by wheel-turned grooves, and the incised stylized foliage has a zigzag infill. The base fragment has a wheel-turned, slightly waisted raised foot-band, a rounded foot-rim, and a partially recessed circular base. A similarly decorated mug was excavated near St. John's Church, Burslem, in 1964. Another was recovered from the Wellfleet Tavern, at Wellfleet, Great Island, Massachusetts.

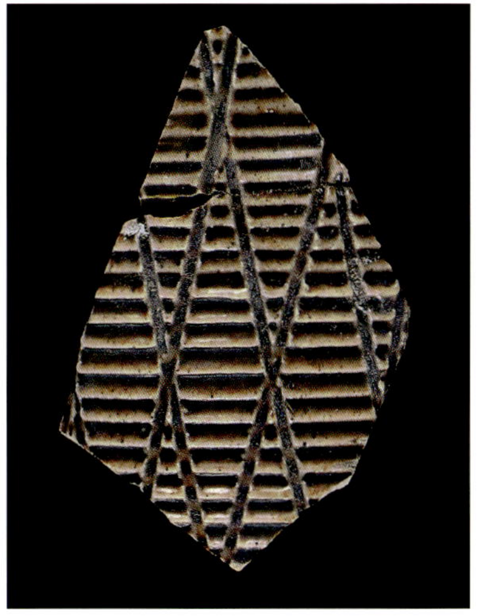

Figure 46 Mug fragment, probably Staffordshire, ca. 1710. This fragment exhibits a mid-brown, iron-rich dip on the exterior and interior. The ground decoration of numerous parallel wheel-turned grooves is hand-incised with straight lines to form an elongated diamond diaper pattern. Other fragments of this type of ware were recovered including one with an impressed partial ale-measure mark that includes the top of a raised unidentifiable royal initial.

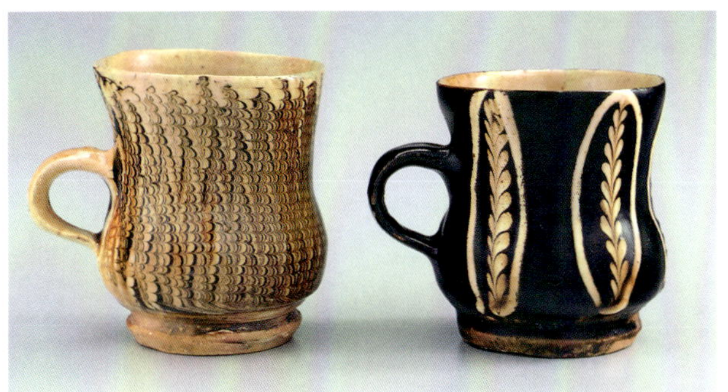

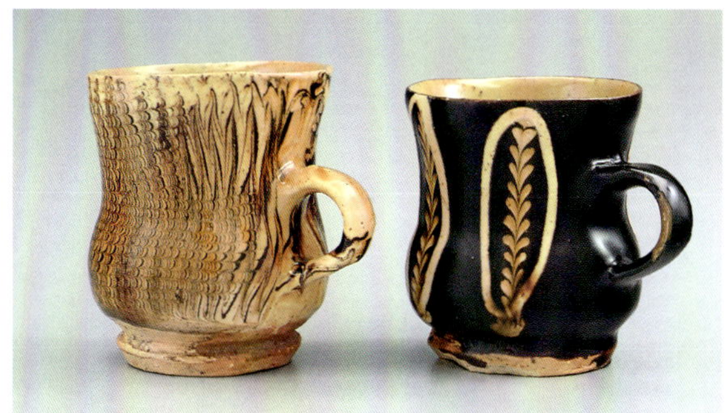

Figure 47 Cups, Staffordshire, 1700. Slipware. H. 2⅞" and 2¾". The cup on the left has a reddish-pink earthenware fabric displaying a white-slip coating. Its exterior is finely combed. The cup on the right has a pale buff earthenware fabric displaying an iron-rich slip coating on the exterior and a white slip coating on the interior. The exterior is trailed in white slip with five stylized vertical leaves, each central vein combed to produce numerous fronds. The slightly concave base is unglazed save for slight glaze flooding. Both cups have been professionally reconstructed and have areas of restoration. A Staffordshire mottled ware cup of similar shape was recovered from the Talbot Hotel site (see fig. 16). Similar cups were recovered from a workman's trench at the present-day Sadler's factory in Burslem.

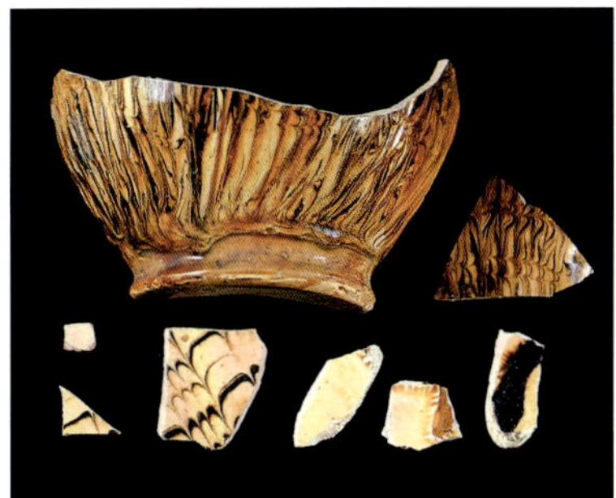

Figure 48 Slipware fragments, Staffordshire, 1700–1720. D. of base fragment: 3¼". The largest fragment represents a cup, or honey pot, with a spherical body and a rounded, angular foot-rim. The pale buff earthenware fabric displays an exterior white-slip coating vertically striped in dark-brown slip with traces of horizontal combing. The small fragments include two dish fragments (bottom left) with combed decoration; three fragments (bottom right) from a press-molded dish, or dishes, with traces of a mid-brown slip infill; and a tiny vessel fragment (left).

Slipware

The small amount of late seventeenth-century slip-decorated earthenware that was recovered from the Talbot Hotel is all apparently of Staffordshire manufacture. Although this group is relatively small, some exceptional examples were found (figs. 47, 48).

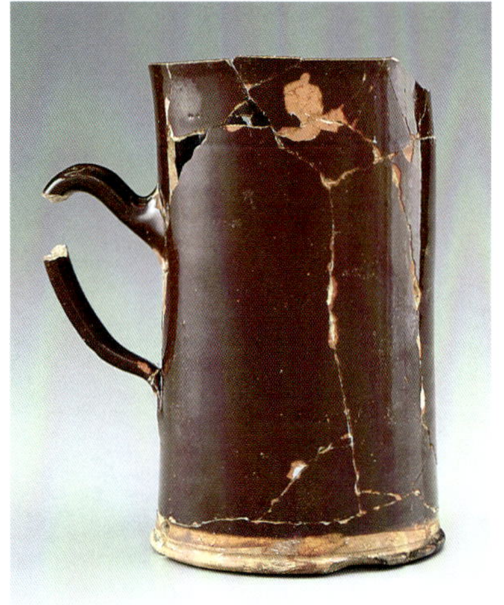
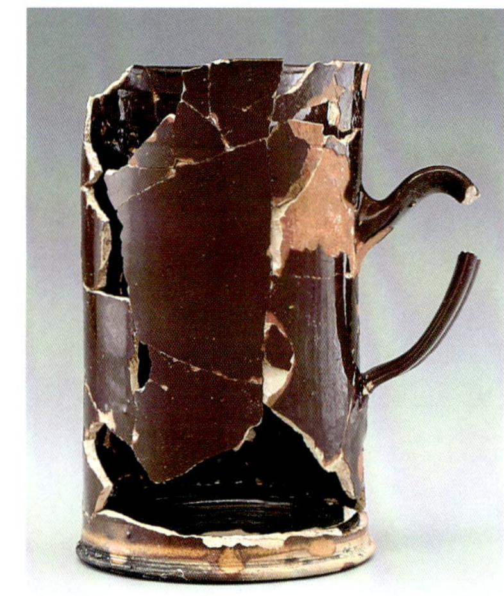

Figure 49 Mug, probably Staffordshire, England, ca. 1720. Slip-coated earthenware. H. 6¾". This quart capacity mug has a tall, cylindrical body with a single wheel-turned groove below the slightly flared rim. The wheel-turned, double-grooved foot-band and the rounded, angular foot-rim are unglazed except for slight glaze flooding. The lead glaze has transformed the slip-coat to a solid dark, reddish-brown color, and the glaze appears translucent yellow where it has flooded over the slip-free foot-band.

Slip-Coated Ware

Only one example of uncommon Staffordshire slip-coated earthenware (also called "chocolate-dipped ware") was recovered, dating from circa 1720 (fig. 49). This type of buff-bodied, once-fired earthenware is characterized by a brown or dark red slip coat beneath a lead glaze. Dated examples of this pottery show that its production was in favor in the 1720s–1740s, although examples have been found in domestic groups of circa 1770. Flatwares tend to be coated and glazed on the inside only, whereas hollow wares are coated and glazed inside and out, with both frequently finishing a little short of the base.

Slip-coated ware is a relatively minor type of pottery, but small quantities have been found on most archaeological sites in Stoke-on-Trent. It is also known to have been made at Buckley, and will probably be found on other sites that produced mottled wares or Staffordshire-type slipwares in the eighteenth century.

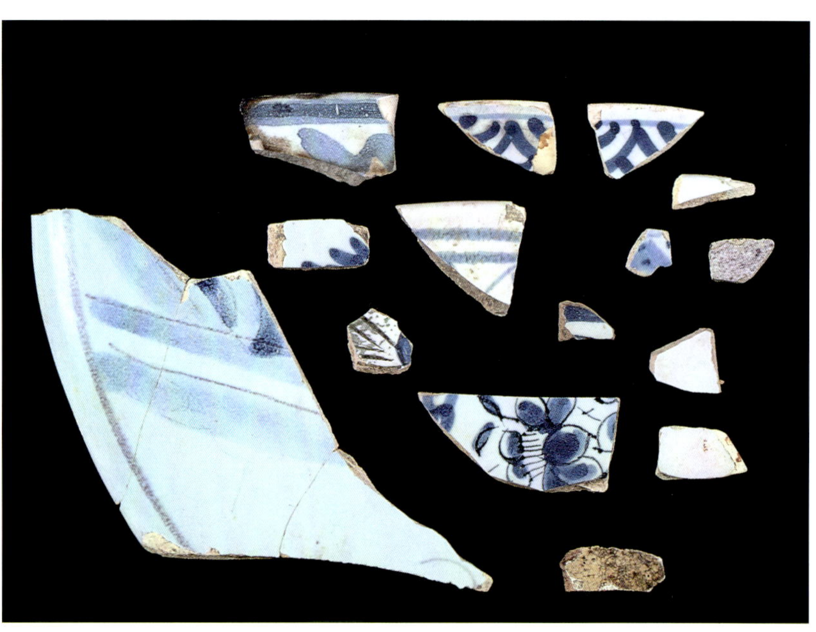

Figure 50 Plate and bowl fragments, England, 1700–1720. Tin-glazed earthenware. The large dish fragment is attributed to Brislington having a plain, shallow, rounded form and a matt, duck-egg blue, tin-glazed ground over a pale buff fabric. The indistinguishable decoration is washed in tones of blue and is delineated in manganese. The majority of the other fragments are attributed to Bristol and painted in blue and, most likely, belong to plates or dishes. The exceptions are a blue-painted fragment from a possible bowl rim; one fragment from a possible drinking vessel, displaying powdered manganese-purple on both interior and exterior; and one fragment with polychrome decoration painted in blue, sponged in green, and delineated in black.

English Tin-Glazed Earthenware

Only a handful of late-seventeenth- and early-eighteenth-century English tin-glazed earthenware fragments was recovered (fig. 50). Such a meager find is in direct contrast to the results of tavern site excavations in the United States, where fragments of British delftware, particularly punch bowls, are found in relative abundance. Recent studies of taverns in Williamsburg, Virginia, and London Town, Maryland, have documented the high frequency of delft punch bowls to the relative low occurrence of stoneware mugs.[16] This discrepancy might suggest a profitable avenue for future transatlantic research concerning the nature and functions of early-eighteenth-century British taverns.

German Salt-Glazed Stoneware

The only continental pottery finds from the Talbot Hotel site were fragments of mid- to late-seventeenth-century Rhenish salt-glazed stoneware, Bellarmine bottles, and two late-seventeenth-century Westerwald mugs (figs. 51–55).

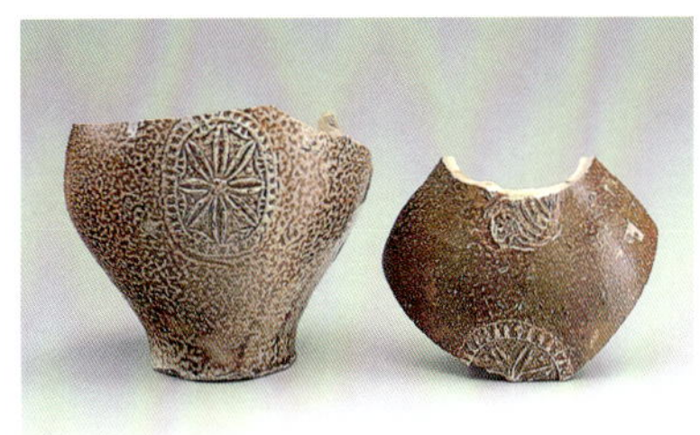

Figure 51 Fragments of two bottles, Germany, ca. 1680. Salt-glazed stoneware. Each of these fragments of Bellarmine bottles have an ovoid body and a freckled, iron-rich exterior dip over a pale gray stoneware fabric. The bottles have a slightly varying oval, relief-molded, rosette medallion applied to the front.

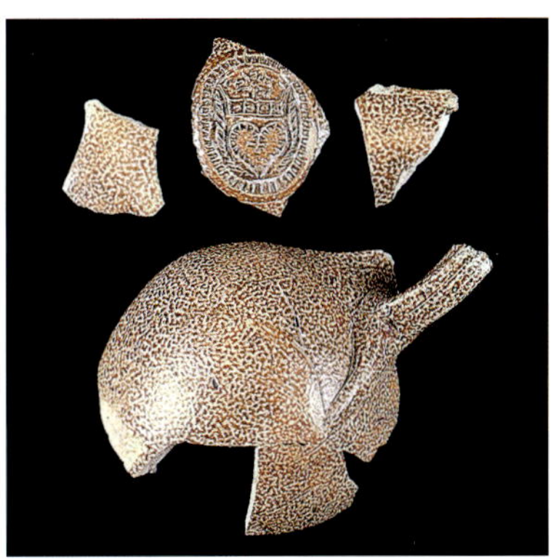

Figure 52 Fragments of Bellarmine bottles, Germany, ca. 1680. Salt-glazed stoneware. One fragment's applied relief-molded, oval medallion depicts a heart encircling a cross beneath a crown. Another fragment (not pictured) displays part of an applied relief-molded medallion, including the initial "H." Similar initialed medallions were found on bottles made at John Dwight's factory in Fulham, London. However, the fragment noted does not correspond with any known Dwight examples.

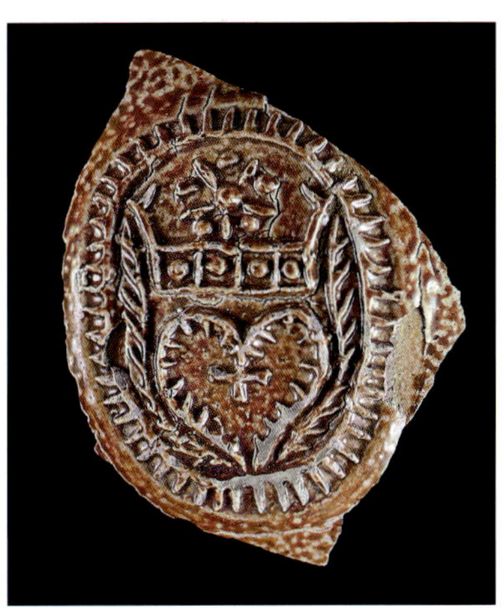

Figure 53 Detail of the heart medallion illustrated in fig. 52.

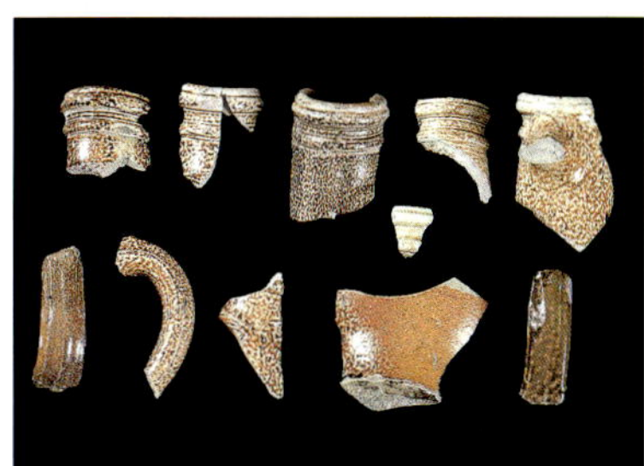

Figure 54 Bottle fragments, Germany, ca. 1680. Salt-glazed stoneware. These various neck, handle, and base fragments may belong to the bottles previously discussed.

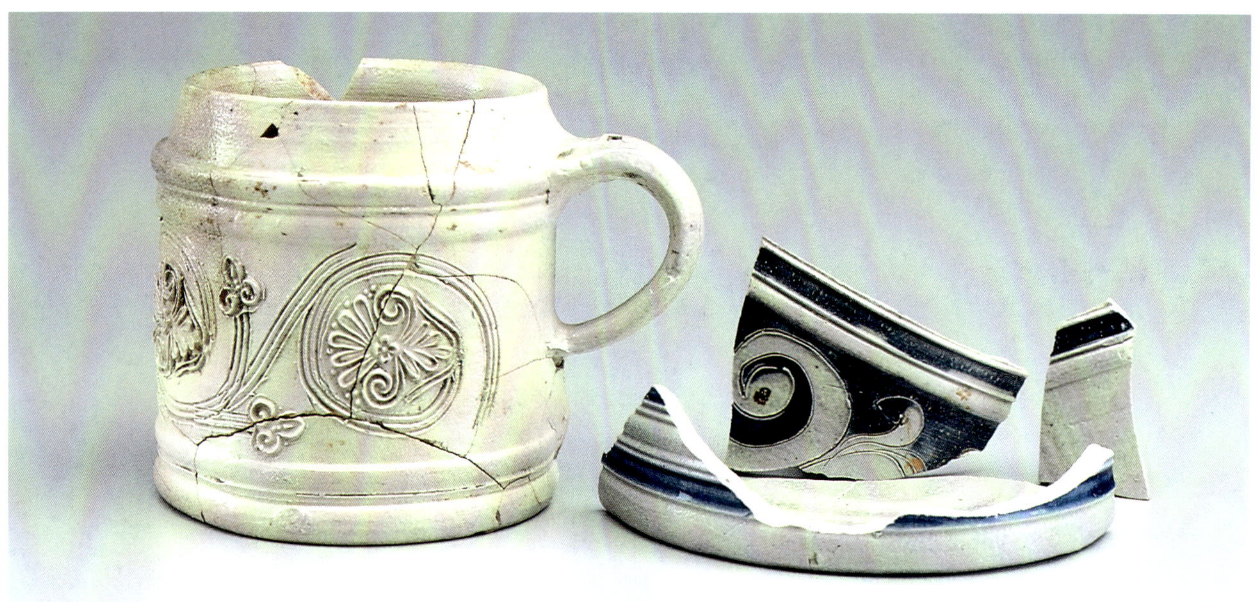

Figure 55 Mug and mug fragments, Westerwald, Germany, 1690–1710. Salt-glazed stoneware. H. 3⅜". The nearly complete example on the left has a loop handle that has an indentation at the top for a metal cover. The stoneware fabric is pale gray, and the base is flat. The mug fragments on the right are incised with foliate scrollwork and display a cobalt-blue background wash.

Observations and Conclusions

The tradition of drinking unhopped ale and hopped beer from pottery mugs flourished from the Middle Ages until at least the beginning of the twentieth century. However, while the "pub culture" achieved a widespread following in England, the development of a ceramic industry was somewhat backward. Robust salt-glazed stoneware drinking vessels were therefore imported continuously from the Rhineland from the fourteenth century until the end of the seventeenth century, when native potters achieved self-sufficiency by producing their own durable drinking vessels, adapting the forms to suit the English taste (fig. 56).

The increasing popularity and complete lack of any regulation of tavern mugs led to William III's Act of 1700 for "Ascertaining the Measures for retailing Ale and Beer," whereby vessels were to be checked during manufacture and stamped with "WR" below a crown. In reality it was not feasible to check the capacity of an unfired clay pot, which would shrink considerably during firing, and it seems that the potters were entrusted with marking their own products. The terms of the Act of 1700 were so poorly understood that the royal cipher was substituted by "AR" by some potters during the reign of Queen Anne, while in Bristol "GR" was consistently used after the accession of George I and throughout the eighteenth century. From a ceramic historian's point of view, the Act of 1700 is invaluable, as the presence of an ale-measure mark provides a date before which a vessel could not have been made.

Relatively few English inns and taverns have been archaeologically investigated.[17] However, such excavated assemblages have been summarized in an American model proposed by Kathleen Bragdon in a comparative study from two colonial sites in Massachusetts: the Joseph Howland farmstead, in Kingston, and the Wellfleet Tavern, at Wellfleet, Great Island.[18] The analysis suggests that tavern assemblages typically include:

1. A large number of vessels, both ceramic and glass.
2. A large proportion of drinking vessels in relation to the whole ceramic assemblage.
3. A large proportion of ceramic fabrics most commonly used for drinking vessels.
4. A large number of wine glasses.
5. A quantity of specialized glassware.
6. And a large number of clay pipes.

The recovered assemblage from the Talbot Hotel conforms to this analysis, and the exploration allows a fascinating insight into the life of the building in the late eighteenth and early nineteenth centuries. It can be deduced that the hotel guests were fed meat from the bone and oysters in their shells, washed down with good English ale and beer in Staffordshire pottery mugs. It appears that these superior utilitarian vessels quickly superseded the somewhat old-fashioned local pottery wares as soon as they had become widely distributed, and therefore readily available, throughout Britain.

After dining, the Talbot Hotel's host would probably have supplied the guests with a "smoke" of tobacco in pre-packed locally made clay pipes–pipes which at that time were disposable as the tobacco was much more expensive than the pipes themselves. The refreshments would then perhaps have concluded with "toddy" of wine or spirit before the guests departed.

Figure 56 Overall view of reconstructed vessels from the Talbot Hotel assemblage.

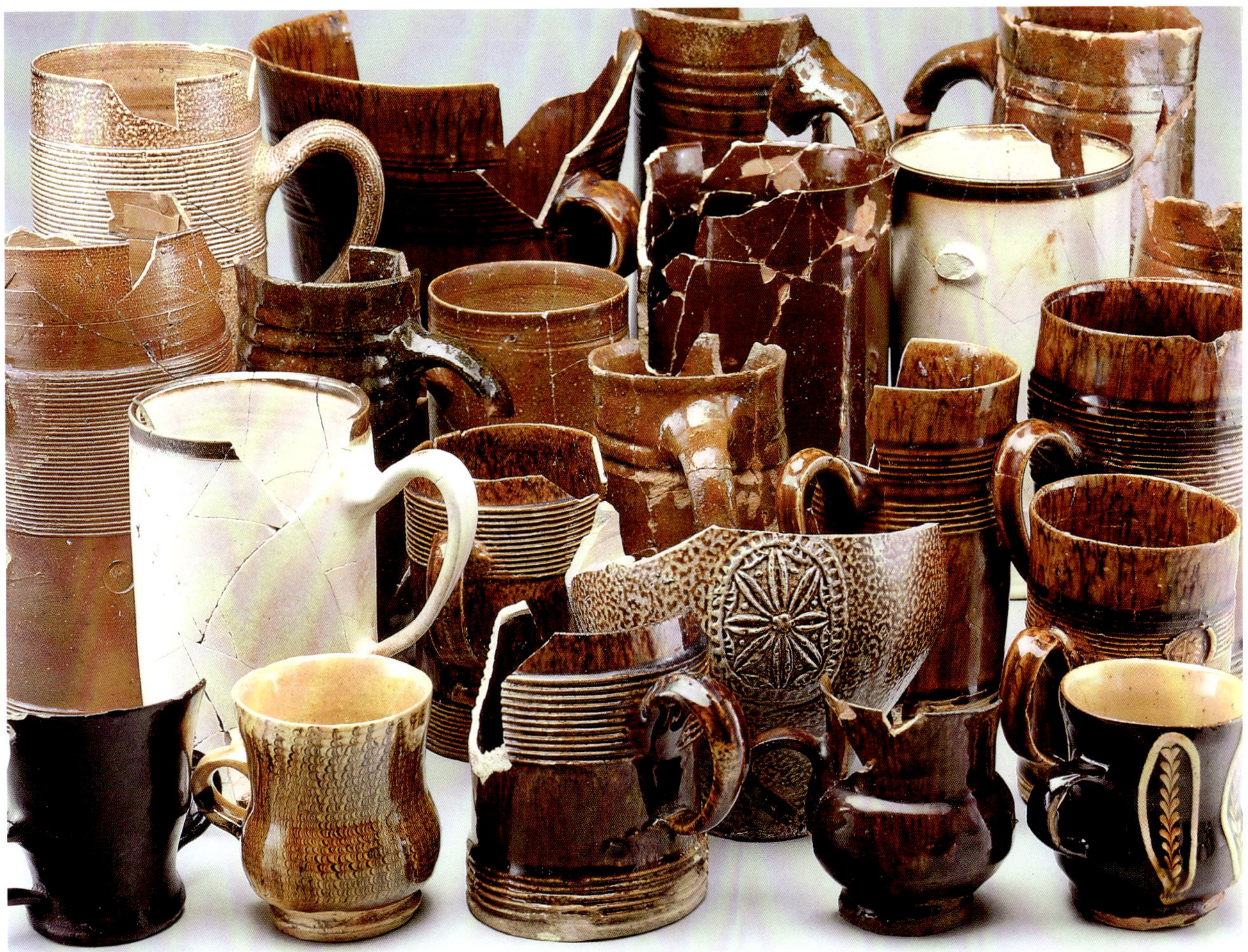

ACKNOWLEDGMENTS

I am grateful for the significant contributions from the following people: Garry Atkins, Kensington Church Street, London, for encouraging me to undertake this project, and for his enthusiasm throughout; David Barker, Senior Museums Officer, The Potteries Museum & Art Gallery Stoke-on-Trent; David Britton and Ashton Keynes of Wiltshire; Geoff Haines, The History of Tetbury Society, Gloucestershire; Mrs. J. V. Thorpe, Archivist & Record Agent, Gloucestershire Record Office; and Peter Wain and the fellow enthusiasts involved in the explorations of the Talbot Hotel cellars.

1. The hills of the Cotswolds are where the long-wooled "Cotswold" breed of sheep originated.

2. A Tudor doorway was revealed when a modern fireplace in the front room of the Talbot Hotel was knocked out in the 1980s.

3. Stroudwater refers to the area in and around the town of Stroud, Gloucestershire, where there was a booming woolen industry.

4. *Victoria History of Gloucestershire,* edited by Nicholas Herbert et al., vol. 11 (London: Oxford University Press for the University of London Institute of Historical Research, 1976).

5. Nigel Spry and Harold Wingham, "Talbot Hotel, Tetbury," *Glevensis, The Gloucester and District Archaeological Research Group Review,* no. 19 (1985): 28–30.

6. The full list of occupations is transcribed by Madge Paterson and Ernie Ward in *Ashton Keynes, A Village With No History* (Chirkbank, Shropshire: Keith Cowley, 1986), p. 120.

7. "Cistercian" ware is the term given to blackware vessels made in the late fifteenth and sixteenth centuries and commonly found near the sites of Cistercian monasteries in England.

8. Arnold R. Mountford, "The Marquis of Granby Hotel Site, Burslem, Stoke-on-Trent, Staffs.," *City of Stoke-on-Trent Museum Archaeological Society Report No. 7* (Stoke-on-Trent: City Museum and Art Gallery, 1975).

9. A similar, three-handled cup is in the Troy D. Chappell Collection. Troy D. Chapell, "An Adventure with Early English Pottery," in *Ceramics in America,* edited by Robert Hunter (Hanover, N.H.: University Press of New England for the Chipstone Foundation, 2001), p. 188, fig. 1, and fragments of similar cups have been found on early-seventeenth-century settlements in the Chesapeake region. A similar mug, commonly known as a "tyg," is illustrated by Ivor Noël Hume in *If These Pots Could Talk: Collecting 2,000 Years of British Household Pottery* (Hanover, N.H.: University Press of New England for the Chipstone Foundation, 2001), p. 129, fig. VI.16a.

10. Robert Plot, *The Natural History of the Countie of Stafford-shire* (Oxford, 1686), p. 123.

11. Arnold. R. Mountford and F. Celoria, "Some Examples of Sources in the History of 17th Century Ceramics," *Journal of Ceramic History,* no. 1 (Stafford, Eng.: George Street Press, 1968), p. 18.

12. F. S .C. Celoria and J. H. Kelly, "A Post-medieval Pottery Site with a Kiln Base Found off Albion Square, Hanley, Stoke-on-Trent," *City of Stoke-on-Trent Museum Archaeological Society Report No. 4* (Stoke-on-Trent: City Museum & Art Gallery, 1973). J. H. Kelly and S. J. Greaves, "The Excavation of a Kiln Base in Old Hall Street, Hanley, Stoke-on-Trent, Staffs," *City of Stoke-on-Trent Museum Archaeological Society Report No. 6* (Stoke-on-Trent: City Museum and Art Gallery, 1974). J. H. Kelly, "A Rescue Excavation on the Site of Swan Bank Methodist Church, Burslem, Stoke-on-Trent, Staffordshire, England," *City of Stoke-on-Trent Museum Archaeological Society Report No. 5* (Stoke-on-Trent: City Museum and Art Gallery, 1973).

13. Eileen Gooder, "The Finds from the Cellar of the Old Hall, Temple Balsall, Warwickshire," *Post-Medieval Archaeology,* vol. 18 (1986): 173–81. David Barker and Mary Holland, "Two Post-medieval Pit Groups from Stafford," *Staffordshire Archaeological Studies,* vol. 3 (1986): 110. Mary J. Kershaw, "An 18th Century Pit Group from Stafford," *Staffordshire Archaeological Studies,* vol. 4 (1987): 80.

14. A "WR" marked mug is illustrated by Gordon Elliott in *John and David Elers and their Contemporaries* (London: Jonathan Horne Publications, 1998), pl. 7A.

15. Arnold R. Mountford, *The Illustrated Guide to Staffordshire Salt-glazed Stoneware* (London: Barrie and Jenkins, 1971), pl. 55, right. Ivor Noël Hume, *If These Pots Could Talk,* p. 199, fig. IX.24.

16. Robert R. Hunter, Jr., "English Delft From Williamsburg's Archaeological Contexts" in John C. Austin, *British Delft in the Colonial Williamsburg Collection* (Williamsburg, Va.: Colonial Williamsburg Foundation and Jonathan Horne, 1994). Al Luckenbach, "Ceramics from the Edward Rummey/Stephen West Tavern, London Town, Maryland, Circa 1725," in *Ceramics in America,* edited by Robert Hunter (Hanover, N.H.: University Press of New England for the Chipstone Foundation, 2002).

17. See Kevin Fryer and Andrea Shelley, "Excavation of a Pit at 16 Tunsgate, Guildford, Surrey, 1991," *Post-Medieval Archaeology,* vol. 31 (1997): 139–230, and Jacqueline Pearce, "A Late 18th-Century Inn Clearance Assemblage from Uxbridge, Middlesex," *Post-Medieval Archaeology,* vol. 34 (2000): 144–86.

18. Kathleen Bragdon, "Occupational Differences Revealed in Artifact Assemblages," in *Documentary Archaeology in the New World,* edited by Mary C. Beandry (Cambridge: Cambridge University Press, 1988), pp. 83–91.

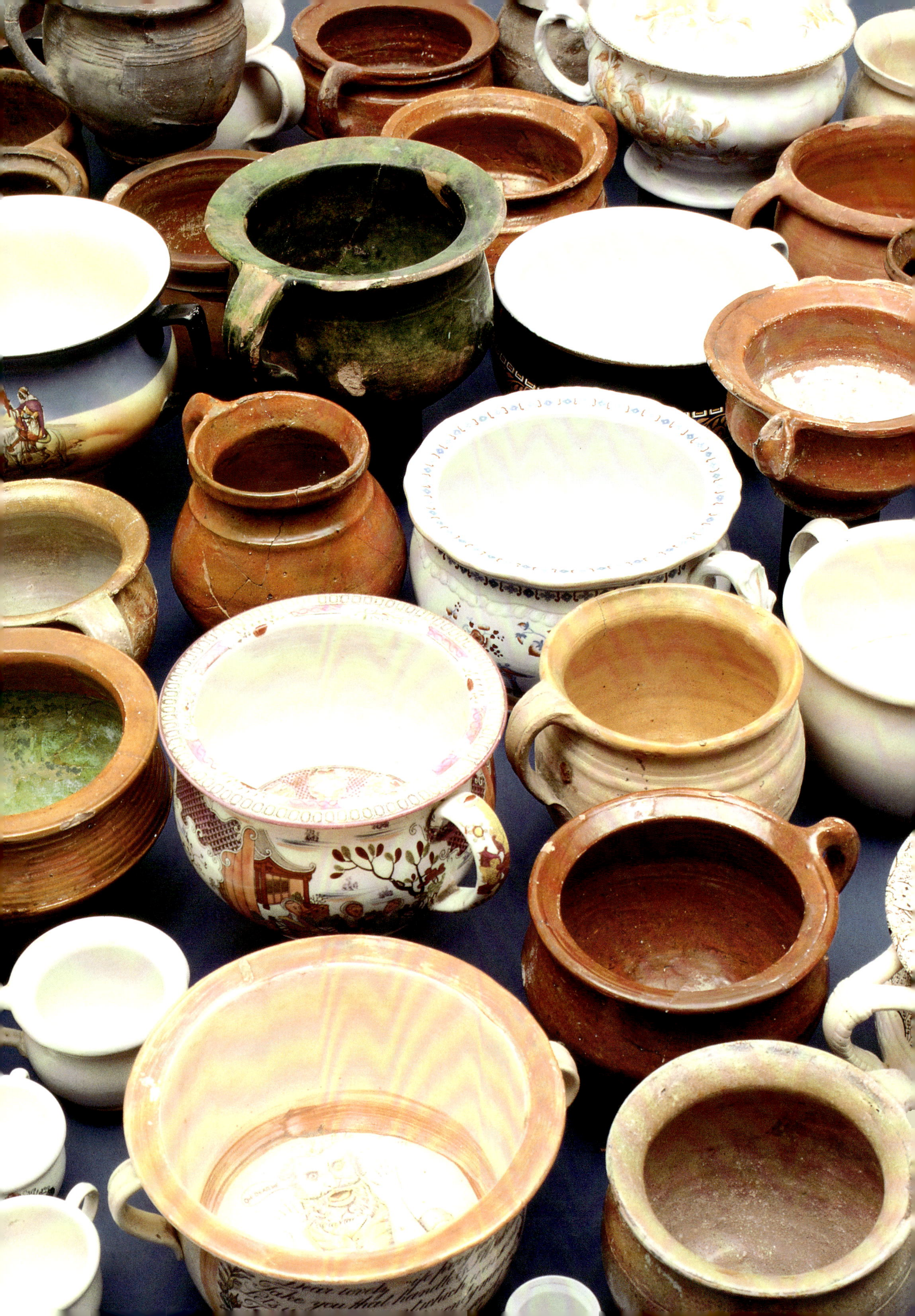

Ivor Noël Hume

Through the Lookinge Glasse: or, the Chamber Pot as a Mirror of Its Time

▼ MANY OF US WISH we had been born with names other than our own, and the mid-seventeenth-century English gentleman Mr. Chamberley may have been one of them. Armorial historian Randle Holme described his heraldic badge thusly:

> He beareth sable, a chamber pot, or a Bed pot Argent. This is by the Jolly crew when met togather ouer a cup of Ale; not for modesty sake, but that they may se their owne beastlynesse, in powering in, and casting out more than sufficeth nature, which if it went not suddenly downwards, would force its way vpwards, is called a Lookinge glasse; But there is nothing neuer so vsefull, but it may be abused, so is this when it is called by such persons a Rogue with one eare, and a pisse pot.[1]

We may safely assume that the history of the chamber pot goes back to the first time hygienists decided that urinating on the floor should be discouraged—at least in polite society.[2] It is equally safe to suppose that the earliest chamber pots were not made specifically for that purpose, but any earthenware pots that came to hand would suffice. When, therefore, were the first pots produced with that evacuatory function in mind?[3]

Limiting myself to English literary sources—which precede British genre paintings by three hundred years and are more accurately datable than are most pots dug from the ground—the earliest seem to date from the first decade of the fifteenth century and refer to chamber pots as "jordans," a term previously applied to glass flasks used by physicians to study the "humors" in urine (figs. 1, 2). I found the illustrated example in a circa 1500 context in London.[4] That pottery vessels were used in the same way is described in *Holinshed's Chronicles* (ca. 1577) wherein "A lewd fellow that took upon him to be skilfull in physicke . . . was set on horsebacke, with his face towards the tail . . . and so was led about the citie . . . with two jorden pots about his neck."[5]

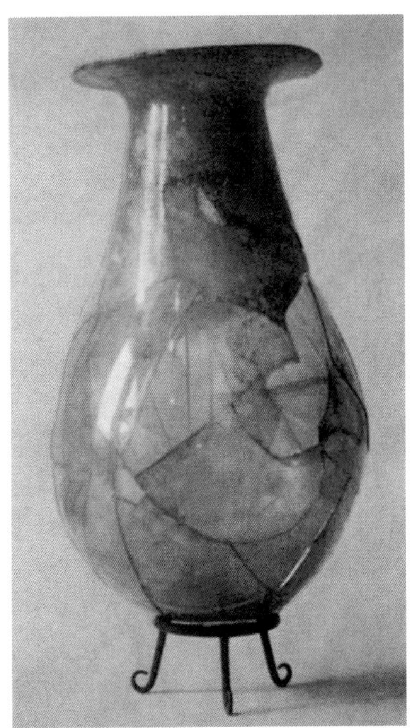

Figure 1 Urinal, English, ca. 1500. Glass. H. 9". (Courtesy, Museum of London.) The original "Lookinge Glasse": A green glass urinal from a Wealden glass house found in a London archaeological context.

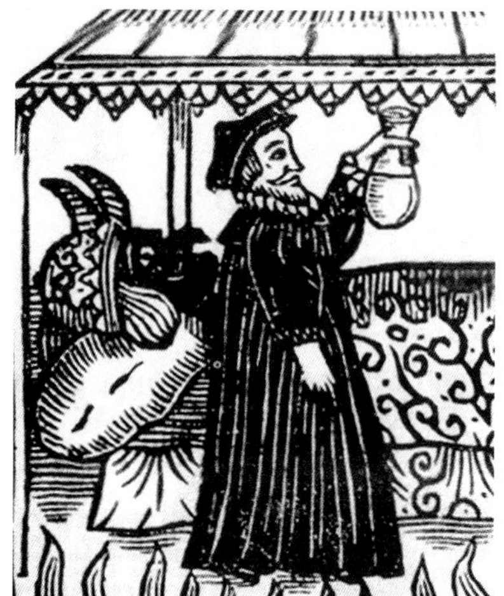

Figure 2 Detail of a woodcut print, 1641. A physician tests the water of Pluto, the Papist devil, in a glass urinal. (Ernst and Johanna Lehner, *Devils, Demons, and Witchcraft* [New York: Dover Publications, 1971], fig. 238.)

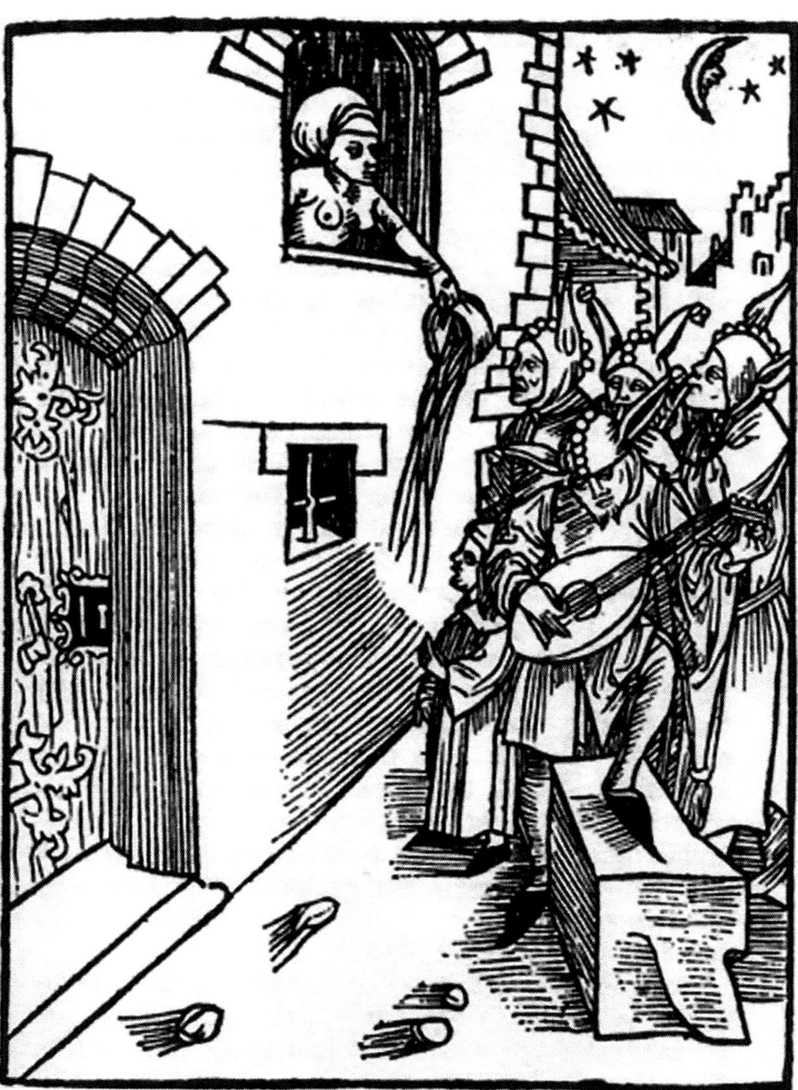

Figure 3 So much for carol singers! The source of this late medieval woodcut is not known, but if it has not been redrawn, it provides one of the earliest renditions of the conventionally shaped chamber pot. (Wallace Reyburn, *Flushed with Pride* [London: Pavilion Books, 1989], p. 49.)

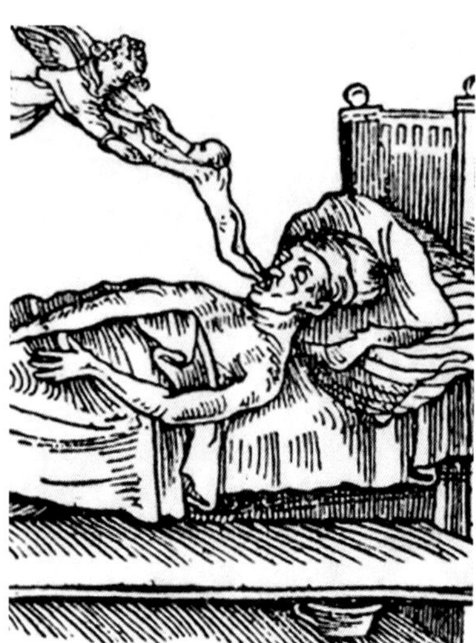

Figure 4 A shallow chamber pan beneath the bed of a dying man. Detail from *Mortilogus,* Augsburg, 1508. (Ernst and Johanna Lehner, *Devils, Demons, and Witchcraft* [New York: Dover Publications, 1971], fig. 182.)

Late medieval woodcuts and engravings sometimes demonstrated the use of the contents as a means of expression, and when others depicted people in bed (fig. 3), they usually provided some kind of pot beside or

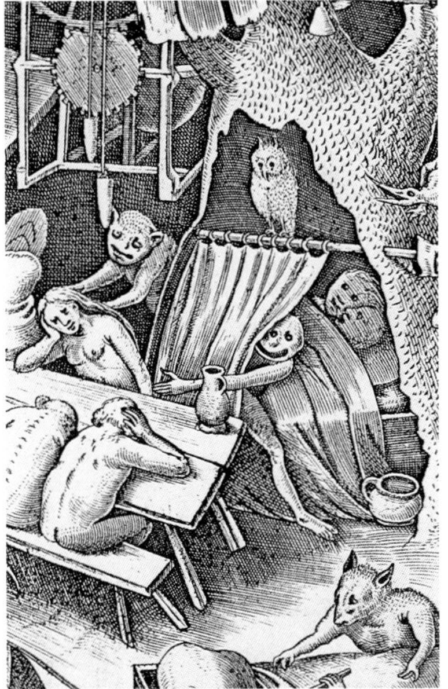

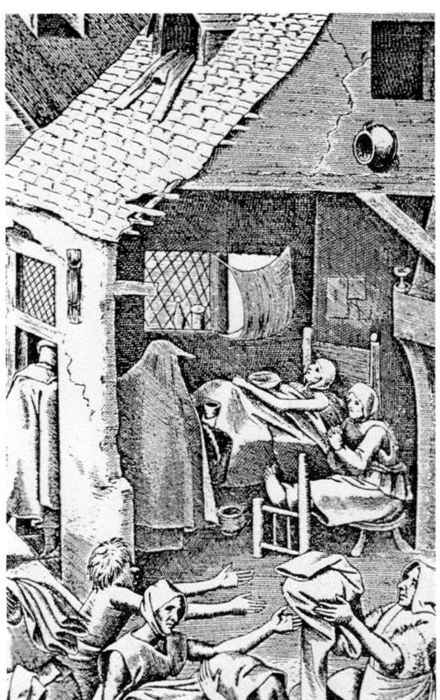

Figure 5 Detail from Peter Bruegel the Elder's *Sloth* in his series of the Seven Sins, 1557. The chamber pot beside the bed of the lazy sinners is a fully developed form with both rim-attached handle and defined foot. (H. Arthur Klein, *Graphic Worlds of Peter Bruegel the Elder* [New York: Dover Publications, 1971], p. 211.)

Figure 6 Detail from Peter Bruegel the Elder's *Charity,* 1559, depicting a carefully drawn and laterally ribbed chamber pot beside a sick bed. Another, whose shape resembles that in his *Sloth,* hangs at the attic level where it serves as a nesting place for insect-eating swallows. (H. Arthur Klein, *Graphic Worlds of Peter Bruegel the Elder* [New York: Dover Publications, 1971], p. 227.)

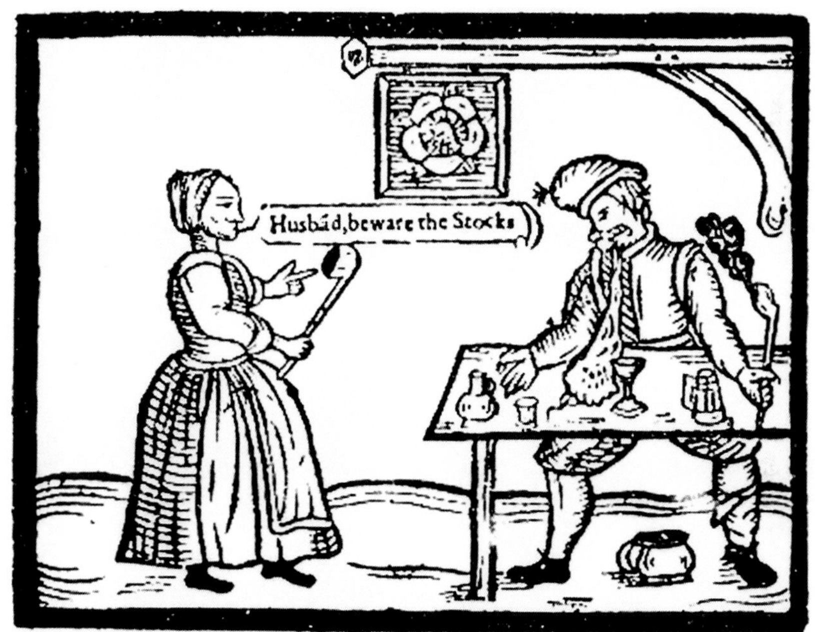

Figure 7 A woodcut illustration from a ca. 1625 English ballad titled "A Statute for Swearers and Drunkards" showing a chamber pot under the tavern table. (*A Pepysian Garland,* edited by Hyder E. Rollins [Cambridge, Mass.: Harvard University Press, 1971], p. 109.)

under it; but woodcuts being as crude as they were, there is not a lot to be learned from them other than that shallow, sometimes handleless pans were so used—which may justify the term "slops" being employed in that connection (fig. 4).[6] By the mid-sixteenth century, and with the availability of engravings copied from genre paintings by Peter Bruegel the Elder and others, we find that chamber pots of now-conventional shapes had become familiar household assets, as, indeed, they were in English taverns at the beginning of the seventeenth century (figs. 5–7). But whether they were of silver, pewter, or common clay is often hard to tell.[7]

The earliest ceramic examples in the Noël Hume Collection reportedly date from the late fifteenth to sixteenth centuries and were found at Bruges in modern Belgium. All three differ from those in contemporary illustrations by having their ear-like handles projecting from their bulbous girths rather than being attached to the rims as are those of most later pots.[8] Reportedly, the earliest of them was made in a hard, brownish, gray ware often described as Flemish proto-stoneware. The pot contains a yellowish sediment in which are imbedded drops of pale pink wax. More clings to the rim at one side and so is suggestive of pouring, and thereby raises doubts that these side-handled vessels were, indeed, chamber pots. The placement of the handle in the upper wall of the pots, rather than attached to the rim, causes the vessel to tip when held by it—a feature undesirable in a chamber pot but right for a milk dipper or skimmer (fig. 8).[9] Dutch collections do include vessels with side handles that are so identified, although in most instances they are of much later dates.[10]

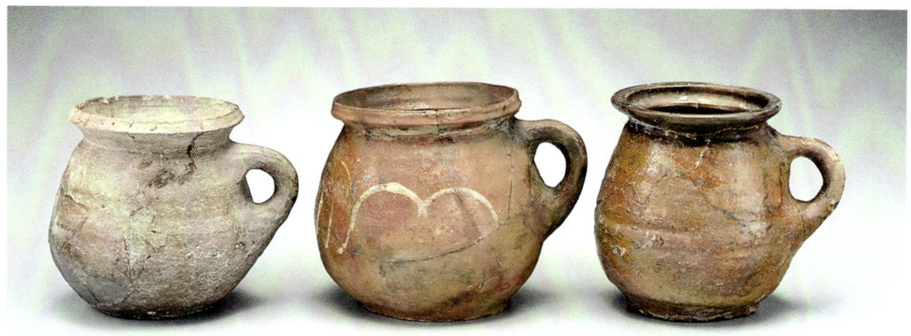

Figure 8 Side-handled dippers. Left: Bruge, early sixteenth century. Gray proto-stoneware. H. 6⅛". Center: Probably Bergen-op-Zoom, mid- to late sixteenth century. Lead-glazed earthenware with white-slip decoration. H. 6¼". Found in Bruge. Right: Bruge, sixteenth century. Lead-glazed earthenware. H. 6¼". (Noël Hume Collection; all photos by Gavin Ashworth unless otherwise noted.)

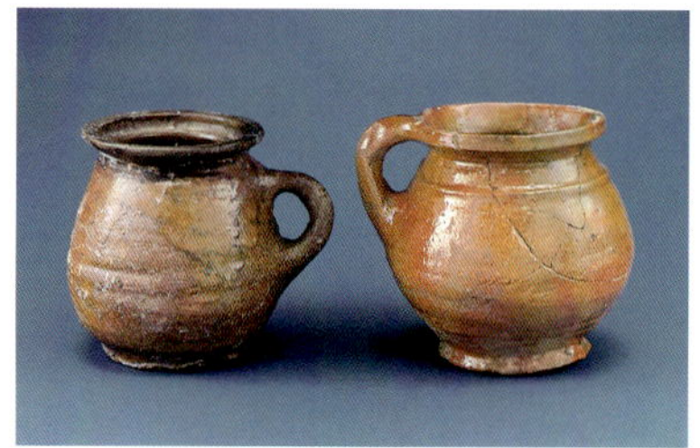

Figure 9 Side-handled dipper and chamber pot. Left: Bruge, sixteenth century. H. 6¼". Right: Rotterdam, sixteenth century. Lead-glazed earthenware. H. 6¾". (Noël Hume Collection.) Similar vessel but with the handle attached to the rim after the potter changed his mind. Note vestigial frilled foot characteristic of sixteenth- and seventeenth-century Dutch chamber pots.

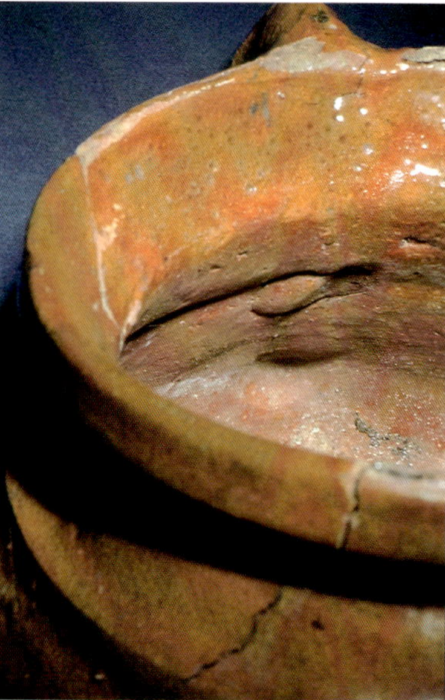

Figure 10 Detail of the pot illustrated on the right in fig. 9 showing plugged indentation where the dipper handle should have been anchored.

The two pots shown in figure 9 are very similar in profile, one having its handle at the shoulder and the other at the rim. Like the other dippers, that on the left exhibits interior indentations (or filled holes) corresponding with the handle's points of attachment. The pot on the right has similar indentations, but that at the top had been plugged with clay when the potter realized that he was applying a handle for a chamber pot rather than for a dipper (fig. 10). So what can this change of intent be telling us?

It implies that Dutch earthenware dippers and chamber pots were being made at approximately the same date. But the evidence of the proto-stoneware example (see fig. 8, left) may be telling us that bag-shaped dippers were in production earlier than were chamber pots. Does this mean that dippers were previously also used as chamber pots until someone discovered that the handle was in the wrong place? If that is true, then the two pots in figure 9 represent the first step in the evolution of the true chamber pot.

The third Bruges dipper differs from the others, being in a hard redware with only rudimentary external glazing, but ornamented with slip-applied swags (see fig. 8, center). This decorative style is attributed to the once-important Netherlandish potting center at Bergen-op-Zoom.[11] All three dippers are bag-shaped, flat bottomed, and lack feet. Indeed, the absence of defined bases on the Bruges pots sets them apart from most Netherlandish chamber pots of the sixteenth century which, even in the rudimentary treatment afforded such pots in Bruegel's paintings and engravings, possess recognizable basal definition.

The Noël Hume Collection's lead-glazed pots found in the Netherlands demonstrate the wide range of shapes used there in the sixteenth and seventeenth centuries (fig. 11). All have crinkled feet, but in every other respect

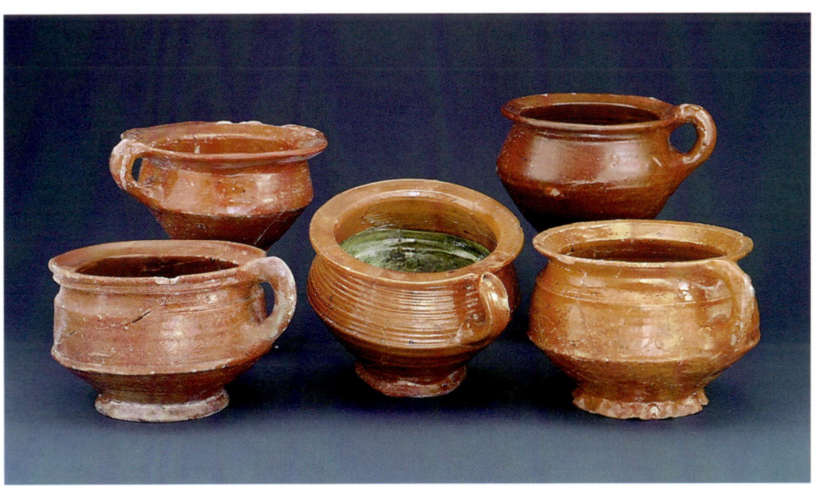

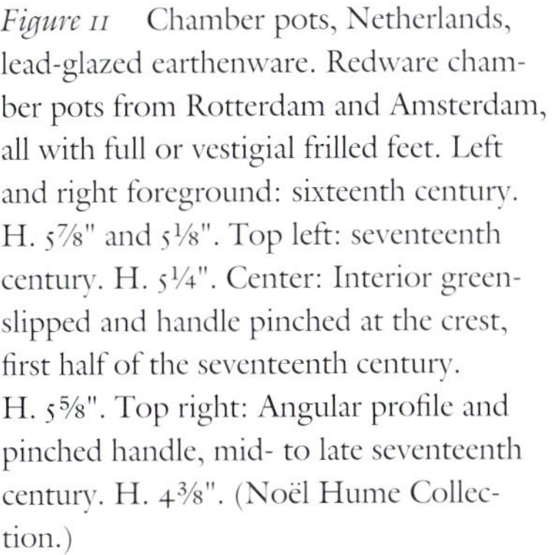

Figure 11 Chamber pots, Netherlands, lead-glazed earthenware. Redware chamber pots from Rotterdam and Amsterdam, all with full or vestigial frilled feet. Left and right foreground: sixteenth century. H. 5⅞" and 5⅛". Top left: seventeenth century. H. 5¼". Center: Interior green-slipped and handle pinched at the crest, first half of the seventeenth century. H. 5⅝". Top right: Angular profile and pinched handle, mid- to late seventeenth century. H. 4⅜". (Noël Hume Collection.)

they differ one from another.[12] Although close dating is not yet possible, it is fair to say that the examples in the left and right foreground belonged to the sixteenth century (the left earlier than the right), and that the green-glazed pot in the center was a product of the first half of the seventeenth century.[13] The flat-rimmed example behind it to the left in most respects appears to stem from the same period, but the flattened and beaded-edged rim would, in England, be consistent with a date as late as the early eighteenth century. The fifth pot (right rear) is of a shape that should date it to the second half of the seventeenth century.

E. M. Ch. F. Klijn's invaluable *Lead-glazed Earthenwares in The Netherlands,* cataloging the collection at the Open Air Museum at Arnhem, illustrates twenty-six chamber pots, five of them attributed to the period

1575–1625, all different, and all from disparate locations.[14] Three questions immediately present themselves: Do the shape variations represent regional differences? How reliable are the dates and what is the documentation for them?

In the study of sixteenth-century earthenwares, we are hampered by the dearth of tightly datable archaeological contexts, and also by the fact that when broken into small pieces, chamber pots can be difficult to identify. Rims that are internally concave or dished (as is one of the Bruges examples) can be mistaken for pipkins which were usually made to receive a lid, were it of earthenware, wood, or even copper alloy.

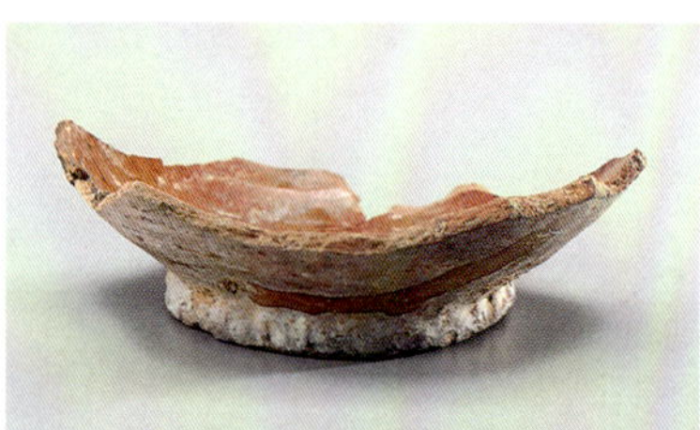

Figure 12 Probable redware chamber pot fragment, Southwark, London, sixteenth century. D. 6½". (Ex-collection Sir David Burnett.) Note the Dutch-style frilled foot.

Very little information is available to identify English chamber pots of the early Tudor era, but a base with a crinkled foot-ring found in the London suburb of Southwark might be from such a pot—but then again it might not (fig. 12).[15] A large, single-handled bowl found in Norwich has a similarly contoured foot, and although having but one handle, it is identified as a Dutch cauldron.[16] However, none of the twenty-seven cauldrons illustrated in E. M. Ch. F. Klijn's previously cited book has single handles, nor crinkled feet.

In writing about the Dutch-type wares found in Norwich, archaeologist Sarah Jennings encapsulated the identification problem when she wrote:

> Local potteries copied extensively the limited range of forms imported into Norwich, and produced vessels indistinguishable from their Dutch counter-parts. They all have some of the distinctive characteristics of the Low Countries products, such as pinched handles, a tripod base, pinched feet, a ring-base or a collar rim.[17]

There can be no denying that the origins of the cited features are Dutch. An example in the Noël Hume Collection excavated in Amsterdam has a pronouncedly crinkled foot and is thought to date from the mid-sixteenth century. The Museum of London's post-medieval ceramics expert, Jacqueline Pearce, is of the opinion that the Southwark fragment is Dutch—which leaves one wondering why an object so easily replicated in England would have been imported.[18]

In spite of the fact that many more archaeological reports providing drawings and descriptions of medieval and later earthenwares have been published in England than abroad, much of the tightest dating for early seventeenth-century wares comes from American excavations on British colonial sites.[19] This is certainly true of chamber pots whose manufacture in Virginia's Martin's Hundred between circa 1620 and 1645 provided a well-dated and documented range and provenance for locally made examples (fig. 13).

We know the name of the potter. He was Thomas Ward whose letters to Nicholas Ferrar in England make it clear that he was resident in the colony as early as 1623.[20] Archaeological evidence leaves no doubt that a potter was at work in Martin's Hundred's Wolstenholme Towne before the Indian massacre of March 22, 1622. It is reasonable to conclude, therefore, that Ward was potting in the Hundred both before and after the attack. As the Wolstenholme township was not established until 1620, we

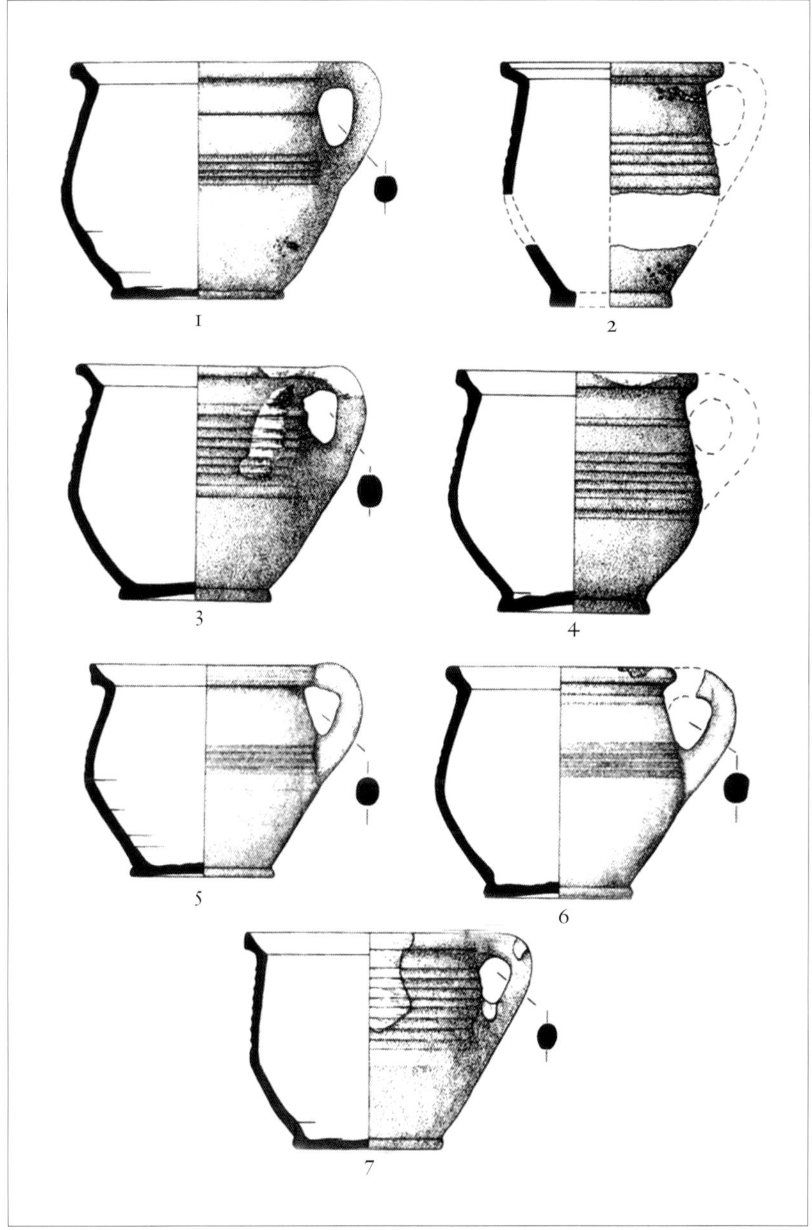

Figure 13 Redware chamber pot profiles from the Thomas Ward kilns at Martin's Hundred, Virginia. (Courtesy, Colonial Williamsburg Foundation.) 1 from the fort well; 2–4 from the potter's pond, all before 1622; 5–6 from the Ward site, ca. 1623–1635; and 7 from the Harwood plantation site but likely to be pre-massacre.

have a *terminus post quem* for chamber pot production there. All that was needed to tie the Thomas Ward chamber-pot package together was to find the same post-massacre type pots on his home site as those discovered in his pre-massacre waster pit in Wolstenholme Towne. But as the drawings show, they were not exactly the same, those made prior to March, 1622, being more heavily grooved that those made after it.

It is tempting in this age of amateur psychoanalysis to read something significant into the change from seven and eight lateral grooves to a modest four. One might see in the former a conscious adherence to Dutch traditions or a desire to replicate the standards of the Old Country in the wilderness of Virginia. But after the massacre, with the chamber pot buying population drastically reduced, and morale low, potter Ward may no longer have had his heart in his work. Ludicrous as reading tea-leaves in a

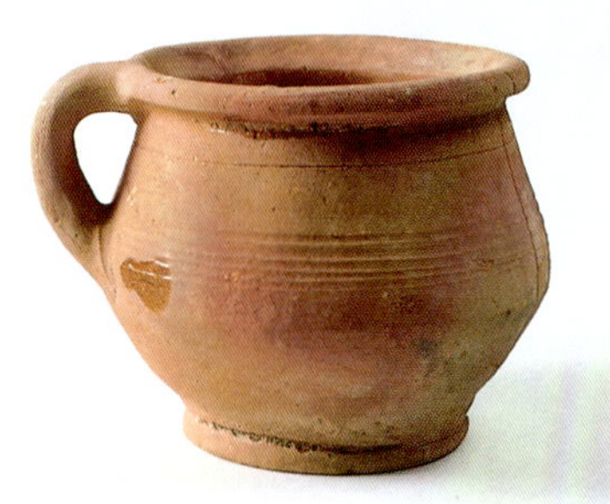

Figure 14 Chamber pot, Virginia, ca. 1620–1622. Unglazed earthenware. H. 6¼". (Courtesy, Department of Archaeological Research, Colonial Williamsburg Foundation.) Unglazed redware chamber pot from the fort well at Wolstenholme Towne in Martin's Hundred, Virginia. See fig. 13, no. 1.

chamber pot may sound, it does seem to be true that pottery-making in Virginia went through a period in the mid-seventeenth century when customers were less demanding, and utility was more important than style.

Lateral ribbing or grooving aside, there is a generic similarity among the Ward products even though rim treatments vary from one to another. It is archaeologically significant that a close parallel to an example from the premassacre "Potter's Pond" was found on the nearby plantation of Martin's Hundred's governor, William Harwood, who is believed to have moved there immediately after the attack on Wolstenholme Towne—presumably taking his chamber pot with him. Less easily explained, however, is the presence of another locally made chamber pot in the well shaft of the fort immediately adjacent to the house Harwood is thought to have occupied before the attack (fig. 14). This pot is larger, the body harder, and unlike the others, unglazed internally, and one questions whether or not it is Ward's work. But if not, then whose? The answer may be that the pot came from Jamestown and was made there between circa 1620 and 1622.[21]

The Thomas Ward chamber-pot series makes it clear that the shapes (though not the ware) coincide with those made in the Surrey-Hampshire kilns and frequently unearthed in London, making everted, squared, and internally dished rims the primary diagnostic factor.[22] A redware example from Southwark that may be dated to the mid-seventeenth century retains the earlier rim features as well as the upper-body cordoning (fig. 15).[23] Key questions, therefore, are when and why did rims change to being flat and wide?

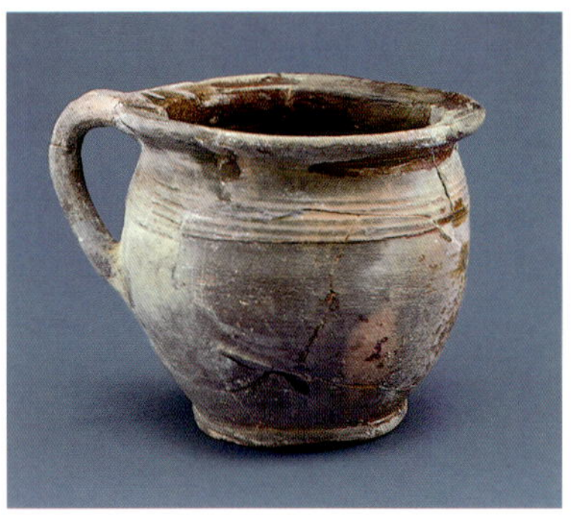

Figure 15 Chamber pot, London, mid- to late seventeenth century. Earthenware. H. 6⅛". (Ex-collection Sir David Burnett.) Typical London redware chamber pot with internal lead glaze and external ornamental lateral grooves similar to those on pots from Martin's Hundred. The well-made handle is vertically channeled and squeezed at the crest, perhaps in the Dutch manner. Found in Southwark.

A clue comes from the Harwood plantation site where an incomplete Rhenish brown stoneware chamber pot was discovered in the post-1625 filling of a cellar (fig. 16). Unique among early colonial-era ceramics, this pot's rim is essentially flat, albeit slightly up-turned. Although plain gray-brown stoneware chamber pots, probably from Frechen kilns, were common in the Netherlands and Germany, there seems to be no firm dating for them prior to 1600. Less angular than the Martin's Hundred example, but otherwise very similar, are two examples in the Noël Hume Collection said to have been found in Amsterdam and attributed by the sellers to the second half of the seventeenth century—but are probably somewhat earlier

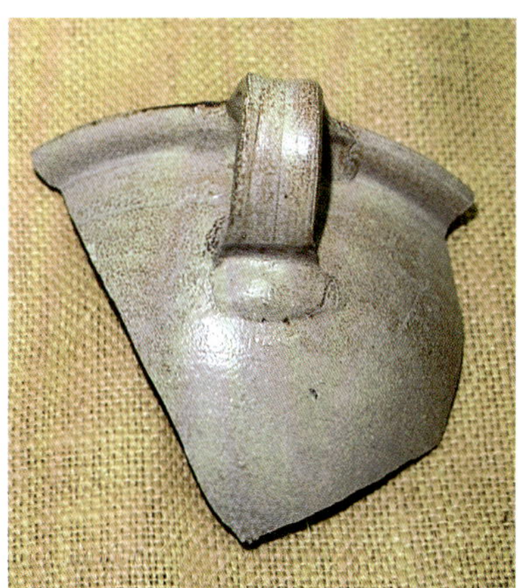

Figure 16 Chamber pot from the Harwood Plantation site at Martin's Hundred, Virginia. (Department of Archaeological Research, Colonial Williamsburg Foundation.) Rim and wall fragment from a Rhenish gray-to-brown stoneware chamber pot, the first of its kind found in America. Recovered from an abandoned storehouse cellar, ca. 1625–1640.

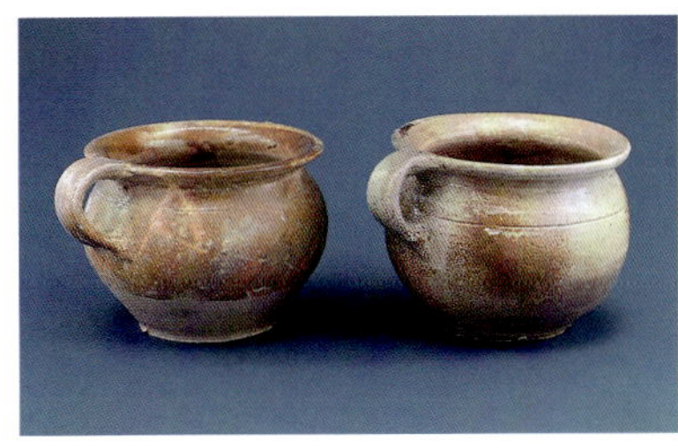

Figure 17 Chamber pots, Germany. Stoneware. H. 5" and 5¼". (Noël Hume Collection.) Excavated in Holland. Left: a close parallel for the Martin's Hundred fragment, ca. 1625–1640. Right: Somewhat taller and more bulbous, and perhaps dating later in the seventeenth century.

(fig. 17).[24] A little known painting depicting another of David Teniers' tavern scenes includes what appears to be a gray-brown stoneware chamber pot in the right foreground. The painting is undated but is comparable to others of the 1640s.[25]

Creating an evolutionary rim-typology would be greatly simplified if it could be established that Rhenish stoneware potters set the fashion for flat rims that would endure through the rest of time. But they didn't.

The beginning of the blue-on-gray stoneware industry in the Westerwald district of the Rhineland heralded the arrival of the heavy duty chamber pot decorated with applied medallions. The earliest often include a 1632 date, at which time the rims were upwardly flaring and internally dished (fig. 18). It was by no means a novel profile, the style being paralleled by

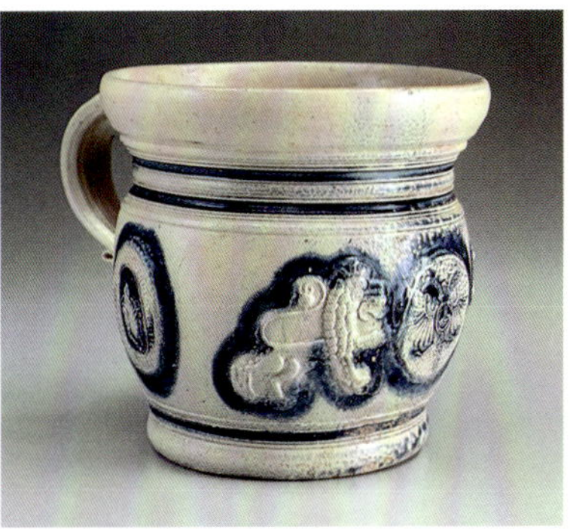

Figure 18 Chamber pot, Westerwald, 1632. Salt-glazed stoneware. H. 6⅛". (Noël Hume Collection.) A gray and blue stoneware chamber pot with everted and internally dished rim, its wall decorated with sprig-applied crowned lions flanking a central double-eagle badge, and oval side medallions featuring a waist length male figure surrounded by a partially legible inscription and the date 1632. Found in Amsterdam.

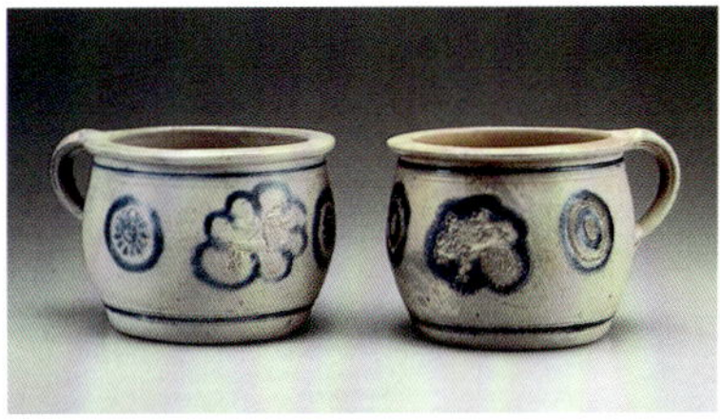

Figure 19 Chamber pots, Westerwald, 1710–1780. Salt-glazed stoneware. H. 5⅜". (Noël Hume Collection; ex-collection Frank Thomas.) Typical of those in the export trade from ca. 1710 to 1780. Left: decorated with sprigged lions and impressed rosettes; Right, less commonly, applied oval medallions with hatched centers. Believed to have been found together, probably in London.

the pewter chamber pot from the 1545 wreck of the *Mary Rose*.[26] Other Rhenish stonewares of the same type bear dates running as late as the 1670s, and it was not until around 1700 that rims were square-cut and flattened. The latter pots, wider than they were tall, became a major Rhenish export through much of the eighteenth century. They are found on most American British colonial sites from modest town houses to great plantations and came with two styles of decoration, namely sprigged lions flanking impressed rosettes or applied, hatched-filled, oval wreathed medallions (fig. 19). There seems to be no dating difference between the two, and the history of the pair in the Noël Hume Collection suggests that they have remained together ever since they were found.[27] Evidence of the Westerwald pots' eighteenth-century mass production is provided by vertical chatter derived from the use of hand-held or post-supported templates—a feature not found on the pots' seventeenth-century predecessors.[28]

Although Rhineland and Dutch ceramic shapes had a considerable influence on English potting in the sixteenth and seventeenth centuries, the English chamber pot—at least in the southeast—developed on different lines exemplified by those from buffware kilns along the Surrey-Hampshire border. In essence, these "border ware" chamber pot bodies were shaped like ribbed pipkins without feet and with strap handles substituting for the kitchen ware's hollow tubes (fig. 20). Those fall into two, very loose groups, early and late, characterized by rims that began upturned and everted and became more square-cut as the seventeenth century progressed.

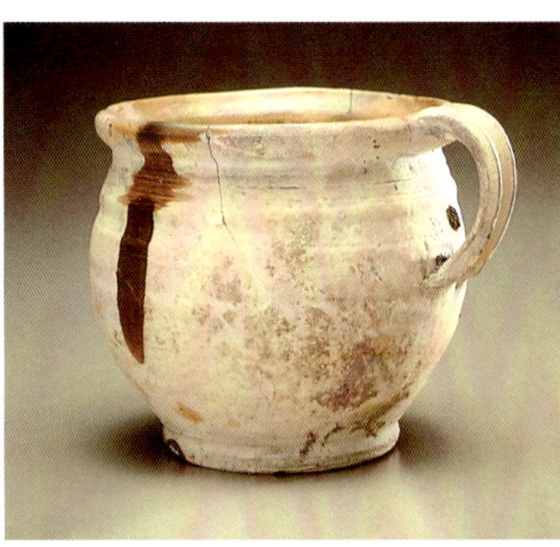

Figure 20 Chamber pot, England, 1600–1650. Earthenware. H. 6⅛". (Noël Hume Collection.) Border ware chamber pot of off-white color, coated internally with a clear lead glaze in contrast to the brown run marring the exterior.

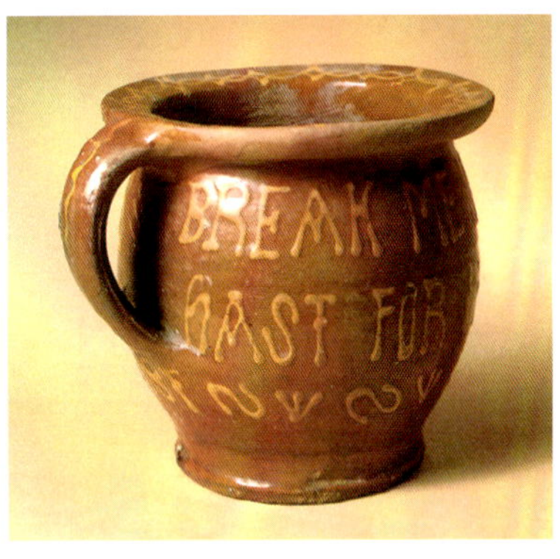

Figure 21 Chamber pot, Essex, England, 1650–1665. Slipware. D. 7". (Photo courtesy Jonathan Horne.) The slip inscription on this "Metropolitan" type chamber pot reads: BREAK ME NOT I PRAY IN YOUER HAST FOR I TO NON WILL GIVE DESTAST. A parallel example in the Museum of London is dated 1651.

Along with border ware chamber pots and some London area redwares, the city's mid- to late-seventeenth-century citizens could buy redware chamber pots elaborately decorated with white slip and inscribed with patriotic and other exhortatory slogans.[29] These were made in the county of Essex near the modern town of Harlow, and because they have been found primarily in London, they are erroneously known as Metropolitan slipware (fig. 21). The earliest dated example is inscribed BREAK ME NOT I PRAY IN YOUER HAST FOR I TO NON WILL GIVE DESTAST 1651.[30] Another's inscription was more to the point, reading BE MERY AND WIS AND PEFF![31] Admonitions of this kind, albeit better spelled, were to continue well through the nineteenth century.

Shifting now from London to the West of England, excavations at Donyatt in Somersetshire have yielded flat-rimmed chamber pots in contexts of the first half of the seventeenth century, their body shapes resembling those from border ware kilns and from the Thomas Ward operation in Virginia. Although numerous examples have been recovered from Donyatt kiln sites, there is no evolutionary consistency among their rim

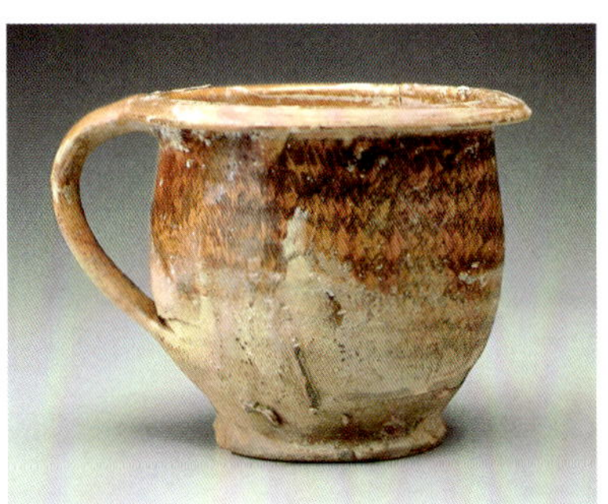

Figure 22 Chamber pot, Donyatt ware, 1680–1700. Earthenware. H. 6¾". (Chipstone Foundation.) The lead-glazed combed slip over a buff body is in a style more characteristic of Staffordshire. The pot was retrieved from a kiln site and is considered to be a waster.

forms, some being merely thickened and everted while others are flat and beaded (fig. 22).[32] From this, one might deduce that rim forms were no more than the potter's choice and were unrelated to seated comfort.[33] Although the majority of chamber pots from Donyatt kilns were taller than they were wide and continued so into the second half of the eighteenth century, there is archaeological evidence that those with sgraffito decoration date from the first half of the seventeenth century, and that others with white slip decoration under an amber lead glaze predominated from the late seventeenth through the first half of the eighteenth century and perhaps beyond.[34]

The earliest dated example of a flat-rimmed, West of England chamber pot was made, not at Donyatt, but in the Barnstaple/Bideford area to the west in Devonshire. This is in the double-fired, white-slipped and sgraffito-decorated, pink-bodied ware characteristic of that area. Found at Jamestown, Virginia, it unfortunately retains only half its date, to wit: 16— (fig. 23). The digits are preceded by the initials WB, and ceramic scholar

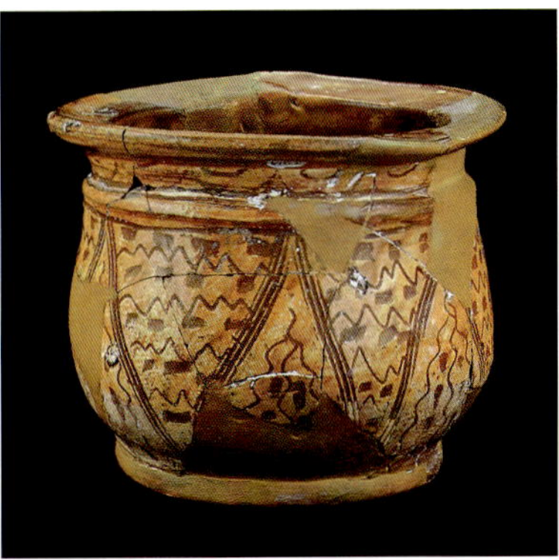

Figure 23 Chamber pot, North Devon, ca. 1670–1680. Sgraffito slipware. H. 5½". (National Park Service, Colonial National Historical Park, COLO J 7369.) The rim is inscribed under the glaze with the initials WB and 16, the rest of the date missing. Probably from a Bideford kiln.

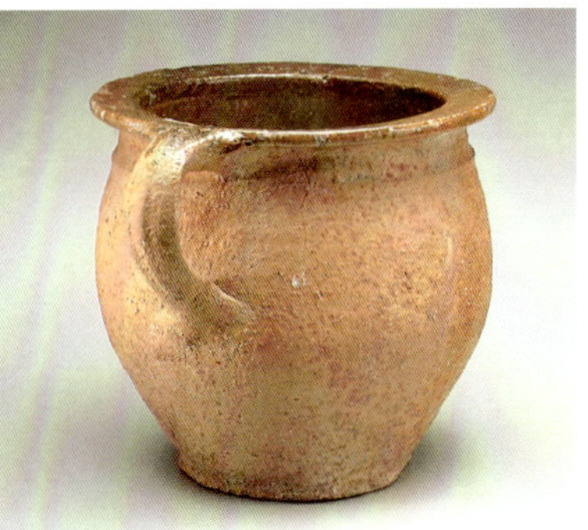

Figure 24 Chamber pot, North Devon, 1660–1700. Lead-glazed earthenware. H. 7¾". (Chipstone Foundation.) This pot's gravel-tempered body is internally lead glazed in mottled green and brown. A product of a Barnstaple or adjacent Fremington kiln.

Merry Abbitt Outlaw has suggested that they may be those of Virginia governor Sir William Berkeley.[35] Also attributable to the Barnstaple area is another flat-rimmed pot with an internal greenish, lead-glaze over a rough-surfaced, gravel-tempered body—a ware exported in large quantities to the American colonies over a long period from about 1620 to the 1750s (fig. 24).

Jamestown's sgraffito-decorated pot retains the basic taller-than-wide proportions common in England throughout the seventeenth century, but Dutch paintings indicate that the reverse was gaining popularity there half

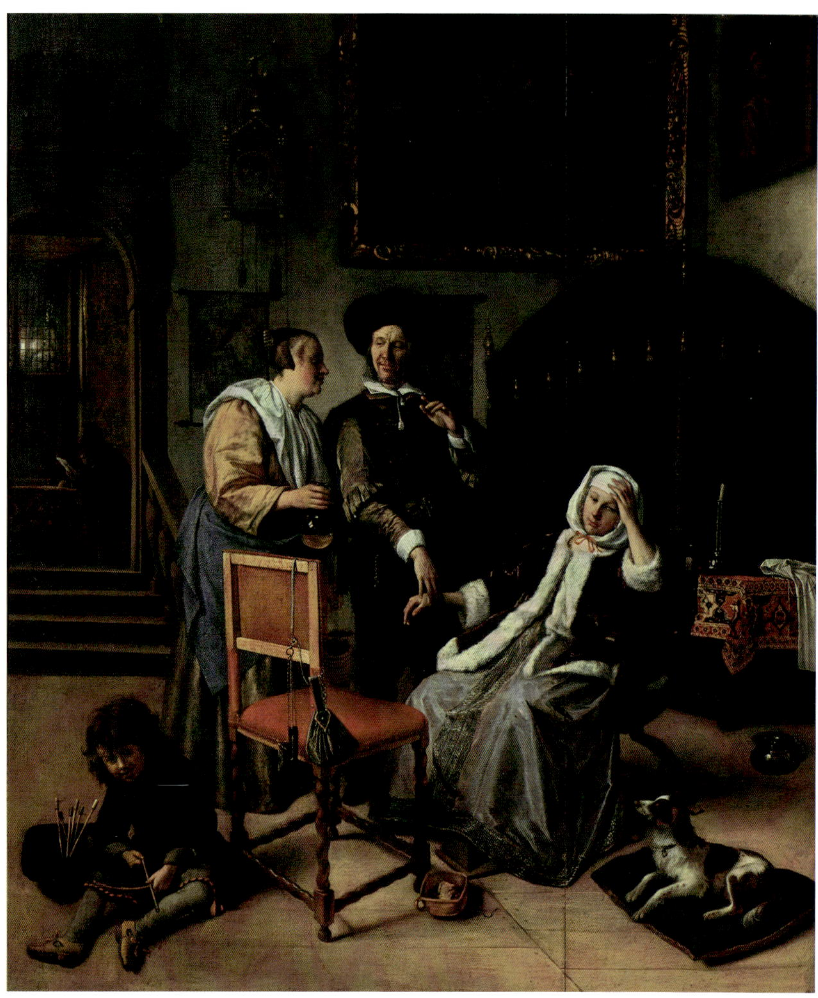

Figure 25 Jan Steen, *The Physician's Visit*, ca. 1655. Oil on panel. (Collection of the Wellington Museum [WM 1525–1948], Victoria and Albert Picture Library, London.) This painting shows a silver or pewter chamber pot, ca. 1655, beside the bed and a glass urinal in the hand of the nurse.

a century earlier. Thus, for example, a chamber pot of those proportions in pewter or silver is to be seen in Jan Steen's *The Physician's Visit* circa 1655, while David Teniers' 1644 painting known as *The Smokers* includes a green-glazed pot with a squat profile and an everted and internally dished rim capable of seating a lid (figs. 25–27).[36] Although there are no comparable English paintings of that period, archaeological evidence leaves no doubt that buff-bodied, green-glazed pots of similar proportions were in use before 1700 (fig. 28). Jacqueline Pearce, in her seminal report on border wares, illustrates two examples, one squatter and earlier than the other, suggesting a comparable shape evolution to be seen among London delftwares.[37] Such pots from the southeast of England are attributed to border ware kilns as are others that came red-bodied and with tortoiseshell lead glazes. Both buff- and red-bodied examples of the early eighteenth century invariably had flat rims, usually with beaded outer edges.

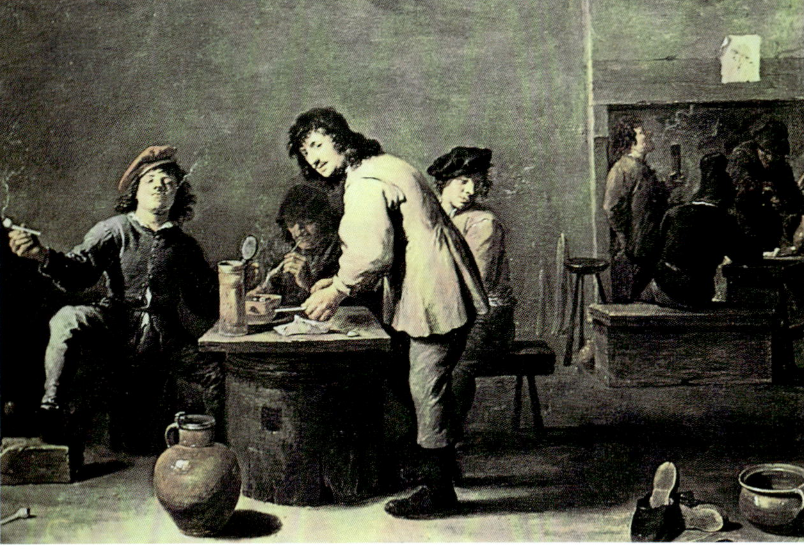

Figure 26 David Teniers, Jr., *The Smokers.* (Photograph and attribution provided by author.) A green-glazed chamber pot is in the right foreground. Although attributable to the mid-seventeenth century, its shape is similar to those in use in southeast England at the beginning of the eighteenth century.

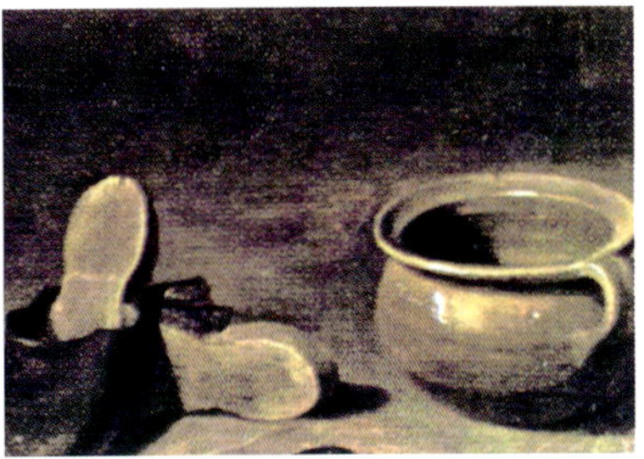

Figure 27 Detail of the painting illustrated in fig. 26 showing chamber pot.

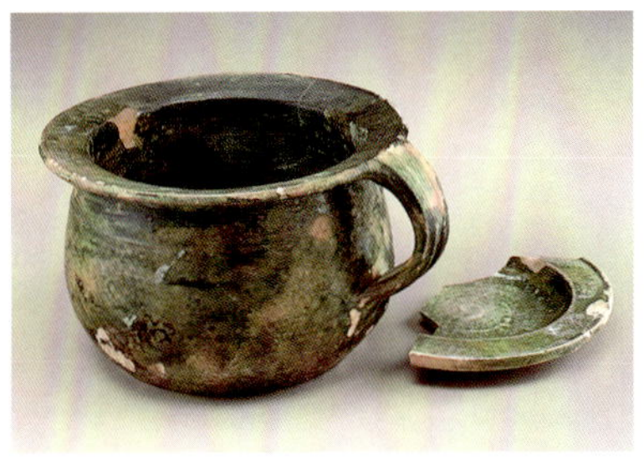

Figure 28 Chamber pot and plate fragment, England, ca. 1700–1720. Earthenware. H. 5½". (Noël Hume Collection; ex-collection Sir David Burnett.) This green-glazed, buff-bodied chamber pot was common in London in the early eighteenth century, characterized by a flat, beaded-edged rim. Shown with it, a small plate of the same ware and rim characteristic; found in Southwark.

Based on all that we know of coarse earthenware chamber pots in the eighteenth century—which is not much—it appears that production declined in proportion to the increasing availability of better quality pots in delftware, white salt-glazed stoneware, creamware, pearlware, and even Chinese porcelain. If there is an evolutionary trend in the coarse wares, it was away from the wide and flat rims of the early eighteenth century toward a narrower and squared form intended primarily to reinforce the upper wall (fig. 29). This would give way later in the century to rims that were outwardly rolled or simply folded. However, as figure 30 demonstrates, a single construction site in Southwark could yield a wide range of

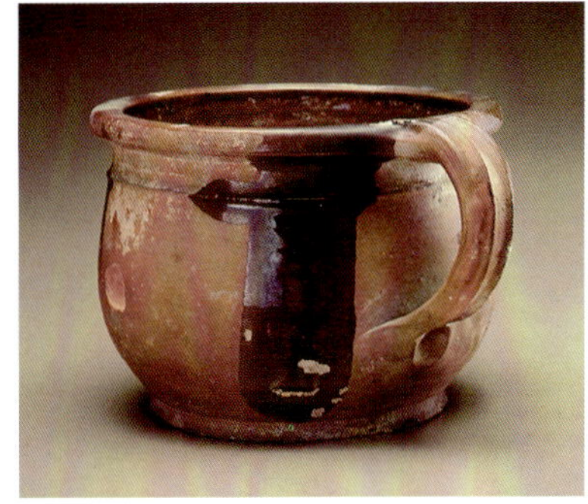

Figure 29 Chamber pot, London, ca. 1750. Earthenware. H. 5½". (Noël Hume Collection.) Probably made in or near London in the mid-eighteenth century, this lead-glazed, redware chamber pot is characterized by a narrow and square cut rim.

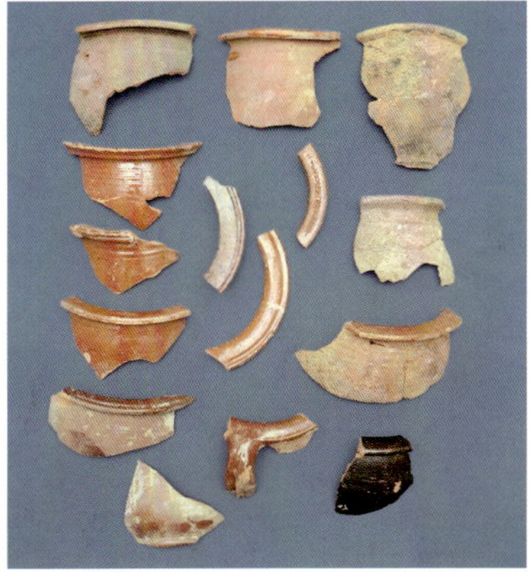

Figure 30 Examples of redware chamber pot rims of the seventeenth and eighteenth centuries, all from a single Southwark construction site. The example at bottom left had been used as a paint pot. (Ex-collection Sir David Burnett.)

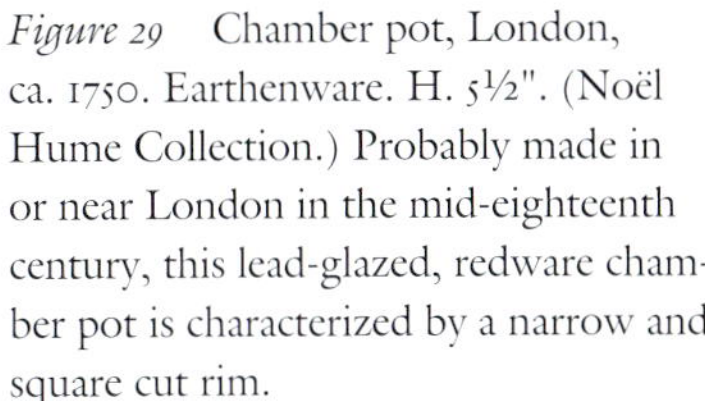

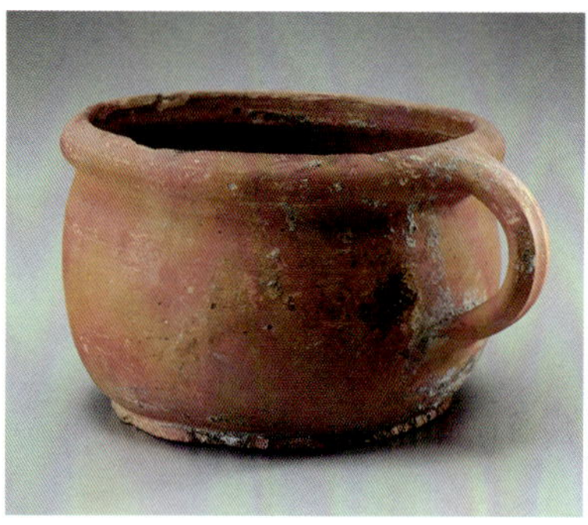

Figure 31 Chamber pot, London, 1820–1860. Earthenware. H. 5⅛". (Noël Hume Collection.) Redware chamber pot internally lead glazed and characterized by a folded and rounded rim. These thick and stolid pots were often made for or used by commercial painters. This example retains traces of both white and green paint.

date-defying rim forms representing the work of different but contemporary potters, separate factories, or entirely different dates.[38] But by no means all later examples were intended as chamber pots, some being sold directly to paint suppliers (colourmen) and used as convenient pots for painters of houses, carriages, and the like (fig. 31). A contemporary portrait of artist William Hogarth shows him at work with one such pot in the foreground, while he, himself, depicted another in his *Strolling Actresses Dressing in a Barn* of 1738—which is very early for a chamber pot form that persisted well through the following century (figs. 32, 33).[39]

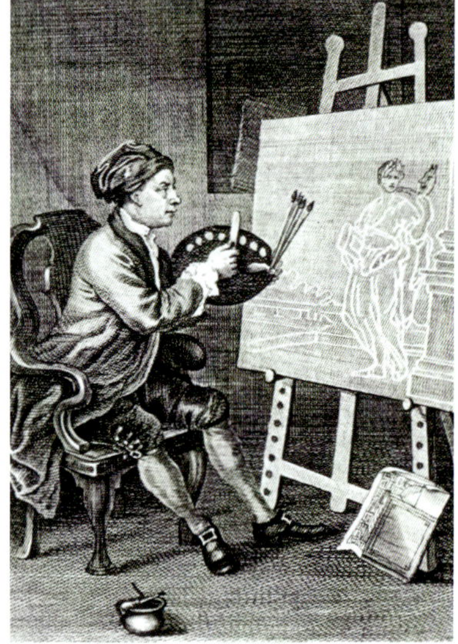

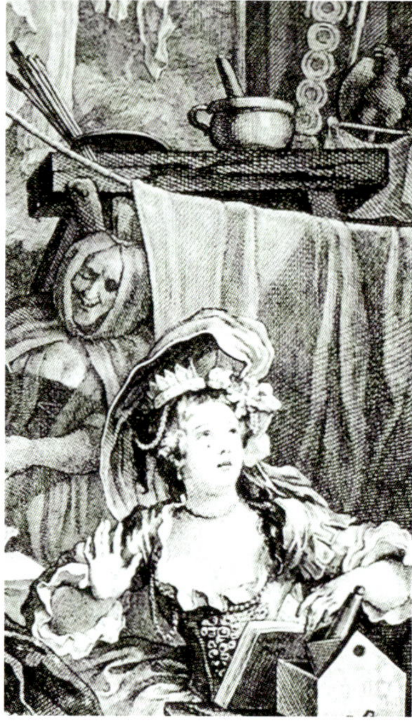

Figure 32 *William Hogarth*, self-portrait, London, 1764. Engraving. (Private collection.) The artist is shown with a paint or oil container of small chamber-pot shape beside him.

Figure 33 Detail of William Hogarth's engraving, *Strolling Actresses Dressing in a Barn*, London, 1738. (Private collection.) This image includes a scene-painter's chamber pot with a pestle (?) resting therein and a pallet and brushes beside it.

A pot of the folded rim variety has been found in a Bermuda harbor, and although it has no more precise context, there is reason to suggest that it may be French and datable to the second half of the eighteenth century (fig. 34).[40] The ware is pink, heavily flecked with red ochre, and the interior lead glaze varies from yellow to a dirty green. The pot's principal characteristic, however, is its outwardly folded and rolled rim.[41] The handle was missing, but the remaining points of contact indicate that it was disproportionately weak. Indeed, the pot's presence in the harbor may have been

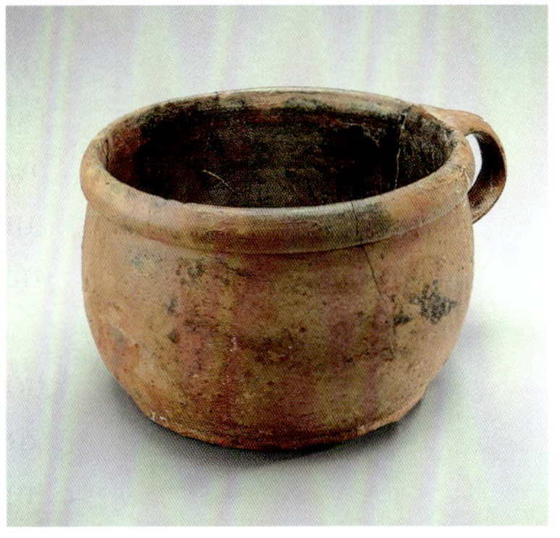

Figure 34 Chamber pot, probably France, late eighteenth century. Earthenware. H. 5¼". (Noël Hume Collection.) This redware pot has a thin internal lead glaze that is dirty green in color. The rim is slightly everted and folded into a weak oval profile. The missing handle (now restored) had been poorly attached and probably broke away when the pot was being emptied from a ship into the harbor at Hamilton, Bermuda.

Figure 35 Chamber pot fragment, London, 1650–1675. Tin-glazed earthenware. H. 4". (Ex-collection Sir David Burnett.) Delftware chamber pot of the earliest shape, the body squat, the rim flattened, and a sharp ridge at the shoulder. The biscuit (once fired) example was found on the site of Christian Wilhelm's Pickleherring factory and dates from the third quarter of the seventeenth century.

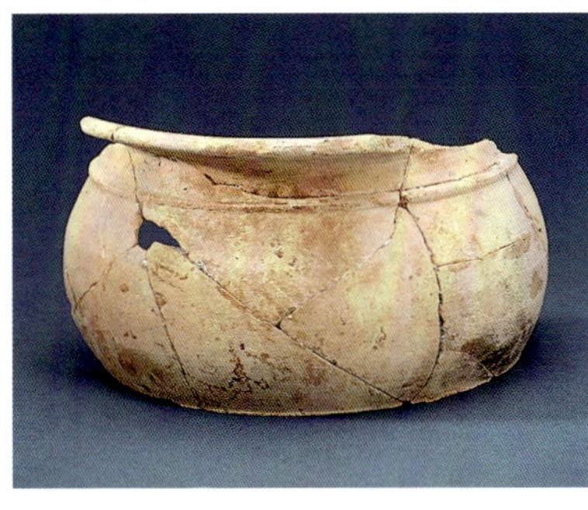

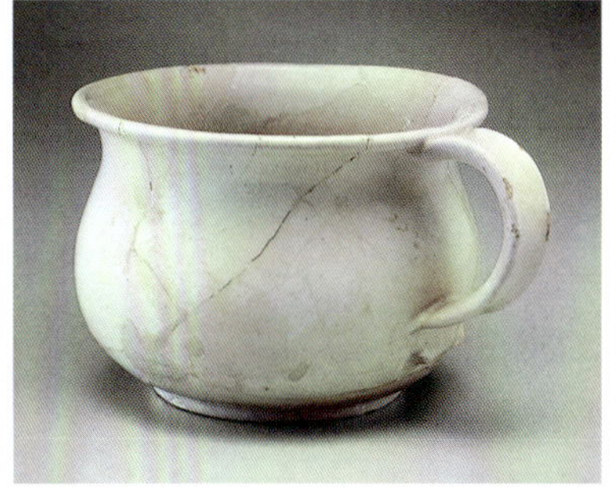

Figure 36 Chamber pot, London, 1700–1725. Tin-glazed earthenware. H. 5⅛". (Noël Hume Collection.) Delftware chamber pot attributable to the first quarter of the eighteenth century.

Figure 37 Chamber pots, England, 1725–1775. Tin-glazed earthenware. H. 4⅝", 5¹⁄₁₆" and 5½". (Department of Archaeological Research, Colonial Williamsburg Foundation.) Examples of delftware chamber pots from excavations in Williamsburg, Virginia, illustrating their evolution from the second to third quarters of the eighteenth century. Their archaeological contexts are post 1750, ca. 1760, and none.

occasioned by handle and pot parting company while being too enthusiastically decanted over the side of a ship.

Lead-glazed redwares did not lend themselves to delicacy or sophistication of ornament, but in England throughout the seventeenth century an ever-widening market for anything in delftware resulted in a new avenue of chamber pot development—and it came with a flat rim (fig. 35). The body shapes were reminiscent of pewter pots from the second half of the seventeenth century. The latters' rims, however, continued to be everted and dished in the manner of the contemporary Westerwald forms. Early in the eighteenth century, pewter rims changed dramatically, being rolled outward and down—the profile by then common among delftware chamber pots.[42] On these, the tin glaze is thick but pink-tinted as a bleed from iron in the clay (fig. 36). Later in the century that tone disappeared, and the glaze acquired, instead, a pale, egg-shell blue tint that is far from attractive (fig. 37). The rims, too, had changed from being boldly flaring and

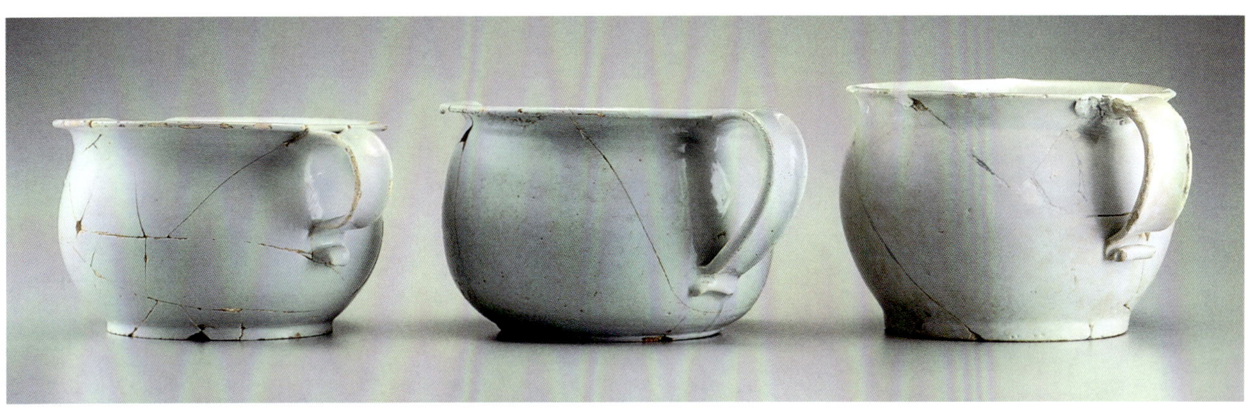

scrolled, to a vestigial outward bend that paid no more than lip service to the earlier styles. Gone, too, was a ridge or cordon at the shoulder, another characteristic of delftware chamber pots from the late seventeenth into the early to mid-eighteenth century.

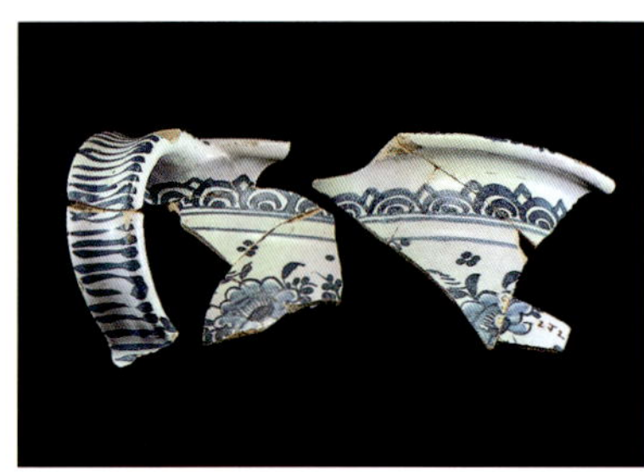

Figure 38 Chamber pot fragment, England, 1710–1730. Tin-glazed earthenware. (Department of Archaeological Research, Colonial Williamsburg Foundation.) Fragments from blue decorated delftware chamber pots found at the Timberlake and Dana site in Williamsburg, Virginia.

Figure 39 Chamber pot fragment, England, 1750–1760. Tin-glazed earthenware. (Department of Archaeological Research, Colonial Williamsburg Foundation.) Fragmentary blue decorated delftware chamber pot from the Roscoe Cole House site in Williamsburg, Virginia.

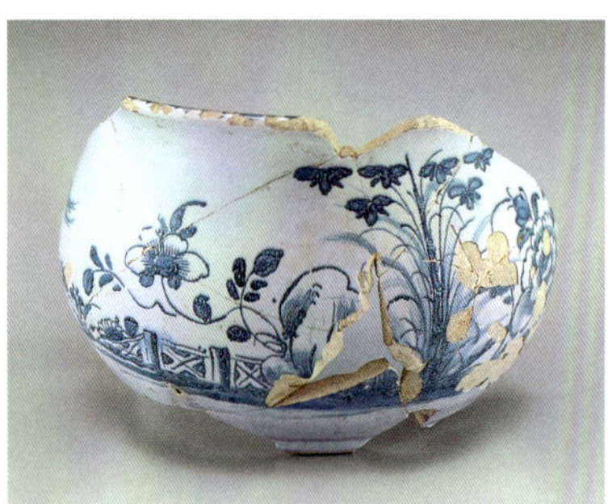

The manufacture of chamber pots was a major facet of the London delftware potters' trade in the late seventeenth century, as is shown by the 1699 inventory of Southwark factory manager John Allen who then had at least 3,000 pots in various stages of production.[43] There is no knowing how many were plain and how many decorated, though the former undoubtedly outnumbered the latter. We do know, however, that ten years later some were being made with the face of the unpopular Jacobite Dr. Henry Sacheverell painted on the interiors.[44] So brisk were the sale of those pots that one potter was able to build himself a mansion at Hackney that came to be known as Piss Pot Hall.[45] Although no Dr. Sacheverell pots survive, the fact that they were being made in 1709 leaves little doubt that they were of delftware—though delftware chamber pots with any kind of decoration would seem to have been in a small minority. Nevertheless, fragments of at least three decorated delftware pots have been found in excavations in Williamsburg, Virginia, one attributable to the first quarter of the eighteenth century and two others to the second and third (figs. 38, 39).[46]

The survival of undecorated anythings, be they chargers or chamber pots, invariably depends on archaeological salvage. Consequently very little has been published (at least in English) on plain European faience and maiolica, and even less on chamber pots. Consequently, my illustrated example from Northern Italy, attributed by the finder/seller to the second half of the eighteenth century, must serve as a reminder of all that we do not know (fig. 40).[47]

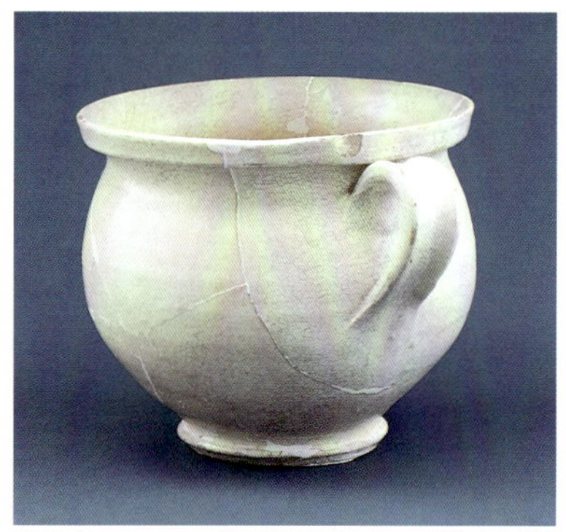

Figure 40 Chamber pot, Italy, 1750–1800. Tin-glazed earthenware. H. 5⅜". (Noël Hume Collection.) An undecorated maiolica chamber pot with everted and square-cut rim. Excavated in northern Italy.

Archaeology at Williamsburg has led to a wide range of unexpected discoveries, among them a trade in hand-shaped chamber pots made on at least one nearby Indian reservation. The illustrated example was discarded around 1770, and it presumably was intended for the use of slaves whose owners were unwilling to provide them with anything better (fig. 41). When I first drew published attention to what I dubbed "Colono-Indian" wares, I suggested that the chamber pot form was derived from contemporary Westerwald stoneware.[48] However, the body shape with its small,

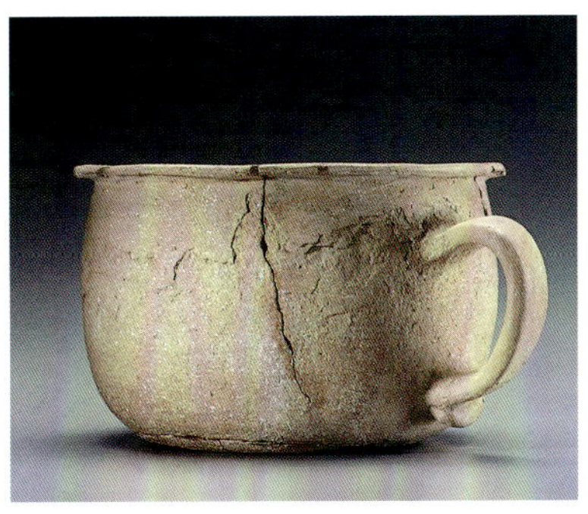

Figure 41 Chamber pot, Virginia, 1750–1770. Unglazed earthenware. H. 4⅞". (Department of Archaeological Research, Colonial Williamsburg Foundation.) This type of ware is referred to as Colono-Indian. The hand-shaped chamber pot is clearly an attempt to copy a European shape in either delftware or white salt-glazed stoneware. The reddish buff body is shell tempered. Note the lower handle terminal created from a separate pad of clay rather than having been drawn out as an extension of the handle. Discarded ca. 1770.

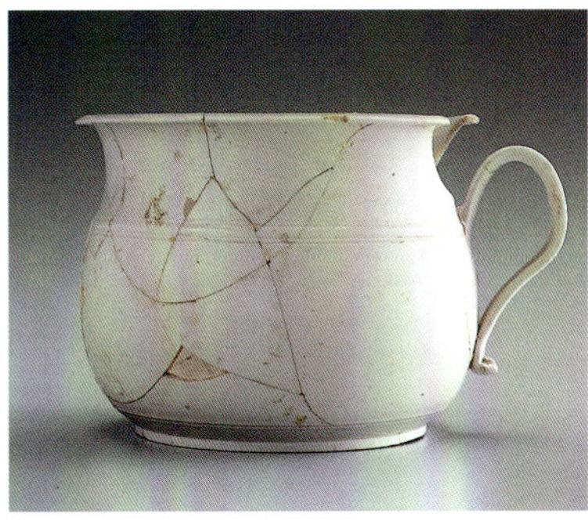

Figure 42 Chamber pot, Staffordshire, 1725–1750. Salt-glazed stoneware. H. 5⅛". (Department of Archaeological Research, Colonial Williamsburg Foundation.) White salt-glazed stoneware chamber pot whose thinness allowed the potter to exercise his talent in a way reminiscent of Hogarth's "Line of Beauty." The pot came from an archaeological context of ca. 1770.

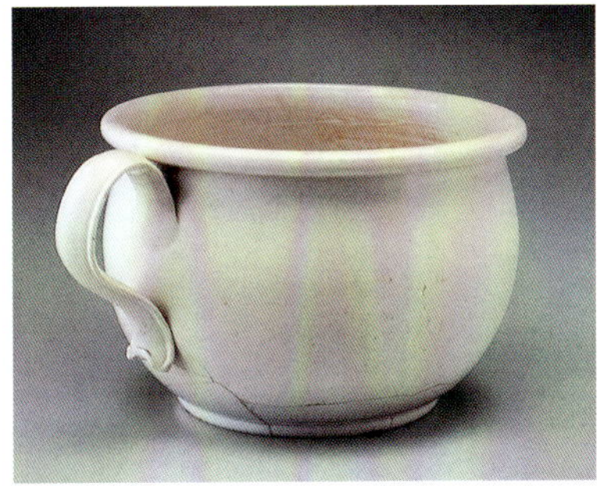

Figure 43 Chamber pot, Staffordshire, 1760–1780. Salt-glazed stoneware. H. 5⅜". (Noël Hume Collection.) The white salt-glazed chamber pot in decline, its early elegance lost and the rim reduced to an everted roll.

flattened rim might equally well have been borrowed from delftware. Unique to these pots is the method of attaching the handles. All are anchored below the rim (in the manner of the Bruge dippers) and plugged through the walls, a technique common among English and European medieval potters.

Returning to the mainstream, the shoulder ridge found on early eighteenth-century delftware chamber pots was also a feature of English white salt-glazed examples in the second quarter of the eighteenth century (fig. 42). Being made in the new, thinner thrown, and more refined clays, they acquired an elegance never attainable in the thickly glazed delft body. They were also more easily cleaned, and although prone to shatter if thrown out of a window, they were less inclined to chip. But, like their coarser cousins, they, too, evolved as the eighteenth century progressed. The sharp shoulder cordon disappeared, and the everted rims became smaller and, in their final evolution, rolled over and bonded with the wall to create a rounded and hollow lip (fig. 43).

Although, by the late 1760s, white salt-glazed stoneware was going out of fashion as table ware, it found a new market in the tap room and bedroom by simulating imported Westerwald stoneware. My late wife Audrey and I coined the term "debased scratch blue" to describe the cobalt-painted and incised mugs, jugs, and chamber pots. The Germans had avoided the temptation to put GR medallions on chamber pots, but the Staffordshire potters were less inhibited. They applied both royal ciphers and profile portraits of George III to their pots and continued to do so into the last

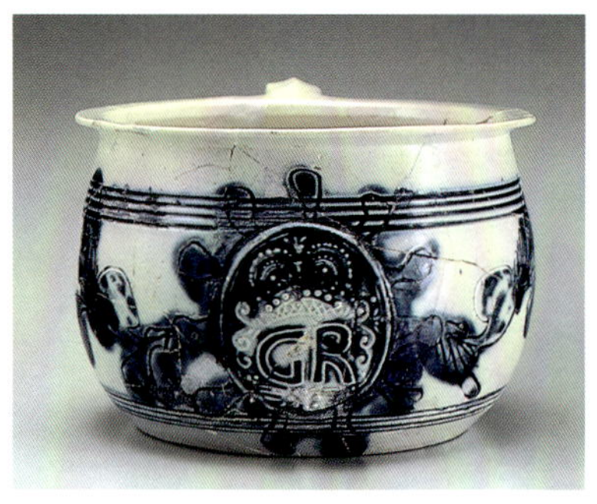

Figure 44 Chamber pot, Staffordshire, 1770–1790. Salt-glazed stoneware. H. 4 11/16". (Department of Archaeological Research, Colonial Williamsburg Foundation.) English debased scratch-blue decorated white salt-glazed stoneware chamber pot, decorated in the style of Westerwald but with the addition of the GR royal initials, an impertinence that the Germans had always avoided.

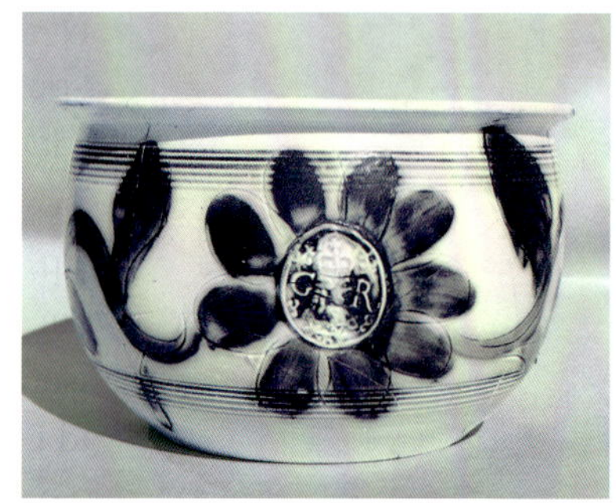

Figure 45 Chamber pot, Staffordshire, 1760–1775. Salt-glazed stoneware. H. 4¾". (Alexandria Archaeology Museums, City of Alexandria, Virginia; photo courtesy Richard Muzzrole.) A similar pot somewhat better painted and decorated with a profile portrait of George III flanked by his GR initials. Found in an Alexandria privy in an early-nineteenth-century context.

decade of the eighteenth century (figs. 44, 45). Their lead would be followed by pearlware potters and by whiteware manufacturers as late as 1837, when one of them indelicately applied a portrait of the young Queen Victoria to a chamber pot exported to Jamaica.[49]

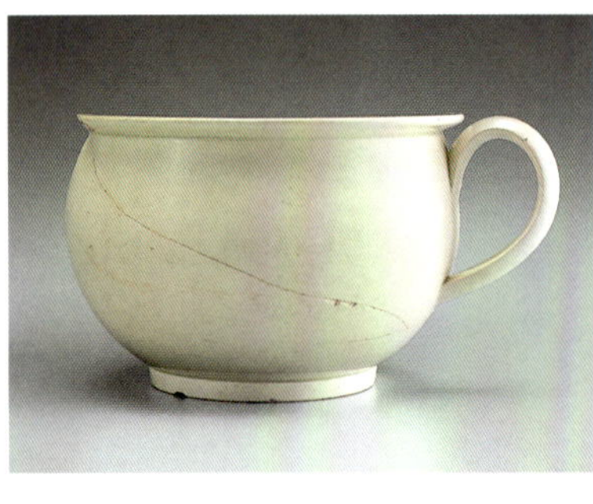

Figure 46 Chamber pot, England, 1775–1800. Creamware. H. 5 5/16". (Department of Archaeological Research, Colonial Williamsburg Foundation.) Undecorated English creamware chamber pots were exported in large numbers. This typical example from Williamsburg excavations features a flat rim and a simple strap handle. Others were more elaborate and came laterally ribbed and with rolled rims.

As we follow the evolution of chamber pot design through the eighteenth century, it is important to remind ourselves that for the most part we are seeing survivors from the lower rungs of English and colonial society. When the property of Virginia's Governor Botetourt was shipped back to England following his death, his silver chamber pot went with it. When, in 1766, the possessions of an unidentified "Noble Personage" were sold in Christie's very first auction, the catalog listed "Two blue and white Nankeen chamber-pots."[50] These may well have been of the variety recovered from the 1752 wreck of the Dutch East India Company's *Geldermalsen,* large numbers of which were sold at Christie's (Amsterdam) in 1986.[51] In short, the higher up the house the lower the grade of chamber pot.

The white stoneware's successor, the ubiquitous English creamware, followed in the later styles, its rims either flat, or rolled and fused, continuing in production to the end of the eighteenth century and beyond (fig. 46). By that time, of course, the blue-tinted pearlware had become the poor

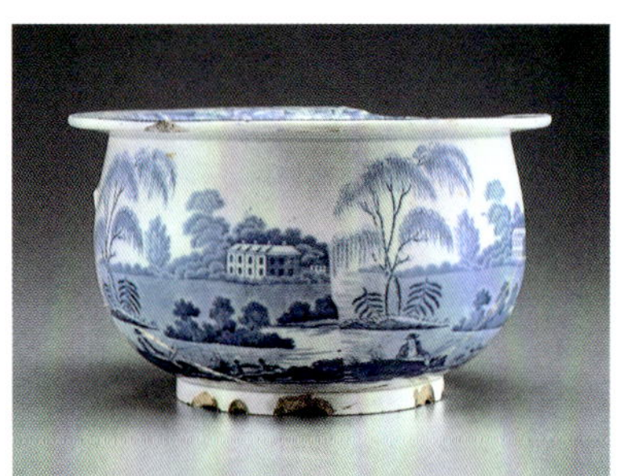

Figure 47 Chamber pot, Staffordshire, 1810–1820. Pearlware. H. 4⅞". (Ex-collection Sir David Burnett.) Blue transfer printed with a widely used print of Nuneham Court in Oxfordshire.

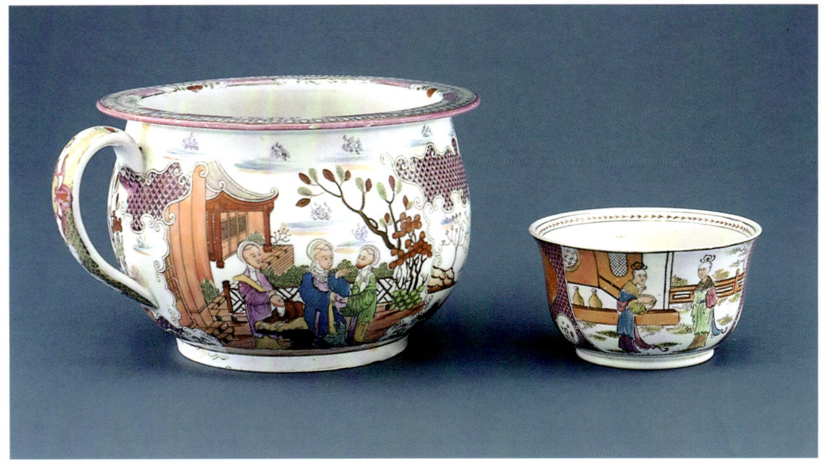

Figure 48 Chamber pot and bowl, Staffordshire, 1800–1810. Pearlware. H. 5³⁄₁₆" and 2⅝". (Noël Hume Collection.) A chamber pot elaborately decorated with a black-transfer print intended as guidance for complex polychrome hand painting in the Chinese manner. Accompanying the chamber pot is a similarly decorated bowl whose very shallow foot suggests that it may have been intended as a shaver's soap dish.

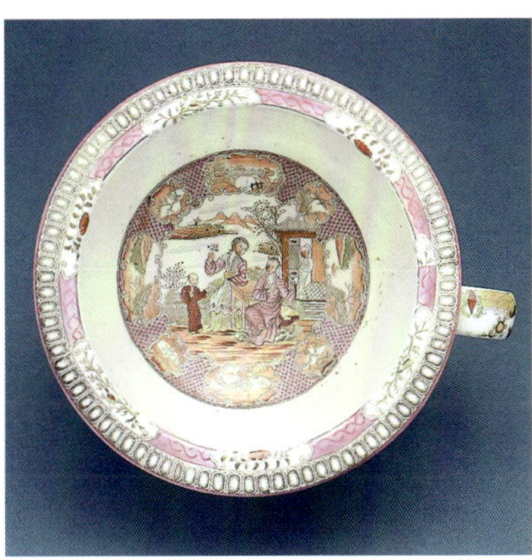

Figure 49 View of the chamber pot illustrated in fig. 48. This interior is richly hand painted onto a transfer design copying that on a bone china plate from the factory of Miles Mason of Lane End, ca. 1805.

man's version of Chinese porcelain, and would continue, generally flat-rimmed and transfer-printed, until ousted by the whiter ironstone china "semi-porcelains" and assorted white wares of the nineteenth and twentieth centuries (fig. 47). Ideally suited to blue transfer printing, chamber pot manufacturing at its simplest called for little decorative skill beyond being sure that the design was the right way up and the transfer joins hidden. At the same time, however, there were high-end designers and decorators who put a phenomenal amount of work into their chamber pots. My figures 48 and 49 with its accompanying soap bowl, combines black-printed outlining with elaborate handpainting characteristic of chinoiserie painting on English porcelain. Particularly surprising is the elaboration of the interior roundel, paralleling that on a bone china plate attributed to Miles Mason of Lane End, circa 1805.[52]

As a cultural signpost, the early nineteenth century's penchant for scatological humor is reflected in chamber pot ornamentation, none perhaps more illustrative than the Sunderland example shown in figure 50 which dates around 1840.[53] Both the pot's twin handles and the exterior doggerel indicate that this was a humorous variation on the popular loving cups of that era, and was made as a gift to newlyweds. One can well imagine the couple's reaction to receiving it—the embarrassed blushing of the bride and the back-slapping guffawing of the groom and his friends that echo from the depths of the pot like the ocean in a seashell. The wide-eyed

Figure 50 Chamber pot, Sunderland, 1830–1850. Pearlware. H. 5". (Private collection.) A double-handled, transfer-printed and hand colored chamber pot designed as a humorous wedding gift. Such pots were relatively common, but their distribution is likely to have been restricted to the rural north of England, such humor not being appreciated in an increasingly straight-laced Victorian urban south. There are several minor variations, some with Sunderland's characteristic luster adornments. As shown in figures 51 and 52, the interior print came as viewers either young or old, perhaps reflecting the age of the newlyweds. Frogs also were optional.

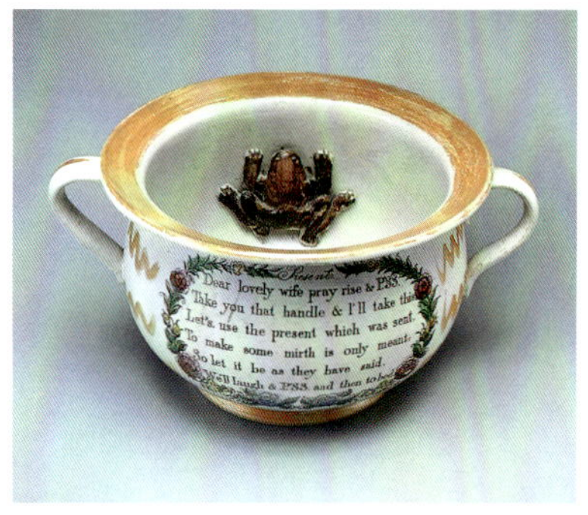

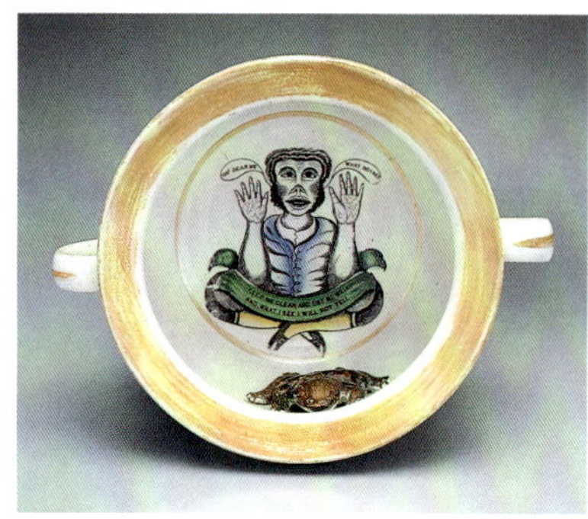

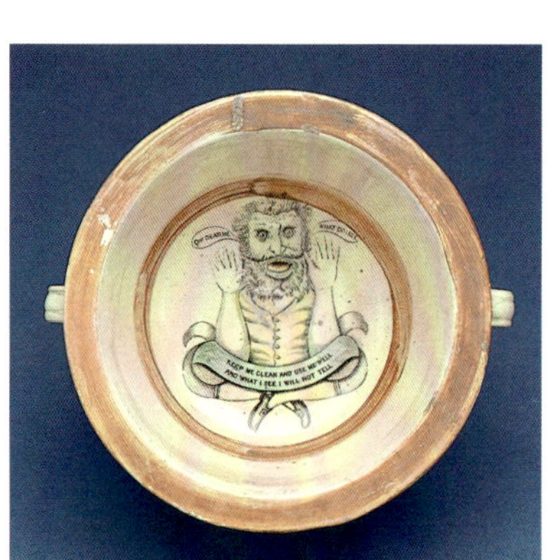

Figure 51 Detail of the interior of the chamber pot illustrated in fig. 50.

Figure 52 Interior view of the Sunderland chamber pot illustrated in fig. 54. (Noël Hume Collection.)

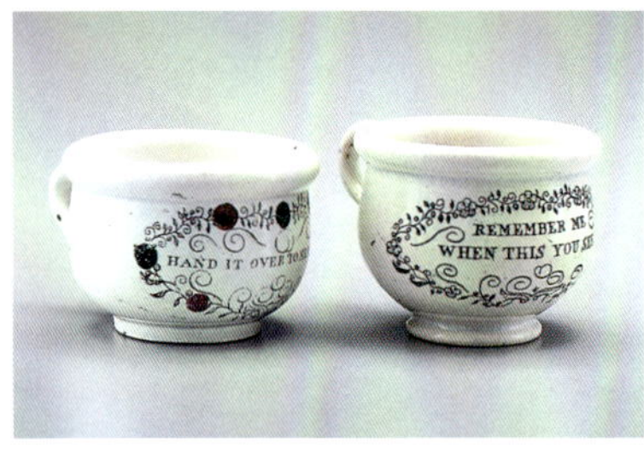

Figure 53 Miniature chamber pots, 1840–1870. Whiteware. H. 2½" and 2¼". (Noël Hume Collection.) Each has a transfer-printed inscription. Both were almost certainly made for sale at fairgrounds or they may have been given away as inducements to purchase more necessary wares.

young man painted on the interior pushes upward with his hands while exclaiming, OH DEAR ME WHAT DO I SEE, and below him KEEP ME CLEAN AND USE ME WELL / AND WHAT I SEE I WILL NOT TELL. Although the lettering came both printed and cursive, inscriptions both inside and out remained fairly consistent, but not so the vigilant voyeur who was supplied both youthful and bewhiskered (figs. 51, 52). The exterior lines emphasize that "Some mirth to make is only meant," while retaining a modicum of modesty by resorting to the letters P.'SS.[54] The line that reads "Remember them who sent you this," harks back to Metropolitan slipware admonitions of the mid-seventeenth century that read WHEN THIS YOU SEE REMEMBER ME.[55] A miniature chamber pot in white earthenware with a comparable inscription probably dates twenty or thirty years later than the wedding gift, as does its companion whose message reads HAND IT OVER TO ME MY DEAR (fig. 53). Just what was to be handed over is left to the imagination, though the dealer who sold the pot referred to it as a salt. He was wrong. The same inscription exists on a full-size, scatological chamber pot in tandem with the words FOR A KISS I'LL HAND YOU THIS.[56]

That the miniaturizing of chamber pots, primarily intended as a joke, persisted into the early twentieth century was demonstrated in a most unlikely location, namely the abandoned mining settlement of Nevadaville in the Colorado Rockies (fig. 54). The one and one-half-inch-tall porcelain pot carries a gilded inscription that reads "There are times when / one desires to be alone."[57] That, in itself, would not prove that this was made as a chamber pot; but the interior removes the doubt (fig. 55). Printed in

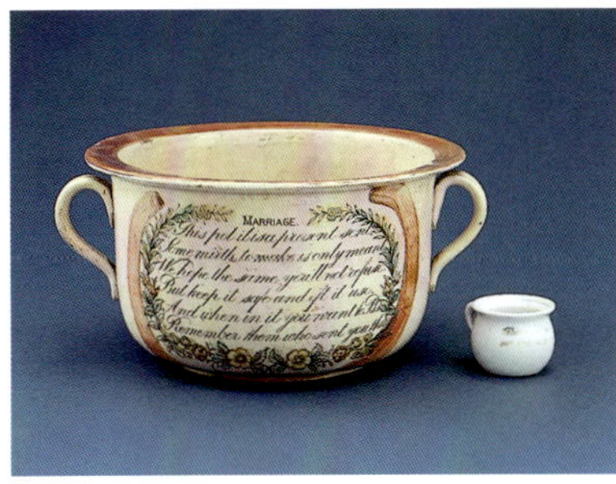

Figure 54 Miniature chamber pot marked GERMANY, early twentieth century. Porcelain. H. 1⅝". (Noël Hume Collection.) The side has a gilded inscription reading: THERE ARE TIMES WHEN / ONE DESIRES TO BE ALONE. The interior bottom is enriched with a transfer-printed and hand-colored human eye beneath a gilded inscription reading "Goo Goo." The full sized pot is included for scale but shows the reverse side of fig. 52.

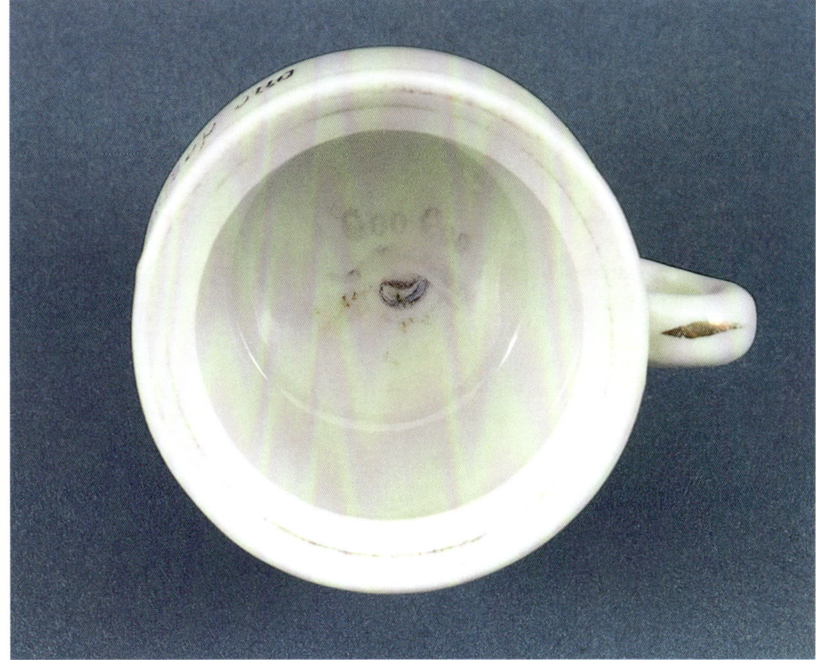

Figure 55 Interior view of the miniature chamber pot illustrated in fig. 54.

polychrome in the bottom is a wide-awake eye under the inscription "Goo Goo." The term "goo goo eyes" became popular around 1900 and was probably close to the date of manufacture for this German miniature.[58] The point, of course, is that it perpetuated the "What do I see?" chamber-pot humor of several earlier generations. It would surface again in the late 1930s inscribed GOOD COMPANION ANTI SPLASH THUNDER BOWL on, and in, a pot marked only MADE IN ENGLAND (fig. 56).[59]

The German invasion of Poland in September of 1939, and "po" being an English sobriquet for chamber pot, prompted several factories to follow in the long-established tradition of putting nasty people in their place. Adolf Hitler was among them, and is to be found in both standard-sized pots and in miniatures like the example made by Lancaster Ltd. of Hanley (1900–1944) and inscribed "ADOLF IN POLAND" (fig. 57).

There can be a significant difference between miniature and small, thereby posing the question: How many small pots of chamber-pot shape were actually used as such? A Westerwald example found in Amsterdam and sold as a small chamber pot is undeniably a small version of the stan-

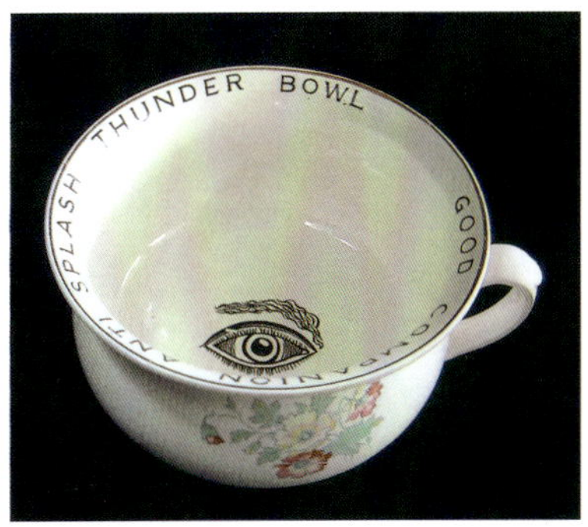

Figure 56 Chamber pot, England, ca. 1935–1940. Whiteware. H. 5¼". (Noël Hume Collection.) Decorated with a weak polychrome floral print on one side. A black eye is printed inside and the rim inscribed GOOD COMPANION ANTI SPASH THUNDER BOWL. Marked "Made in England."

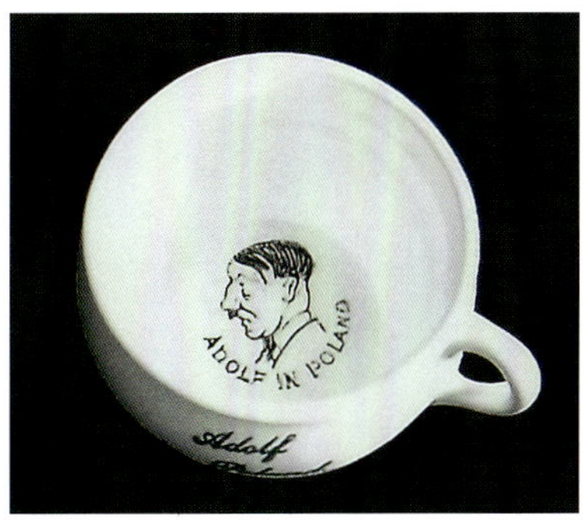

Figure 57 Chamber pot, miniature, Lancaster Ltd., Hanley, England, 1939–1940. Whiteware. H. 1½". (Noël Hume Collection.) A morale-building, humorous toy printed internally with a profile of Adolf Hitler and inscribed both inside and out ADOLF IN POLAND. Maker's mark on base.

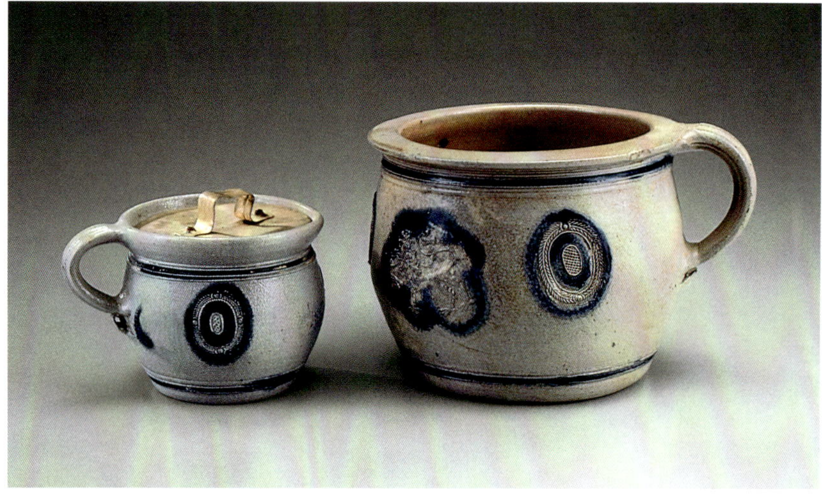

Figure 58 Soap dish and lid, Germany, ca. 1750. Salt-glazed stoneware. H. 3¾". (Noël Hume Collection.) Westerwald gray and blue stoneware vessel of small chamber pot shape, but thought to have been intended as a shaver's soap dish. The sprigged cartouche parallels those on some full-sized Rhenish chamber pots like the example on the right. Both the pot and its brass lid were found *in situ* in an Amsterdam privy.

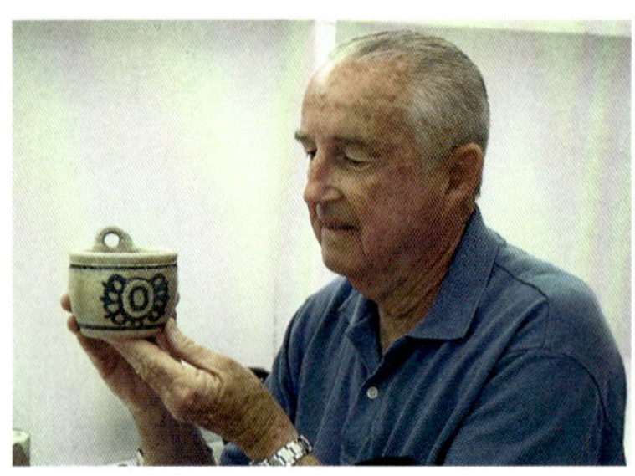

Figure 59 A loop-handled Westerwald stoneware parallel for figure 58 found by diver-conservator William Gillies on an unidentified Bermuda shipwreck of ca. 1740–1750. H. approx. 3⅝". (Courtesy, William Gillies.)

dard Rhenish export of the mid-eighteenth century (fig. 58). Having been found with its flat brass lid *in situ* it seemed proof that chamber pots sometimes came with metal lids. But having acquired it, questions began to nag. Why did small people need proportionately small pots to pee in? And what had this one contained that caused its flat brass lid to remain in place even when it was thrown into a pit? The likely answer came from two widely separated sources, a Bermuda shipwreck and an 1839 painting by J. Rentinck of a Westphalian pot-pedlar trying to sell his wares to a Netherlandish farmer's wife. Among the products laid out on the floor is a small Westerwald stoneware cup or bowl with a looped side handle. Illustrated by Klijn, it shares catalog space with two earthenware vessels of similar shape identified as soap cups and attributed to the second half of the nineteenth century.[60] That such cups were being produced in Westerwald stoneware a hundred years earlier is demonstrated by an example found by Bermudian diver William Gillies on a mid-eighteenth-century shipwreck (fig. 59).[61] The decoration on his cup matches that of the lidded vessel and ties the two to date, while the now-established purpose of the Bermuda soap cup strongly suggests that they came both wall-mounted and portable. It makes much more sense, therefore, to explain the *in situ* lid as having being secured by dried soap than by any less attractive substance. The lesson in all this is simple: If it looks like a too-small chamber pot, it probably was not expected to be so used.

A small delftware vessel recently sold as a child's chamber pot is only three inches in height and is clearly too small for that purpose (fig. 60). However, it is matched in size by Dutch redware, single-handled vessels there described as mustard pots.[62] The delftware pot's body shape with its everted rim and single ridged shoulder resembles English delftware chamber pots of circa 1700–1725. Not yet having traced the pot to a Dutch dealer (which I later did), I was prompted to return to John Robbins' 1699 Pickleherring factory inventory to see whether he had been making delftware mustard pots. He had. There were 360 in the category of "White and Painted Perfect Ware" and listed as "white & painted Mustard potts."[63] So far, so good. However, today we think of mustard being dispensed in

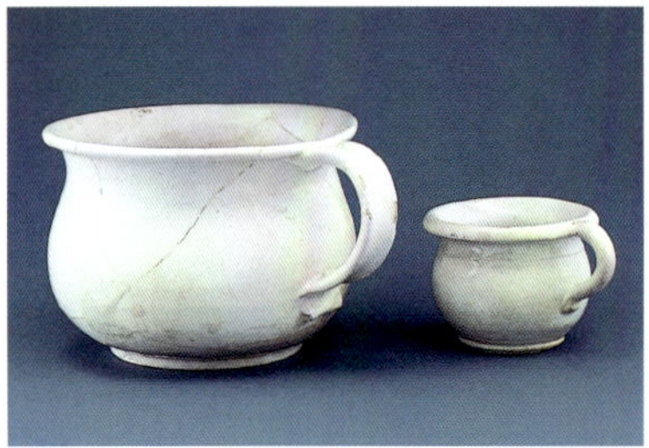

Figure 60 Miniature chamber pot, Netherlands, 1700–1730. Tin-glazed earthenware. H. 3". (Noël Hume Collection.) A full sized chamber pot illustrated in figure 36 is included for scale next to the Dutch delftware vessel of chamber-pot shape.

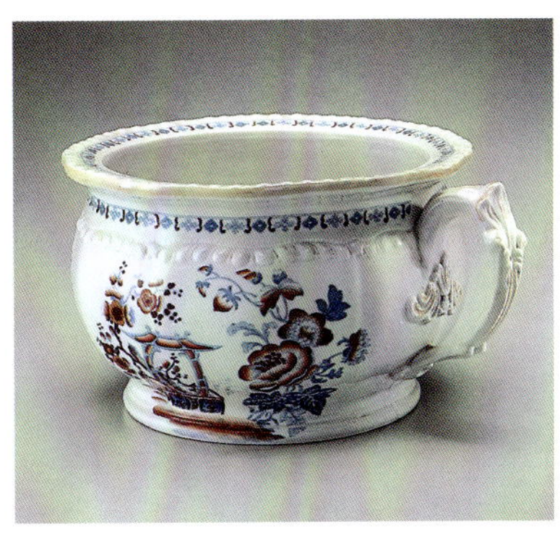

Figure 61 Chamber pot, Staffordshire, ca. 1825. Stone china. H. 5¾". (Noël Hume Collection.) This chamber pot was cast in a two-piece mold whose junction lines have not been removed; it is transfer printed in blue overlaid in hand-applied red. The chinoiserie pattern is reproduced internally, and the exterior rim and shoulder are molded in a bead-and-reel design reminiscent of white salt-glazed stoneware plate rims. The elaborately molded and gilded handle is enriched with a separately applied upper terminal. The base is marked with the kind of badge allowed to companies that had been granted its usage by Royal Appointment.

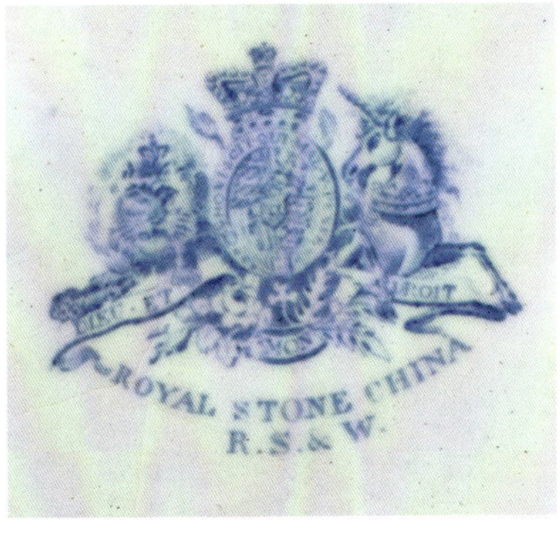

Figure 62 Detail of the printed mark on the base of the chamber pot illustrated in figure 61. The associated inscription declares itself to be that of a manufacturer of ROYAL STONE CHINA from the factory of R. S. & W. The company is believed to be that of Stevenson and Williams, a short-lived Cobridge partnership of ca. 1825, but there is no known evidence that it enjoyed royal patronage. The English royal arms are charged with the cap or crown of Hanover and therefore date prior to the accession of Queen Victoria in 1837.

quantities far smaller than could be served in a three-inch chamber pot. So was this always so? The 1725 edition of a *Family Dictionary* suggests otherwise, describing under the heading "Mustard" how, by augmenting it with "verjuice, Sugar, Claret-wine and juice of Lemon, you have an excellent Sauce to any sort of Flesh or Fish." The writer also advocated that one "should put it all into a glazed mug."[64]

Although the delftware pot's general body shape is comparable to contemporary London chamber pots, the handle is round-sectioned and the rim is pronouncedly undercut. The latter feature may have been designed for a paper, bladder, or a parchment cover to be secured over the mouth if the mustard sauce was to be stored. The *Oxford English Dictionary* quotes from Wyclif's Sermons (1380) wherein mustard was to be "covered with parchment to exclude the air."

One might argue, therefore, that neither the delftware pot, nor some of the nineteenth-century white ware "miniatures" were made as amusing if embarrassing toys, but were condiment pot shapes in common use in working class homes. I have to allow, however, that I have not as yet found any documentary or pictorial evidence to support that premise. Furthermore, this initially beguiling thesis has serious flaws. French faience mustard pots of the eighteenth century (and later) were cylindrical and had no handle, while English stoneware versions were miniature versions, not of chamber pots but of brown stoneware pitchers.[65]

By the early- to mid-nineteenth century the proliferation of factories and burgeoning populations both in the Old World and the New, rendered the evolutionary pursuit of chamber-pot shapes an exercise in futility. Molded mass production offered an elaboration of forms hitherto unavailable, and while some are datable through marks and factory design catalogs, the styles have more to do with paralleling a factory's production in other shapes such as pitchers, wash basins, and planters than with customers' finely focused taste in chamber pots. The example illustrated in figure 61 fits well within the nineteenth century's transition from handsome to horrible. Made around 1825 by the Hanley firm of Ralph Stevenson and Aldborough Lloyd Williams, and cast in "Royal Stone China," its rim and shoulder decoration recall the bead-and-reel border motifs of eighteenth-century white salt-glaze (figs. 61, 62).[66] Both its inside and outside are decorated in a restrained (albeit transfer-printed) Chinese peony-and-pagoda pattern highlighted in over-glaze red and the rim and handle in a pale orange simulation of gold. The latter had been separately cast, and after being manually attached, an individually sprig-molded fleur-de-lis upper terminal was added to obscure the junction. This degree of elaboration was a far cry, for example, from the unadorned stone china chamber pots in use at the Williamsburg mental institution when it burned in 1885.

Virginia's first mental institution opened in Williamsburg in 1773, and archaeological excavations on the site prior to the building's reconstruction, revealed, along with much else, a chronology of chamber pots throughout its life. Whereas the hospital's pre-Revolutionary War ceramic needs were served by imports from England, the last decade of the eighteenth century

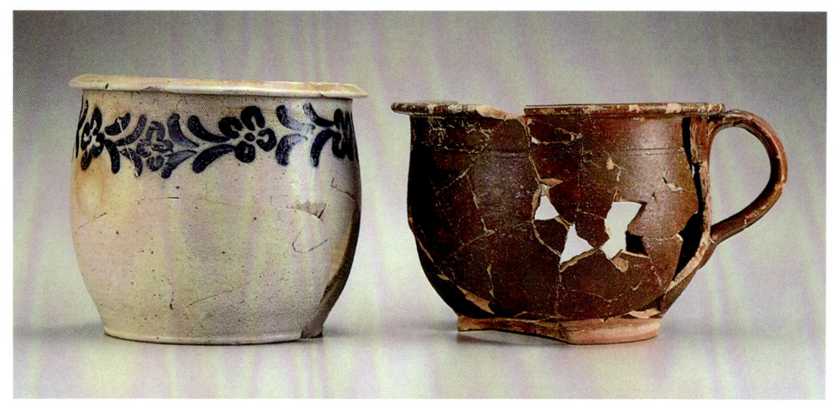

Figure 63 Chamber pots, American, 1790–1810. Salt-glazed stoneware and lead-glazed earthenware. H. 6¾" and 6¼". (Courtesy, Department of Archaeological Research, Colonial Williamsburg Foundation.) Examples of American chamber pots used in the lunatic asylum at Williamsburg, Virginia, ca. 1790–1810. The redware pot is possibly from the factory of Henry Piercey in Alexandria, whereas the stoneware example is likely to have been made either in Philadelphia or Baltimore.

saw a turn to domestic suppliers, significantly, it seems, to potteries in Alexandria, Virginia, and in Baltimore, Maryland. Figure 63 shows the principal choices: coarse, lead-glazed earthenware, like those produced in the factory of Henry Piercy between 1792 and 1809, and gray and blue stoneware in imitation of the old Westerwald wares. As the nineteenth century progressed, we find a return to English sources—remarkably to a specific shipment of thin, whiteware chamber pots bearing the initials W. L. H. (Williamsburg Lunatic Hospital), the initials applied in re-fired overglaze black (fig. 64). Although it is possible that the institution's ini-

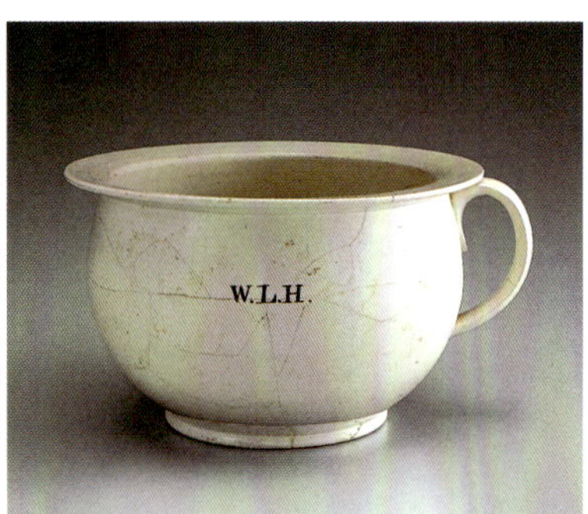

Figure 64 Chamber pot, England, ca. 1838. Whiteware. H. $5\frac{15}{16}$". (Courtesy, Department of Archaeological Research, Colonial Williamsburg Foundation.) This chamber pot was initialed specifically for the Williamsburg Lunatic Hospital whose name was changed in 1838. Believed to be English, but the initials may have been added by an American importer.

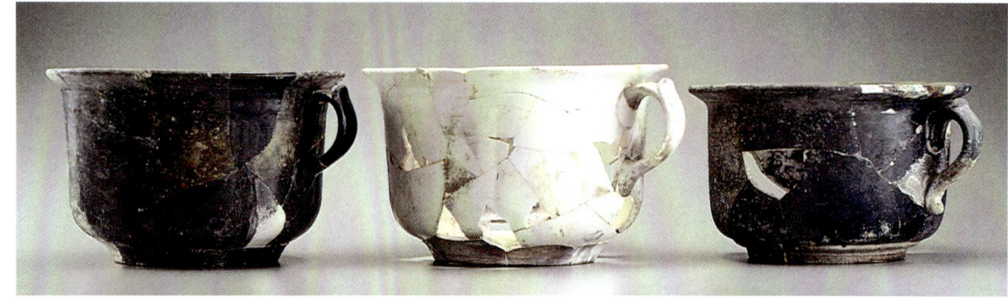

Figure 65 Chamber pots, England, 1860–1885. Whiteware. H. of tallest: 5⅞". (Courtesy, Department of Archaeological Research, Colonial Williamsburg Foundation.) Three among several fire-blackened, heavy-duty ironstone-type chamber pots found in the debris of the 1885 fire that destroyed the Williamsburg asylum.

tials were part of a direct English order, it is more likely that the identification was applied by an American wholesaler. A circa 1825–1838 date for the historically important chamber pot stems from the institution's own evolution from Lunatic Hospital to Lunatic Asylum. The change was more than semantic. It marked a profound philosophical shift from a hospital rigorously intent on mending repairable minds, to a haven—a compassionate asylum—for the incurably insane.[67]

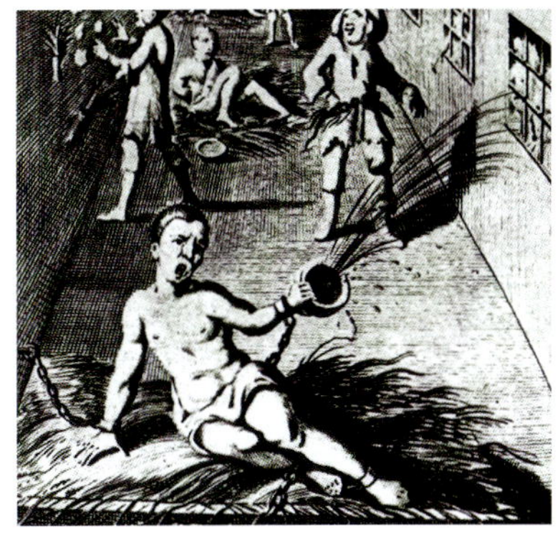

Figure 66 Detail from an engraving illustrating Jonathan Swift's *A Tale of a Tub* (1751 edition), showing the chamber pot as a means of expression.

The transition had brought inmate comfort up from a chain in the wall and straw on the floor to simple furnishings whose scope mirrored the dependability of the confined individual. Nevertheless, the asylum remained a Spartan institution reflected in the industrial strength chamber pots found burned in the debris from the 1885 fire (fig. 65). However, the much earlier illustration from Jonathan Swift's *A Tale of a Tub* reminds us that in demented hands a chamber pot could become a formidable weapon (fig. 66).[68] That possibility had not been overlooked by the warden of the Eastern State Hospital who provided vulcanized rubber pots for the dangerously insane (fig. 67).

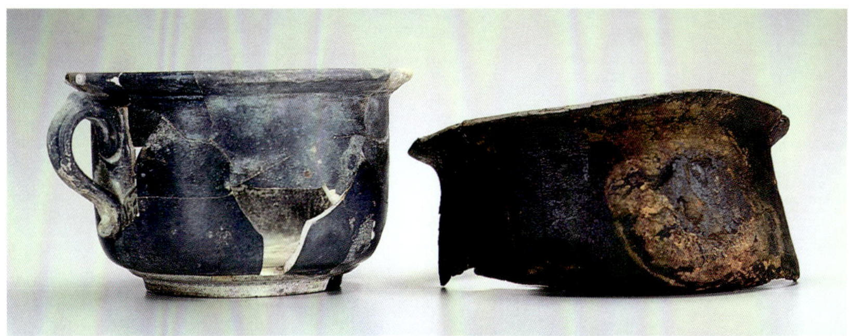

Figure 67 Chamber pots, England, ca. 1880. Whiteware and vulcanized rubber. H. 5⅜". (Courtesy, Department of Archaeological Research, Colonial Williamsburg Foundation.) Another ironstone-type chamber pot from the Williamsburg asylum's 1885 fire shown alongside the remains of a vulcanized chamber pot intended for the use of unruly patients.

The circumstances that once generated the need for rubber chamber pots can be seen in modern parlance as a "reality check." Setting aside the grace of a white salt-glaze rim, the cuteness of a two-handled wedding gift, or the delicate chinoiserie of Messrs. Stevensen and Williams' Royal Stone China (marred inside by a telltale yellow stain), one cannot escape the fact that their function, though familiar, is not one to contemplate—any more than were their immediate contexts. The adage about the relative values of words and pictures is exemplified by the photograph in figure 68. The glass-plate negative seems to have been made around 1900, perhaps shot in

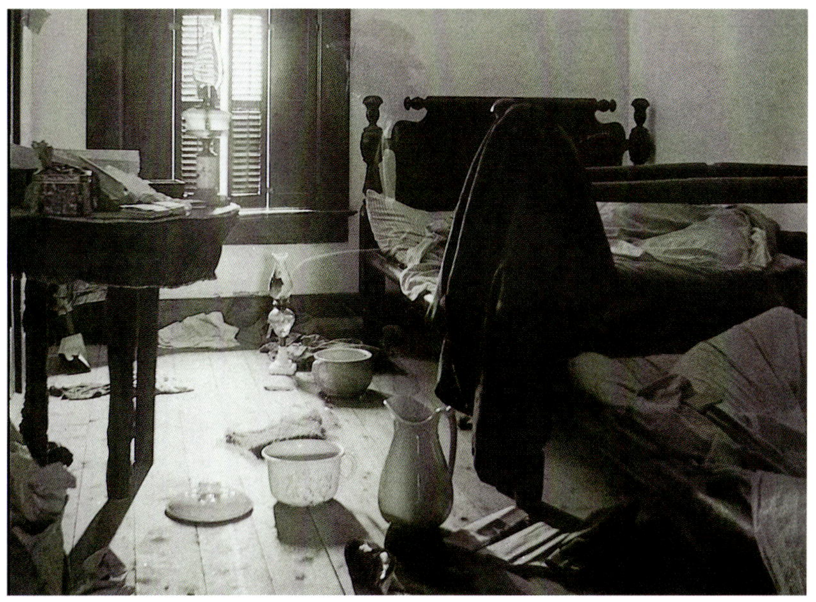

Figure 68 Print from a glass negative. (Courtesy, David Doody and the Image Alchemy Inc. Collection.) This photograph, perhaps shot in a New Orleans flop house, shows typical turn of the twentieth-century chamber pots more or less in use. Note the ghost image of one of the room's occupants seated on the bed.

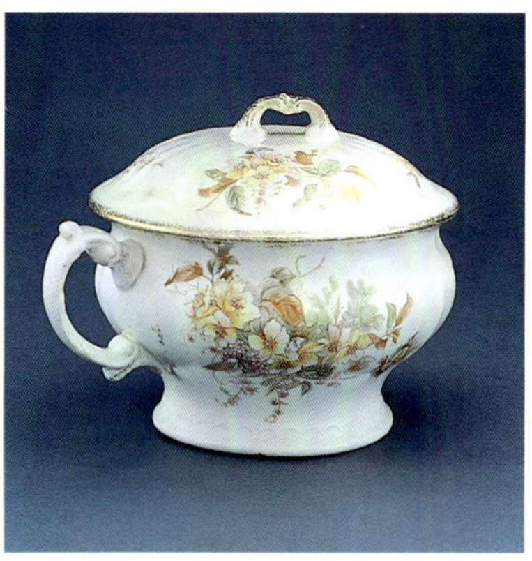

Figure 69 Chamber pot and lid, Maddock's Lamberton Works Royal Porcelain, Trenton New Jersey, ca. 1892. H. 5¾". (Noël Hume Collection.) A massive, lidded chamber pot of hotel-china whiteware, gadroon molded and decorated with transfer-printed polychrome floral sprays and spatter gilding. Though moldmade, the marks have been almost entirely erased. There are tripod stilt marks scarring the interior base suggesting that the pot was fired upside down.

a New Orleans flop house, and shows two heavy-duty chamber pots of different shapes and wares in use in a single, two-bed room. The ghostly figure seated on the far bed may have been relieved that at least one pot came with a lid.

The lidded example illustrated in figure 69 serves as a reminder that in the second half of the nineteenth century, hotel-quality sanitary wares became a mainstay of ceramic production on both sides of the Atlantic. Among the Staffordshire leaders in the American trade was the firm of John Maddock which began export production in the 1850s. But although this example bears a Maddock mark, it comes from the factory of a namesake, Thomas Maddock of Trenton, New Jersey, who took over the nearby Lamberton Works in 1892.[69]

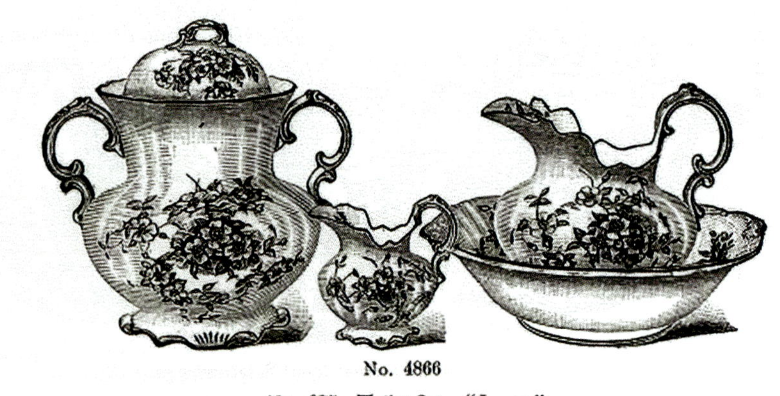

Figure 70 Catalog illustration, Messrs. Higgins & Seiter, New York, 1899. In the late nineteenth century chamber pots were commonly sold in sets of a dozen, though social sensitivity kept them from being pictured in the ads.

The lidded Lamberton pot, though imposing in its profile, and described as "Royal Porcelain," is in reality a ponderous off-white ware, spatter gilded and polychrome transfer-printed with floral sprigs that belie the pot's industrial strength durability. It undoubtedly came en suite with jug, basin, and other toiletry essentials (fig. 70).[70] Horrid though it may be to modern eyes, it nevertheless remains a reflection of turn-of-the-century taste. Far more pleasing are two further examples of changing fashion: first, an 1880s reflection of a penchant for Japanese fans and bamboo that

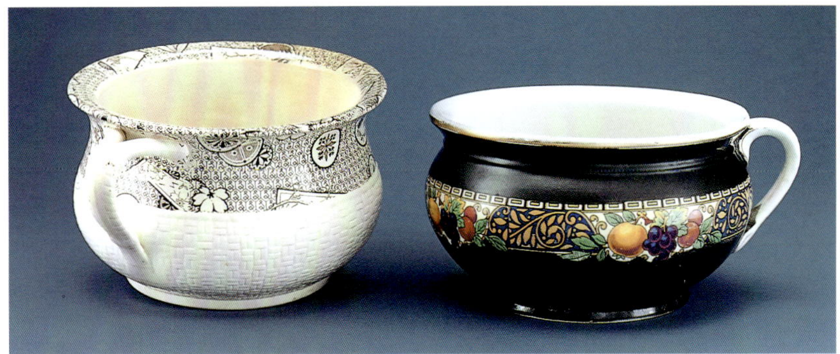

Figure 71 Chamber pots, England, ca. 1880 and 1900. Whiteware. H. 5¾" and 5½". (Noël Hume Collection.) Examples of diverse late Victorian chamber-pot taste. The left hand cream-colored example is molded below the girth with a basketry pattern that continues onto the unusual bifurcated handle. The upper wall and rim are transfer printed in sepia in an elaborate pattern of storks, fans, twigs, flowers, and a boy apparently pursuing a butterfly. However, the pattern is inverted and presumably intended to complement an equally decorative lid. No maker's mark, but printed with a diamond-shaped design registration mark for August, 1880. The pot recalls the enthusiasm for Japanese textiles and ceramics that burgeoned in the late nineteenth century. The unmarked example on the right is a whiteware reminder of a paralleling taste for contrasting colors and fluid lines loosely related to the art nouveau movement.

Figure 72 Chamber pot, England or possibly North Germany, ca. 1920–1930. Whiteware. H. 5¼". (Noël Hume Collection.) Titillating dreams of Bedouin tents, Arab sheiks, and fates definitely not worse than death, may have been fostered by transfer-decorated pots like this from the 1920s.

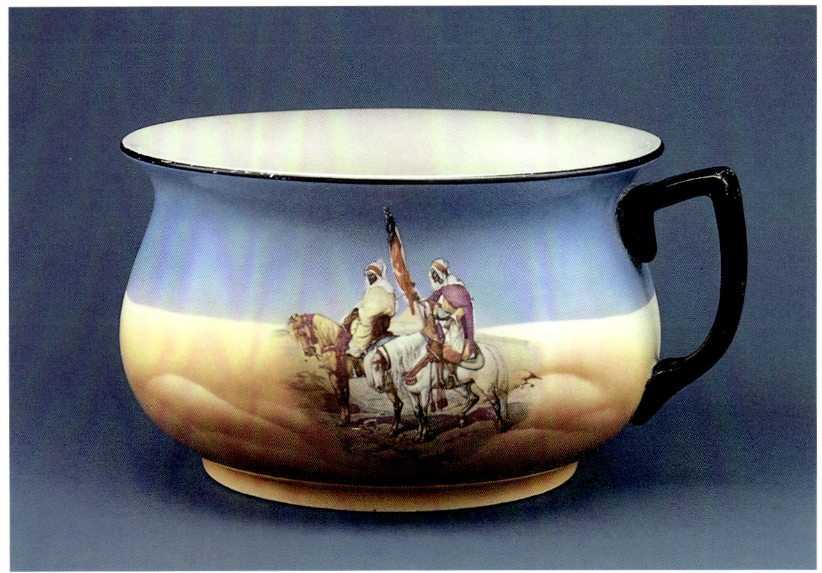

survives in W. S. Gilbert's lyrics for *The Mikado* (1885); and second, in a surprisingly pleasing representative of the art nouveau movement of the 1890s where dramatic black contrasts with florid fruit reminiscent of polychrome Renaissance maiolica (fig. 71).

It may well take another hundred years for early twentieth-century chamber pots to be collected as legitimate antiques. In the meantime, they still have their place in the artifactual history of their time—providing we are not too late to "read" them correctly. My last example is already an enigma (fig. 72). Unmarked, save for a painter's device, its decoration

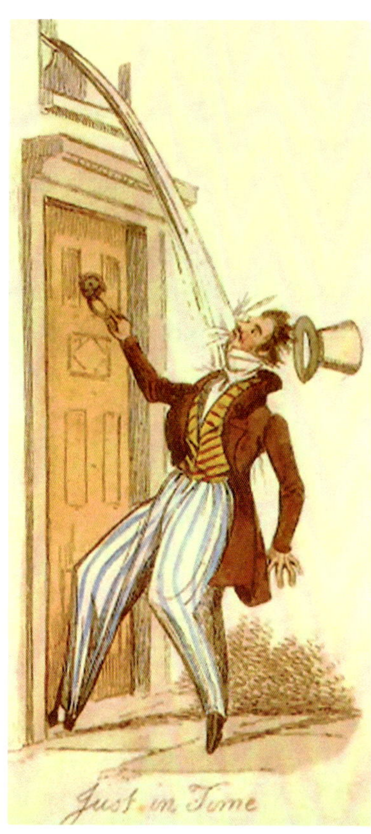

Figure 73 "Just in Time." Hogarth would have called this a "Tail Piece." (Mary Evans Picture Library.)

is equally divided between azure sky and yellow desert sand, together an evocative background for a transfer of two horse-mounted Arabs.[71] Why, we may ask? The enormous international success of Rudolph Valentino's 1921 silent movie *The Sheik* may be the answer, as may Stuart Romburg's 1927 musical *The Desert Song*. Either way, tucked under the bed, the pot may have been the catalyst for exotic and heart-palpitating dreams. But whose bed, and where? Then again, perhaps neither connection is valid, and the pot was a joke that invited the user to create her own oasis in the desert?

To some readers this inquiry may seem frivolous, childishly scatological, and unwarranted in a journal devoted to the serious study of ceramic history. But before coming to that conclusion, we need to ask ourselves how old a pot must be before we should attempt to deduce its maker's intent or its owner's taste. Were those questions being asked, say, of a seventeenth-century slipware chamber pot with a "naughty" inscription, research into contemporary literature and art would be an essential facet of cataloging. Is an enigmatic eighty-year-old pot any less deserving? I think not.

And another thing: Suppose these handled vessels were not for sanitary use but were, instead, posset pots, fruit bowls, or wine coolers. How, then, would museums, connoisseurs and collectors regard them (fig. 73)?

A C K N O W L E D G M E N T S
The author is indebted to ceramic authority Garry Atkins; John Austin, retired curator of ceramics at the Colonial Williamsburg Foundation; David Gaimster late of the British Museum; *Ceramics in America* editor Robert Hunter for information and specimens that have contributed to this article; ceramics collector Marco Maas in Holland; Jaqueline Pearce, ceramics specialist at the Museum of London's Archaeology Service; Colonial Williamsburg archaeology curator William Pittman; and Chipstone Foundation executive director Jonathan Prown.

1. Randle Holme, *An Academie or Store House of Armory & Blazon,* vol. 2 (Chester, 1682; reprint, London: the Roxburghe Club, 1905), p. 2. The "looking glass" sobriquet remained in use into and through the eighteenth century. Nathaniel Bailey's *Etymological English Dictionary,* vol. 2 (1737) cites it in its collection of "Canting Words and Terms," and in 1811 a new edition of a *Dictionary of the Vulgar Tongue* (reprint, London: Bibliophile Books, 1984) defined "looking-glass" as "A chamber pot, jordan, or member mug." The *Oxford English Dictionary*'s first reference to chamber pots occurred in 1570 in a Durham inventory listing "Fyue chamber pottes of pouther vs."—five chamber pots of pewter, five shillings.

2. Before you remind me of all the pots I have omitted, it may be helpful to understand that this survey focuses primarily on the European evolution of the form beginning in the Netherlands and transferring to Britain and Virginia in the early seventeenth century. The spectrum of wares produced by virtually every American redware and stoneware pottery through the nineteenth century remains a rich field for another writer to plow.

3. The pseudonymous P. Amis in his pioneering paper "Some domestic vessels of southern Britain: a social and technical analysis," *Journal of Ceramic History,* no. 2 (1968): 7, noted that in the Greek colony of Sybaris in southern Italy, the well-heeled inhabitants were "the first people to invent chamber pots which they carried to parties." Dr. Amis was citing Athenaeus, *Deipnosophistae,* XII, 519e. However, in 1825 the Reverend Thomas Dudley Fosbroke in his *Encyclopedia of Antiquities* had another explanation, stating that the Sybarites "would not be at the trouble of moving." Cited by Lucinda Lambton in *Temples of Convenience and Chambers of Delight* (New York: St. Martin's Press, 1995), p. 8. There are several references to chamber pots in classical literature, e.g. Flavius Arrianus' commentaries on the books of Epictetus (ca. A.D. 95–180) wherein the philosopher asked whether it was beneath a man's dignity to hold another's chamber pot. Slightly earlier was Petronius Arbiter's *Satyricon* (Chap. V) wherein he described games in the reign of Nero and noted that one elderly ball player had a eunuch on hand "clutching a chamber pot of solid silver." We have to remember, however, that a vessel quite unlike the standard post-medieval chamber pot may have been so termed by the translator to equate with the Latin or Greek for a urinal.

4. Ivor Noël Hume, "Medieval Bottles from London," *Connoisseur* 139, no. 560 (March 1957): 105, fig. 2.

5. Raphael Holinshed's *Chronicles* (1577), 1807 ed., vol. 2, p. 751, cited by the *Oxford English Dictionary.*

6. An illustration derived from *Der Geistliche Auslegung des Lebens Jesu Christi,* Ulm, ca. 1480–1485 was republished by P. Amis in "Some domestic vessels of southern Britain," p. 14, fig. 8.

7. The earliest pewter example found in Britain was recovered by Dr. Margaret Rule from the wreck of the *Mary Rose* (1545) and published in *Country Life* (May 24, 1979): 1638.

8. A bag-shaped pot in this gray ware, with a similarly located handle, is illustrated in H.J.E. van Beuningen's *Verdraaid goed gedraaid* (Rotterdam: Museum Boymans-van Beuningen, 1973), pp. 70–71, fig. 384, and there attributed to the first half of the fifteenth century. Another vessel with a comparable ear-like handle is made as a bird's nesting bottle. It dates from the seventeenth century and is illustrated in E. M. Ch. F. Klijn, *Lead-glazed Earthenwares in The Netherlands* (Arnhem: Netherlands Openluchtmuseum, 1995), p. 290.

9. A black-glazed redware vessel of chamber pot shape was found in a ca. 1730–1775 deposit of kiln waste in Albion Square, Hanley, and although described as such, its handle was attached at the girth and not at the rim, suggesting that this, too, was a dipper. F.S.C. Celoria and J. H. Kelly, *A Post-medieval pottery site with a kiln base found off Albion Square, Hanley,*

Stoke-on-Trent, Staffordshire, England, Archaeological Society Report no. 4 (Staffordshire, Eng.: City of Stoke-on-Trent Museum, 1973), p. 27, no. 128, p. 68.

10. Ibid., p. 94, ca. 1700.

11. Ibid., p. 248. Examples with conventional rim-attached handles are attributed to ca. 1475–1525.

12. No. 1 was found near Amsterdam, and the rest in Rotterdam.

13. Ivor and Audrey Noël Hume, *The Archaeology of Martin's Hundred* (Williamsburg, Va.: Colonial Williamsburg Foundation, 2001), pt. 1, p. 166, pl. 63.

14. Leiden, Amsterdam, Dordrecht, Paardenveld in Utrecht, and unrecorded.

15. The London fragment's foot is smaller than those of the larger Dutch chamber pots (but comparable to others) and lacks the overall lead glazing characteristic of most Dutch chamber pots.

16. Sarah Jennings et al., "Eighteen Centuries of Pottery from Norwich," *East Anglian Archaeology,* Report no. 13 (Norwich, Eng.: Norfolk Museums Service, 1981), pp. 137–38, no. 954. This "cauldron" is overall half an inch smaller than the Dutch chamber pot shown in fig. 6, no. 2.

17. Ibid., pp. 134–36.

18. There are moments when one doubts one's sanity at debating so abstruse a point and wonders whether this exercise is perhaps the apex of pointless pedantry. In short: Who gives a damn whether sixteenth-century chamber pots had frilly bottoms? The answer, of course, is that ceramic history and research are fascinating fields of discovery for those of us whose daydreams are set amid the antimacassars of 221B Baker Street .

19. It may well be that British archaeologists knew much more about the dating of their ceramics finds than became available through their publications. It remains true, nonetheless, that the earlier writers were generally content to describe the vessel, show a drawing of it, and state on which site it was found. Such dating as is afforded (and often there is none) stems from undocumented opinions or conventional wisdom (which may well be valid) rather than from stratigraphic associations. In consequence, one has to be cautious about relying on such potentially sand-seated evidence.

20. Noël Hume and Noël Hume, *The Archaeology of Martin's Hundred,* pt. 1, pp. 40–41.

21. A chamber pot of Martin's Hundred type was found in Structure 110 at Jamestown in a stratum attributed to ca. 1630–1650, but lay adjacent to Structure 111 believed to have been associated with potting in the period 1620–1650. John L. Cotter, *Archaeological Excavations at Jamestown* (Washington, D.C.: U. S. National Park Service, 1958), pp. 102–12.

22. A redware chamber pot of this general type was found in a pit while rebuilding the deanery of Westminster Abbey in 1951. Published nine years later, the pot was said to have been deposited around 1525, making it one of the earliest known. However, drawings of other vessels from the same group suggest a date in the first years of the seventeenth century, and point to the hazards of reliance on dating arrived at when knowledge of post-medieval ceramics was still in its infancy. J. G. Hurst, "A Late Medieval Pit at Westminster Abbey," *The Antiquaries Journal* 11 (July–October 1960): 293–94, fig. 3, no. 16.

23. Coarser than the white clay "border ware" pots, the London pot's ridges are sharper and therefore less pleasingly undulating.

24. Another found in London and described as "stoneware chamber-pot; grey internally, brown externally," was published with the comment that "most archaeologists consulted wisely insist that a date range of '18th–19th cent' is the only one possible." Amis, "Some domestic vessels of southern Britain," p. 20 and p. 28, no. 26. David Gaimster has drawn my attention to yet another found in Canterbury's Linaire Gardens (1979), now in the collection of the Canterbury Archaeological Trust, No. 115.542, and attributed to Frechen.

25. Advertised on eBay, Oct. 24, 2002, by Groupe Union Française de Gestion.

26. See note 6.

27. These pots had been bought at auction and were in the Frank Thomas Collection in 1952. They were culled from it and given to the author as being culturally unworthy of a place in a collection of Rhenish ceramic art.

28. Evidence of template chatter is to be found on most, if not all, Westerwald hollow wares after ca. 1680 and is indicative of mass production.

29. The white slip appears yellow beneath the redware's overall lead glaze.

30. J. E. and Edith Hodgkin, *Examples of Early English Pottery Named, Dated, and Inscribed* (London, 1891), p. 9. Wolf Mankowitz and Reginald Haggar in their *The Concise Encyclopedia of English Pottery and Porcelain* (New York: Frederick A. Praeger, 1968), p. 149, state that at

the time of writing, dated Metropolitan slipwares ranged from 1638 to 1659. They cited also an undated chamber pot in the Hanley Museum inscribed EARTH I AM ET TES MOST TRU DISDAN ME NOT FOR SO ARE YOU.

31. This pot, once in the Guildhall Museum, is now in the Collection of the Museum of London.

32. The combed slip decoration on the illustrated pot is a technique one usually associates with Staffordshire beginning in the second half of the seventeenth century. However, comparable fragments from Donyatt kilns reportedly date as early as the fourteenth century. See R. Coleman-Smith and T. Pearson, *Excavations in the Donyatt Potteries* (Chichester, Eng.: Phillimore & Co., 1988), pl. 2.

33. Ibid., pp. 306–11.

34. Ibid.

35. Merry A. Outlaw, "Scratched in Clay: Seventeenth-Century North Devon Slipware at Jamestown, Virginia," in *Ceramics in America,* edited by Robert Hunter (Hanover, N.H.: University Press of New England for the Chipstone Foundation, 2002), p. 34. As the inscribed pot was found in a Jamestown ditch and not at the governor's Green Spring home, one wonders how and why it strayed so far from the Berkeley bedroom. The pot was first published by C. Malcolm Watkins in his "North Devon Pottery and Its Export to America in the 17th Century," *United States National Museum Bulletin 225* (Washington D.C.: Government Printing Office, 1960), p. 38, fig. 15, where he interpreted the initials as WR and suggested a royal relationship.

36. Jan Steen painted several versions of another bedroom scene titled *The Morning Toilet,* each with a metal chamber pot beside the bed. One of these paintings is in the British Royal Collection at Buckingham Palace. *Dutch Pictures from the Royal Collection,* The Queen's Gallery Buckingham Palace (London: Lund Humphries, 1971), No. 38. In using paintings as parallels, it is important to remember that while shapes can be relied on (at least in general), old varnish and the accuracy of photographic reproduction can darken and significantly distort colors.

37. Jaqueline Pearce, *Border Wares* (London: Her Majesty's Stationary Office, 1992), early: pl. 11, bottom left; late: p. 33, fig. 13, right.

38. The only means of narrowing dates is to find examples in tightly sealed and reliably datable archaeological contexts. But even then there is no certainty of the pot's age at the time it entered the ground. All that can be said with confidence is that it was discarded at a date no later than that of the deposit, in archaeological parlance, a *terminus ante quem*.

39. A second chamber pot appears in the lower left corner of the latter engraving. Its curiously squat shape suggests that Hogarth had not taken great care in its rendering and with posterity not a concern, it was enough that the object should be recognizable as a chamber pot. This is a point worth bearing in mind whenever we look for stylistic nuances in the works of painters and engravers.

40. Amis, "Some domestic vessels of southern Britain," p. 25, nos. 20 and 21.

41. Rims of this type and wares of this color are present among sherds from a French wreck of ca. 1760 off the coast of Bermuda. For contextual details see Ivor Noël Hume, *Shipwreck! History from the Bermuda Reefs* (Hamilton, Bermuda: Capstan Publications, 1995), pp. 18–24.

42. Amis, "Some domestic vessels of southern Britain," p. 25, no. 19, with pewterer's mark TM 1716. Resembling the 1545 *Mary Rose* pot, another dished and everted rim form is to be seen on a pewter chamber pot recovered from the wreck of the Dutch ship *Batavia* that foundered off the west coast of Australia in 1629. Myra Stanbury, *Batavia Catalogue* (Perth, Australia: Dept. of Maritime Archaeology, Western Australian Museum, ca. 1975) p. 34, no. 3031, there described only as a "round pewter pot."

43. Frank Britton, "The Pickleherring Potteries: An Inventory," *Post-Medieval Archaeology* 24 (1990): 61–92.

44. The notion of painting or printing the faces of unpopular people on the interiors of chamber pots was to continue until World War II when portraits of Adolph Hitler accompanied such inscriptions as HAVE THIS ON "OLD NASTY" and ANOTHER VIOLATION OF POLAND, Po being one of many sobriquets for chamber pot. Another on the side reads N^{O} 1 "JERRY," Hitler being the number one German. Lambton, *Temples of Convenience and Chambers of Delight,* p. 151. An unlikely place to find another, but there just the same, is the ZAM (Center for Unusual Museums) in Munich, Germany.

45. Cited in *Dictionary of the Vulgar Tongue*. Further evidence of the ubiquitousness of chamber pots is illustrated by the fact that a temporary tavern built on the Thames during the

great Frost Fair of 1696 was named the Flying Piss Pot. An anonymous tract titled *Christ Exalted, and Dr. Crisp Vindicated* (1698), p. 63, asks the question "Hath not the Potter power over the Clay, of the same lump, to make a hundred Chamber-pots, and but five drinking Vessels?"

46. John C. Austin, *British Delft at Williamsburg* (Williamsburg, Va.: Colonial Williamsburg Foundation, 1994), p. 290. There are no examples in Michael Archer's *Delftware* (London: Stationery Office City, 1997), a catalogue of the collection at the Victoria and Albert Museum. This may demonstrate their rarity on the one hand or, on the other, previous curators' reluctance to find artistic merit in anything so humble.

47. Purchased on eBay from an Italian dealer.

48. "An Indian Ware of the Colonial Period," *Quarterly Bulletin, Archeological Society of Virginia* 17, no. 1 (September 1962): 9. The term has since been corrupted to "Colono Ware" meaning any pottery made by non-whites in the colonial era.

49. Ivor Noël Hume, "Collectors' Notes," *Antiques* 90, no. 4 (October 1966): 521.

50. *A Catalogue of the Genuine Household Furniture . . . Late the Property of a Noble Personage (Deceas'd), Fryday December, 5, 1766*, p. 7, lot 24, that sold for £1.2*s*.0*d*. Two more pots were sold on that day, described as "Two flower chamber-pots and covers" (p. 3, lot 14) that fetched 15*s*.0*d*. The material was not identified, but they may have been floral-decorated delftware. The unidentified owner evidently had been in the East India trade and had spent time in Bengal as a person of consequence.

51. Christie's, *The Nanking Cargo*, Amsterdam, April 28–May 2, 1986, lots 1094–1221.

52. Impressed mark M. MASON. Mankowitz and Haggar, *The Concise Encyclopedia of English Pottery and Porcelain*, pl. 65b.

53. Pots of this type continued to be made into the 1880s at the Garrison Pottery in Sunderland, albeit with less ribald inscriptions. See Lambton, *Temples of Convenience and Chambers of Delight*, p. 81.

54. Recalling the Metropolitan slipware chamber pot slip-inscribed BE MERY AND WISE AND PEFF. See note 32, and Ivor Noël Hume, *If These Pots Could Talk: Collecting 2,000 Years of British Household Pottery* (Hanover, N.H.: University Press of New England for the Chipstone Foundation, 2001), p.78, fig. IV. 3.

55. On a Metropolitan slipware jug. Hodgkin and Hodgkin, *Examples of Early English Pottery Named, Dated, and Inscribed*, p. 53, no. 193.

56. Lambton, *Temples of Convenience and Chambers of Delight*, p. 117. Another example (p. 121), also of mid-nineteenth century date, is inscribed around the rim: FILL [?] ME UP AND USE ME WELL AND WHAT I SEE I WILL NEVER TELL. HAND IT TO ME MY DEAR.

57. Two small, false-fronted "antique" stores are all that remains of Nevadaville.

58. Webster's *Ninth Collegiate Dictionary* (1983), variation of "goggle-eyed."

59. The suggested dating is based on the similarity of lettering found on several anti-Hitler pots of the early 1940s.

60. Klijn, *Lead-glazed Earthenwares*, p. 57, fig. 48; p. 247, top.

61. Noël Hume, *If These Pots Could Talk*, p. 89, figs. IV. 23–24, there described but not identified.

62. Klijn, *Lead-glazed Earthenwares*, p. 235.

63. Britton, "The Pickleherring Potteries: An Inventory," pp. 70–71.

64. M. Chomel revised by Mr. R. Bradley, *Dictionaire Oeconomique or The Family Dictionary* (London: D. Midwinter at the Three Crows in St. Paul's Church-Yard, 1725).

65. Noël Hume, *If These Pots Could Talk*, p. 170, fig. VIII.8. Late English delftware decorated with GR medallions in the manner of debased scratch blue stoneware were made for the London purveyor William Wyatt and stenciled under the glaze PREPARED MUSTARD. Supplied with pairs of horizontal shell-shaped handles, they bear no resemblance to chamber pots. Alec Davis, *Package & Print, The Development of Container and Label Design* (New York: Clarkson N. Potter, Inc., 1967), fig. 3, following p. 112.

66. Geoffrey A. Godden, *Encyclopaedia of British Pottery and Porcelain Marks* (New York: Crown Publishers, 1964), p. 598, no. 3713. The recorded mark differs from that on the pot which reads R. S. & W rather than R. S. W.

67. In 1841 the name was changed yet again, this time to the Eastern State Asylum. See Shomer S. Zwelling, *Quest for a Cure: The Public Hospital in Williamsburg, 1773–1885* (Williamsburg, Va.: Colonial Williamsburg Foundation, 1985), p. 30.

68. Zwelling, *Quest for a Cure*, fig. 3.

69. Beginning in 1850, Trenton was to become America's principal source of white granite wares for sanitary use, and by 1883, more than twenty potteries were producing it. The New

Jersey factory of Thomas Maddock and Sons continued under that name until 1923 when it was acquired by partner D. William Scammell and became the Scammell China Company.

70. Chamber pots came en suite with ten or eleven other pieces comprising one large water pitcher, one basin, one slop jar (two handled with lid), one chamber pot with lid, one small water pitcher, one shaving brush vase, one mug, and one soap dish in three parts. In 1899 prices ranged from $4.00 to $16.50 per set. *Higgins & Seiter Catalog, New York* (1899; reprint, Princeton, N.J.: Pyne Press, 1971).

71. A chamber pot with similar characteristics is illustrated in Manfred Klaunda, *Geschichte und Geschichten vom Nachttopf* (Munich: Zentrum für Anssergewöhnliche Museen, 1992), p. 26 and described as "stoneware with a kitschy painting of an 'evening mood,' North German, around 1930" (trans.).

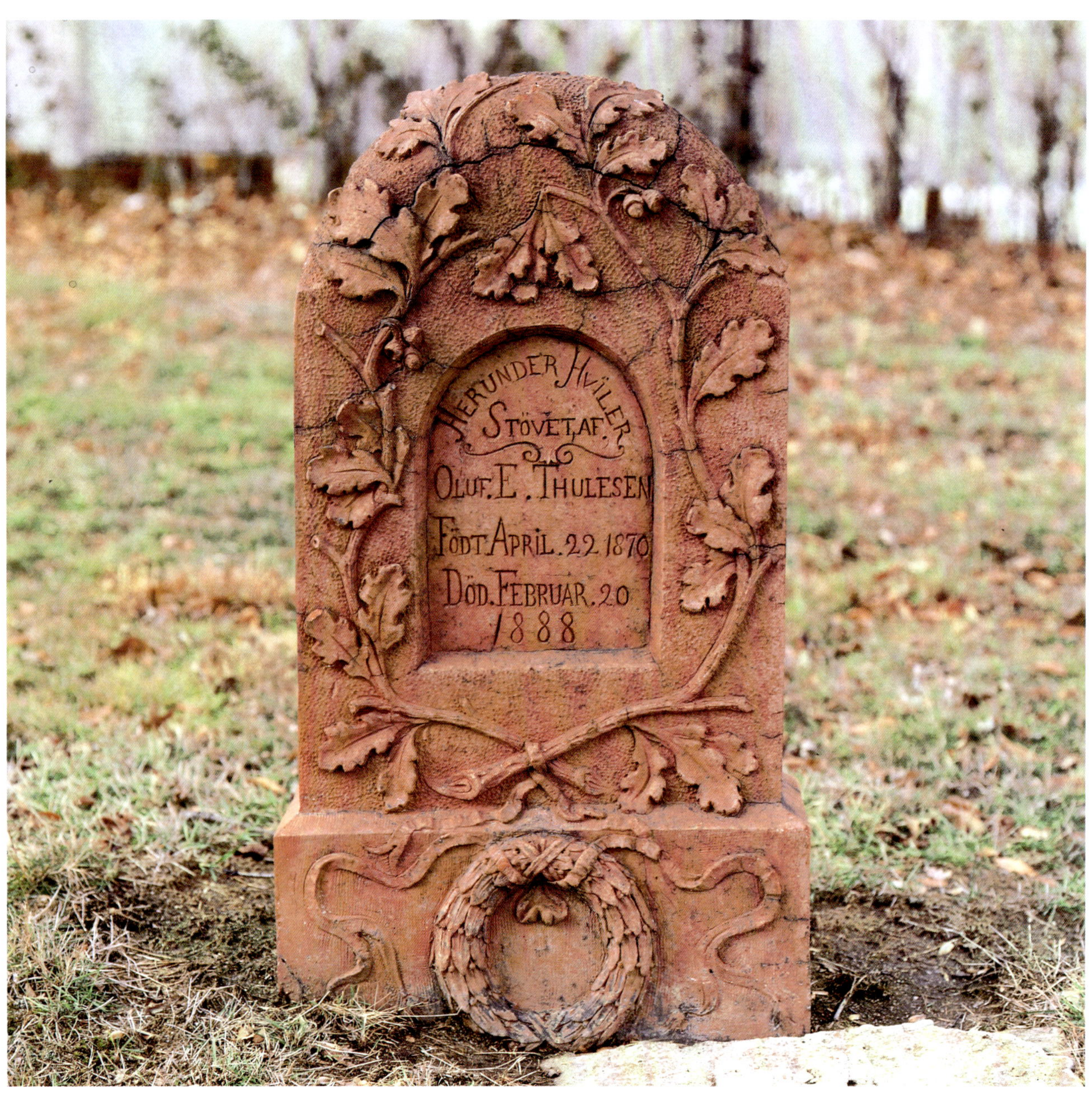

Figure 1 Gravemarker, Perth Amboy, New Jersey, 1888. Terracotta. H. 34½". (Photographs by Gavin Ashworth unless otherwise noted.) The Oluf Thulesen marker is made from a single piece of unglazed red terracotta. It is decorated with carefully sculpted oak boughs, complete with acorns. The marker is located in Alpine Cemetery, Perth Amboy.

Richard Veit and Mark Nonestied

Taken for Granite: Terracotta Gravemarkers from New Jersey and New York

▼ VICTORIAN AND EARLY-twentieth-century urban cemeteries are generally filled with hundreds, and sometimes thousands, of gray granite and white marble memorials. In the cemeteries of central New Jersey's Clay District, this rather homogenous picture is punctuated by nearly two hundred colorful red, green, blue, and brown ceramic gravemarkers (figs. 1, 2). Produced from architectural terracotta, they are reminders of a once thriving industry and the people who worked in it. At the same time, they provide a material record of the ceramicists' skills, the potential of their material, and, even more importantly from an archaeological standpoint, dated examples of their work. Terracotta markers are found in a band running diagonally across New Jersey between Woodbridge in the north and Trenton in the south. A handful of examples are also found in nearby Staten Island, New York. The markers' distribution reflects the presence of rich clay deposits associated with the Raritan Formation and, more specifically, the location of turn-of-the-century terracotta factories (fig. 3).

The terracotta these markers were made from is not simply the brick red stuff of flowerpots and utilitarian redwares; rather, it is architectural terracotta. This is a form of ornamental ceramic cladding used in architecture, made from sculpted and molded clay. The clay body has a fine texture that allows it to be molded, sculpted, and glazed. Terracotta was often made in the form of hollow blocks with internal webbing or supports that allowed it to be both strong and light (fig. 4).

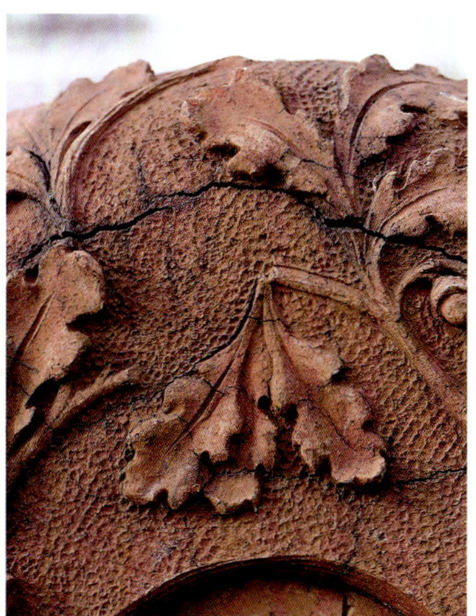

Figure 2 Detail of the oak boughs on the gravemarker illustrated in figure 1. The tree of life cut down was a common Victorian gravemarker design. This snapped twig conveys the same idea, a life cut short. Oluf Thulesen was only eighteen when he died.

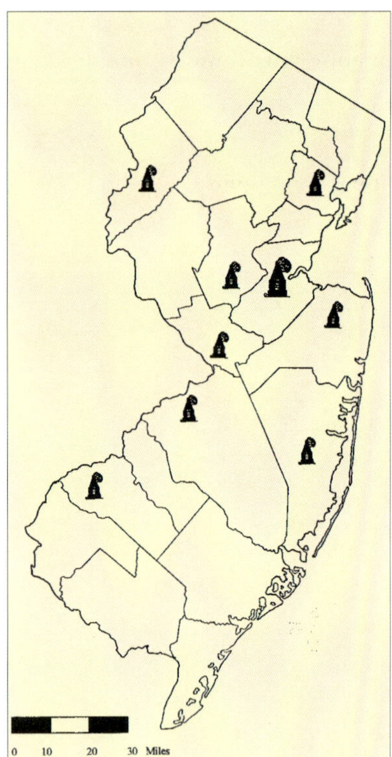

Figure 3 The kilns on this map show the approximate location of New Jersey's major terracotta manufacturers. (Courtesy, *IA: The Journal of the Society for Industrial Archaeology*.) The Raritan Formation of Cretaceous clays runs transversely across New Jersey from northeast to southwest.

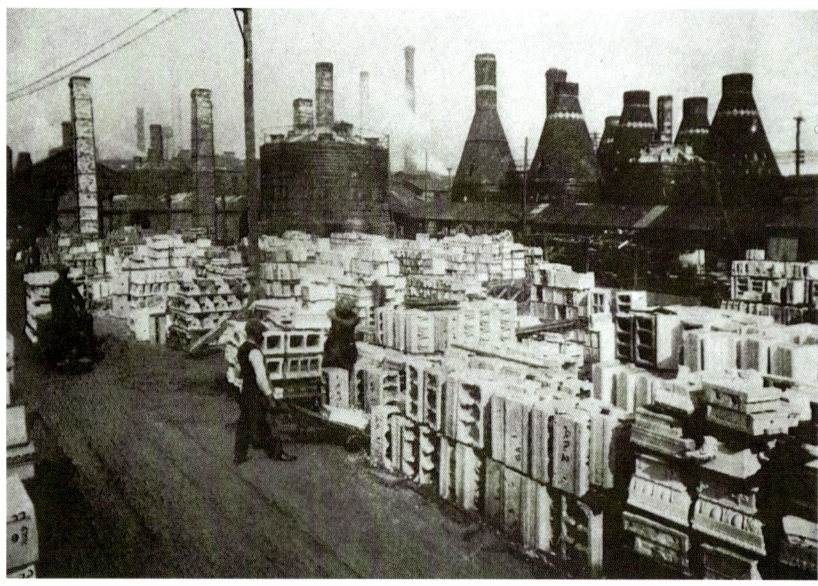

Figure 4 Photograph of the Atlantic Terracotta Company's Perth Amboy factory. (Collection of Richard Veit.) This early-twentieth-century photograph gives a good idea of the size of typical pieces of architectural terracotta. Note that almost all of the blocks are hollow.

The Rise and Fall of New Jersey's Terracotta Industry

Although terracotta is an ancient material, used by cultures as distinct as the Romans and the Qin Dynasty Chinese, it fell out of use after the fall of the Roman Empire and was not revived until the Renaissance. The noted architect Andrew Jackson Downing introduced terracotta to Americans in the mid-nineteenth century. James Renwick and Richard Upjohn, Sr., also influential architects, seconded Downing's call for terracotta in architecture. By the 1880s Charles Thomas Davis, an authority on the ceramics industry, was writing that:

> The largest terracotta works in this country [the United States] are located at Perth Amboy in New Jersey. Woodbridge and Perth Amboy both owe their prosperity to the manufacture of terracotta, fire-brick and tiles, and the traveler journeying westward in New Jersey, from either of these thrifty towns, will find his way skirted by frequent hollows and excavations stretching irregularly on either hand . . . this section should become to us what the Staffordshire district is to England.[1]

Nineteenth-century architects viewed terracotta as a sort of wonder material. It was less expensive than stone; it could be mass produced to exacting specifications; it easily took a glaze; it was fireproof; it could be sculpted and molded; it was easy to clean; and it was billed as lasting forever. Moreover, it was associated with several innovative architectural tastemakers, ranging from the aforementioned Renwick and Upjohn to Stanford White, Cass Gilbert, and Henry Furness.

The first individual to attempt the manufacture of terracotta in New Jersey was Diedrich Winnter of Newark. A potter by training, Winnter and his associates made a terracotta cornice for the Corn Exchange Building in New York City in 1853. Sadly, it failed after only one winter's frosts.[2] One wit later noted:

> This company was owned and operated by several educated Europeans (Winnter, Haefeli, Huber, and Schrag) who during the hours of labor . . . used to sweeten their tasks by reflections upon the Renaissance—classical conversations in Latin, Greek, French, and German . . . and it is assumed that if they had been possessed of less mental culture, if they had been poorer scholars and better terracotta makers, success would not have eluded them.[3]

Despite this failure, other manufacturers in Trenton, Burlington, and Gloucester City began to manufacture architectural terracotta in small quantities.

This changed in 1873 when Alfred Hall, a successful brickmaker and yellow ware potter from Perth Amboy, decided, at his nephew William's suggestion, to start manufacturing terracotta. Alfred Hall sought the advice of James Taylor, former superintendent of a British terracotta factory, who had spent the last five years helping establish terracotta factories in Chicago, Boston, and New York. Taylor suggested his brother Robert as a technical advisor to Hall. With Robert Taylor on board, Hall reincorporated his firm as the Perth Amboy Terracotta Company.[4] Shortly thereafter, Hall bombastically claimed, "This new terracotta industry (of which I was the founder) brings into the state about three hundred thousand dollars per annum, and with proper aid from capital would soon bring in more than one million per annum, and eventually will bring in more wealth than all the crockery business in Trenton"(fig. 5).[5]

Figure 5 Photograph of the Perth Amboy Terracotta Company. (Courtesy, Princeton Historical Society.) This photograph shows Alfred Hall's original brickworks/yellow ware pottery turned terracotta factory on Buckingham Avenue in Perth Amboy as it appeared in 1879.

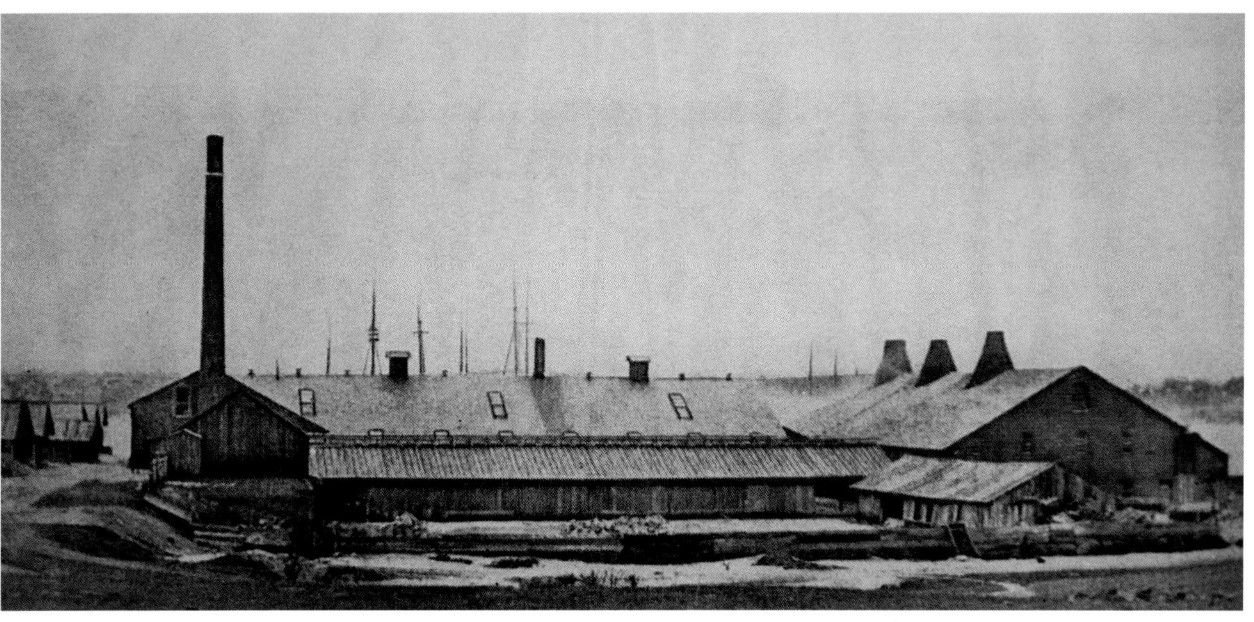

As Hall predicted, the industry continued to grow. He, however, left the company he had founded following a disagreement with his co-owners. Nevertheless, the Perth Amboy Terracotta Company rose to preeminence in the field. By 1898 it had forty-six kilns and dominated the Perth Amboy waterfront. Charles DeKay, writing for *Harper's Weekly,* noted:

> An early riser in the ancient village of Tottenville, Staten Island, glancing across the narrow Achter Kull, shall see on a misty morning the white low-lying sea fog pierced by singular yet picturesque forms. They are truncated cones of brick with lighter bands running around them. They stand near the water's edge, and might readily be taken for something Egyptian or otherwise Oriental, for Indian tepes [*sic*] or saints' tombs in some queer country of Indo-China.[6]

Early ceramic historian Edwin Atlee Barber described these kilns, as "among the largest of the kind on this continent, if not the world"(fig. 6).[7]

Other companies followed the lead of the Perth Amboy Company and established themselves in and around Perth Amboy. Noteworthy producers included the New Jersey Terracotta Company, the Standard Terracotta Company, the Excelsior Terracotta Company, and the South Amboy Terracotta Company (fig. 7). As competition increased, profits fell. In reaction, four companies—Atlantic Terracotta of Staten Island, the Perth Amboy Terracotta Company, the Excelsior Terracotta Company of Rocky Hill, and the Standard Terracotta Company of Perth Amboy—merged in 1906–1907 to form the dominant player in the marketplace, Atlantic Terra-

Figure 6 Photograph of the Perth Amboy Terracotta Company's factory from *Geological Survey of New Jersey, Vol. IV, Clay Industry,* 1904. Notice the enormous kilns.

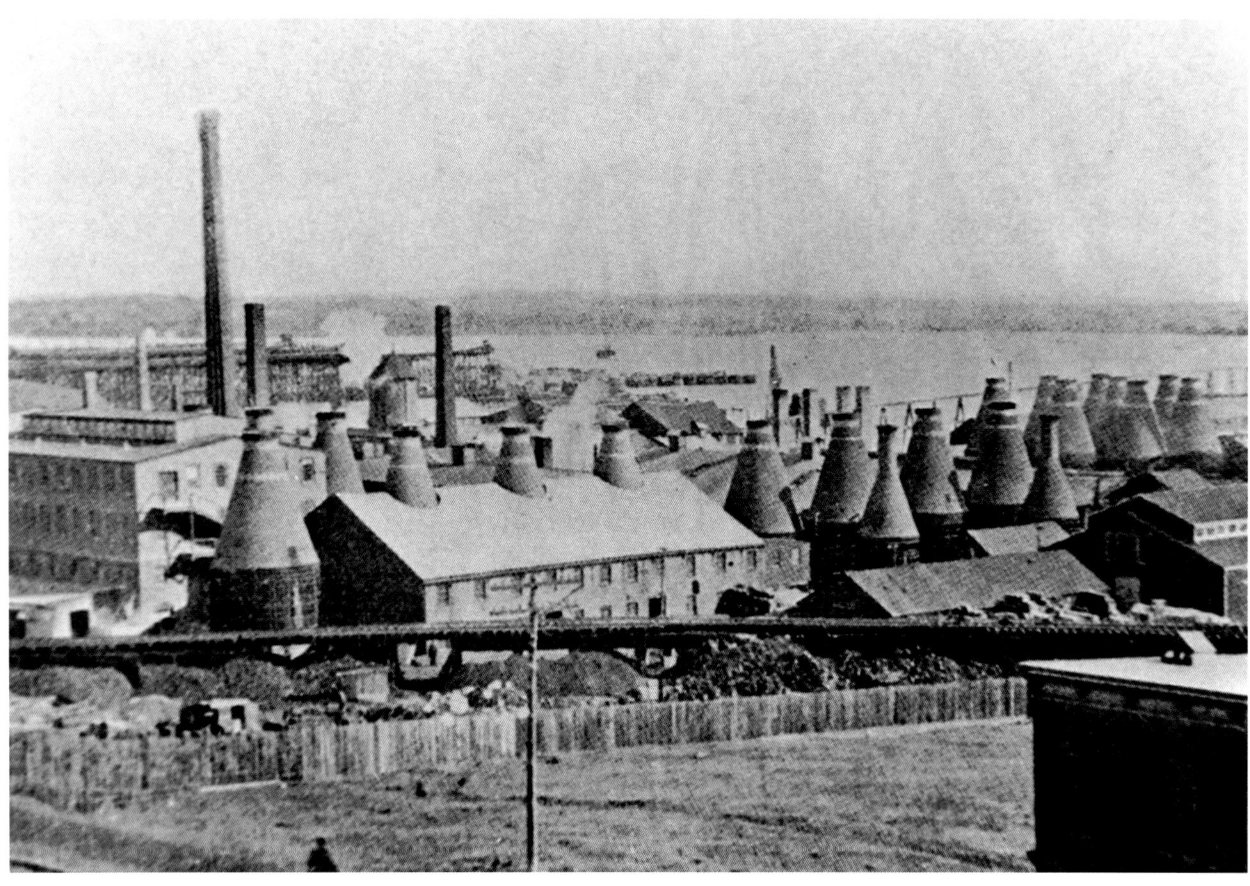

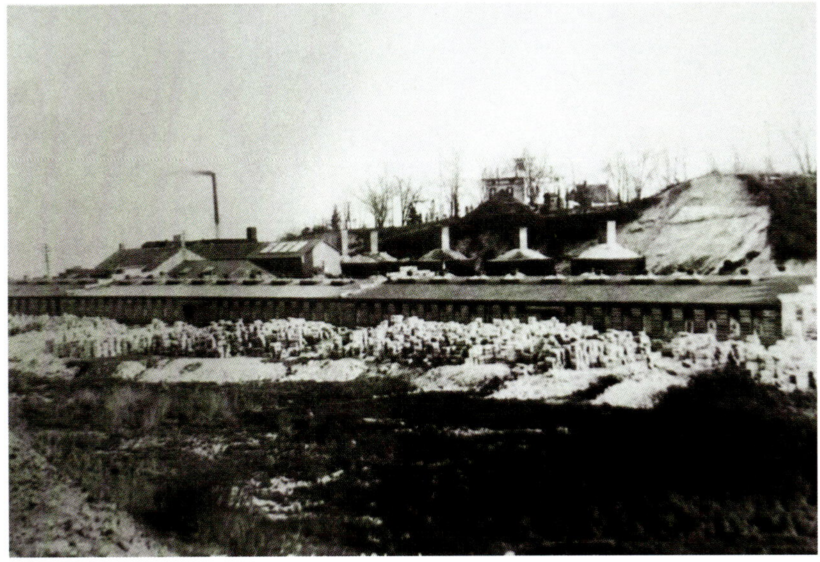

Figure 7 Postcard photograph of the South Amboy Terracotta Company, later part of the Federal Seaboard Terracotta Corporation. (Collection of Richard Veit.) Note the line of kilns and the extensive stock of finished ware.

cotta. All four plants remained in operation. In 1912 the company produced 7,500 tons of terracotta cladding for what was then the tallest building in the world, New York City's Woolworth Tower. Later, in 1932, it produced the stunning polychrome terracotta façade for the Philadelphia Museum of Art.[8]

In 1909 Charles Geer, the first president of the newly reorganized Atlantic Terracotta, left and formed a competing firm, Federal Terracotta in Woodbridge. In 1928 Federal merged with the South Amboy Terracotta Company and the New Jersey Terracotta Company to form the Federal Seaboard Terracotta Corporation. During World War I, Federal Terracotta manufactured terracotta practice bombs for the Army Air Corps.[9] Later, the company became an important producer of extruded wall ashlars and swimming pool blocks. Their most famous buildings are the McGraw Hill Building in New York City and Asbury Park's Convention Hall (fig. 8).

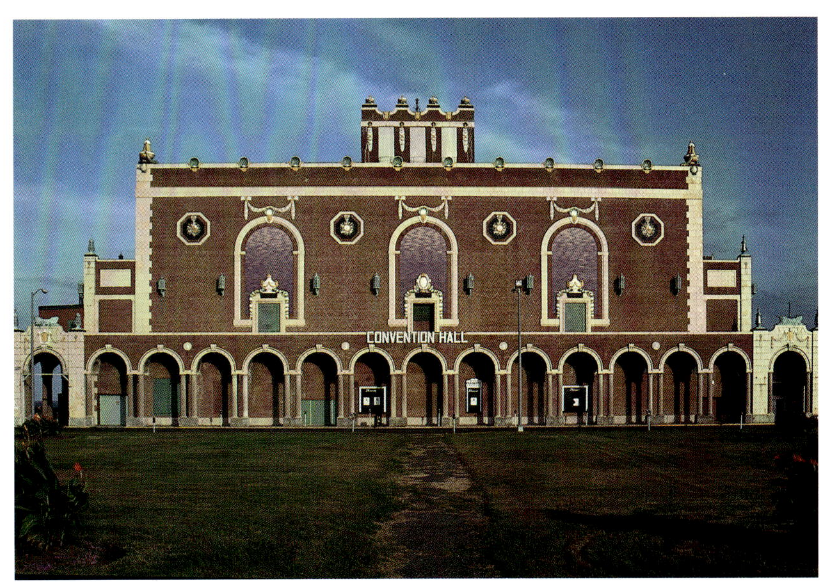

Figure 8 Asbury Park Convention Hall, 1928–1930, New Jersey. (Photo, Richard Veit.) The building features buff and polychrome terracotta details. The terracotta employed in it was produced by the Federal Seaboard Terracotta Corporation.

The Depression of the 1930s led to a contraction in the industry. Atlantic closed down its Rocky Hill plant, and by 1941 Federal Seaboard had shut down its Woodbridge Plant. During World War II, the number of local workers in the industry dropped below 800 for the first time since 1900.[10] After the war, architects turned to new, less expensive materials; by 1968 the last remaining company, Federal Seaboard, had closed its doors. The end had been a long time coming. In 1932 E. V. Eskesen, president of Federal Seaboard Terracotta, wrote with prescience, "The dream of the modern architect is to build houses entirely out of metal, glass, and cement. In this construction, brick, tile, or terracotta has no place."[11]

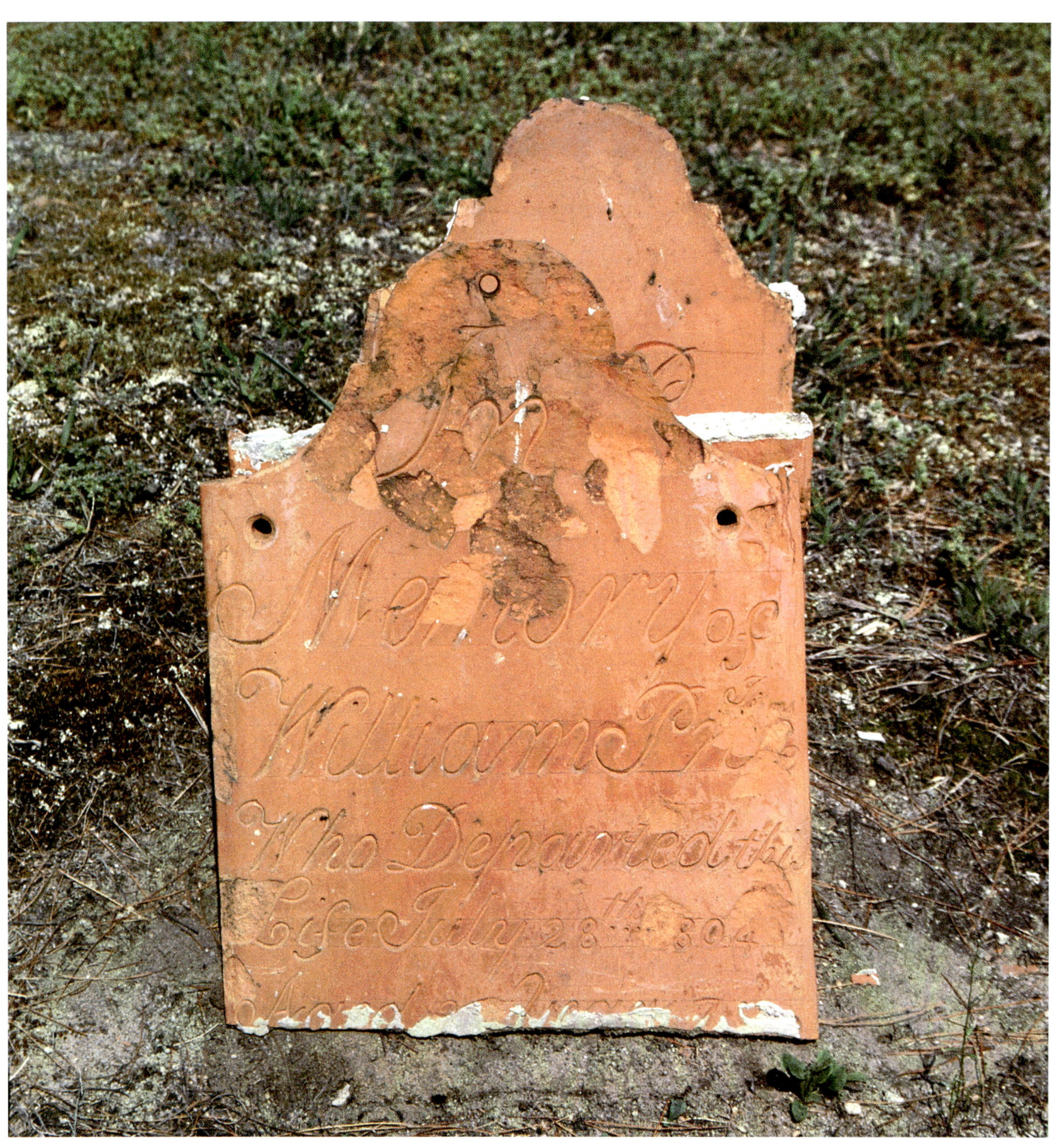

Figure 9 Gravemarker, Mount Holly, New Jersey, 1804. Terracotta. H. 18". (Photo, Richard Veit.) This early ceramic gravemarker marks the final resting place of William Price. Presumably it was produced by a local potter. Apparently it broke in two and was repaired, unsuccessfully, with some sort of adhesive. An accompanying footstone also survives.

Terracotta Gravemarkers

One little known product of the terracotta works was gravemarkers. Although gravemarkers are generally assumed to be made from stone, many other materials have been used for memorials. Wooden memorials have been used in the United States since colonial times. During the nineteenth century, iron gravemarkers were occasionally produced. Cast zinc markers, sold under the trade name Monumental Bronze, are common in late-nineteenth-century cemeteries. Homemade concrete gravemarkers are also common in twentieth-century ethnic cemeteries.

Even earlier, the Qin Dynasty Chinese (221–207 B.C.) buried a magnificent army of terracotta workers with their emperor, and the ancient Romans made gravemarkers out of terracotta. Later, in seventeenth-century England, enterprising potters were producing gravemarkers, and in the nineteenth century, a variety of monuments were made from a ceramic material called Coade's Stone.[12]

The first ceramic gravemarkers in New Jersey date from the early nineteenth century and predate the terracotta industry. There is an 1804 redware marker in Mount Holly (fig. 9) and a pair of stoneware markers in Port Elizabeth. The latter are associated with a nineteenth-century glassworks and were apparently produced from the clay used to make crucibles. These early clay markers are, however, nearly unique and cannot be considered part of a larger local tradition of gravemarker production.

Ceramic memorials made up only a small portion of the terracotta plant's products. To date 175 have been found in New Jersey and adjacent parts of New York State. Other examples have been reported from upstate New York, near the site of a terracotta factory, as well as from California, Louisiana, and Ireland. The markers were produced in a variety of forms, most of which fall within the standard canon of Victorian mourning art. They include crosses, tablets, pedestals surmounted by urns, obelisks, and statues. Some were simply made, while others are quite elaborate. This variation is intentional. In the words of Edmund Gillon, "The Victorians, with their great sense of the personal, felt that individual achievement should be recognized. It did not seem to them that a child should have the same stone [or in this case terracotta] as a war veteran, or that the minister or ship captain should lie, as they do today, under nearly identical markers."[13] Size and ornamentation were particularly important. Kenneth Ames has pointed out that "Most planners of America's rural cemeteries apparently accepted social class and hierarchy as a fact of nineteenth-century life. The major rural cemeteries are graphic registers of social significance and status."[14] Rural cemeteries were not, in fact, located in rural areas, but were products of the rural cemetery movement, which advocated situating cemeteries outside urban centers and designing them so that they presented a pleasing, park-like setting. Most of the gravemarkers discussed here are found in small Roman Catholic cemeteries associated with new eastern and southern European immigrants, but some are found in Alpine Cemetery, a local example of the rural cemetery movement, located in Perth Amboy.

Figure 10 Gravemarker, Perth Amboy, New Jersey, 1879. Terracotta and sandstone. H. 120". The Ellen Falvey Royle gravemarker is located in St. Mary's Cemetery, Perth Amboy. It dates from 1879 and employs both buff and red terracotta. The core of the marker, which has survived less well than the terracotta, is sandstone. The roof and cross are yellow, unglazed terracotta; the columns are red, unglazed terracotta.

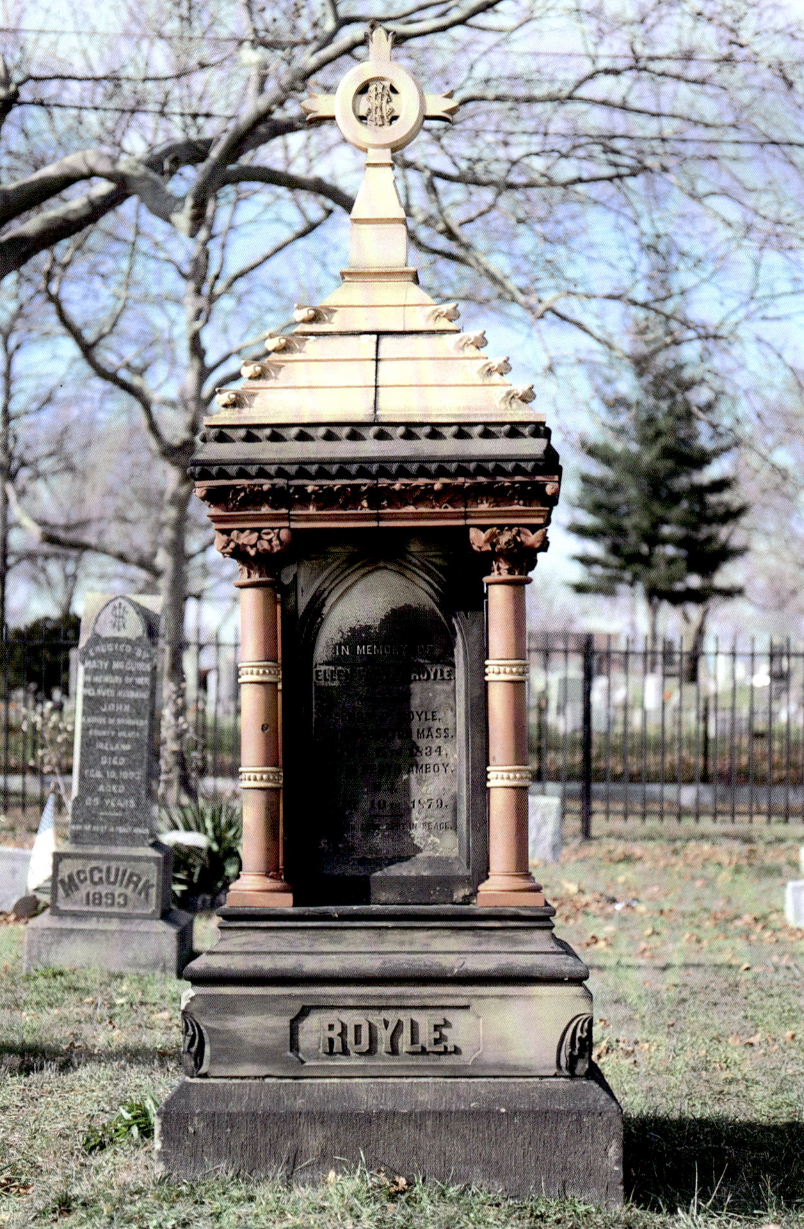

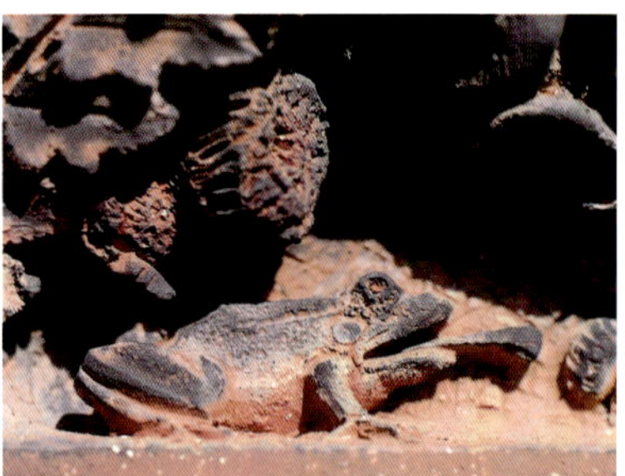

Figure 11 Detail of the frieze on the south side of the gravemarker illustrated in fig. 10. The frieze depicts a menagerie of small animals, including flies, spiders, frogs, and birds. One wonders whether they were intended for the gravemarker or reused from some other project. The frog seen here is about to swallow a spider. The frog is approximately two inches tall.

The markers vary considerably in size. Some are less than six-inches tall, while others reach seven or eight feet in height. One of the largest and most impressive is for Ellen Royle, who died in 1879 (figs. 10, 11). The marker's central core was made from brown sandstone used to support a large terracotta cap with columns. The effect is stunning. Another fine composite marker is the Sofield family memorial (fig. 12). It is dated 1873 and was made from several pieces of yellow terracotta. Spaces where small marble tablets were once attached with personal information about the deceased are clearly visible; unfortunately, some have eroded and others are missing.

The earliest terracotta gravemarkers date from the 1870s and 1880s. The latest examples date from the 1930s. Crosses were the single most popular style of gravemarker, making up forty-two percent of all dated examples.

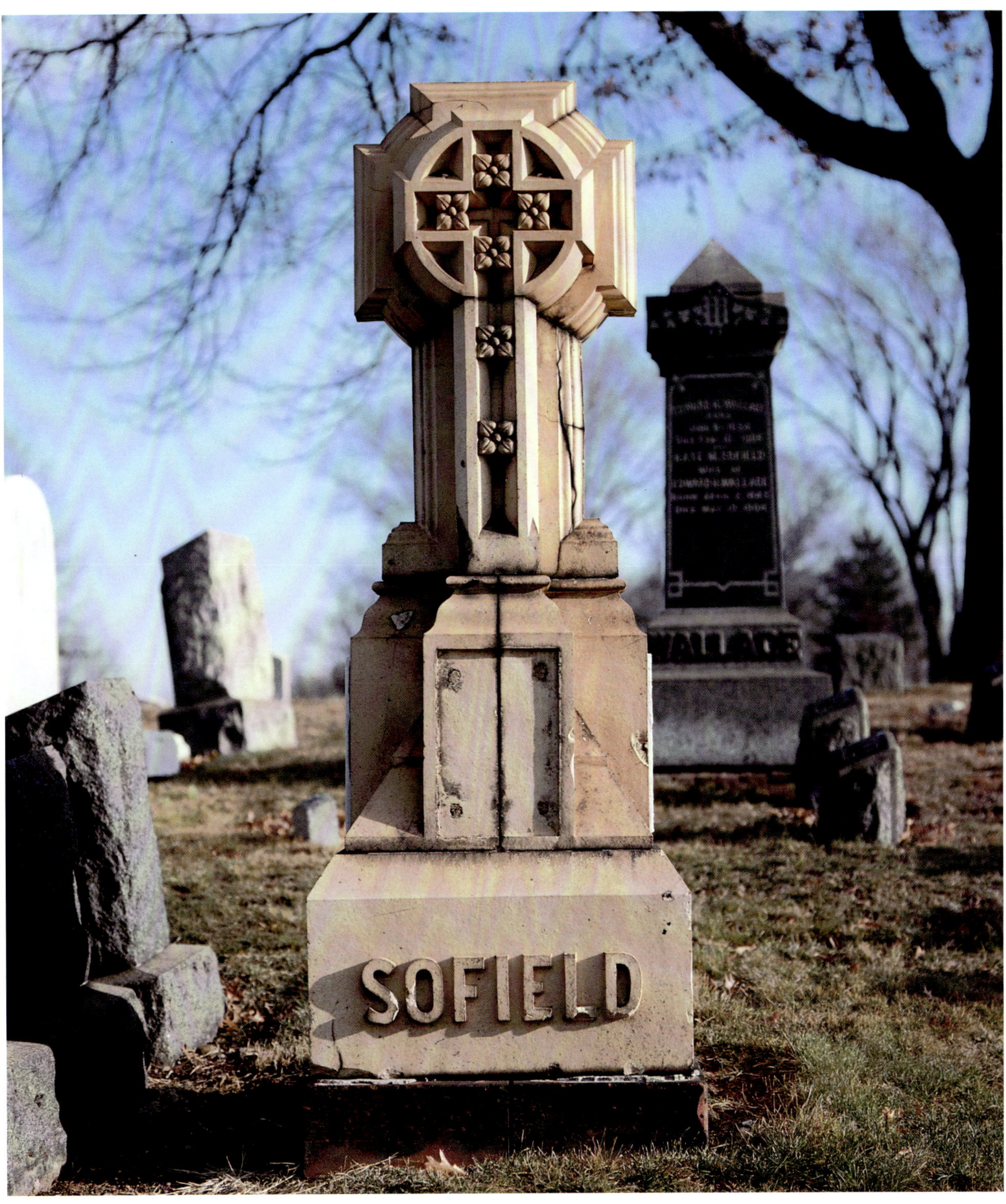

Figure 12 Gravemarker, Perth Amboy, New Jersey, ca. 1870. Terracotta and marble. H. 88". The Sofield family memorial, located in Alpine Cemetery, is one of the larger surviving terracotta monuments. When erected it was ornamented with four marble plaques inscribed with personal information about the deceased. Only two of these remain: one for David Sofield, age 76, and another for his wife, Mary, age 70. David died in 1873, his wife in 1870. Either the marker is backdated or it was erected after other family members passed on, as there were no terracotta producers in Perth Amboy in 1870.

Figure 13 Gravemarker, Perth Amboy, New Jersey, 1878. Terracotta. H. 57". The C. Madsen marker, made from buff-colored unglazed terracotta, is located in Alpine Cemetery. Made for a six-month-old child, it shows amazing attention to detail.

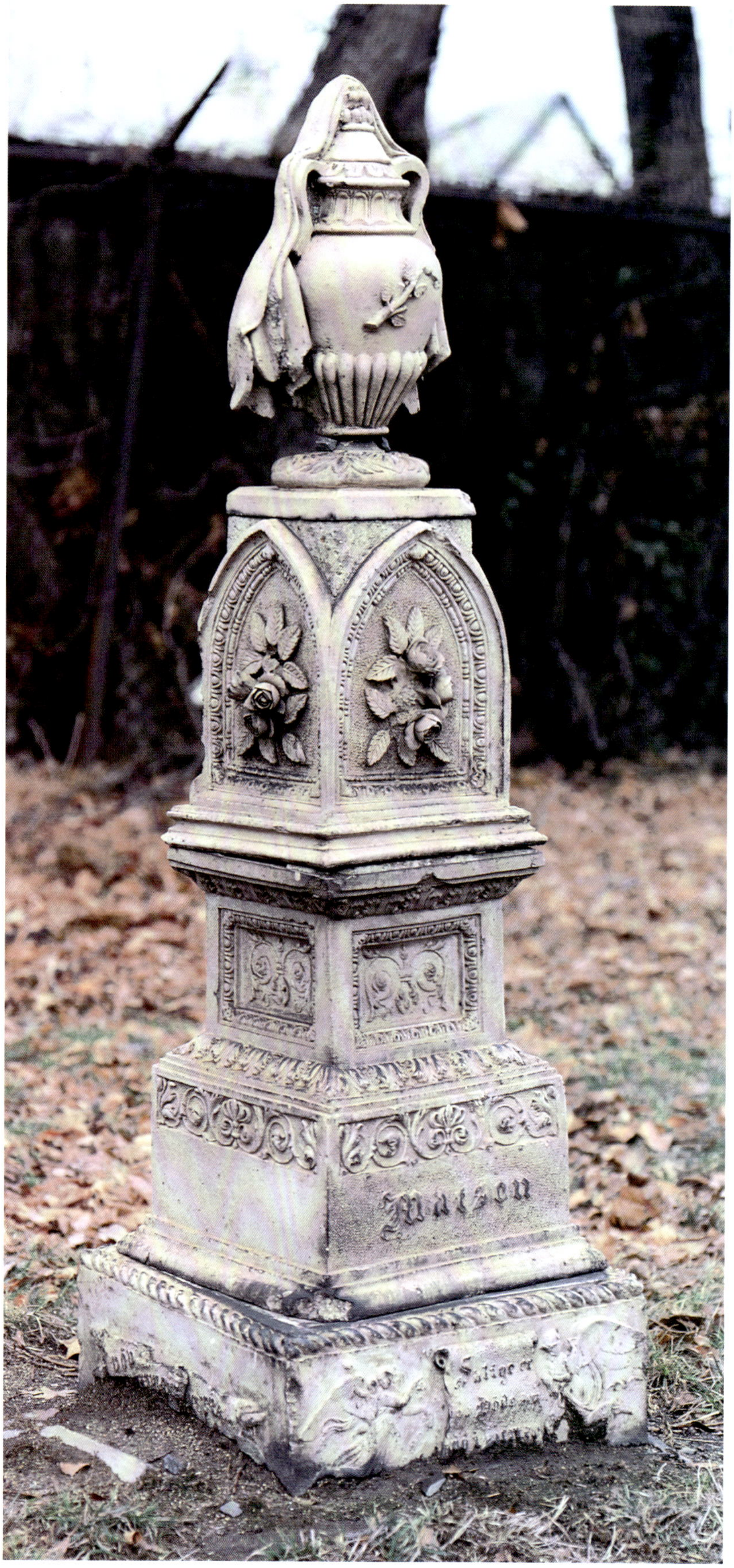

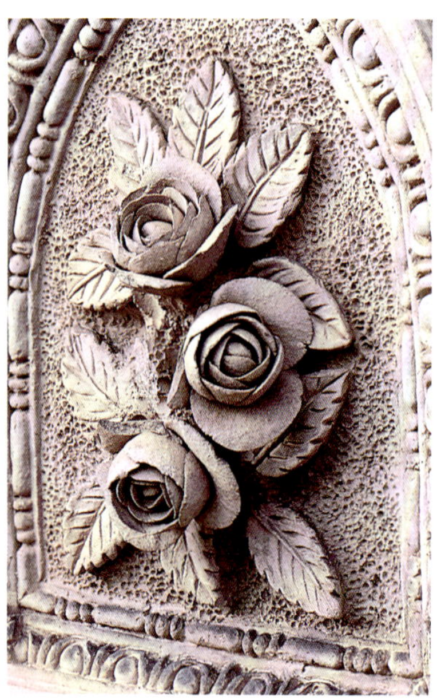

Figure 14 Detail of the gravemarker illustrated in fig. 13. One of four clusters of roses applied to the faces of the Madsen marker. Note the similarities between the stippled background on this marker and that of the Thulesen marker (see fig. 1). Although neither piece is signed, one wonders if the same craftsman produced them.

Figure 15 Gravemarker, Perth Amboy, New Jersey, ca. 1880. Terracotta. H. 32". This uninscribed baluster, molded from red, unglazed terracotta, is a good example of the architectural pieces that were employed as gravemarkers. It is located in Alpine Cemetery.

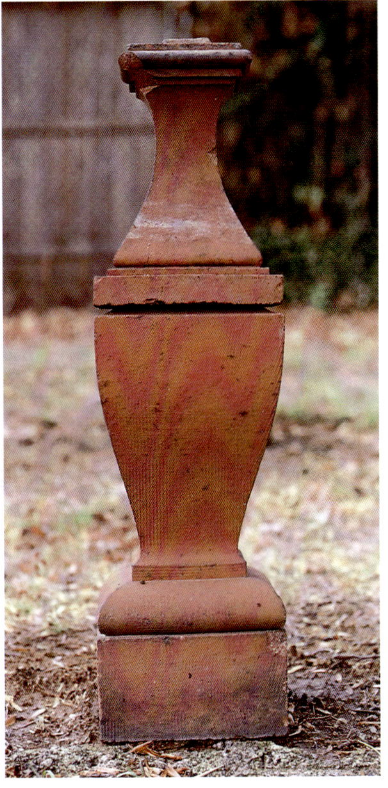

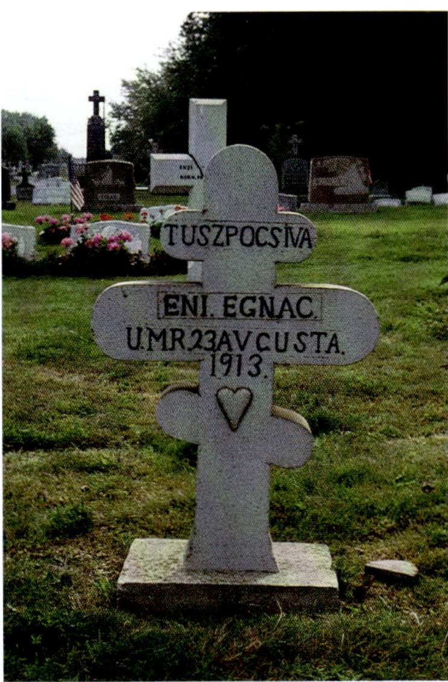

Figure 16 Gravemarker, Woodbridge, New Jersey, 1913. Terracotta. H. 29". The Eni Egnac marker is located in St. John the Baptist Greek Catholic Cemetery. This three-bar cross marker is made from white glazed terracotta.

Markers in the form of urns, tablets, columns, obelisks, and sculpture or statuary were also made (figs. 13, 14), and in a handful of cases, architectural elements were recycled as gravemarkers (fig. 15). The greatest variability in gravemarker forms occurred in the 1890s.

Although crosses as a generic category are quite common, the form of the crosses varies tremendously (figs. 16, 17). Some are in the form of Orthodox crosses, a few resemble tree trunks, and others imitate carved granite. Several show the cross bar of the Eastern Orthodox Church.

Many of the markers use color to good effect. This is true of both glazed and unglazed examples. Glazed terracotta came into widespread use after 1894.[15] On some of the later markers, the lettering was accentuated with color, and white or gray markers were ornamented with gold, black, blue, or red details. Particularly colorful markers include an unusual cruciform marker in the Hillside Cemetery, Metuchen, which sports a shield showing St. Christopher surrounded by a band of azure blue tiles and a cross in the same color (fig. 18). Another colorful marker commemorates Joseph Bauman who is buried in St. Mary's Cemetery, Perth Amboy. It is a simple one-piece cross and tablet in red terracotta with a golden Star of David. The question of Herr Bauman's religion remains unresolved (fig. 19).

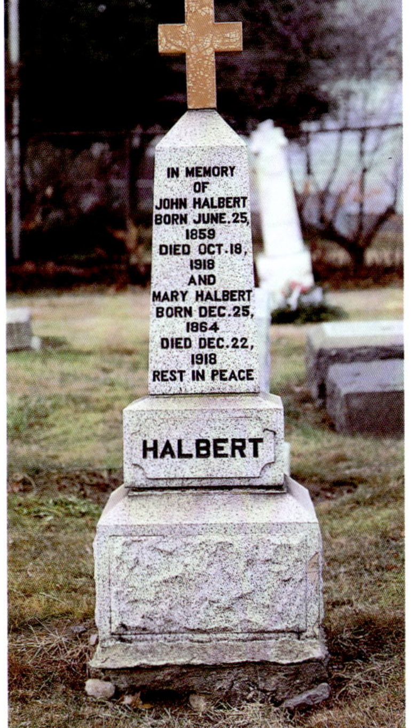

Figure 17 Gravemarker, Perth Amboy, New Jersey, 1918. Terracotta. H. 75". The John and Mary Halbert marker is a good example of mass-produced terracotta gravemarkers with faux granite finish. The granite-like texture was produced using a sprayed on glaze and was marketed under the trade name Granitex. The marker dates from 1918 and is located in Alpine Cemetery.

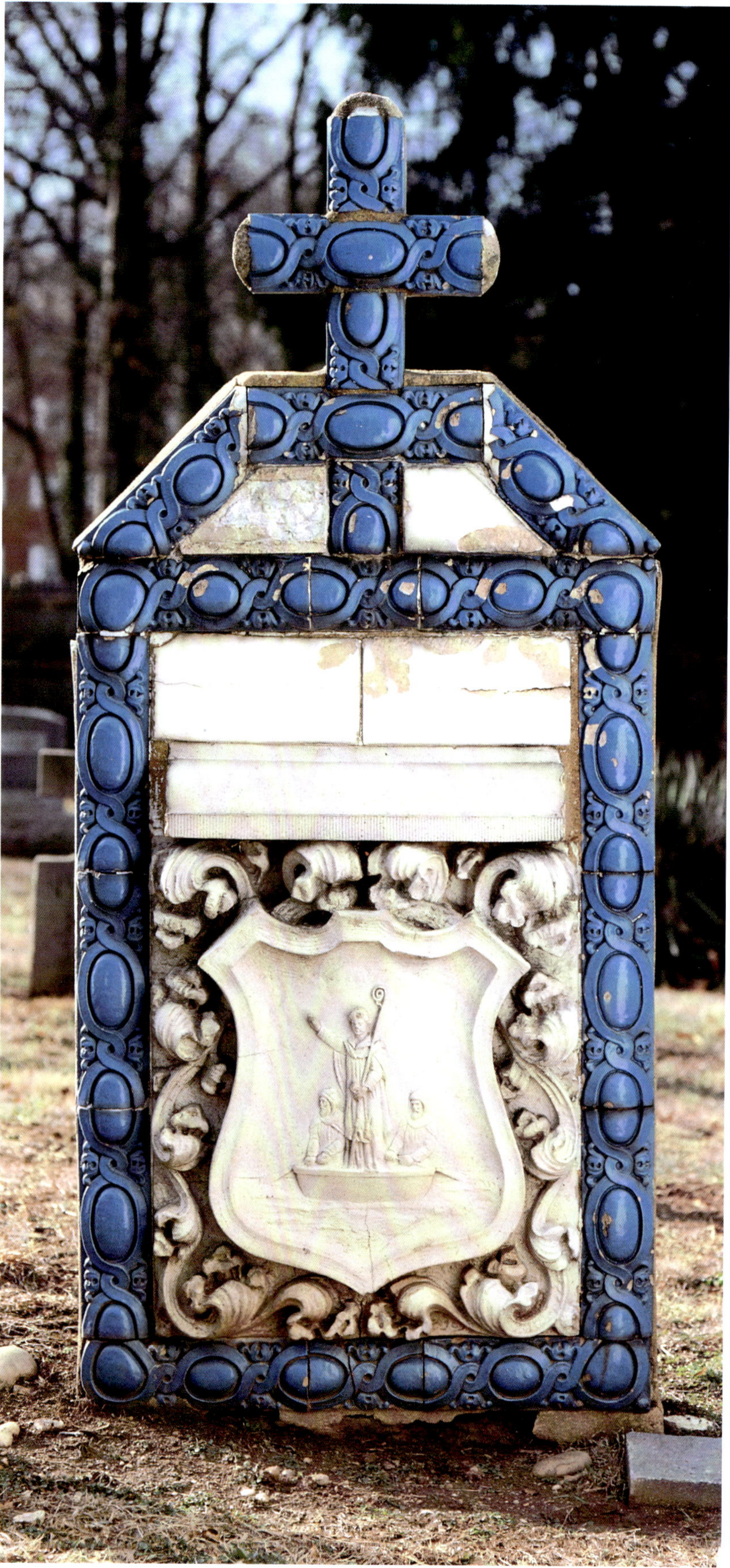

Figure 18 Gravemarker, Metuchen, New Jersey, ca. 1920. Terracotta. H. 70". This is an uninscribed polychrome gravemarker from Hillside Cemetery. It incorporates deep blue tiles for the border and cross around a centerpiece shield that shows St. Christopher. These pieces may have been scavenged from other projects. Together they form a remarkable composition.

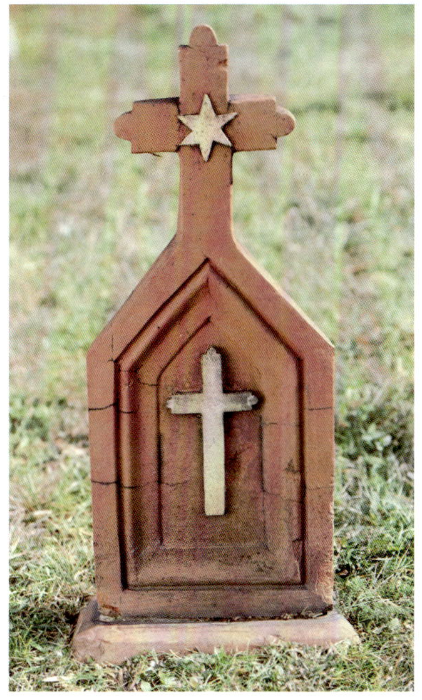

Figure 19 Gravemarker, Perth Amboy, New Jersey, 1900. Terracotta. H. 27". The Joseph Bauman marker is made of brick red terracotta and combines a cross motif with a golden Star of David. It is located in St. Mary's Cemetery, and dates from 1900. This is the back of the marker.

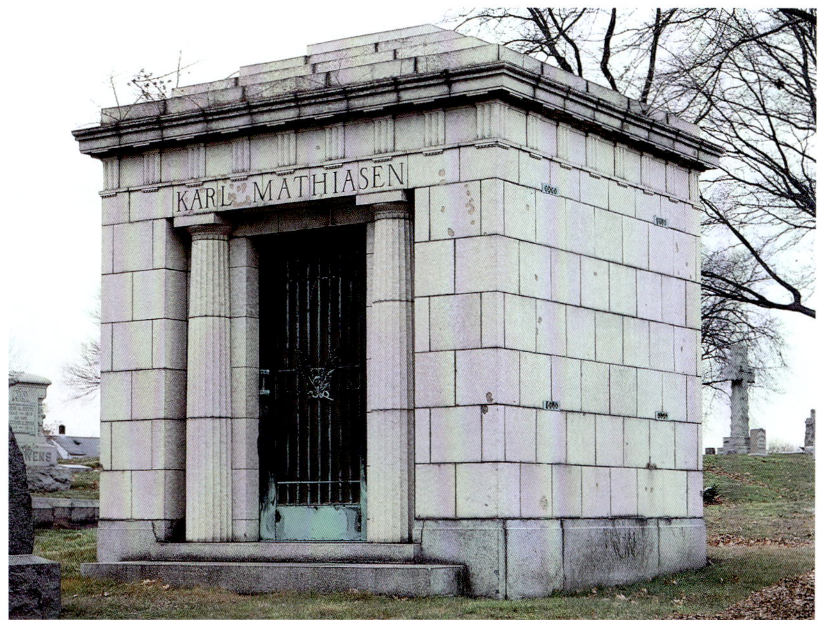

Figure 20 Mausoleum, Perth Amboy, New Jersey, 1920. Terracotta. H. approx. 144". Karl Mathiasen was a motivating force behind the development of New Jersey's terracotta industry. A Danish immigrant, he worked as a potter for Alfred Hall after coming to America. Later, he worked for terracotta manufacturer Robert Taylor in Boston, and subsequently at the Perth Amboy Terracotta Company. In 1888 he and his brother-in-law Otto Hansen founded their own firm. In 1893 it became the New Jersey Terracotta Company, later part of Federal Seaboard. His mausoleum, which appears to be made from granite is, of course, terracotta.

The simplest markers recorded, and presumably the least expensive, were the aforementioned recycled architectural elements, and simple, uninscribed one-piece memorials. However, elaborate mausoleums were also made of terracotta. Appropriately enough, Karl Mathiasen (died 1920), the first president of the New Jersey Terracotta Company, had one erected to his memory (fig. 20) as did the Hansen family, who were associated with the same company.

In the second decade of the twentieth century, mass-produced, standardized markers with granite finishes, produced in three basic forms, crosses, obelisks, and tablets, became popular. These markers employed a finish known as Granitex, which has the look and appearance of granite.

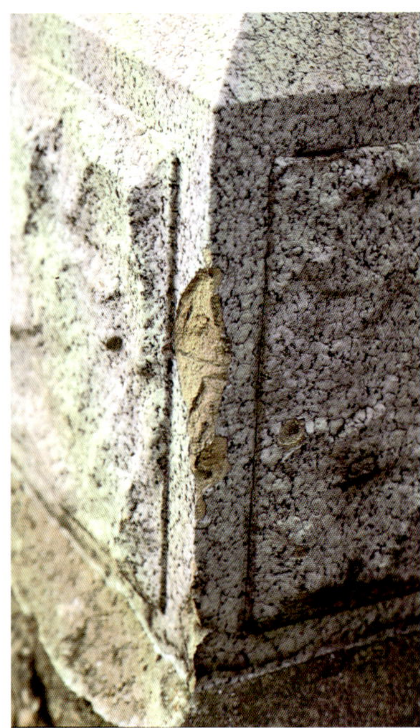

Figure 21 Detail of the gravemarker illustrated in fig. 17. This close up of the Halbert marker shows the terracotta body underneath the granite-like glaze.

Unless chipped, they can be very hard to distinguish from real stone. They show just how closely terracotta could mimic other materials, and they are much less conspicuous than the colorful earlier markers (fig. 21). They probably reflect an attempt at commercial production by the factories.

The gravemarkers highlight the ethnic diversity of Perth Amboy and the Clay District. The 1910 census reveals that seventy-seven percent of Perth Amboy's inhabitants were foreign born or the children of foreign-born parents. This figure correlates well with what we know of the terracotta industry. In 1881 Alfred Hall noted that he had "Men of all nations familiar with working clay in his employ."[16] Although most of the lettered gravemarkers have English inscriptions, epitaphs in Danish (fig. 22), German, Italian, Hungarian, and Russian were also noted. Factory documents indicate that expatriate Englishmen provided the technical know-how that got the fledgling industry off the ground. Danish émigrés rapidly assumed management positions in many of the companies, and Italians and some Danes came to dominate the modeling departments. Hungarians, and in later years Puerto Rican immigrants, also figured prominently in the factories. Arguably the most moving memorial is that of Bruno Grandelis. It dates to 1905 and was sculpted from white glazed terracotta by a highly skilled craftsman. The marker depicts, just smaller than life size, a casket with its lid ajar set between two truncated pillars topped by lit torches. From the casket an angel is rising carrying in her arms a young boy, probably four-year-old Bruno, dressed in a sailor's suit (figs. 23, 24). Inscribed on the marker's reverse (fig. 25) is a single line in Italian, *Tuo padre fece,* which translates as "your father made this." It represents the height of Victorian mourning iconography realized in terracotta. Unfortunately, Mr. Grandelis has yet to be identified in factory or census records. He was clearly an extraordinarily talented craftsman.

Another common gravemarker form, though never dated, was the "DBS" tablet (fig. 26). Although many of the markers discussed so far are

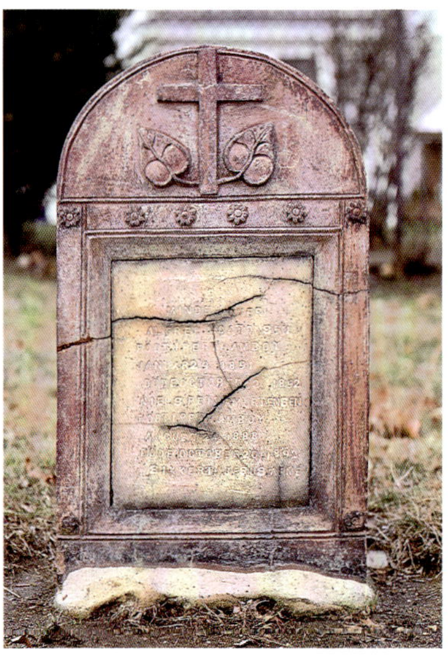

Figure 22 Gravemarker, Perth Amboy, New Jersey, 1892. Terracotta. H. 29". This pastel colored terracotta gravemarker commemorates two children: Alfred Mortensen (1891–1892) and Niels Peter Mortensen (1888–1892). The inscription is in Danish. The gravemarker is located in Alpine Cemetery.

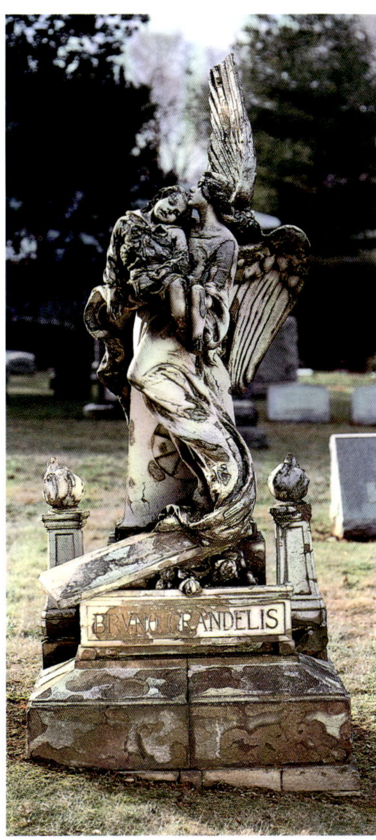

Figure 23 Gravemarker, Metuchen, New Jersey, 1905. Terracotta. H. 80". The Bruno Grandelis marker is arguably the most artistic terracotta monument produced. It is also the only marker that depicts an actual individual. The monument is located in Hillside Cemetery.

Figure 24 Detail of the gravemarker illustrated in fig. 23.

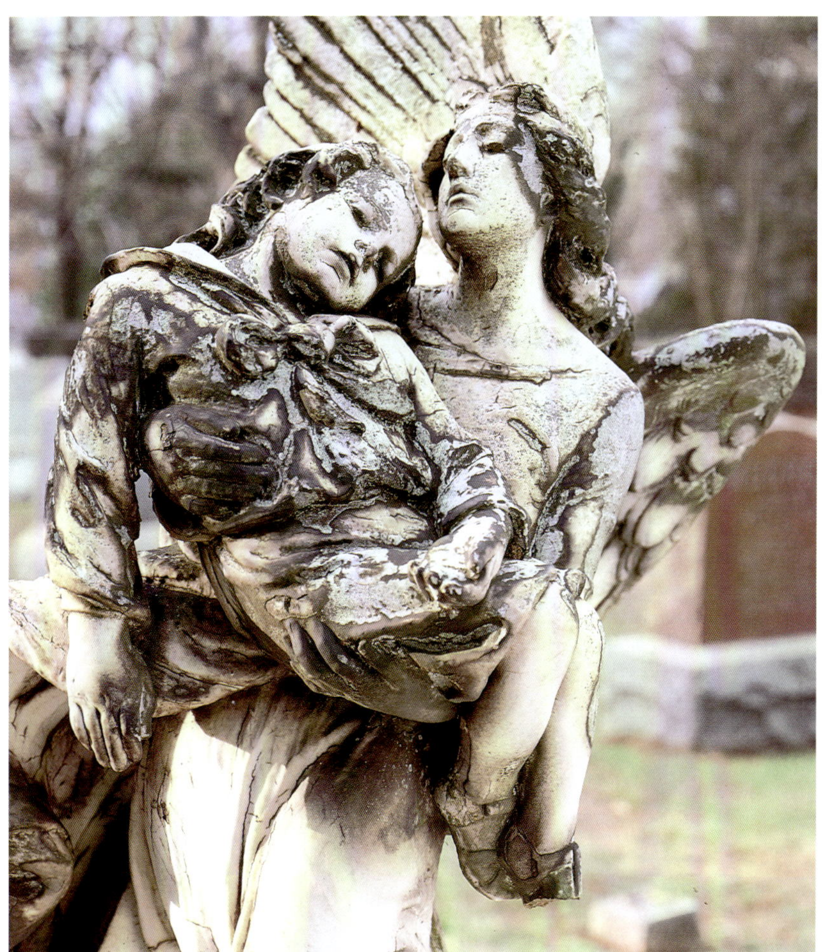

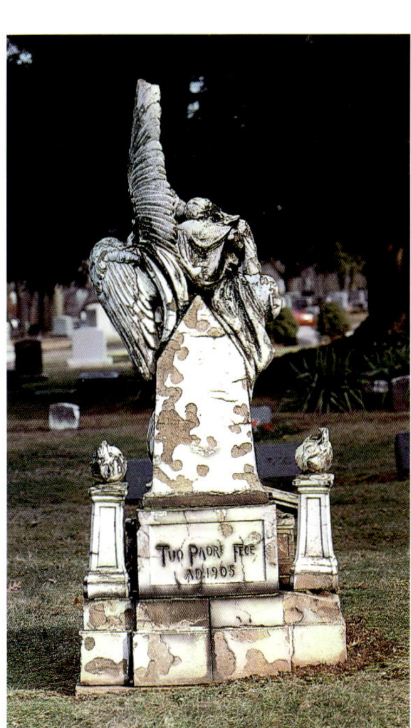

Figure 25 Reverse of the gravemarker illustrated in fig. 23.

unique, these tablet markers were quite literally stamped from the same mold, or, at most, a couple of very similar molds. They are associated with the Danish Brotherhood in America, a fraternal order founded in 1882 by Danish veterans of the American Civil War.[17] In 1893 an accompanying Danish Sisterhood was founded, hence the initials DBS for Danish

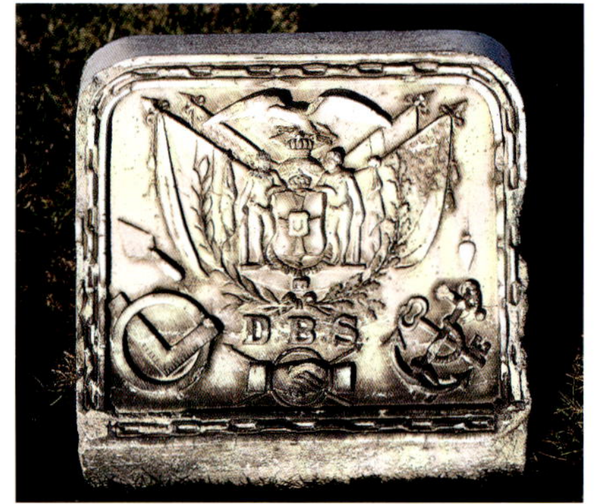

Figure 26 Fraternal marker, Perth Amboy, New Jersey, ca. 1900. Terracotta. H. 14". These mass-produced ceramic gravemarkers were erected by members of the Danish Brotherhood and Sisterhood, a fraternal organization begun by Danish-American Civil War veterans. The gravemaker is located, as are many just like it, in Alpine Cemetery.

Brother and Sisterhood. This organization provided its members with an array of benefits including life insurance, help in old age and sickness, and burial aid. The mass-produced DBS terracotta gravemarkers are associated with the local chapters of these organizations. In truth they are not gravemarkers but fraternal markers, sometimes used with and sometimes in place of regular gravemarkers.

Graphing the markers by decade reveals an interesting distribution. The first inscribed markers bear dates in the 1870s, around the time the first factories were formed. They gradually grew in popularity from the 1870s until roughly 1910. Then, they exploded in popularity. After 1920, they rapidly fell to their nadir (fig. 27). Breaking down the distribution by year reveals the cause of this newfound popularity. More gravemarkers were produced in 1918 than in any other year. This was the year that a devastating influenza epidemic struck the nation. In New Jersey, 300,000 cases were reported in October, November, and December, and over 17,000 people died. Although exact statistics are unavailable, deaths from the flu occurred so

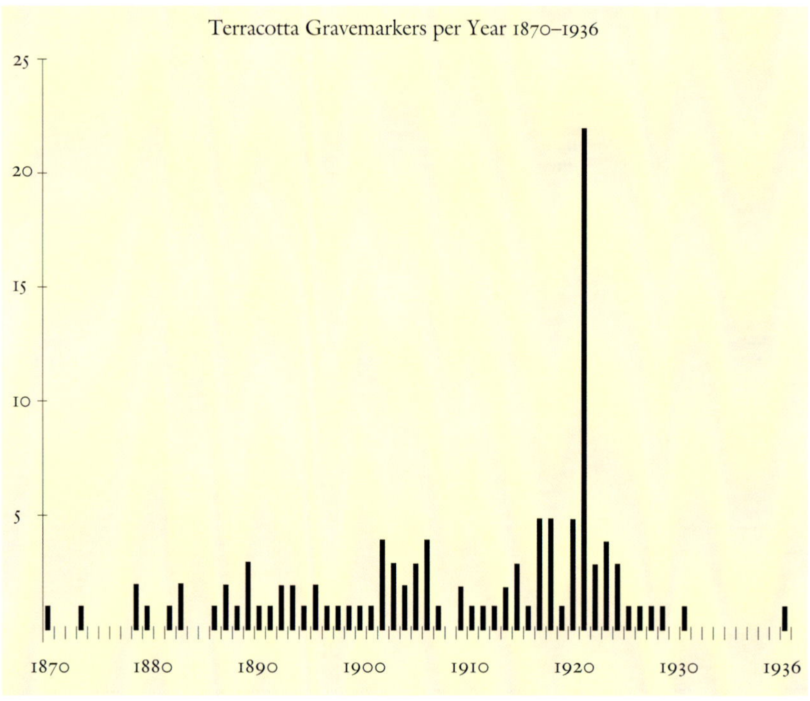

Figure 27 A bar chart showing dated terracotta gravemarkers and the years in which they were erected. (Courtesy, Richard Veit.) Notice the strong peak in 1918 that coincides with the influenza epidemic brought home by troops returning from World War I.

rapidly in Perth Amboy that mass graves were dug to hold the bodies. The catastrophe was compounded by an explosion at the nearby Morgan munitions factory, which left hundreds of individuals homeless at the height of the epidemic. Lacking adequate shelter and provisions, they were even more susceptible to the flu. Alpine Cemetery set aside land for burial of these victims. Many of the gravemarkers in this section of the cemetery were made from terracotta, although other graves have small numbered marble markers. The undulating landscape, largely devoid of gravestones, probably indicates that many graves were never marked at all.

In the 1920s and 1930s the markers decreased in popularity. The latest one recorded dates from 1936. Although it might seem that more, not less, terracotta gravemarkers should have been made during the Depression, many terracotta workers were laid off and therefore in no position to make gravemarkers or anything else.

Manufacture

For a roughly sixty-year period, terracotta gravemarkers were made in New Jersey and New York. Although we have documented their distribution and cataloged their forms and inscriptions, questions remain. How were the markers made? Who produced them? Why did they make them and why did they stop?

The manufacture of architectural terracotta is well understood and continues today at a handful of factories: Gladding McBean in Sacramento, California; the Boston Valley Terracotta Company in Orchard Park, New York; and Ibstock Hathenware in Normanton-on-Soar Loughborough, England, are the industry leaders. A basic overview of how terracotta was made is provided below; however, the process varied from place to place and changed over time. Presumably the process employed to make gravemarkers was similar.

As mentioned earlier, central New Jersey is rich in clays. In Middlesex County, where the Amboys and Woodbridge are located, the Raritan Formation, a rich Cretaceous deposit suitable for stoneware and terracotta, is found close to the ground surface.[18] Easily mined, it was considered the best clay available for terracotta. In fact, Charles Davis felt it necessary to add the following caveat to his 1884 volume *A Practical Treatise on the Manufacture of Bricks, Tiles, Terracotta, etc.*, "In devoting so much space to the description of New Jersey terracotta clays, no slight is intended to the terracotta productions of other sections of the country as . . . they seem to take great care in the execution of all architectural terracotta."[19]

The clay was generally mined by hand in open pits, using shovels and carts. It was then allowed to weather and oxidize. Then it was washed or mixed down with water until it was the consistency of cream.[20] It was then strained and allowed to settle in a drying pan. Next grog, generally "scrap terracotta, fire brick, saggers, scrap pottery, sanitary ware, hollow tile, or specially calcined terracotta clays," was added.[21] Up to thirty percent of the final mixture might be grog, which helped eliminate shrinkage in the kiln. The clay was then put through a pug mill and aged. Now it was ready for molding. Architects supplied drawings to the factories, which would be interpreted in clay or plaster (fig. 28).

The modelers and sculptors used a thirteen-inch long ruler in their work to make up for shrinkage in the kiln. The clay body was either sculpted or pressed into a plaster mold. In 1913 Harry Lee King, an officer with several New Jersey companies, wrote:

> The modeling shop is a component part of the plant with a pervading atmosphere scarcely akin to inert clods of clay and dull plastic forms . . . . Here the pliant modeling clay, under the skillful manipulation of artists, takes on many forms, perhaps . . . the graceful sweep of some festooned panel, a stately caryatid, a graceful capital, or . . . a fanciful grotesque.[22]

Our only contemporary description of the manufacture of a terracotta gravemarker comes from an 1895 newspaper article, where a journalist described seeing a "boy carving in the soft brown clay the inscription for a memorial plaque."[23]

Some gravemarkers appear to have been sculpted, whereas others were molded. The latter were made in plaster molds, reinforced with strap iron or wires, which could be reused over and over. Pressing the clay into the molds took great strength. After a mold was filled, the pressers would set it aside to dry. The piece was then removed and allowed to sit for several days. Next it was finished by rubbing and trimming. It was then taken to a drying room heated to about eighty-five degrees Fahrenheit. After two days of drying, glazes and slips were applied to the hardened unfired body. Red, buff, and gray was the triumvirate of colors on which the industry initially built its strength. In the 1880s a variety of new colors were introduced. White, a popular color for gravemarkers, was first produced in 1889.[24] A correspondence-school textbook on the manufacture of terracotta, printed in the early twentieth century, noted ". . . granite, with its mottled or speckled coloring [and] limestone and sandstone with various toolings of the surface can be closely copied".[25]

The ware was then stacked in the kiln, with sandy clay wads known as bearings placed between the pieces, forming compartments. These bear-

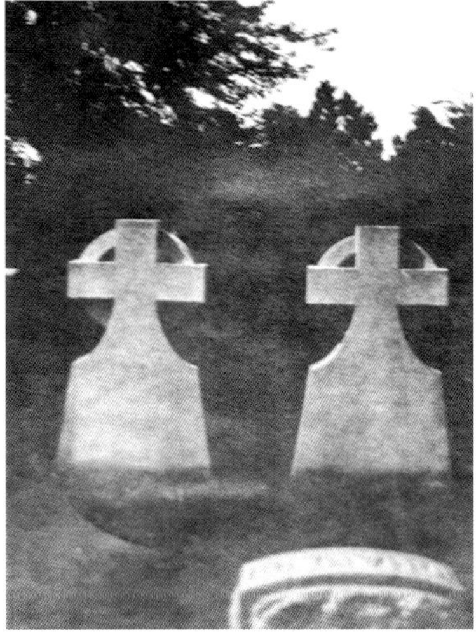

Figure 28 A photograph showing plaster models of proposed terracotta gravemarkers. (Courtesy, Columbia University, Avery Architectural Library and the Friends of Terracotta Collection.) These were made by the New York Architectural Terracotta Company, working at the request of a Mr. Henry Hiss, from Woodlawn Cemetery, New York, and date from 1915. It is not clear that the New York company pursued the idea any further, though markers had long been made informally by many firms.

ings served to distribute the weight of the wares and also helped contain explosions within the kiln. Muffle kilns, which kept the hot gases separate from the ware, were particularly common. Many New Jersey manufacturers preferred updraft kilns. At first, charcoal was the fuel of choice; later, coal, oil, and even gas were employed. The firing process itself lasted between one and two weeks. Peter C. Olsen, president of the Federal Seaboard Terracotta Corporation, accurately described terracotta as "a piece of granite that's been made in two weeks."[26] Temperatures inside the kilns reached 2300 degrees Fahrenheit, and were measured using Seger or pyrotechnic cones, which melted once the desired temperature had been reached. After cooling, sometimes for as long as five days, the ware was removed from the kilns and shipped to its final destination. Pieces were assembled using wooden dowels, iron bars, and metal anchors, all of which tend to decay and cause failure. After installation, the terracotta was cleaned using a dilute solution of oxalic or sulfuric acid.[27]

Very few specifics can be added regarding the production of terracotta gravemarkers. Out of those examined, only a handful of gravemarkers were marked. One in Trenton is marked Lamberton, a pottery manufacturer; another in Alpine Cemetery is marked with the logo of the South Amboy Terracotta Company; and a third, found in South Amboy, is stamped with the mark of the Excelsior Terracotta Company, South Amboy. This last marker is curious, as there is no record of an Excelsior Terracotta Company in South Amboy. Many of the markers in Perth Amboy are believed to have been the work of Nels Alling, a talented Danish émigré sculptor.[28] Sadly, Mr. Alling also failed to sign his work.

Interpretations and Conclusions

Terracotta gravemarkers, much like the glass chains and canes made at day's end by glassblowers, seem to have been a natural byproduct of the industry. They were inexpensive to manufacture, colorful, and personal. Writing in the 1920s, a cemetery superintendent in Bridgeport, Connecticut, decried the gravemarkers chosen by new immigrants and complained of the "weird taste of the foreign element for freakish monuments and such."[29] He undoubtedly would have been appalled by the colorful ceramic gravemarkers of the Clay District. Nevertheless, they provide us with an unusual material avenue for understanding this industry and the people who worked in it. Given the steps in the manufacturing process, the workers could not have produced the markers without management's tacit approval at the least. Interestingly enough, attempts to formalize their production under the trade name Tanagras seems to have failed. The markers appear to be a form of small-scale craft production occurring within and taking advantage of the larger industrial setting.

Many of them are incredibly elaborate (fig. 29), true showpieces of the sculptor's talents. The terracotta industry produced a highly visible product in architectural elements and was a source of considerable pride for the people of the Clay District. Buildings throughout Perth Amboy display some of the finest and most imaginative terracotta in the United States.

Figure 29 Gravemarker, Perth Amboy, New Jersey, 1912. Terracotta. H. 50". The Owen Revell marker is located in Alpine Cemetery. Made from unglazed tan terracotta, it is inscribed "Erected by his sorrowing relatives and friends of Lambeth England." Lambeth was a center of ceramic manufacture, and one might speculate that Revell had learned his trade there.

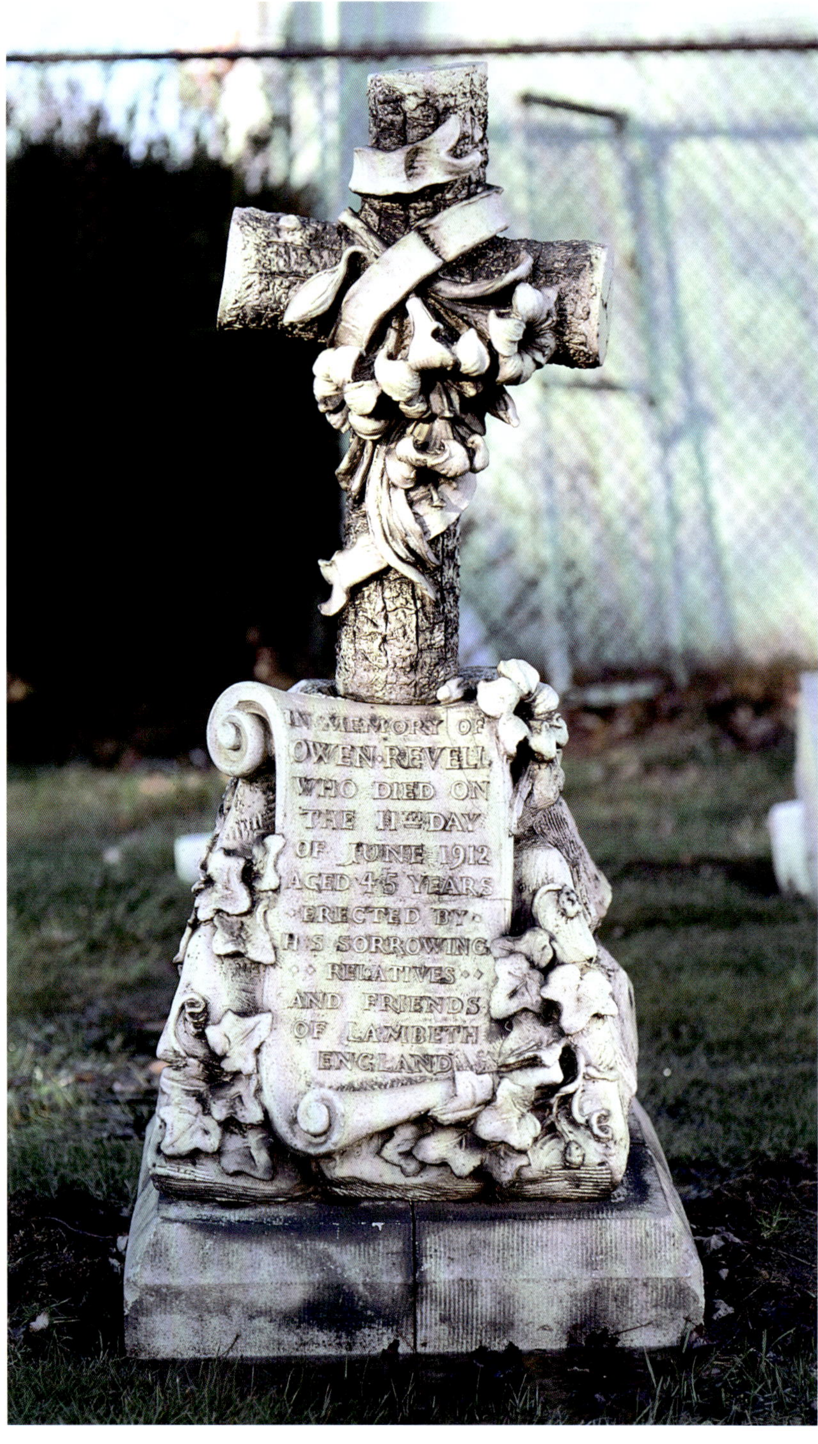

Ornaments as diverse as race cars, dancing pastries, and a miniature Statue of Liberty decorate local buildings (fig. 30). This pride seems to have spilled over into the cemeteries as well.

At the same time, many of the gravemarkers are associated with new immigrants and the children of immigrants, individuals who may have been quite poor. Except for the most skilled workers, wages in the Clay District were low. A ceramic gravemarker may have been an economical substitute for a granite or marble memorial.

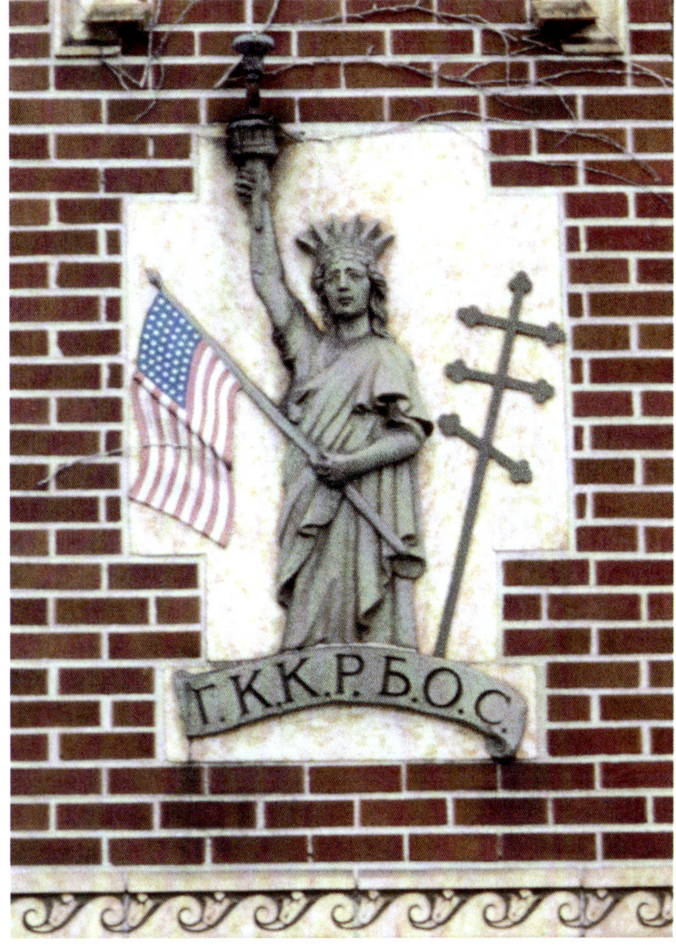

Figure 30 Wall plaque, Perth Amboy, New Jersey, ca. 1928. Terracotta. H. approx. 36". A miniature polychrome Statue of Liberty adorns the façade of the former Greek Catholic Carpatho-Rusin Benevolent Association on Broad Street. It shows, on a small scale, the skill of the clayworkers. Note the interesting juxtaposition of the American flag, the three-bar cross, and the socket for an electric bulb in Liberty's hand.

As previously noted, many of these gravemarkers are located in ethnic cemeteries and are often associated with inexpensive plots. Their neighbors are often wooden, metal, and concrete gravemarkers, all homemade. Terracotta was an improvement on all these materials as it was much more long lasting. However, in one instance, we found evidence that a terracotta gravemarker had been discarded when the family could afford a more traditional granite memorial.

During the influenza epidemic of 1918, ceramic memorials stood in for stone. However, later in the 1930s they petered out and eventually disappeared. Again, no single factor seems to account for their decline. During the 1930s the factories were declining, and there may have been fewer opportunities to make gravemarkers. Companies may also have looked askance at using up raw materials and time on the job for personal items. Skilled workers lost their jobs, reducing the opportunity to make anything from terracotta. At the same time, some of the older markers may have been showing their age, as the dowels that held them together failed and urns toppled off obelisks. Similarly, more acculturated immigrants may have disapproved of the colorful memorials of their predecessors.

For roughly sixty years, terracotta gravemarkers were made and used in the Clay District of New Jersey and New York. These colorful markers provide a glimpse of the incredible craftsmanship found in the terracotta industry, commemorate some of the individuals who worked there, and highlight the potential of this ceramic medium. Today, New Jersey's terracotta industry is a memory, but the gravemarkers remain to remind us of its glory.

ACKNOWLEDGMENTS

The authors thank Rob Hunter for the opportunity to include this article in *Ceramics in America*. Gavin Ashworth's photographic skills helped bring the markers to life. Two institutions have supported our research on terracotta and gravemarkers in particular: Monmouth University and the Middlesex County Cultural and Heritage Commission. Numerous individuals at local historical societies in New Jersey and New York, as well as Susan Tunick, the dean of terracotta studies, have shared their knowledge, photographs, and artifacts with us. The title of this article was inspired by her New York City walking tour, "Terracotta: Don't Take It For Granite." Robert Schuyler, from the University of Pennsylvania, greatly encouraged Richard Veit's initial research on terracotta in Perth Amboy.

1. Charles T. Davis, *A Practical Treatise on the Manufacture of Bricks, Tiles, Terra-Cotta, Etc.* (Philadelphia: Henry, Carey, Baird, and Co., 1884), p. 310.

2. Walter Geer, *The Story of Terracotta* (New York: Tobias A. Wright, 1920), p. 37.

3. Anonymous, *The Pottery and Porcelain of New Jersey* (Newark, N.J.: Newark Museum, 1947), p. 3.

4. William C. McGinnis, *History of Perth Amboy, 1651–1958,* 4 vols. (Perth Amboy, N.J.: American Publishing Company, 1962), 4: 13.

5. Alfred Hall of Perth Amboy to the organizers of an exposition in Louisiana, October 1, 1884, Special Collections and Archives, Rutgers Univ., New Brunswick, N.J.

6. Charles DeKay, "What Terra Cotta May Do," *Harpers Weekly* 39 (1895): 655–58.

7. Edwin Atlee Barber, *The Pottery and Porcelain of the United States,* 2d ed. (New York: G. P. Putnam's Sons, 1901), p. 386.

8. Michael Stratton, *The Terracotta Revival: Building Innovation and the Image of the Industrial City in Britain and North America* (London: Victor Gollancz, 1993), p. 203.

9. Richard Veit and Mark Nonestied, "Bombs Away! Unearthing a Cache of Terracotta Practice Bombs From the First World War," in *Ceramics in America,* edited by Robert Hunter (Hanover, N.H.: University Press of New England for the Chipstone Foundation, 2002): pp. 227–31.

10. Richard Veit, *Skyscrapers and Sepulchers: A Historic Ethnography of New Jersey's Terracotta Industry* (Ph.D. diss., Univ. of Pennsylvania, 1997), pp. 31–43.

11. Gary F. Kurutz and Mary Swisher, *Architectural Terracotta of Gladding McBean* (Sausalito, Calif.: Windgate Press, 1989), p. 10.

12. Allison Kelly, *Mrs. Coade's Stone* (Upton-on-Severn, Eng.: Self Publishing Assoc., 1990), pp. 243–45.

13. Edmund V. Gillon, *Victorian Cemetery Art* (New York: Dover, 1972), p. ix.

14. Kenneth L. Ames, "Ideologies in Stone: Meanings in Victorian Gravestones," *Journal of Popular Culture* 14, no. 4 (1981): 651.

15. DeKay, "What Terracotta May Do," p. 655.

16. John P. Wall and Harold Pickersgill, *History of Middlesex County, New Jersey in Three Volumes* (New York: Lewis Historical Publishing Company, 1921), p. 393.

17. Varick A. Chittenden, *The Danes of Yates County: The History and Traditional Arts of an Ethnic Community in the Finger Lakes Region of New York State* (Penn Yann, N.Y.: Yates County Art Council, 1983).

18. J. Volney Lewis and Henry B. Kummel, *Geological Survey of New Jersey. Bulletin 14. The Geology of New Jersey* (Union Hill, N.J.: Dispatch Printing Company, 1915), p. 126.

19. Davis, *A Practical Treatise on the Manufacture of Bricks, Tiles, Terra-Cotta, Etc.,* p. 310.

20. Frank G. Matero, Elizabeth A. Bede, and Albert Tagle, "An Evaluation of the Effects of Cleaning Methods on Unglazed Architectural Terracotta: With Notes on the Manufacture and Characterization of Nineteenth-Century American Production" (Architectural Conservation Laboratory, Graduate School of Fine Arts, Univ. of Pennsylvania, 1995), pp. 8–9.

21. Hewitt Wilson, "Monograph and Bibliography on Terracotta," *American Ceramic Society Bulletin* 5, no. 2 (1926): 98.

22. Harry Lee King, "A History of Architectural Terracotta," *Architecture and Building* 45, no. 1 (1913): 311–15.

23. DeKay, "What Terracotta May Do," p. 657.

24. Walter Geer, *Terracotta in Architecture* (New York: Gazlav Brothers, 1892), p. 56.

25. William S. Lowndes, *Plastering and Architectural Terracotta* (Scranton, Pa.: International Text Book Company, 1920), p. 29.

26. "Federal Plant was Organized 60 Years Ago," *Perth Amboy Evening News,* December 4, 1948.

27. Matero, Bede, and Tagle, "An Evaluation of the Effects of Cleaning Methods on Unglazed Architectural Terracotta," p. 18.

28. McGinnis, *History of Perth Amboy,* p. 43.

29. John Matturi, "Windows in the Garden: Italian-American Memorialization and the American Cemetery" in *Ethnicity and the American Cemetery,* edited by Richard E. Meyer (Bowling Green, Ohio: Bowling Green University Popular Press, 1993), p. 30.

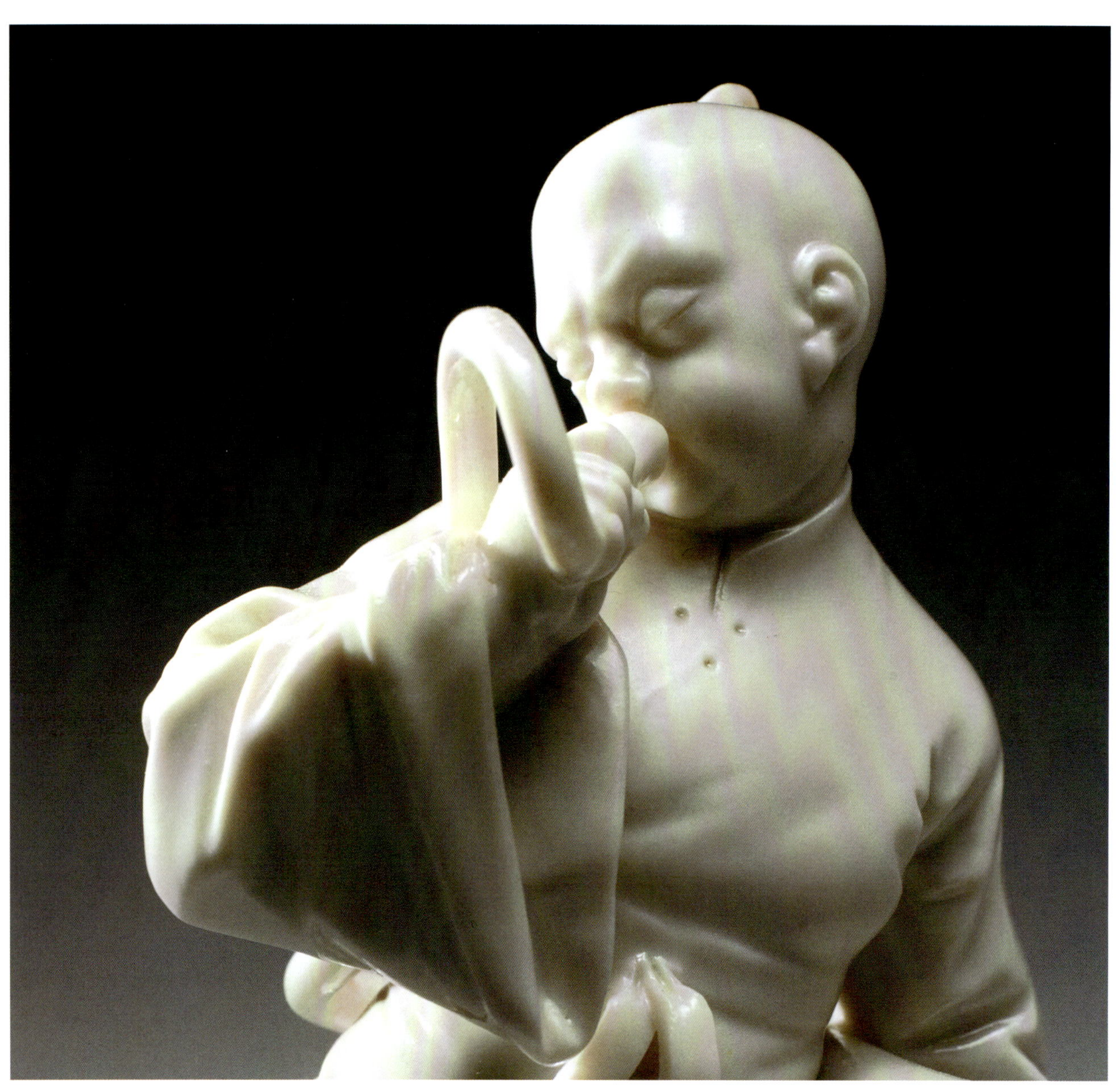

Figure 1 Franz Anton Bustelli, detail view of a Chinese musician figure, Nymphenburg, Germany, twentieth century after a ca. 1750 original from the Nymphenburg factory. Porcelain. H. 4 15/16". (Hood Collection, photos by Gavin Ashworth unless otherwise noted.)

Graham Hood

Meditations on a Chinese Musician

▼ OVER FORTY YEARS ago I took up my first curatorial post, assuming responsibility for a wide-ranging collection of European decorative arts. It included notable groups of eighteenth-century Meissen figures and fine French porcelains from the J. P. Morgan Collection, early English porcelains, as well as Chinese ceramics from the sixth century onward. I have to admit that my knowledge and experience of such objects then, without putting too fine a point on it, was absolutely nil. They constituted a branch of art history and collecting history of which I was wholly ignorant.

Although my parents were born, as was I, on the edge of "The Potteries" in England, I recall nothing of the far-flung and beneficent influence of that region on our breakfast, dinner, or tea tables. No fond light did I ever see come into my parents' eyes, no faint smile of proud possession relax their lips when they handled teapot or platter. Even as I matured, through three years of history at Oxford and two years of art history at the Courtauld Institute in London, I cannot recall "porcelain" ever being mentioned as a subject worthy of attention.

So it is a matter of some retrospective surprise that I have found these things, of such little consequence in my background and in the estimate of serious historians and art historians of that time, so intriguing, charming, beautiful. What follows is a personal testament to the power of ceramics to arouse the deepest feelings of delight and of curiosity—their fragile loveliness capable of producing the same kind of awe as a beautiful bird's wing, their durable constituents able suddenly to bring to life a moment of civilization, of human beings' aspirations and needs, long gone.

This essay is also a paean, in part, to the power and importance of "aesthetic incest," as scornfully defined by Walter Muir Whitehill in the 1960s. An influential historian of his day, Whitehill wrote that "no amount of the aesthetic incest of sitting and gazing at a chair, or a pot, will tell one anything of value about the object, beyond its existence." I strongly disagreed then, and I still do. But more than that, I suppose I have felt sorry for people like him who could not derive deep spiritual nourishment from something of great beauty. There is a well-known ode by the English Romantic poet John Keats addressed to a Grecian urn that contains some immortal and oft-quoted lines. One, rarely quoted, is as follows: "Thou, silent form, dost tease us out of thought / As doth eternity." Whether it be a classical urn of great purity of line and complexity of decoration, or a rococo figurine that is amazingly evocative of human beauty, gazing at a pot can be as profoundly moving and restorative as, I believe, prayer can be.[1]

As a curator in charge of more than two hundred of his creations, my discovering the nature of German sculptor Johann Joachim Kaendler's genius was akin to the way it must have been to meet his little figures on an eighteenth-century dessert table for the first time. Sir Charles Hanbury-Williams expressed it most happily in 1749: "When the Desert was set on, I thought it was the most wonderful thing I ever beheld. I fancy'd myself either in a Garden or at the Opera." Like Sir Charles I have been able to enter into the garden or walk about on the stage. As a curator I have been able to pick the figures up, turn them around at will, and examine them from every angle. Some of them are grave, others are frankly pictorial, some have an intended German pompousness, while others, especially the commedia dell'arte figures, are so full of animation, their gestures so large, their dress so distinctive, that they invariably evoke a warm smile. The best of them do not seem small. As you focus and gaze on them intently, they grow in size; they are no longer decorative whimsies or baubles, they are sculpture.[2]

During this period of discovery I shared an office with a fellow curator, who had started his first museum job the very same day as I. He was in charge of paintings and sculpture and was passionate about contemporary art. Yet he had unusually wide-ranging taste and a most perceptive eye. He also registered the same delight at these little figures that I did. We visited other collections, especially the Metropolitan Museum's expansive holdings of similar objects. In doing so, I became aware of the work of Franz Anton Bustelli of Nymphenburg and admired his great playfulness. His figures, I thought, without analyzing it at length then, were more expressive and more sharply modeled than Kaendler's. They seemed to me to represent the next stage of development in the art.[3]

One day my colleague told me he had been looking at examples of Bustelli's work and had been particularly moved by some all-white Chinese figures. He spoke of them with great animation and genuine admiration. I went to see them as soon as possible. I was spellbound by these Chinese musicians. My colleague had noted how the modeler appeared to have crafted the costumes with unusual speed and breathtaking sureness, taking off broad slices of clay with a knife and creating an extraordinary and most vivid sense of movement, a sense only enhanced by their pure whiteness. They were a revelation to me.

A couple of years later, through the kind agency of another colleague, I became the proud possessor of a facsimile of one of these Chinese figures. It had been made at the Nymphenburg factory, using (it was claimed) the same clay and molds that Bustelli had used in the late 1750s (figs. 1–3). I have looked at and held this little treasure thousands of times and still marvel at how so small a thing can be so expressive. In the perfection of its replication it continues to suggest the essence of the ineffable grace of a superb musical phrase.[4]

The small form also has a delicious fluidity of movement in the languid turns and twists of its body. But I had never articulated to myself this aspect of its genius quite so well as the art historians, John Fleming and

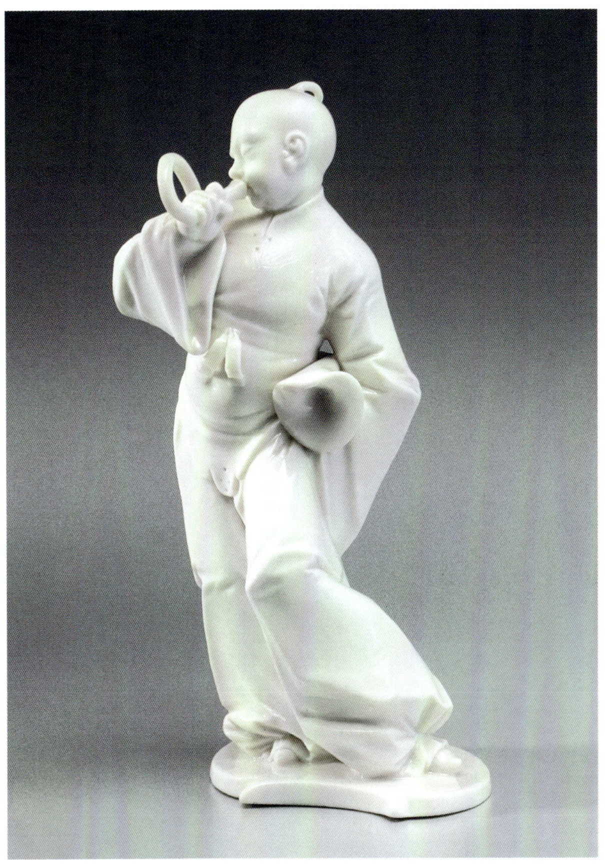

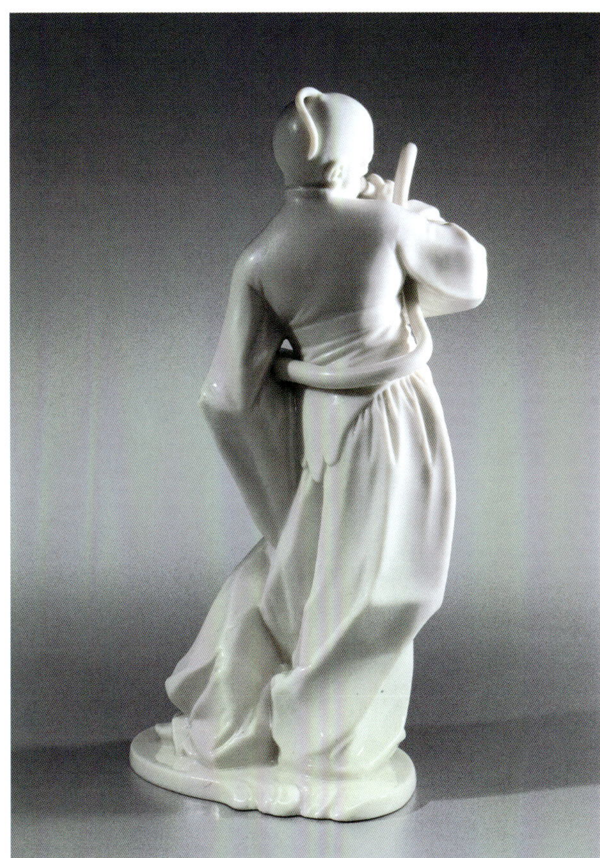

Figure 2 Side view of the figure illustrated in fig. 1.

Figure 3 Back view of the figure illustrated in fig. 1.

Hugh Honour, in a phrase written long ago, but which I have discovered only recently: "[Bustelli's figures] are represented in attitudes which could not physically be held for more than a split second, caught in movement at the moment of supreme grace. No sculptor and, indeed, no medium less delicate than porcelain, has ever succeeded in catching the fleeting movements of the human figure with greater sensitivity."[5] To which I can only add that the more I have gazed at this piece over the years, the more poignant its allusions to the fleetingness of human grace have become.

While discovering the pleasures of early Meissen at my museum, I was also coming to appreciate the beautiful elegance of form and refinement of color of Vincennes and early Sevres porcelains, and the incomparable whiteness of St. Cloud. At the same time, I was most fortunate to be introduced to oriental ceramics (as they used to be called). Another of my colleagues had lived in Korea for some years, and he played a key role in this joyful development. A gruff New Englander, he placed these wares on a pedestal of purity and restraint that seemed unequaled, though he would not have said so in as many words. His discovery of them had been intuitive and by practical experience. As a result of what I picked up from him, I spent as much time as possible in the oriental galleries of major museums, and had my aesthetic awareness of the wondrous subtleties of form and color expanded and enriched beyond anything I could have imagined. An hour of quietude in a museum in Boston, New York, or Philadelphia nourished me spiritually for months.[6]

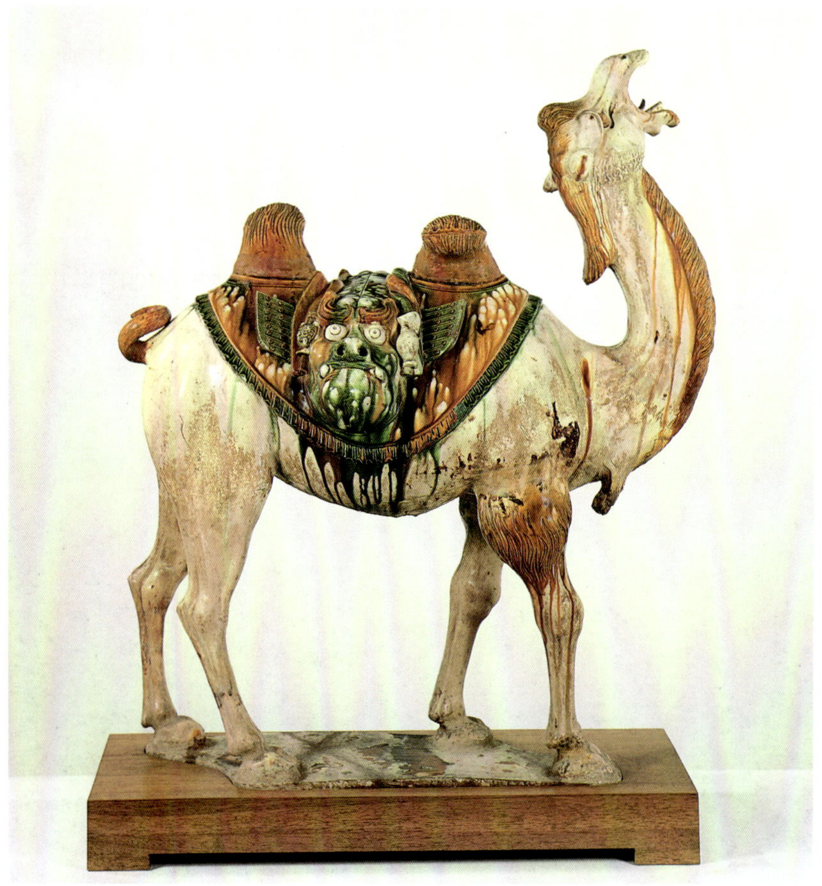

Figure 4 Sepulchral figure of a Bactrian camel, China, T'ang period, eighth century. Glazed earthenware. H. 34½". (Courtesy, Wadsworth Atheneum, Hartford, gift of James Junius Goodwin.)

I was to discover, however, that not all oriental ceramics are the essence of restraint and purity. In my recollection of American museums of forty years ago, it seems that most T'ang figures on display were small and rather statuesque, so it was with astonishment that one day I came upon a figure almost three feet high, almost as long, and of tremendous expressiveness and power (fig. 4). It was a Bactrian camel, in the familiar green, brown, yellow, and cream T'ang colors. On its back was a large cloth over which hung a highly ornate warrior's saddlebag, modeled with great detail. The colors cascaded down from the cloth and bag under the animal's belly, from its shoulders down the front legs, and from the head and forelock down the arched neck. They gave the impression that the animal was enduring enormous stress—they might almost have been blood—a sense only accentuated by the upward and sideways lift of the creature's head, the mouth wide open as if in a huge scream.

Monumental T'ang figures have become a more frequent sight in museums since then, but almost always I am amazed by their sculptural power. The camel is as expressive as any T'ang figure of its size I've ever seen. I came on it in the private room of a highly reputed dealer, and I'm proud that I was able to play a role in bringing it to the public. It was the first of many museum acquisitions over the next four decades.

I have met many collectors in my career, but only a small handful of them impressed me as collecting for the love of the object, rather than for the love of themselves reflected in the objects they think they have been so smart to buy. In my early curatorial days I was fortunate to meet Forsyth Wickes, whose collection of brilliant seventeenth- and eighteenth-century French art was the object of many a museum director's avarice. I visited him twice in his Newport, Rhode Island, home, the second time to pick up an exquisite Pater he was lending to my museum. (This French painting showed me figures that equaled Bustelli's in their grace and beauty.) I was alone on this trip and had the privilege of a personal tour of the main parts of the house from the collector himself. Wickes was very elderly and couldn't get up or down without assistance, but he managed to totter through the rooms and point out his favorite things. He was also blind, but he knew his way through his own rooms and could point out exactly where some truly exquisite things were.

We finished the tour in a small inner room, lined with shelves, on which stood French porcelains. I helped him down onto a sofa in the middle of the room. He noted that I'd seemed interested in porcelains, and he wanted me to look at his choice things, and handle them. He started by saying, "If you look at the upper shelf to the left of the fireplace, on the extreme left you'll see a lovely Vincennes dish of a very rare yellow. You'll also note that the back has a most interesting feature." For the next couple of hours he took me through his superb collection, piece by piece, his knowledge far outstripping mine, pointing out wonderful details though he was unable to see a single one of them. Clearly, he had looked at them so intensely when he had his sight, they were burned into his memory. And he relived their beauty for an appreciative audience.

In the early days of my tenure at a second museum, after I had changed fields and entered the realm of American arts, another colleague took me through some rarely visited vaults at Yale University. Among numerous, rather inconspicuous ceramics stood a little blue and white pot to which my colleague pointed and said, "And that's a piece collectors genuflect over." At the time, it hardly seemed worth the trouble. Two or three months later, on my first visit to the Winterthur Museum, our guide stopped in front of a small table on which stood a pleasant blue and white dish that looked English, about 1770. He went on to say it was a recent accession, one of only about half a dozen known and made in Philadelphia before the Revolution. He turned it over and I saw it was marked with the letter "P" in underglaze blue. A distant bell rang, and within a few hours I remembered the same mark on the piece I had seen in the Yale vault a couple of months earlier.

So began a four-year quest to understand these two ordinary-looking pieces as well as a small group of their relatives. This was not a case of gazing (Walter Whitehill could have relaxed over this one); it was a case of worrying and teasing their past out of them, of confidently placing them in the historical continuum. It was a part-time quest, full of intriguing leads that led nowhere, false scents, cul-de-sacs, and a lot of very nice and very helpful people. The exercise culminated in a small, professional dig on the site of an eighteenth-century Philadelphia factory. I clearly recall the

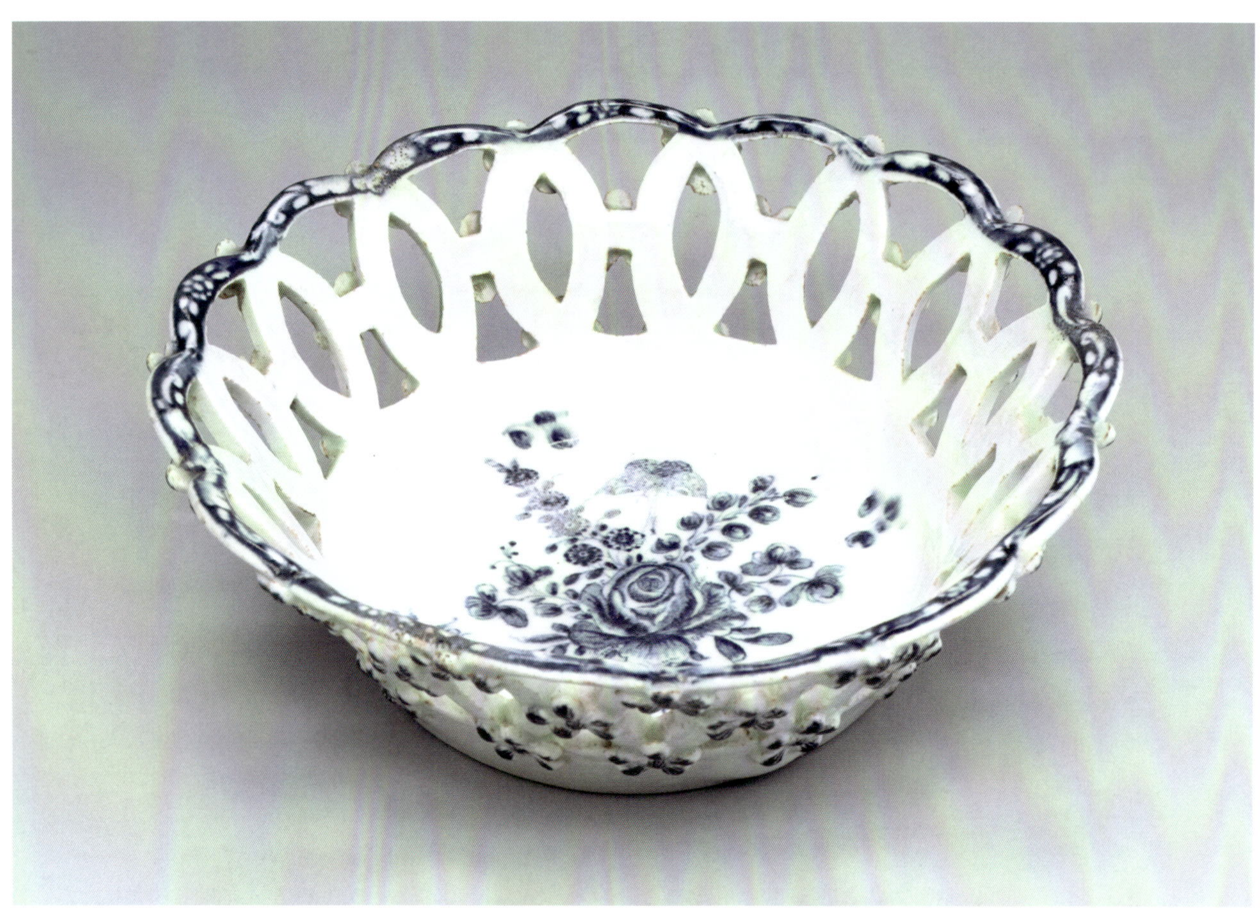

Figure 5 Fruit basket, American China Manufactory (Bonnin and Morris), Philadelphia, 1770–1772. Soft-paste porcelain. D. 6⅞". (Courtesy, Detroit Institute of Arts, Founders Society Purchase, Gibbs-Williams Fund; photo © 2002.)

deep glow of satisfaction I felt, standing knee-deep in the ground, surrounded by urban debris in a distinctly unscenic part of the city, as sherds appeared that precisely matched the molded and painted elements of the attributed pieces.

I was also able to play a role in steering several of the known, whole pieces into the public domain, including the handsome dish illustrated in figure 5. And later I persuaded a publisher to produce my account of this exciting project.[7]

While I was curator of American art at one of America's finest old city museums, the Detroit Institute of Art, I found almost daily inspiration in the superb collections of Dutch and Flemish art, the legacy of the great German-American museum director Wilhelm Valentiner. It was then customary for art historians to poke fun at some of his over-ambitious attributions, Rembrandt in particular. But in talking with people who had come under the spell of his intelligence and legendary charisma, and by reflecting on his achievements, it was clear that he was an extraordinary man, an achiever on a grand scale.

So it was a surprise to me one day in the museum storerooms to discover a collection he had put together, an inconspicuous little group that seemed to be dwarfed by the outsize legend of the man. It was a small number of ceramic fragments, all colorful Italian majolica, and all bearing some original inscription—perhaps the painter's signature, perhaps some

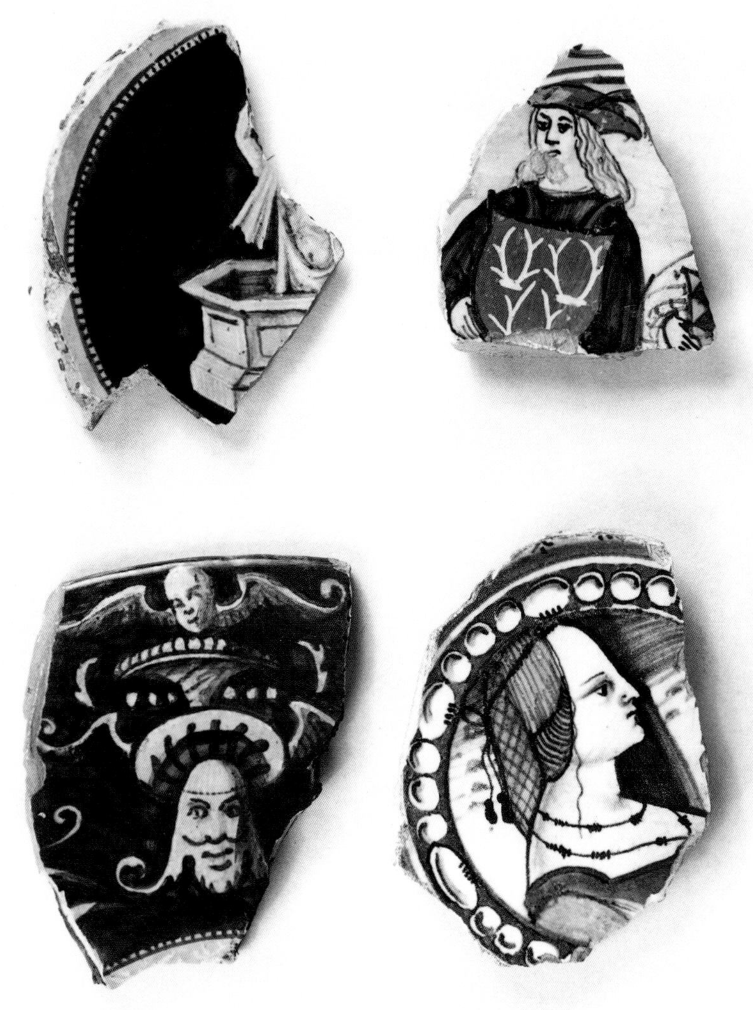

Figure 6 Majolica fragments, Italy, fifteenth century. Tin-glazed earthenware. (Courtesy, Detroit Institute of Arts, gift of Dr. Wilhelm R. Valentiner; photo © 1975.)

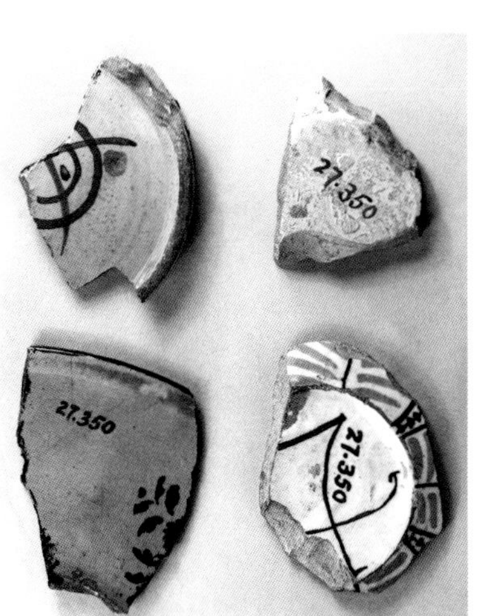

Figure 7 Back view of the majolica fragments illustrated in fig. 6.

identification of the person who had commissioned or would own the piece. All the fragments were small. These were not the complete, "important" pieces that I had been led to believe were the sine qua non of "important" collectors, certainly of museum collections. Perhaps some of the pieces were key documents, I don't know, but suddenly this little collection, which Valentiner had given to the museum, made perfect sense to me—intriguing, enchanting, delightful to the experienced museum-goer, and making the great man, after all, seem quite human (figs. 6, 7).

What I did not know at the time was that Valentiner had been interested in ceramics since his youth. For him they were another, and very appealing, aspect of man's endless creativity. He had put together, for example, a collection of Dutch delft tiles about 1905, when he had spent some time studying in the Netherlands. This collection he apparently gave to the Metropolitan Museum of Art some years later.[8]

I was most fortunate to spend the next twenty-five years of my career with the truly great collection of seventeenth- and eighteenth-century

British ceramics at Colonial Williamsburg—a large assemblage of whole objects and a vast number of fragments. I worked alongside a curator who was a restless acquisitor, and I was a colleague of one of the foremost historical archaeologists of his day. This was a time when gazing raptly at the particular felicities of a pot took second place to determining and explaining its historical context. Furthermore, I have to confess that for breathless beauty of color, design, and texture these pots also took second place in my heart to an array of splendid and gorgeous textiles of the same period that I was also privileged to work with.[9]

Nevertheless, there were some standout moments when the unique appeal of a piece of pottery or porcelain swept the scales off my eyes and fixed itself forever in my memory. "Mr. Nobody" seems to me a remarkable achievement for the seventeenth-century delft potters (fig. 8). Yet I

Figure 8 "Mr. Nobody," London, 1682. Tin-glazed earthenware. H. 8½". (Courtesy, Colonial Williamsburg Foundation.)

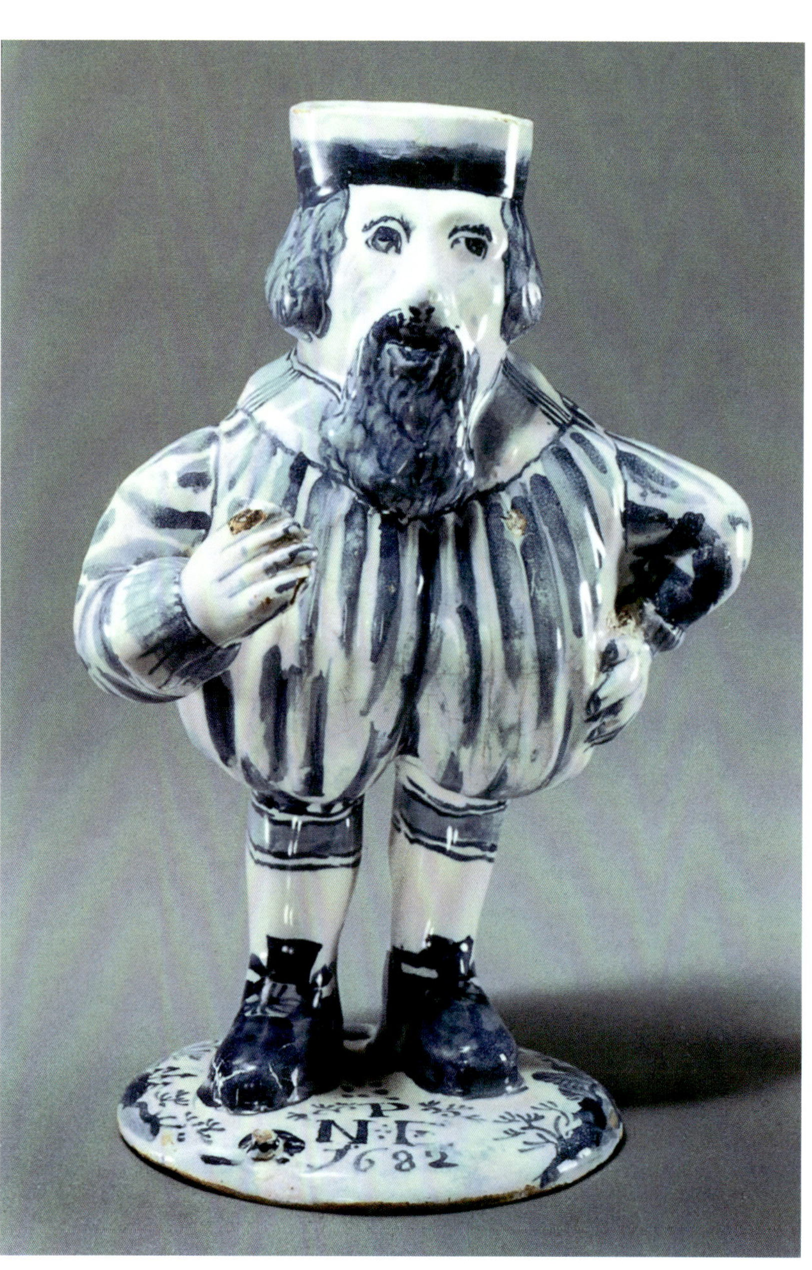

Figure 9 Harlequin figure, Bow Porcelain Factory, London, ca. 1760. Soft-paste porcelain. H. 7¾". (Courtesy, Colonial Williamsburg Foundation.)

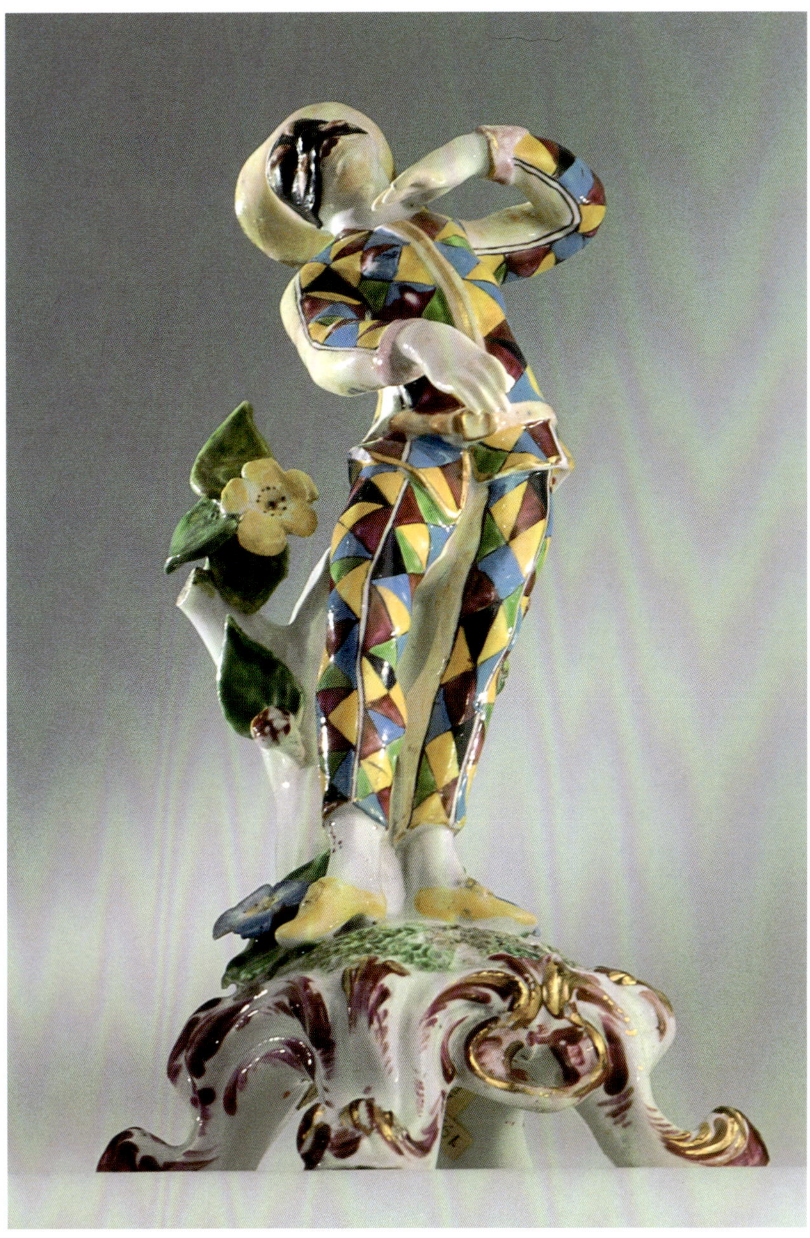

wonder if the men who made and painted this disembodied fellow did anything more than chortle over it. Did it stop them for a moment in their busy lives and make them consider some fundamental questions about the nature of existence? It certainly struck me that way when I paused to consider it in its original context.

One day, for a special exhibition on style, we placed the Bow Harlequin figure (fig. 9) on a shelf about six and one half feet above floor level. The effect on me was electrifying. Suddenly, all of the marvelous vitality of the figure became apparent. Although it was undoubtedly based on other prototypes, the subject's inherent animation had still been brilliantly captured by the Bow modeler. Up to that time I'd thought the piece a little tame—a northern figure, lacking the southerner's true zest for life. In this instance it took an unusual viewpoint to make its real genius evident to me.

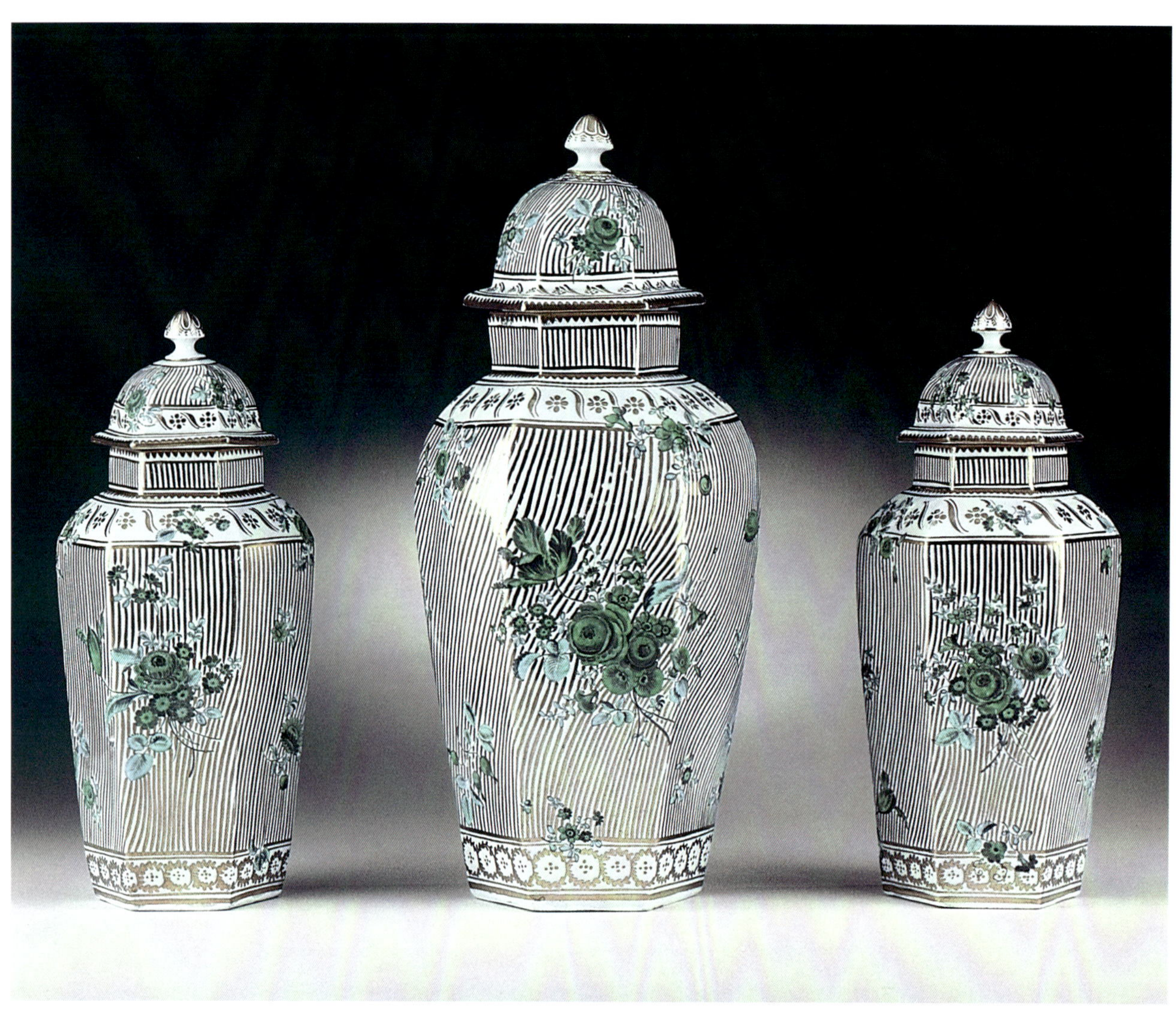

Figure 10 Garniture, Worcester Porcelain Manufactory, Worcester, ca. 1770. Soft-paste porcelain. H. of tallest: 15⅜". (Courtesy, Colonial Williamsburg Foundation.)

Figure 11 Detail of bowl, Worcester Porcelain Manufactory, Worcester, ca. 1770. Soft-paste porcelain. D. 11." (Courtesy, Colonial Williamsburg Foundation.)

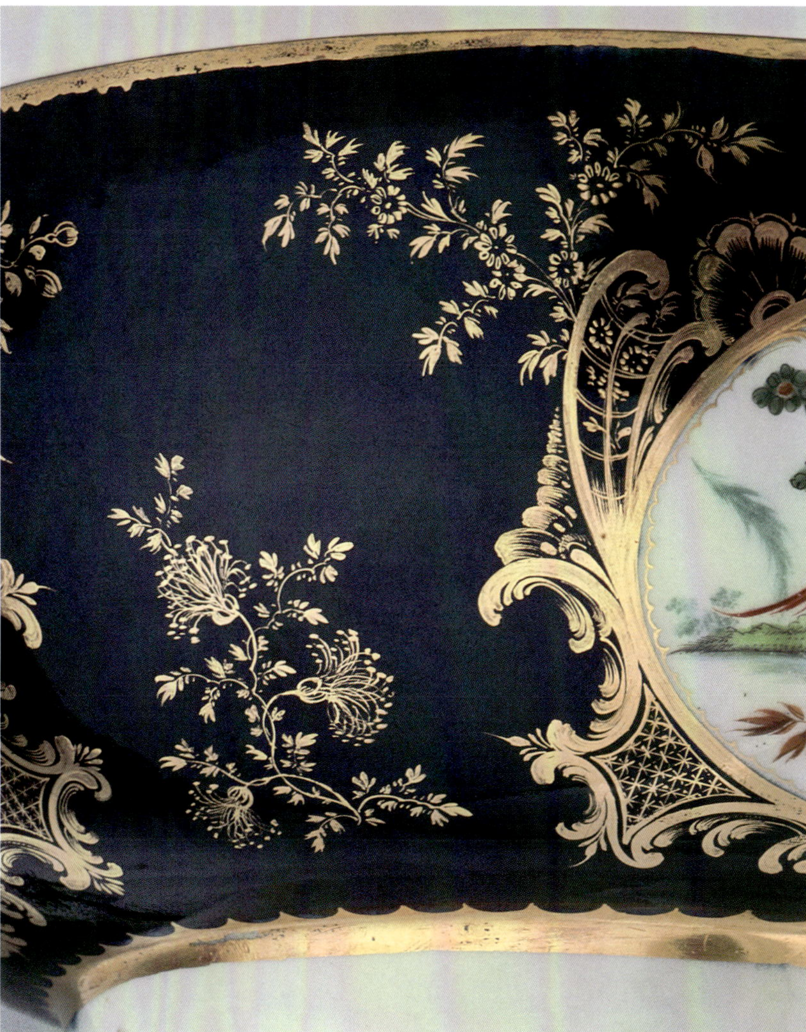

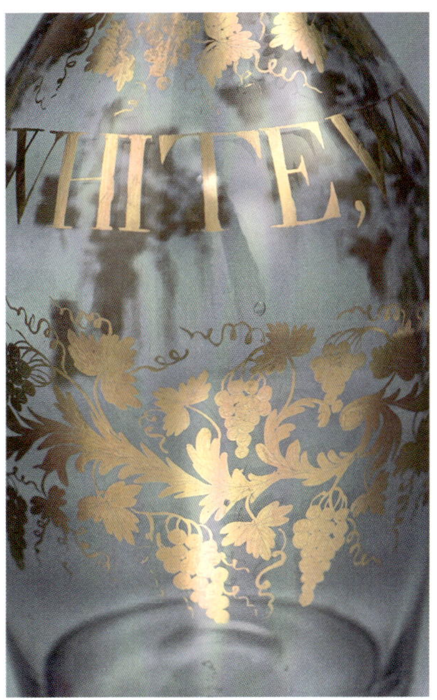

Figure 12 Detail of one of a pair of gilt decorated lead glass decanters, England, ca. 1770. H. 11¾". (Courtesy, Colonial Williamsburg Foundation.)

The illustration of the Worcester garniture (fig. 10) in the auction catalog made the group seem remarkable enough, but when I set my eyes on the actual objects, I think my heart missed a beat. I've long been partial to the octagonal form, but here it was the combination of colors and motifs that was breathtaking. The transfer-printed floral groups in a kind of light green-aqua are set against pale gold stripes that curve subtly down the body. I would have expected the stripes to be as precisely articulated as the flowers, but since they were applied by hand, all the hand's wonderful irregularities, however skillfully and painstakingly done, lend an extra liveliness and the most subtle vibrations to the forms.

Gilding on English porcelain of the 1760–1790 period is not uncommon and is generally of a good, workmanlike standard. But the gilding I spotted on one particular bowl attained a rare degree of precision and elegance (fig. 11). It kindled a new appreciation for this decorative art, which soon led to the acquisition of two particularly lovely glass decanters, objects that delighted me whenever I looked at them (fig. 12).

For most of the years I was interacting with specialists in ceramics, and involved in collecting, here and in England, the subject of Dutch delft

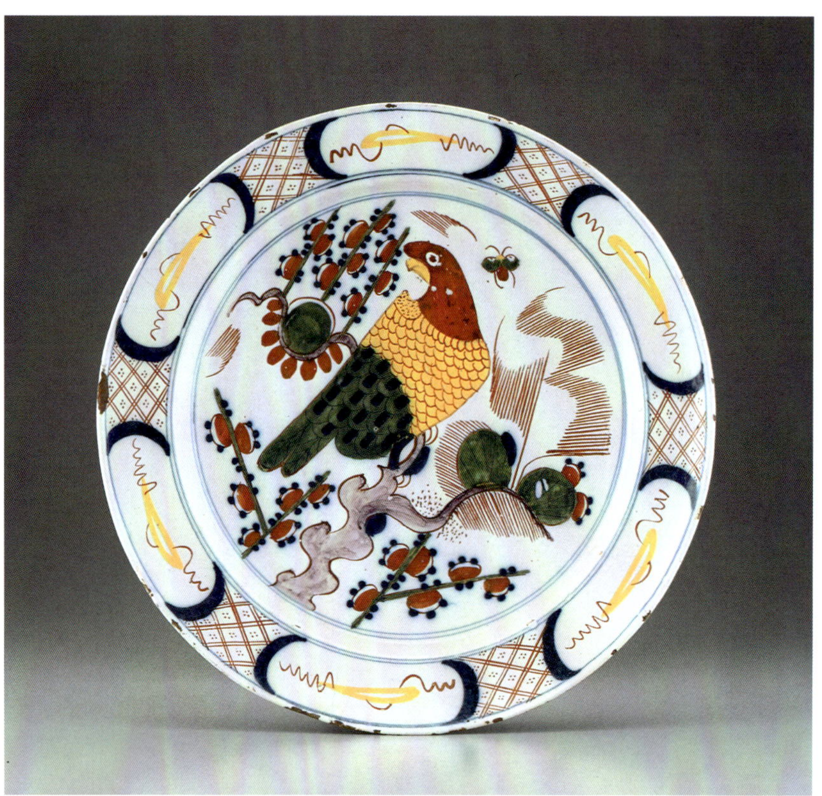

Figure 13 Dish, Netherlands, 1720–1740. Tin-glazed earthenware. D. 13½". (Hood Collection.)

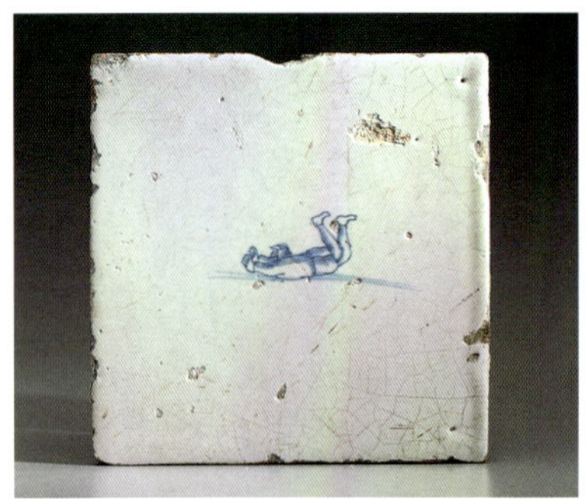

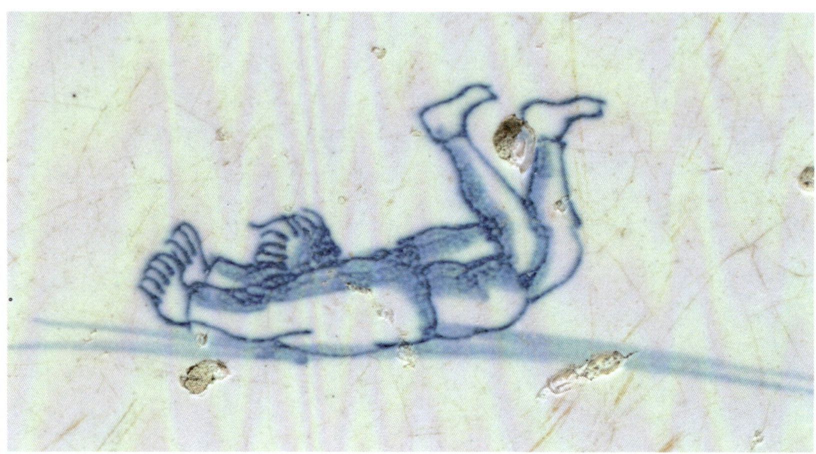

Figure 14 Tile, Netherlands, ca. 1700. Tin-glazed earthenware. W. 5⅛". (Hood Collection.)

Figure 15 Detail of the tile illustrated in fig. 14.

seemed always to be of secondary, even tertiary interest, except for tiles, and these were judged to be inferior in importance to plates, dishes, bowls, hollow wares, and so on. But who could not find the imperial hauteur of a Dutch (East Indian?) parrot enormously appealing (fig. 13)? And who could resist smiling at the animal or human figures engaged in an endless range of activities, painted with the most disarming directness in blue on simple cool-white squares (figs. 14, 15)? Then to see almost 30,000 of them—all different as far as I could tell—in their original location on the walls and ceiling in a room in the Menshikov Palace in St. Petersburg was staggering. And then to see as many, if not more, in the next room, this time embellished at each corner join with a small gilt-metal rosette, was to see something truly amazing, and beautiful.

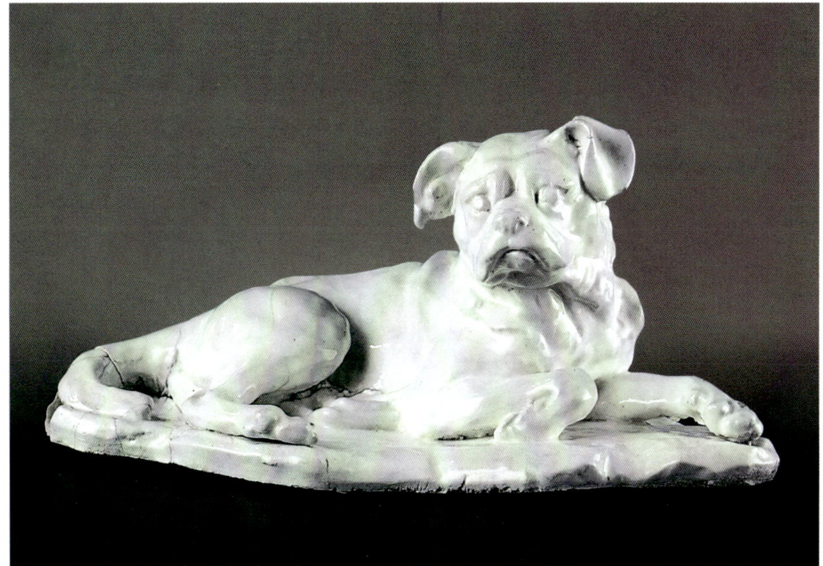

Figure 16 Étienne-Maurice Falconet, *Trump*, Chelsea, 1745–1750. Soft-paste porcelain. L. 11½". (Courtesy, Colonial Williamsburg Foundation.)

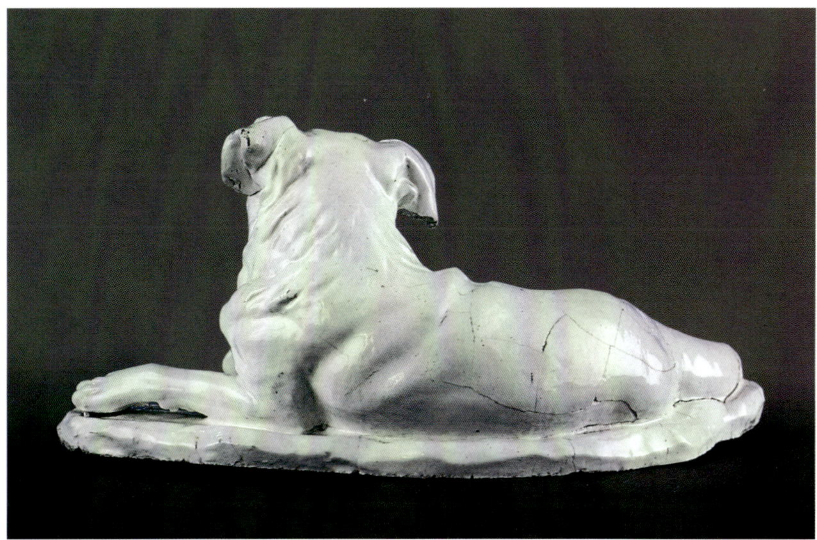

Figure 17 Back view of *Trump*, illustrated in fig. 16.

When the opportunity arose to bid on one of the three known Chelsea figures of Trump, the favorite pug of the renowned English artist, William Hogarth, I was very excited (figs. 16, 17). The ceramic medium was a rare product of the artistic genius of Étienne-Maurice Falconet, who made such an important contribution to the development of the rococo style in England, and the personal taste of the greatest English painter and engraver of his day. For me, the little porcelain dog seemed a charming symbol of the freedom that Hogarth claimed for his art and the defiance of accepted artistic tenets that Falconet represented. That Hogarth had posed Trump in the foreground of his self-portrait leaves no doubt about the role that Hogarth saw for his pet.

When I was finally able to hold the figure of Trump and saw with what an extraordinary sense of life the Frenchman had invested him, I was sure that my sense of the little sculpture as much more than a curio or token of friendship had been right.

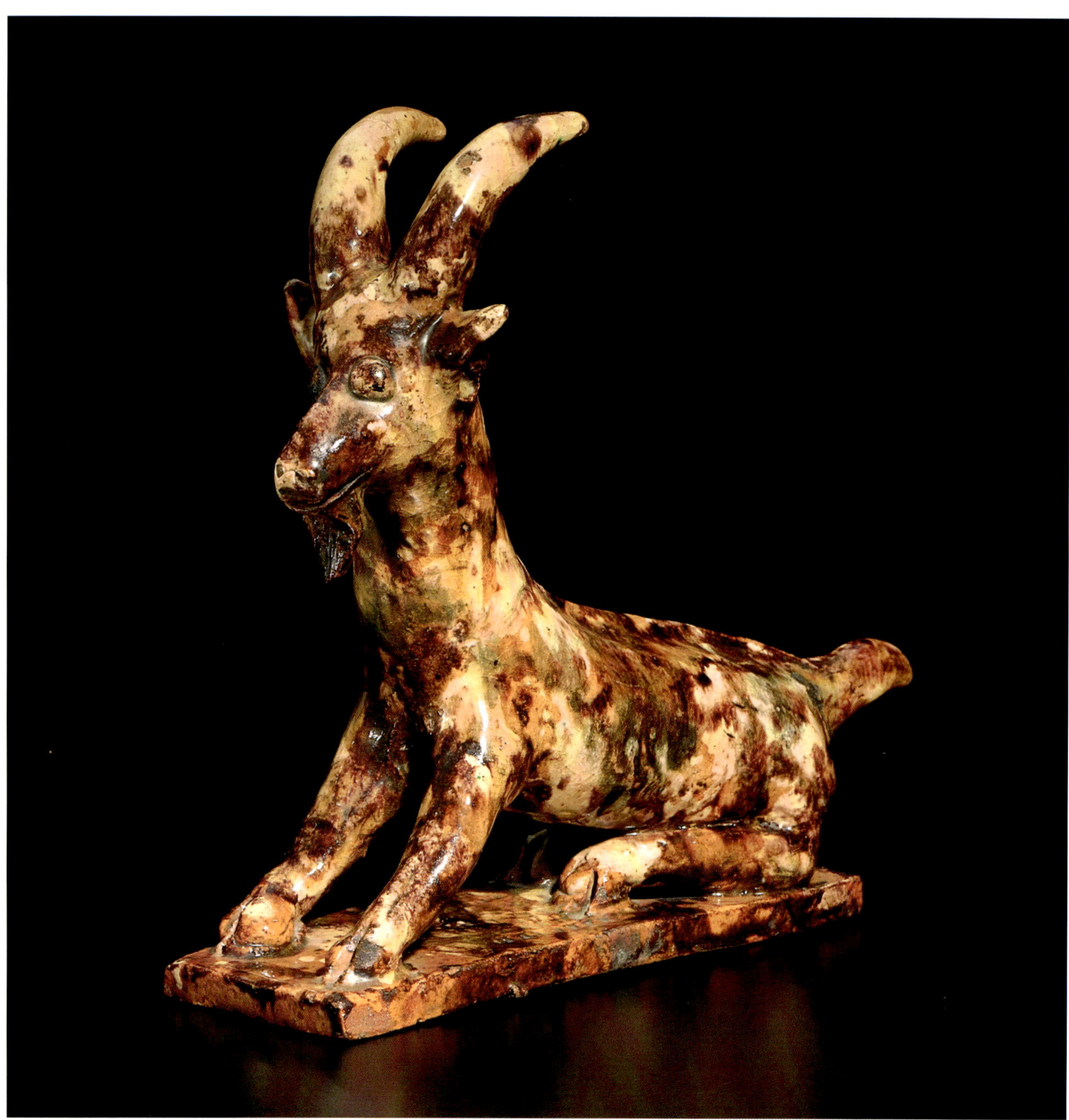

Figure 18 Anthony Baecher, seated goat figure, Winchester, Virginia, ca. 1880. Lead-glazed earthenware. H. 6⅞". (Courtesy, American Folk Art Museum, promised gift of Ralph Esmarian; photo, John Bigelow Taylor © 2000).

In May 1995 a well-known collection of southern material was auctioned by Sotheby's. There were many items of interest to Colonial Williamsburg. Several curators went to make a pre-auction inspection. They came back with rave reviews of a glazed redware figure of a goat, made and signed about 1880 by Anthony W. Baecher of Winchester, Virginia (fig. 18). Although it is unpretentious in size—only seven inches high and six and one half inches long—they praised it so enthusiastically and had such a high estimate of its likely sale price that I thought they had collectively lost their minds. The day before the auction I went to see for myself. I think I examined all the other items the curators were recommending before I came to the goat. When I did, it swept me off my feet with its dynamism, its bril-

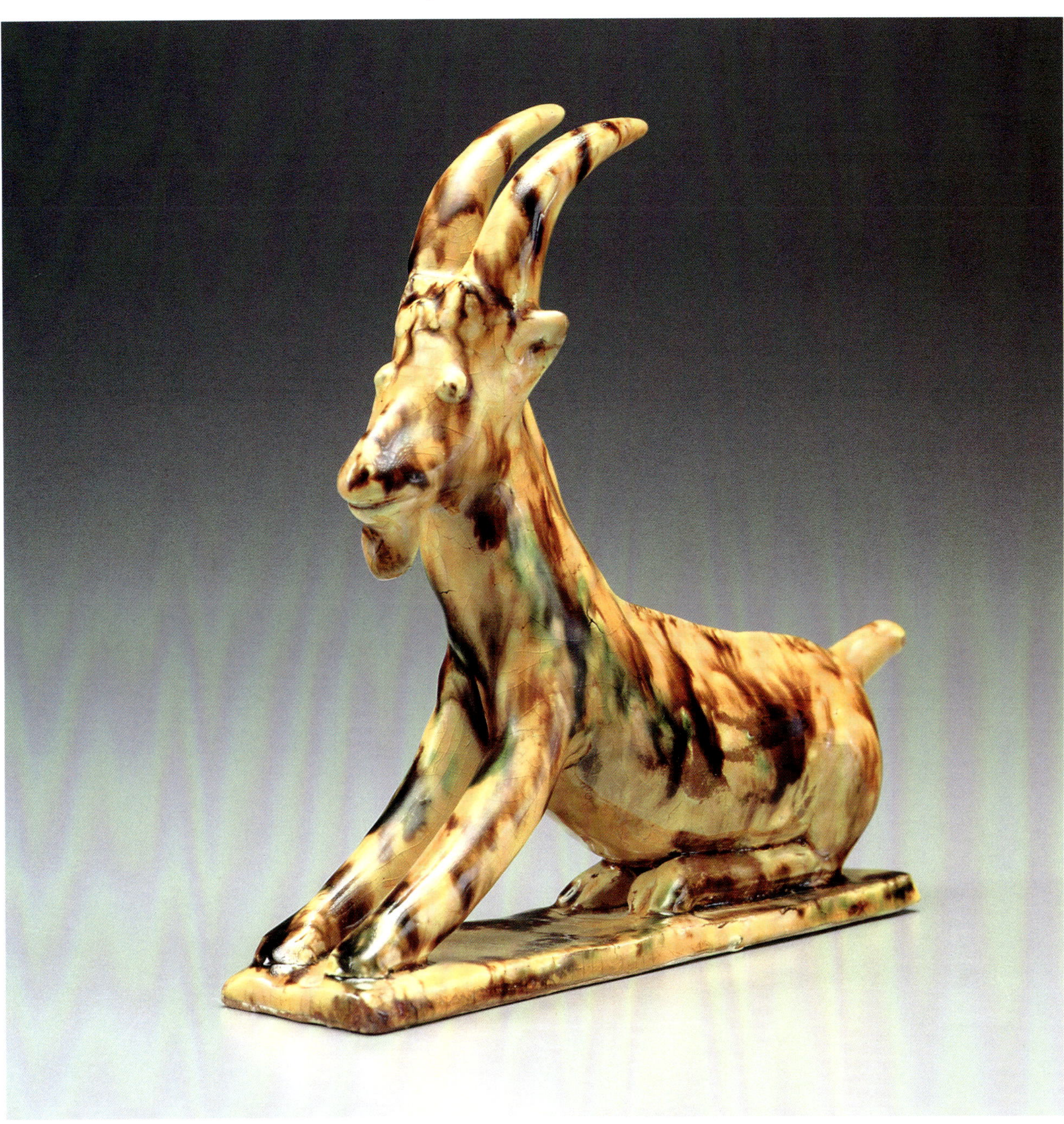

Figure 19 Michelle Erickson, seated goat after Anthony Baecher, 1995. Glazed earthenware. H. 6⅞". (Hood Collection.)

liant sense of life, its immense appeal. There and then I decided I was going to bid higher than my colleagues had recommended. I did so, but reluctantly dropped out when the bidding reached almost seven times the low estimate. There was another item later in the sale that was even more important for our collection, and I was forced to husband what resources I had.

The change in my attitude from skepticism to enthusiasm clearly amused some of my junior colleagues, and they persuaded one of today's most gifted potters, Michelle Erickson, to make a copy. This she did from a photograph, and with remarkable speed, but she was still able to imbue it with such vitality that I gasped when I took it out of the box (fig. 19). For a split

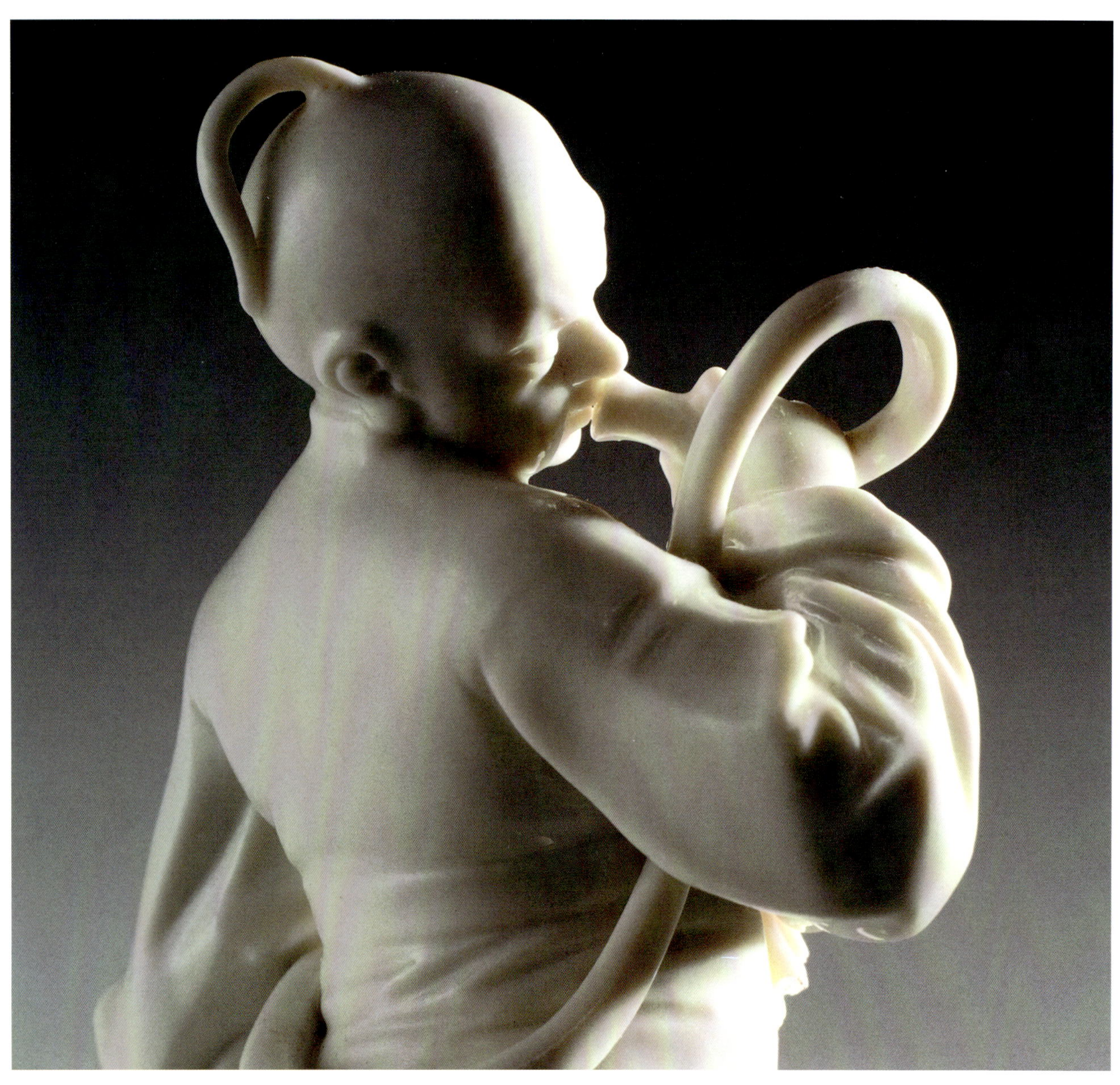

Figure 20 Detail of the Chinese musician illustrated in fig. 1.

second—though I knew it could not possibly be—I thought I was holding the actual piece! It, too, like the Chinese musician, now occupies a very special place in my life and in our house.

I believe in all that material culturalists have written about the many roles that ceramics, even ordinary mass-made ones, have occupied in people's lives. But more than that, I believe in the power of contemplating a piece of glazed clay, which has been invested with the true spirit of human creativity and discipline, to add something immeasurable to our lives (fig. 20).

1. Walter M. Whitehill, Wendell D. Garrett, Jane N. Garrett, *The Arts in Early American History* (Chapel Hill, N.C.: University of North Carolina Press, 1965), p. 22.

2. William B. Honey, *Dresden China* (London: A & C Black, 1934), p. 101.

3. This colleague was Samuel J. Wagstaff, Jr., who brought modern and avant-garde art to Hartford, Connecticut, in the 1960s through his innovative exhibits at the Wadsworth Atheneum. After a few years subsequently as Curator of Modern Art at the Detroit Institute of Art, from 1968 on (again we arrived to take up new posts the same week), Sam retired to New York where he became conspicuous as a full-time collector of considerable ambition, and as patron and companion of Robert Mapplethorpe. While curator of this porcelain collection, I made the acquaintance of a local ear, nose, and throat surgeon, who was most interested in the two-hundred-year-old German and English figures in my charge, because he had made an extended study of noses. He claimed that noses were an important, though little noted, part of national characteristics. He said he thought he could tell the two groups apart. I invited him to the museum, and gave him a test. There were no labels, and he was not allowed to pick up any of the figures. He got them all right!

4. Jules D. Prown bought this figure at the Nymphenburg factory in the summer of 1965 and gave it to me. For this, for his steady encouragement and wise counsel, as well as several years of mentoring, I owe him an enormous debt of gratitude.

5. John Fleming and Hugh Honour, *Dictionary of the Decorative Arts* (New York: Harper and Row, 1977), pp. 133–34.

6. Henry P. Maynard, Curator of American Art at the Wadsworth Atheneum in Hartford in the 1960s and 1970s, to whose kind and unassuming tutelage I owe much.

7. I've written about this project at length in *Bonnin and Morris of Philadelphia; the First American Porcelain Factory, 1770–1772* (Chapel Hill, N.C.: The University of North Carolina Press, 1972). A shorter version, with some valuable additions kindly supplied by Michael K. Brown, is my essay, "The American China," in *The American Craftsman and the European Tradition, 1620– 1820* (Minneapolis, Minn.: The Minneapolis Institute of Arts, 1989), pp. 240–56.

8. Margaret Sterne, *The Passionate Eye: The Life of William R. Valentiner* (Detroit, Mich.: Wayne State University Press, 1980).

9. My colleague as curator of ceramics for twenty years was John C. Austin, who energetically expanded the already very strong collection. The archaeologist was Ivor Noël Hume. I must also pay my tribute to the editor of this journal for the extraordinary things he teased out of (seemingly) nowhere in his too brief stint as assistant curator of ceramics at Colonial Williamsburg. The collection became even stronger and more interesting because of his efforts. The objects he recommended for acquisition included the Chelsea figure of *Trump*, which I describe later in this article (figs. 16, 17).

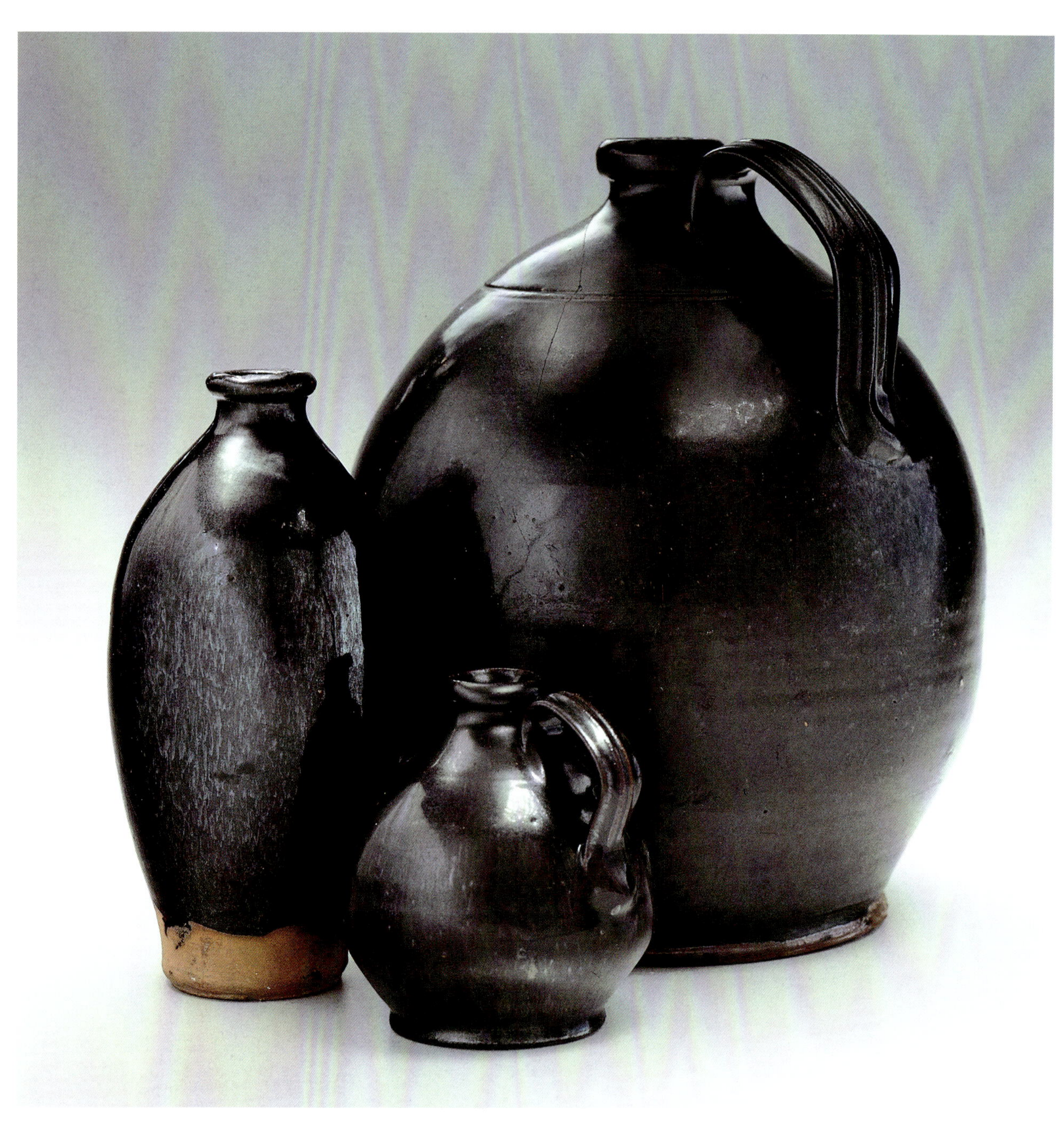

Anthony W. Butera, Jr.

"Informed Conjecture": Collecting Long Island Redware

Figure 1 Jugs and flask, probably Huntington, New York, late eighteenth/early nineteenth century. Manganese enriched lead-glazed earthenware. H. of tallest: 10⅛". (All objects from the Anthony W. Butera, Jr. Collection; photos by Gavin Ashworth unless otherwise noted.) The attribution to Huntington is based on a jug that descended in a Huntington family. These objects are thought to date from the 1780s when Jonathan Titus owned the property until it sold on February 27, 1805. The lip on the flask matches the lips on the other two vessels. All three vessels were acquired locally. It should be noted that this kind of attribution is not foolproof; however, the importance of local knowledge and provenance becomes important when no other evidence is available.

▼ BEING A YOUNG pottery collector has its rewards and challenges. I began seriously collecting only about twelve years ago. In this relatively short time, I have found myself playing all sorts of roles in order to achieve my goals. Sometimes I am a student, scholar, detective, traveler, photographer, archaeologist, psychologist, banker, book collector, spy, beggar, writer, and often a pain-in-the-neck!

My process of collecting is evolving, providing the opportunity to discover what I really want and need. This, of course, leads to the question which most collectors attempt to answer: Why do I collect? For me, the answer is intertwined with the Huntington, Long Island, redwares that are the focus of my collection.

As a child growing up in an historic area on Long Island, I formed an appreciation for pottery. Although there were no collectors in the family, my parents always served formal dinners on fine china. I remember admiring and handling their wedding gifts, modern pieces of Wedgwood. Colonial Williamsburg was always mentioned in our family, especially since my parents lived near there when they were first married. I was familiar with the colonial style as our home was decorated in that manner. In the early 1970s, I was given *The Flower World of Williamsburg* by Joan Parry Dutton.[1] Among the illustrations are photographs of some of Colonial Williamsburg's fine ceramics collections. When I first visited Colonial Williamsburg in 1975, these illustrations inspired me to photograph the ceramics in many of the historic buildings. These are the first pictures I took of ceramics.

As a high school student, I enjoyed all of my activities and studies, having a particular love of history, Latin (which included Roman history), and music. My major in college was music. After college I returned home to work in the family business of mason contracting. Living in a historic area occasionally meant working on historic homes, and I found I needed to know how to treat these homes properly. The magazines *Colonial Homes* and *Early American Life* provided a resource at that time. While looking through these magazines, I would come across photographs of redware, which piqued my curiosity. On our frequent trips to a summer place in upstate New York, I never saw this mysterious redware, so I began a search. When I finally found a fluted redware mold in an antique shop in Rockland, New York, I bought it. Although I have since learned that this first piece was of European origin, I still enjoy having it in my collection.

Living near Manhattan gives a budding collector a great advantage. Many great museums, auction houses, and antique shows are nearby. With

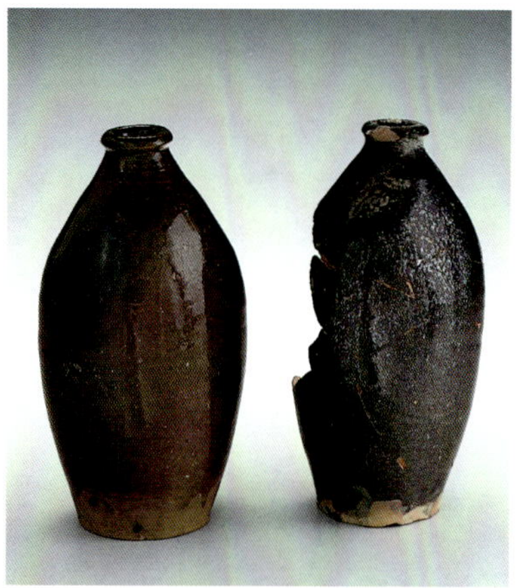

Figure 2 Flasks, probably Huntington, New York, late eighteenth/early nineteenth century. Right: Manganese enriched lead-glazed earthenware. Left: Lead-glazed earthenware daubed with manganese oxide. H. of both: 7⅛". The black-glazed flask fragment was discovered underneath the floor of a ca. 1810 house in Miller Place, Long Island. The lip of the flask is similar to several known Huntington vessels, including a straight-sided black manganese lead-glazed earthenware jar attributed to the Titus period in an early Huntington collection, and a rim waster found at the pottery site.

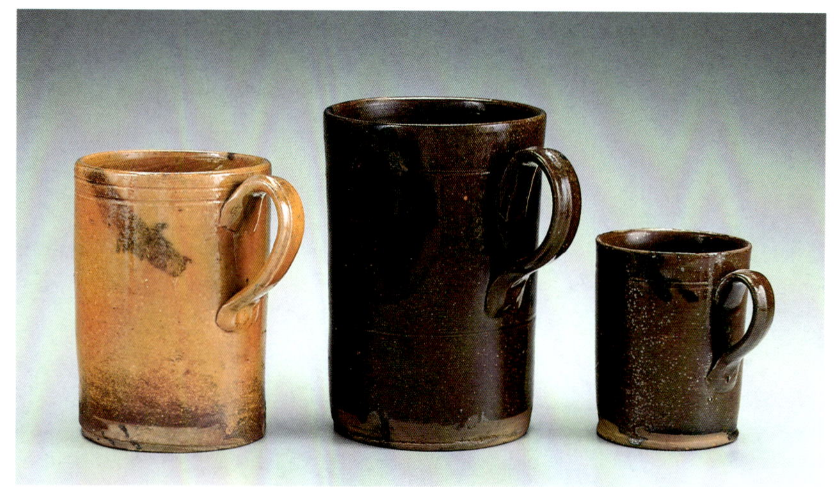

Figure 3 Mugs, probably Huntington, New York, 1805–1860. Lead-glazed earthenware daubed with manganese oxide. H. (left to right): 5 7/16", 6½", and 3 15/16". This is a rare graduated group of tankards attributed to the Huntington pottery. The tankard on the far right came from a local source. The other two vessels did not, but both match the first almost perfectly. It is interesting to note the color difference which should not always be a guideline for attribution since the color of fired red earthenwares can be affected by conditions inside or outside the kiln, contaminants in the glaze, or different conditions of the clay source. The style of the extruded handles and their attachments has been found at the site of the Huntington pottery.

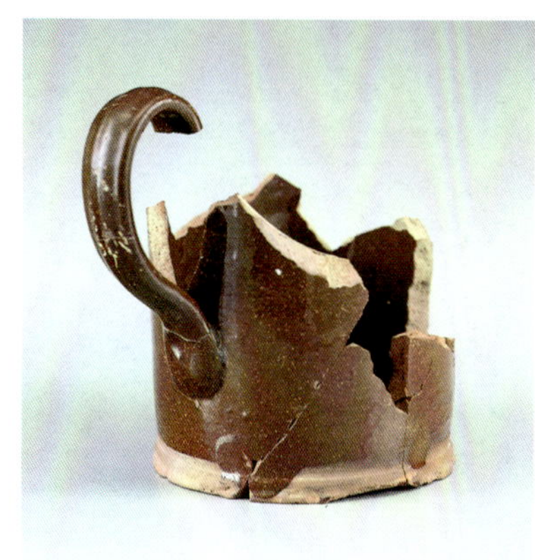

Figure 4 Mug fragment, probably Huntington, New York, 1805–1860. Lead-glazed earthenware daubed with manganese oxide. D. 3½". This fragment of a tankard was found during the removal of a Victorian porch from a ca. 1680–1700 house in Mt. Sinai, Long Island. It is similar in all ways to the mugs illustrated in fig. 3. A similar tankard appears in the 1837 William Sydney Mount painting *The Long Story*.

my growing interest in redware, I began to attend more and more shows to educate myself. The first time I attended the International Fine Arts and Antiques Show in New York City, dealers Kinneman and Ramaeker were exhibiting. The focal point of their booth for me was a very large, slip-decorated American redware charger. Although I did not purchase it, the experience inspired me to start my hunt in earnest. While antiquing with family and friends, I came across the dealers Jack and Maryellen Whistance who have a small shop that specializes in American antiques, includ-

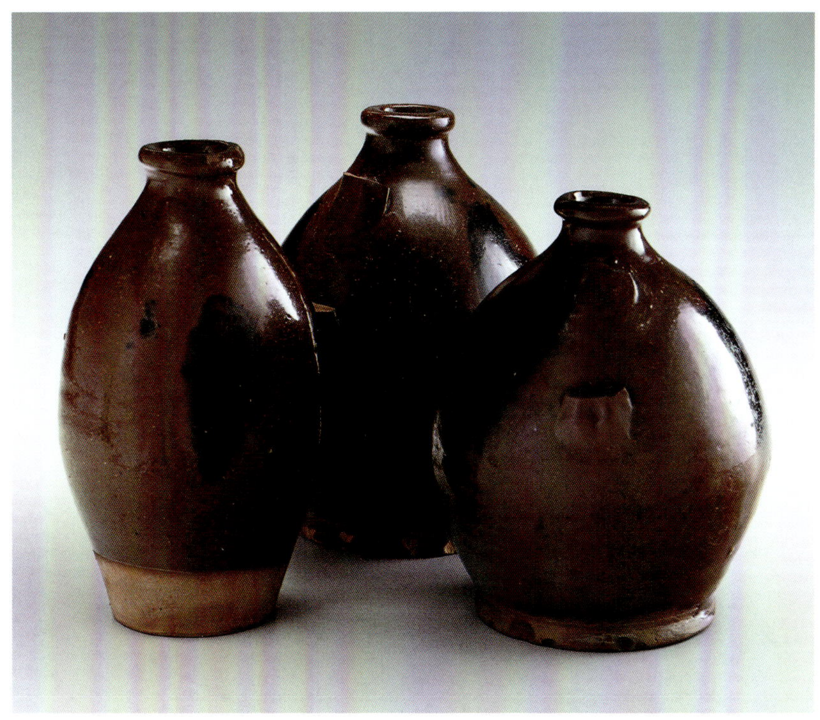

Figure 5 Jugs and flask, probably Huntington, New York, 1805–1860. Lead-glazed earthenware daubed with manganese oxide. H. of tallest: 6⅞". These three pots were purchased at auction from the Charles Embree Rockwell estate in Nissequogue, Smithtown, Long Island. This was a rare opportunity to purchase redware directly from a Long Island estate. The handle attachments are similar to the tankards illustrated in fig. 3. Also the same attachment of the handles on the jugs has been found at the pottery site. Although these examples are similar to wares produced at the Norwalk potteries, these pots have a local history and have been attributed to the Huntington pottery.

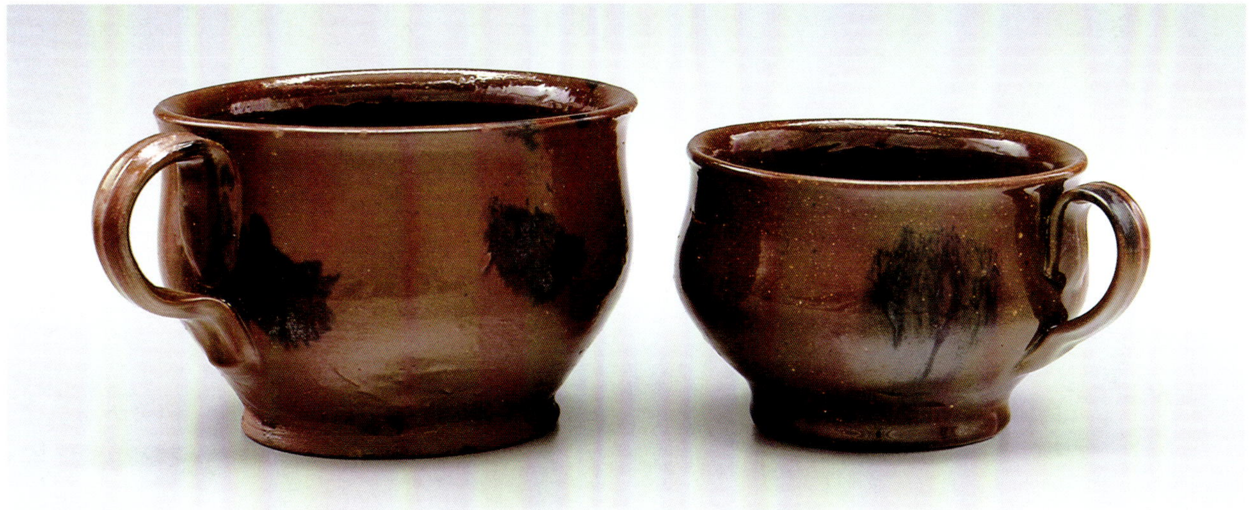

Figure 6 Porringers, possibly Huntington, New York, 1805–1860. Lead-glazed earthenware daubed with manganese oxide. H. 3¾" and 3½". These two porringers are without any local provenance. However, identical handles have been found at the Huntington pottery site. Another example is in a local collection.

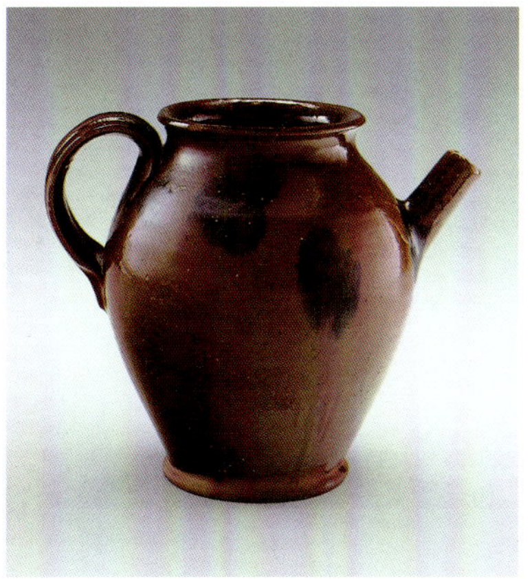

Figure 7 Syrup or oil jar, possibly Long Island, New York, ca. 1840. Lead-glazed earthenware daubed with manganese oxide. H. 8½". Although this pot has a New England provenance, an identical extruded handle has been found at the Huntington pottery site. Two other pots of this form made in salt-glazed stoneware are known and are believed to be from the Hudson River Valley. The Huntington pottery shares a continuum with the Hudson River Valley potteries through the Caire and Brown families. Wet drug jars in continental tin-glazed earthenwares appear in this form.

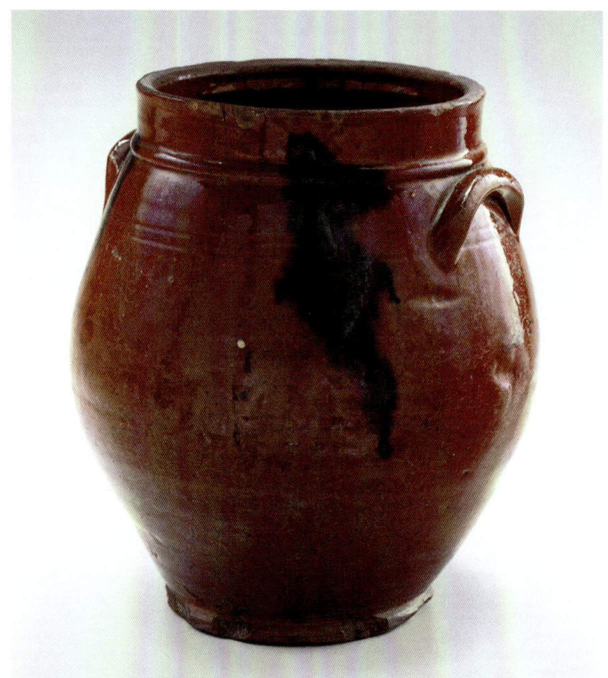

Figure 8 Jar, attributed to Huntington, New York, 1805–1860. Lead-glazed earthenware daubed with manganese oxide. H. 8". This is a form traditionally attributed to Huntington.

Figure 9 Jar and lid, possibly Long Island, New York, 1805–1860. Lead-glazed earthenware daubed with manganese oxide. H. to top of lid. 10⅝". Another variation on the form illustrated in fig. 8. It is possible that some of these pots were made in the Hudson River Valley, although there is no evidence yet to prove this.

Figure 10 Jar, possibly Long Island, New York, 1840–1860. Lead-glazed earthenware daubed with manganese oxide. H. 8¾". This jar descended in a Riverhead, Long Island, family and was found with a salt-glazed stoneware butter churn bearing the mark of Fredrick J. Caire Huntington who came to Huntington in the 1840s.

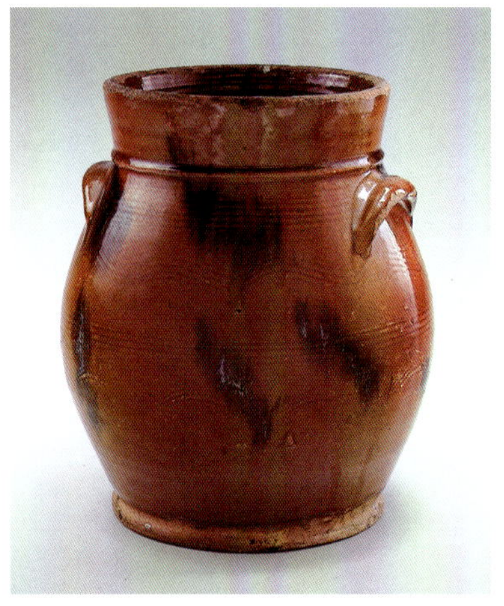

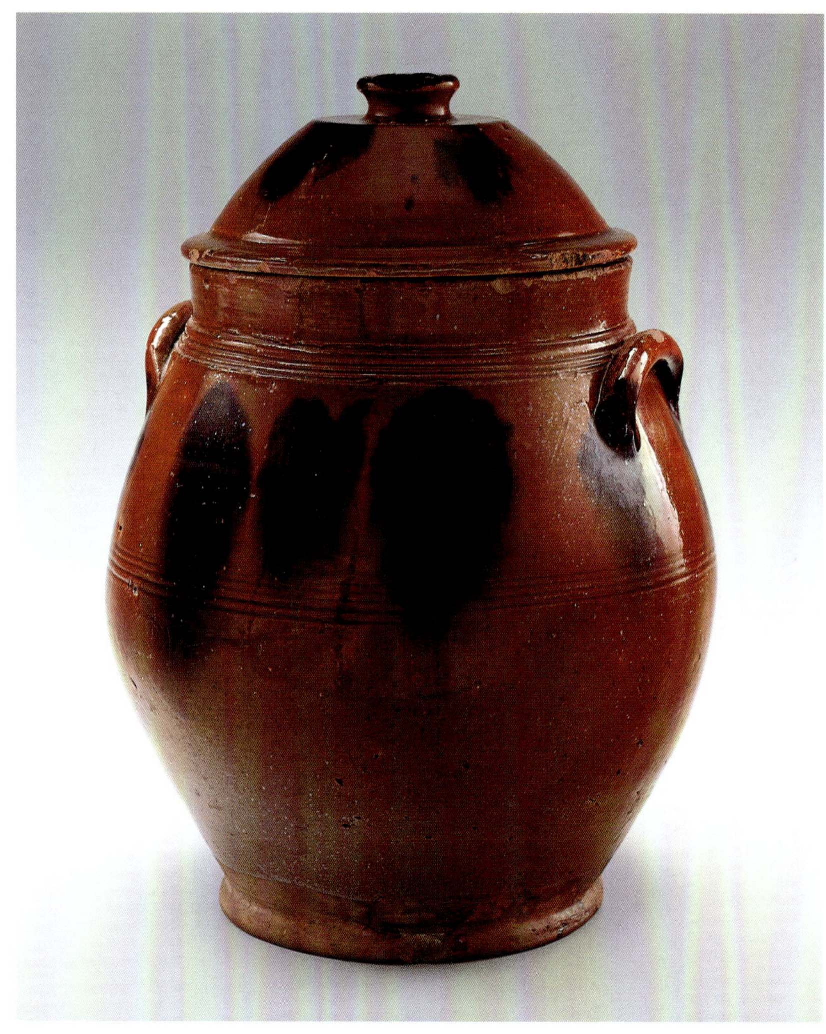

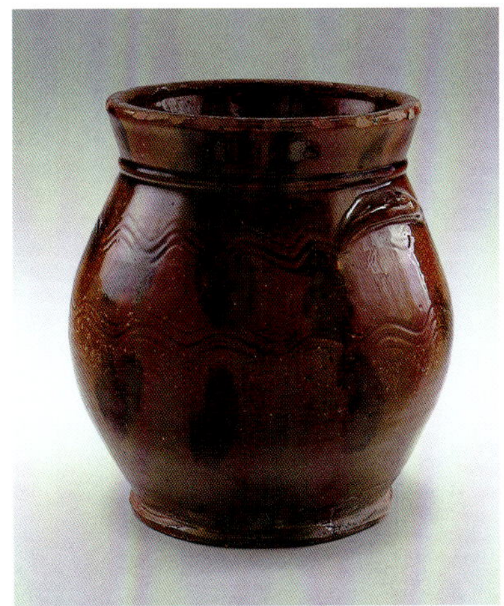

Figure 11 Jar, possibly Long Island, New York, 1805–1860. Lead-glazed earthenware daubed with manganese oxide. H. 8½". This pot came from a collection formed on Long Island in the 1950s. It is slightly smaller than the jar illustrated in fig. 10, making the two pots look different at first glance. Further examination reveals similar features, and it is possible that they both were made by the same potter.

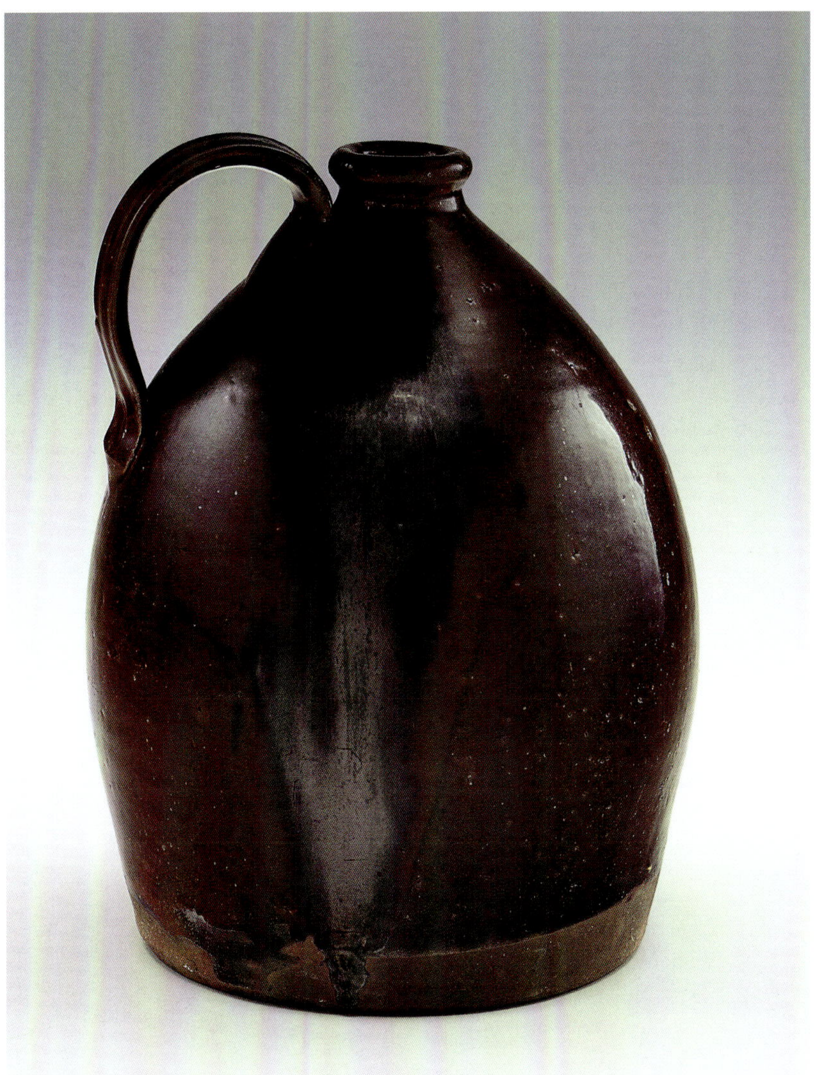

Figure 12 Jug, probably Long Island, New York, 1835–1860. Lead-glazed earthenware daubed with manganese oxide. H. 10". This handled jug comes from an early Setauket, Long Island, collection formed before 1950. A handled jug of this form appears in the painting illustrated in fig. 13. Traditionally, collectors of American pottery have believed that this form was produced later. This painting establishes an earlier date.

ing a fine selection of redware. I have often returned to their beautiful shop to listen to their advice on collecting and to buy many pieces of redware, some of which are illustrated here.

The magazine *Antiques* is a necessary tool for any collector. After seeing Jeannette Lasansky's article on Pennsylvania pottery in the October 1990 issue, I attended redware potter Lester Breininger's annual porch sale, since most of the pieces illustrated in the article were from his personal collection.[2] The sale included demonstrations of throwing pots and slip-decorating. After meeting Lester Breininger and viewing his collection, which focused on locally made pottery, I was motivated to collect what was made in my area of Long Island at the Huntington pottery. This decision coincided with a newly published book by Cynthia Corbett for the Society for the Preservation of Long Island Antiquities (SPLIA), *Useful Art: Long Island Pottery*.[3]

What initially struck me in reading Corbett's book were the illustrated geometric designs on plates attributed to the Huntington pottery. These designs were described as being first incised, then having slip applied over the incising. This technique fascinated me and provided another good reason to collect these plates. Here was something not only unique among the many American redwares but also something made and used in my area.

The history of the Huntington pottery, or more accurately, the potteries, extends over a century. The Huntington community was rich in clay resources with easy water access to New York City and the Connecticut market. Although the clay sources of the area were used in brick making as early as 1751, it is uncertain exactly when the first pottery arose. It has been speculated that Jonathan Titus may have operated a pottery in conjunction

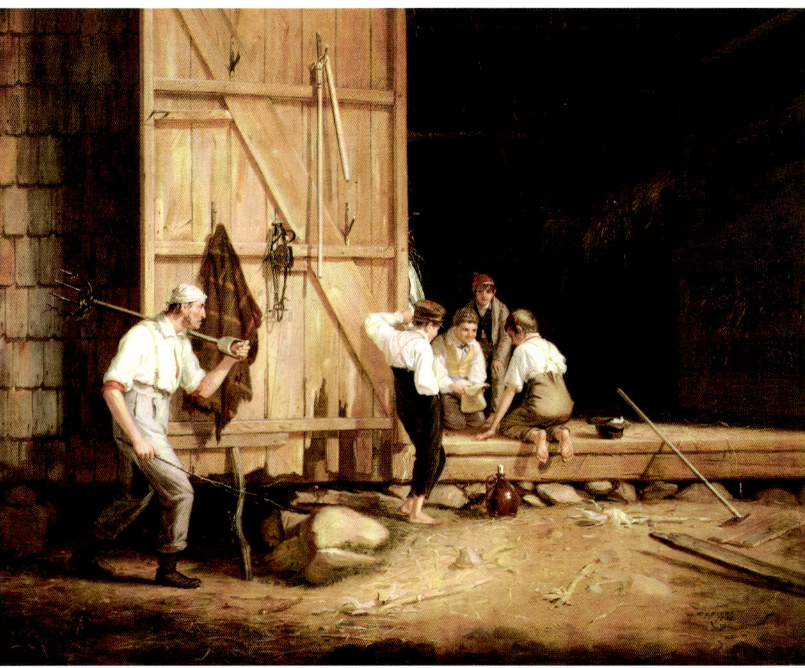

Figure 13 William Sydney Mount, *Truant Gamblers (Undutiful Boys)*, 1835. Oil on canvas. 24" x 30". (Courtesy, New-York Historical Society, acc. no. 1858.)

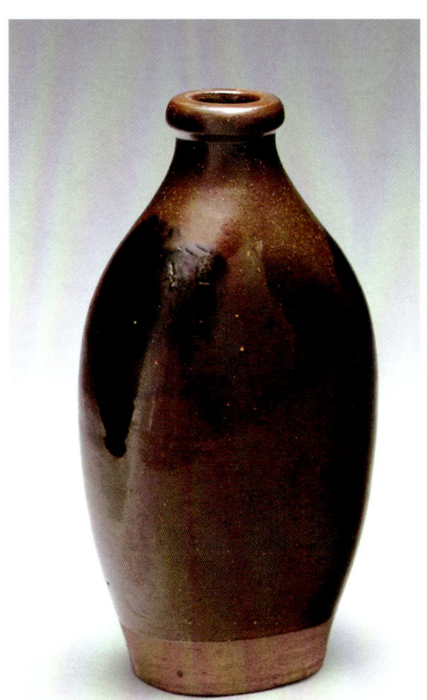

Figure 14 Flask, probably Huntington, New York, 1835–1860. Lead-glazed earthenware daubed with manganese. H. 8". This flask has the same lip as the jug illustrated in fig. 12 . Although glaze should not always be used as a guideline for attribution, it sometimes helps when a group of wares are compared. This flask was found concealed in the wall of a house in the Port Jefferson area.

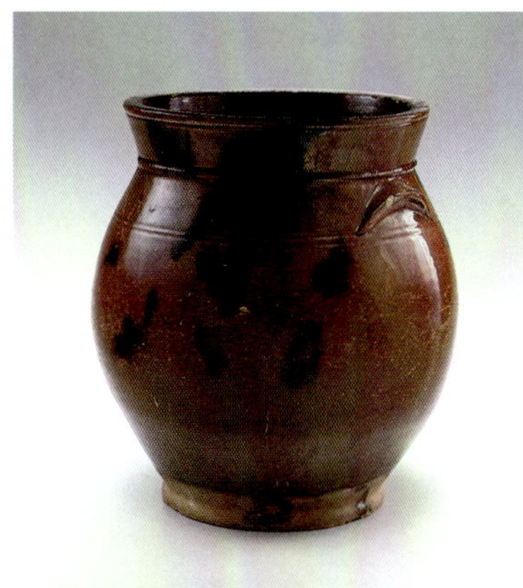

Figure 15 Jar, possibly Long Island, New York, 1805–1860. Lead-glazed earthenware daubed with manganese oxide. H. 9½". This jar has a credible Long Island provenance.

Figure 16 Pitcher, possibly Huntington, New York, 1805–1860. Lead-glazed earthenware daubed with manganese oxide. H. 9½". The form, color, and decoration of this pitcher are similar to the jar illustrated in fig. 15. The pitcher's extruded handle has been found at the pottery site.

Figure 17 Jar and lid, probably Long Island, New York, 1805–1860. Lead-glazed earthenware daubed with manganese oxide. H. to top of lid 10½". This jar came from an early collection formed in Port Jefferson. It was found together with a straight-sided jar probably made by the same potter.

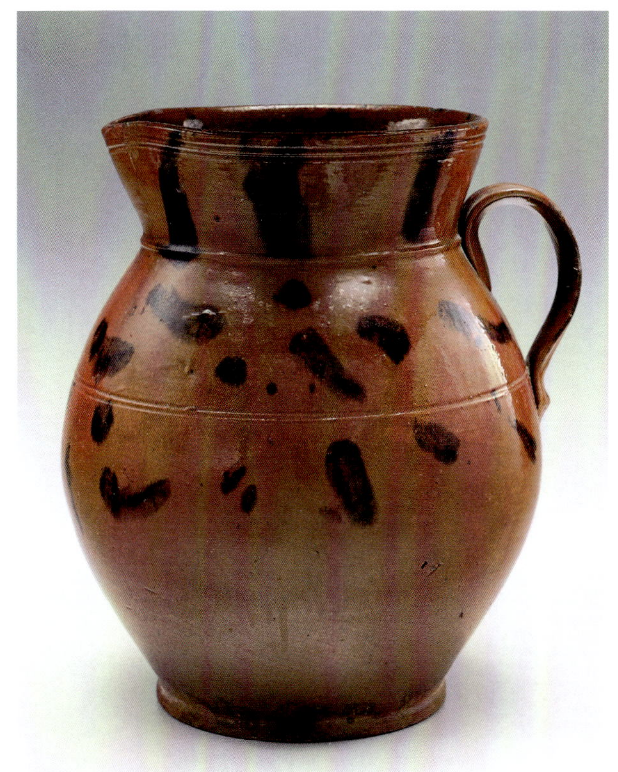

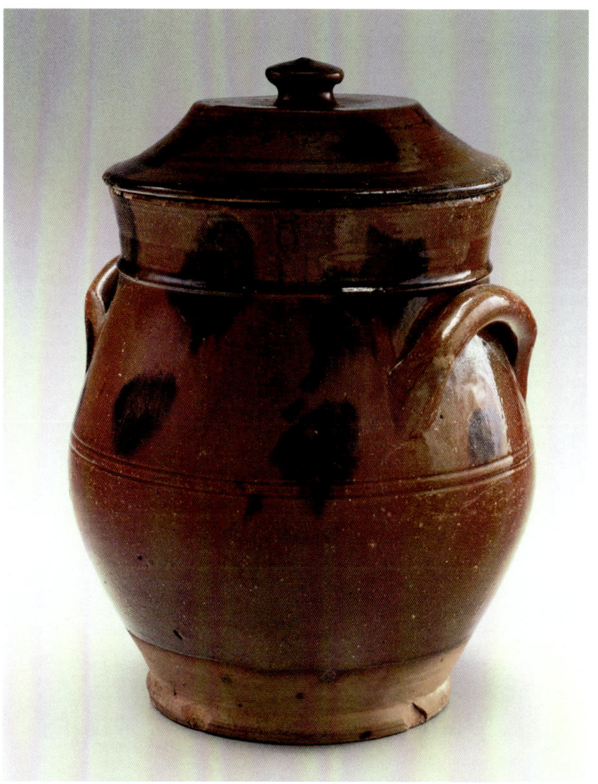

with his tavern operation in the late eighteenth century. The first historical mention of a pottery on the site occurs in 1805 when a firm known as Samuel J. Wetmore and Company took over the property. From that point on, documentation of the pottery varies in detail, as various owners and workmen are known to have been associated with the operation. A number of historical accounts shows the range of earthenware and stoneware produced there. The best documentation for the pottery comes with the tenure of the Brown brothers from 1863 until 1905 when operations ceased.[4]

The redware from this one hundred-year-old pottery operation, which served the everyday needs of nineteenth-century Long Island communities, has been the focus of my collecting efforts. In spite of the availability of documents and other evidence, surprisingly little information has been published about the actual redware products of Huntington, and after collecting a fair number of redware plates, I became increasingly dissatisfied with the few published descriptions of their manufacture I could find. Why would such a labor intensive process have been em-

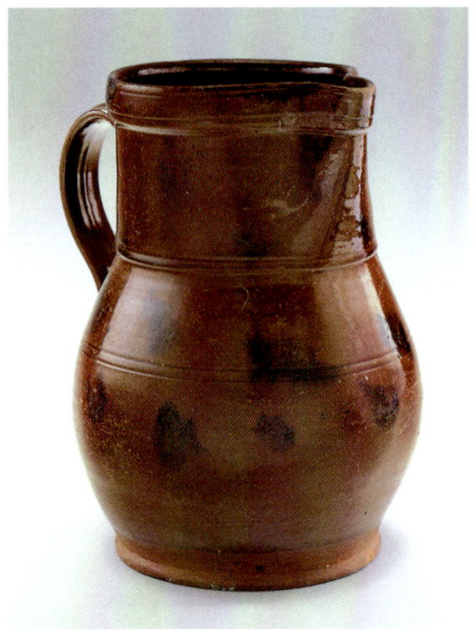

Figure 18 Pitcher, possibly Huntington, New York, 1805–1860. Lead-glazed earthenware daubed with manganese oxide. H. 10⅛". This pitcher has been attributed to Huntington on the fact that this type of extruded handle and its attachment have been found at the pottery site. The belly of the pitcher also matches the belly of the pot in fig. 17, suggesting that the two were made by the same potter. Another pitcher of a different form, but with the same handle and attachment, appears in the painting illustrated in fig. 19.

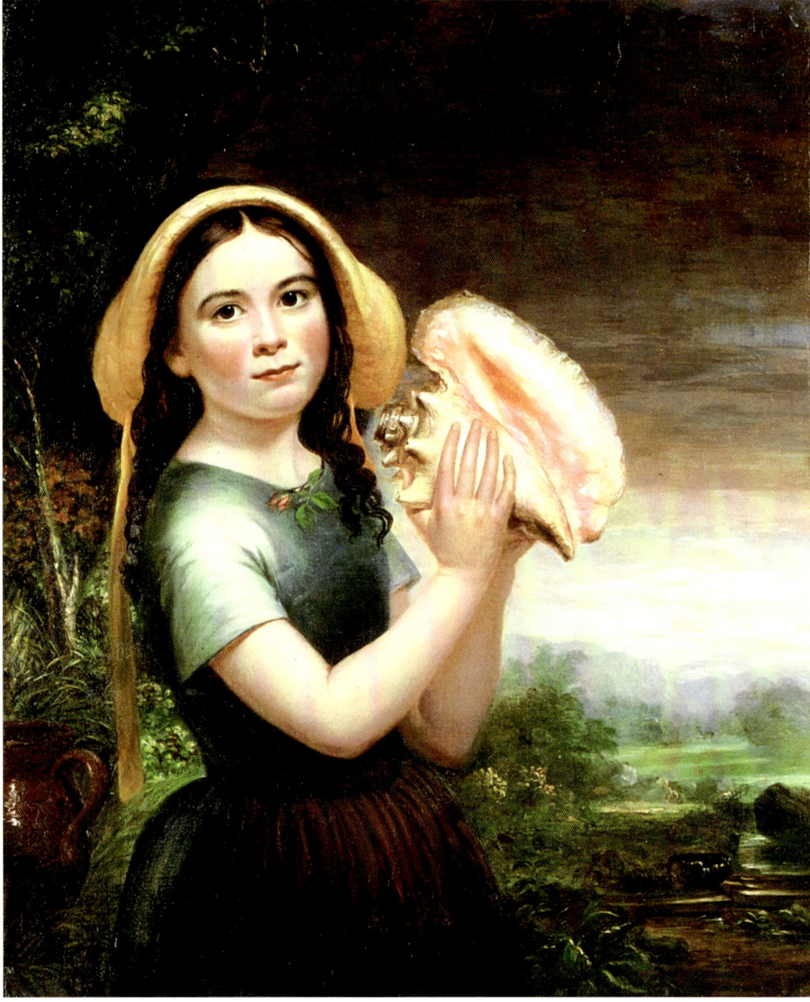

Figure 19 Shepard Alonzo Mount, *The Breakfast Call,* 1852. Oil on canvas. 24" x 30". (Courtesy, Long Island Museum of American Art, History and Carriages; gift of Mr. and Mrs. Ward Melville, 1976.)

ployed? Why did so many of these redware plates have missing areas of slip? Why did some plates have more slip applied than others? Most importantly, why did Greg Shooner, a well-versed modern redware potter, refuse to accept this labor intensive process when he decorated his own red earthenware?

In 1996 technology historian Don Carpentier held the first of his annual workshops on ceramics at Eastfield Village near Albany, New York. This was a good opportunity for me to bring this question of slip decorating to scholars and, more importantly, to potters. When I arrived at Eastfield on the morning of Greg Shooner's lecture, I noticed tin welding equipment which had been used recently at the back of the room. As the day progressed, Greg and Don kept asking me what I thought about the Huntington plates and how did I think they were made. At the end of Greg's lecture, he and Don surprised me by demonstrating how the plates were really decorated. A tin stamp was made, dipped in the slip, and then pressed onto the rolled-out slab of clay. The slip came off the stamp onto the clay. In addition, the stamp left a faint impression in the clay. Don had known about this technique through his study of English mochaware, and he had published a demonstration of its use on mocha ware.[5]

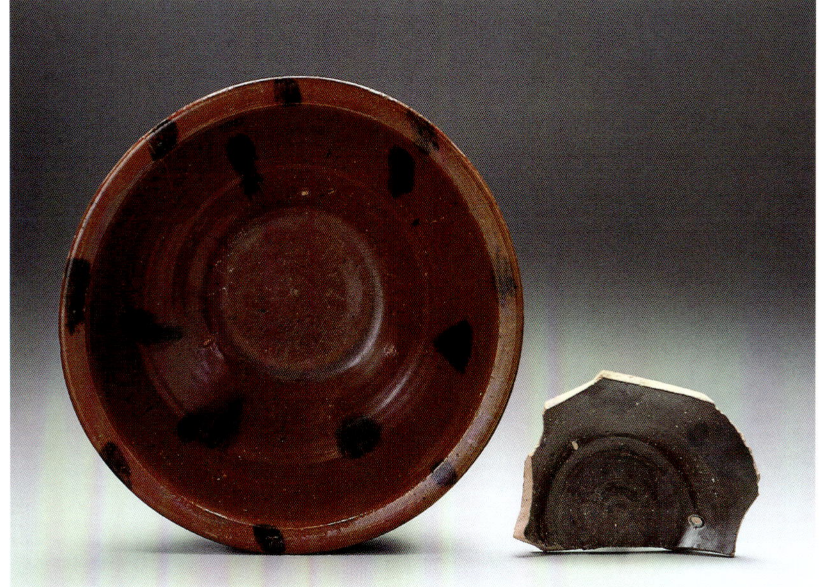

Figure 20 Bowl and archaeological fragment, Huntington, New York, 1805–1860. Lead-glazed earthenware daubed with manganese oxide. D. 13". Wasters of these bowls have been found at the pottery site. Matching rims have also been found along with the kiln furniture needed to stack the bowls in the kiln. Sherds of these bowls have also been found in Port Jefferson and Mt. Sinai, Long Island.

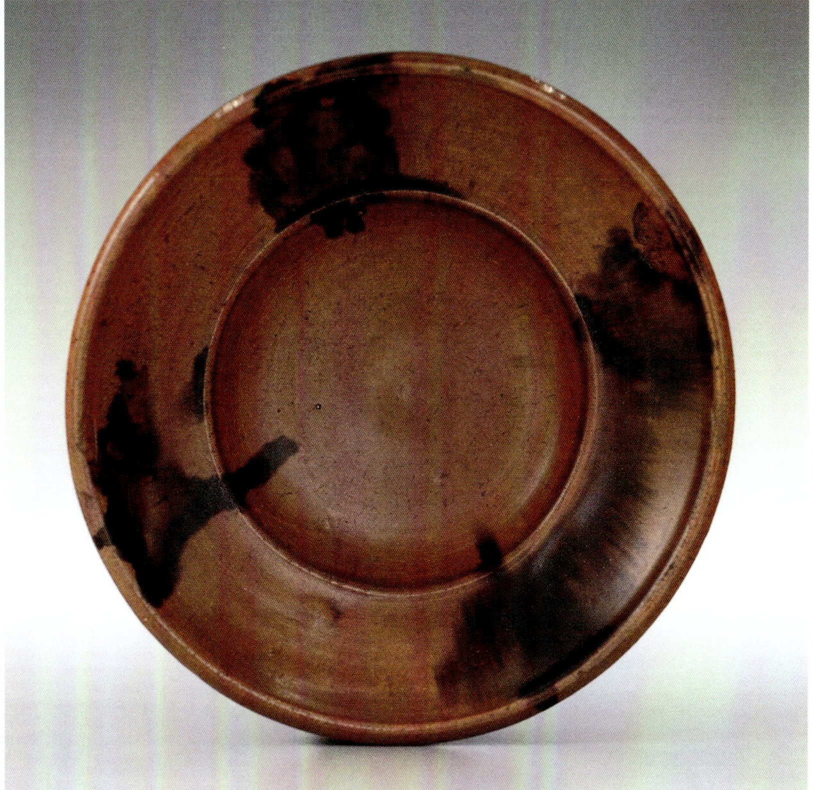

Figure 21 Bowl, Huntington, New York, 1805–1809. Lead-glazed earthenware daubed with manganese. D. 5⅝". Two other examples of this form are owned by the Huntington Historical Society. This is a technically difficult form to produce. The small bowl has been thrown on a wheel, probably bisque fired, decorated, glazed on both sides then fired perhaps in a saggar. This form may be a tobacco dish, which is listed as one of the most expensive forms that Samuel J. Wetmore and Company produced ca. 1808–1809.

After discovering that this method of stamping was used at the Huntington Pottery, I became interested in exploring the sources of the designs used for the tin stamps. Some designs were similar to those found on English medieval paving tiles. They are commonly found on wrought iron from all periods, including contemporary factory-made wrought iron. They are also similar to designs on Gothic Revival encaustic tiles, which are interesting because the Gothic Revival period coincides with

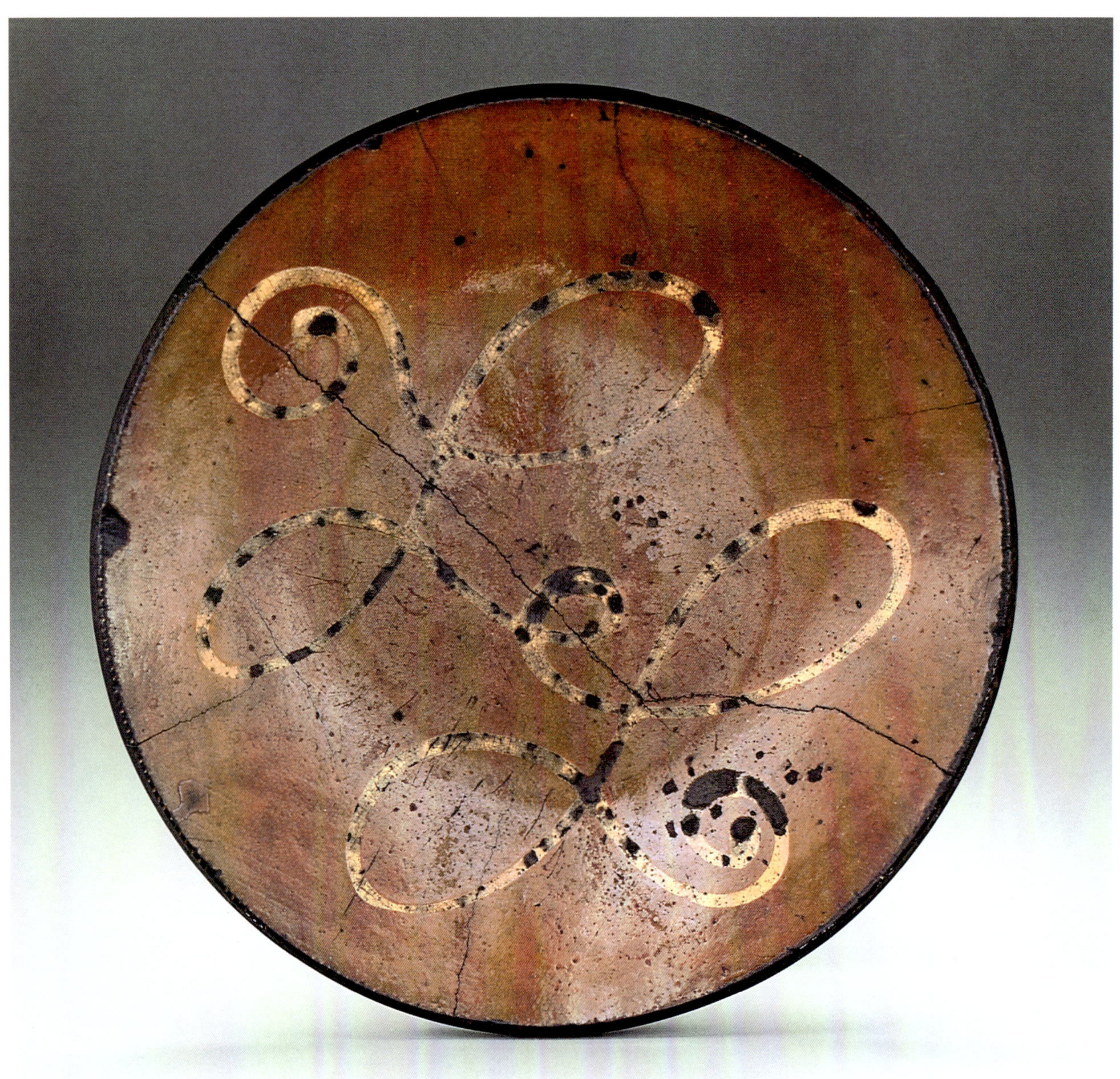

Figure 22 Dish, Huntington, New York, 1805–1860. Lead-glazed earthenware with slip decoration. D. 13¼". The slip decoration on this plate matches the cobalt blue decoration on a salt-glazed stoneware pot that descended in the Brown family and was probably made in Huntington before the Brown's ownership. It is interesting to find a decorator who worked on stoneware and redware. Although the condition of this plate is poor, the large size and decoration are quite rare.

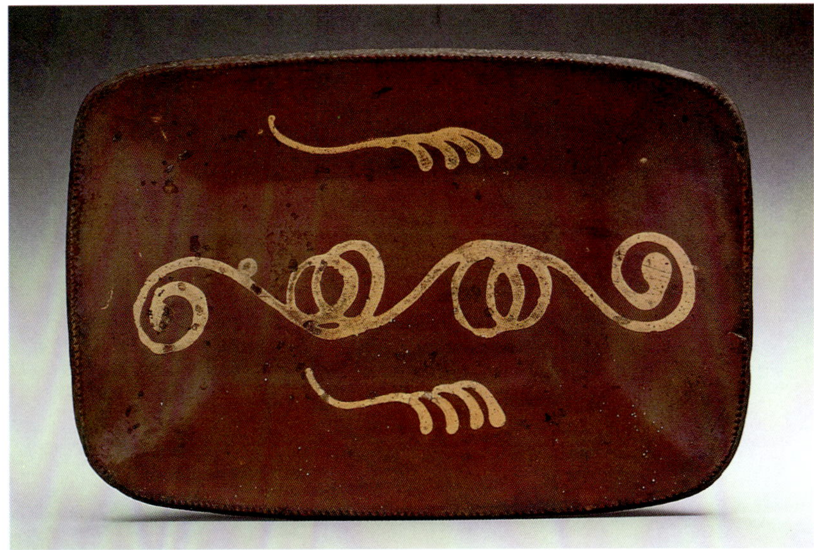

Figure 23 Loaf dish, Huntington, New York, 1805–1860. Lead-glazed earthenware with slip decoration. L. 14⅜". This is another variation by the same decorator who ornamented the dish illustrated in fig. 22. The central curvilinear design occurs in cobalt on salt-glazed stoneware from the pottery site. The feather type design on the top and bottom of the loaf dish have been found at the pottery site in slipware and cobalt blue salt-glazed stoneware. A signed F. Caire Huntington stoneware jug in a private collection has a similar design. This loaf dish was recently discovered in a barn on Long Island.

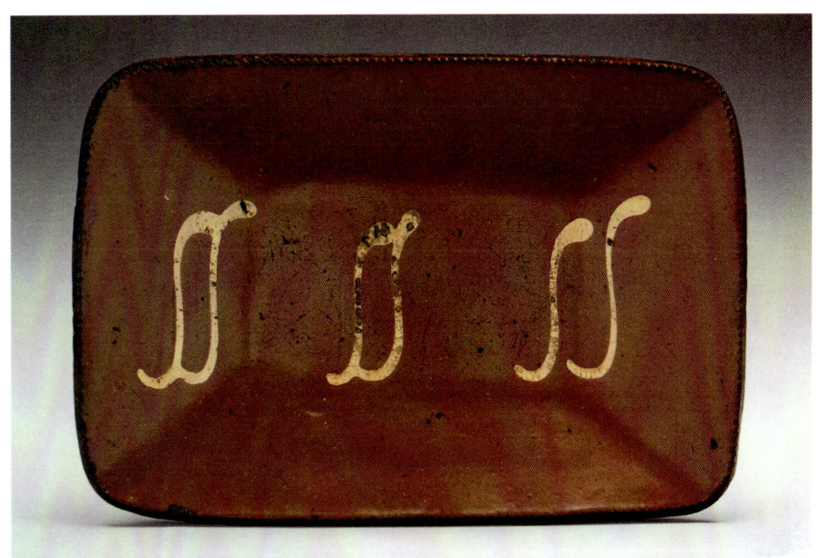

Figure 24 Loaf dish, Huntington, New York, 1805–1860. Slip-decorated lead-glazed earthenware. L. 11³⁄16". This loaf dish is decorated by the same skilled decorator who applied the slip on the dishes illustrated in figs. 22 and 23. Much practice is needed to execute these designs, as the slip tends to clog and has to be mixed frequently.

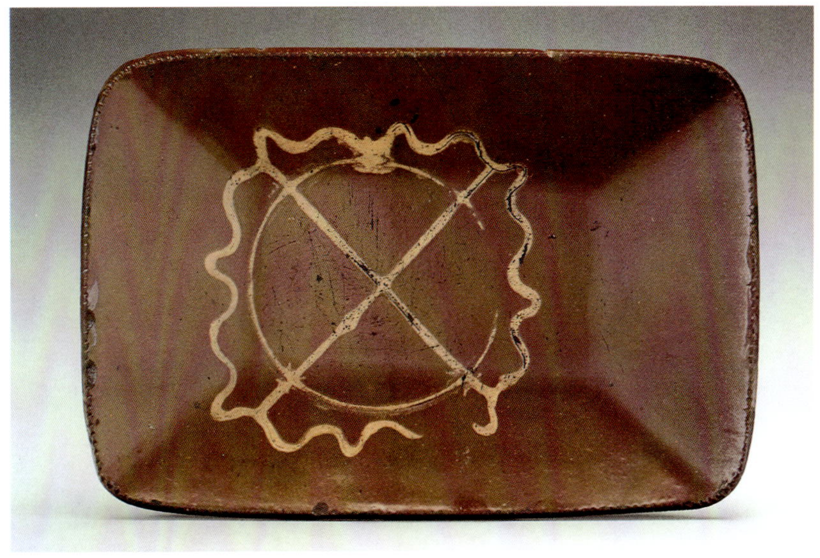

Figure 25 Loaf dish, Huntington, New York, ca. 1840–1860. Lead-glazed earthenware with slip decoration. L. 11½". This stamped pattern was found at the pottery site.

Figure 26 Demonstration by Greg Shooner of the stamping techniques used to decorate Huntington redware. (Photo, Anthony W. Butera, Jr.) This tin stamp was fashioned during the annual ceramics conference at Eastfield Village. Here the stamp is being dipped into white slip.

Figure 27 A series of stampings applied to a red clay slab illustrating the speed and repetitive nature of this method of slip decorating. (Photo, Anthony W. Butera, Jr.)

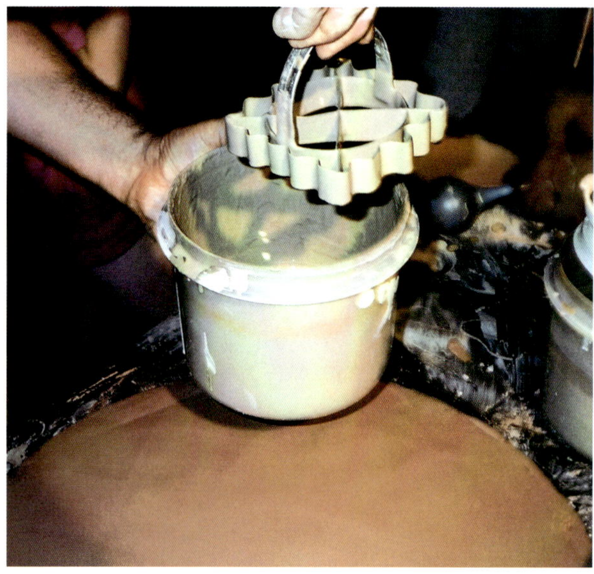

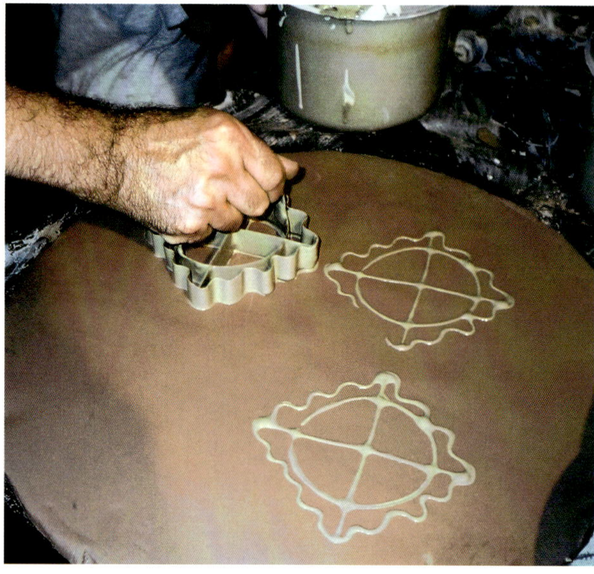

Figure 28 Border tile, England, fourteenth century. Earthenware. L. 4¾".

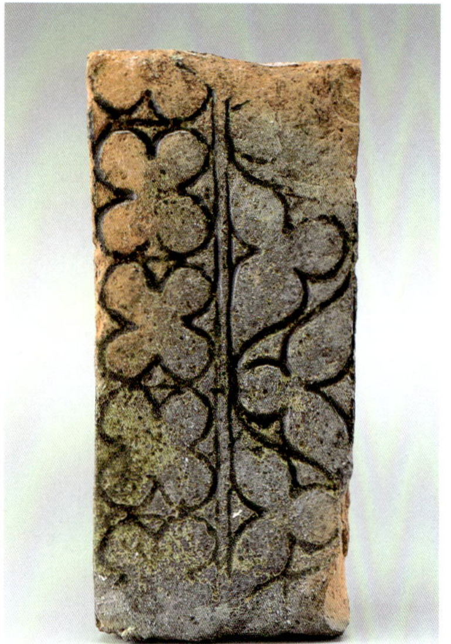

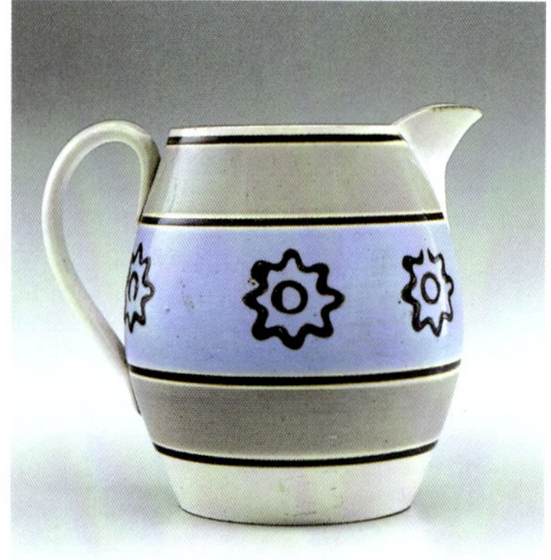

Figure 29 Jug, Britain, ca. 1840. Whiteware. H. 6". The star-like slip decoration has been applied with a stamp in a manner analogous to the Huntington pottery examples.

the same period that the Huntington stamped plates were produced. I have tried to somehow connect these trades, but so far I can only agree with this quote: "Although slip decorations probably derive from multiple and unconsciously chosen sources . . . [they] resemble gothic design elements, such as a rose window, crockets, quatrefoils, and the wheel of life . . . these designs were devised as something aesthetically familiar and easily worked."[6]

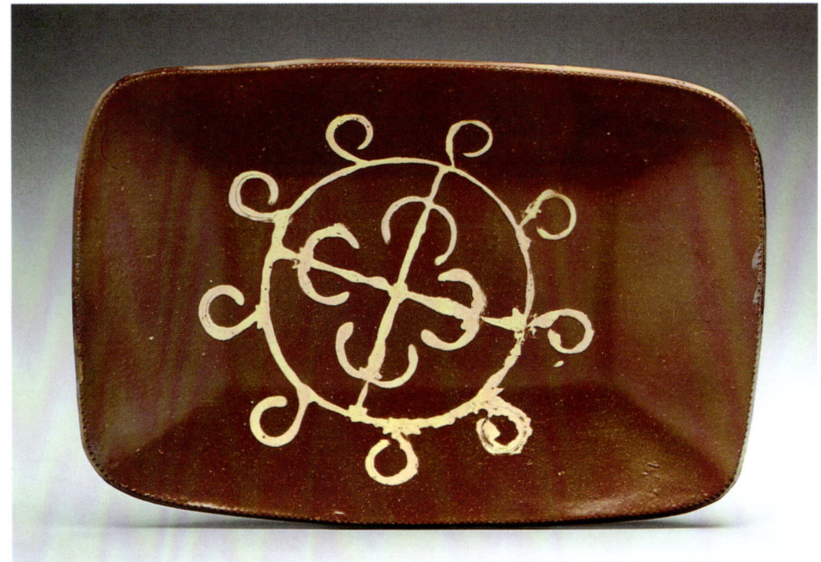

Figure 30 Loaf dish, Huntington, New York, 1840–1885. Lead-glazed earthenware with slip decoration. L. 14½". Only two loaf dishes with this stamped design survive. This pattern has been found at the Huntington pottery site.

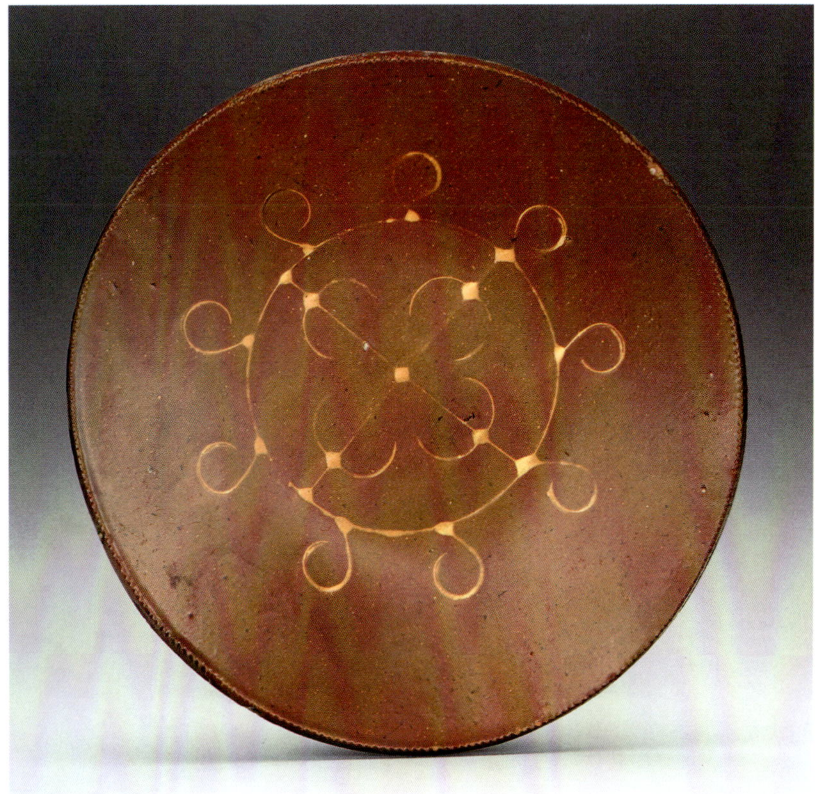

Figure 31 Dish, Huntington, New York, 1840–1885. Lead-glazed earthenware with slip decoration. D. 12". The slip may be lighter from using the stamp repeatedly without redipping in the slip. This would increase decorating speed and conserve slip.

So far, all of these stamped plates have been attributed to Huntington, Long Island. Such attributions, however, must be made with caution. To date, I have counted at least thirteen designs that were used. Some of these patterns might have been altered by changes made in the tin stamp by removing or adding pieces of tin. But another explanation for the large number of patterns is that some stamped plates might have been made elsewhere. Since there is little published archaeology to support attribution, I

Figure 32 Loaf dish, Huntington, New York, 1840–1885. Lead-glazed earthenware with slip decoration. L. 12⅞". This loaf dish and all other plates with the stamped star design have some sort of staining or muddiness in the glaze. This muddiness also appears commonly on other Huntington stamped patterns. This effect may have occurred through contamination due to experimentation with glazes or from the making of Rockingham-type glazed pots. Fragments of Rebekah-at-the-Well teapots have been found at the site including parts of saggars associated with their manufacture.

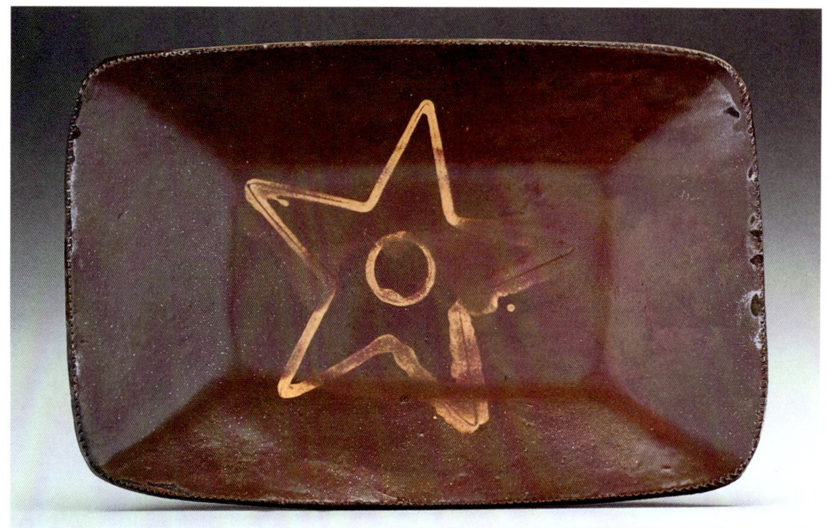

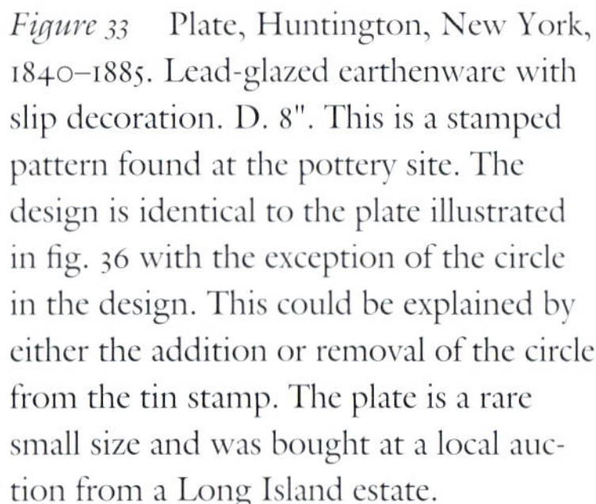

Figure 33 Plate, Huntington, New York, 1840–1885. Lead-glazed earthenware with slip decoration. D. 8". This is a stamped pattern found at the pottery site. The design is identical to the plate illustrated in fig. 36 with the exception of the circle in the design. This could be explained by either the addition or removal of the circle from the tin stamp. The plate is a rare small size and was bought at a local auction from a Long Island estate.

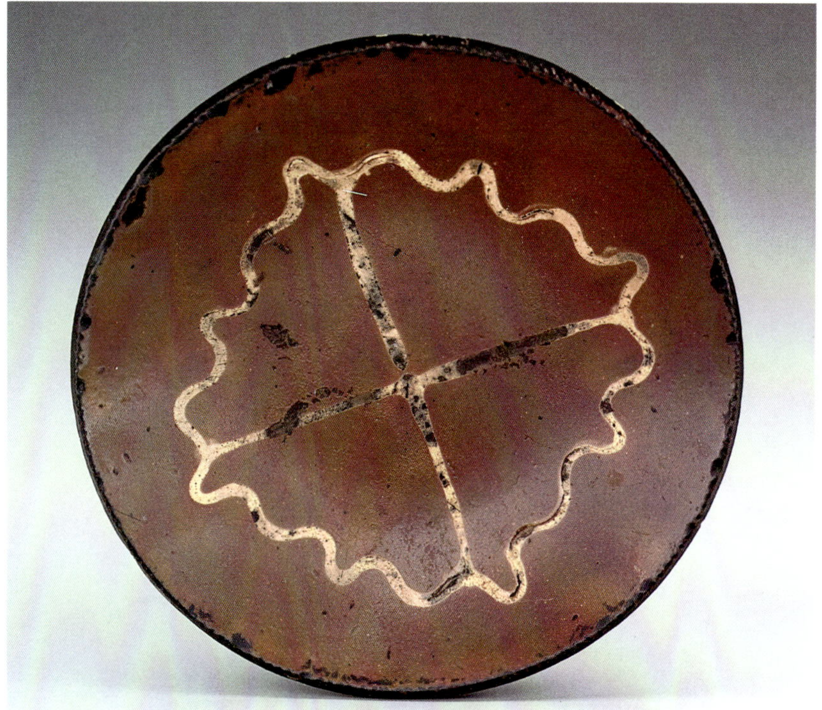

have had to rely upon my own guidelines based on the collection of sherds that I have found at the actual site of the Huntington pottery. In addition, I consider attributes such as plate sizes and shapes. Furthermore, the provenance of the pieces is a major factor in supporting my findings. Unscientific as this may seem, I realize that all of the questions cannot be answered until we have more archaeological data. Until then, we have to rely on our instincts and the understanding of the potters and their culture.

Slip-script red earthenware plates have always been popular with collectors. On a visit to an antique shop on Oyster Bay, Long Island, I came across a plate with the name "Nettie," in slip-script. Knowing the dealer and his sources, I thought that the plate was possibly a Huntington piece.

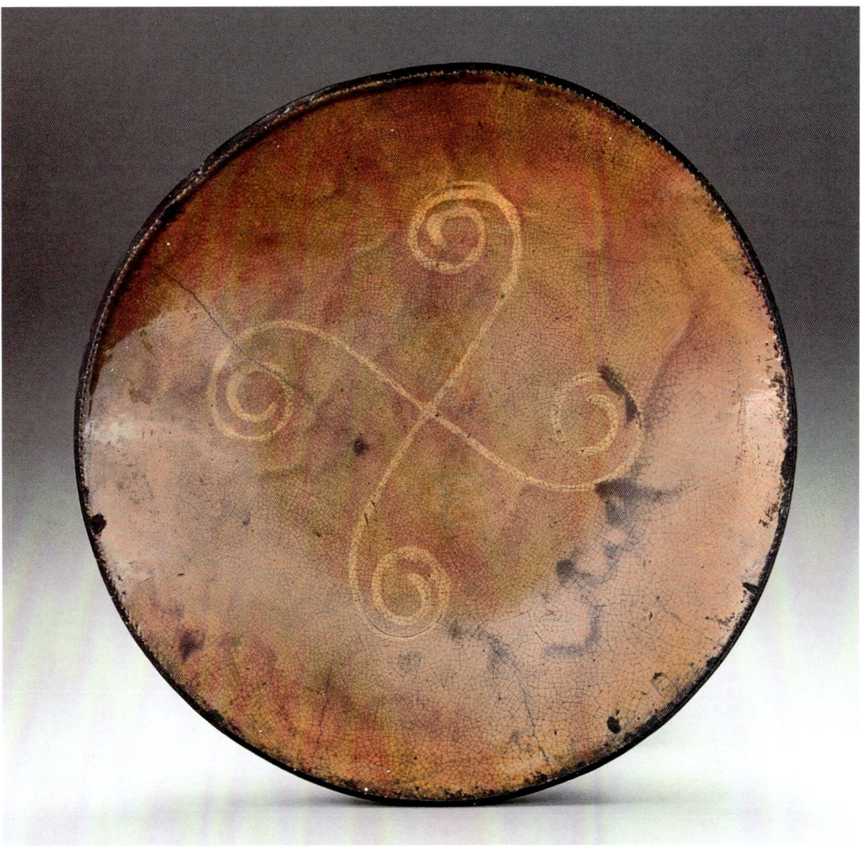

Figure 34 Dish, Huntington, New York, 1840–1885. Lead-glazed earthenware with slip decoration. D. 13". Example of a stamped design found at the pottery site in a very rare large size.

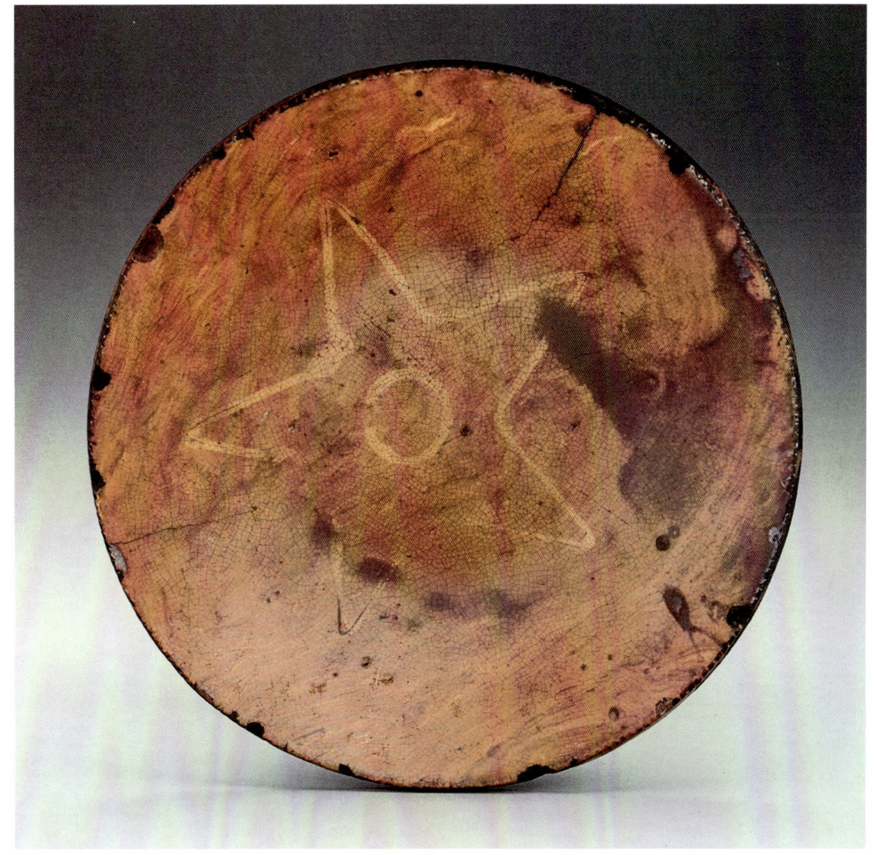

Figure 35 Plate, Huntington, New York, 1840–1885. Lead-glazed earthenware with slip decoration. D. 9⅞". Like the loaf dish illustrated in fig. 32, this plate has staining in the glaze, which is typical of plates with the stamped star design. In addition, the clay used in this plate has an agateware look. This may have been clay left over from the manufacture of a "variegated" ware. Sherds of a scroddled-type ware have been found at the site.

Without additional information, I was not able to attribute the plate, so I did not buy it. A few years later it came up for auction and was advertised together with a salt-glazed stoneware pot with the Brown Brother mark circa 1870–1885 and, in the same hand, "butter" in cobalt blue slip. This was enough information for me to attribute the "Nettie" plate to Huntington, and I was the winning bidder.

Shortly afterwards I met a Southampton dealer who owned a slip-script plate in the same distinctive script which said "Long Island." I then remembered seeing a slip-script plate advertised in *Maine Antique Digest* that said "Flying Cloud." Luckily, I had seen this plate at the Winter Antiques Show in New York, and as it was still available from the dealer, I purchased it. To accompany the traveling exhibit of the Bertram and Nina Little Collection, which was given to the Society for the Preservation of New England Antiquities (SPNEA), a small catalog was published.[7] Catalog illustration number fifty-eight is a slip-script plate in the same hand as the three previously mentioned plates. The plate in the Little collection is inscribed "America" for, I believe, the schooner *America* that won the

Figure 36 Plates, Huntington, New York, 1840–1888. Lead-glazed earthenware with slip decoration. D. of all: 10⅛". These three plates with a stamped design were probably made on the same mold.

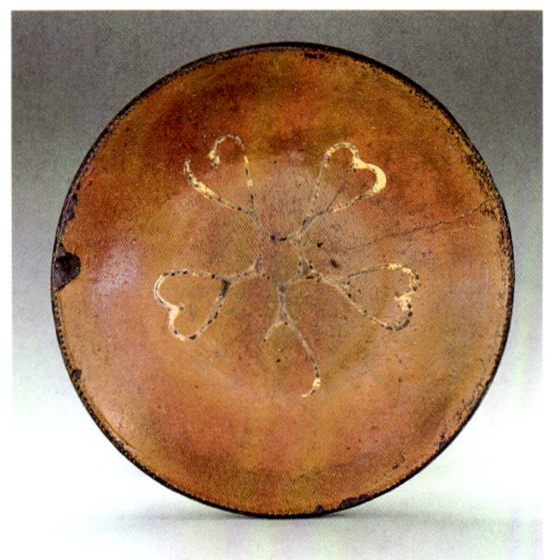

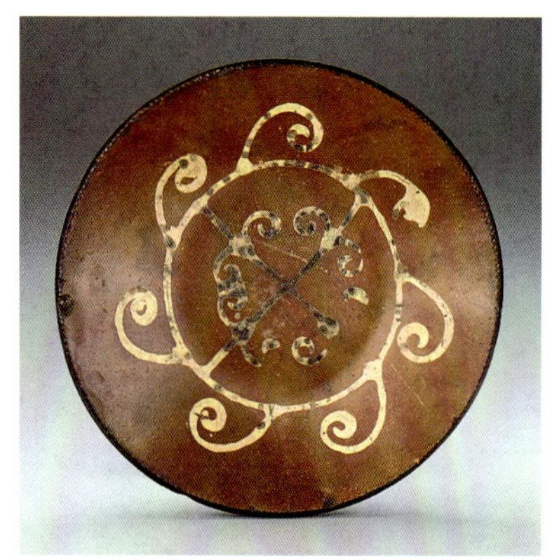

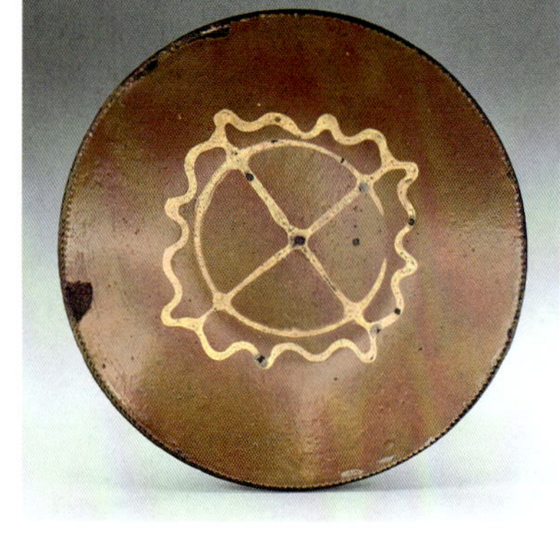

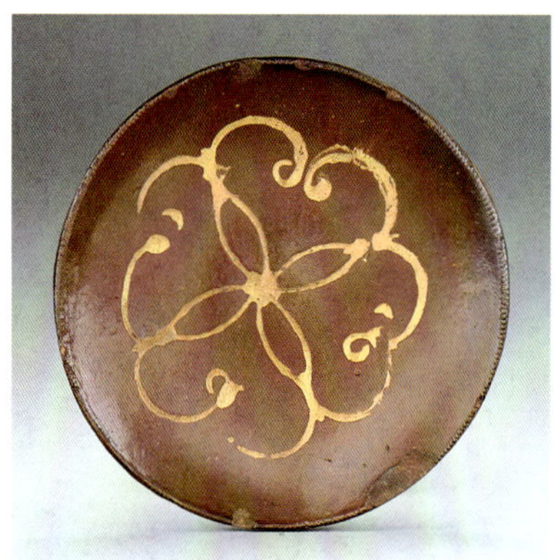

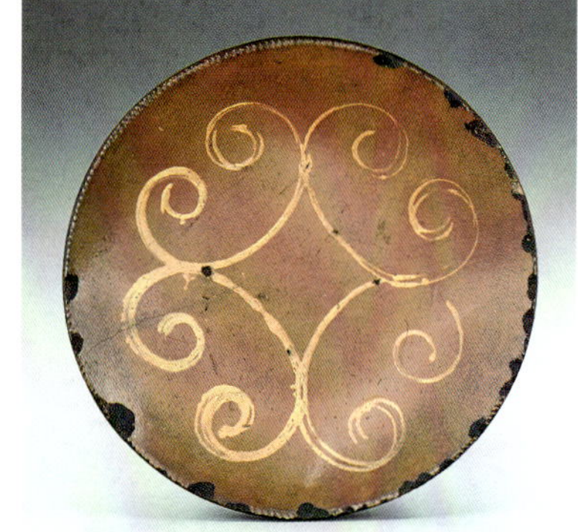

Figure 37 Plates, New England, 1840–1885. Lead-glazed earthenware with slip decoration. D. 10¾" and 9⅛". Much caution must be used in attributing all stamped plates to Huntington. The designs on these two plates have not been found at the Huntington pottery site. They could have been made at one of the Norwalk potteries. In this collection there are other examples of plates with stamped designs which have not come from Huntington or Norwalk. Stamping technology surely must have been used at other American potteries from the same period.

Figure 38 Plate, Huntington, New York, 1851–1885. Lead-glazed earthenware with slip decoration. D. 8". This plate, along with another plate of the same size in a Long Island collection which says "Long Island," has been attributed to the Huntington pottery. The "Nettie" plate was purchased at auction with a salt-glazed stoneware pot having the Brown Brother mark ca. 1870–1885. The stoneware jar was decorated with the word "Butter" in the same distinctive script that appears on this redware example in cobalt blue.

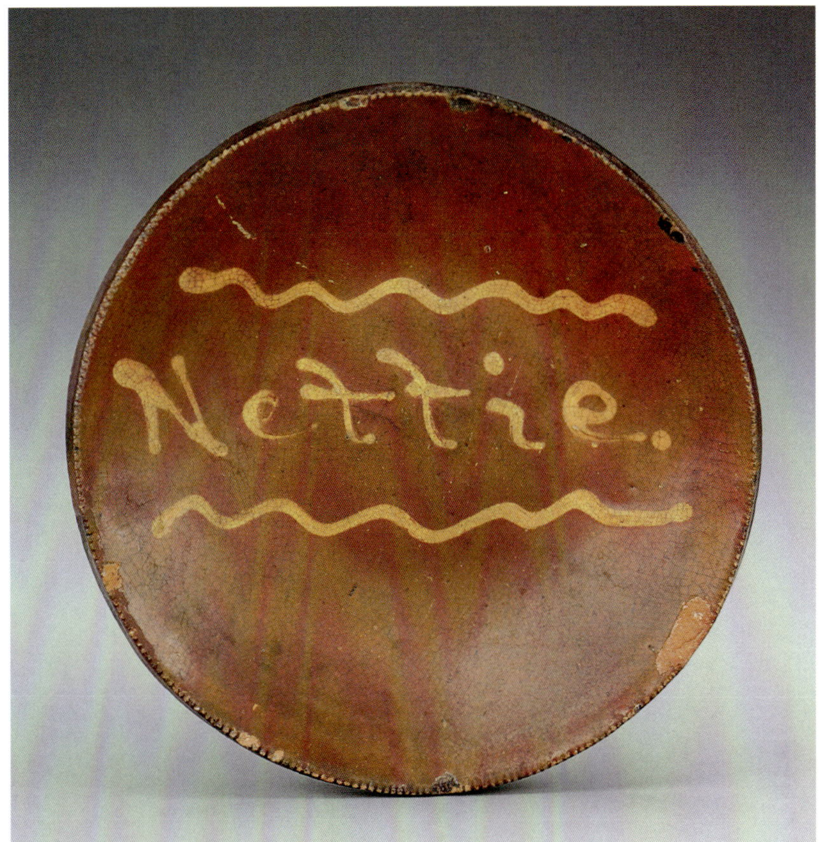

Figure 39 Dish, Huntington, New York, ca. 1851–1885. Lead-glazed earthenware with slip decoration. D. 11½". *Flying Cloud* was a famous clipper ship launched on April 15, 1851. Another slip-decorated plate by the same decorator with the name "America" is in the Nina Fletcher Little collection. The latter plate commemorates the schooner for which the America's Cup race was named. The sails for the *America* were made in Port Jefferson by Reuben H. Wilson. George Brown, the last owner of the Huntington pottery, was an original member of the local yacht club and built and sailed boats.

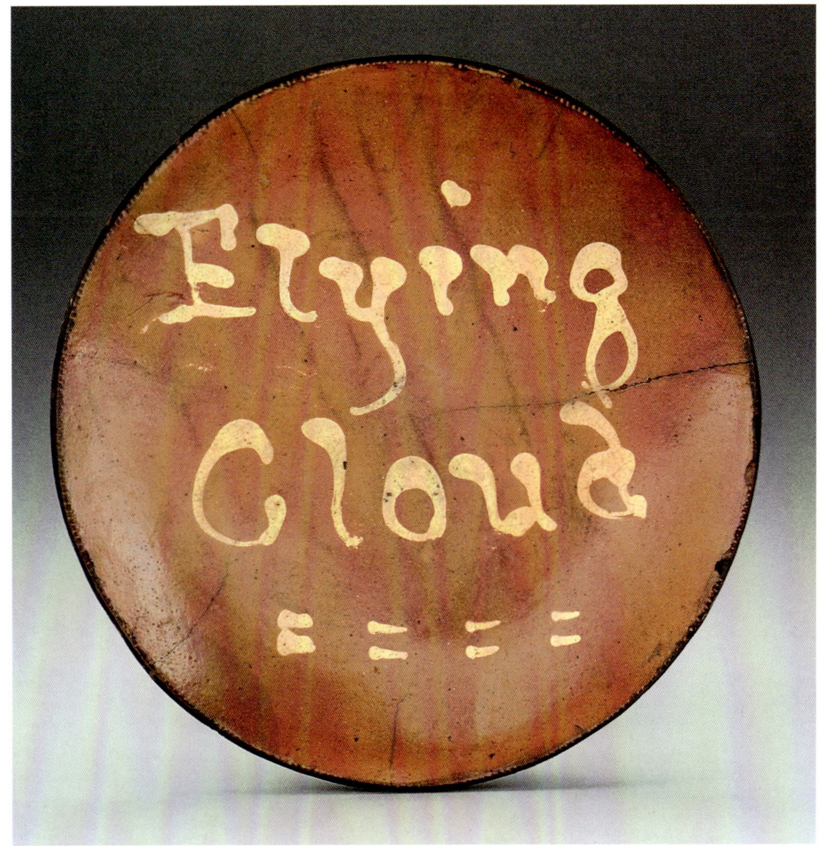

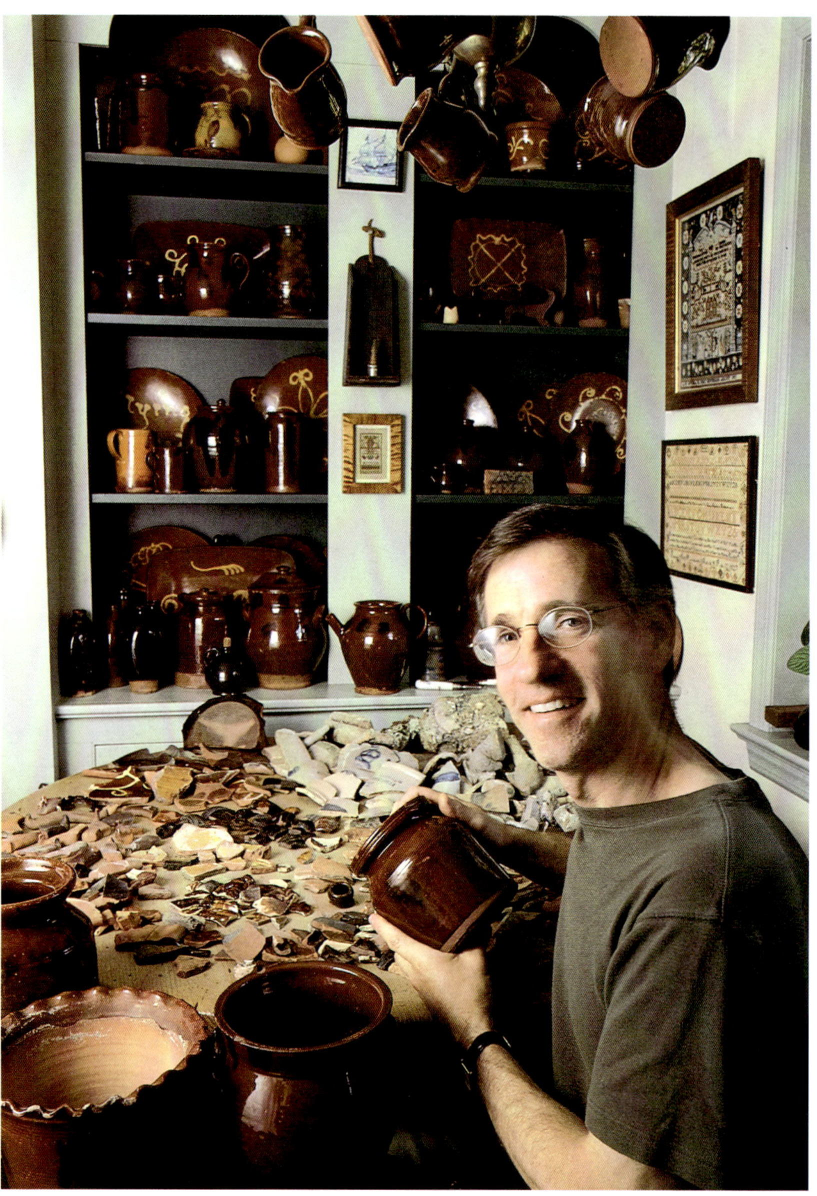

Figure 40 Anthony W. Butera, Jr.

Hundred Guinea Cup on August 22, 1851. As a collector, I was pleased to have a slip-script plate closely connected to one in the Little collection, a collection that I have admired greatly and from which I have learned a great deal.

The slip-script on these plates deserves more discussion. Both the "Flying Cloud" plate and the "America" plate are highlighted with a double dash line. Since the "America" plate is obviously decorated with a two-quilled slip cup, it is safe to assume that the two-quilled cup was also used to decorate the "Flying Cloud" plate, even though the name is a single line of slip. The decorator would have to turn the cup so that only one line of slip could be formed. To form the double dotted line of slip, which is on the bottom of the plate, the decorator would once again quickly turn the cup, and a double line would be formed. When you closely examine the dot on the letter "i" in "Flying Cloud," you can almost see two dots.

Since a great deal of skill was needed to competently use the free-flowing slip-trailing method of decoration, we can readily see why stamping the plates with slip was developed. The stamping technique for creating decoration on ceramics can be found in early fourteenth-century English tiles, redware sherds from the James Kettle Pottery in Danvers, Massachusetts (1687–1710), and even English mochaware. Stamps permitted decoration to be applied as quickly as possible using relatively unskilled labor.

We have to wonder why slipware potters did not resort to the stamping technique more often, since it seems to have been around for centuries. Was it part of the apprenticeship to learn how to use the slip cup, and taboo not to learn this technique? Which kind of decoration did consumers prefer, or were they able to tell the difference? Were consumers only interested in getting the product as quickly and cheaply as possible? Did a potter have a bad day and break all his slip-cups on hand and have to come up with a quick way to decorate? Although it may be impossible to answer these questions, they need to be asked to increase our understanding.

American genre painter William Sydney Mount has been a great resource for me as a collector of Long Island pottery. For years I have admired his pictures at the Long Island Museum (formerly the Carriage House Museum) and his prints in the homes of friends and family. In the SPLIA book, several paintings illustrate pottery in a period setting. When Deborah J. Johnson's *William Sydney Mount* was published in 1998, I studied the paintings and the pottery included in them.[8] A good sized redware jug is at the center of the painting *The Truant Gamblers,* 1835 (fig. 13). Intrigued that this form existed at such an early date, I hoped to find a similar form. Much to my surprise, on a visit to a dealer in Southampton, Long Island, I found a nearly identical jug. The dealer told me that the jug had come from an early collection from Setauket, Long Island, just a few miles from where William Sydney Mount had painted the picture. The jug, and other items in the collection, had been moved off the island in 1950, was later sold at an auction in North Carolina, traveled to Southampton with the dealer, was bought by me, and returned to within two miles from where it had started. That would qualify the jug as a favorite piece, since it practically found me.

At the Long Island Museum's exhibition on William Sydney Mount's brother, Shepard Alonzo Mount, I was delighted to see the original painting *The Breakfast Call* (fig. 19). The only published photograph I knew of was in Deborah Johnson's *Shepard Alonzo Mount: His Life and Art*.[9] The photograph in this book is very small and in black and white. The actual painting is quite large, thirty-six by twenty-nine inches, and in the lower left hand corner is a red earthenware pitcher with the handle painted beautifully, the same type of extruded handle which I had always associated with the Huntington Pottery. It is a unique piece, and I am fortunate to have these well-known artists who painted red earthenware pottery represented in the locale where I collect. However, I have yet to find an American period painting that includes a picture of American slip-decorated earthenware.

As a collector with limited resources, I have tried to educate myself as much as possible, and books are a ready resource. When I first started buying books on American red earthenware, they were mostly older publications with poor photography and hit-or-miss research. But there were exceptions. Besides the SPLIA book on Long Island pottery, good information could be found in Lura Woodside Watkins' *Early New England Potters and Their Wares.* In addition, William C. Ketchum's *Potters and Potteries of New York State, 1650–1900* had a very good chapter on the Huntington pottery.[10] However, even though Ketchum quotes Richard M. Bayles' *Sketches of Suffolk County, Historical and Descriptive* (1874), he does not include the entire eyewitness account of Bayles' visit to the Brown Brother operation at the Huntington Pottery. Finally, here it is:

> Brown Brother's Pottery, located among the settlement on the east side of the harbor, is one of the interesting features of the place. Its origin is ancient, some part of the establishment having been running since the pre-revolutionary period—so says tradition. The buildings in which the business is carried on are not in a shape to be easily described but they probably embrace some seven or eight thousand square feet of floor room, for the most part being two floors in height. The Brown Brother's manufacture a great variety of "stone" and earthenware such as jugs, jars, butter-pots, pie platters, sauce pans, flower pots, hanging baskets &c. Six or eight men are kept at work, two wagons are all the time traveling up and down the island, and during the busy seasons of the spring and autumn sloops are chartered, loaded with goods and sent away to different ports along the Connecticut shore as well as other places. The process of making the specialties of this establishment is very simple, yet could be much better described by the hands of the potter with the clay, than with pen and ink upon paper. The first thing, however, to be done is to mix and temper the clay. For the different articles different qualities of material are used and for most of the articles clay from different mines have been mixed together. This mixing is done in a huge bin. The clay is then placed in the tempering machine, which is an upright iron cylinder with an arrangement inside which being turned by horse power grinds up the clay and squeezes it out through holes about two inches in diameter, near the bottom of the mill. Inside these holes a fine wire sieve is placed so as to keep back any sticks or small stones that may be in the clay. The doughy mass is then stowed away in a damp cellar where it will keep for weeks without losing its temper, and from which it is taken as it is needed for use. Nearly all the kinds of ware made here are turned on a sort of lathe. This is simply a disk, say a foot or more in diameter, made of two inch plank, and fastened in a horizontal position on the end of a spindle which is kept whirling around by a foot treadle. On the center of this disk a lump of clay is placed, and as it spins round the hands of the skilled workman are pressed against it from outside and inside so as to draw it up to the desired shape. In making jugs the handle is made separate and stuck on after the jug is finished. Some of the ware is cast in molds of plaster of Paris. This process is more tedious and consequently about twice as expensive. After the ware is formed and sufficiently dried to allow it to be handled with safety it is stacked up in large ovens or kilns, to be baked. These kilns, of which there are two here, are made of brick, of circular form, ten or twelve feet across them and six to eight feet high and arched over the top. When they are filled, a hot fire is started in the pit below, and the heat and flames pass up through the mass of ware until it becomes of a white heat. The glazing on the outside of stone ware is produced by throwing salt into the kiln while the heat is greatest. This baking process

> consumes three hundred cords of wood per annum. The Pottery is located immediately on the shore and a dock is connected with it, so sloops can float up to the premises to land wood or load with ware.[11]

This is the only eyewitness account of the Huntington pottery that I know of. Even though it is a late account, it does describe the making of earthenware. Most important here is the use of plaster of Paris molds, which probably indicates the making of Rebekah-at-the-Well tea pots, corresponding with sherds found at the site and kiln furniture associated with their manufacture. This account gives us a glimpse of the scale and the activities conducted at the pottery in the third quarter of the nineteenth century.

My study of Huntington, Long Island, red earthenware has led me to consider all kinds of ceramics. As a result, I have read books on different types of pottery and porcelain, and after attending lectures at Eastfield Village every year, I have had the opportunity to talk to authors and collectors whose collections have been published. As my understanding grows, my collecting skills improve.

The title for this article comes from one of my favorite quotes in the book *Iznik, The Pottery of Ottoman Turkey.*[12] "Informed conjecture" is perhaps a polite term for what many collectors employ in the process of rationalizing a collection. When empirical facts are few and far between, we have to make the best use of the smallest available evidence. Hopefully, the publication of these examples presented here will add to the information about Huntington redwares and reduce the conjecture.

One of my favorite stories about collecting is from the *Bowles Collection of 18th-Century English and French Porcelain.* When Henry Bowles takes delivery of a very rare Chelsea strawberry dish, the customs agent shakes his head in disbelief when he sees the price paid for the rather stained piece.[13] I have experienced this same reaction many times after showing friends and family pieces of redware that I have bought, and this is true of other collectors and scholars. Although Iznik pottery, Chelsea porcelain, and Huntington, Long Island, red earthenware are from completely different areas in the world and span different centuries, they share a continuum in the world of ceramics and the struggles of the potters who made them.

One issue common among ceramic collectors is that of condition. Condition can be a problem when dealing with the relatively fragile red earthenware, which was usually subject to heavy use. My standards have always been to keep repaired objects out of the collection. Repairing one of these humble pots is like stripping the original finish off an antique piece of furniture. No matter what has happened to a piece, whether fortunate or unfortunate, it adds to the truthfulness of the object, and it is dishonest to make it something that it is not.

Subjects for debate are plates that have an excessive amount of rim chipping. Some of these chips may have been the result of plates fused together in firing and then broken apart. This may be one reason for the use of coggling, where the interstices created by tooling the rims make it easier to separate fused plates. Without these flaws, however, we could not study how plates were placed in the kiln and fired. This roughness must have been acceptable to consumers who bought inexpensive red earthenware by the dozens and therefore should be acceptable to modern day collectors.

My collection now includes sherds I have found from a site on the shore of Huntington Harbor where wasters were dumped. On my first visit I had some bittersweet feelings. The site is a massive jumble of wasters from at least one hundred years of pottery manufacture, which have tumbled in the tides since they were discarded. As I began to pull these wasters from the sand and mud, I was amazed at the great variety. I found slip-decorated redware with stamped patterns, slip-cup decorated redware, combed redware, slip with copper oxide green, fragments of plates completely covered in slip, bisque-fired redware, a great variety of extruded redware handles, fragments of redware hollow ware vessels, salt-glazed stoneware with cobalt blue decoration, Albany-slip stoneware, Rebekah-at-the-Well teapot sherds, scroddleware or agateware, possibly black-glazed teapots, and the kiln furniture associated with their manufacture such as setting tiles, stilts, and many stoneware spacers. The diversity here represents the success of the industry for over a century, and I now realize the huge amount of history waiting here to be studied.

Another dimension of my collection, not illustrated here, are reproductions. Some of my reproductions are as pleasing to me as the originals: they can be used, they are easy to find, and, most of all, they are cheap. Reproductions can make good learning tools. Through the mistakes I have made handling them (in other words breaking them), I have learned how fragile this pottery can be. I have also found that treated correctly, it can readily survive. From speaking with the potters who make reproductions, I have also learned a great deal. I once asked one of the Shooners why they put slip cyma curved designs on a pair of redware candlesticks, hoping that the answer would be that they had seen them on English slipware. Instead, the answer was, "I was using them to fill space." Disappointed at first with this response, I then realized that Greg and Mary Shooner have studied and worked with redware pottery from Europe as well as America—and that helped explained it. Although they did not really invent the design when they used it, they had probably seen it, and subconsciously added it to their repertoire. We see many designs cutting across cultures and centuries, like an unspoken language, communicated through pottery and its apprentices.

My collecting continues and probably will not stop, since it is now incorporated into who and what I am. Yet, I sometimes ask myself what am I really collecting? Are these just plain pots with no souls or are they objects hiding tremendous wealth in potting history? Once the potter Michelle Erickson told me she greatly admired red earthenware potters because the type of clay they used was so difficult to work. How interesting this is, since redware was the most common pottery, and yet only the most skilled potters could make it. Listening to the piano waltz D.145, No. 2 by Franz Schubert, which lasts only about forty-eight seconds, I noticed the similarities of this waltz to red earthenware pottery. They are both very simple on the surface, made quickly, made for everyday use for the common people, and yet they are a shadow of the past. They both walk the fine line between simplicity and complexity. What collectors are really looking for is not perhaps the objects but the people behind them, the source of that shadow. I have always been curious to know what has happened in the past and to connect with that community. This is what good scholarly collections should be about. I hope my collection is one of these and can be shared on these pages.

1. Joan Parry Dutton, *The Flower World of Williamsburg* (Williamsburg, Va.: Colonial Williamsburg Foundation, 1973).

2. Jeannette Lasansky, "Pennsylvania Pottery in Berks County Collections," *Antiques* 138, no. 4 (October 1990): 810–19.

3. Cynthia Arps Corbett, *Useful Art: Long Island Pottery* (Setauket, N.Y.: Society for the Preservation of Long Island Antiquities, 1985).

4. Ibid., pp. 20–25.

5. Lynne Sussman, "Mocha, Banded, Cat's Eye, and Other Factory-made Slipware," *Studies in Northeast Historical Archaeology Monograph Series,* no. 1 (Boston: Council for Northeastern Archaeology, 1997).

6. Corbett, *Useful Art: Long Island Pottery,* p. 29.

7. Exhibition catalog, *A Passion for the Past: The Collection of Bertram K. and Nina Fletcher Little at Cogswell Grant* (New York: The American Federation for the Arts, 1996).

8. Deborah J. Johnson, *William Sydney Mount: Works in the Collection of The Long Island Museum* (New York: Museums at Stony Brook, 1998).

9. Deborah J. Johnson, *Shepard Alonzo Mount: His Life and Art* (New York: Museums at Stony Brook, 1988).

10. Lura Woodside Watkins, *Early New England Potters and Their Wares* (Cambridge, Mass.: Harvard University Press, 1950); William C. Ketchum, Jr., *Potters and Potteries of New York State, 1650–1900* (Syracuse, N.Y.: Syracuse University Press, 1987), pp. 88–103.

11. Richard M. Bayles, *Sketches of Suffolk County, Historical and Descriptive* (Port Jefferson, N.Y.: privately printed, 1874).

12. Nurhan Atasoy and Julian Raby, *Iznik, The Pottery of Ottoman Turkey* (London: Alexandria Press, 1989), p. 49.

13. Simon Spero, *The Bowles Collection of 18th-Century English and French Porcelain* (San Francisco: Fine Arts Museum of San Francisco, 1995), p. xxi.

Merry Abbitt Outlaw

New Discoveries—Introduction

▼ PORCELAIN AND POTTERY—*they are my mystery. The world exists in order that we may create from it their excellence; and so that I—I myself—can communicate to others that beauty which else they might never see. I should understand something now, should I not, of that grace and those forms, dug from and shaped to transcend this dreary place where we scratch about and wait to die? Clay scrabbled out of the dungy earth, mixed with water, with sand, with flint, with ashes of bones; kneaded, caressed and moulded by patient hands; fired in the kiln and put to work to ease our lot, to add comfort and a little style to our necessity to eat, to drink, to wash, to excrete; or set up simply to be admired like music, for our dignity and pleasure; and like our own flesh, doomed at last to be shattered and discarded, rubbish trampled back into the ground whence it came. What else thus bodies forth the nature of life and manifests, from the finite, the infinite?*

Richard Adams, *The Girl in a Swing*, 1980

Around 1618, a potter working in the Westerwald region of Germany applied intricate molding to the midgirth panel of a stoneware jug depicting the parable of the Prodigal Son. From Luke 15:11–32, the chronicle was commonly used in the seventeenth century to symbolize themes of extravagance, repentance, and forgiveness. When the wasteful, wayward son repented and returned to his family, his compassionate father forgave him. He told his servants to "… bring hither the fatted calf, and kill it; and let us eat, and be merry; For this my son was dead, and is alive again; he was lost, and is found. And they began to be merry."

Soon after it was brought to Virginia, a jug of this type was shattered and discarded in an early-seventeenth-century well at Jamestown, the first permanent English settlement in the New World. Recently found in the course of archaeological excavations, the broken sherds have been reassembled, bringing the magnificent lost vessel back to life. Once again it shares its enduring lesson, just as it did with those who long ago helped establish the European foothold in America.

Whether made "to ease our lot in life" or "simply to be admired like music," the New Discoveries reported this year are linked by a common theme—ceramics that incorporate the human figure. Most are archaeological, ranging in time from circa 1618 to 1900, and their subjects vary from the heavenly to the earthly. The Prodigal Son jug from Jamestown is the oldest figural object included in this year's array of New Discoveries. Next oldest is another exciting find from Jamestown. Excavated in the

1950s, it is part of a seventeenth-century mold for a toy soldier made of clay. White ball clay or terracotta toys or figurines are often recovered from seventeenth-century English, Continental, and American sites. But the discovery of a mold used to manufacture them domestically is exceedingly rare, perhaps unique.

Dating from the seventeenth to nineteenth centuries, the recently excavated Lewis pottery complex in Buckley, Wales, is reported. Included in the report is another figural object—a molded bearded face that was recovered from the site. Analyses of artifacts and features from this significant site are ongoing, and have the potential to reveal that vessels made there may have reached America.

Unquestionably reaching America from England is an amazing assemblage of Staffordshire slipware vessels discarded in Philadelphia, Pennsylvania, in the second quarter of the eighteenth century. This important assemblage was recovered during 1976 excavations. The author identifies several dishes made by Samuel Malkin, a well-known Staffordshire potter, including the bat-molded sunface dish that illustrates the cover of this year's journal.

An important eighteenth-century figural discovery are the five English soft-paste porcelain figures handed down in a family directly descended from the Ogle governors of Annapolis, Maryland. Documentary evidence suggests that Benjamin Ogle may have purchased them when he was a young student in England in the mid-1760s. Purely decorative, these figurines illustrate the sophisticated consumer behavior of elite Americans toward the end of the colonial period.

The products of two American pottery kiln sites dating to the late eighteenth century are presented this year. One article examines the Bellarmine-type faces recently recovered from the 1770s Richards stoneware kiln in Lamberton, New Jersey. Briefly mentioned in *Ceramics in America* 2001, these sherds have since been associated with small jug fragments also found at the site. It is argued that rather than remnants of a "Bellarmine-like" tradition, the faces are reflective of pottery styles of the period.

The other late-eighteenth-century kiln products article presents some of the circa 1793–1799 Jacob Meyer, Jr. earthenware forms found at Mount Shepherd, North Carolina. Moravian born and raised, Meyer was trained by the master potter Gottfried Aust in Salem, North Carolina. Since the Moravian religion strongly promotes peace, archaeologists were surprised to find that this independent minded craftsman was turning out stove tiles bearing military motifs.

Representing the only hand-molded New Discovery figure is a unique terracotta skull dating circa 1830–1860. It appears to have been made on a domestic site in Loudoun County, Virginia, where it was found. The author convincingly argues that it was an element of a malevolent curse stemming from African-American or German-American folk religion.

Finally, three recent nineteenth-century American discoveries demonstrate the importance of recovering and analyzing pottery waster deposits. Dating between 1863 and 1868, yellow ware and Rockingham ware wasters

from the Coxon Clinton Street Pottery in Trenton, New Jersey, comprise one deposit. Although most of the collection is undecorated, the recovered relief-molded figural sherds supply the dates for the assemblage. On the other hand, reexamination of Anthony Baecher's 1864–1889 shop site in Winchester, Virginia, exposes the faceless everyday earthenware products of a potter who is exceptionally well known for his figural folk art creations. Of the thousands of sherds examined from the site, only two appear to be fragments of figurines. Lastly, analysis of wasters from the Baynham site near Trenton, South Carolina, made it possible for one archaeologist to identify an intact Albany-slipped stoneware face jug auctioned on the internet site eBay.com. The maker's mark and distinctive neck and handle reveal not only that Mark Baynham made the vessel, but also, for the first time, that he made face jugs!
<Xkv8rs@aol.com>

William B. Liebeknecht, Rebecca White, and Richard W. Hunter

A Coxon Waster Deposit of the Mid-1860s Sampled in Trenton, New Jersey

▼ IN SEPTEMBER 2000, archaeological monitoring conducted by Hunter Research, Inc. prior to the construction of the recently opened Marriott Hotel in downtown Trenton, New Jersey, included sampling of a waster deposit of plain yellow ware, Rockingham ware, and related kiln furniture.[1] The deposit, observed in the side of a construction trench, was roughly twenty feet in length and up to two and half feet thick, and consisted of a densely packed lens of several thousand sherds and kiln fragments. Analysis of these materials and of the land use history of the hotel site has enabled the assemblage to be attributed to Charles Coxon's Clinton Street Pottery and assigned a manufacturing date between 1863 and 1868.[2]

Several vessel forms are represented in the assemblage, with the most common being shallow undecorated pie plates and nappies of various sizes. The majority of the sherds consist of plain yellow ware, but some pieces display distinctive relief-molded decoration. Approximately forty percent of the sherds have a clear alkaline glaze, with roughly half of this material being covered with the streaked or mottled brown manganese glaze that is characteristic of Rockingham ware. The remaining sherds are bisque-fired and show a range of yellow ware body types, most likely the result of multiple clay sources or impurities in the clay. No makers' marks are in evidence, which is not surprising since "some 90% of all yellow ware is unmarked."[3] Dating and attribution of this ware has long been the subject of frustrating speculation; in this instance, however, there is sufficient evidence to pinpoint both an approximate date and likely manufacturer.[4]

Dating of the waster deposit was accomplished in part through the archaeological stratigraphy and known history of the site. The lens containing the sherds and kiln furniture was sealed approximately one foot beneath a thick layer of flint nodules and chunks of quartz and feldspar, materials that derive from the use of the site by the Golding & Company flint and spar mill, a supplier of tempering materials to the Trenton potteries. The Golding Company was in operation at this location from 1868 until the late 1920s, thereby providing a *terminus ante quem* of 1868 for the waster deposit.[5]

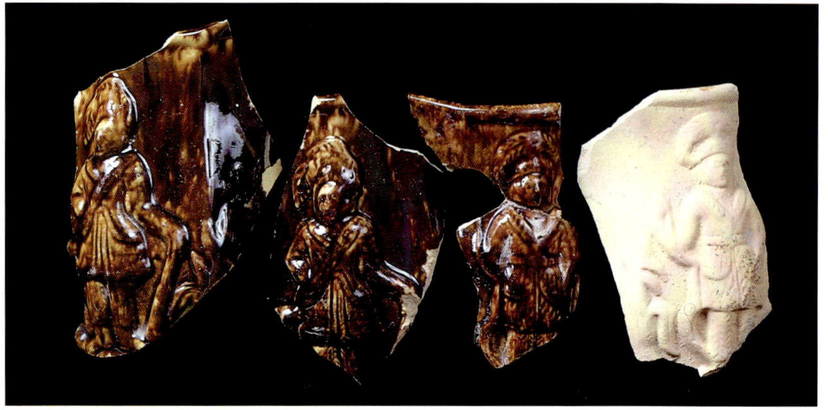

Figure 1 Sherds, Clinton Street Pottery, Trenton, New Jersey, 1863–1868. Rockingham-type ware. (All photos, Gavin Ashworth.) These sherds are from small pitchers with a molded plumed cavalier on opposing sides.

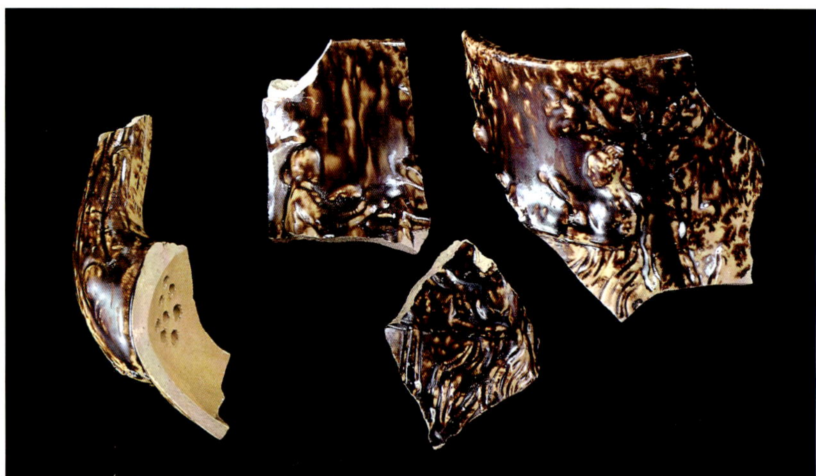

Figure 2 Sherds, Clinton Street Pottery, Trenton, New Jersey, 1863–1868. Rockingham-type ware. Sherds from a teapot with a molded scene of two ladies having tea.

Assignation of the ceramic materials in the waster deposit to Charles Coxon's Clinton Street Pottery stems in part from the dating of the deposit, but is based primarily on the attributes of the sherds showing relief-molded decoration. Among the Rockingham ware motifs identified are: a cavalier figure, typically found on creamers (fig. 1); two ladies having tea, typically found on teapots (fig. 2); a hunt scene, found on handled pitchers where a stag and hanging bird are molded on the body and the handle is formed as an outstretched hound (figs. 3, 4); a small Toby pitcher (fig. 5); and a corn cob impression, found on food molds (fig. 6). Several Trenton pottery experts, among them Jay Lewis and the late David J. Goldberg, agree that these relief patterns are most likely the product of the Clinton Street Pottery. The clarity of the design and attention to detail suggest that the molds were probably the work of John Coxon, rather than his better-known father, Charles.

Charles Coxon founded the Clinton Street Pottery, a two-kiln facility, in 1863 in the Coalport section of Trenton. Coxon, a native of Longton, Staffordshire, immigrated to the United States in 1849, working first in the Bennett Pottery in Baltimore (1849–1858) and then the Swan Hill Pottery in South Amboy (1858–1861), before relocating to Trenton and working for the firms of Millington & Astbury and William Young & Sons. In the year following the establishment of the Clinton Street Pottery, John S. Thomp-

Figure 3 Sherds, Clinton Street Pottery, Trenton, New Jersey, 1863–1868. Rockingham-type ware. These fragments are from a hound-handled hunt scene pitcher depicting a running stag and a hanging game bird around the body over a small standing bird and a running rabbit near the base.

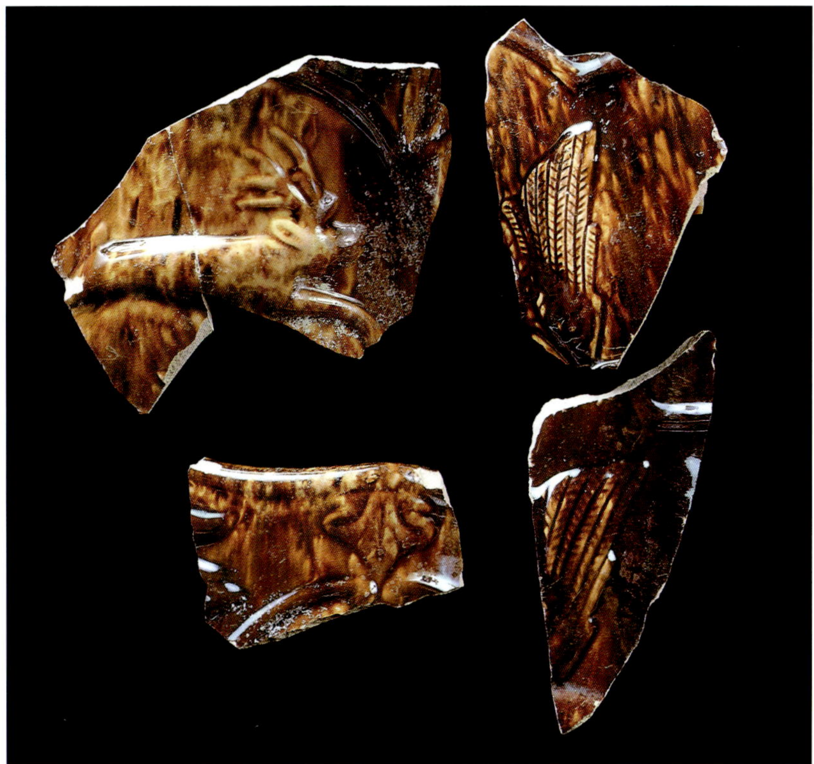

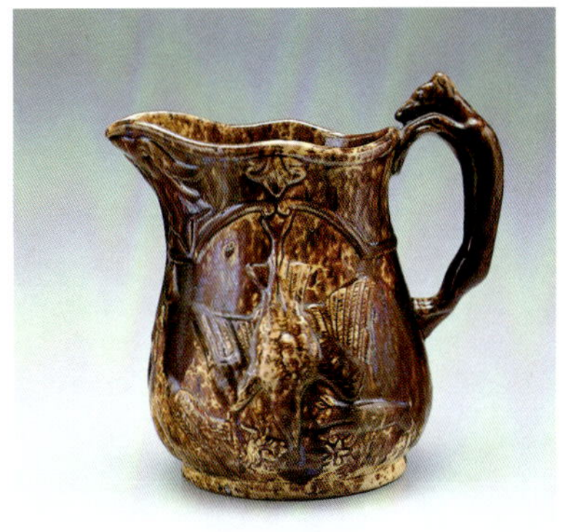

Figure 4 Pitcher, Clinton Street Pottery, Trenton, New Jersey, 1863–1868. Rockingham-type ware. H. 10". (William B. Liebeknecht collection.) An antique example of a Rockingham glazed hound-handled hunt scene pitcher. Note the eagle head that forms the spout.

Figure 5 Sherds, Clinton Street Pottery, Trenton, New Jersey, 1863–1868. Biscuit fired earthenware from a small Toby pitcher with a scowling face.

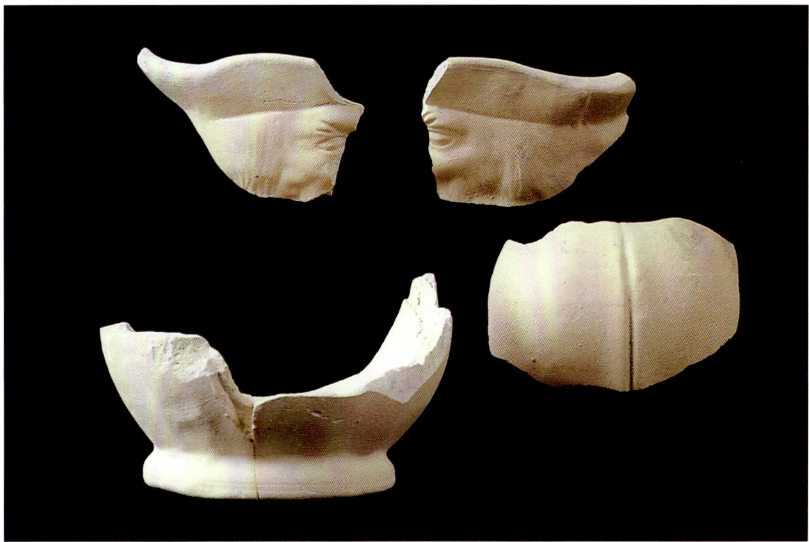

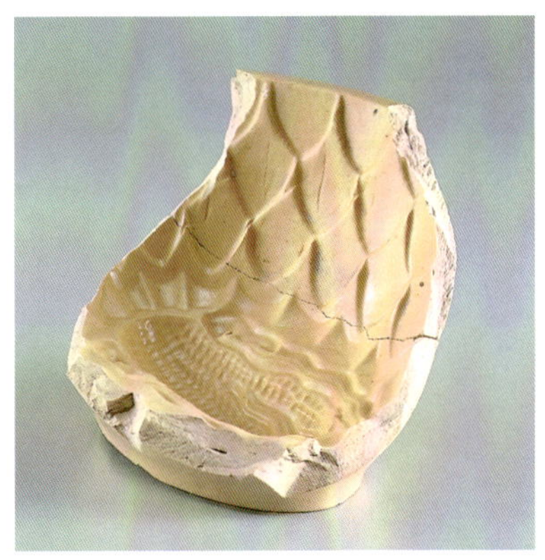

Figure 6 Sherds, Clinton Street Pottery, Trenton, New Jersey, 1863–1868. Yellow ware. A yellow ware corncob food mold fragment with overlapping scaled sides.

son joined with Coxon to form the company "Coxon & Thompson," and the firm began concentrating on the manufacture of "creamware and white graniteware." Yellow ware and Rockingham ware were likely also being produced during these early years, as this is the material for which Charles Coxon is best known. Coxon died of sunstroke in July of 1868, but his widow and sons reorganized the pottery under the name Coxon and Company. This firm thrived in the production of hotel china until 1883 when it was sold to the firm of Alpaugh and McGowan. The pottery was eventually renamed the Empire Pottery and in 1900 became absorbed by the Trenton Potteries Company.[6]

The identification of the yellow ware and Rockingham ware materials from the Marriott Hotel site as products of Charles Coxon's Clinton Street Pottery in the mid-1860s supplies a useful benchmark for ceramic historians, collectors, and archaeologists. This find demonstrates the value of documenting and analyzing ceramic waste deposits in major industrial pottery centers, even when these are located some distance from the manufacturing site.

William B. Liebeknecht
Principal Archaeologist
Hunter Research, Inc.
<wbl@hunterresearch.com>

Rebecca White
Archaeologist
Hunter Research
Laboratory Supervisor
<rwhite@hunterresearch.com>

Richard W. Hunter, Ph.D.
President and Principal Archaeologist
Hunter Research, Inc.
<rwhunter@hunterresearch.com>
<http://hunterresearch.com>

1. An initial archaeological study of the Marriott Hotel site was completed in 1998. See Hunter Research, Inc., "Phase I Archaeological Investigation, Proposed Marriott Hotel Conference Center, City of Trenton, Mercer County, New Jersey" (report on file, New Jersey Historic Preservation Office, Trenton, 1998). An expanded article on the Coxon waster deposit is to appear in *Trenton Potteries,* the Newsletter of the Potteries of Trenton Society, Volume 3, Issues 1 and 2. A full report on all aspects of the archaeological monitoring at the Marriott Hotel site, including a detailed inventory of the Coxon ceramic waste, is forthcoming in 2003.

2. In the case of this deposit, waste was carted just over a mile from the Coxon kilns down to the mouth of Assunpink Creek on the Delaware River, where it was used as fill. Much of the Delaware River shoreline below Assunpink Creek, especially in Lamberton, is composed of similar waste from a range of Trenton's industrial potteries.

3. Joan Leibowitz, *Yellow Ware: The Transitional Ceramic* (Clinton, Mass.: Colonial Press, Inc., 1985), p. 9.

4. John Spargo, *Early American Pottery and China* (New York, N.Y.: Garden City Publishing Company, 1926), pp. 196–97.

5. Trenton Historical Society, *A History of Trenton, 1679–1929: Two Hundred and Fifty Years of a Notable Town with Links in Four Centuries* (Princeton, N.J.: Princeton University Press, 1929), pp. 920, 955; "Golding Sons Company Build New Feldspar Mill," *Trenton Magazine* (September 1928): 2–3, 20.

6. For further detail on the Coxon family and their potteries, see Edwin Atlee Barber, "Early Ceramic Printing and Modeling in the United States," *Old China* 3, no. 3 (1903): 51–52; David J. Goldberg, "Charles Coxon: Nineteenth-Century Potter, Modeler-Designer and Manufacturer," *Journal of the American Ceramic Circle* 9 (1994), pp. 28–64; Hunter Research, Inc., "The Trenton Potteries Database" (Electronic Database, Property of New Jersey Department of Transportation, Trenton, 1999).

Leigh J. Dodd

Excavations on the Site of the Lewis Pottery Complex, Buckley, North Wales, United Kingdom

▼ IN MARCH 2000, an archaeological evaluation was carried out by Earthworks Archaeological Services on the site of a proposed residential development in Buckley, Flintshire, North Wales. At the time of the evaluation the site was unoccupied waste ground but had been used as a timber yard until recently. Archaeological investigations elsewhere within the Buckley area have produced evidence of structures associated with the pottery industry dating from the seventeenth to nineteenth centuries.[1] Documentation relating to the site indicated occupation over time by various members of the Lewis family, a local family of potters. Further, several maps from the mid-eighteenth and nineteenth centuries clearly show the presence of a circular kiln structure and adjacent building, probably a cottage or workshop.

Four linear trenches were excavated as part of the evaluation exercise. Two trenches were positioned strategically in order to evaluate the presumed location of the kiln structure and associated building; the remaining two trenches were located speculatively. The well-preserved remains of the base of a circular brick-built kiln and the stone foundations for a second structure were positively identified. The results clearly warranted full excavation prior to construction, and during the summer of 2000, an area measuring approximately 65.6' x 131' was excavated.

The base of the kiln was almost totally exposed during full excavation; the small part left unexposed was not threatened by the development. The kiln structure, probably of beehive type, consisted of a circular brick-built firing chamber, 3.2' in diameter, with an internal floor of baked clay and a single walk-in entrance. Six fireboxes, each protruding a further 4.6' from the chamber, were spaced evenly around its circumference. Alternating brick and clay floors lay between the fireboxes, the brick flooring presumably used to provide a working surface upon which to stock fuel for firing (fig. 1). An outer circular stone-built wall foundation, the hovel wall, surrounded the firing chamber and measured 38.7' in diameter.

To the northwest of the kiln lay the remains of the associated building visible on cartographic sources and identified during the field evaluation. This structure measured 72.2' x 18.4' and consisted of four individual rooms with a possible fifth at its southern end. This fifth room, or annex, contained a number of rows of brick laid upright on their sides; the clay deposit beneath them showed signs of heating (fig. 2). This enigmatic feature may have formed part of a drying floor on which the pottery was gradually and partially dried before being transferred to the kiln for firing. Comparisons need to be sought in order to assist in the interpretation of this feature. The remaining rooms would have formed both accommodations—a brick and stone hearth was encountered—and workshop/storage space to prepare and stock the pottery vessels produced.

The remains of a second brick-built kiln of diminutive proportions were found to the east of the potters' workshop (fig. 3). This kiln measured a mere 8.2' in diameter and displayed evidence of six fireboxes each protruding approximately 2' further. This small kiln may have been used for experimental firing purposes or to produce finer products.

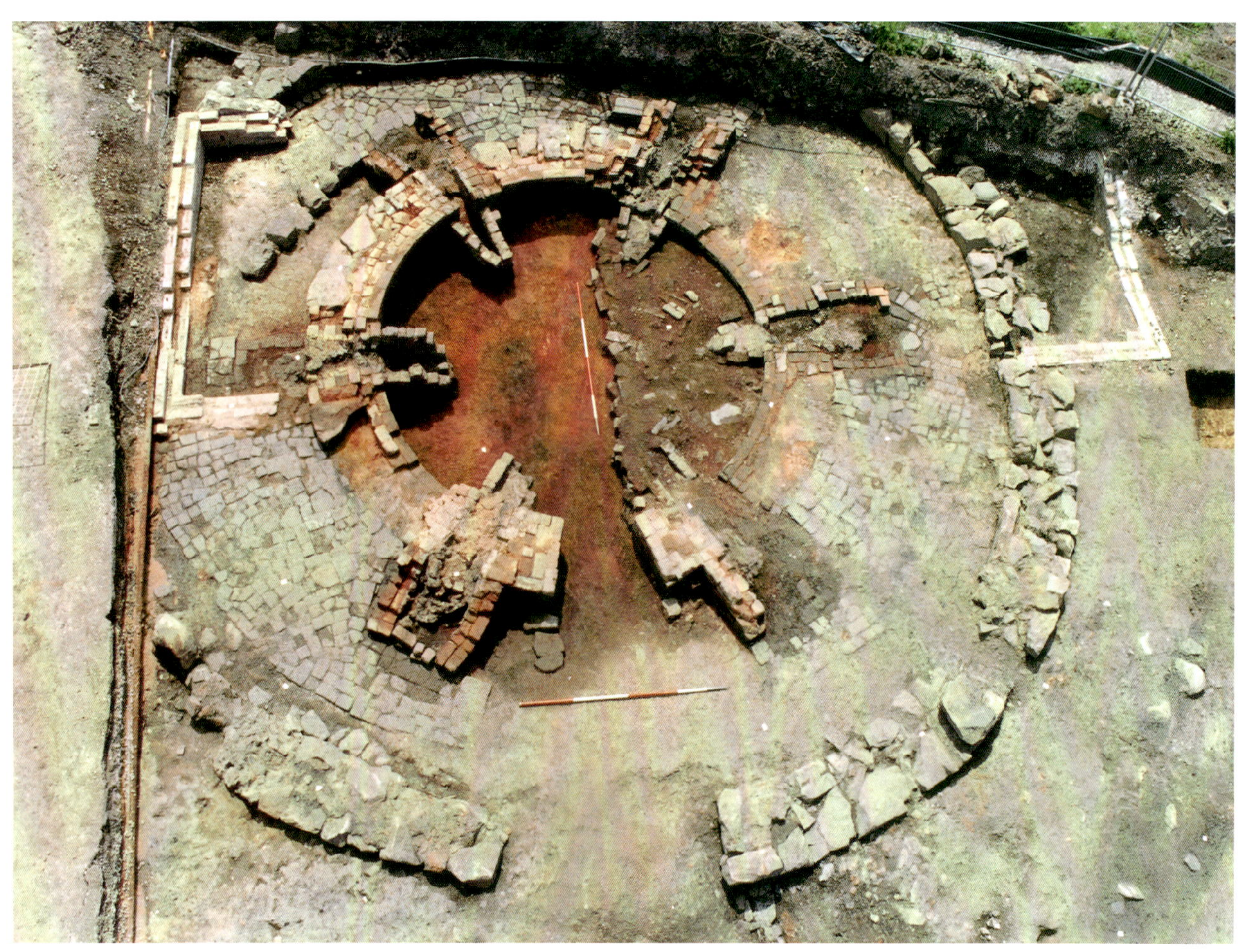

Figure 1 Oblique view of the Lewis kiln, Buckley, showing walk-in entrance, fireboxes, alternating brick flooring, and surrounding hovel wall base. Scale bars each measure 2m (approximately 6.5'). (All photos, courtesy Earthworks Archaeological Services.)

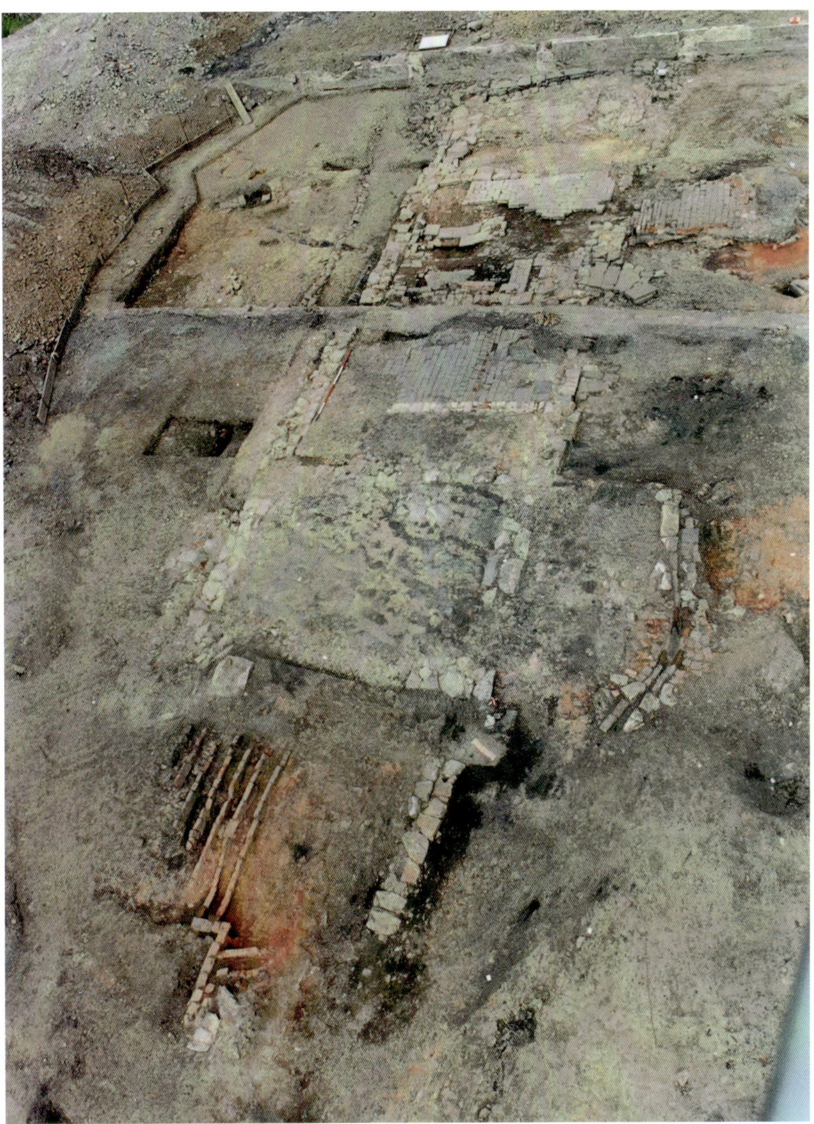

Figure 2 The potters' cottage and workshop, comprising five individual rooms. The possible drying floor lies at the bottom left of this photograph. Scale bar measures 2m.

A large quantity of pottery wasters and kiln furniture was recovered from the soils within the pottery complex; this material has allowed the characterization of the vessel types and forms produced on the site and the means by which they were both stacked and fired. The Lewis pottery manufactured a variety of black and brown lead-glazed red fabric vessels that included large bowls and dishes, round-bodied and straight-sided mugs, storage jars, and chamber pots, together with white slip decorated bowls, dishes, and mugs. Industrial vessels in the form of white lead extraction pots were also recovered from the site, as well as molded architectural fragments and glazed roofing ridge tiles.

Of the more unusual ceramic items recovered was a fragment from a possible ornamental vessel with an applied molded face of a bearded man with a high forehead and longish hair (fig. 4). This unusual vessel had been biscuit fired and coated in a white slip but had never reached its second, or glost, firing. Only a single example of this type was found, and it may be reasonably assumed that it was not typical of the vessel types being pro-

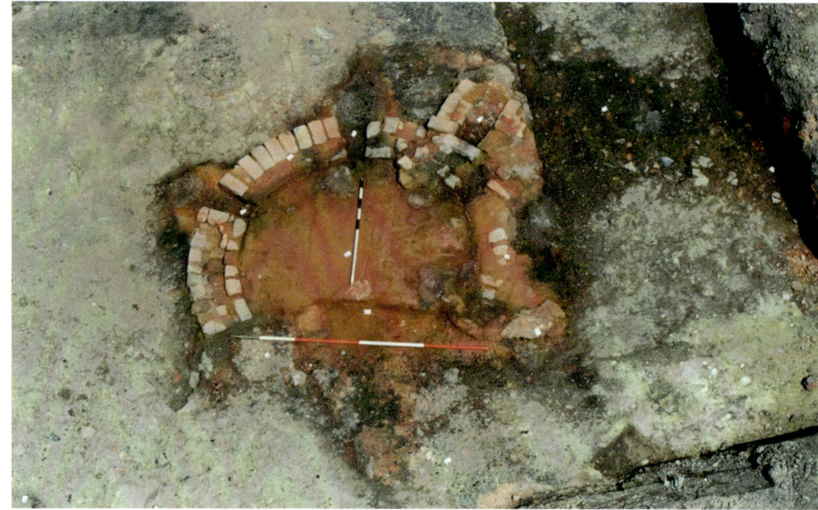

Figure 3 The remains of the second kiln uncovered during the excavations. Scale bars measure 1m (approximately 3.3') and 2m.

duced. The kiln furniture recovered included large cylindrical saggars with pierced walls, crescent-shaped spacers, small pyramid-shaped spacers, and crude pillow spacers formed by merely squeezing a piece of clay within the fist. Many examples still bear the fingerprints and nail marks of the potters.

Activity on the site earlier than the mid-eighteenth century also became evident during the course of the excavation. Encountered was a small circular hearth-like feature, together with possibly contemporary and associated wall foundations. The hearth feature was subject to archaeomagnetic dating techniques returning a "last firing" date of between 1660 and 1690. Gullies were also found containing black-glazed and trailed slipware vessels (although seemingly not wasters), together with stamped clay tobacco pipes datable to the latter decades of the seventeenth century. A pit, partially sealed beneath the hovel wall of the large kiln, produced wasters that included a black-glazed bowl and a spouted pipkin suggestive of earlier manufacture on the site, possibly during the late seventeenth or early eighteenth century.

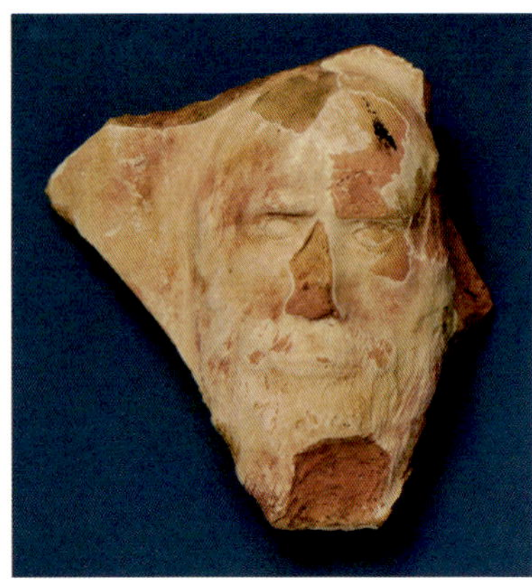

Figure 4 Face fragment, Lewis Pottery Complex, Buckley, North Wales, mid-eighteenth to nineteenth century. Biscuit-fired earthenware. One of the most unusual sherds recovered during the excavations, it bears an applied molded bearded face and is coated with white clay slip.

Following completion of the archaeological excavation, much of the pottery complex, including the remains of the kiln, was re-buried and preserved beneath a protective layer of stone. Examination of the remains of the Lewis pottery by future generations will thus be possible. Meanwhile, work continues upon the data recovered, not least the sheer volume of pottery, and it is anticipated that the forthcoming report will add to our understanding of the vessel forms, kiln technology, distribution (perhaps even across the Atlantic), and the techniques and skills employed by the Buckley potters of yesteryear.

Leigh J. Dodd, BSc.AIFA
Senior Archaeologist
Earthworks Archaeological Services
<L.Dodd@btinternet.com>

1. Robina McNeil, "Excavations at Buckley," *Archaeology in Clwyd* 7 (1984): 20–21.

Stephen E. Patrick

A Maryland Grouping of Bow and Derby Figures of the 1760s

▼ DOCUMENTARY EVIDENCE for the use of ceramic figures in eighteenth-century American households is extremely rare—much less the actual survival of such pieces. Recently, however, five English soft-paste porcelain figures dating from the 1760s have come to light that provide an important illustration of elite choices by early American consumers in acquiring and displaying decorative ceramics. The figures now belong to the City of Bowie Museum's Belair Mansion, a 1745 plantation house first owned by a colonial governor of Maryland, Samuel Ogle (1690–1752), and then by his son, Benjamin Ogle (1749–1809), a state governor. The figures, which had remained in the possession of direct descendants of the Ogle governors, were rediscovered during the restoration and research for furnishing the house as a museum.

The five pieces consist of three groupings: two Bow goats with putti (fig. 1), a Derby gardener paired with his female counterpart (fig. 2), and a lone Derby figure of the Roman god Mars (fig. 3). The Bow figures date to circa 1760, and have pad bases with raised flowers and a square potting hole in the back. On one, three cherubim frolic on a billy goat (fig. 4). On the other, two cherubim sit on a nanny goat with her kid (fig. 5).[1]

The Derby gardener figures stand on rococo bases full of C-scrolls and floral motifs, and carry baskets of flowers and vegetables. Their dress is not that of working gardeners but rather the frivolous costuming associated

Figure 1 Pair of goats with putti, Bow Porcelain Factory, London, 1759–1769. Soft-paste porcelain. H. 7" and 6½". (Courtesy, City of Bowie Museums; all photos, Richard Rohlfing.)

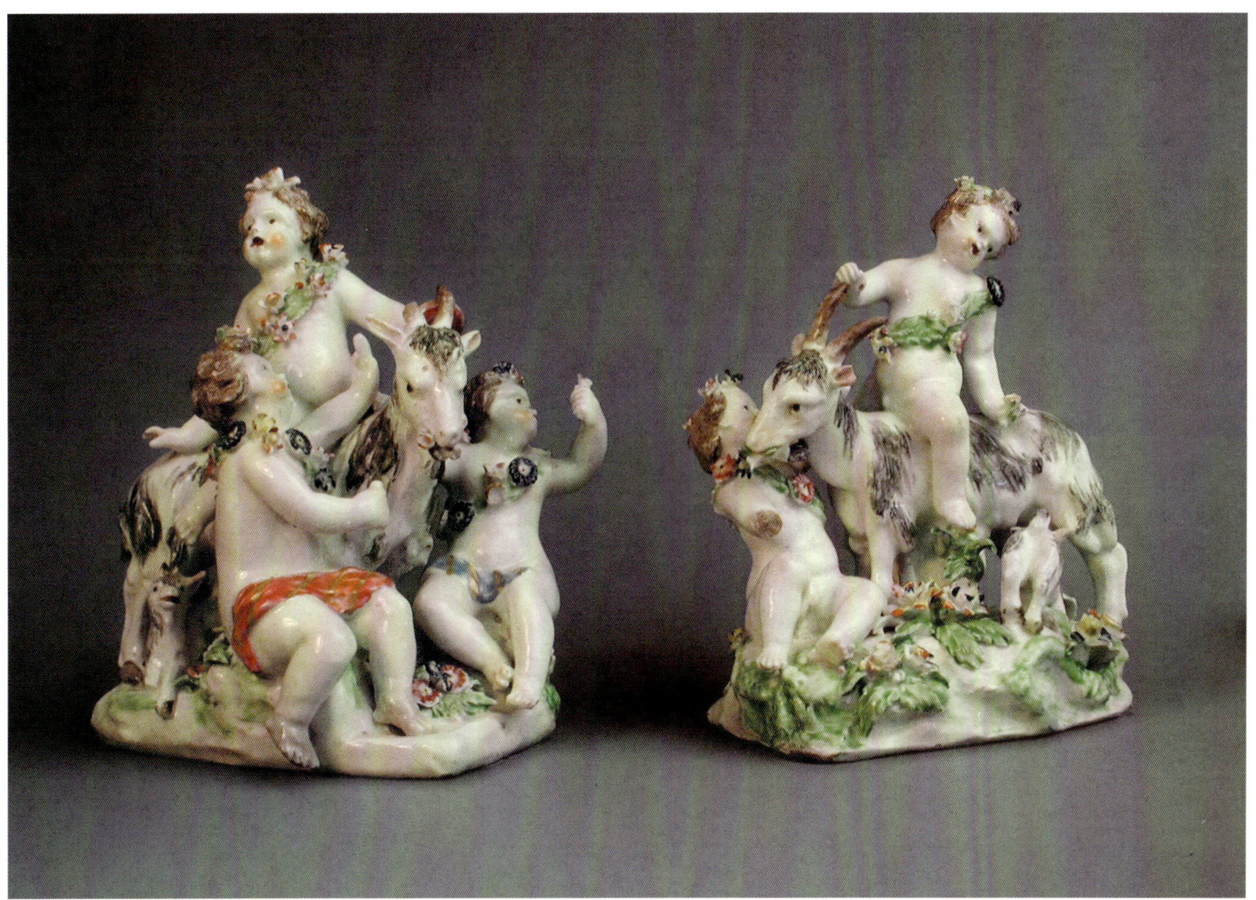

Figure 2 Pair of gardeners, Derby Porcelain Works, Derby, 1759–1769. Soft-paste porcelain. H. 9½".

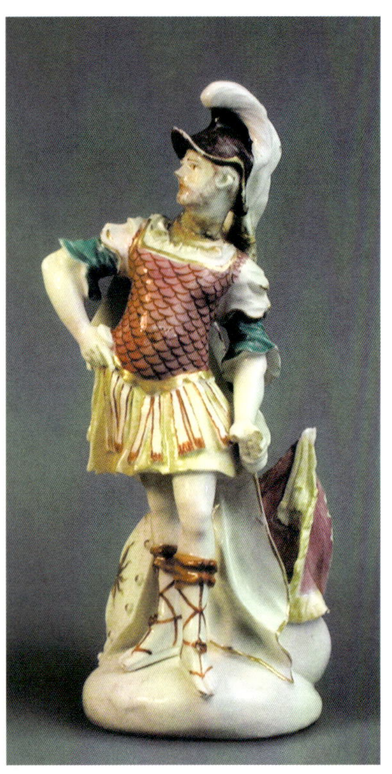

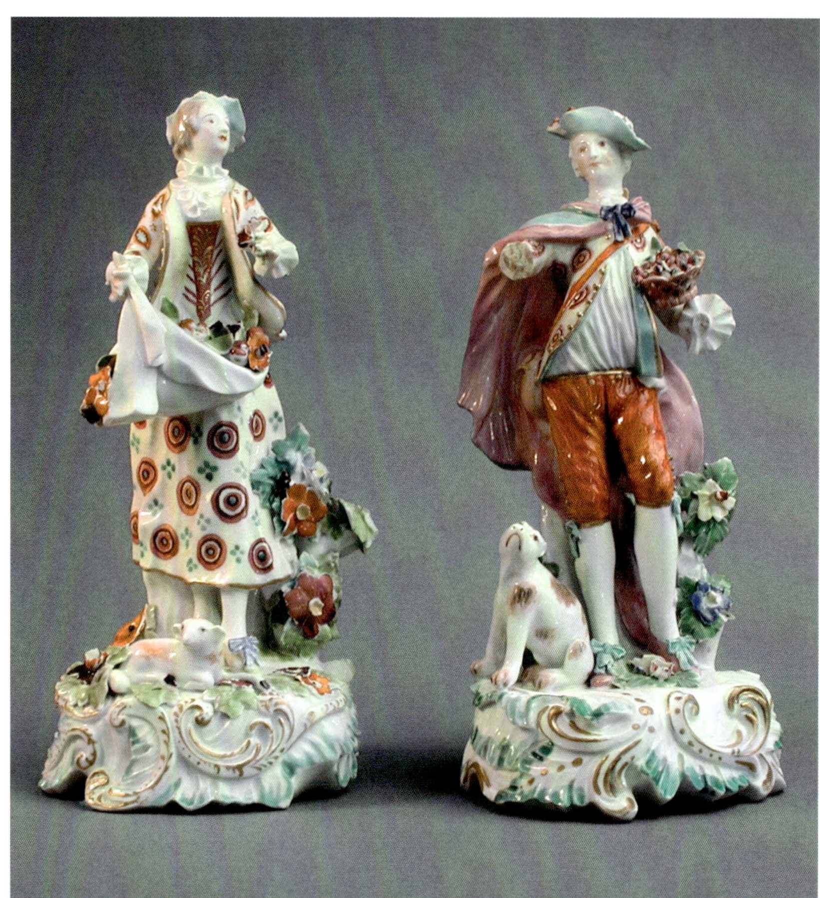

Figure 3 Figure of Mars, Derby Porcelain Works, Derby, 1759–1769. Soft-paste porcelain. H. 7".

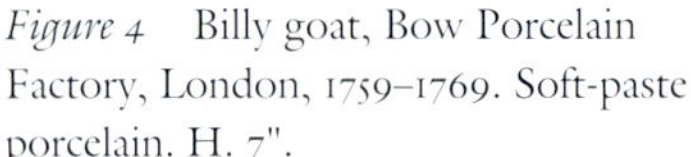

Figure 4 Billy goat, Bow Porcelain Factory, London, 1759–1769. Soft-paste porcelain. H. 7".

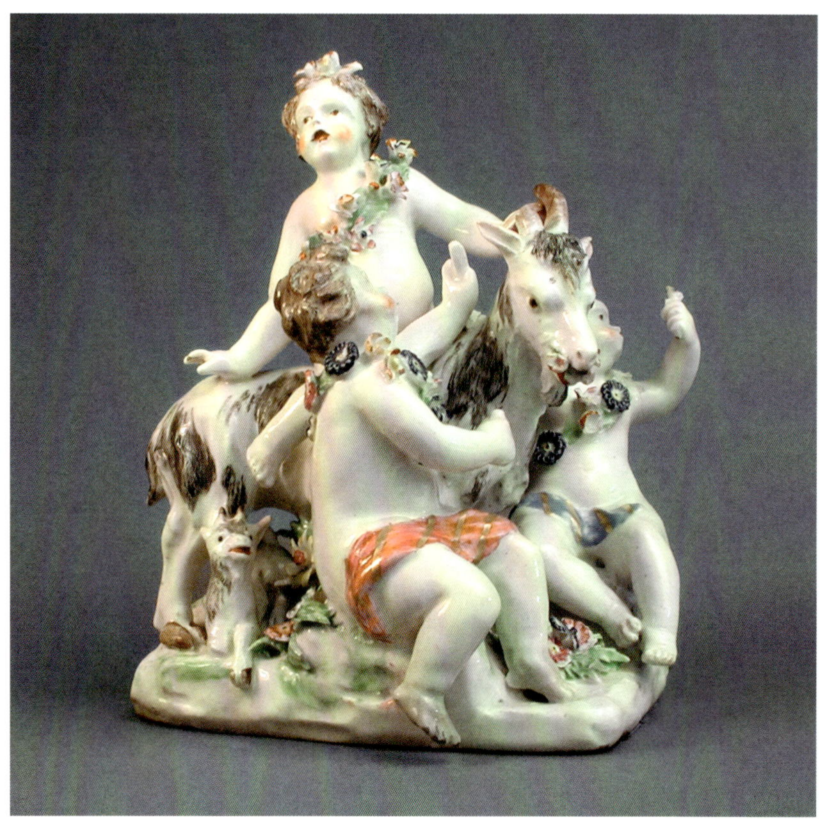

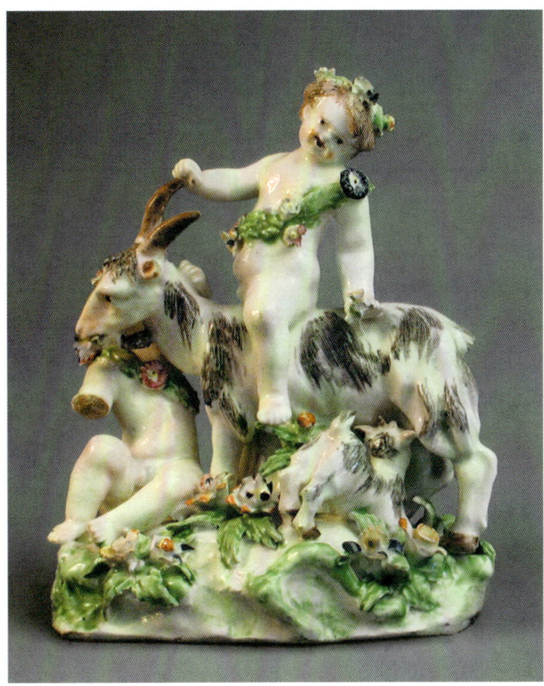

Figure 5 Nanny goat with putti, Bow Porcelain Factory, London, 1759–1769. Soft-paste porcelain. H. 6½".

with the rococo taste. With his *contraposto* pose, the Mars figure speaks less of war and more of classically inspired art.

The porcelain figures represent a type often used as mantle garniture in the eighteenth century. Importantly, family descendants can attribute their purchase to Governor Benjamin Ogle. The figures cumulatively can be traced to a narrow range of dates between 1759 and 1769. This coincides with the period in the mid-1760s when young Benjamin was studying at Eton in England, where he very possibly may have purchased them. An examination of contemporary merchant records for Annapolis, where the Ogles owned a townhouse from the 1740s to 1815, reveal that no examples of this type appeared on shop shelves in the capital city.[2]

Intriguingly, the probate inventory for Benjamin's son, Benjamin Ogle II (1796–1844) who died at Belair, lists "5 china mantle ornaments . . . 25¢," suggesting that the figures, eighty years after their original purchase, were not highly valued by the inventory taker.[3] This listing, however, combined with the fact that the donor is a direct descendant of Benjamin Ogle, provides invaluable evidence to support the family tradition that these pieces were at Belair in the 1760s.

Stephen E. Patrick
Director, City of Bowie Museums
<spatrick@cityofbowie.org>

1. Peter Bradshaw, *18th Century English Porcelain Figures* (Woodbridge, Suffolk, Eng.: Antique Collectors' Club, 1981), p. 105.

2. Stephen Patrick, "Class and Consumerism: Ceramic Purchases in the Colonial Chesapeake," *Ars Ceramica* 10 (1993).

3. Benjamin Ogle II probate, Prince George's County, Maryland, Administration 400, Docket 1810, April 30, 1844.

David G. Orr

Samuel Malkin in Philadelphia: A Remarkable Slipware Assemblage

▼ DURING THE WINTER of 1976, Charles E. Hunter and Herbert W. Levy conducted archaeological excavations on historic sites located between Market and Church Streets and between Front and Second Streets in downtown Philadelphia to mitigate highway construction in the area.[1] Among the many colonial features excavated, a well on Market Street was one of the most significant. Sealed around 1760, it yielded a rich harvest of early eighteenth-century ceramics, including a remarkable assemblage of slipware vessels made in Staffordshire, England (figs. 1, 2).

Neither subtle nor especially ground breaking, this article is to inform readers about one small group from the vast collections of material unearthed during the seminal years of historical archaeology. Like Pompeii, where I have labored for almost forty years, Philadelphia possesses an immense collection of archaeological data that sorely needs description and

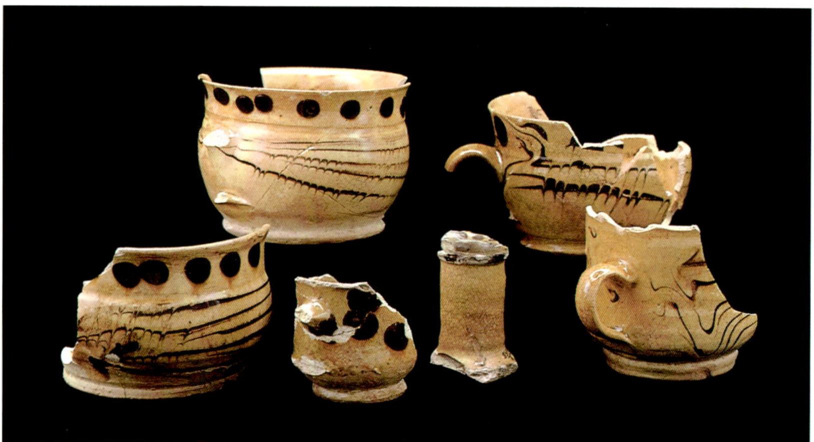

Figure 1 A group of hollow ware vessels, Staffordshire, 1720–1740. Slipware. (All objects courtesy, State Museum of Pennsylvania; photos, Gavin Ashworth.) A grouping of some of the ceramics recovered from the Market Street excavations. The candlestick fragment in the center is the only object not recovered from the well.

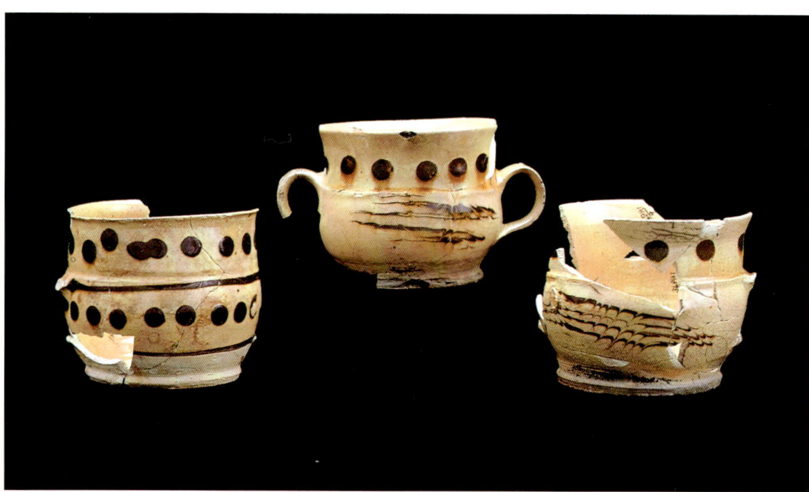

Figure 2 Double and single-handled cups, Staffordshire, 1720–1740. Slipware. These large drinking vessels were recovered from the Market Street well.

further study.[2] As the Market Street slipware assemblage illustrates, the unreported ceramic heritage from our historic past is extremely significant and intrinsically exciting (figs. 3, 4).

Most notable among the slipware vessels in the Market Street assemblage are several dishes manufactured by Samuel Malkin (1688–1741) of Burslem in Staffordshire, England. Malkin's distinctive relief-decorated

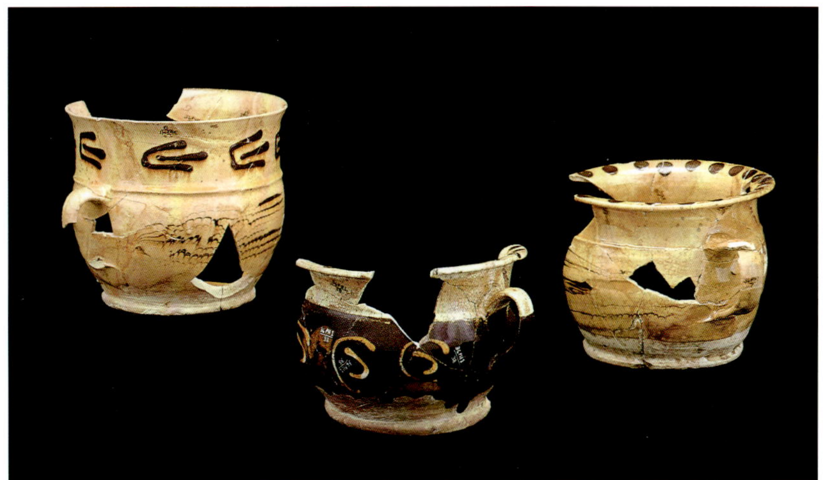

Figure 3 Two chamber pots, center and right, and a posset pot, left, Staffordshire, 1720–1740. Slipware. Posset pot H. 5¾".

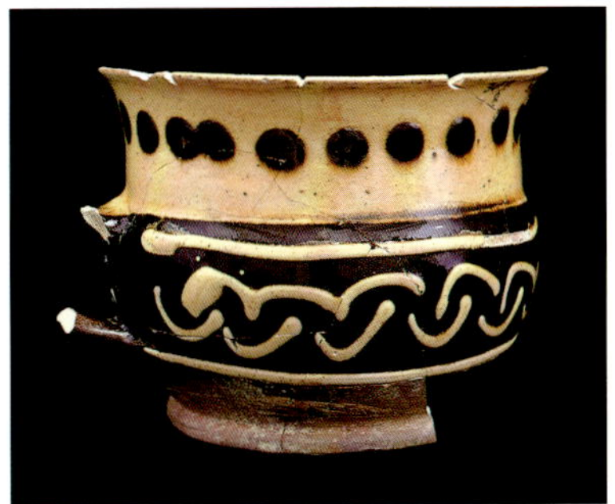

Figure 4 Large cup, Staffordshire, 1720–1740. Slipware. H. 4". A striking slipware cup decorated on the exterior with brown slip below the rim, and in reverse on the bowl.

and press-molded earthenware is well recognized.[3] He was one of the last important Staffordshire slipware potters to employ press molding, which by the end of the eighteenth century had declined there considerably.[4] In 1939, excavations of Malkin's factory site in Burslem yielded a number of important fragments of his labors, including molds for making slipware. Among his many signed pieces are examples that display the initials "SM" in molded relief.

Two important small dishes from the Market Street assemblage parallel the examples recovered in Burslem. They carry the initials "SM" in relief flanking a central dot of slip decoration and four small crosses (figs. 5, 6).

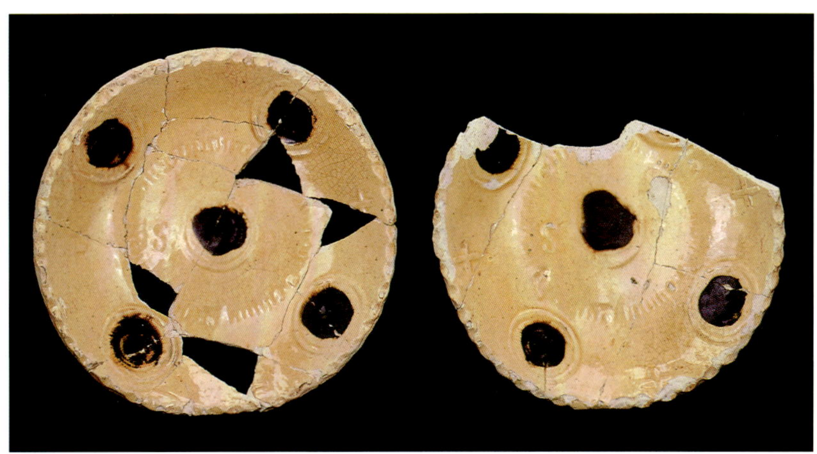

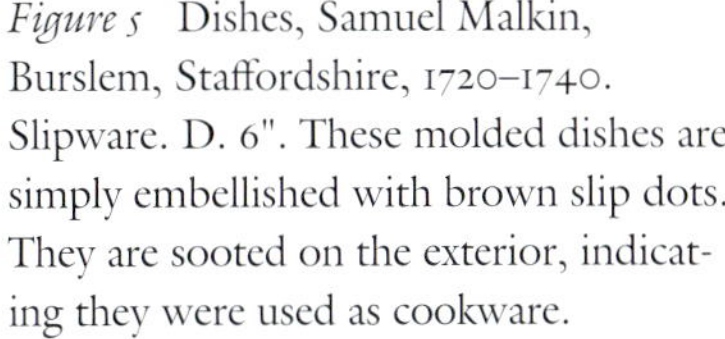

Figure 5 Dishes, Samuel Malkin, Burslem, Staffordshire, 1720–1740. Slipware. D. 6". These molded dishes are simply embellished with brown slip dots. They are sooted on the exterior, indicating they were used as cookware.

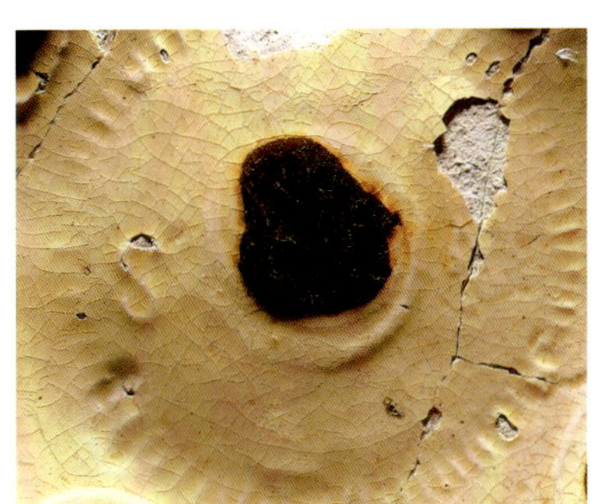

Figure 6 Detail of "S M" initials from a dish illustrated in fig. 5.

Also in the collection are two almost intact sunface dishes and sherds from two others (figs. 7, 8). It is believed that Malkin made these impressive large dishes.[5] Press-molded, they are emblazoned in relief with a sun's radiating countenance, magnificently achieving the ancient Renaissance desire for "filling the tondo." The fragmented sunface dishes are tantalizing because they are decorated much differently. For example, the possible eye sherd may belong to an undocumented sunface design (fig. 9).

All together, this remarkable collection brings to mind the familiar words of Henry Glassie, "Pottery works in the world. Displaying the complexity

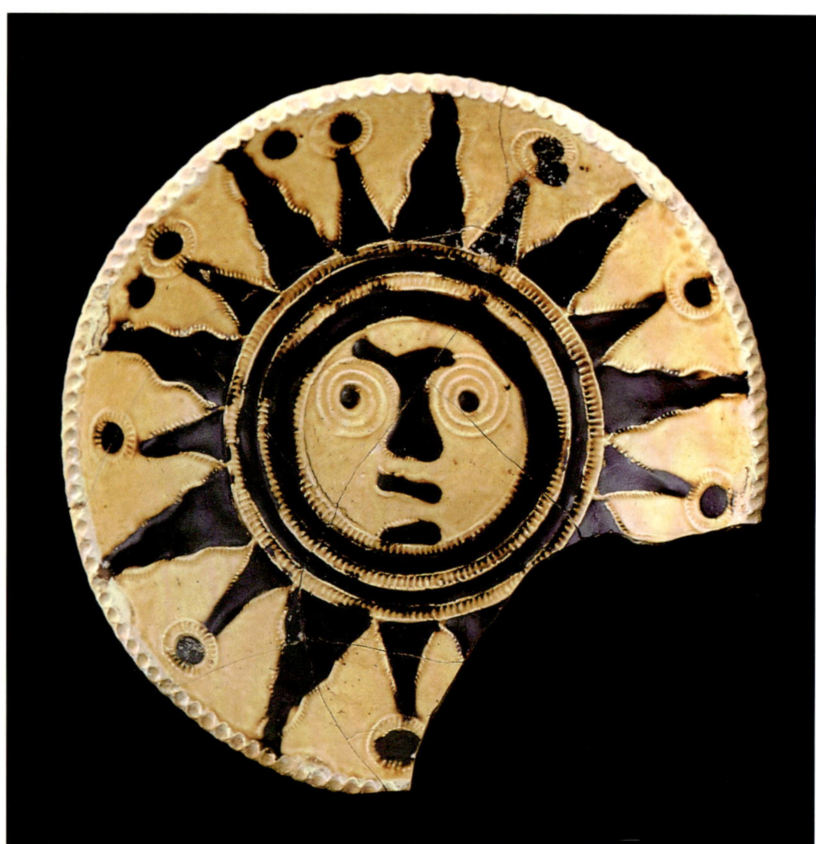

Figure 7 Sunface dish, probably Samuel Malkin, Burslem, Staffordshire, 1720–1740. Slipware. D. 11⅛". The sooted exterior of this dish evidences its use in the oven.

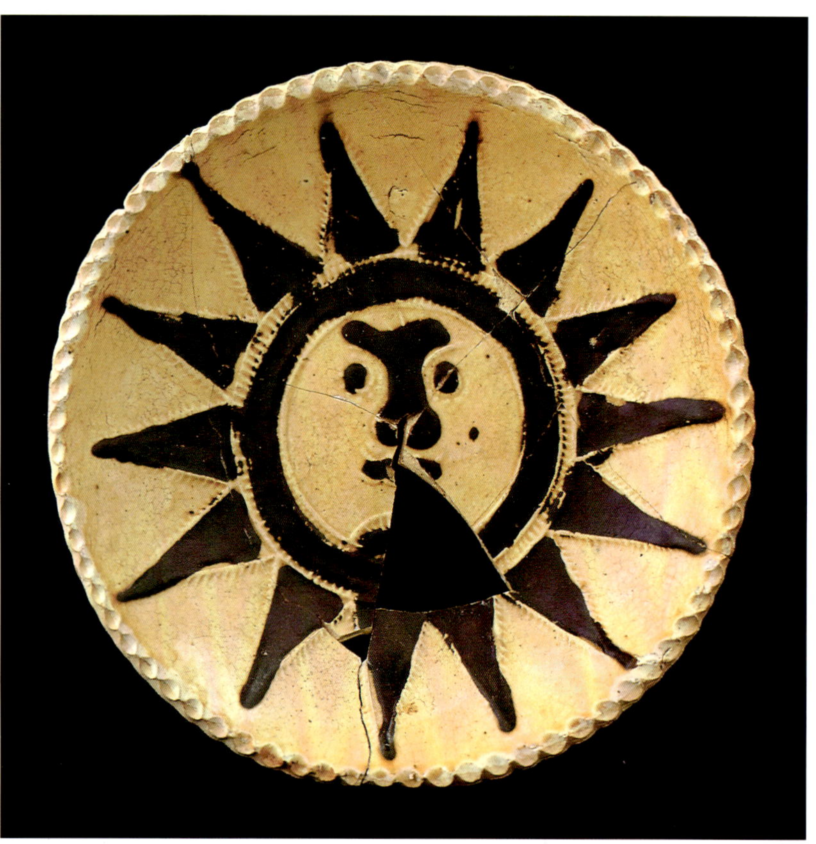

Figure 8 Sunface dish, probably Samuel Malkin, Burslem, Staffordshire, 1720–1740. Slipware. D. 7½". This dish displays no evidence of oven use.

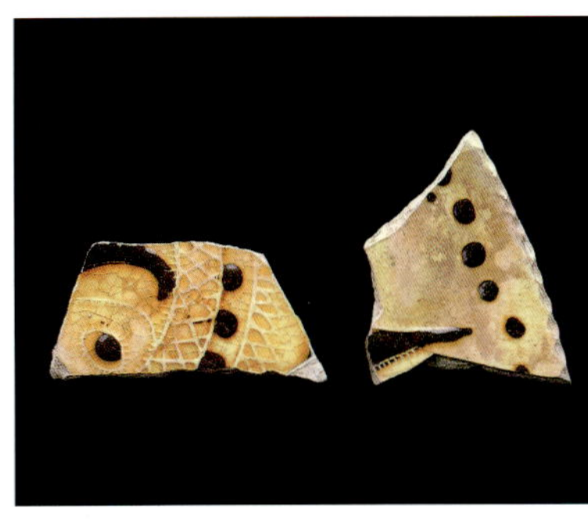

Figure 9 Fragments of other sunface dishes. Probably Burslem, Staffordshire, ca. 1720–1740. Slipware. These fragments, also from the Market Street well, are from sunface dishes most likely made by Samuel Malkin.

of the human condition, it brings the old and the new, the personal and the social, the mundane and transcendent into presence and connection."[6] Archaeologically, its story awaits a full contextual examination of its provenience before its significance can be fully addressed.

For Philadelphia, with its own thriving earthenware factories in operation, this Staffordshire slipware assemblage raises a number of questions. For instance, what did these vessels mean to the Philadelphia consumers? Were they specially selected for their curious iconography? Did they have religious connotations, as did some signed Malkin dishes with biblical illusions that promoted a virtuous life? Did they carry political overtones, as did other Malkin examples that illustrated Jacobite political references? Or, were they simply the products of a flourishing Atlantic trade in which an enormous variety and quantity of pottery arrived regularly from the homeland?

Much historical archaeology has been carried out in the city of Philadelphia over the last half century.[7] Could more sunfaces or slipware with other messages and images still slumber in the relative oblivion of collections from these excavated sites? Future studies of these archaeological materials promise to lead us into new avenues of understanding and interpreting the social and economic history of Philadelphia and its surroundings.

ACKNOWLEDGMENTS First, kudos and a golden Marshalltown trowel are awarded to the excavators who, in 1976, with their accurate recording and interpretative drawings, helped put this material into the proper context. Second, the staff of the State Museum of Pennsylvania is thanked for its outstanding job in conserving this material and for graciously permitting its publication. Assistant curator Janet Johnson, ably assisted by Elizabeth Wagner and Rich Petyk, is to be warmly thanked not only for her cooperation with the author, but for her boundless enthusiasm for these objects as well. Janet is also acknowledged for mercifully encouraging me to fully analyze this feature in the future.

David G. Orr, Ph.D.
Senior Regional Archaeologist
Northeast Region, National Park Service
<DLORR44@msn.com>

1. Charles E. Hunter and Herbert W. Levy, "Report on the Archaeological Salvage Excavations on the Northwest Side of Market and Front Streets, Philadelphia, Pa. Winter, 1976" (report for the Pennsylvania Department of Transportation, on file Pennsylvania State Museum, Harrisburg, Pa.). Herbert Levy, a graduate student at the American Civilization Department at the University of Pennsylvania, brought some of this material to my attention at that time while I was on the faculty. I attributed several of the objects to the Staffordshire potter Samuel Malkin, and used them in various unpublished works, including a paper I presented in the fall of 1999 on early archaeology in Philadelphia at "The Arts of Baroque Pennsylvania: a Symposium" sponsored by the Philadelphia Museum of Art. The assemblage is published for the first time in this journal.

2. A group called the Philadelphia Archaeological Forum was founded in Philadelphia recently. Among its goals is to provide support and funding for Philadelphia's "orphan collections," as well as those of the major institutions.

3. See especially Leslie B. Grigsby, *The Longridge Collection of English Slipware and Delftware*, 2 vols. (London: Jonathan Horne Publications, 2000), and Michelle Erickson and Robert Hunter, "Dots, Dashes, and Squiggles: Early English Slipware Technology," in *Ceramics in America*, edited by Robert Hunter (Hanover, N.H.: University Press of New England for the Chipstone Foundation, 2001) pp. 94–114. The latter article provides an outstanding description of exactly how these decorative dishes were made and decorated.

4. David Barker, *Slipware* (Princes Risborough, Eng.: Shire Publications Ltd., 1989), p. 18.

5. Other sunface dishes are known and most are attributed to Malkin. Michael Cooper illustrates one larger than figure 3 (13" in diameter), and another was discovered in the excavations at the Wetherburn Tavern site in Colonial Williamsburg. Ronald G. Cooper, *English Slipware Dishes, 1650–1850* (London: Alec Tiranti, 1968), fig. 248. Leslie B. Grigsby, *English Slip-Decorated Earthenware at Williamsburg* (Williamsburg, Va.: Colonial Williamsburg Foundation, 1993), p. 44.

6. Henry Glassie, *The Potter's Art* (Bloomington and Indianapolis: Indiana University Press, and Philadelphia: Material Culture, 1999), p. 17.

7. John Cotter, Daniel G. Roberts, and Michael Parrington, *The Buried Past: An Archaeological History of Philadelphia* (Philadelphia: University of Pennsylvania Press, 1992). See especially p. 470, where the authors state: "Conserving archaeological data and making them readily accessible are among other top priorities for future Philadelphia archaeology."

Christopher T. Espenshade

The Two Faces of Anthony Baecher

▼ ANTHONY W. BAECHER was an earthenware potter in Pennsylvania, Maryland, and Virginia in the nineteenth century. His work has been widely hailed as among the best folk pottery of the Shenandoah Valley based on a wide variety of surviving masterpieces.[1] The recent archaeological testing of the Anthony Baecher site in Frederick County, Virginia, highlights the two faces of Anthony Baecher.[2] Baecher was a highly skilled, highly creative ceramic artist, but he also made many rather

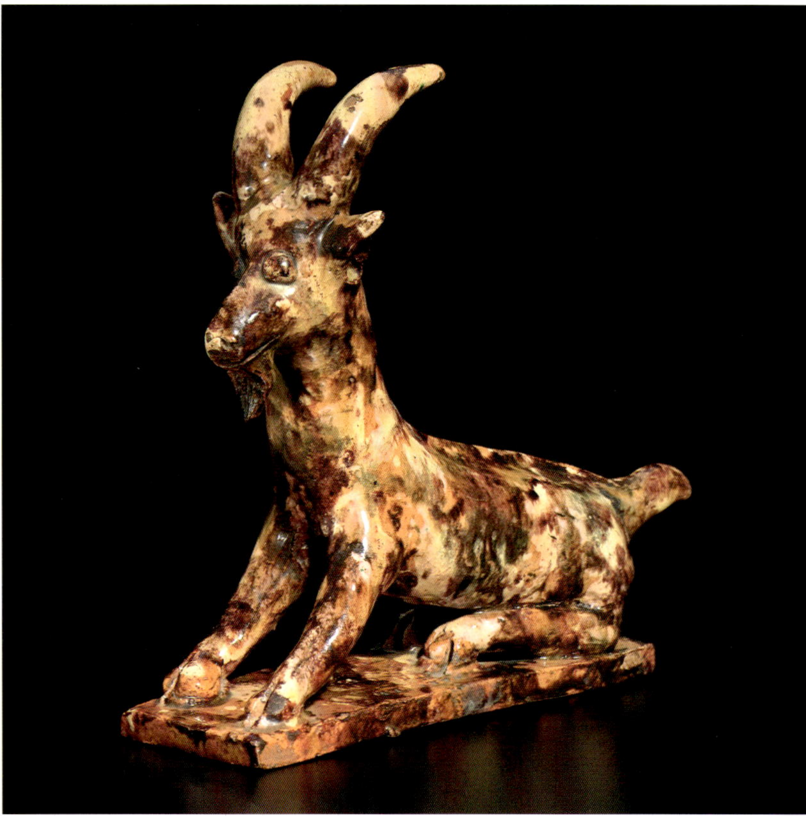

Figure 1 Goat, Anthony Baecher, ca. 1880. Lead-glazed earthenware. H. 6⅞". (Courtesy, American Folk Art Museum, promised gift of Ralph Esmarian; photo, John Bigelow.) This figurine exhibits Baecher's command of glazes by using manganese over slip. Marked three times: BAECHER/WINCHESTER VA.

pedestrian pots. This contrast underlines the inherent biases in personal and museum collections versus the pots found in the archaeological record.

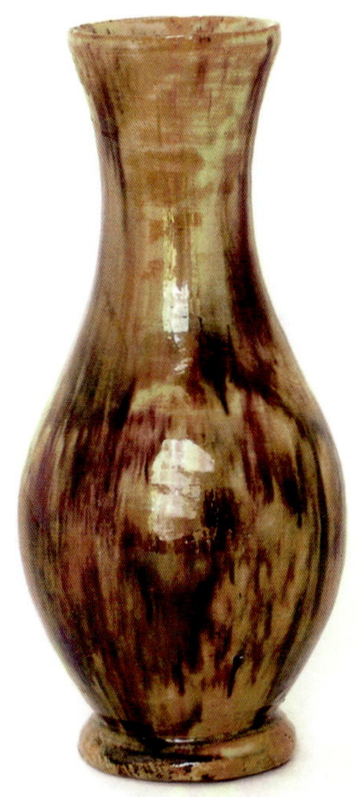

Baecher is generally recognized for three strengths: his palette of glaze/underglaze combinations; his use of applied decoration; and his skill in making animal and human forms as stand-alone items or accents on ornate pieces (figs. 1–2). Ceramic historian Gene Comstock observes: "Of all the pottery produced in the Valley, Bacher's is the most likely to be characterized as a true representation of American folk art in spite of his resurgent rococo and strong German influences."[3] Likewise, early historians Alvin Rice and John Stoudt were impressed with Baecher's potting: "A. W. Bacher was, without a doubt, the most skilled of the master potters of the Shenandoah Valley, and his influence is apparent in the later products of both S. Bell and Son, and the Eberly Pottery."[4] The 2002 preliminary testing of Baecher's Virginia shop provided a very different view. Skelly and Loy, Inc., conducted limited testing at Baecher's 1864–1889 shop near Winchester (fig. 3), and also examined material from earlier work at the site by

Figure 2 Vase, Anthony Baecher, Winchester, Virginia, ca. 1865–1880. Lead-glazed earthenware. H. 9". (Courtesy, Dr. and Mrs. George E. Manger Collection.) This vessel demonstrates his striking glaze effects resulting from the use of manganese, copper, and lead oxides over a slipped engobe. Stamped twice: BACKER.

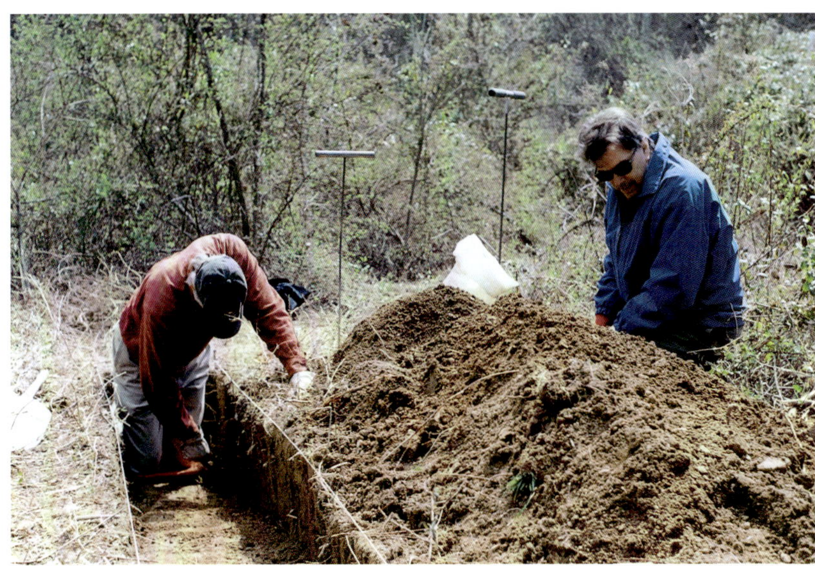

Figure 3 David Hazzard (left) and Gene Comstock completing the 3.5 x 0.5 m trench at the site of the Baecher Shop, Frederick County, Virginia. (Photo, Christopher T. Espenshade.)

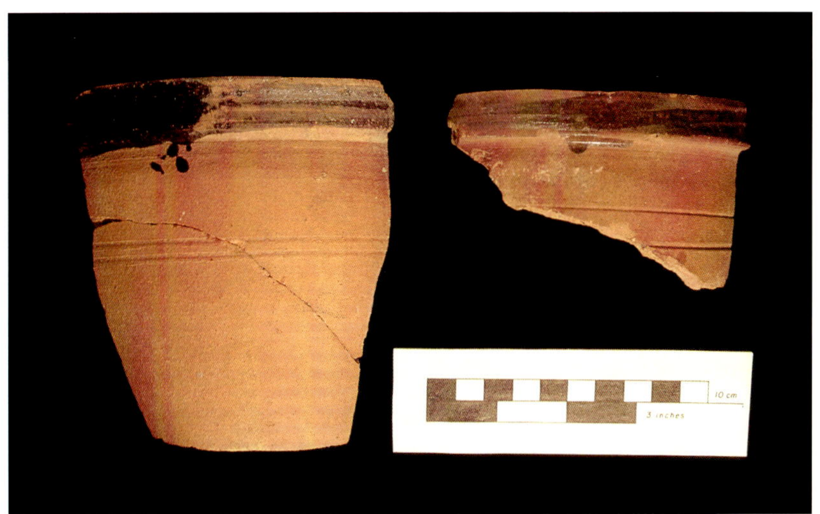

Figure 4 Storage jar fragments, Anthony Baecher Shop, Frederick County, Virginia, 1864–1889. Lead-glazed earthenware. (Photo, Alain C. Outlaw.) These fragments are characteristic of Baecher's lesser-known utilitarian vessels. The rims are squared on the exterior, and the interior glazes are dark brown to black. Note the sandy texture of the unglazed exterior.

others.[5] A total of 2,252 sherds was analyzed (fig. 4). The collection is dominated by simple storage jar forms with interior lead glazing, generally unadorned bases, heavy rims, and incised lines on their shoulders. There is a high degree of variability in the width and thickness of rims, and there is no evidence that templates were used in forming the rims. Less than 0.5 percent of the assemblage has glaze/underglaze combinations other than basic lead glaze. No slip-trailing, applied decoration, or sgraffito is evidenced. Handles are pulled, rather than extruded. Only two possible figurine fragments are encountered. In general, the day-to-day vessels made at the Baecher shop are less than spectacular and do not reflect the artistic skills of the potter. Indeed, it could be argued that, aesthetically, Baecher's utilitarian ware shows devolution from earlier regional traditions.[6]

Overall, the archaeology of the Baecher site reminds us of the biases in our databases. Museums and private collectors tend to hold the most unusual, most ornate, and least utilitarian pieces made by a potter. Archaeological samples may not capture the full range of production at a site, are biased toward failures, and tend to emphasize exactly those items for which the least care was taken. These contrasting databases can yield a somewhat complete picture only when taken together. In the current case, both faces of Anthony Baecher are legitimate. Baecher was an extremely skilled folk artist, but the competitive demands of the Valley market forced him to simplify his bulk production. Baecher balanced his occasional tours de force against his day-to-day economic baseline of mundane vessels.

Christopher T. Espenshade
Archaeologist
Skelly and Loy, Inc.
<cespenshade@monroeville.skellyloy.com>

1. H. E. Comstock, *The Pottery of the Shenandoah Valley* (Chapel Hill, N.C.: University of North Carolina Press for the Museum of Early Southern Decorative Arts, 1994).

2. During his career, Baecher also spelled his name Packer, Bacher, and Backer.

3. Comstock, *The Pottery of the Selnandoah Valley,* p. 164.

4. Alvin H. Rice and John Baer Stoudt, *The Shenandoah Pottery* (Strasburg, Va.: Shenandoah Publishing House, 1929), p. 88.

5. Dr. Gene Comstock, Robert Jolley of the Winchester Regional Preservation Office of the Virginia Department of Historic Resources (VDHR), and David Hazzard of the Threatened Sites Program (VDHR) assisted Skelly and Loy, Inc. in the excavation. Robert Jolley has been conducting research concerning the longevity of the earthenware tradition in Frederick County, Virginia, and has noted this apparent devolution in much of the late nineteenth-century earthenware.

6. Christopher T. Espenshade and Linda Kennedy, "Skilled Potters, Mundane Pots: Preliminary Archaeological Testing of the Anthony Baecher Pottery Shop (44FK550), Frederick County, Virginia, 2002." Report for the Threatened Sites Program, Virginia Department of Historic Resources, Richmond, Va.

William B. Liebeknecht and Richard W. Hunter

The Richards Face—Shades of an Eighteenth-Century American Bellarmine

▼ IN MAY 2000, during reconstruction of New Jersey Route 29, remains of a stoneware pottery kiln were documented on the banks of the Delaware River in Lamberton, the historic port of Trenton, New Jersey. The kiln was part of a pottery complex established by William Richards in the early 1770s that stayed in operation at least into the Revolutionary War years.[1]

Among the roughly 14,000 sherds and items of kiln furniture recovered during emergency excavations conducted at the kiln site are three sherds that display distinctive bellarmine-like applied faces on their exterior surfaces (fig. 1). Although it is not possible to obtain full profiles of the vessels decorated in this manner, analysis of the kiln assemblage allows these faces to be linked with a series of small, tan-bodied stoneware jugs, some of which have a dark brown slip coating on their exteriors. The jugs in question are of gallon size or smaller, with an interior rim diameter of only about one inch.

Matching the body and surface treatment of the face sherds with other sherds reveals that several of the jugs had pierced handles, implying that they had metal (perhaps silver or pewter) lids. Furthermore, a number of the rim sherds with the matching body and surface treatment exhibit an external lid seat. Base sherds show no evidence of pedestals, which corroborates their typing as bulbous jugs rather than serving vessels, such as

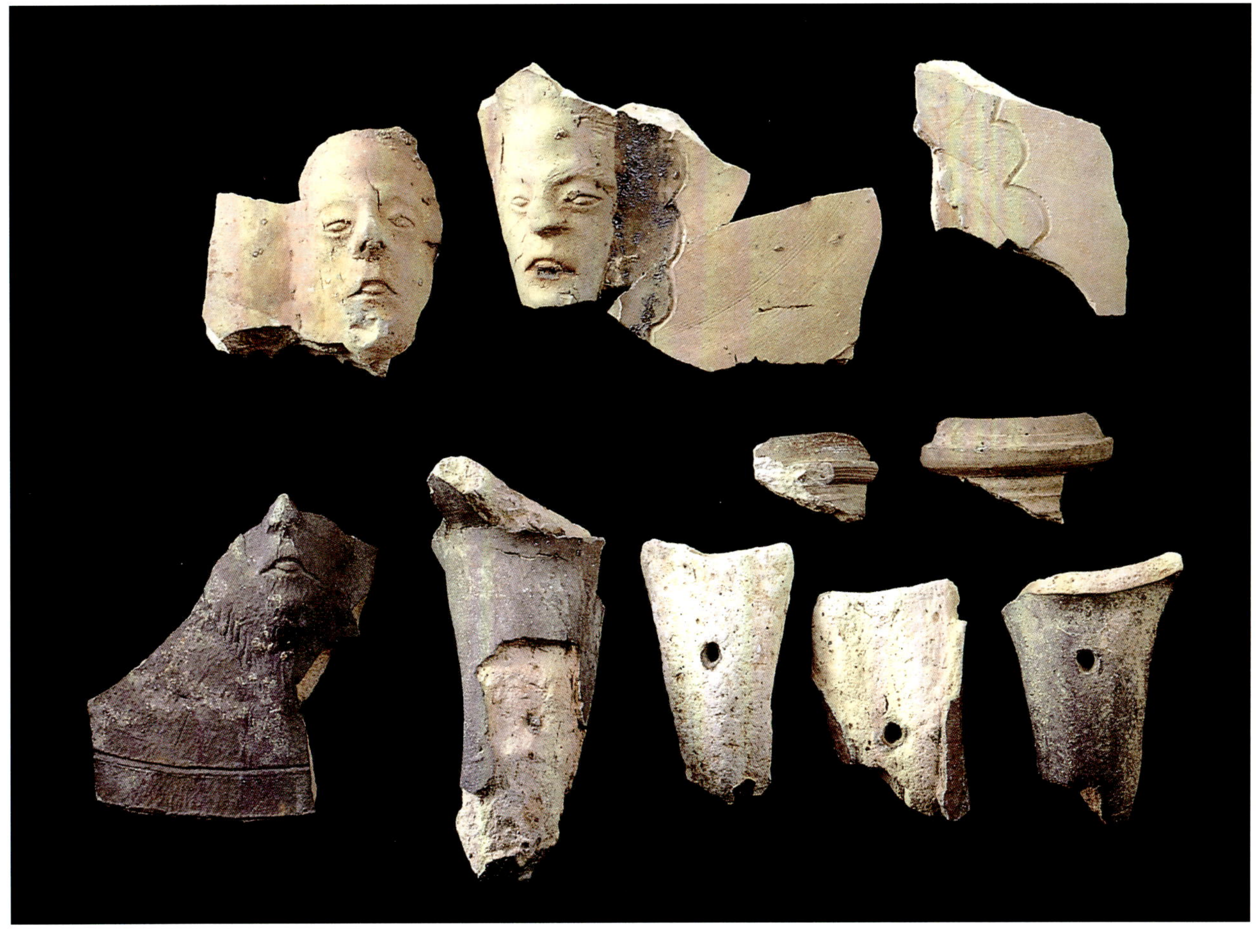

Figure 1 Bellarmine-like faces from the Richards stoneware site, Lamberton, New Jersey, ca. 1774–1787. Stoneware. (Photo, Gavin Ashworth.)

bottles, flagons, or tankards. The three sherds have the faces encircled within an incised scalloped border, a Richards pottery signature decorative motif used especially in the definition of lobed flowers on chamber pots, tea bowls, and tankards.

Although it is possible to link the face sherds with a particular vessel type, it is difficult to better characterize the jugs. For instance, it is unclear if the bodies of these vessels exhibited any further decoration, or whether they had an otherwise plain brown exterior. It is clear, however, that the faces are applied high on the vessel shoulder, in much the same fashion as on Bellarmine vessels, and were not, for example, positioned on a pouring spout.

To date, no other American-made colonial stoneware vessels with applied facial decoration have been found, making the Richards examples unique.[2] That only three out of several thousand sherds were identified as face-decorated suggests limited production of a special order item, which—if true—means that these vessels will be sparsely represented in ceramic collections and archaeological assemblages. All three faces are made from the same mold, further stressing their uniqueness.

The influences behind the Richards jugs with applied face decoration are unclear. While the term "bellarmine" is hoisted in the banner headline for this brief article, there are substantive differences between the Richards face and those found on typical European bellarmine vessels.[3] The latter, also referred to as "graybeards" or "bartmännern," generally depict abundant, boldly formed facial hair and frequently bear an oval medallion. Neither trait is evident on the Richards specimens, although what appears to be a rudimentary beard-like growth (possibly the result of scoring to attach the sprig-molded face to the vessel body) is a distinguishing characteristic on these jugs.

The expressive faces on European bellarmine vessels—smiling, frowning, or challengingly fierce—are also absent. The Richards face is more naturalistic, but blank, somewhat akin to a death mask, and notable for its very slightly sticking-out tongue. One presumes that the face is intended to be male, but this is not entirely certain. Indeed, the protruding tongue is reminiscent of the currently popular line of American Girl dolls. More believably, the peeping tongue was intended to "cock a snook" at the British Crown, a sentiment entirely in keeping with William Richards' patriotic service as ships' husband to the Pennsylvania Navy during the Revolutionary War.[4] It is relevant that one of the few broadly datable items in the assemblage is a sherd sprig molded "GR" (a reference to Georgius Rex, King George III), implying that the final kiln firing and waster deposition took place before the British imperial yoke had been fully unharnessed.

A more secure, if non-committal, conclusion is that the Richards face does not seek to imitate the European bellarmines exactly and probably owes little to this German, Low Countries, and English tradition that was in somewhat of a lull in the second half of the eighteenth century. This visage is more likely inspired by contemporary taste for the pseudo-classical as seen in the use of naturalistic anthropomorphic decoration on jugs and other wares in a variety of ceramic fabrics. The Richards face should thus be viewed perhaps less as a continuation of ceramic tradition and more as an expression of social commentary in the vein of Hogarthian or Diderotist illustration.[5]

ACKNOWLEDGMENTS The authors in particular wish to acknowledge Ivor Noël Hume for stimulating our thought processes in the preparation of this article and for drawing our attention to relevant comparative material. We have also appreciated the input and comment of many of our colleagues, notably Ian Burrow, George Cress, Damon Tvaryanas and Rebecca White at Hunter Research, Inc., Meta Janowitz at URS, and David Zmoda at the New Jersey Department of Transportation.

William B. Liebeknecht
Principal Archaeologist
Hunter Research, Inc.
<wbl@hunterresearch.com>

Richard W. Hunter, Ph.D.
President and Principal Archaeologist
Hunter Research, Inc.
<rwhunter@hunterresearch.com>
<http://hunterresearch.com>

1. Richard W. Hunter, "Eighteenth-Century Stoneware Kiln of William Richards Found on the Lamberton Waterfront, Trenton, New Jersey," in *Ceramics in America*, edited by Robert Hunter (Hanover, N.H.: University Press of New England for the Chipstone Foundation, 2001), pp. 239–43.

2. A single example of applied face decoration was identified among the wares produced by the mid-eighteenth-century Philadelphia stoneware potter Anthony Duché, but the specimen in question was fashioned in green-glazed earthenware (Robert Giannini, personal communication). See also Robert L. Giannini III, "Anthony Duché, Sr., Potter and Merchant of Philadelphia," *Antiques* 119, no. 2 (January 1981): 198–203. Another applied face may be noted on a red earthenware garden planter found at Green Spring plantation in James City County, Virginia; see Audrey Noël Hume, *Archaeology and the Colonial Gardener*, Colonial Williamsburg Foundation No. 7 (Williamsburg, Va.: Colonial Williamsburg Foundation, 1974), pp. 54–57.

3. For typical European Bellarmine faces, see David Gaimster, *German Stoneware 1200–1900* (London: British Museum Press, 1997); Chris Green, *John Dwight's Fulham Pottery, Excavations 1971–79* (London: English Heritage, Archaeological Report 6, 1999), pp. 220–22; Ivor Noël Hume, *If These Pots Could Talk: Collecting 2,000 Years of British Household Pottery* (Hanover, N.H.: University Press of New England for the Chipstone Foundation, 2001), pp. 117–26.

4. William Richards was appointed ships' husband for the Pennsylvania Navy in May of 1776; see *Naval Documents of the American Revolution*, 8 vols. (Washington, D.C.: Naval History Division, Department of the Navy, 1996), 5: 192.

5. For example, *Engravings by Hogarth*, edited by Sean Shesgreen (New York: Dover Publications, Inc., 1973), pls. 10, 13, 23, 45; *A Diderot Pictorial Encyclopedia of Trades and Industry: 485 Plates Selected from L'Encyclopédié of Denis Diderot*, edited by Charles C. Gillispie (New York: Dover Publications, Inc., 1959, 1987), pls. 308, 318, 336, 418, 429, 445, 449, 458.

Beverly A. Straube

The Prodigal Son Returns to Jamestown

▼ BREATHLESS FROM THE 300-yard dash from the well he had been digging, the archaeologist appeared at the laboratory door. "Look what I found!" he exclaimed as he opened his muddy fingers and presented a sherd of blue and gray stoneware. The blue was so brilliant it appeared as if it had been made yesterday. "I think it's a horse's ass," the archaeologist gasped. Sure enough, the sprig-molded design on the sherd showed the hindquarters of an animal with a long tail. This was just the first of seventy-one pieces of the same vessel—a stoneware jug manufactured in Germany—that was excavated from a well on Jamestown Island, Virginia, site of the English colony that was first established in 1607 (fig. 1).

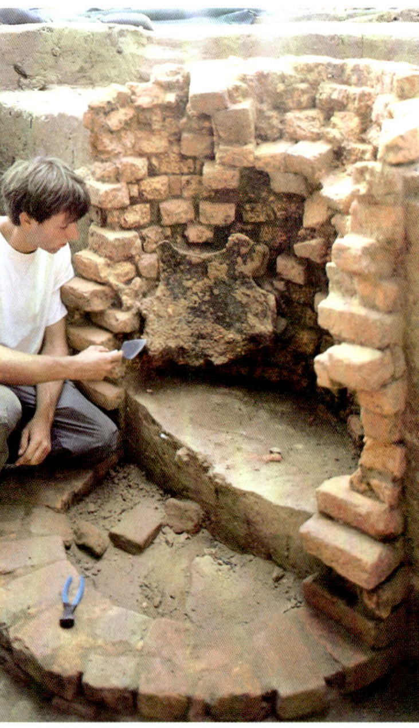

Figure 1 Association for the Preservation of Virginia Antiquities archaeologist Danny Schmidt excavating a breastplate from the top of an early seventeenth-century brick-lined well at Jamestown, Virginia. The well was full of military and domestic iron objects. Sherds of an early Westerwald stoneware jug depicting the biblical story of the Prodigal Son were found scattered throughout the well. (Courtesy, Association for the Preservation of Virginia Antiquities.)

Although located in the center of a Confederate earthwork erected during the Civil War, the well was built in the first quarter of the seventeenth century. This was determined by the dates of the artifacts unearthed in the trench surrounding the well that the colonists had dug as they constructed the brick-lined shaft. The objects found within the well itself suggest that it had ceased functioning as a source of water by the mid-1620s and was then quickly filled with debris.

The jug, which was discovered in pieces from top to bottom of the well, was produced in the Westerwald region of Germany near Cologne. Also known as the *Kannenbackerland* or "pot firing region" of Germany, the Westerwald "contains some of the richest sources of fine pottery making clays in north-west Europe."[1] Its prominence in the production of stoneware blossomed at the end of the sixteenth century with the migration to the area of many potters escaping political unrest in Raeren (now Belgium) and Siegburg.

Westerwald products are common finds on American colonial sites through the seventeenth and eighteenth centuries. They were prized for their lightness, durability, and attractive decoration. After the Revolutionary War, however, American stoneware production in city centers such as Alexandria and Philadelphia and in the Valley of Virginia was able to compete with the Westerwald imports and eventually replaced them.

The Jamestown jug is a form known as a baluster jug. Sprig-molded friezes, derived from pattern books of designs used by the potters, decorate the neck and paneled body. The neck is ornamented in the Raeren style with grotesque masks in ovoid frames interspersed with relief floral strapwork. The midgirth reflects one of the biblical themes that became so popular in the Westerwald in the early seventeenth century. Seven panels, of which only fragments remain, depict the New Testament story of the Prodigal Son.

A complete "Prodigal Son" jug pictured in Otto von Falke's *Das Rheinische Stein zeug* is a close parallel to the Jamestown jug (figs. 2, 3).[2] Besides the date of December 1618, a legend over the arcaded panels reads *Historia von dem verloren Sohn wie Sant Lucas davon dut schriben* ("History of the Prodigal Son according to Saint Luke").

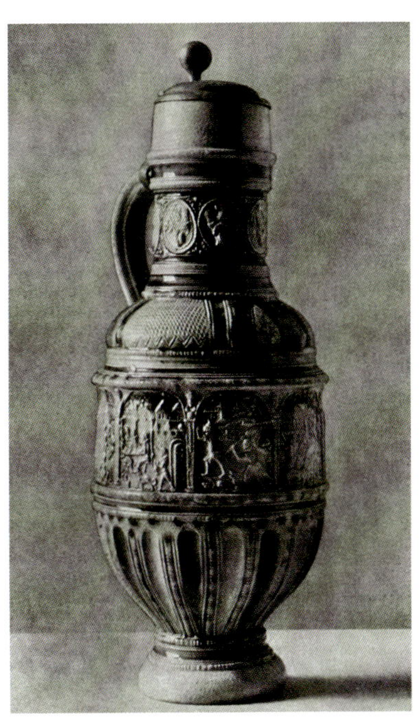

Figure 2 Jug, Grenzau, Germany, 1618. Salt-glazed stoneware. This example parallels the archaeological Jamestown jug. The legend indicates that it was produced in 1618 in Grenzau.

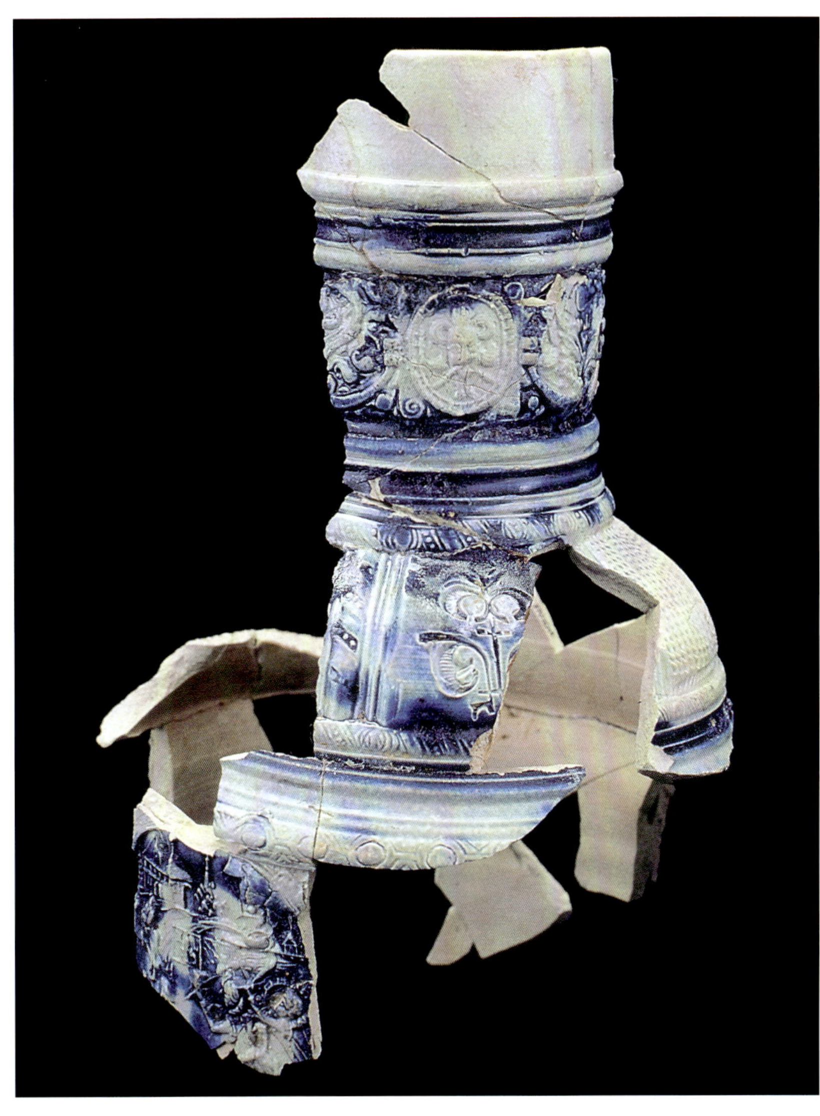

Figure 3 Jug, probably Grenzau, ca. 1618. Salt-glazed stoneware. (Photo, Gavin Ashworth.) This archaeological jug is comprised of sherds recovered from the early seventeenth-century well at Jamestown.

Parts of this legend can also be seen on the Jamestown fragments, such as the word *Historia* on the first panel in the narrative (fig. 4). It depicts the Prodigal Son on horseback, leaving home with his inheritance. Also recovered from the well was the final panel, which shows the Prodigal Son reconciling with his older brother who had been angered by all the fuss being made over the return of his errant sibling (fig. 5).

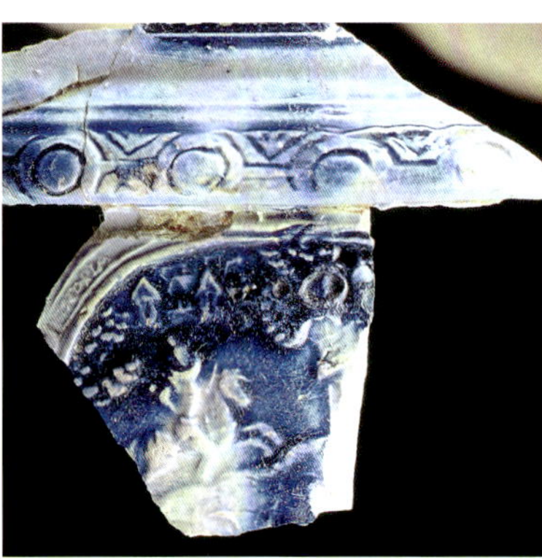

Figure 4 Fragment of the jug illustrated in fig. 3. This is part of the first panel in the narrative showing the Prodigal Son departing on horseback with his inheritance. The German word *Historia* (history) appears in the arcade over the panel.

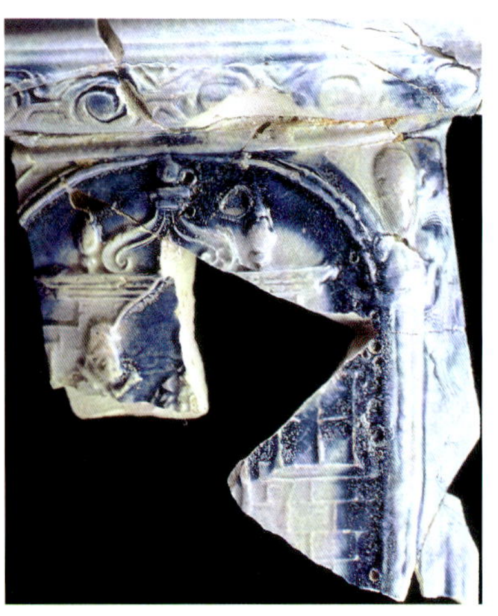

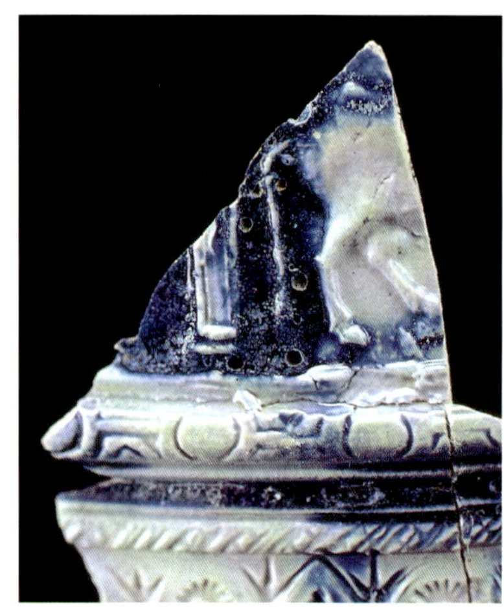

Figure 5 Fragment of the jug illustrated in fig. 3. The final panel on the jug, it depicts the Prodigal Son making amends with his brother.

Figure 6 Fragment of the jug illustrated in fig. 3. The first sherd of the jug found in the well, it shows the rear end of an animal, which later proved to be the fattened calf being led to slaughter for the Prodigal Son's welcome-home feast.

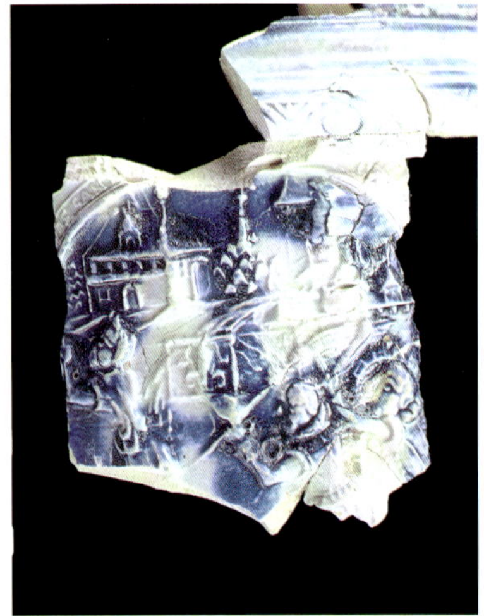

Figure 7 Fragment of the jug illustrated in fig. 3. This panel displays the initials "Z L" on a plaque. Once thought to represent the initials of the jug's maker, they are now recognized as being on a sign indicating the way to the brothel (*Zur Lilie*) in the Prodigal Son narrative.

The "horse's ass" that had excited the archaeologist is, in reality, the rear end of the fattened calf that is being slaughtered for the welcoming-home feast for the Prodigal Son. Parts of the legend as described above (. . . *ie Sa*. . .) are visible on this panel (fig. 6).

One of the recovered panel sherds raised much excitement, as it appeared to have the initials "Z L" and perhaps part of a date (fig. 7). Surely, it was thought, this must be the mark of the maker who could possibly be identified. Research soon proved that other scholars had been mislead by the same mark and that Otto von Falke had indicated in 1908 that the initials are part of the design.[3] "Z L" stands for *Zur Lilie* which means "to

Lily's house." The initials are on a sign identifying the brothel from which the Prodigal Son had just been expelled.

The "Prodigal Son" jug has been retrieved from its watery grave and has returned to Jamestown. Just as the father in the Prodigal Son narrative states, "let us eat, and be merry . . . for he was lost, and is found."[4]

ACKNOWLEDGMENTS The author thanks Reinhard Straube for patiently translating and interpreting German texts.

Beverly A. Straube
Curator, *Jamestown Rediscovery*™
Association for the Preservation of Virginia Antiquities (APVA)
Jamestown, Virginia
<bly@apva.org>

1. David Gaimster, *German Stoneware 1200–1900* (London: British Museum Press, 1997), p. 251.
2. Otto von Falke, *Das Rheinische Steinzeug* (1908; reprint, Osnabrüch: Otto Zeller Verlag, 1977), pp. 90–92.
3. Ibid., p. 91.
4. Luke 15: 32.

Alain C. Outlaw

Backcountry Sophistication: Anthropomorphic Elements from a Piedmont North Carolina Kiln

▼ A BACKYARD OF 532 ACRES of woodlands in the rolling hills of central North Carolina—what more could two preteen brothers ask for in 1968, when the outdoors and imagination played central roles in entertainment? The explorations of Jeffery and Lee Farlow, ages eleven and nine respectively, led to their discovery of pottery fragments, bearing "silver looking stuff . . . wagon wheel designs . . . and elbow type legs" on a small upland near their home at the Mount Shepherd Methodist Camp, eight miles northwest of Asheboro.[1] When I was introduced to the site several years later, it reminded me of my 1961 visit to the caves of Lascaux, discovered by five boys in central France in 1940. There, too, the secret and unexpected finds from a remote wooded area were eventually, reluctantly, revealed to grownups.

But unlike the Lascaux caves, the finds at Mount Shepherd were visible on the surface. Ceramic sherds were discovered on top of the ground, and the remnants of stone footings for the pottery manufactory were under slight mounds of stone rubble. As well, clay pits or cellars appeared as depressions on the forest floor. Under the auspices of the North Carolina Historical Potters Exploration, Inc., created by the late Mr. and Mrs. Walter Auman of Seagrove, these topographic irregularities in the woods were excavated in 1974 and 1975, revealing the remains of a stone-walled kiln with brick-lined flues (fig. 1), brick heating stove base, workshop floor defined by a clay lens, clay extraction pits, and various stone pier and foundation traces.[2] All the major elements of the pottery manufactory, including clay extraction, clay processing, turning and molding, firing, and storage, were archaeologically investigated.[3]

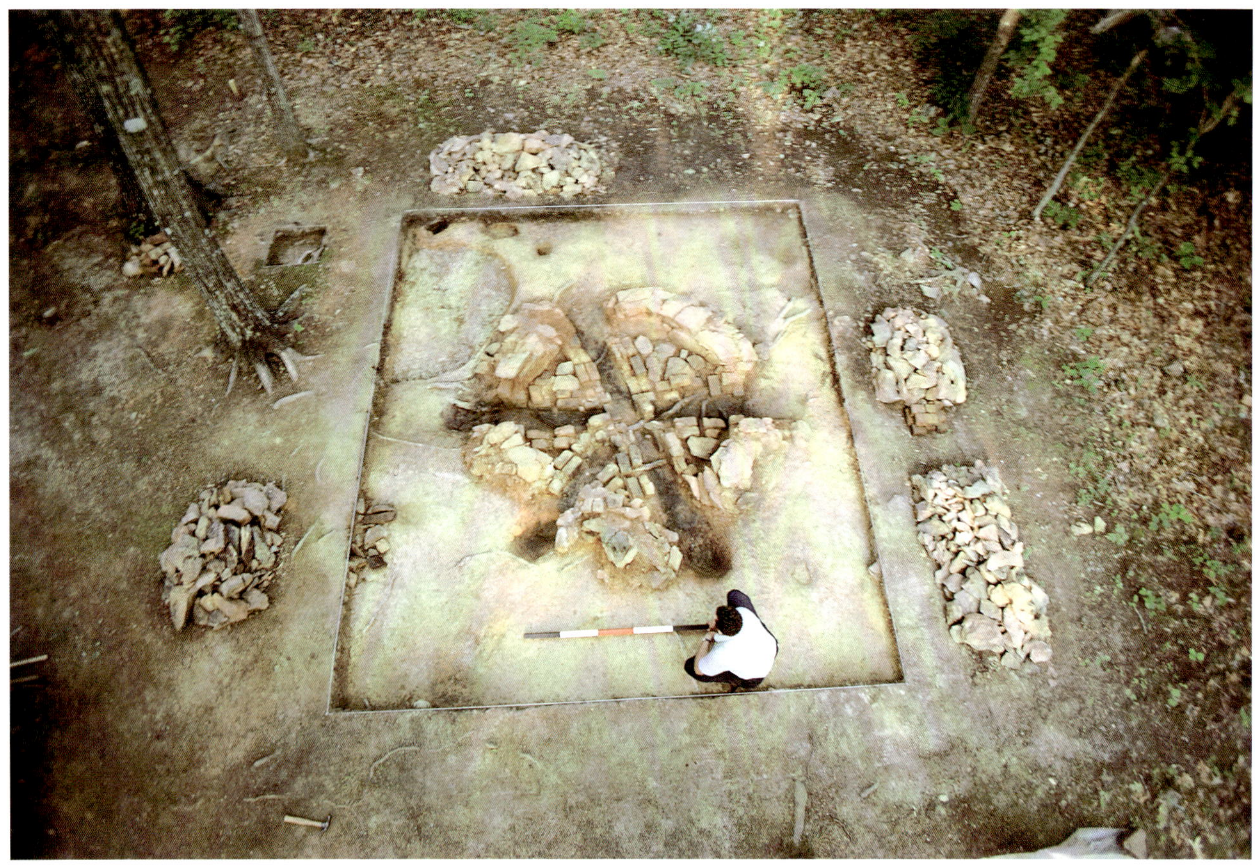

Figure 1 View of completed 15' x 18' excavation encompassing a five-flued kiln. Scale in feet. (All photos, Alain C. Outlaw.)

Excavations of the relatively small and remote operation revealed that a surprisingly large and sophisticated range of pottery was produced at Mount Shepherd (fig. 2). Both wheel thrown and press molded objects manufactured at the site served the needs of the local market, and they included forms for food storage and serving, household heating, and leisure activities. By far, the most prolific vessel form was the undecorated, interior-glazed, utilitarian food storage jar found throughout the entire site, including the last firing of the kiln. A pit contiguous to the kiln was filled with biscuit fired dishes extensively decorated with slip-trailed geometric and floral motifs. Found elsewhere were fragmentary and complete examples of molded reed smoking pipe bowls, bearing fine, crisply detailed faces (fig. 3). Serving a functional as well as a decorative role, press molded biscuit fired stove tiles were also made at Mount Shepherd. The relief motifs include a soldier standing at attention with a musket at his left shoulder and wearing a waistcoat, coat, and tricorn hat (fig. 4).[4] Another reminder of Lascaux, a small headed, long bodied, short-legged horse decorates the surface of other stove tiles (fig. 5). In contrast to its rider who sports a long braided queue, the walking horse's tail is close cropped. The rider is outfitted in a short tailed coat and a jockey-style hat common to those worn by mounted soldiers, or dragoons, in the period.

The discovery of the Mount Shepherd site in 1968 came on the heels of important excavations carried out by Stanley South on Moravian pottery making sites at Bethabara and Salem, North Carolina, from 1963 to 1968.[5]

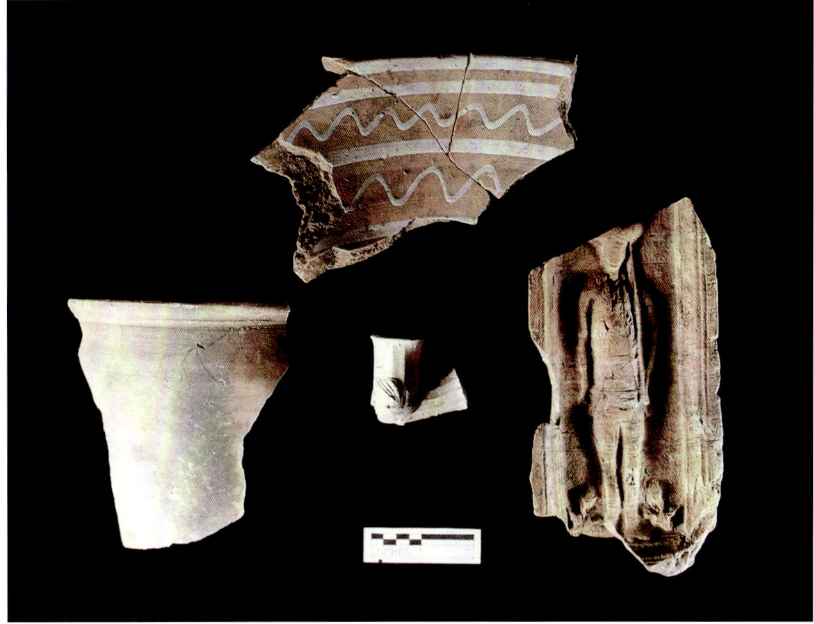

Figure 2 Range of wares produced at Mount Shepherd, North Carolina, 1793–1799. Biscuit fired earthenware. Left to right: storage jar, slipware plate, stove tile. Center: reed pipe bowl. Scale is in inches and centimeters.

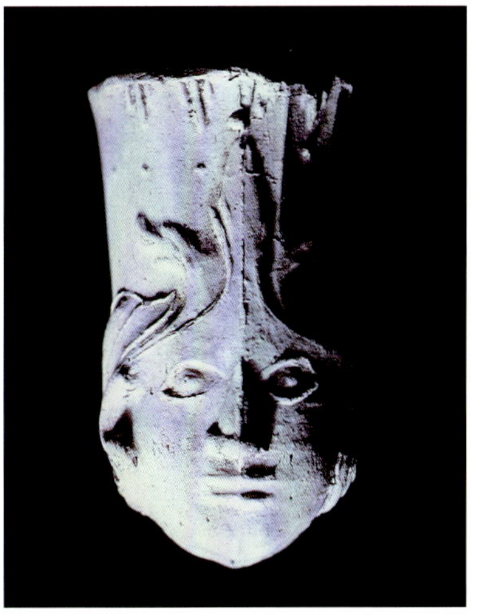

Figure 3 Detail of the anthropomorphic smoking pipe illustrated in figure 2.

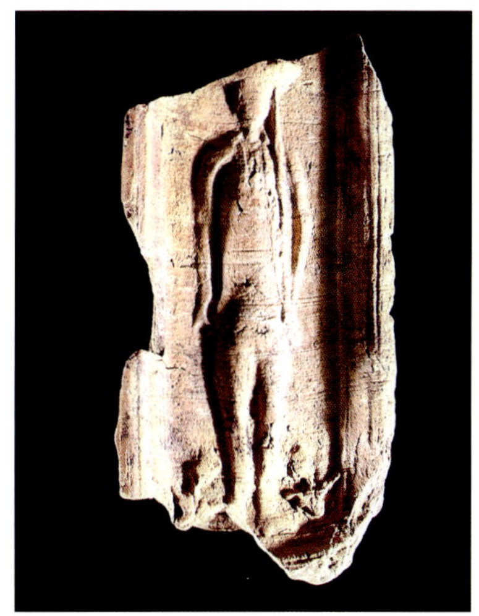

Figure 4 Detail of the soldier stove tile illustrated in figure 2.

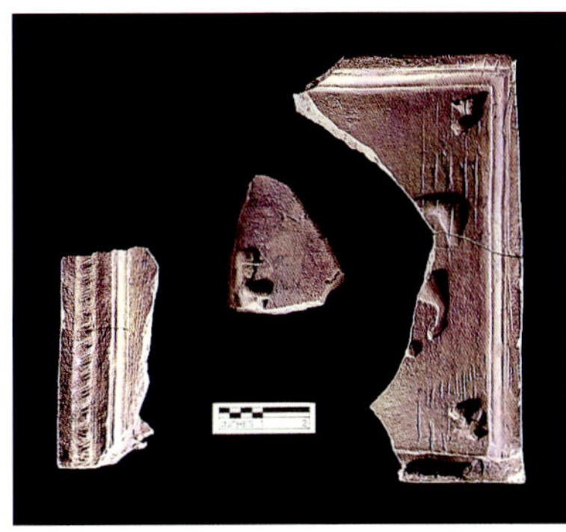

Figure 5 Fragments of a mounted soldier stove tile and border. Scale is in inches and centimeters.

Although the Mount Shepherd wares closely resembled ceramics made by Gottfried Aust from 1755 to 1771, the few non-locally made artifacts recovered dated the site to circa 1775–1800. Obvious from the onset that the Mount Shepherd pottery was manufactured in the Moravian tradition, later artifact and documentary research by L. McKay Whatley divulged the link and name associated with the site. Whatley presented conclusive evidence that a former Aust apprentice, Philip Jacob Meyer (aka Jacob Meyer, Jr.) owned the land and ran the pottery between circa 1793 and 1799.[6]

It is clear from the investigations at this site that sophisticated wares in the region were not exclusively made in the principle Moravian settlements. Not only could these diverse forms be found in the hinterlands, but, like the militaristic motifs unknown in the Moravian pacifist tradition, they could take an unexpected course. This diversity points out that there is yet much to be learned about non-English pottery traditions in North America.

Alain C. Outlaw
Principal Archaeologist
Archaeological & Cultural Solutions, Inc.
Williamsburg, Virginia
<Outlaw@archaeologist.us>
<http://archaeologist.us/>

1. James Wicker, "Archaeologists Explore Old Pottery Site in Randolph," *The Randolph Guide* (North Carolina), Wednesday, April 23, 1969.
2. Alain C. Outlaw, "Preliminary Excavations at the Mount Shepherd Pottery Site," *The Conference on Historic Site Archaeology Papers* 9 (Columbia, S.C.: University of South Carolina, 1974), pp. 2–12.
3. Alain C. Outlaw, *Mount Shepherd Pottery Site,* National Register of Historic Places Inventory–Nomination Form (May 30, 1979).
4. Lowell McKay Whatley, Jr., "Moravian Tile Stoves of the American Colonial Period," (presented to the Department of Fine Arts in Partial Fulfillment of the Requirements for the Degree of Bachelor of Arts with Honors, Harvard College, Cambridge, Mass., April 1, 1977).
5. John Bivins, Jr., *The Moravian Potters in North Carolina* (Chapel Hill, N.C.: The University of North Carolina Press, 1972). Stanley South, *Historical Archaeology in Wachovia–Excavating Eighteenth-Century Bethabara and Moravian Pottery* (New York: Kluwer Academic/Plenum Publishers, 1999).
6. L. McKay Whatley, "The Mount Shepard Pottery: Correlating Archaeology and History," *Journal of Early Southern Decorative Arts* 6, no. 1 (1980): 21–57.

L. Madison Washburn

Toy Story

▼ AMONG THE MORE PRACTICAL accoutrement for shaping a new nation—from mousetraps to weapons—an unexpected rediscovery on Jamestown Island reminds us of history's more playful side. Fitted tightly in a drawer of miscellaneous metals, the buff-colored mold for making toy soldiers was hard to miss.

In the 1950s, National Park Service (NPS) archaeologists recovered the tiny form in Jamestown, Virginia's "New Town" from a mid- to late-seventeenth-century trash pit "containing large quantities of goodies"—an apt characterization for this rare find. In fact, historical documentation of the island's playthings is sparse.[1] The passage of time takes its toll on transient materials; frequently, however, the distinction between adult diversions and children's toys is simply a difficult call.[2] Made of a durable composition, an amalgam of materials like plaster of Paris, sawdust, bran, and glue, the mold is neither altogether fragile nor its intent ambiguous.

Toy soldiers have been found in the ancient tombs of pharoahs and emperors and, most likely, anywhere else sticks, stones, and bits of cloth could be assembled. Thousands of years later children still played soldier, but perhaps waged war with an army of clay. Diminutive wares made from two-part molds, such as toy soldiers and figurines of people and animals, were popular in the seventeenth century. Recovered examples are often made from the same fine-grained and malleable white ball clay that was used to manufacture smoking pipes, an important seventeenth-century industry in England and Holland.

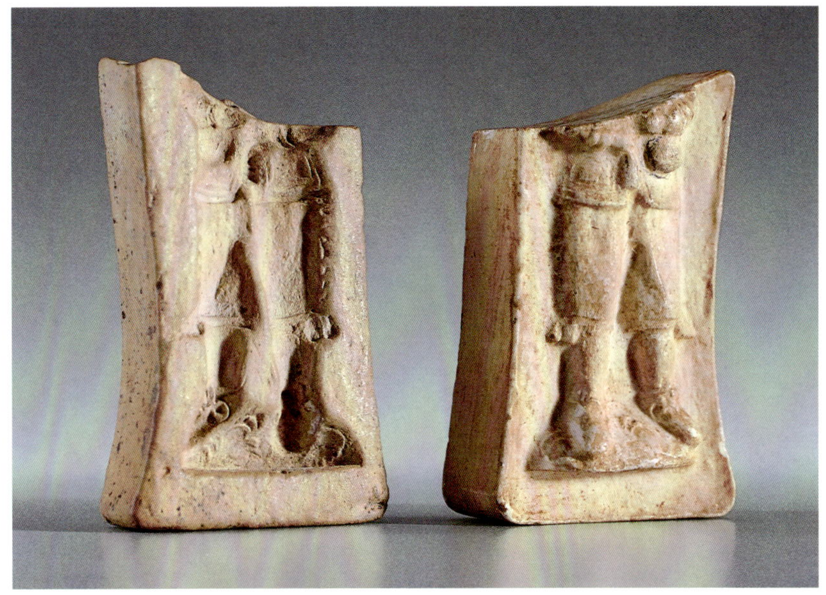

Figure 1 Fragment of a two-part intaglio mold and an impression of a toy soldier found at Jamestown, Virginia. Left: Mold, English, 1650–1700. Composition. H. 1.6". Right: Impression, Harpers Ferry, West Virginia, 1976. Dental plaster. (Courtesy, Colonial National Historical Park, COLO J 7084 and COLO J 30409; photo, Gavin Ashworth.) After cutting away the excess clay, a complete mold would have shaped a tiny figure in three dimension.

By 1625 artisans in the Virginia colony and upper reaches of the Chesapeake, having adapted to the local clays, were also skillfully turning out tobacco pipes. Since the fashionable introduction of smoking and the commercialization of tobacco, pipe making had become a successful enterprise in both the Old World and the New. And the New World, with its growing population and economy, had become an attractive new market for a secondary product. Probably a broken reject from a pipe maker's kit, the mold from Jamestown suggests that toy figurine production—or at least the required tools—had reached America by the second half of the seventeenth century.

Although only a little more than twenty-five percent intact, the mold's negative revealed "the lower half of the soldier (two legs and portion of body as high as the stomach) in intaglio."[4] Almost a quarter of a century after its retrieval, intellectual curiosity got the better of Jamestown's curatorial staff; the fragment was forwarded to the NPS museum laboratory at Harpers Ferry, West Virginia, literally, to fill in the gaps. Dental plaster was employed to produce the positive, accentuating beribboned breeches, lace-up shoes, a simple coat, and a leather pouch strapped securely around the waist. The left hand grasps what appears to be the grip of a regimental flag. Imagination, and a little research, would have to outfit the rest. A breastplate and helmet might have finished off this soldier's garb, creating a more military look and a figure about two inches tall (fig. 1).

The Greek philosopher Plato believed that "you can discover more about a person in an hour of play than in a year of conversation." The same could be said about a nation and its playthings. Perhaps it is fitting that this nation, so much at war—nearly three million killed or wounded in military action since America's declaration of independence—should point to toy soldiers as one of the country's earliest amusements. At least, says one modern-day sage, "in the world of toys, blood is never spilled, the odds are never too high, and the good guys will always win."[5]

L. Madison Washburn
Freelance Writer
Assistant Curator, James River Institute for Archaeology
<Wren946@cs.com>

1. Colonial National Historical Park (CNHP) fieldnotes, Project 102, Structure 17, Refuse Pit 2 (p. 21).

2. Personal communication, 2002, Beverly Straube, Curator, Jamestown Rediscovery™.

3. Ivor Noël Hume, *A Guide to Artifacts of Colonial America* (New York: Alfred A Knopf, 1969), p. 314.

4. John L. Cotter, Chief Archeologist, CNHP (1950–1953), catalog card number COLO J 7084.

5. http://toycollecting.about.com/library/weekly/aa011800a.htm.

Christopher C. Fennell

Molded Malevolence: Instrumental Symbolism Rendered in Clay

▼ EXCAVATIONS AT AN early-nineteenth-century house site in Loudoun County, Virginia, uncovered an artifact that was likely created and used as a material component of a malevolent curse. Such objects, which were typically created and deployed in secret, are rarely found. The artifact is a small clay likeness of a human skull (fig. 1), three-fourths of an inch in height, which was hand sculpted using the red-yellow clay available from the subsoils of the area. The anatomical features of the skull are very well defined and proportioned. On the upper back of the skull is a raised figure of crossed lines or a large "X" (fig. 2). The initials R, M, S, and D appear in raised clay between the arms of the "X" (fig. 3). The initial M is more eroded than the others and could be an H. X-rays reveal that the object has a small loop of iron wire as an internal core (fig. 4). The person who made this figure likely used the wire as a base to hold the clay, sculpting the material when it was partially hardened. This artisan shaped the single form of the skull with its raised inscription and then fired the unglazed figure at a relatively low temperature. The object was not made in a physical mold, but its complex design was likely influenced and shaped by particular religious beliefs and practices.

This skull was uncovered six inches below the soil surface underlying the floorboards of a small house (fig. 5), roughly halfway between the north and south doorway entrances. The object was located in association with other artifacts dating to the period of approximately 1780–1860. The house is located several miles to the south of Harpers Ferry, West Virginia, in a heavily wooded, upland area to the east of the Shenandoah Valley. The surviving structure is one and one-half stories tall, one room deep, two rooms wide, with a central chimney for stoves, and it was constructed of thick, hand-hewn timbers interwoven in a cross-notch fashion. German settlers in this region were primary users of this type of floor plan and building method. However, the region was inhabited by a diverse population, including settlers of Scots-Irish, English, African, German, and Irish heritage. Census, tax, and land ownership records indicate that an Anglo-American family named Demory acquired and settled this property in the early 1800s. An unrecorded occupancy of the site by a family of German heritage may have preceded the Demory family settlement.

Figure 1 Skull, Loudoun County, Virginia, probably ca. 1830–1860. Low-fired earthenware. H. ¾". (All images, Christopher C. Fennell.)

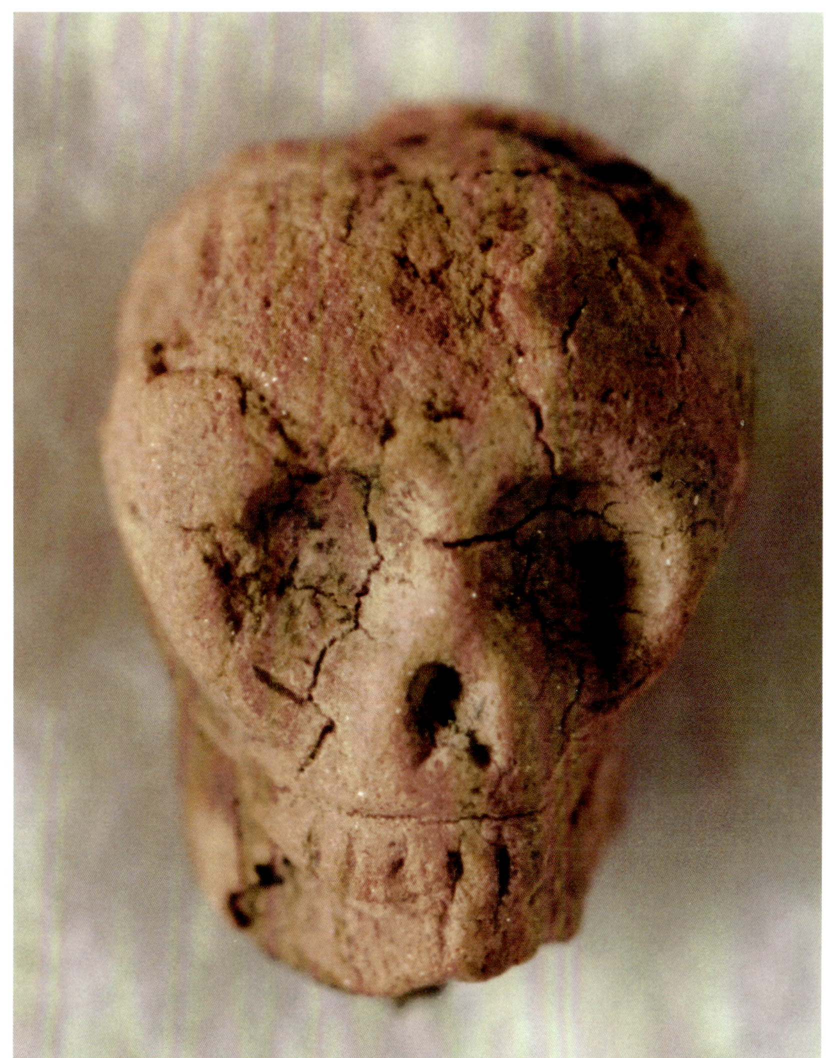

Figure 2 Rear view of the clay skull illustrated in figure 1. This view shows the inscriptions on the sculpted surface.

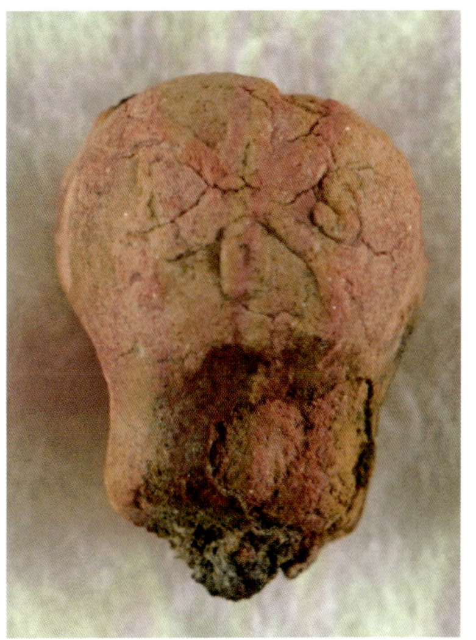

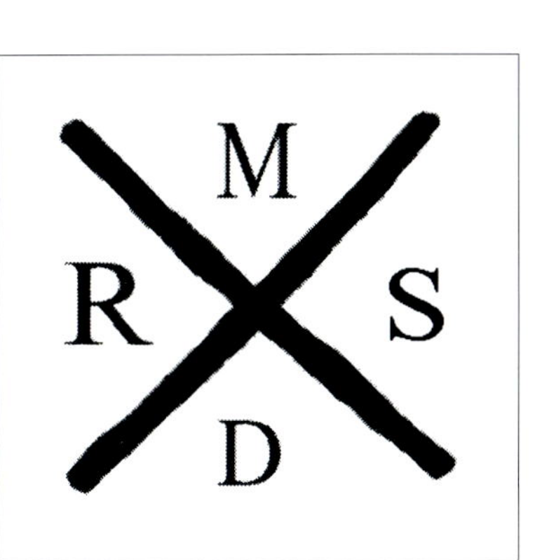

Figure 3 Diagram of the inscription on the back of the skull illustrated in fig. 2.

Figure 4 X-radiograph of the skull, revealing the iron wire used as base for holding the clay.

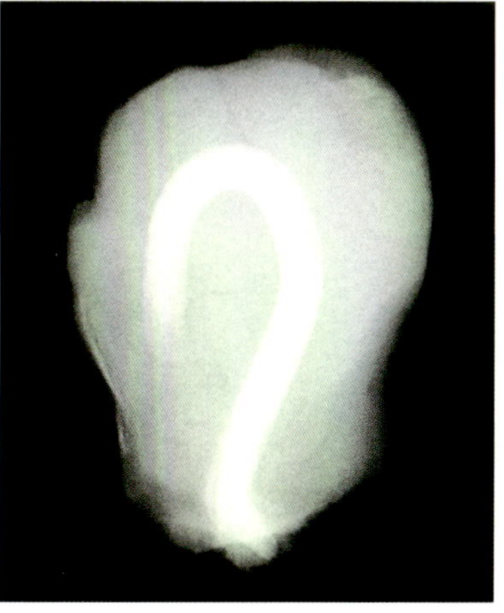

A variety of possible explanations for the artifact's design includes its creation and use as a toy or gaming piece, an icon of a family's armorial crest, an icon of a guild or secret society, or a form of memento mori. However, these interpretations prove unconvincing because none of them can

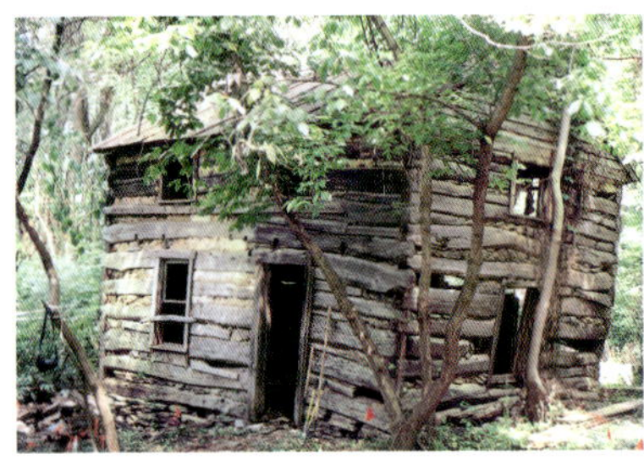

Figure 5 House site in Loudoun Valley, Virginia, where the clay skull was found.

account for all of the object's attributes. The most persuasive explanation is that this object was part of a malevolent curse created pursuant to the beliefs and practices of an African-American or German-American folk religion.

Within certain African-American folk religion beliefs dating to this time period, one would invoke spiritual powers with an instrumental symbol of crossed lines to signify the intersection of the spiritual world with the land of the living. The purpose of the invocation would be communicated by the use of the accompanying symbol of the skull to signify death. The initials would be used to identify the person targeted by the curse. Placing the object in a pathway frequently traversed by the targeted person would facilitate the activation of the curse. Recently discovered documentary evidence indicates that in the 1840s the Demory family owned two enslaved African-American men named Joseph and Henry, one of whom may have been knowledgeable about such beliefs and practices. The initials of "MD" or "HD" also match the names of members of the Demory family. However, the initials "RS" cannot be explained as identifying a targeted person. Detailed census and tax records reveal no one with those initials living in the area during the relevant time periods.

Persons of German-American heritage possessed similar beliefs and practices, often called hexerei or "powwowing," which were the product of a separate history and independent development. Here, too, the crossed lines invoked the summoning of spiritual powers, and the skull figure would communicate a focus on death. The name of the targeted person would be inscribed onto the object, again providing an explanation for the "MD" or "HD" initials. An object with such imagery related to a targeted person could be buried in the ground to symbolize the demise of that individual.

Notably, this German-American tradition also provides an explanation for the "RS" initials. A palindrome square of *rotas* or *sator* was a prominent form of written charm within this belief system, as were inscriptions employing Latin initials, such as "INRI," in geometric patterns. This invocation was created by writing or inscribing a square of five-letter words in Latin:

S A T O R
A R E P O
T E N E T
O P E R A
R O T A S

This translates roughly as "the sower Arepo holds steady the wheels," thus invoking a creative force that controls the wheels of the cosmos and the vicissitudes of fortune. In emphasizing the symmetrical quality of this magic square, inscriptions would often place the word *rotas* first and *sator* last. Protective uses of this charm date back to the late Roman Empire's expansion throughout western Europe and were included in folk religion traditions used by German-Americans in the nineteenth century. The "RS" initials on the clay figure therefore could represent an abbreviation of the *rotas* palindrome, set within a geometric inscription, to provide a further invocation of spiritual forces. This explanation of the purpose and use of the clay skull remains the most persuasive at this juncture because it best accounts for all of the attributes and context of the artifact.[1]

Christopher C. Fennell, Ph.D.
Historical Archaeologist
Department of Anthropology, University of Virginia
<cfennell@alumni.virginia.edu>

1. An extended analysis and related bibliography concerning this subject are available in the author's article entitled "Conjuring Boundaries: Inferring Past Identities from Religious Artifacts," *International Journal of Historical Archaeology* 4, no. 4 (2000): 281–313. Additional details concerning the history of the Loudoun Valley house site and its occupants over time are presented in the author's dissertation, "Consuming Mosaics: Mass-Produced Goods and Contours of Choice in the Upper Potomac Region" (Ph.D. diss., University of Virginia, 2003).

Mark M. Newell

Making His MARK

▼ IN 1996, THE Georgia Archaeological Institute (GAI) began researching Joseph Gregory Baynham, a potter who worked in the Edgefield alkaline-glaze tradition near Trenton, South Carolina, in the 1870s. Begun in 1997, excavations of his pottery production site have surprisingly revealed two sites: the 1870s Joseph Baynham site, situated above the older,

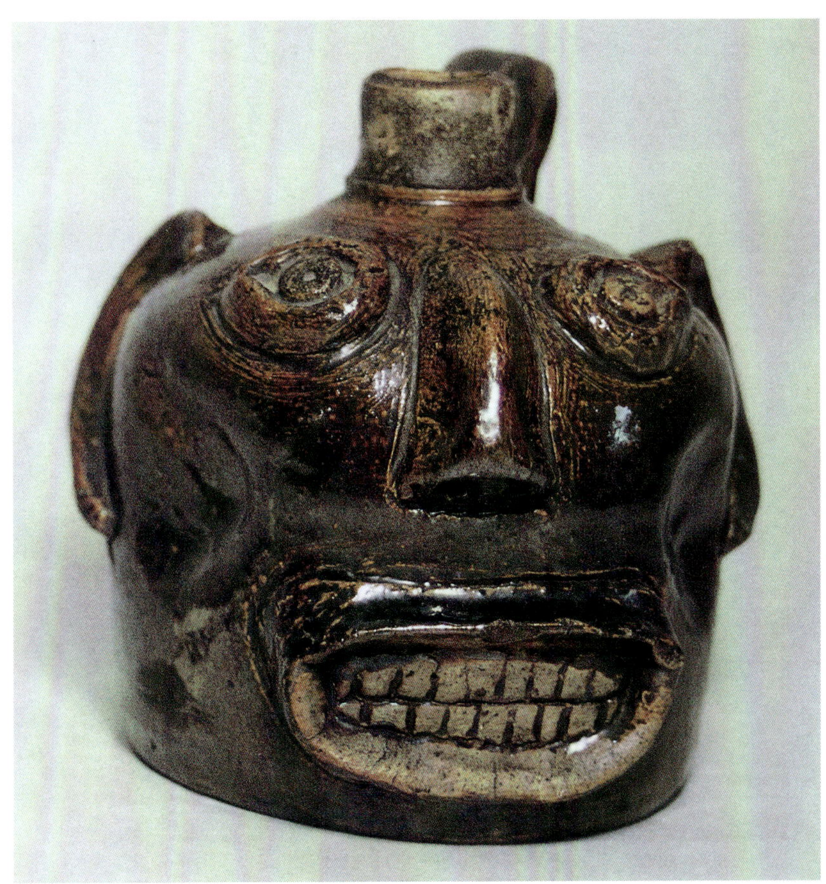

Figure 1 Face jug, Mark Baynham, Trenton, South Carolina, ca. 1900. Albany-slipped stoneware. H. 5". (All photos, courtesy Robert Girouard.) The style shows distinct connections with the face vessels made by African slave potters working in the area since the late 1850s.

Figure 2 Back view of the face jug illustrated in fig. 1. The maker's stamp, MARK• contains a distinct period after his name. This period appears to be an addition to the stamp from earlier versions, and imitates the style of his father's pottery, Joseph Baynham, which is marked JGB•.

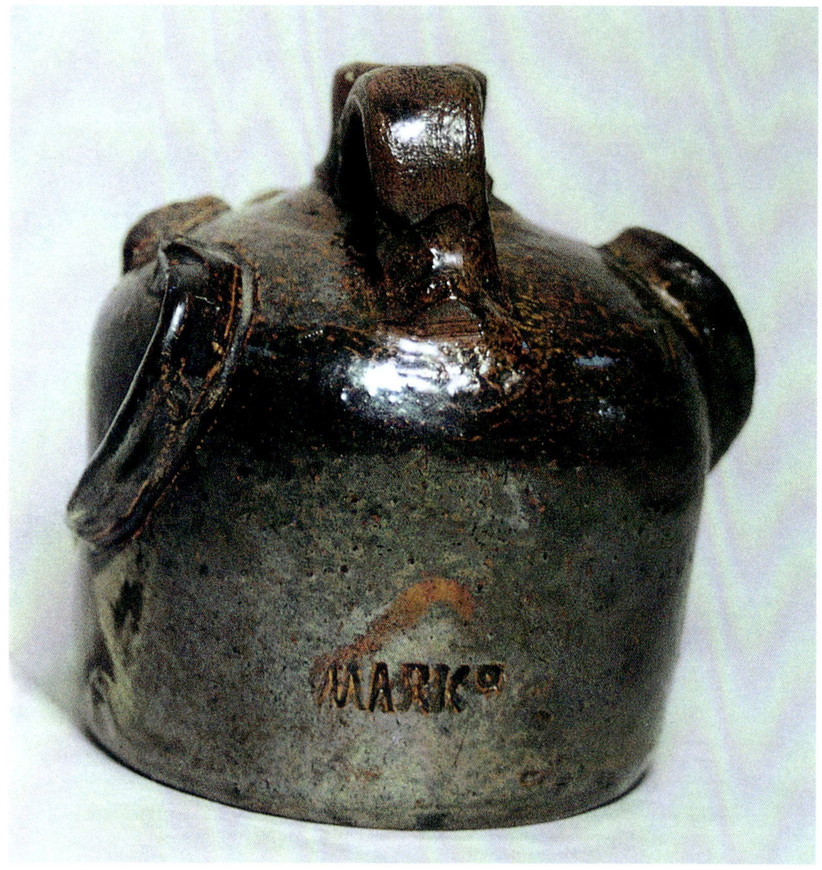

Figure 3 Side view of the face jug illustrated in fig. 1. This view reveals Mark Baynham's distinctive tubular neck and curvaceous neck to shoulder handle.

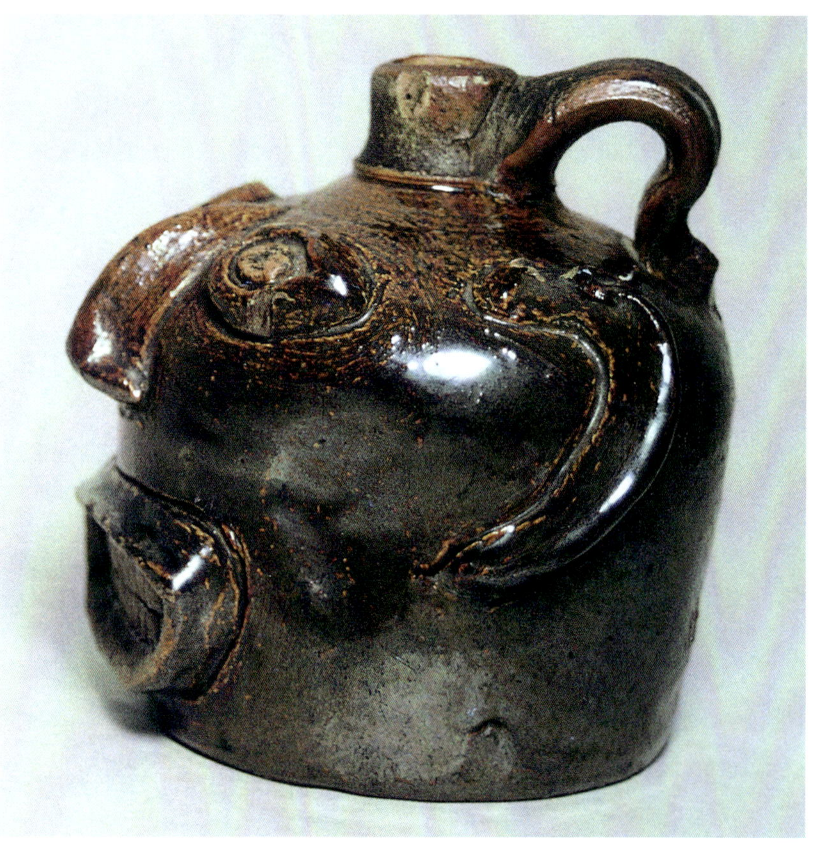

ca. 1862–1872, Lewis Miles site.[1] Differences in styles, glazes, and fabrics have made it possible to attribute the hundreds of vessels recovered to different periods of manufacture, and even to some of the potters who worked there.

In 2002, on the Internet site eBay.com, a small Albany-slipped stoneware face jug was auctioned (fig. 1). The exterior above the base was stamped "MARK•" (fig. 2), and I instantly recognized the marker's mark of Mark Baynham! As well, I could see that the diminutive vessel exhibited Baynham's distinctive tubular neck and gracefully curved neck-to-shoulder handle (fig. 3).

Born in 1878, Mark was the eldest son of Joseph Baynham, and by age nineteen was making his own pottery at his father's Trenton works.[2] During excavations of the site, his stamp "MARK" was found on three whole jugs in a gully filled with intact wasters.[3] A fourth documented example is in a private collection. Now the fifth known complete "MARK" jug, the eBay vessel, is the first evidence that he made face jugs.

Undoubtedly, slave-made face jugs manufactured in Edgefield and dating from the late 1850s influenced Mark, as his jug appears to be directly modeled on those examples. The ears and nose are applied, as are the lips and eyelids. The eyes and teeth are modeled into the unglazed body of the vessel, the teeth being especially reminiscent of the African style vessels. Though not of kaolin as are the African-American face jugs, the teeth and eyeballs are unglazed, implying very careful application of the glaze, again copying the African-American practice.

Fortunately, GAI is continuing investigations at the Baynham/Miles complex site. Artifact studies are enabling scholars to confidently identify products from the site in the archaeological record as well as in aboveground collections. As this research continues, more remarkable new discoveries are sure to follow.

Mark M. Newell, Ph.D.
Director
Georgia Archaeological Institute
<mnewell@yahoo.com>

1. Mark M. Newell, "A Spectacular Find at the Joseph Gregory Baynham Pottery Site," in *Ceramics in America*, edited by Robert Hunter (Hanover, N.H.: University Press of New England for the Chipstone Foundation, 2001), pp. 229–32.

2. Nancy Baynham, *Baynham: A South Carolinian Family* (Augusta, Ga.: Hamburg Press, 2000).

3. Newell, "A Spectacular Find," p. 232.

Book Reviews

Geoffrey H. Priestman. *An Illustrated Guide to Minton Printed Pottery, 1796–1836*. Sheffield, England: Endcliffe Press, 2001. 373 pages, 600 bw illustrations, 115 color plates. $78.00.

Many years ago I was privileged to visit the storeroom for the engraved copper printing plates of Minton's manufactory in Stoke-on-Trent. Joan Jones, the curator of the Minton Collection, estimates that there are some 30,000 copper plates. They include not only table and toiletware patterns for printing in monochrome but also printed outline designs for hand coloring. There are engraved plates for tiles and acid patterns for the rich embellishment of fine bone china, as well. Packed very tightly into pens stretching from floor to ceiling, the plates present a formidable challenge to anyone wishing to research them. Geoffrey Priestman, who undertook this task with determination and dedication, has given us a comprehensive book that should be in the library of every Minton collector and of most collectors of blue-and-white, transfer-printed earthenwares.

Thomas Minton's career as a skilled engraver and entrepreneur is outlined in the first chapter. With the support of his family, Minton was dedicated to producing earthenware and bone china of the highest quality. Personal reminiscences of printers and transferers provide a delightful insight into the factory scene. The naming of patterns by printers is of particular interest, especially those named after the craftsmen who produced them, even if these names never reached the official lists. For example, one Copeland pattern had been christened "Jam Tart," a pattern name that clearly would have made advertising difficult. Instead, it became known as the more marketable "Royal Bracelet," then "Majestic." After this contextual chapter, the book focuses on patterns and shapes attributed to the Minton factory.

A useful Pattern Reference Guide illustrates all of the Minton patterns in full color, enabling the reader to appreciate the delicate differences in the tonal quality of blue. The "Broseley" pattern is the principal Chinese landscape printed in the paler ultramarine blue, whereas most of the other oriental-style designs are printed in the darker royal blue.[1]

The chapter titled "Early Landscapes" (perhaps more aptly called "Early Chinese Landscapes") is a comprehensive catalog of designs, providing valuable comparisons between identical patterns produced by different manufacturers. The same detailed attention has been given to subsequent chapters. One section illustrates the subjects that were used on black prints and bat-printed wares, each one helpfully numbered.

Priestman's attribution to Minton of previously unattributed patterns like "Roman," "Bewick Stag," "Camel and Giraffe," and the "Monk's Rock" series is of the greatest satisfaction. (*The Dictionary of Blue and White Printed Pottery* will need to be updated.[2] And I wonder if a further examination of the reverse of some of the copper plates might reveal indisputable proof of the author's claims?) Despite the enormous number of existing copper plates, it is nevertheless surprising that Priestman was unable to find any for a number of Minton patterns, including "Roman," "Shepherd," "Monk's Rock," and "English Scenery," and only two for "The Hermit" pattern, one of which was engraved on the reverse of another pattern. It seems probable that some of the Minton copper plates were sold in the mid-nineteenth century.

The earliest list of Minton printed patterns is thought to have been made about 1870, at the start of the Franco-Prussian war when the demand for copper for munitions would have affected their value. Other mid-century conflicts that may have affected the disposition of copper plates were the Crimean War from 1853 to 1856 and the Indian Mutiny in 1857. Priestman does not mention the inclusion of the previously named patterns in the 1870 record book, so it seems likely that the copper plates had been sold already. (Copeland produced a similar book about 1865 which recorded all, or nearly all, of the patterns. Some were marked "Engravings destroyed," which meant that copper plates of redundant patterns were "knocked up"—the reverse surface was leveled by knocking up deeply engraved areas so that a new design might be engraved thereon.)

Collectors might wonder why manufacturers did not keep paper records of transfer-printed patterns that were printed in only one color. Keeping records of one color patterns was believed unnecessary because the engravings were almost always available. Pattern books were introduced to record those designs that were either entirely hand decorated or were embellished with extra color applied by hand, known as print and paint. These books usually only recorded patterns that were decorated on top of the glaze, sometimes called "enamel" decorations.

One factor affecting the thickness of the copper plates was the variation in cobalt colors. The early, thin plates were appropriate for the strong, deep color of cobalt blue, so the depth of the engraving was slight. Ceramic historian Paul Holdway has pointed out that the strength of cobalt lessened through time, requiring deeper line engraving and stipple punch work to achieve a comparable result. Hence, thicker copper plates were needed.[3]

For patterns for which no engraved copper plates have been found, Priestman has made use of his extensive collection of ceramic objects, linking their shapes to archival sources and identifying the patterns with those named in the lists retained in the archive collection. In this endeavor, he acknowledges the valuable and dedicated work of the late Alyn Giles Jones, the archivist appointed by John Hartill, the factory's last managing director before Royal Doulton acquired Minton. Jones created and maintained an enormous index of irreplaceable material.

One reason for the book's focus on pattern identification is revealed in the chapter "Early Minton Factory Marks." Nonetheless, one wonders why Minton was so reluctant to link his name to his early transfer-printed wares, only inscribing a modest scripted M instead of the formal printed marks that show such ingenuity of design.

The detailed photographs of printed workmen's marks with the accompanying patterns are especially useful and must have taken a great deal of study to assemble. These marks are distinctive and should help collectors authenticate an attribution to Minton. As Priestman cautions, however, workmen's marks cannot be any more than a guide since workers moved from one manufactory to another, and similar marks could have been used by others.

The chapter illustrating various shapes is quite helpful and, in the finer points of detail, should be of great assistance in attributing unmarked objects to Minton. In particular, the reproduction of part of the 1827 dinnerware factory book showing thirty different hollow ware shapes will be useful to collectors of blue-and-white, transfer-printed pottery.

One criticism, though minor, is the omission of various cup sizes. The inventory of January 1817 (p. 15) lists "London handled teacups @ 5/- dozen, Norfolk handled cups @ 4/6 dozen, and Irish handled cups @ 6/6 dozen." London-size cups were the most common. Today, as in 1817, a teacup holds about seven to eight fluid ounces, so the most expensive Irish-size cup probably relates to today's breakfast-size cup, which holds nine to ten fluid ounces. The Norfolk cup may be equivalent to the coffee cup, holding five and one-half fluid ounces. As late as 1872, an industry *Foreign Price List* records only Norfolk-, London-, and Irish-size cups.

Also, the sizes of hollow ware (p. 257) are misrepresented. Numbers like 12s, 24s, 36s, and so forth, represent the number of clay objects to be counted carried on a six-foot ware board into the "greenhouse" (where the unfired, or "green," clayware was collected and placed into the biscuit oven). A 12s pitcher, while being the basis for pricing a "potter's dozen," was also about five to five and one-half inches in diameter and would have held about two and one-half to three pints of fluid. A 36s pitcher holds one pint of sixteen fluid ounces. The "sizes" refer to dimensions, rather than to capacity. A clay maker needed to make, say, thirty-six pitchers of that size in order to earn the price per dozen. These sizes have been abandoned because the present staff in retail shops no longer understands the peculiarities of the pottery counts.[4]

Illustration captions are clear and detailed, including measurements in millimeters and approximate dates. The photographs are distinct and of a size that makes it easy to distinguish important features. Pictures of the plate's and saucer's reverse are unusual, but helpful. Use of the term foot *ring* is to be applauded, instead of the more widely used, and incorrect, term foot *rim*.

At the end of each chapter there is a list of references, 186 altogether, many attributed to the Minton archive collection. There is no separate bibliography. The two indexes—one solely for pattern names—complete this truly remarkable, thoroughly researched, and superbly illustrated publication.

The book's importance as a record of the Minton factory heritage is accentuated by the pending loss of some of the material products of that tradition. The Minton manufactory site has been vacated and, as I write in May 2002, is being offered for sale along with most of the ceramic collection. Joan Jones has succeeded in retaining a small number of representative pieces for display in the Minton Room at the Royal Doulton Visitor Centre in Stoke-on-Trent. The copper plate archive collection and the paper archive collection are accommodated at the Nile Street site of Royal Doulton in Burslem, Stoke-on-Trent.

Robert Copeland
Historical Consultant to The Spode Museum Trust, Stoke-on-Trent

1. Robert Copeland, *Spode's Willow Pattern and Other Designs after the Chinese*, 3rd ed. (London: Studio Vista/Cassell, 1999), opposite p. 70.

2. A. W. Coysh and R. K. Henrywood, *The Dictionary of Blue and White Printed Pottery, 1780–1880* (Woodbridge, Suffolk, Eng.: Antique Collectors' Club, 1982). A. W. Coysh and R. K. Henrywood, *The Dictionary of Blue and White Printed Pottery, 1780–1880*, vol. 2 (Woodbridge, Suffolk, Eng.: Antique Collectors' Club, 1989).

3. David Drakard and Paul Holdway, *Spode Printed Ware* (London: Longman, 1983), p. 25.

4. Robert Copeland, *Spode and Copeland Marks and Other Relevant Intelligence*, 2nd ed. (London: Studio Vista, 1997), pp. 142–43.

Henry Glassie. *The Potter's Art*. Philadelphia, Pa., and Bloomington and Indianapolis, Ind.: Material Culture and Indiana University Press, 1999. 149 pages; 76 bw and 25 color illustrations; bibliography, index. Photography and design by the author. $10.40 (softcover).

"It is good to be a potter. At work, the potter manages the transformation of nature, building culture while fulfilling the self, serving society, and patching the work together with pieces of clay that connect the past with the present, the useful with the beautiful, the material with the spiritual" (p. 116). In *The Potter's Art*, Indiana University folklore professor Henry Glassie has given us simple explanations for complicated mechanisms that define the intersection of ceramic objects and human society from the potter's point of view. This is a global story, enriching our view of the craftsman with portraits of dignity, nobility, and sincerity, and exposing the complexity of a simple, traditional utilitarian pot. Based on his wide-ranging fieldwork carried out over a lifetime of looking at pottery and talking to potters, Glassie's treatise explores the nature of art and demonstrates the common links that join potters across diverse cultures.

Henry Glassie likes potters. He wants us to share his enthusiasm. And, frankly, it is hard to resist his passion in *The Potter's Art.* In this slim volume, we meet a mix of potters from around the world: the Pals of Bangladesh who make *kalshis* (common utilitarian pots of all kinds) and *murtis* (images of the deities for worship); traditional stoneware potter Lars Andersson of Raus in Skåne, Sweden; the Meaders and Hewell families, figural stoneware potters of Georgia; Acoma, New Mexico, potters Lilly Salvador and Marvis and Wanda Aragon, who base their contemporary collectible pottery on ancient patterns and practices; the master potters and decorators of Kütahya, Turkey; the Tatebayashi family of Kakiemon potters in Arita, Japan; and the potters of *yaki* ware working in Hagi, Japan. This diversity is reflected in their wares, which have been carefully chosen to exhibit both sacred and secular goals, ranging from the Bangladeshis' *murtis* to the Georgians' face jugs.

For students just learning about ceramics, the insights presented here will likely be a revelation about goods that most people ignore. As Glassie notes, his "goal is to illustrate how common clay is made to carry value" (p. 19). For collectors who have loved these pots for years, his words are confirmation of long-held beliefs. Those readers who fall in between these extremes, however, will likely be struck by his narrow definition of value in clay. Glassie's potters make things by hand in traditional forms and glazes; Glassie, the folklorist, values folk over fine, handmade over machine made. He explains that hand work takes time out from the "rush for modernity," that "technological process divides people from the earth and separates the mind from the hands, reducing art to design" (pp. 54–56). Ergo, we will not find English shell-edge pearlware or Russel Wright's famous *American Modern* dinnerware discussed in this book. But that should not keep us from embracing Glassie's point of view, at least for the duration of his narrative. Indeed, readers who choose to follow along are rewarded by Glassie's inspiring insights into pottery. The section on transformations, for example, is pure poetry. Here he rhapsodizes on pottery as it goes from wet to dry, soft to hard, dull to bright, and useless to useful.

On the central issue of his treatise, however, Glassie waffles. He explains that art is a cultural phenomenon in which the object's value is defined by its integration into society, rather than its rarity or monetary value. "Art disturbs nature to embody values," he writes, "the object's worth lying in its ability to provoke and sustain argument" (p. 18). He cautions that this definition of art is not a market phenomenon; it is not defined as the part of the marketplace where art equals higher prices (or even the reverse, that high price equals art). He blames the market for skewing the production values of potters through the buyer's misunderstanding of what art is: "Conditioned by ideas from art-appreciation classes so suffused with the idea of the pictorial that the craft of photography has been embraced as an art, and the art of pottery is still called a craft, today's buyers want few churns and many face jugs" (p. 39). He laments that many potters shift from utilitarian ware to ornamental in order to see their work gain higher monetary value. In a modern society that uses plastics, machine-made ceramics, and metals for utilitarian purposes, we want our handmade pots to be decorative. Finally, he admonishes us to see things differently: "Where use meets beauty, where nature transforms into culture and individual and social goals are accomplished, where the human and numinous come into fusion, where objects are richest in value—there is the center of art" (p. 34).

On the other hand, he cherishes the ability of potters to pursue their art by adapting to new markets, for we are also shown how the execution and interpretation of selected wares have changed positively over time. For example, Glassie demonstrates how Acoma pots once used to carry water are now valued for the high prices they can attain in Santa Fe art galleries. Because of these shifts in value, the art of decoration is driven toward greater perfection. In Kütahya, Turkey, the number of ateliers (and pottery workers) actually increased during the twelve-year period that Glassie studied them, from the mid-1980s to the late 1990s, because the city's art has gained global recognition. This new value gives the potters and decorators confidence in their skills and in themselves to carry forward in other aspects of their lives. Similarly, families of traditional stoneware potters continue to work in Georgia because buyers see art in their face jugs and are willing to pay prices that keep the potters in business.

Glassie would rather that the work of these potters was integrated into their societies as it had been in the old ways, but he's willing to accept their current successes as an opportunity to meet and study them as living beings. If their work had been completely eclipsed by modern society, if they were no longer living and working as potters, he would have had only their historic wares at hand. He yearns for potters of the past, but welcomes the company of potters in the present. This is not a bad thing, although one wonders why Glassie, with all his passionate embrace of potters, has not taken to the wheel himself.

If you like pots, *The Potter's Art* is a "feel good" book. After reading it you will feel good about the potters. You will feel good about their pots. And you will feel good about yourself for being able to appreciate it all. You might even learn a thing or two. All of which makes it a worthwhile book to read, despite its limited range of appreciation for the ceramic arts.

One final note regarding the origins of *The Potter's Art*. The book is a revision and slight expansion of the fourth chapter of *Material Culture,* Glassie's textbook study of material culture, a concept which he defines as the "place" where history and art connect.[1] For those who know this chapter entitled "The Potter's Art," the book *The Potter's Art* will seem very familiar and may not need to occupy space on your shelf. On the other hand, those who are attracted to the study of pottery in the context of material culture studies may find that *Material Culture* is a more appropriate purchase than *The Potter's Art.*

Ellen Paul Denker
Museum consultant and writer

1. Henry Glassie, *Material Culture* (Bloomington, Ind.: Indiana University Press), 1999.

Charles L. Venable, Ellen P. Denker, Katherine C. Grier, and Stephen G. Harrison. *China and Glass in America, 1880–1980: From Tabletop to TV Tray.* Dallas: Dallas Museum of Art, 2000. Photography by Tom Jenkins. 496 pp., 345 illustrations (255 in color), catalog documentation, references, index. $49.50.

From Tabletop to TV Tray takes a comprehensive look at a century of changes in dining and the American market as reflected by tableware. Packed with information and illustrations, this fine book is recommended for collectors, archaeologists, museum curators, historians, and others interested in American culture, tablewares, the pottery industry, and material culture from 1880–1980.

The book presents 209 catalog entries from the more than 500 objects in the collections of the Dallas Museum of Art and the Newark Museum, both of which hosted the accompanying exhibit. Focusing on objects made for household use in the American market, the collection includes American and foreign manufacturers such as Wedgwood, Spode, Homer Laughlin, Lenox, Haviland, Rosenthal, and Noritake.

Despite the central role of tableware in many cultures, most art museums do not seriously collect "dishes." Connoisseurship, recent age, mass production, and utilitarian function have worked against the collection and study of modern tablewares, as has the perceived superiority of twentieth-century modernism over more conservative revival designs. On the other hand, thriving online auctions, mass-market antiques publishing, ceramic collectors clubs, and flea market economies show that plenty of collectors put serious time and money into collecting dishes. Groups such as the Friends of Blue, Transferware Collectors Club, White Ironstone China Association, and Tea Leaf International abound, competing for every known maker, vessel form, pattern, or shape.

The authors bring to the tabletop not only their professional experiences in the museum, history, American studies, and anthropology fields but also their collecting interests as self-described "dishaholics." All four admit to home cupboards bulging with tablewares bought at department stores and antique stores or acquired as gifts and travel souvenirs. In addition, the charming introduction to chapter 1 includes descriptions of family dish legacies that each author will inherit—from Franciscan Ware's "Woodside" pattern to Limoges porcelain in a floral and gilded pattern, and from Bavarian china in a rose pattern edged in gold to the "Ballerina" shape of Universal Potteries.

Design, production, marketing, and consumption aspects of tableware are all considered in this book. Chapter 1 by Kasey Grier with Stephen Harrison provides a social history of modern tableware in the American market, delightfully illustrated with contemporary advertisements and photographs. This chapter touches on a variety of issues, such as mail order catalogs, open stock purchasing, specialty tableware, and cocktails and drinking in the home. The placement of this consumption-oriented chapter at the book's beginning gives substance to a diverse and changing American market. Among the chapter's wealth of information is a citation from Lucy Allen's 1915 book, *Table Service,* indicating the relationship between middle-class family tableware sets of the late Victorian/Edwardian era and cheap domestic labor. According to this book's guidelines, a four-course dinner for six diners called for a total of 151 service dishes, place settings, and flatware pieces to be washed, or twenty-five pieces per diner.[1]

The focus of the next two chapters is on tableware production. Chapter 2 by Lenox archivist Ellen Denker with Charles Venable covers American production, and chapter 3 by Charles Venable with Stephen Harrison describes foreign (primarily British and Japanese) production. Case studies in both chapters also include useful information on design and marketing. Data presented in chapter 3 on British imports, critical to the American market until the end of the nineteenth century, could have been summarized better graphically. The description of post-World War II British production is extremely useful.

Chapter 4 by Charles Venable describes marketing. Chapter 5 by Charles Venable and Stephen Harrison focuses on design but also covers marketing. Intriguing trends include the end of open stock selling and the shift to sales of place settings in the late 1930s and especially after World War II; adversely, set sizes and the variety of sizes and shapes offered to department stores and consumers shrank considerably. Sidebars sketch histories of importers Ebeling & Reuss of Philadelphia, designers Frank Graham Holmes of Lenox and contract designer Belle Kogan, the Pittsburgh trade show, retailer Marshall Field, and bridal registries.

Tom Jenkins' stunning photography provides its own narrative of changes in the American market, reducing the light to avoid glare on whitewares, while using the transparent qualities of glass to make the subjects sparkle. Photographs are balanced with a variety of advertisements and other ephemera to provide context for the great variety of wares.

Most of the catalog entries were written by Venable and Harrison with contributions by Denker. Information includes shape and pattern names, dates, makers, designers, size, and marks. Catalog illustrations are integrated seamlessly into the body of the text. No marks are illustrated. The integration of porcelain, earthenware, and glass objects into a single catalog makes good sense on a consumption level, as well as in terms of design and marketing.

I offer a few notes on the exhibit, which I saw at the Newark Museum. I enjoyed the "Great Wall of China," displaying an array of plate decorations, and I really appreciated the use of the Vernon Kilns "Our America" pattern, featuring a map of the United States with an accompanying panel describing the American market. Another attentive touch: the exhibit invited those people who actually used these dishes to interact by jotting down their tabletop memories in a handy notebook for visitors.

The part of the exhibit that I kept coming back to was the video area set up in the front hall of the Newark Museum. It featured a living room setting with a 1950s-vintage television showing "Choice in China," a post-World War II trade film by the American Fine China Guild. Despite the film's premise (the ghost of an old potter guides his descendant in selecting her china pattern, with scenes at home, at the china store, and in the factory), which seems campy to twenty-first-century eyes, the video touched on important aspects of production, marketing, and consumption.

In addition to factory images of chemistry, filling clay presses, batting out and jiggering, slip casting, fettling, lining, applying decals, and applying handles, three scenes portrayed the competition between American and British manufacturers, porcelain versus earthenware, and problems of glaze crazing. In one of these scenes a china salesman was pushing the young lady to purchase American china by disparaging British bone china as heavy, while an older (hilariously British) couple urged her not to buy the British ware.

Another scene set up a not-so-subtle demonstration of the stain-resistant properties of earthenware and porcelain plates. Each ware was dipped into dye, which completely washed off the porcelain plate, but left the earthenware plate stained. As crazing was a problem for British and later American white granite wares when first introduced, the video demonstration showed that earthenware crazes, porcelain does not. (The crazed earthenware plate was promptly dropped into the trash can!) This video reminded me strongly of the promotional booklet, *The Potter's Wheel,* published by a Trenton pottery in the 1880s.[2] The booklet's premise involved an unfortunate accident with a folding table, a lot of broken china, and a tour through the Burroughs & Mountford factory in Trenton for replacements. The booklet, despite its clichéd premise, like the video provides a wealth of good description and illustrations of contemporary pottery manufacture and decoration.

There must have been compelling reasons to place the video area at the exhibit's front and center. Perhaps it was because the TV tray symbolized the exhibit's title, but the location and technical limitations detracted from the video's impact. The main problem was the video location in a noisy open area between the front door and the atrium, which meant street noise (including a fire engine parade) drowned out the audio. The vintage television was visually perfect, but the screen size was small and the video quality poor. The use of an authentic set probably limited potential for improving sound that could have been remedied by headphones with adjustable volume controls. The slide show nearby had headphones and was perfectly audible, but it was the video that intrigued me, and I stayed through several showings until I had heard the entire clip.

The exhibit and book successfully bridge the gap between museum and popular interests in a century's worth of wares on the American table. The unified multiauthor voice helps make this publication successful as a research contribution, museum catalog, and collector book. The result is a book suited, fittingly enough, for both nostalgic coffee-table browsing, as well as for serious reading about pottery, china, and glass in America.

Amy C. Earls
Ceramics in America

1. Lucy G. Allen, *Table Service* (Boston: Little, Brown, 1919).
2. W. S. Harris, *The Potter's Wheel and How It Goes Round in the Nineteenth Century* (Trenton, N. J.: Burroughs and Mountford, [1886]).

Amanda E. Lange. *Delftware at Historic Deerfield, 1600–1800.* Deerfield, Massachusetts: Historic Deerfield, Inc., 2001. 165 pp.; 169 color illus., bibliography. $50.00.

Deerfield's extensive collection of English tin-glazed earthenware, commonly called delftware, is the basis for the catalog *Delftware at Historic Deerfield, 1600–1800* and major exhibition "Delicate Deception." As the first in a series of decorative arts catalogs planned by Deerfield, this thoroughly researched and beautifully illustrated publication showcases not only the museum's collection but also the scholarship of curator Amanda Lange and her staff.

The majority of delft objects in the museum's collection were given by two couples, Henry and Helen Flynt, Deerfield's founders, and Reginald and Rachel French. The Flynts purchased many rare and spectacular examples from major dealers, while the Frenches concentrated on more common pieces with local histories. It is unusual for two such different collecting philosophies to be represented in one collection, but Lange wisely has combined them with recent acquisitions and loans to display a broad spectrum of tin-glazed wares. Three essays introduce the catalog. "Collecting Delftware at Historic Deerfield" focuses on the Flynts, who were influenced by Colonial Williamsburg and especially Winterthur to enhance their carefully assembled interiors with ceramics. Of the dealers who supplied the Flynts with ceramics, John Kenneth Byard and Millie Manheim are profiled in this chapter. Although it is understandable that the Flynts should have top billing, it is disappointing that less than one paragraph was devoted to the Frenches. As Lange says in her final sentence, "The French collection's breadth of ceramic patterns virtually makes it an encyclopedia of delftware exported to the New England region" (p. 10).

The second essay covers the history and manufacture of delftware, concentrating on the introduction and development of the ware in the British Isles. In 1567, two potters arrived in Norwich from Holland, founding an industry that continued for more than two centuries. Lange attributes delftware's popularity to the passion for Chinese porcelain, so easily imitated by delft, and the change in dining and drinking patterns requiring specialized ceramics; its fragility, especially when used for hot liquids, was the reason for its decline. This is an abbreviated version of a well-documented history. Lange does not address the similarities between the early English and Dutch delftwares nor the histories of the individual pottery centers.

"Delftware in the Connecticut River Valley," the third essay, is the most valuable for students of U.S. ceramic consumption. Much has been written about delftware in the mid-Atlantic region, most notably John Austin's comprehensive volume on Williamsburg. However, aside from the catalog of the China Students Club of Boston's fiftieth anniversary exhibit, little research has been published on delftware in New England.[1]

Lange's presentation of evidence from probate inventories and merchants' accounts in the Connecticut River Valley, combined with family artifacts from the Dr. John Williams household, reveals that the most commonly listed items were plates and bowls, with gallipots and ointment jars appearing archaeologically. The inhabitants of Deerfield were slow to replace pewter and treen with earthenware, so delftware did not enjoy the same popularity there as it did in New England seaports. Considering the difference in terminology between eighteenth-century accounts and current names for ceramic forms, and the fact that smaller items were frequently combined in inventories, it may well be that Deerfield households had a greater variety of delftware than previously realized. The catalog is organized by functional category: dining wares, flower containers, lighting devices, and an impressive collection of ointment pots. Some of the more unusual items in the collection, although not specified in Connecticut River Valley inventories, have been noted in other New England locations. Flower containers, stands or salvers, draining bowls or colanders, salts, and monteiths are among them.

It is important to remember that the most common utilitarian vessels are least likely to survive. While the London-made bottle and basin (fig. 90) are beautiful examples of toilet articles, hand-wash basins and plain chamber pots far outnumbered any other forms in sanitary wares. Similarly, small, undecorated ointment pots are common archaeologically but were too unimportant to appear in inventories.

Lange introduces each functional category with a brief history of the customs of the times relating to ceramic use. She then describes each object, adding historical or archaeological data concerning the related pieces. For example, figures 15 and 16, punch bowls decorated with blue fish on powdered manganese ground, are accompanied by an explanation of the fish as a symbol of drinking and with references to other fish bowls in North American contexts. This is extremely valuable research information.

The publication of *Irish Delftware* by Peter Francis has drawn attention to delftware production in other locations in the British Isles.[2] New England ships were calling regularly at Scottish and Irish ports, so it should be no surprise that ceramics were included in the trade; however, this exhibit is the first to display pieces with New England histories. The French collection contains examples with local histories from Delftfields in Glasgow and possibly from Dublin. Both Irish and Scottish sherds have been identified recently in Portsmouth, New Hampshire. Lange has correctly attributed these pieces when possible and has explained the difficulty in distinguishing between Liverpool and Dublin examples.

Mounting a major ceramics exhibit presents challenges for many museums. It is especially difficult to create an exhibit that will appeal to both the general museum audience and to specialists in the field. Highly ornamental wares, like Meissen porcelain, present well in exhibit galleries, but delft, with its inexpensive, utilitarian forms, is much more difficult to display. Although Lange's research has produced an impressive teaching experience, and she draws from an extensive collection, the objects themselves lack the drama of high-style ceramics, and a large gallery space tends to diminish rather than enhance their impact. The space does allow for more use of partial room settings with appropriate accessories, such as the dining table arrangement. This type of presentation could have also been used for other categories and would have worked well with Historic Deerfield's large collection of related objects. A video of contemporary potter Michelle Erickson making delftware reproductions not only helped to explain the potting process but also provided a connection with the people who originally produced these pieces.

In complete contrast to the exhibit gallery are the visible storage study galleries, where most of the French collection resides. Here, the ceramics enthusiast can find case upon case of objects, each carefully identified. The catalog combines the best of both presentations. The dust jacket, with its multiple plates, is as enticing as the study of galleries, while the catalog entries give a thorough analysis of each significant object.

Delftware at Historic Deerfield is a valuable reference in a compact volume. It deserves a place in the library of anyone with an interest in English delftware exported to North America.

Louise P. Richardson
Research Associate for Ceramics, Strawbery Banke Museum

1. John C. Austin, *British Delft at Williamsburg* (Williamsburg, Va.: Colonial Williamsburg Foundation in association with Jonathan Horne Publications, 1994); China Students Club of Boston, *Unearthing New England's Past: The Ceramic Evidence* (Lexington, Mass.: Scottish Rite Masonic Museum of Our National Heritage, 1984).

2. Peter Francis, *Irish Delftware: An Illustrated History* (London: Jonathan Horne Publications, 2000).

Nancy E. Owen. *Rookwood and the Industry of Art: Women, Culture, and Commerce, 1880–1913*. Athens, Ohio: Ohio University Press, 2001. 355 pp.; color plates, b/w figures, appendix, notes, bibliography, index. $24.95.

Rookwood enthusiasts might compare reading *Rookwood and the Industry of Art* to a train ride. Those readers already interested in American art pottery, china painting, international expositions, and decorative arts at the turn of the twentieth century will enjoy the trip immensely. Written by Nancy E. Owen, a lecturer in American art and women's studies at Northwestern University in Evanston, Illinois, the well-designed and generously illustrated text (many familiar images) focuses on running the Rookwood pottery business. At departure, the author announces the journey's route: "This book explores the ways in which the production, marketing, and consumption of Rookwood pottery reflect and inflect the commercial and cultural milieu in the United States from 1880 to 1913" (p. 2). Owen arrives at her destination after concluding that Rookwood was so successful at marketing itself as art that it failed commercially in the years before World War I.

There are some interesting meanderings and important stops during the trip. Chapter 1 introduces the 1876 Philadelphia Centennial Exhibition, the American aesthetic movement, American ceramics at the Centennial, and the American art pottery movement. Chapter 2 addresses women in middle-class American culture during the late nineteenth century and their role in the arts, in Cincinnati (where the Rookwood industry originated), and at Rookwood. In chapters 3 and 4 readers learn valuable information about the pottery's labor history, the ideal aesthetic of the arts and crafts workshop, and the impracticality of that model for Rookwood, although its pottery operators used romance to ensconce all of its output as art. In her discussion of Rookwood and its participation in international expositions of the late nineteenth and early twentieth centuries in chapter 5, Owen addresses the question posed to institutions and individuals attending these exhibits: "What's so American about Rookwood?" Chapter 6 tackles the difficult task of placing a name, face, and class on the pottery's consumers, and the epilogue lists the changes in technology and world order that helped end Rookwood's elite position in the national market.

Readers meet some fascinating individuals along the way. Photographs of seated women—each with a paintbrush in hand—gazing at a decorated Rookwood pot are interpreted rightly as portraits "reminiscent of a long tradition of representations of male painters in their studios" (p. 94). Former pottery manager William Watts Taylor, who was given the Rookwood business by founder Maria Longworth Nichols Storer, reveals himself in a complaint to colleague Charles Fergus Binns, "The Pottery has been written about to a rather tiresome degree from the 'woman's standpoint' and . . . you can imagine how this has been rather written to death. . . . Of course you know Rookwood so well that you appreciate how its characteristic development has been the work of the other sex to at least a controlling extent" (p. 16). Owen also introduces the thorny personality of decorator Laura A. Fry and recounts the lawsuit she brought against the pottery for alleged patent infringement of a Fry-developed atomizer used for decorating ceramics. (Rookwood won the suit.) Another decorator, Patti Conant, expresses a laborer's point of view as she reminisces about her career at the pottery: "The prestige of being a Rookwood decorator and the 'love of art for art's sake' was supposed to compensate for the very low pay, which is just unbelievable today"(p. 78). All the while, readers learn about people deeply engaged in the art and business of the pottery industry.

There are some snags in the line. Owen states that her book is based on her dissertation. Such a document usually includes a review of the literature, as well as the author's contribution to the overall scholarship of the topic. *Rookwood and the Industry of Art* would have done well to include such a review since there has been so much written on the pottery hailed as a "dominating force in the pottery market." Authors of dissertations also typically state what is original about their inquiry. While not addressed in this publication, I venture to say that Owen's book-length focus on Rookwood attempts to expand a strictly art history perspective to include a cultural history context, including commerce and consumerism.

Readers understand that Owen knows the Rookwood literature, but the author still needs to provide references for many statements, which she assumes are familiar to her readers. In some cases, quotations and paraphrases are not attributed at all, while others are attributed incorrectly. As a result, the reader is advised to use the book's endnotes with caution.

The author provides plenty of directions in the main body of the text: "This chapter [6] imagines the intended audience for various Rookwood wares by examining the ways in which Rookwood management attempted to influence consumption through advertising, mail-order sales, and selection of retail agencies" (p. 80). And again on page 81: "The second part of this chapter argues that the consumption of Rookwood can be understood in terms of the mechanisms by which demand shaped supply." But such signposts may lead to unwelcome intrusions into the text. For Owen, repetition becomes an occupational hazard for choosing a topic that defies strict chronological chapter organization: the subject involves a relatively brief era with overlapping theories of aestheticism, arts and crafts, and art nouveau. Such difficulties might have been addressed by more careful editing; perhaps a second edition could incorporate improvements.

Ultimately, readers have the sense that everyone in the book is acting true to form. There are no surprises. Rookwood is a vehicle to view the tension between culture and commerce, and it is a good and familiar one. Owen does place the pottery in its cultural milieu, but it may be helpful to examine other art industries and other potteries. Further informative queries might include: What were other ceramic manufacturers doing as points of comparison? Did Rookwood mirror other art industries born around the time of the 1876 Philadelphia Centennial Exhibition? Why was Rookwood operated as a business under Taylor despite its loud claims of art for art's sake? Does the culture versus commerce polarity bring ceramic historians closer to understanding the complexities of gender, business, art, consumerism, and American culture? If so, how?

In summary, Owen is a new conductor whose enthusiasm for her topic is apparent on every page. She tracks the Rookwood story, places it within a business context, and searches for feeder lines, or story sidelights. Some, such as chapter 4's discussion on American collectors, are intriguing; others, such as the discussion of the novella *The Yellow Wallpaper* by Charlotte Perkins Gilman (p. 17), are mere digressions. Yet there is enough inherent interest in the Rookwood story for readers to join this one in saying, "All aboard!"

Cynthia Brandimarte
Southwest Texas State University and Texas Parks and Wildlife Department
San Marcos and Austin, Texas

Christiaan J. A. Jörg and Michael Flecker. *Porcelain from the "Vung Tau" Wreck: The Hallstrom Excavation*. Singapore: Oriental Art, 2001. 172 pp.; 273 color illus. $60.00.

The study of Chinese porcelain has been transformed during the past two decades by the discovery and excavation of shipwrecks. Each wreck encapsulates the trade of a specific period, and many of the wrecks are datable by means of objects found on board other than porcelain. Many of these wrecks have been excavated by commercial salvagers, rather than by underwater archaeologists, and art historians are dependent on their results whether or not we approve of their methods.

It is far more expensive to carry out underwater excavations than excavations on land, although often the underwater excavations yield more valuable artifacts. This is particularly true in the case of ships transporting Chinese porcelain since, unlike other trade goods such as silks or lacquer, some types of porcelain can remain in seawater for a significant period of time and retain their decoration. The clear glaze on blue-and-white wares may be degraded by seawater, but the underglaze blue decoration will remain.

The *Vung Tau* (named for the nearby south Vietnamese province where it was found) was a Chinese junk loaded with porcelain and other cargo. The ship was most likely bound for Batavia when it burned and sank off Vietnam's coast around 1690. A fisherman found the wreck in 1986, and soon local divers had pulled a large number of porcelain pieces from the foundered vessel (p. 103). Of the 48,000 pieces recovered from the site, many went to antique dealers in Vietnam, Hong Kong, and Singapore. Eventually these activities were stopped by the Vietnamese government, which arranged for Sverker Hallstrom, a commercial salvager, to excavate the wreck. The expectation was that the sale of salvaged porcelain would be profitable, and it was. After the Vietnamese selected a few hundred pieces for their museums, the remaining 28,000 pieces were sold at Christie's, Amsterdam, on April 7–8, 1992, where they realized a return of $7.3 million.

Porcelain from the "Vung Tau" Wreck is divided into two sections. The first section, by Christiaan Jörg, concerns the porcelain. Jörg is one of the world's premier scholars of Chinese porcelain, and his extensive knowledge of the Dutch East India Company (Verenigde Ooost-Indische Compagnie, or VOC) trading records makes him uniquely qualified to discuss inter-Asian trade and to analyze the porcelain from the *Vung Tau*.

Jörg begins with a thorough discussion of the Dutch China trade in the seventeenth century and uses engravings of porcelain rooms by Daniel Marot to illustrate Europe's "passion for porcelain." It was a revolutionary time for the China trade, as the Dutch took over from the Portuguese, and the VOC began, in 1635, ordering tableware made in specifically Western shapes from the Chinese. (No hard-paste porcelain had, as yet, been produced in Europe.) Most important in this section is Jörg's discourse on the Chinese junk trade and the founding of Batavia in 1619 to "attract junks and create facilities for Chinese settlers. . . . Chinese merchants joined forces with the Company [VOC] to develop and expand trade networks throughout Southeast Asia" (p. 23). Although the book's locator map helpfully pinpoints the wreck, an additional map showing the trade routes between China and the Indonesian archipelago would have been useful.

Blanc de chine pieces, storage jars, and porcelain figures were included among the ship's cargo. The majority of the collection, however, was made up of blue-and-white porcelain hollow and flatwares composed of two main groups: (1) the finer quality wares fired in the kilns of Jingdezhen, and probably intended for Batavia, then the Netherlands or Islamic markets, and (2) a group of blue-and-white wares made in provincial kilns and destined for Southeast Asia. Each shape is discussed in the context of function. For example, the discussion of cups and saucers is particularly interesting because it involves the evolution of tea and coffee drinking in seventeenth-century Europe.

It is not possible to know whether the porcelain was intended for the Dutch or Islamic market or both. Although Jörg mentions that there are many cups and saucers from the Kangxi period (1662–1722) in the Netherlands, he cautions against assuming that their presence rules out an Islamic connection (p. 57). The pieces' painted floral designs would be acceptable to Islamic patrons, who could not accept decorations incorporating human or animal figures. The cargo also included hookah bases, kendis, and ewers, which were "not primarily for the Dutch market" (p. 74).

The publication's photographs are taken from the Christie's catalog and are generally clear, each item dramatically silhouetted against a white background. The layout is arranged effectively so that featured pieces and relevant text are usually on the same page. Unfortunately, the images do not include accompanying dimensions, and, inconsistently, some illustrated pieces are mentioned in the text, but others are not.

The second part of the book concerns the actual excavation and is written by archaeologist Michael Flecker. Since I am an art historian, not an archaeologist, I am not qualified to judge his report. However, Flecker seems to have organized the excavation properly. He writes: "Commercial salvage outfits have in the past earned a bad reputation, and rightly so, for tearing out everything of financial value without bothering to record anything of the site" (p. 109). Further, he was determined to approach the excavation "systematically, thoroughly, and pragmatically" (p. 109). In spite of his resolve, his collaboration with Hallstrom taints his work in the eyes of the underwater archaeology community. As one of the ethical positions of the Society for Historical Archaeology states: "The collecting, exchanging, buying or selling of archaeological artifacts and research data for the purpose of personal satisfaction or financial gain . . . are declared contrary to the purposes of the society."[1]

The archaeological community feels strongly about cooperating with for-profit excavations. The Convention on the Protection of the Underwater Cultural Heritage, organized by UNESCO and held in Paris in November 2001, dealt with this issue as follows: "The commercial exploitation of underwater cultural heritage for trade or speculation or its irretrievable dispersal is fundamentally incompatible with the protection and proper management of underwater cultural heritage. Underwater cultural heritage shall not be traded, sold, bought or bartered as commercial goods."[2] It is a difficult issue, since it is unrealistic to expect significant funds to be allocated for proper underwater excavations in less-developed countries. Countries without the financial resources to excavate shipwrecks on their own can be tempted to make such arrangements with salvagers.

The loss of ceramic information through shipwreck salvage can be devastating. Typical of such loss is the *Nuestra Señora de la Concepcion,* which was wrecked off the Dominican Republic in 1641. Commercial salvagers have excavated this site over several decades, and many pieces of blue-and-white porcelain have been found. The Dominican government made an agreement with the salvage company that the ceramics from the wreck would be shared equally. The pieces that the salvagers kept have probably been sold, along with any record of their existence. Some of these pieces may have been unique and important for porcelain dating, but this information is now lost.

In comparative terms, the *Vung Tau* wreck is less of a loss because we have the Christie's catalog, and a large number of pieces remain in Vietnam. Even so, Jörg discusses the impact of this particular for-profit excavation on the availability of knowledge. Because 28,000 of the 48,000 pieces of porcelain were sold, our record relies on the Christie's auction catalog (p. 95), which did not depict all of the collection's various shapes and decorations. The porcelain sold by the auction house has been dispersed all over the world and is lost to scholarly study. Furthermore, there is no information available on the pieces owned by the Vietnamese government. And who knows what the divers left behind?

This book is essential for anyone interested in Chinese porcelain of the late seventeenth century. The thoughtful discussion of each vessel type's function and the coverage of inter-Asian trade make it an invaluable reference.

Linda R. Shulsky
Parsons School of Design

1. UNESCO, *Convention on the Protection of the Underwater Cultural Heritage* (Paris, November 2, 2001), Rule 2, p. 16.

2. *Ethical Positions of the Society for Historical Archaeology,* Bylaws, Article VII (March 30, 2001).

Compiled by
Amy C. Earls

Checklist of Articles and Books on Ceramics in America Published 1998–2002

▼ THE FOLLOWING LIST includes publications about ceramics made or used in America from the time of European colonization through the present day and published from 1998 through 2002. Many of the references were compiled through online library database searches at Princeton University. Databases used include *World Catalog First Search* (Online Computer Library Center) and *Global Books in Print* (R. R. Bowker) for books; *America: History and Life* and also *Historical Abstracts* (ABC-CLIO), *Arts and Humanities Index* (Thomson Institute for Science Information's Web of Science), *Art Index* (H. W. Wilson), and *International Bibliography of the Social Sciences* (Educational Resources Information Center, WebSPIRS5) for journal articles; and SCIPIO (Research Libraries Group) for auction catalogs. The burden is on the reader to examine and select the references that may be of interest.

The print publications listed below are only part of the rapidly growing body of data on ceramics in America. Online resources include virtual museum exhibits and type collections. Fiesta ware on CD-ROM (see the entry by the Huxfords in last year's checklist) is the first publication by a major American collectibles publisher (Collector Books) in this format. Electronic publications with search engines could help the reader find information more quickly, and an enlargeable text feature could increase access by a sight-impaired audience. Perhaps the greatest potential for online research stems from the tremendous quantity of images available, some organized by ware and type on websites, but most in the ceramics section of online auctions and sales. The sales data may be found in tens of different websites, text descriptions often are misleading or inaccurate, and the data may be ephemeral, disappearing after the sale is made. However, the images alone can be enough to identify patterns and shapes and to trace these through time and space. Victorian majolica shapes described as British can be matched exactly with wasters from late-nineteenth-century Trenton production sites, and the Chinese House pattern can be identified on pots ranging from nineteenth-century painted pearlware to twentieth-century decal hotelwares. And, unlike print publications, image reproduction in color is cheap, and worldwide access through computers at home, library, or school is instantaneous. Truly global research is now feasible. Although images can never substitute for actually handling the pots, they can indicate which pots are worth taking the time and effort to handle.

The quantity of data being published constantly challenges the completeness of this checklist. I would welcome your help in alerting me to publications in print or electronic format relating to ceramics in America. Please address all communications to the Book and Exhibit Review Editor, *Ceramics in America,* P. O. Box 121, Florence, New Jersey, 08518, U.S.A. <trentonpots@yahoo.com>.

Adams, Elizabeth. *Chelsea Porcelain.* London: British Museum Press, 2001.
Adams, Yvonne. *Meissen Figures, 1730–1775: The Kaendler Years.* A Schiffer Book for Collectors. Atglen, Pa.: Schiffer, 2001.
Adamson, Glenn. "Michelle Erickson." *American Craft* (August/September 2002): 56–59.
Akveld, Leo, and Els M. Jacobs. *The Colourful World of the VOC: National Anniversary Book VOC, 1602–2002.* Exhibit catalog, Netherlands Maritime Museum, Amsterdam, March 16–October 27, 2002, and the Rijksmuseum, Amsterdam, October 12–February 2, 2003. Bussum, Netherlands: Thoth, 2002.
Allen, Benjamin L. "The 'Pretzel' Shaped Pad Mark—An Unrecorded Pad Mark?" *Northern Ceramic Society Newsletter,* no. 128 (2002): 37–40.
Amouric, Henri, Florence Richez, and Lucy Vallauri. *Vingt mille pots sous les mers: Le commerce de la céramique en Provence et Languedoc du Xe au XIXe siècle.* Exhibit catalog, Musée d'Istres, May 27–November 28, 1999. Aix-en-Provence, France: Edisud, 1999.
Ash, Michael David. *Bretby Art Pottery: A Collector's Guide.* Swadlincote, Derbyshire, Eng.: David Ash Publishing, 2001.
Atterbury, Paul. *Cornish Ware and Domestic Pottery by T. G. Green of Church Gresley, Derbyshire.* 2nd ed. Shepton Beauchamp, Eng.: Richard Dennis, 2001.
Austin, John C. "British Delft at Williamsburg." In *Wedgwood: Art, Design, & Production,* edited by Keith A. McLeod, 41–45. Proceedings of the Wedgwood International Seminar, nos. 43, 44, and 45. Quebec: Wedgwood International Seminar, 2002.
Ayers, John, with an essay by Yuan Bingling. *Blanc de Chine: Divine Images in Porcelain.* New York: China Institute Gallery/China Institute in America, 2002.
Banks, Catherine. "Enoch Wood Ceramics Excavated in Burslem, Stoke-on-Trent." *Ceramics in America* (2001): 233–36.
———. "'for the gratification of future antiquaries . . .': Enoch Wood's Caches at the Potteries Museum & Art Gallery." *Northern Ceramic Society Newsletter,* no. 125 (2002): 37–43.
Barclay, Katherine. *Scientific Analysis of Archaeological Ceramics: A Handbook of Resources.* Oxford: Oxbow Books, 2001.
Barker, David. "'The Usual Classes of Useful Articles': Staffordshire Ceramics Reconsidered." *Ceramics in America* (2001): 72–93.
Barnes, Donna R., and Peter G. Rose with Charles T. Gehring and Nancy T. Minty. *Matters of Taste: Food and Drink in Seventeenth-Century Dutch Art and Life.* Albany and Syracuse, N.Y.: Albany Institute of History and Art and Syracuse University Press, 2002.
Bassett, Mark. *Understanding Roseville.* A Schiffer Book for Collectors. Atglen, Pa.: Schiffer Books, 2002.
Baumann, Timothy E. "From Pottery Kilns to People of Color: Industrial and African-American Archaeology in Arrow Rock, Missouri." *Features and Profiles* (December/January 1998/1999): 4–10.
Bedell, John. "Delaware Archaeology and the Revolutionary Eighteenth Century." *Historical Archaeology* 35, no. 4 (2001): 83–104.
Bedell, John, and Gerard P. Scharfenberger. "Ordinary and Poor People in 18th-Century Delaware." *Northeast Historical Archaeology* 29 (2000): 23–48.
Berg, Maxine. "From Imitation to Invention: Creating Commodities in Eighteenth-Century Britain." *The Economic History Review* 60, no. 1 (2002): 1–30.
Bieling, Karen. "Replicating Redware Dishes Using Delaware Valley Clays." Paper presented at annual meeting, Council for Northeast Historical Archeology, Wilmington, Del., October 18–20, 2002. (www.Bielings.com)
Bimson, Mavis, and Ian C. Freestone. "Phosphatic Porcelain from the Vauxhall Site." *English Ceramic Circle Transactions* 18, pt. 1 (2002): 91–95.
Black, Harding. "Opening the Door to Copper-Red Glazes." *Ceramics Monthly* (February 2002): 104–5. (orig. pub. January 1953.)
Black, John. *British Tin-Glazed Earthenware.* Shire Album 390. Princes Risborough, Buckinghamshire, Eng.: Shire Publications, 2001.
Blair, Munroe. *Bathroom Ceramics.* Shire Album 391. Princes Risborough, Buckinghamshire, Eng.: Shire Publications, 2002.
Blakey, Harold. "Newcastle Potters and the Export of Earthenware from Newcastle upon Tyne, 1739 to 1796." *Northern Ceramic Society Journal* 18 (2001): 113–52.
Brassard, Michel, Myriam Leclerc, Marcel Mousette, and Réginald Auger. "Identifier la céramique et la verre anciens au Québec: Guide a l'usage des amateurs et des professionels." *Cahiers d'archeologie du CELAT* 12. Québec: CELAT (Université Laval, Centre d'études sur la langue, les arts et les traditions populaires des francophones en Amérique du Nord), 2001.
Bressey, Stephen. "Attribution of the Angel and Banner Mark to Hicks and Meigh." *Northern Ceramic Society Newsletter,* no. 126 (2002): 25–30.
Brighton, Stephen A. "Prices that Suit the Times: Shopping for Ceramics at The Five Points." *Historical Archaeology* 35, no. 3 (2001): 16–30.
Britt, John. "Oil-Spot Glazes." *Ceramics Monthly* (June/July/August 2002): 64–67.
Brown, Chris. "A Caughley Muffin Plate?" *Northern Ceramic Society Newsletter,* no. 128 (2002): 33–35.
Brown, Roxanna M. *The Ceramics of South-East Asia: Their Dating and Identification.* Chicago: Art Media

Resources, 1989: reprint, 2000.
Bùi, Minh Trí, and Kerry Nguyên Long. *Gôm hoa lan Viêt Nam: Vietnamese Blue and White Ceramics.* Hanoi, Vietnam: Nhà Xuât Ban Khoa Hoc Xã Hôi, 2001.
Burdess, Sheryl. *Shelley Tea Ware Patterns.* A Schiffer Book for Collectors. Atglen, Pa.: Schiffer Books, 2002.
Buttemir, Yvonne. "Ceramic Celebrations of the 1839 Eglinton Tournament." *Northern Ceramic Society Newsletter,* no. 127 (2002): 39–40.
Cabak, Melanie, and Stephen Loring. "'A Set of Very Fair Cups and Saucers': Stamped Ceramics as an Example of Inuit Incorporation." *International Journal of Historical Archaeology* 4, no. 1 (2000): 1–34.
Cantwell, Anne-Marie, and Diana diZerega Wall. *Unearthing Gotham: The Archaeology of New York City.* New Haven, Conn.: Yale University Press, 2001.
Cardew, Michael. *Pioneer Pottery.* Rev. and enlarged ed. Westerville, Ohio, and London: American Ceramic Society and A. and C. Black, 2002.
Carney, Margaret. "The History of Glidden Pottery." *Studio Potter* (December 2001): 80–86.
Carpentier, Donald, and Jonathan Rickard. "Slip Decoration in the Age of Industrialization." *Ceramics in America* (2001): 115–34.
Casey, Andrew, and Ann Eatwell, eds. *Susie Cooper: A Pioneer of Modern Design.* Woodbridge, Suffolk, Eng.: Antique Collectors' Club, 2002.
Cerioni, Imelda. *Who Made This Teapot?* Stafford, Eng.: Staffordshire Partnership, 2001. (Children's book with 40 color illustrations of Burgess, Dorling and Leigh's Middleport Pottery.)
Chaimov, John. "Hummel Figurines: Molding a Collectible Germany." *Journal of Material Culture* 6, no. 1 (2001): 49–66.
Chappell, Troy D. "An Adventure with Early English Pottery." *Ceramics in America* (2001): 186–207.
Cheng, H. S., Z. Q. Zhang, H. N. Xia, J. C. Jiang, and F. J. Yang. "Non-Destructive Analysis and Appraisal of Ancient Chinese Porcelain by PIXE." *Nuclear Instruments and Methods in Physics Research Section B-Beam Interactions with Materials and Atoms* 190 (2002): 488–91.
Chinese Arts Auction Records. *2002 Antiques, 1/1/01–12/31/01.* Taipei, Taiwan: Chinese Arts Auction Records, 2002.
Chinese Yixing Teawares from the Collection of the Mai Foundation [Gu hu zhi mei]. Taipei: Cheng yang yi shu wen hua ji jin hui, 2000.
Christie's. *European Ceramics, Dutch Delftware and Glass.* Auction catalog, Christie's Amsterdam, May 15, 2002. Amsterdam: Christie's, 2002.
———. *European Ceramics, Dutch Delftware and Glass: Including a Collection of Meissen Porcelain.* Auction catalog, Christie's Amsterdam, October 30, 2001. Amsterdam: Christie's, 2001.
Clark, Garth. *The Artful Teapot.* New York: Watson-Guptill Publications, 2001.
———. "Going for the Gold: The Marketplace for Ceramic Art." *Ceramics Monthly* (October 2001): 36–40.
Cochrane, Rosemary. *Salt-Glaze Ceramics.* North Pomfret, Vt.: Crowood, dist. in the U.S. by Trafalgar Square Books, 2001.
Cockerill, John. "Warburtons—Potters of Tyneside." *Northern Ceramic Society Journal* 18 (2001): 59–76.
Coe, Debbie, and Randy Coe. *Liberty Blue Dinnerware.* A Schiffer Book for Collectors. Atglen, Pa.: Schiffer, 2002.
Connell, Diana. "Delftfield Excavation—An Appraisal of the Sherds." *Northern Ceramic Society Newsletter,* no. 126 (2002): 31–37.
Cooper, Emmanuel. *Ten Thousand Years of Pottery.* London: British Museum Press, 2000.
Cordell, Ann S. *Continuity and Change in Apalachee Pottery Manufacture.* Center for Archaeological Studies Monograph 9. Mobile, Ala.: Center for Archaeological Studies, University of South Alabama, 2001.
———. "Continuity and Change in Apalachee Pottery Manufacture." *Historical Archaeology* 36, no. 1 (2002): 36–54.
Cosentino, Peter. *The Encyclopedia of Pottery Techniques.* New York: Sterling, 2002.
Cox, Alwyn. "Don Pottery Blue-Printed 'Named Italian Views' and the Abbé de Saint-Non's 'Voyage Pittoresque.'" *English Ceramic Circle Transactions* 18, pt. 1 (2002): 1–28.
———. "Recent Excavations at the Swinton/Rockingham Pottery: Early Brameld Transfer-Printed Earthenwares." *English Ceramic Circle Transactions* 17, pt. 3 (2001): 390–412.
Cox, Alwyn, and Angela Cox. *Rockingham, 1745–1842.* Woodbridge, Suffolk, Eng.: Antique Collectors' Club, 2001.
Cunningham, Jo, and Darlene Nossaman. *Homer Laughlin China: Guide to Shapes and Patterns.* A Schiffer Book for Collectors. Atglen, Pa.: Schiffer, 2002.
Curry, Kevin. "William Dargan and the Worcester Shakespeare Service." *Irish Arts Review Yearbook* 17 (2001): 70–79.
Darling, Trevor. "Limehouse Potting Pots." *Northern Ceramic Society Newsletter,* no. 124 (2001): 23–27.
———. "Liverpool Porcelain—The Profile Bud Pattern." *Northern Ceramic Society Newsletter,* no. 128 (2002): 14–29.
Dawson, Aileen. *French Porcelain: A Catalogue of the British Museum Collection.* London: British Museum Press, 2000.
———. "Josiah Wedgwood I and Figure Sculpture: A Brief Survey." In *Wedgwood: Art, Design, & Production,* edited by Keith A. McLeod, 128–42. Proceedings of the Wedgwood International

Seminar, nos. 43, 44, and 45. Quebec: Wedgwood International Seminar, 2002.

Deagan, Kathleen. "La Vega *Céramica Indo-Hispano*—An Early Sixteenth-Century Caribbean Colono-Ware." *Ceramics in America* (2002): 195–98.

Deblander, Robert, and Sylvie Girard. *Robert Deblander: L'œuvre céramique, 1951–2001.* Exhibit catalog, Musée National de Céramiques de Sèvres, Sèvres, November 6, 2001–February 4, 2002. Vendin-le-Vieil, France: La revue de la céramique et du verre, 2001.

DeMuth, Mary Ann. "David Greenbaum." *Ceramics Monthly* (June/July/August 2002): 78–81.

Denker, Ellen Paul. "Parian Porcelain Statuary: American Sculptors and the Introduction of Art in American Ceramics." *Ceramics in America* (2002): 62–79.

DeWaal, Edmund. "Modern Things." *Ceramic Review* (March/April 2002): 18–21. (Lucie Rie's work.)

Drakard, David, and Paul Holdway. *Spode: Transfer Printed Ware, 1784–1833.* Enlarged and updated 2nd ed. Woodbridge, Suffolk, Eng.: Antique Collectors' Club, 2002.

Dubay, Debby. *Antique Limoges at Home.* A Schiffer Book for Collectors. Atglen, Pa.: Schiffer, 2002.

———. *Living with Limoges.* A Schiffer Book for Collectors . Atglen, Pa.: Schiffer, 2001.

du Boulay, Anthony. "English Ceramics in National Trust Houses." *English Ceramic Circle Transactions* 18, pt. 1 (2002): 169–81.

Duffy, Henry J., ed. *Paul St. Gaudens (1900–1954): Ceramic Artist.* Exhibit catalog, Saint-Gaudens National Historic Site, August 25–October 31, 2001. Cornish, N. H.: Saint-Gaudens National Historic Site, 2001.

Edmundson, Roger S. "A Caneware Jug Marked 'Jackfield Co Salopian.'" *Northern Ceramic Society Newsletter,* no. 124 (2001): 33–42.

———. "Shropshire Potters, and Their Associates, Insured with the Salop Fire Office." *Northern Ceramic Society Journal* 18 (2001): 39–57.

Elliott, Gordon. *The Design Process in British Ceramic Manufacture, 1750–1850.* Stafford, Eng.: Staffordshire University Press, 2002.

Elwood, Marie. "Colonial Wares in British North America—'Their Few Possessions.'" In *Wedgwood: Art, Design, & Production,* edited by Keith A. McLeod, 46–54. Proceedings of the Wedgwood International Seminar, nos. 43, 44, and 45. Quebec: Wedgwood International Seminar, 2002.

Epps, Joyce. "Two Neale and Wilson Porcelain Tureens." *English Ceramic Circle Transactions* 18, pt. 1 (2002): 29–32.

Erickson, Michelle, and Robert Hunter. "Dots, Dashes, and Squiggles: Early English Slipware Technology." *Ceramics in America* (2001): 94–114.

Espir, Helen, J. van Dam, J. Ressing-Wolfe, Errol Manners, Christiaan Jörg, Susan Miller, Eva Ströber, Hillary Young. "East Meets West: Oriental Porcelain Decorated in Europe." *Transactions of the Oriental Ceramic Society* 65 (2001).

Farnsworth, Paul, ed. *Island Lives: Historical Archaeologies of the Caribbean.* Tuscaloosa, Ala.: University of Alabama Press, 2001.

Ferguson, Patricia F. "Wedgwood & Bentley's Bulbous Root Pots: Refining and Reviving an Eighteenth-Century Floral Fashion." In *Wedgwood: Art, Design, & Production,* edited by Keith A. McLeod, 55–70. Proceedings of the Wedgwood International Seminar, nos. 43, 44, and 45. Quebec: Wedgwood International Seminar, 2002.

Fermo, P., F. Cariati, C. Cipriani, G. Padeletti, B. Brunetti, and A. Sgamellotti. "The Use of Small Angle X-ray Scattering (SAXS) for the Characterisation of Lustre Surfaces in Renaissance Majolica." *Applied Surface Science* 185, nos. 3–4 (2002): 309–16.

Feuerfarben: Majolia aus Sizilien, 1550–2000/Colori del fuoco: Maiolica di Sicilia, 1550–2000. Nürnberg: Germanischen Nationalmuseum, 2000.

Findlen, Suzanne R. *Taste and Choice in Early Portsmouth, New Hampshire, as Seen through Ceramic Archaeological Evidence, 1700–1860.* Master's thesis, University of Delaware, 2001.

Fischer, Felice. "The Centennial Exhibition, The Philadelphia Museum of Art, and Hector Tyndale." *Antiques* (March 2002): 96–103.

Fisher, Judith. "Sussex Pottery." *Ceramics Monthly* (December 2001): 73–76.

Forbes, Sheila. "Lieutenant Munro." *Northern Ceramic Society Newsletter,* no. 127 (2002): 44–47.

Fowler, Sandra, and Wendy Harvey. *Art Nouveau Tiles, c. 1890–1914.* A Schiffer Book for Collectors. Atglen, Pa.: Schiffer, 2001.

Fraser, Harry. "Thermal Shock Resistance." *Ceramic Review* (January/February 2001): 58–59.

Fraser, James H. *The Bottle Hill Pottery Studio of Arthur W. Rushmore and Delight Rushmore Lewis.* N.p.: Tideline Press, 2002.

Frost, Harry E. "A Retrospective of Twentieth-Century Worcester Porcelain." In *Wedgwood: Art, Design, & Production,* edited by Keith A. McLeod, 176–87. Proceedings of the Wedgwood International Seminar, nos. 43, 44, and 45. Quebec: Wedgwood International Seminar, 2002.

Fuchs, Ronald W., II. "Chinese Export Porcelain from the Leo and Doris Hodroff Collection at Winterthur." *Antiques* (January 2002): 200–205.

———. "Eighteenth-century Tiled Fireplaces in the Delaware Valley." *Ars Ceramica,* no. 16 (2000): 50–61.

Fuller, Lance. "Messrs. Boote's Patent: The Manufacture of Pottery and Such Like Wares." *Northern Ceramic Society Newsletter,* no. 124 (2001): 6–8.

Gerhauser, Leslie E. *Delftware in New York, ca. 1664–1776.* Master's thesis, Cooper-Hewitt, National Design Museum, New York City, 2001.

Giblin, John, and Jenifer Giblin. *Langley Mill Pottery: Its History and Its Wares.* Heanor, Derbyshire, Eng.: J. and J. Giblin Publishing, 2002.

Glaser, Sylvia. *Majolika: Die italienischen Fayencen im Germanischen Nationalmuseum Nürnberg.* Nürnberg: Germanischen Nationalmuseum, 2000.

Glenn, James. "Brown Mugs and Jugs: A Personal Foray into the Field of Collecting." *Ceramics in America* (2002): 170–90.

Glosband, Merrily. "Indian Market: New Directions in Southwestern Native American Pottery." *Ceramics Monthly* (April 2002): 62–66.

Goodby, Miranda F. "The Road to Longton Hall: New Evidence for William Littler's Early Career." *English Ceramic Circle Transactions* 17, pt. 3 (2002): 366–82.

Goodwin, Jonathan. "American Export Wares Excavated in Tunstall, Stoke-on-Trent." *Ceramics in America* (2002): 218–21.

Gordon, Maddy. *Head Vases Etc.: The Artistry of Betty Lou Nichols.* A Schiffer Book for Collectors. Atglen, Pa.: Schiffer, 2001.

Gray, Jonathan. "The Ridgways in Swansea." *English Ceramic Circle Transactions* 17, pt. 3 (2001): 413–19.

Grigsby, Leslie B. "'Drink Fair Don't Swear': Winterthur's Punch Bowls and Punch Drinking in America." *Antiques* (January 2002): 176–83.

Gums, Bonnie L. "Earthfast (Pieux en Terre) Structures at Old Mobile." *Historical Archaeology* 36, no. 1 (2002): 13–25.

———. *Made of Alabama Clay: Historic Potteries on Mobile Bay.* Center for Archaeological Studies Monograph 8. Mobile, Ala.: Center for Archaeological Studies, University of South Alabama, 2001.

Gums, Bonnie L., and George W. Shorter, Jr. *Archaeology at Mobile's Exploreum: Discovering the Buried Past.* Center for Archaeological Studies Monograph 3. Mobile, Ala.: Center for Archaeological Studies, University of South Alabama, 1998.

Gustafson, Eleanor H. "A Rare Pair." *Antiques* (April 2002): 40–42. (Bonnin & Morris pickle dishes.)

Hanes, Joyce. "Two Eighteenth-Century Vanity Plates." *Ceramics in America* (2002): 216–18.

Hanley, Colin. "The Location of the Plymouth Factory (Part 1)." *English Ceramic Circle Transactions* 18, pt. 1 (2002): 37–44.

Harkey, Linda. "Will Ruggles and Douglass Rankin's Rock Creek Pottery." *Ceramics Monthly* (September 2002): 42–47.

Harman, M. A. *Collecting Blue Willow: Identification and Value Guide.* Paducah, Ky.: Collector Books, 2001.

Harrison-Hall, Jessica. *Catalogue of Late Yuan and Ming Ceramics in the British Museum.* London: British Museum Press, 2001.

Haslam, Malcom. "Michael Cardew: A Centenary Exhibition, Paul Rice Gallery, London." *Crafts* (September/October 2001): 63–64.

Henrywood, R. K. *Staffordshire Potters, 1781–1900.* Woodbridge, Suffolk, Eng.: Antique Collectors' Club, [2003].

Higby, Wayne. "The Qing Is Dead, Long Live the Qing." *American Ceramics* 14, no. 1 (2002): 46–47.

Hillis, Maurice. "An Introduction to Ceramic Raw Materials, Bodies and Glazes." *Northern Ceramic Society Journal* 18 (2001): 77–111.

———. "The Liverpool China Manufactory of Wm. Reid & Co.—A Survey of the Wares." *English Ceramic Circle Transactions* 18, pt. 1 (2002): 58–90.

Hofer, Margaret K. "A Rediscovery at The New-York Historical Society." *Ceramics in America* (2001): 218–20.

Horn, Barbara. "Ceramic Accounts Found among the Seafield Muniments." *English Ceramic Circle Transactions* 18, pt. 1 (2002): 189–96.

Howell, John. "Lowestoft Porcelain: The Final Decade." *English Ceramic Circle Transactions* 17, pt. 3 (2001): 332–59.

Hunter, Richard. "Eighteenth-Century Stoneware Kiln of William Richards Found on the Lamberton Waterfront, Trenton, New Jersey." *Ceramics in America* (2001): 239–43.

Hunter, Robert. "The Stylistic Works of Michelle Erickson." *Ceramics: Art and Perception,* no. 46 (2001): 46–51.

Hunter, Robert, and George L. Miller. "All in the Family: A Staffordshire Soup Plate and the American Market." *Ceramics in America* (2001): 222–25.

Hurry, Silas D., with Martin E. Sullivan, Timothy B. Riordan, and Henry M. Miller. *". . . once the Metropolis of Maryland": The History and Archaeology of Maryland's First Capital.* St. Mary's City, Md.: Historic St. Mary's City Commission, 2001.

James, A. Everette, with Rodney Leftwich. *North Carolina Art Pottery, 1900–1960.* Paducah, Ky.: Collector Books, 2002.

Johnson, Christopher. "Developments in Pottery Manufacturing Technology in the Twentieth Century." In *Wedgwood: Art, Design, & Production,* edited by Keith A. McLeod, 151–62. Proceedings of the Wedgwood International Seminar, nos. 43, 44, and 45. Quebec: Wedgwood International Seminar, 2002.

Jörg, Christiaan J. A., and Michael Flecker. *Porcelain from the "Vung Tau" Wreck: The Hallstrom Collection.* Singapore: Suntree Publishing, 2001.

Kerr, Ann. *Collector's Encyclopedia of Russel Wright.* 3rd ed. Paducah, Ky.: Collector Books, 2002.

Kerr, Rose. "Chinese Porcelain in the Wernher Collection." *Apollo* (May 2002): 44–46.

———. "Missionary Reports on the

Production of Porcelain in China." *Oriental Art* 47 (2001): 35–39.
———. "'A Passionately Immoderate and Incurable Addiction to Buying Porcelain': The Collection of Augustus the Strong at Dresden." *Orientations* (November 2001): 39–44.
Kerr, Rose, and John Ayers. *Blanc de Chine: History and Connoisseurship Reviewed.* London: Routledge Curzon, 2002.
Kerr, Rose, John Ayers, Chuimei Ho, Kenson Kwok, Eva Ströber, and Heidi Tan. *Blanc de Chine: Porcelain from Dehua, A Catalogue of the Hickley Collection, Singapore.* Chicago: Art Media Resources, 2002.
Kiser, Taft. "Seventeenth-Century Donyatt Pottery in the Chesapeake." *Ceramics in America* (2001): 220–22.
Kline, Barbara S., Margaret C. Wehrspaun, and Jerry Kline. *The Complete Book of Florence Ceramics.* A Schiffer Book for Collectors. Atglen, Pa.: Schiffer, 2002.
Kockelmann, W., A. Kirfel, and E. Hahnel. "Non-Destructive Phase Analysis of Archaeological Ceramics Using TOF Neutron Diffraction." *Journal of Archaeological Science* 28 (2001): 213–22. (Rhenish stoneware.)
Krajewski, A., and L. Paci. "True Three-Colour Photoceramic." *Journal of Materials Science* 36 (2001): 3467–78.
Kyushu Ceramic Museum. *Shibata Collection Part VII: Arita Porcelains Produced in the 17th Century, The Essence of Arita Porcelain.* Kyushu: Kyushu Ceramic Museum, 2001.
Lange, Amanda E. *Delftware at Historic Deerfield.* Deerfield, Mass.: Historic Deerfield, Inc., 2001.
Ledes, Allison E. "Meissen for Royalty." *Antiques* (July 2001): 22–24.
Lin, Anthony. "Glorious Innovations: Imperial Porcelains of the Kangxi Era." *Arts of Asia* (July/August 2001): 28–42.
Lister, Florence C., and Robert H. Lister. *Maiolica Olé: Spanish and Mexican Decorative Traditions.* Santa Fe, N.M.: Museum of New Mexico Press, 2001.
Luckenbach, Al. "Ceramics from the Edward Rumney/Stephen West Tavern, London Town, Maryland, Circa 1725." *Ceramics in America* (2002): 130–52.
———. "The Seventeenth-Century 'Lloyd Plate' from the Broadneck Site in Maryland." *Ceramics in America* (2002): 205–6.
Lukacs, George H. *Poughkeepsie Potters and the Plague.* Charleston, S.C.: Arcadia, 2001.
Mackay, James. *Antiques at a Glance: Ceramics.* London and New York: PRC, dist. Sterling, 2002.
Maisels, Catriona, and David Maisels. "James King—A Dundee Chinaman." *Northern Ceramic Society Newsletter,* no. 128 (2002): 30–32.
Mallet, J. V. G. "Engine-turning on Chelsea Porcelain, with Considerations on Its Previous Use at Meissen and Vincennes/Sèvres." *English Ceramic Circle Transactions* 17, pt. 3 (2001): 420–29.
Margolin, Sam. "'And Freedom to the Slave': Antislavery Ceramics, 1787–1865." *Ceramics in America* (2002): 80–109.
Markin, Trevor. "An Update on Thomas Fletcher, Engraver and Black Printer." *Northern Ceramic Society Newsletter,* no. 127 (2002): 41–43.
Marple, Leland, and Carol Marple. *R. S. Prussia: The Formative Years.* A Schiffer Book for Collectors. Atglen, Pa.: Schiffer, 2002.
Martin, Ann Smart. "Magical, Mythical, Practical, and Sublime: The Meanings and Uses of Ceramics in America." *Ceramics in America* (2001): 28–46.
Martz, Karl. "Decorate with Engobes!" *Ceramics Monthly* (May 2002): 86–89. (Orig. pub. February 1953.)
Mason, Lark E., Jr. *Asian Art.* Woodbridge, Suffolk, Eng.: Antique Collectors' Club, 2002.
Massey, Roger. "Bovey Tracey Potteries Revisited." *English Ceramic Circle Transactions* 18, pt. 1 (2002): 114–21.
———. "Nicholas Crisp at Bovey Tracey." *English Ceramic Circle Transactions* 18, pt. 1 (2002): 96–113.
———. "The Size and Scale of Eighteenth-Century English Porcelain Factories." *English Ceramic Circle Transactions* 17, pt. 3 (2001): 442–66.
Mathieson, John. *Raku.* Westerville, Ohio, and London: American Ceramic Society and A. and C. Black, 2002.
Matos, M. A. P. "Christian Iconography in Chinese Porcelain." *Oriental Art* 47, no. 5 (2001): 27–34.
Maurer, Christopher, with Maria Estrella Iglesias. *Dreaming in Clay on the Coast of Mississippi: Love and Art at Shearwater.* New York: Doubleday, 2001.
McErlain, Alex. *The Art of Throwing.* N. Pomfret, Vt.: Trafalgar Square, 2002.
Miller, George L., with Patricia Samford, Ellen Shlasko, and Andrew Madsen. "Telling Time for Archaeologists." *Northeast Historical Archaeology* 29 (2000): 1–22.
Miller, George L., and Robert Hunter. "How Creamware Got the Blues: The Origins of China Glaze and Pearlware." *Ceramics in America* (2001): 135–61.
Miller, Lynn. "Wedgwood & Nature in the Nineteenth Century." In *Wedgwood: Art, Design, & Production,* edited by Keith A. McLeod, 85–101. Proceedings of the Wedgwood International Seminar, nos. 43, 44, and 45. Quebec: Wedgwood International Seminar, 2002.
———. "Wedgwood & Nineteenth-Century Creamware." In *Wedgwood: Art, Design, & Production,* edited by Keith A. McLeod, 24–40. Proceedings of the Wedgwood International Seminar, nos. 43, 44, and 45. Quebec: Wedgwood International Seminar, 2002.
Miller, Susan. "Images of Asia in

French Luxury Goods: Jean-Antoine Fraisse at Chantilly, c. 1729–36." *Apollo* (November 2001): 3–12.

Mitchell, Laurence. *The Meissen Collectors' Catalogue*. Woodbridge, Suffolk, Eng.: Antique Collectors' Club, 2001.

Molina-Rodriguez, Rafael. "The Potter's Shed at Old City Park." *Ceramics Monthly* (June/July/August 2002): 68–69.

Mueller, Shirley M. "Surface Silver Decoration on Chinese Export Porcelain: A Survey." *Oriental Art* 47, no. 3 (2001): 56–64.

Nadler, Daniel. *China to Order: Focusing on the 19th Century and Surveying Chinese Polychrome Export Porcelain Produced During the Qing Dynasty 1644–1908*. Paris: Vilo International, 2001.

National Academy of Design, Caskey-Lees, and Sha-Dor. *The New York Ceramics Fair*. Exhibit catalog, New York Ceramics Fair, January 17–20, 2002. New York: National Academy of Design, 2002.

Newbound, Betty, and Bill Newbound. *Best of Blue Ridge Dinnerware*. Paducah, Ky.: Collector Books, 2002.

Newell, Mark M. "The Search Continues: New Insights into Old Edgefield Folk Potters." *Ceramics in America* (2002): 224–26.

———. "A Spectacular Find at the Joseph Gregory Baynham Pottery Site." *Ceramics in America* (2001): 229–32.

Nicholson, Nick, Marilyn Nicholson, and Jim Thomas. *Rookwood Pottery: Identification and Value Guide*. Paducah, Ky.: Collector Books, 2002.

Nissen, Craig, Margaret Hanson, and Bob Hanson. *McCoy Pottery Collector's Reference and Value Guide*. Vol. 3. Paducah, Ky.: Collector Books, 2001.

Noël Hume, Ivor. *A Guide to Artifacts of Colonial America*. Philadelphia: University of Pennsylvania Press, 1970; reprint, 2001.

———. "A Pot Potpourri." *Ceramics in America* (2002): 1–16.

———. "Potsherds and Pragmatism: One Collector's Perspective." *Ceramics in America* (2001): 3–27.

Noël Hume, Ivor, and Audrey Noël Hume. *The Archaeology of Martin's Hundred, Parts 1 and 2: Interpretive Studies; Artifact Catalog*. Philadelphia: University Museum Publications, 2001.

Northeast Auctions. *The Estate of Madeline Whitney Shea, Including a Large Collection of Chinese Export Porcelain with Many Examples of Armorial Porcelain*. Auction catalog, Northeast Auctions, Portsmouth, N. H., March 4, 2001. Portsmouth, N. H.: Northeast Auctions, 2001.

———. *New Hampshire Weekend Auctions, Including The Roger T. Powers Collection of Anglo-American Transfer-printed Ceramics and Lustreware*. Auction catalog, Northeast Auctions, Manchester, N. H., August 21–22, 1999 (Part 1); November 21, 1999 (Part 2); March 4–5, 2000 (Part 3). Portsmouth, N. H.: Northeast Auctions, 1999–2000.

———. *New Hampshire Weekend Auctions, Including The Sheila Saul Collection of Delft with Collections of Wedgwood and Sunderland Lustre*. Auction catalog, Northeast Auctions, Manchester, N. H., November 3–4, 2001. Portsmouth, N. H.: Northeast Auctions, 2001.

———. *Portsmouth Weekend Auction: Featuring a Selection of Oriental Artifacts . . . Ceramics Including Sunderland Lustre and Liverpool Jugs . . . Chinese Export Porcelain, Including Canton and Armorial . . .* Auction catalog, Northeast Auctions, Portsmouth, N.H., August 18–19, 2001. Portsmouth, N.H.: Northeast Auctions, 2001.

———. *The Sherwood Smith Estate Collection of American Furniture and Chinese Export Porcelain*. Auction catalog, Northeast Auctions, Portsmouth, N. H., March 2, 2002. Portsmouth, N. H.: Northeast Auctions, 2002.

Olin, Jacqueline S., M. James Blackman, Jared E. Mitchem, and Gregory A. Waselkov. "Compositional Analysis of Glazed Earthenwares from Eighteenth-Century Sites on the Northern Gulf Coast." *Historical Archaeology* 36, no. 1 (2002): 79–96.

Outlaw, Merry Abbitt. "A Collection of Curious 'Canns.'" *Ceramics in America* (2002): 206–8.

———. "Scratched in Clay: Seventeenth-Century North Devon Slipware at Jamestown, Virginia." *Ceramics in America* (2002): 17–38.

Owen, J. Victor. "Antique Porcelain 101: A Primer on the Chemical Analysis and Interpretation of Eighteenth-Century British Wares." *Ceramics in America* (2002): 39–61.

———. "Geochemical and Mineralogical Distinctions between Bonnin and Morris (Philadelphia, 1770–1772) Porcelain and Contemporary British Phosphatic Wares." *Geoarchaeology* 16 (2001): 785–802.

Parks, Dennis. *Living in the Country Growing Weird (A Deep Rural Adventure)*. Reno: University of Nevada Press, 2001.

Patrick, Stephen E. "The American Foundation of the Chelsea Porcelain Manufactory, 1745–1784." *Ceramics in America* (2002): 213–16.

Pearce, Jacqueline. "Ceramics for Refined Taste: Chinese Porcelain from London Excavations." *Oriental Art* 47 (2001): 55–60.

Pearce, Jacqueline, and Beverly Straube. "The Double Dish Dilemma." *Ceramics in America* (2001): 215–17.

Perkins, Dorothy W. "Emphasize Form with Slip Combing." *Ceramics Monthly* (September 2002): 119–22. (orig. pub. August 1953.)

Pierson, Stacey, and Amy Barnes. *A Collector's Vision: Ceramics for the Qianlong Emperor*. London: Percival David Foundation of Chinese Art, 2002.

Pilcher, Don. "Looking at Kenzan." *Ceramics Monthly* (September 2002): 60–64.

Pitman, Jennifer. "China's Presence at the Centennial Exhibition, Philadelphia, 1876." *Studies in the Decorative Arts* 10, no. 1 (Fall/Winter 2002–2003): 35–73.

Pittman, William, and Robert Hunter. "A Cache of Eighteenth-Century Flowerpots in Williamsburg." *Ceramics in America* (2002): 209–13.

Polick, Terri. *Modern Fiesta: 1986–Present.* A Schiffer Book for Collectors. Atglen, Pa.: Schiffer Books, 2002.

Polikoff, Muriel. "The Portland Vase: The Wedgwood Copies & Other English Portland Vases." In *Wedgwood: Art, Design, & Production,* edited by Keith A. McLeod, 102–14. Proceedings of the Wedgwood International Seminar, nos. 43, 44, and 45. Quebec: Wedgwood International Seminar, 2002.

Pomfret, Roger. "George Harrison: His Partnership with William Hyatt and Their Dealings with Abbot & Simpson of Philadelphia." *Northern Ceramic Society Newsletter,* no. 126 (2002): 40–45.

Poole, Julia. "Ceramics in the Household of the 4th Duke of Bedford—Bills and Other Evidence." *English Ceramic Circle Transactions* 18, pt. 1 (2002): 122–68.

Pope, Rex. "A Consumer Service in Interwar Britain: The Hotel Trade, 1924–1938." *Business History Review* 74, no. 4 (2000): 657–82.

Popp, Andrew. "Barriers to Innovation in Marketing in the Mid-Nineteenth Century: Merchant-Manufacturer Relationships." *Business History* 44, no. 2 (2002): 19–39.

———. *Business Structure, Business Culture, and the Industrial District: The Potteries, c. 1850–1914.* Aldershot, Eng.: Ashgate, 2001.

———. "Specialty Production, Personal Capitalism and Auditors' Reports: Mintons Ltd., c. 1870–1900." *Accounting, Business and Financial History* 10, no. 3 (2000): 347–70.

———. "Trust in an Industrial District: The Potteries, c. 1850–1900." *Journal of Industrial History* 3, no. 1 (2000): 29–53.

Powell, E. A. "Quality Cargo." *Archaeology* (November/December 2001): 9. (Italian majolica from 16th-century Spanish shipwreck off the Scottish coast.)

Pratt, Michael. *Mid-Century Modern Dinnerware.* A Schiffer Book for Collectors. Atglen, Pa.: Schiffer, 2002.

Priestman, Geoffrey H. *An Illustrated Guide to Minton Printed Pottery, 1796–1836.* Sheffield, Eng.: Endcliffe Press, dist. in the U.S. by Bradshaw and Whelan Ceramic Reference Books (Asheville, N.C.), 2001.

Prown, Jonathan, Glenn Adamson, Katherine Hemple Prown, and Robert Hunter. "'The Very Man for the Hour': The Toussaint L'Ouverture Portrait Pitcher." *Ceramics in America* (2002): 110–29.

Pulver, Martin. "An Early 19th Century American Merchant's Ledger." *English Ceramic Circle Transactions* 18, pt. 1 (2002): 182–88.

Rago Auctions, David. *Estate Auction: American Porcelain, Tiffany, Toys, Pens, Bibelots.* Auction catalog, David Rago Auctions, Lambertville, N. J., June 9, 2002. Lambertville, N. J.: David Rago Auctions, 2002.

———. *Roseville/Collector/Stangl Auction Weekend.* Auction catalog, Lambertville, N. J., April 20–21, 2002. Lambertville, N. J.: David Rago Auctions, 2002.

———. *20th Century Modern Auction.* Auction catalog, Lambertville, N. J., October 26–27, 2002. Lambertville, N. J.: David Rago Auctions, 2002.

Ramsay, W. H. R., A. Gabszewicz, and E. G. Ramsay. "'Unaker' or Cherokee Clay and Its Relationship to the 'Bow' Porcelain Manufactory." *English Ceramic Circle Transactions* 17, pt. 3 (2001): 474–99.

Redstone, David. "Kishere's Mortlake Pottery." *English Ceramic Circle Transactions* 18, pt. 1 (2002): 45–57.

Reslewic, S., and J. H. Burton. "Completely Nondestructive Technique for Measuring Lead Isotope Ratios in Glazed Pottery and Implications for Understanding Majolica Production in New Spain." *Abstracts of Papers of the American Chemical Society* 222 (August 2001): 4.

Rice, Dennis. *Cats in English Porcelain of the 19th Century.* Woodbridge, Suffolk, Eng.: Antique Collectors' Club, 2002.

———. *Dogs in English Porcelain of the 19th Century.* Woodbridge, Suffolk, Eng.: Antique Collectors' Club, 2002.

Richardson, Louise. ". . . And the Find!" *Ceramics in America* (2001): 238.

Ritchie's. *Ceramics from the Estate of Elizabeth Collard, Ottawa.* Sale 678. Auction catalog, Ritchie's, Toronto, December 2, 2002. Toronto: Ritchie's, 2002.

Roberts, Claire, and Michael Brand, eds. *Earth Spirit Fire: Korean Masterpieces of the Choson Dynasty (1392–1910).* Aldershot, Eng.: Powerhouse, 2000.

Roberts, Gaye B. "Basalt and Jasper." In *Wedgwood: Art, Design, & Production,* edited by Keith A. McLeod, 115–27. Proceedings of the Wedgwood International Seminar, nos. 43, 44, and 45. Quebec: Wedgwood International Seminar, 2002.

———. "Wedgwood & Eighteenth-Century Creamware." In *Wedgwood: Art, Design, & Production,* edited by Keith A. McLeod, 8–23. Proceedings of the Wedgwood International Seminar, nos. 43, 44, and 45. Quebec: Wedgwood International Seminar, 2002.

———. "Wedgwood & Nature in the Eighteenth Century." In *Wedgwood: Art, Design, & Production,* edited by Keith A. McLeod, 71–84. Proceedings of the Wedgwood International Seminar, nos. 43, 44, and 45. Quebec: Wedgwood International Seminar, 2002.

Roberts, Lois M. "Blue Painted Creamware and Pearlware." *Northern Ceramic Society Journal* 18 (2001): 1–37.

———. "John and George Rogers—Underglaze Blue Painted Wares." *Northern Ceramic Society Newsletter*, no. 128 (2002): 10–13.

Robinson, Delia. "Comment: Mug Shots—Going on eBay." *Ceramics Monthly* (May 2002): 92–96.

Rockwell, Dean. *Antique Knife Rests: The History, Manufacture and Use of English, American and Continental Knife Rests in Metal, Glass and Ceramic.* Ypsilanti, Mich.: Proctor, 2000.

Rogers, Phil. *Salt Glazing.* Philadelphia: University of Pennsylvania Press, 2002.

Rousmaniere, Nicole C., ed.. *Arts of Kazari: Japan on Display, 15th–19th Centuries.* New York: Harry N. Abrams, Inc., 2002.

Rubenstein, Leonard. "A Ceramic Vocabulary." *Ceramics Monthly* (October 2001): 50–52. (Personal reminiscences of Alfred University and a career in studio ceramics.)

Sargent, William R. "'Send Us No More Dragons': Chinese Porcelains for the Western Market." *Studio Potter* (December 2001): 18–21.

Saunders, Julie. "Eighteenth-Century Worcester." In *Wedgwood: Art, Design, & Production,* edited by Keith A. McLeod, 163–75. Proceedings of the Wedgwood International Seminar, nos. 43, 44, and 45. Quebec: Wedgwood International Seminar, 2002.

Savill, R. "Sèvres Porcelain in the Wernher Collection." *Apollo* (May 2002): 40–43.

Scarlett, Timothy J. *Potting in Zion: Craft and Industry in Utah, 1848–1930.* Ph.D. diss., Anthropology Department, University of Nevada, Reno, 2002.

Scherer, John L. "The Weitsman Stoneware Collection at the New York State Museum." *The Magazine Antiques* (February 2002): 88–93.

Schiffer, Nancy N. *Figural Japanese Export Ceramics.* A Schiffer Book for Collectors. Atglen, Pa.: Schiffer, 2002.

———. *Shape and Decoration in Japanese Export Ceramics.* A Schiffer Book for Collectors. Atglen, Pa.: Schiffer, 2002.

Scott, Rosemary E. "Two Collectors: Emperor and Baronet." *Orientations* (January 2002): 50–56.

Sessions, Billie, Elaine Levin, and Richard Johnston. *Ripples: Marguerite Wildenhain and Her Pond Farm Students.* Exhibit catalog, California State University, San Bernardino, January 24–March 13, 2002. San Bernardino, Calif.: California State University, 2002.

Sharp, Rosalie W. Ceramics, Ethics, and Scandal: The Rosalie and Isadore Sharp Collection of Porcelain and Pottery. Toronto: Key Porter Books, 2002.

Shimizu, Christine. *La porcelaine japonaise/Japanese Porcelains.* Paris: Charles Massin, 2002.

Shinn, William. "The Versatile Extruder." *Ceramics Monthly* (December 2002): 54–58.

Shipkowitz, Davida, and Irving Shipkowitz. *The ABC's of ABC Ware.* A Schiffer Book for Collectors. Atglen, Pa.: Schiffer, 2002.

Shorter, George W., Jr. "Status and Trade at Port Dauphin." *Historical Archaeology* 36, no. 1 (2002): 135–42.

Sloan's. *Americana.* Auction catalog, Sloan's, North Bethesda, Md., March 9, 2002. North Bethesda, Md.: Sloan's, 2002.

———. *Asian Ceramics and Works of Art.* Auction catalog, Sloan's, North Bethesda, Md., April 8, 2002. North Bethesda, Md.: Sloan's, 2002.

———. *The Autumn Auction, Including Property from the Collection of Elizabeth duPont Bayard Weedon.* Auction catalog, Sloan's, North Bethesda, Md., September 20–21, 2002. North Bethesda, Md.: Sloan's, 2002.

———. *Furniture and Decorative Arts Auction.* Auction catalog, Sloan's, North Bethesda, Md., July 19–20, 2002. North Bethesda, Md.: Sloan's, 2002.

———. *Gordon Estate Sale.* Auction catalog, Sloan's, North Bethesda, Md., March 16, 2002. North Bethesda, Md.: Sloan's, 2002.

Smith, John, Nancy Smith, and Brooke Smith. *Antique Toothbrush Holders.* A Schiffer Book for Collectors. Atglen, Pa.: Schiffer, 2002.

Smith, Marjorie. "Frances Senska." *Ceramics Monthly* (September 2002): 50–54.

Snyder, Jeffrey B. *Collecting Oyster Plates.* A Schiffer Book for Collectors. Atglen, Pa.: Schiffer, 2001.

———. *Depression Pottery.* Rev. and exp. 2nd ed. A Schiffer Book for Collectors. Atglen, Pa.: Schiffer, 2002.

———. *Fiesta: Homer Laughlin China Company's Colorful Dinnerware.* Rev. and exp. 4th ed. A Schiffer Book for Collectors. Atglen, Pa.: Schiffer, 2002.

———. *Hall China.* A Schiffer Book for Collectors. Atglen, Pa.: Schiffer, 2002.

———. *McCoy Pottery: A Field Guide.* A Schiffer Book for Collectors. Atglen, Pa.: Schiffer, 2002.

Sotheby's. *European Ceramics, Delftware and Glass.* Auction catalog, Sotheby's Mak van Waay, April 3, 2001, Amsterdam. Amsterdam: Sotheby's, 2001.

———. *European Ceramics, Delftware and Glass.* Auction catalog, Sotheby's Amsterdam, June 5, 2002. Amsterdam: Sotheby's, 2002.

Spain, David H. *Noritake Fancywares A to Z: A Pictorial Record and Guide to Values.* A Schiffer Book for Collectors. Atglen, Pa.: Schiffer, 2002.

Sprague, Roderick. "China or Prosser Button Identification and Dating." *Historical Archaeology* 36, no. 2 (2002): 111–27.

Steen, Carl. "Industrial Pottery in the Old Edgefield District." *Ceramics in America* (2001): 226–29.

Stephenson, Roy. "The Ceramic

Finds." In Kieron Tyler, "The Excavation of an Elizabethan/ Stuart Waterfront Site on the North Bank of the River Thames at Victoria Wharf, Narrow Street, Limehouse, London E14." *Post-Medieval Archaeology* 35 (2001): 53–95.

Stradling, Diana, and J. Garrison Stradling. "American Queensware—The Louisville Experience, 1829–1837." *Ceramics in America* (2001): 162–85.

Straube, Beverly. "European Ceramics in the New World: The Jamestown Example." *Ceramics in America* (2001): 46–71.

———. "A Peacock's Flight . . . Across 100 Years." *Ceramics in America* (2002): 199–201.

Ströber, Eva. *"La maladie de porcelaine . . .": East Asian Porcelain from the Collection of Augustus the Strong.* Berlin: Edition Leipzig, 2001.

Swann, C. P., and C. H. Nelson. "Böttger Stoneware from North America and Europe: Are They Authentic?" *Nuclear Instruments and Methods in Physics Research Section B-Beam Interactions with Materials and Atoms* 161 (March 2000): 694–98.

Teicholz, Nina. "Sotheby's Sells Storied Porcelain." *Art and Auction* (January 2002): 34. (Porcelain collection that inspired Bruce Chatwin's novel, Utz.)

Therrien, Monika, Elena Uprimny, Jimena Lobo Guerrero, María Fernanda Salamanca, Felipe, Gaitán, and Marta Fandiño. *Catálogo de cerámica colonial y republicana de la Nueva Granada: Producción local y materiales foráneos (Costa Caribe, Altiplano Cundiboyacense-Colombia).* Bogotá: Fundación de Investigaciones Arqueológicas Nacionales, Banco de la República Bogotá, 2002.

Tourtillott, Suzanne J. E. *500 Teapots: Contemporary Explorations of a Timeless Design.* Asheville, N. C.: Lark Books, 2002.

Trent, Robert. "Richard Schalck, Stoneware Potter of Marblehead, Massachusetts." *Ceramics in America* (2002): 153–69.

Tuck, James A., and Barry Gaulton. "*Terra Sigillata* from a Seventeenth-Century Settlement in Newfoundland." *Ceramics in America* (2002): 202–4.

Tung, Wu. *Earth Transformed: Chinese Ceramics in the Museum of Fine Arts, Boston.* Boston: Museum of Fine Arts, Boston, 2001.

Twitchett, John. *Derby Porcelain, 1748–1848.* Woodbridge, Suffolk, Eng.: Antique Collectors' Club, 2002.

VanBuskirk, William H. *Late Victorian Flow Blue and Other Ceramic Wares: A Selected History of Potteries and Shapes.* A Schiffer Book for Collectors. Atglen, Pa.: Schiffer, 2002.

van Lemmen, Hans. *Architectural Ceramics.* Shire Album 395. Princes Risborough, Buckinghamshire, Eng.: Shire Publications, 2002.

Veit, Richard, and Mark Nonestied. "Bombs Away! Unearthing a Cache of Terra Cotta Practice Bombs from the First World War." *Ceramics in America* (2002): 227–32.

Veith, B. "Edward Lycett and the Faïence Manufacturing Company." *Antiques* (July 2001): 84–91.

Vince, Alan. "Ceramic Petrology and Post-Medieval Pottery." *Post-Medieval Archaeology* 35 (2001): 106–18.

Volk, Joyce Geary. "A Warner House Search . . ." *Ceramics in America* (2001): 236–38.

Walford, Tom. "The Search for Thomas Whieldon's Creamware." *English Ceramic Circle Transactions* 17, pt. 3 (2001): 430–41.

Waller, Jane. *Colour in Clay.* Marlborough, Eng.: Crowood, dist. in the U.S. by Trafalgar Square, 1998.

Walker, Barbara, and Dave Williamson. *Quest for Quimper.* A Schiffer Book for Collectors. Atglen, Pa.: Schiffer, 2002.

Wang, Cheng-hua. "The Qianlong Emperor and His Legacy: The National Palace Museum's 2002 October Exhibition." *Orientations* (October 2002): 60–68.

Wang, Qingzheng. *A Dictionary of Chinese Ceramics [Zhongguo tao ci ci dian].* Singapore: Sun Tree, 2002.

Waselkov, Gregory A. *Old Mobile Archaeology.* Mobile, Ala.: Center for Archaeological Studies, University of South Alabama, 1999.

Waselkov, Gregory A., and Bonnie L. Gums. *Plantation Archaeology at Rivière aux Chiens, ca. 1725–1848.* Center for Archaeological Studies Monograph 7. Mobile, Ala.: Center for Archaeological Studies, University of South Alabama, 2000.

Waselkov, Gregory A., and John A. Walthall. "Faience Styles in French Colonial North America: A Revised Classification." *Historical Archaeology* 36, no. 1 (2002): 62–78.

Watson, Wendy. *Italian Renaissance Ceramics from The Howard I. and Janet H. Stein Collection and the Philadelphia Museum of Art.* Philadelphia: Philadelphia Museum of Art, 2001.

Watts, Andrew. "Three Kilns." *English Ceramic Circle Transactions* 18, pt. 1 (2002): 33–36.

Welch, Matthew. *Body of Clay, Soul of Fire: Richard Bresnahan and the Saint John's Pottery.* Afton, Minn.: Afton Historical Society Press, 2001.

"Weldon Creamware." *Ceramic Review* (March/April 2002): 32–33. (www.peterweldon.co.uk.)

White, Carole B. *The Collector's Guide to Made in Japan Ceramics: Identification & Values,* vol. 4. Paducah, Ky.: Collector Books, 2002.

———. *Glass and Ceramic Baskets Identification and Value Guide.* Paducah, Ky.: Collector Books, 2001.

Whittaker, Dick, and Jack Goody. "Rural Manufacturing in the Rouergue from Antiquity to the Present: The Examples of Pottery and Cheese." *Comparative Studies in Society and History* 43, no. 2 (2001): 225–45.

Wilcoxen, Charlotte. "Journey of Discovery: A Retrospective." *Ceramics in America* (2001): 212–14.

Wilkinson, Vega. *Spode-Copeland-Spode: The Works and Its People,*

1770–1970. Woodbridge, Suffolk, Eng.: Antique Collectors' Club, 2002.

Williams, Nigel. *Porcelain Repair and Restoration: A Handbook*, rev. by Loretta Hogan and Myrtle Bruce-Mitford. London: British Museum Press, 2002.

Wilson, Gillian, and Catherine Hess. *Summary Catalogue of European Decorative Arts in the J. Paul Getty Museum*. Los Angeles: Getty Publications, 2001.

Wilson, Richard L. *The Potter's Brush: The Kenzan Style in Japanese Ceramics*. Exhibition at the Freer Gallery of Art, Washington, D.C. London: Merrell Publishers, dist. in the U.S. by Rizzoli International (New York), 2001.

Wilson, Timothy, and David Williams. "An Italian Maiolica Albarello from Merstham, Surrey." *Post-Medieval Archaeology* 35 (2001): 119–21.

Wittwer, Samuel. *A Royal Menagerie: Meissen Porcelain Animals*. Los Angeles: J. Paul Getty Museum, 2001.

Wondrausch, Mary. *Mary Wondrausch on Slipware*. Westerville, Ohio: American Ceramic Society, 2001.

Wood, John K. "Encaustic Tiles." *Ceramic Review* (May/June 2002): 56–57.

Wright, Russel, Dianne H. Pilgrim, Malcolm Holzman, and Ian L. McHarg. *Russel Wright: Good Design Is for Everyone: In His Own Words: Designs for Living, Home, Woodland Garden*. St. Paul, Minn.: MBI Publishing, 2001.

Zusy, Catherine. "Archaeology at the United States Pottery Company Site in Bennington, Vermont." *Ceramics in America* (2002): 221–23.

Index

Chipstone Foundation Publications

Order Form

Title	*Code*	*Qty*	*Price*
American Furniture 2002	AF2002	____	$55
American Furniture 2001	AF2001	____	$55
Back Issues Available 1994 – 2000	AFback	____	$55
American Furniture – *2 year subscription*		____	$100
American Furniture – *3 year subscription*		____	$145
Ceramics in America 2002	CA2002	____	$55
Ceramics in America 2001	CA2001	____	$55
Ceramics in America – *2 year subscription*		____	$100
Ceramics in America – *3 year subscription*		____	$145
If These Pots Could Talk	IFTHCL	____	$75
____________	______	____	____
Shipping		____	____

U.S. Shipping $5.00 for first book; $1.25 for each additional book.
Foreign Shipping $6.50 for first book; $2.00 for each additional book.

TOTAL ________

Name ______________________________
Tel ______________________________
Address ______________________________
____
City State ZIP ______________________________

❏ Check payable to "UPNE"

Credit Card

❏ AMEX ❏ Discover ❏ Mastercard ❏ VISA

CC# ______________________ Expires ________

Please send to:
University Press of New England
37 Lafayette Street
Lebanon, NH 03766
University.Press@Dartmouth.edu
603/643-7110 • 800/421-1561 FAX 603/643-1540 www.upne.com

www.chipstone.org

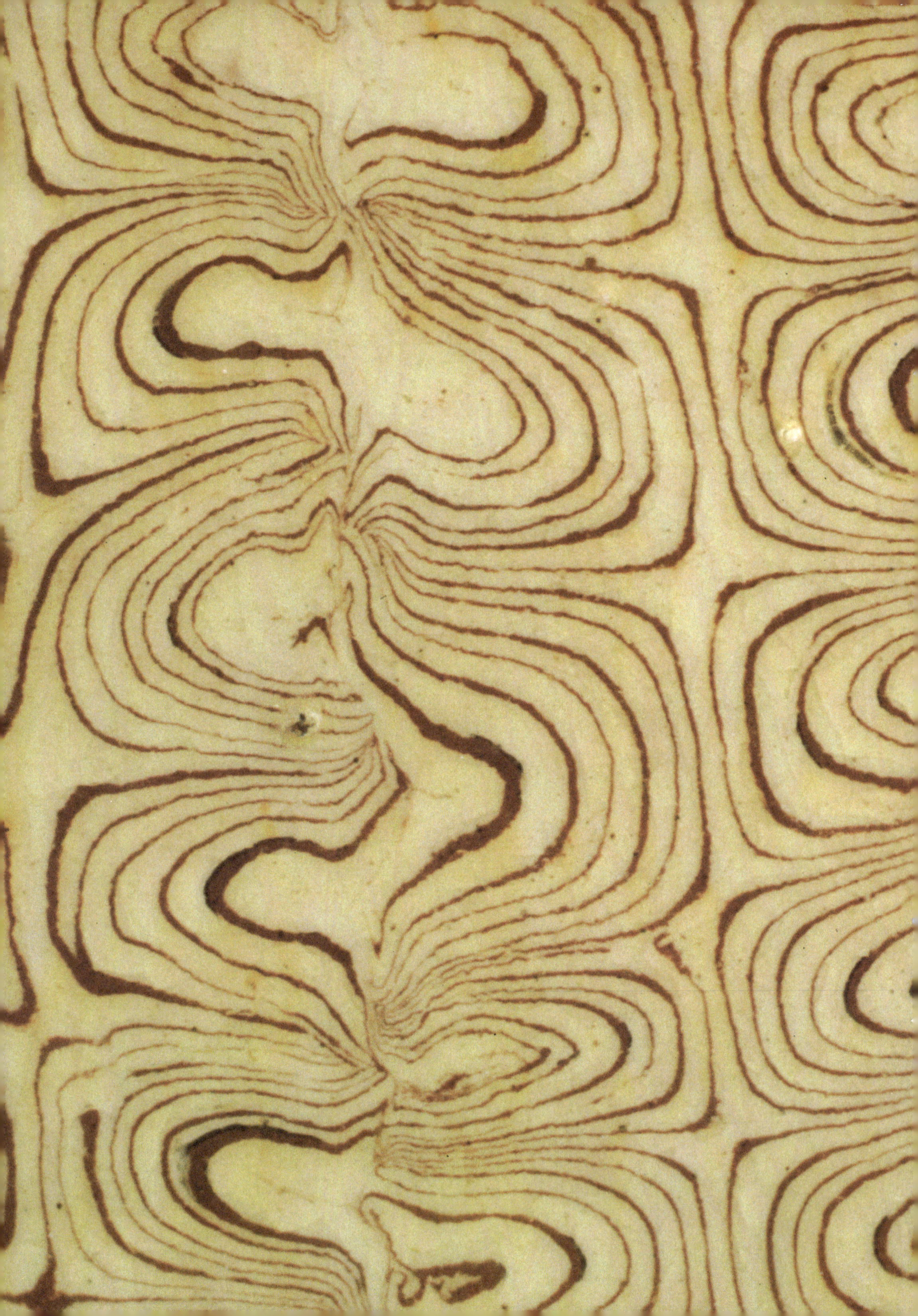